T0394542

The Art of Language

Brill's Studies in Language, Cognition and Culture

Series Editors

Alexandra Y. Aikhenvald (*Centre for Indigenous Health Equity Research, Central Queensland University*)
R.M.W. Dixon (*Centre for Indigenous Health Equity Research, Central Queensland University*)
N.J. Enfield (*University of Sydney*)

VOLUME 32

The titles published in this series are listed at *brill.com/bslc*

In Honour of Alexandra Y. Aikhenvald

The Art of Language

Edited by

Anne Storch
R.M.W. Dixon

BRILL

LEIDEN | BOSTON

Cover illustration: Max Beckmann, *Stillleben mit Türkenbund*, oil on canvas, 50.2 × 47.2 cm. Painted in Frankfurt in 1926. Public Domain.

Library of Congress Cataloging-in-Publication Data

Names: Aĭkhenval'd, A. I͡U. (Aleksandra I͡Ur'evna) honouree. | Storch, Anne, editor. | Dixon, Robert M. W., 1939- editor.
Title: The art of language / edited by Anne Storch, R.M.W. Dixon.
Description: Leiden ; Boston : Brill, [2022] | Series: Brill's studies in language, cognition and culture, 1879-5412 ; volume 32 | Includes bibliographical references and index.
Identifiers: LCCN 2022000464 (print) | LCCN 2022000465 (ebook) | ISBN 9789004510388 (hardback ; acid-free paper) | ISBN 9789004510395 (ebook)
Subjects: LCSH: Linguistics. | LCGFT: Essays.
Classification: LCC P125 .A65 2022 (print) | LCC P125 (ebook) | DDC 410–dc23/eng/20220217
LC record available at https://lccn.loc.gov/2022000464
LC ebook record available at https://lccn.loc.gov/2022000465

Typeface for the Latin, Greek, and Cyrillic scripts: "Brill". See and download: brill.com/brill-typeface.

ISSN 1879-5412
ISBN 978-90-04-51038-8 (hardback)
ISBN 978-90-04-51039-5 (e-book)

Copyright 2022 by Anne Storch and R.M.W. Dixon. Published by Koninklijke Brill NV, Leiden, The Netherlands.
Koninklijke Brill NV incorporates the imprints Brill, Brill Nijhoff, Brill Hotei, Brill Schöningh, Brill Fink, Brill mentis, Vandenhoeck & Ruprecht, Böhlau and V&R unipress.
Koninklijke Brill NV reserves the right to protect this publication against unauthorized use. Requests for re-use and/or translations must be addressed to Koninklijke Brill NV via brill.com or copyright.com.

This book is printed on acid-free paper and produced in a sustainable manner.

Contents

PART 2
How to Imbue Words with Power

PART 3
How to Keep Languages Strong

Preface

The idea for this volume emerged during a tea break on a workshop in Cairns. The vibrant atmosphere there and the great hospitality of Sasha Aikhenvald, one of the convenors, were the conditions under which our secret plan to edit a volume for Sasha was developed. Since then, we have been supported in a most special way by a large of group of colleagues. We remain deeply grateful to all contributors of this volume for their great chapters that were wonderful to read and to bring together in this book. And we are greatly indebted to Mary Chambers for the fantastic job she did in proofreading and commenting on the entire volume, and to Paulin Baraka Bose and Max Grötzinger who so competently assisted us in formatting—without the three of them we would have had a tough time. Our heartfelt thanks are due, last but not least, to Elisa Perotti for looking after our volume so well. It was a good experience, which leaves us contented and grateful, hoping the addressee of it all will love this book too.

Anne Storch and *R.M.W. Dixon*
September 2021

Figures and Tables

Figures

Tables

Notes on Contributors

Anne Storch
University of Cologne

R.M.W. Dixon
Central Queensland University, Cairns

Kate Burridge
Monash University, Melbourne

Katarzyna I. Wojtylak
University of Warsaw

Simon Overall
University of Otago, Dunedin

Rosita Henry
James Cook University, Cairns

Michael Wood
James Cook University, Cairns

Helma Pasch
University of Cologne

Felix Ameka
University of Leiden

Willem Adelaar
University of Leiden

Nerida Jarkey
University of Sydney

Sihong Zhang
Heifei University of Technology

Maarten Mous
University of Leiden

Isabelle Bril
Lacito, CNRS, Paris

Luca Ciucci
James Cook University, Cairns

Jovino Brito
Tariana community Brazil

James Sesu Laki
Manambu community Papua New Guinea

Hannah Sarvasy
Western Sydney University

Dineke Schokkin
University of Canterbury, Christchurch

Lars Johanson
Gutenberg University of Mainz

Éva Á. Csató
Uppsala University

Carol Genetti
New York University, Abu Dhabi

Carlos M. Nash
University of Kansas, Lawrence

Angeliki Alvanoudi
Aristotle University of Thessaloniki

Junwei Bai
James Cook University, Cairns

Pilar Valenzuela
Chapman University, Irvine

N.J. Enfield
University of Sydney

Bernd Heine
University of Cologne

Christa König
Goethe University, Frankfurt am Main

Elena Skribnik
Ludwig-Maximilians-Universität, Munich

CHAPTER 1

Linguistics as Art, Language as Joy

Anne Storch and R.M.W. Dixon

1 Diversity

The perceptive reader will recognize that the title of this book imitates and complements that of another. It is Alexandra Aikhenvald's *The Art of Grammar: A Practical Guide* (2015), a classic study, which was the stimulus for the present collection of examinations of language at large, and of reflection on what linguists do. Her introduction to descriptive linguistics was the focal inspiration for this volume. It is a text on linguistics that invites the reader to engage with language in a special way: like much of Aikhenvald's work, *The Art of Grammar* offers numerous approaches to her topic that reach way beyond conventional methodologies which tend to see language as a self-contained entry, static and self-serving. Reflecting on why a language is the way it is, Alexandra Aikhenvald (2015: 303) remarks:

> Language is not some kind of algebraic-type system. It only has existence as a tool through which its community of users interact with each other and with the world around them. In keeping with this, external factors may be partly responsible for language change. […] Further factors may include attitudes to the use of one's own and others' languages, types of political organization, economic practices […] and socio-cultural attitudes of all kinds. […] These factors may allow us to explain some things. But we will hardly ever be able to precisely predict which way a language will develop.

In other words, linguists are encouraged to approach a language in a holistic way and to treat it with humility. Studying and describing a language takes us beyond the boundaries of linguistics per se. It involves immersion into a distinctive community, learning and thinking in a new language, trying to view the world in the way that its speakers do. In this manner, a researcher achieves perspective and insight into the fundamental character of the language and its community of users, something that goes way beyond the scope of a text-book grammar.

In pursuing such rewarding goals one may have to struggle against bureaucracy, such as 'ethics approvals' demanded by people with no understanding of

© ANNE STORCH AND R.M.W. DIXON, 2022 | DOI:10.1163/9789004510395_002

the type of work involved (and in a form which may be offensive to Indigenous people). One can follow a safe but hollow path for a staid academic career. Or one can step into left field, embrace diversity, throw off the blinkers of western orthodoxy, and get to the heart of the matter.

Thus, when Alexandra Aikhenvald (2015: xv) explains that 'linguist' can mean either a polyglot or an analyst who studies language, she seems to hint that being both at the same time might indeed be an asset—to not only know about the diverse and dynamic ways in which people express themselves and interact with the world around them, but to turn such knowledge into living experience.

Her continued struggle for an acceptance of diversity instead of bureaucratic duress is also reflected in the ways in which, in her many talks, Alexandra Aikhenvald presents her own experiences of becoming a part of a language community. Often, she begins by inviting her audience to join her on an imaginary journey: first, we take a plane, then we hop on a bus, then there will be a ship, and finally a canoe. The vessels become smaller and smaller, until we stand face to face with another person, encountering them and interacting. To many audiences—including some from Indigenous communities—such a way of storytelling and of intricately weaving academic knowledge together with personal experiences is a form of art. This art is done so well in Aikhenvald's work that it often feels spontaneous and unassuming.

But it isn't. It is linguistics as an art that involves practices other than just making use of established methodologies, often outspoken and challenging, always open and hospitable. It is an offer to converse and interact, bringing all there is into the discussion. Linguistics as art is not a linguistics that moves along mainstream certainties. It raises difficult issues and has space for dispute. At the same time, it always demonstrates how much Aikhenvald—and those who share her vision—are able to enjoy diversity and the experience of difference. It is how a scholarly discipline, in a very personal and unique way, comes to be filled with life. Not easy to achieve.

2 Biography

While her own experiences with languages and their academic and non-academic communities always form part of Alexandra Aikhenvald's contributions to linguistics, her biography is often not brought to the fore.

She was named after her paternal grandfather, Alexander Y. Aikhenvald, a leading economist who was arrested in 1932 for opposing Stalin concerning the wisdom of collectivization. He was executed in 1941, although it was more than forty years before his family found out exactly what had happened to him and when. His wife was sent off for eight years of hard labour and then indefinite exile, based on a spurious report and also because she was his wife. Her maternal grandfather was a high officer in what was later called the KGB, and had played a role in the prosecution of the paternal grandfather. In April 1937 he was arrested as part of Stalin's purge and executed four months later, although the family didn't find out about this for another fifty years (and Alexandra was able to pinpoint his place of execution and burial only in 2006). Her maternal grandmother was also sent off for eight years' hard labour and then exile, just for being the wife of 'an enemy of the people'.

Alexandra's father and mother were, perforce, brought up by friends and relatives. Both were then exiled in 1949 (when about twenty years of age), simply by virtue of being the children of 'enemies of the people'. They met in exile, in Karaganda, Kazakhstan. In 1951 her father, Yuri Aikhenvald—who became an outstanding poet, writer, and literary critic—was then arrested as part of an anti-Semitic campaign. Like many others, he feigned mental illness to avoid being sent to a forced labour camp. Alexandra's parents were reunited only in 1955, after Khrushchev rolled back the carpet of repression a little following Stalin's demise. She was born in 1957.

Alexandra Aikhenvald was one of brightest students in her school and intended to study Classics at the Moscow State University. But the head of that department, A.A. Takhogodi, stated that with such a Jewish name she would not be accepted. So—to our eternal benefit—she enrolled in the Department of Structural and Computational Linguistics, obtaining excellent results in her BA and MA examinations. Then she was denied a PhD scholarship, again because she was Jewish. So she got a job as Research Assistant in the Institute of Oriental Studies, within the Soviet Academy of Sciences, and did a PhD (on Berber languages, from North Africa) in her spare time.

But in what circumstances? Sharing a small apartment of two rooms plus kitchen with parents, aunt, husband (who didn't get on with her parents), and baby son. One would be listening to BBC World Service radio broadcasts in one room, another watching television in the other room. Amongst this, with child on lap, Alexandra typed out a fine PhD dissertation. It was published, in three parts, and won First Prize in the National Competition for Publications in Oriental Languages in 1988 and again in 1990. At the early age of thirty-one, she was appointed Senior Research Fellow in the Institute of Oriental Languages.

Then came escape from that awful country. Escape to anywhere. To Brazil, at that time nothing much academically, but a free country. And with lots of Indigenous languages, which the Brazilian linguists themselves had most certainly not done justice to. She undertook intensive fieldwork in the north-west—across a river border from Colombia—on several languages from the Arawak family.

And then on to Australia. Alexandra applied for a Senior Research Fellowship from the Australian Research Council and was awarded one in September 1993. There were only ten that year, across all Australian universities. Both in Russia and in Brazil she had published prolifically—high-quality books and papers, including a grammar of Modern Hebrew (published in 1990) and also one on Biblical Hebrew (which had been accepted for publication but was wallowing within the system). She took up the Senior Research Fellowship, at the rank of Professor, at the Australian National University in February 1994. Together with Bob Dixon, Alexandra founded the Research Centre for Linguistic Typology at the ANU and in 2000 moved with it to La Trobe University in Melbourne.

She continued intensive fieldwork on Tariana and other languages from the Arawak family in Brazil, with her 729-page monograph *A Grammar of Tariana, from Northwest Amazonia* being published by Cambridge University Press in 2003. On coming to Australia, Alexandra embarked on immersion fieldwork in neighbouring New Guinea, with her 728-page monograph *The Manambu Language of East Sepik, Papua New Guinea* being published by Oxford University Press in 2008. She was also active on the theoretical front, making seminal contributions to typology with hefty volumes on *Classifiers: A Typology of Noun Classification Devices* (2000), *Evidentiality* (2004), *Imperatives and Commands* (2010), *The Art of Grammar: A Practical Guide* (2015), and *Serial Verbs* (2018).

Alexandra was Director of the Language and Culture Research Centre at James Cook University in Cairns from 2009, and in 2012 was awarded a prestigious ARC Laureate Fellowship. The range of her interests and publications continued to broaden, with monographs, and many papers, on language contact, the language of well-being, language maintenance and revitalization, and cross-cultural communication. She has been outspoken in her demands for justice and fair treatment for her colleagues and students. *I Saw the Dog: How Language Works*, a book intended for a general audience, was published in 2021. In 2021 Alexandra Aikhenvald relocated to the Cairns campus of the Central Queensland University, as a founder member of the 'Language, Culture, and Social and Emotional Well-being' research hub within the timely and innovative Centre for Indigenous Health Equity Research.

Alexandra Aikhenvald's stellar achievements in grammar writing and typological theory have been well acknowledged. In this book we are celebrating those of her endeavours which extend beyond such central areas but have always been part of her thinking about language. They include investigating the pragmatic power of words, the linguist's role in promoting language retention and documenting generational shift, and working with communities in maintaining their languages. Alexandra is unstinting in her generosity and hospitality towards students and colleagues from near and far, which resonates with the chapters in the first part of this volume.

3 Reflection

In honour of Alexandra Aikhenvald, this volume contains a selection of chapters that illustrate how linguists—with whom she worked over the years and whose ways of doing linguistics she often inspired—approach language. Their contributions are also informed by critical and multifaceted ways of reflection.

One of the motivations for this book was the interest shared by Alexandra Aikhenvald with many of her colleagues in finding ways in which linguistics could contribute in appropriate ways to the acknowledgement of non-Northern, often marginalized, knowledge and languages. The various critical debates of recent years—such as on the history of linguistics, its relevance for society, and the particular texts and images it produces—have to some extent obscured the discussion on what the tasks of linguists in this complex setting might actually be. It is surely a timely task to provide a more open and diverse text as a reply to such debates—taking knowledge from and on languages of the Tropics and the Global South more seriously. This involves exploring different ideas of what language does and what is done with language, considering different ways in which hospitality and humanity are expressed, and asking about more integrative ways of keeping languages—other than the world's dominant colonial ways of communication—relevant. In order to raise awareness of the various important and often critical and original contributions that linguists make, and the potential of deep knowledge about linguistic diversity and Indigenous intellectual wealth, this book is intended to bring together new insights into the tasks and responsibilities of linguists and their discipline.

Very much inspired by Alexandra Aikhenvald's work, this volume is informed by our interest in opening up disciplinary knowledge and offering connections between different approaches to language in contemporary linguistics. Rather than focusing on a particular single methodology or theoretical assumption, the book is intended to present part of the wealth of linguistic knowledge as an intertwined project, which combines numerous practices, positionalities, and perspectives. We believe, together with the contributors to this volume, that it is a crucial and timely task to emphasize the relevance of linguistic knowledge on power, hospitality, social class, marginalization, mobility, history, secrecy, the structures of discourse, and the construction of meaning. This is a gamut of knowledge that needs to be brought together—as it is brought together in personal discussions, conversations and encounters. To work along the traces of linguistic connectivity, marginalized narratives, in and on lesser studied (often stigmatized) language practices, and to shed light on the tasks of linguistics in making diverse knowledges transparent—this offers space for critical discussions on the ethics of linguistics, its challenges, contributions and tasks.

We remain critical about forecasting the development of linguistics. In this book, we prefer to explore where we are now, being concerned with some of the most central problems in contemporary linguistics, and at the same time with some of the most marginalized languages of the time and world we live in. While the publication of such research is mostly in English, much of the knowledge shared in it hardly ever reaches the institutions in our own environment. Institutions of learning—schools, university departments representing national philology, immigration and integration policy makers—hardly seem to have accepted the findings of linguists working on marginalized and minority languages. Knowledge from the tropics hardly ever seems to count. The advantages of multilingualism, of more open language concepts, decolonial language ideologies, and Indigenous philosophies seem to have gone unnoticed where they should have been relevant. And yet: our engagement with the diverse possibilities of expressing the experiences of humans changes our perspective on the world. What is needed is an open linguistics that concentrates on the multitude of possibilities offered through languages to make sense of reality, and that takes the creativity and sovereignty of speakers seriously. This will fill the study of language with life and agency. It might therefore be no coincidence that Alexandra Aikhenvald has pioneered the studying of evidentiality. Her focus on epistemic language, together with classifiers (that help to categorize referents) and taboo (that helps to normalize practices), provides a glimpse into the diverse ways in which language allows us to see the world. Instead of forcing us to look at colonial languages and imposing their norms and standards on others, her work invites us to learn about other possibilities.

4 Composition of This Book

The contributions assembled in this book offer multiple insights into how linguists engage with epistemology, creativity, hospitality and critique in language. They also do something more than this: they move aside colonial languages, national philology and European monolingualism, and say something about the true wealth of linguistics that becomes discernible once we turn our gaze on what has sometimes been considered marginal but is in fact an intrinsic part of the organism which is language.

As a collection of gifts offered to Alexandra Aikhenvald, this book also investigates the impact of her work on ours and on our views on language and its social context. The contributors to this volume have thereby been invited to create a balanced and yet polyphonic text that will offer diverse perspectives, not a uniform picture. The volume is organized into four main sections. The first one is comprised of contributions on hospitality and generosity, as an aspect of both Aikhenvald's work and personal attitude. It begins with Kate Burridge's chapter on 'truthiness', the belief that something is true on the basis of one's gut feeling, regardless of the evidence or facts. Kate Burridge gives copious examples of her experience over decades of work on radio and TV, during which she has invited diverse publics to learn more about linguistics. This invitation has not always created hospitable encounters between the linguist and her audiences: language was often perceived as national as well as personal property and the linguist seen as a transgressive, dangerous person putting established belief into question.

The second chapter in this section is a study of an alternative to the inhospitable neoliberal conceptualization of language and feeling. Kasia Wojtylak explores the various meanings of 'heart' in Murui, a language spoken in Colombia and Peru. The Murui heart is constructed in at least two different ways, namely as a physical organ of a particular shape, thus relating to the natural world that contains similarly shaped objects (fruits), and as the seat of interiority, relating to other forms of context in which the individuum operates. The integration of the natural environment and individual emotional life offers fascinating perspectives on how we can also conceive the world, as an entangled, living place in which humans are connected to other beings, for example through the shape of the heart. In the following chapter, Simon Overall demonstrates that a hospitable, life-giving integration of humans and their environment can also be understood via a careful study of creative language. He analyses the language of drinking songs in Kandozi, spoken in Peru. A recurrent motif is the role of birds in the songs, particularly the red-throated caracara, the yellow-rumped cacique, and the oropendola, all of which are gregarious and noisy. The birds are symbolic of human sociality, due to their preference for forest-edge habitats near human settlements, their communal nesting habit reminiscent of human settlements, and their consistent vocalization reminiscent of human speech and song. The effect is striking: artistic language and poetry here are not connected to correct speech and orderly practice, but to the shrill and often disturbing cries of the birds. Language here is a very powerful form and concept that refers to nature and contingency, instead of to control through humans.

The next chapter, written by Rosita Henry and Michael Wood, helps us to turn the gaze to the possibilities of researchers to encounter and create hospitality in fieldwork contexts. Hospitality and how this applies between the researcher and members of the Kumula and Penambi Wia (Papua New Guinea) is here based on reciprocity and how it is constructed as a concept and lived as a practice. Exchanging dances, names, and stories all helps in drawing participants into mutual exchanges of promises, on which dynamic and sustainable relationships are built. The following chapter, by Helma Pasch, describes crucial aspects of Indigenous politeness concepts. Writing about Zande, spoken in various countries in central Africa, Helma Pasch demonstrates how multiple language ideologies and ascriptions of linguistic identity in a multilingual, diverse society result in rationalizations of the Self as hospitable. The concept of Zande speakers as being particularly polite is also shown to be a powerful and sovereign reply to experiences of marginalization and colonization.

The continuities of colonial power relations and imperial formations are also what underlies Anne Storch's chapter on the meanings of smell in Luwo, a language of South Sudan. Luwo is one of the world's languages that exhibit an unusually large vocabulary of smell words. These are not only used in order to refer to the natural environment, but also to concepts of relationships one shares with others. The grammar and practice of hospitality is closely connected to scents and transcends the boundaries of single languages, thereby binding together people who share violent pasts and presents. Hospitable language, having the potential to express retained sovereignty in a marginalized setting therefore also focuses on the powers of reciprocity.

The penultimate chapter in this section is Felix Ameka's study of concepts of Othering in various West African languages, including Ewe, Ga, and Wolof. The chapter's fascinating case studies on the various verbs that encode 'speak' illustrate how tone, voice, stance etc. are perceived and constructed as something that the Other does differently. Together with his observations on how 'I' and 'you' are put in a different order in different societies, these analyses help to understand how Othering is practised and rationalized in different ways, namely to exclude, or to include.

The concluding chapter of the section, Willem Adelaar's study of Quechua, offers a fascinating perspective on how we can describe and theorize politeness in a language that has no obvious expression of it. Social deixis however is manifested in indirect and subtle ways in Quechua, with semantic extensions into aspect and other non-directional meanings.

The second part of this book is about how words are imbued with power. Alexandra Aikhenvald's studies of the ways in which taboo and secrecy are created and used in language are some of most fascinating aspects of her work, and the chapters brought together in this section relate to her contributions in many ways. The section begins with Nerida Jarkey's chapter on social relations in White Hmong, spoken in China and adjacent south-east Asia. In a language spoken in an egalitarian society, Hmong kin terms function to reinforce understanding of the type of relationship between the interactants and consequently the expectations concerning rights and duties within this relationship. The words imbued with power are those used for one's closest kin: when a woman marries, she undergoes a loss of personal identity in that she is now expected not to use affinal terms for referring to her natal family, since she must now see them from the perspective of her husband and children. The following chapter, by Sihong Zhang, offers insights into other ways in which the power of the word can be associated with a particular part of the speakers' repertoires: in Ersu, spoken in Sichuan, China, different classes of words and grammatical forms, namely imperatives, prohibitives, causatives, a persuasive marker, and interrogative forms are predominantly associated with power. They all interact and play a role in politeness practices, and by carefully studying the ways in which this happens, Zhang is able to shed more light on the diverse resources people use to create powerful words and ways of speaking.

The third chapter of this section, by Maarten Mous, describes and contrasts curses and blessings in Iraqw, a language of Tanzania. Curses are directed to the god who is asked to inflict bad things on the person designated. Blessings, in turn, are directed at people and these use imperatives. The interesting way in which imperatives are used in blessings (but hardly ever in curses) not only illustrates typological and structural complexities, but also the complex indexicality of imperatives, giving further evidence on the multiple meanings and constructions of such categories. Imperatives are also in the focus of the next chapter, by Isabelle Bril. Her study is concerned with directive speech acts in Northern Amis, a Formosan language. An important feature of the language is its four voices: active voice, nonactive voice, undergoer voice, and locative voice. The way in which these voices interact with imperative mechanisms is revealing. It relates to a cline of politeness: undergoer voice is most polite for addressing deities and aged persons, locative voice is of intermediate politeness, while the other two voices are less polite, being used to address children, equals, and inferiors. Bril thus explains how imperative forms often express other types of speech acts than commands, such as imprecations, admonitions, entreaties, invitations, and phatic speech acts with illocutionary force.

In the final chapter of this section, Luca Ciucci takes a different approach. He explores the power in a particular form of language that is considered to heal. In Ayoreo, spoken in Paraguay and Bolivia, the word itself can exert magic power on reality, and this manifests itself in the taboo genres of myths and magic formulas. The latter are called *sarode* and are mainly used for healing purposes. The importance of these formulas and the language concept enshrined in them remains highly relevant: when the Ayoreo have come into contact with outsiders they have always paid a high death toll owing to diseases for which they do not have antibodies, a situation that seems to recur.

The third part of the book is devoted to the question of what the role of linguists might be in promoting language retention and documenting generational shift. This is one of the key areas for understanding the meaning and impact of Aikhenvald's work, which is also reflected in the two contributions by members of the communities in which she works, the first in Amazonia and the second in the Sepik region of Papua New Guinea. The meanings of integrity and participation are reflected in these chapters, which are both written by community members who have actively participated in the study of their languages, working with Alexandra Aikhenvald over many years. In a letter written in Tariana (directed to and translated by R.M.W. Dixon), Jovino Brito writes about how he perceived Aikhenvald's integration in his community through immersion fieldwork. She was adopted by his family and continues to be seen as a dear family member. Brito explains why the so-called 'side products' of linguistic fieldwork, such as ABC books, have helped him and many other Tariana speakers to become interested in keeping their language alive. This also includes addressing Aikhenvald by her Tariana name, *Kumatharo*, as well as keeping in contact with her—these days via WhatsApp. Brito makes clear that Aikhenvald should be presented to the academic audiences of this book not simply as a linguist, but as a special person to the Tariana. In his appreciation of Alexandra Aikhenvald, James Sesu Laki recalls her frequent stays among the Manambu. He describes what makes a good linguist from his perspective: the ability to learn a new language quickly, the willingness and interest to live with the community and share daily-life experiences, openness and kindness, the ability to establish lasting friendships, and something that he, referring to words of his late wife, Pauline Yuaneg Luma-Laki, calls 'glowing'. To really engage with each other's language and lifeworld requires more than one's previously acquired knowledge on fieldwork methodology and linguistic theory, Laki suggests; it must be based on a glowing interest in others.

The section continues with Hannah Sarvasy's study on child language and language used with children in Nungon, spoken in Papua New Guinea. This chapter provides a detailed study of the use of the near future tense by Nungon children. Interestingly, the near future appears in children's speech several months later than the other four verbal inflections, and once acquired, it appears to have a wide role: (a) for immediate context, (b) for hypothetical events with plausible hodiernal time-frames, and (c) for threats. Understanding the complex pragmatics of this form and how it is acquired by small children impressively illustrates the importance of shared efforts in keeping Indigenous languages alive. In the subsequent chapter, Dineke Schokkin is interested in subsistence practices as an important aspect of how a language is kept alive. Writing about the Idi-speaking people in southern New Guinea, Schokkin brings out the fundamental nature of fieldwork—becoming a part of a community and sharing their ways of thinking about the world around. In the setting she explores, the coconut is a multi-purpose plant. In addition to eating its flesh and drinking its water coconut oil is used for hair and skin care. Palmfronds are used as ground cover and as sleeping mats. The fronds are used to make brooms and baskets are made from the leaves. There is also coconut wine, and coconut trees are planted to signify special events. Throughout the chapter, the voices of speakers expand on the meanings and uses of coconuts. By engaging with the rich knowledge on coconut farming and the language connected to it, Schokkin demonstrates how Indigenous methodologies can be applied by linguists.

A different take on the issue of language vitality is employed by Lars Johanson and Éva Á. Csató in their chapter on what is usually referred to as 'code copying'—a complex process that provides insights into how speakers creatively make use of linguistic resources, but also into how minority languages are perceived as lacking in stability when this process becomes very strong. The example of Turkic languages and the huge variety of code-copying strategies that can be described and analysed in these languages also helps us to understand "the communicative functionality of the language that keeps it alive". Sharing this insight, Carol Genetti and Carlos M. Nash describe, in their subsequent chapter, how languages are strengthened by enhancing their speakers' interest and engagement in retaining their functionality. The authors document eight InField/CoLang workshops. These were intended to enhance collaboration between linguists and speakers of endangered languages. The biennial meetings, all held at universities in the USA and each taking about six weeks, focused on up to four languages each. The nature of the topics discussed in these intensive workshops was continually rethought and expanded over the years. The biographical sketches of six notable participants, which follow the instructive description of the project itself, describe how they progressed through the sequence of workshops, what they learnt, and what they contributed.

The last contribution to Section Three focuses on the importance of sustainable and balanced personal relationships and how these do more than just help to retain knowledge about endangered languages. They also, as bonds between speakers and linguists, help to build connections between different participants and locations of knowledge production. In this chapter, R.M.W. Dixon writes about his experiences of working with the last guardians of Wargamay, Nyawaygi, and Mbabaram. In what he describes as 'salvage fieldwork', Improvisation and a creative use of methodologies is crucial. Dixon argues for 'real' fieldwork: not something superficial like a quick interview in a café, but something that creates bonds, a relationship, and a deeper understanding. Asking for integrity, encouraging readers to take the time that is needed and consider the wellbeing and dignity of the people they work with, this contribution helps us to understand that linguistics is not only about one's knowledge of the discipline, but also about one's involvement in the field.

The fourth section of the book deals with the art of making language transparent, exploring the intricacies of epistemic grammar and the deep meanings of particular fields in the lexicon. Here, the contributions refer to Alexandra Aikhenvald's masterly studies in evidentiality and her outstanding descriptive work. The first chapter of the section does so by looking at a still poorly understood strategy, namely the expression of counter-expectance. Angeliki Alvanoudi's contribution on the particle *ba* in Modern Greek, based on a rich corpus of recordings from phone calls and conversations, demonstrates that the particle is used in a wide range of functions and meanings, such as indicating surprise, unprepared mind, emotional disruption, and negation. This greatly helps in understanding the highly complex indexicalities and meanings of mirative markers, their pragmatics and discursive usage. This is also the aim of Junwei Bai's study of the ways in which grammar encodes knowledge in Munya, a language of China. The markers for evidentiality, egophoricity, and mirativity are first explained carefully, before Bai turns to the relationship between these three categories. He demonstrates how the inferential evidential can have a mirative overtone in certain circumstances, how the mirative particle can be used with evidentials but not with an egophoric marker, and various other ways in which these markers are entangled.

In the following chapter, Pilar Valenzuela discusses nominal classification in Shiwilu, a language of Peru. A noun, a classifier, or the 'deceased' marker *-ku* (referring to someone who is no longer alive) may be incorporated into a verb; the valency does not change. It is not very common that free-standing nouns can be incorporated, and whereas in most languages incorporation is restricted to terms in O or S/O function, classifiers and the deceased marker may occur in A and in S/A functions. At the same time, Valenzuela addresses one of the most fascinating aspects of systems of nominal classification, namely classifiers that refer to the realm of taboo, the netherworld, and potentially harmful objects. In the subsequent chapter by N.J. Enfield, the focus is on the underlying meaning of such practices, asking about why people use particular terminologies, categories and expressions, and what the context of their practices is. Investigating the contrast between a 'utilitarian' view (after Eugene Hunn) and the 'intellectualist' view (after Brent Berlin), Enfield offers a detailed discussion of colour terminology and of names for smells across a fair range of literature. He concludes that the two views are not opposed, but blended. He finishes by quoting from his own work: "to truly understand the word, we must ask not what it means. Instead, we must ask: what are people's reasons for using it?"

This is also an important aspect of the contribution by Bernd Heine and Christa König. They explore the meanings and functions of discourse markers in Akie, spoken in Tanzania. The authors characterize Akie as a discourse-marker prominent language. Twenty five discourse markers are identified, including such fascinating forms as *nayái* 'so it be!', a concluding agreement, and *ntán(o)* 'you should know', drawing attention to what follows. The chapter focuses on a case study: an intensive investigation of the discourse marker *aríí kas ira* 'you understand?', making sure that the hearer has understood the speaker's account. The last chapter of the section deals with three major Mongolic languages, Khalkha, Buryat, and Kalmyk. Elena Skribnik explores the parameters set in a 2009 volume, *The semantics of clause linking*, linking these to the notion of 'evaluation', i.e. 'good' versus 'bad'. After a typological sketch she offers discussions of anteriority, posteriority, simultaneity, causal constructions, purposive constructions, and manner and attendant constructions. Interesting insights include a construction for coding succession contrary to expectations, and another one for expressing precedence with unexpected succession. The chapter ends with a question: "Why do Mongolic languages encoding events and their sequences constantly evaluate and compare them to social norms and individual expectations?"

It is our hope that the collection of articles brought together in this volume will result in many more questions, leading to more integrative, original and sustainable linguistic work.

References

Aikhenvald, Alexandra Y. (1990). *Sovremennyj Ivrit.* (*Modern Hebrew.*) Serija: Jazyki narodov Azii i Afriki (Series: Languages of the peoples of Asia and Africa). Moscow: Nauka.

Aikhenvald, Alexandra Y. (2000). *Classifiers: A typology of noun categorization devices.* Oxford: Oxford University Press.

Aikhenvald, Alexandra Y. (2003). *A Grammar of Tariana, from Northwest Amazonia.* Cambridge: Cambridge University Press.

Aikhenvald, Alexandra Y. (2004). *Evidentiality.* Oxford: Oxford University Press.

Aikhenvald, Alexandra Y. (2008). *The Manambu language of East Sepik, Papua New Guinea.* Oxford: Oxford University Press.

Aikhenvald, Alexandra Y. (2010). *Imperatives and commands.* Oxford: Oxford University Press.

Aikhenvald, Alexandra Y. (2012). *The languages of the Amazon.* Oxford: Oxford University Press.

Aikhenvald, Alexandra Y. (2015). *The art of grammar.* Oxford: Oxford University Press.

Aikhenvald, Alexandra Y. (2018). *Serial verbs.* Oxford: Oxford University Press.

Aikhenvald, Alexandra Y. (2021). *I saw the dog: How language works.* London: Profile Books.

Dixon, R.M.W. and Alexandra Y. Aikhenvald (eds.) (2009). *The semantics of clause linking: A cross-linguistic typology.* Oxford: Oxford University Press.

PART 1

How to Be Welcoming and Hospitable

CHAPTER 2

Truthiness and Language—Popular Perception and Fall-Out

Kate Burridge

1 Introduction—Truthiness

> It used to be, everyone was entitled to their own opinion, but not their own facts. But that's not the case anymore. Facts matter not at all. Perception is everything. Truthiness is 'What I say is right, and [nothing] anyone else says could possibly be true.'
>
> STEPHEN COLBERT, interview with *The A.V. Club*

The notion of truthiness here is not the short-lived nineteenth century truthiness (a colloquial synonym for truthfulness). This more recent creation arose in the context of twenty-first century US politics, the brainchild of comedian Stephen Colbert in a 2005 episode of his mock TV news show, *The Colbert Report*. Colbert's truthiness encompasses more than the approximation of truth—it is the belief that something is true on the basis of one's gut feeling regardless of the evidence or facts. There is no doubt that the word captured the ethos of the time, and in that same year, the American Dialect Society declared *truthiness* their 'Word of the Year'.

Truthiness has long been associated with political misinformation. An early example occurred in Australia on 10 September 1996, when newly elected Member of Parliament, Pauline Hanson, declared that "Australia is in danger of being swamped by Asians." As the then Secretary of the Department of Foreign Affairs and Trade, Philip Flood later wrote, "Hanson revived a false image of Australia as a nation opposed to Asian immigration and to strong links with Asia. She also had a warped idea of evidence" (2008: 75). During an interview on the topic, Hanson was challenged to support her assertion that one million illegal immigrants were entering Australia each year, to which she replied: "But you are just asking for 'book facts'. We don't need 'book facts': we know it is happening." Book facts was the label Hanson coined for evidence that appeared in books—as Stephen Colbert later put it, "[t]ruth comes from the gut, not books" (*The Colbert Report*, 17 October 2005). It joins *post-truth*, *fake news*, *alternative facts* and *truthful hyperbole*, just some of the other contributions to this century's Orwellian word-hoard.

© KATE BURRIDGE, 2022 | DOI:10.1163/9789004510395_003

It was in 2004 that I had my eyes opened to the existence of truthy accounts of language. *The Age* newspaper had published an opinion piece *Too much speech-junk? Yeah-no!* in which former English teacher David Campbell listed what he saw as various "speech junk developments", one of which was *yeah-no*. After outlining some of the research findings that Margaret Florey and I had published on this newly identified discourse particle (Burridge and Florey 2002), he then dismissed them—he knew that *yeah-no*, just like the other features he had identified in other people's speech, served "no useful purpose". I found it fascinating that David Campbell could write so clearly about the complicated semantics of discourse particles like *yeah-no*, acknowledging their roles in conversational interaction and politeness, and yet go onto reject these outright simply because his commonsense told him otherwise.

My many years of engaging with the general public have shown me that people are generally fascinated by their language, and most feel free to voice their opinions on linguistic matters. There is nothing wrong with that—we all have intuitions, insights, visions. The problem is when these gut feelings are then put above intellectual examination, in this case well-researched linguistic evidence. Language issues are "hot button" issues involving matters of privilege and power, traditional values and stereotypes, and these are of course compelling shapers of the gut feelings that feed our opinions. Worldviews affect people's ability to think rationally (see Cook and Lewandowsky 2011 on debunking myths)—even when linguists think they are getting the linguistic message across, people can fall back on their comfortable knowledge, what they "know" to be true. *Yeah-no* is "yet another example of speech junk—unnecessary words that clutter up our language."

Those in the linguistics profession are well aware that many things commonly believed to be true about language are in fact false, and linguists are constantly raining on people's parades. These parades can involve trivial notions of etymology (no, babies weren't thrown out with the bathwater in medieval times), but they can be more serious. In a lengthy two-page opinion piece in *The Age* newspaper, Dean Frenkel (2015), with no background in the relevant disciplines of historical linguistics or phonetics, described how the Australian accent arose from the drunken speech of the first convicts. His account of Australia's "national speech impediment" began:

> Let's get things straight about the origins of the Australian accent. Aussie-speak developed in the early days of colonial settlement from a cocktail of English, Irish, Aboriginal and German—before another mystery influence was slipped into the mix.

> The Australian alphabet cocktail was spiked by alcohol. Our forefathers regularly got drunk together and through their frequent interactions unknowingly added an alcoholic slur to our national speech patterns. For the past two centuries, from generation to generation, drunken Aussie-speak continues to be taught by sober parents to their children.

Research going back to the 1970s is clear on the sorts of speech errors brought about by the consumption of alcohol (e.g. Lester and Skousen 1974; Chin and Pisoni 1997; Cutler and Henton 2004), but these aren't the ones featured in this piece. What Frenkel was describing here is the result of universal processes that shape sounds and sound systems—well-trodden paths of phonological change, not the dysfluencies accompanying slow drunken speech. But journalists had no interest in listening to linguists and the press around the world lapped the fiction up. As Crystal (2015) described in his blog, even after his long conversation with the *Daily Mirror* journalist, the story was presented "as if it were gospel." He concluded, "[t]his kind of journalism makes the job of a linguist so much harder."

In this chapter, I explore the ways that people think about language and value, and the fall-out of this thinking. The views can be ferociously passionate and confident but, as is clear from the example just given, are often woefully lacking in the norms and standards of evidence we have come to expect of public debate on other topics (*post-truth*, *alternative facts* and *fake news* aside!). As I show, the social consequences of this can be far-reaching.

For some time, sociolinguists have been researching public opinion about language (e.g. Cameron 2012; Curzan 2014). The work I am reporting on here piggybacks on this research; it also draws on the research by those linguists who have been playing a vital role in raising public awareness of the complex consequences of culture and language difference within such settings as education, health and the law (e.g. Eades 2018; Fraser 2018a,b; Aikhenvald 2020). It is also based on personal letters, emails, online commentary and general feedback I have received during my now more than thirty years involvement with language programs for radio and television; e.g. weekly language segments for public and commercial talkback radio around Australia and (from 2006–2011) the TV program *Can We Help* (http://www.abc.net.au/tv/canwehelp/).

2 The Challenge of Getting the Message Across

> [Linguists] are categorically the dullest people on the face of the earth. [...] Rather than trying to present and explain information, they seem to be going in the opposite direction. They try to shield people from knowing anything useful about the language.
>
> LAURENCE URDANG, interview with Colin McEnroe, 13 January 1992

As a lexicographer, and editor of *The Language Quarterly Verbatim* (a publication on "language and linguistics for the layperson"), Laurence Urdang would have known what linguists do. So his attack on what the interviewing journalist described as "the pointed headed abstruse strudel of academic linguistics" does suggest there is a 'brand image problem' here. The piece originally appeared in *The Washington Post*, and was picked up by newspapers around the world. Admittedly, it was some time ago, and linguistics these days is much more in the public arena, in ways that presumably Urdang would have supported. However, I maintain that the discipline still has something of an image problem, and this continues to stymie effective dialogue between linguists and the wider community. Urdang's message was certainly clear at the time—if you want to know something about language, do not ask a linguist.

A number of things can damage a brand: bad communication practices and bad management of negative reviews are among them. Of course, in the case of linguistics, it may even be that there is little to no awareness of the actual brand itself (do people really know what linguists do?), and, as I go on to discuss, this can be a real barrier to the involvement of linguists in fields such as the law and education. Much of the problem stems from the object of study, namely, language. The fact that linguistics deals with the everyday gives the impression that the profession doesn't involve a sufficient level of expertise. While a deep interest in quantum mechanics or thermodynamics, for example, would never qualify me to write a book on the subject, there are many highly successful publications on the English language written by people with no background in the science of language (e.g. Lynne Truss' blockbuster book *Eats, Shoots and Leaves*). A lack of 'brand identity' causes all sorts of problems when it comes to getting the facts of language across—too complex and it looks like quackery, or worse 'junk science' (see below); too simple and it looks like anybody can do it.

Consider the following email I received on 15 May 2020 (from a lecturer in Academic English at an Australian university). It was prompted by a radio segment on ABC's *Overnights* (14 May 2020), and the topic was pronunciation, variation and change. The message I hoped to get across was that language issues are never a simple matter of a tick or a cross by a linguistic form, but are more complex, and way more interesting, than this. For example, one talkback question had to do with loanwords, and I gave the different adaptations of originally French words like *homage* and *garage* (e.g. ['hɒmədʒ] versus [gə'raʒ]) to illustrate how variation sometimes stems from the length of time the words have been in the language. Here is an extract of one response I received that day:

> Dear Ms Burridge,
>
> I cringed every time I heard you on ABC radio (14 May) pronounce 'pronunciation' 'pronounciation'. There is no such word.
>
> You threw in the occasional correct pronunciation of 'pronunciation' but kept reverting to 'pronounciation'. You said it about 15 times.
>
> Mischievous does not end in 'ious'. Why would you condone it? Why would you say that people are pronouncing it that way because they are familiar with words such as 'devious'? Does that make it correct? [...] You are encouraging what is happening to the English language and are contributing to its demise. You are contributing to those of us over the age of 50 needing an interpreter within the next 10 years.
>
> I understand that language changes but to hear a so-called linguist speak so poorly is very disconcerting. It is just a matter of time until we can expect you to say 'impordant' for 'important' or 'allephant' for 'elephant' or 'ostraya' for 'Australia' and then say that these pronunciations are acceptable.
>
> You actually condoned the pronunciation of 'homage'. Unbelievable! 'Homage' is derived from the French but in English-speaking countries it is pronounced 'homage', not 'homarge'. Shame on you Ms Burrardge.
>
> When I heard you say 'yep' on the radio, I realised there is no hope.
>
> No doubt you would justify the examples I am giving. Clearly, to gain the qualifications you have acquired, speaking correctly is not a requirement. There is a great irony here.
>
> I shall be changing to another station next time you're on the radio.

The 45-minute segment covered (in a light-hearted and I thought convincing manner) some of the powerful drivers of change, such as analogy and phonological processes like palatalization and voicing. However, nothing I offered convinced this listener to shift from her clear commonsense distinction between what is 'right' and what is 'wrong'. The university lecturer, with presumably a commitment to education, was still not open to the possibility of an alternative way of viewing these language features. It is also telling that the audio from the radio segment confirmed that on no occasion did I pronounce the word *pronunciation* as "pronounciation" (except when I was illustrating the change). A number of similar complaints have convinced me that speakers become so consumed with their pet hates that they hear them even where they do not exist.

There is a lot of doublethink that underpins our linguistic beliefs and our behaviour. People's own writing is frequently at odds with their public pontificating on language; many emails and letters I receive abound in grammatical and typographical errors (examples below). Dictionaries that fail to update cease to be used; and yet if dictionary makers and handbook writers admit current usage, there are howls about declining educational standards (Stockwell and Minkova 2001: 191 f.). Euphemistic exclamations like *shucks* and *fudge* are camouflaged cuss words, expressing the same emotions as full-blown obscenities; tabooed concepts can be acceptably uttered by using euphemisms but not direct terms (Allan and Burridge 2006). The fact that *to be* is a linguistic mongrel comprising verb forms from three, possibly four, other verbs is interesting, but for *bring* and *buy* to collide in this way is calamitous; change is fine only if it remains a historical curiosity (Burridge 2010a). Finally, despite the legendary attachment to the vernacular in Australia, there is a well-attested and thriving linguistic complaint tradition, one that even exceeds what has been observed in other major English-speaking nations (Lukač 2018). Australians place a high value on larrikinism ('bad (disorderly) behaviour'), while at the same time Australia is a society that is exceedingly rule-governed (Hirst 2004), and, according to the Australian component of the most recent World Values Survey, even "open to *'strongman' and technocratic styles of government"* (Sheppard, McAllister and Makkai 2018: 4; their emphasis).

This ability of individual human beings to hold contradictory points of view on a common entity or phenomenon is necessary to permit an intelligent organism to pragmatically adapt to its environment. But it is something that upsets rationalists—and it makes the challenge of exposing truthiness about language even more difficult and complex. As Cook and Lewandowsky (2011: 1) emphasize at the start of their *Debunking Handbook*, "[i]t's not just what people think that matters, but how they think."

Linguists clearly cannot ignore or condemn speakers for saying "pronounciation" instead of "pronunciation", any more than zoologists can denigrate dromedaries for having only one hump and not two; yet this is precisely the sort of activity the public expects of them. Linguists find this expectation ill-informed and narrow-minded; the public feels let down. The fall-out is mutual suspicion and skepticism. Linguists who come out and challenge false beliefs about language are often misinterpreted as pushing an 'anything goes' agenda. They might also be criticized for spouting this agenda from their position of privilege, which they attained via an education that taught them the importance of the finer points of pronunciation and grammar (as shown by the complaint aired in Coddington 2008; see below). Consider one of the 192 comments following something I wrote for *The Conversation* with developmental psychologist Cammie McBride; the piece emphasized the complexities surrounding the history of /h/, and also the recognized benefits of the acrophonic letter name *haitch* (over *aitch*) for children learning sounds and letters (see Burridge and McBride 2018).

> So according to linguists it's perfectly fine to call apples oranges, even worse, orangas. [...] I am concerned that linguists are effectively dumbing down our speech skills in their mission for relevance; and to sully our collective value system that values communication skills.

Time and time again people's pet hates do not conform to linguistic reality, and the story of *haitch* in Australia is another example. The pronunciation of the letter name has become a social password—*aitch* carries the stamp of approval, and aitchers' reactions are often visceral (see for example Enfield 2018). The strong stigma surrounding *haitch* derives from its long association with Irish Catholic Education. Despite the anti-British sentiment that was around in early times, there was general antagonism towards the Irish and an accompanying low prestige of Irish varieties (see Hickey 2004: 110).[1] Irish *haitch* is a widespread popular etymology for this letter name, even though there is no real evidence for it, as lexicographer Sue Butler points out (2014). But never let facts get in the way of a good shibboleth.

As Cameron (2012: 227) writes, "[l]inguists are apt to suppose that facts about language would, in any rational argument, speak for themselves. This supposition is false, both in theory and in practice." When the findings of linguistic

1 For the important role the Irish played in modern Australia's love-hate relationship with the vernacular, see Musgrave and Burridge (to appear).

research are carefully laid out, as they were in that *Conversation* piece, linguists imagine that they are getting the message across. And yet people still fall back on their comfortable knowledge—what they 'know' to be true. Let me quote from one the many exchanges I had on this issue (15 May 2018; errors are original).[2]

> Let's cal a spade a spade and haitch the Irish version of aitch used in the Catholic Church in Australia, hence in its educations system and hence by the many Catholics who went into teaching. When's the next re-run of this topic? I can't wait. [...] My point is, it's not a shibboleth to speak of the Irish connection, it's a fact. And let's give it a rest

It is as Cameron goes on to describe (2012: 227): certain things might be factually true but that does not make them desirable. And this is all the more so in the current climate of general distrust of and skepticism towards experts, attested by the flourishing of headlines following the shock of the two epoch-making events Brexit and Trump: "Britain has had enough of experts, says Gove", "The real reason that we don't trust experts anymore", and "'Had enough of experts?' Anti-intellectualism is linked to voters' support for movements that are skeptical of expertise". Facts and figures do not speak for themselves. "Knowing stuff isn't enough", as one subheadline put it (Shaw 2016).

3 Getting to the Bottom of People's Assumptions about Language

> You don't look up truthiness in a book, you look it up in your gut.
> STEPHEN COLBERT, 13 January 2006

Severin and Burridge's (2020) investigation of a database of usage queries attests to the booming complaint tradition downunder (this was a sample of 880 pieces of correspondence received over a roughly six-month period). Their research highlights the extent to which Australians seek out confirmation of 'correct' usage (in forums such as letters to the editor, radio talkback, and television programs)—in fact, as mentioned above, Lukač (2018) suggests these verbal hygiene activities exceed those found in other English-speaking nations:

2 I should add here that these exchanges also involved phone calls from a number of grateful haitchers, happy to now know the background to a feature in their speech that had made them feel inadequate for so long—not only does *haitch* have the pedigree, it has definite benefits for letter sound learning.

> In my analysis of letters to the editor published across the English-speaking world (Lukač, 2016), I found that the practice of publishing letters on language use is not limited to a particular country. It is, however, the most popular in Australia and New Zealand, followed by Ireland and the UK, and least established in the US and in Canada. (Lukač 2018: 8)

Severin and Burridge's study also reveals that this opposition to non-standard usage is not confined to the older listeners and viewers of Australia's national broadcaster—the complaints came from all age groups, including younger Australians who have experienced the 'language in use' approach at school (emphasizing variation and change). Not all areas of the language attracted the same degree of criticism, however, and they proposed the following cline of 'unacceptability':

> orthography/pronunciation > morphosyntax > lexis/semantics

Spelling and pronunciation are what speakers had squarely in their sights; this was also Curzan's finding (2014: 29) and is also supported by Severin's earlier usage survey, which demonstrated similar results (see Severin 2013).

Australians' preoccupation with the more superficial aspects of speaking and writing reflects the fact that, as predicted by Labov's (1993) 'sociolinguistic monitor', this linguistic knowledge is more socially salient and therefore open to attracting more evaluative attention; by comparison, syntactic knowledge is less observable and largely flies under the radar. Also relevant here is the English education received in schools. As in many countries across the English-speaking world (see Crystal 2006b), the move away from the explicit teaching of linguistic awareness in the latter half of the twentieth century left the general public in Australia with a limited knowledge of the complexities of grammar. Just as Curzan (2014: 73) has described for American English, the Australian school system, especially in the early years, targets punctuation and spelling—those most standardized elements. The use of spelling bees, spelling tests, dictionaries and computer spell-checkers in English education reinforces the notion that variation in spelling is unacceptable, and where it exists, Americans are typically held responsible—students are usually instructed that one of these forms is 'correct' and the other is 'American' (i.e. 'correct' UK *honour* versus 'incorrect' US *honor*). For example, in one email I received (9 May 2008), the person queried the correct spelling of the word meaning 'to send out goods'—"is it *dispatch* or *despatch*?":

> All my googling is suggesting that one is an English term and the other is American. I loathe Americanising of English words and would rather like to be able to write "The Queens English" with confidence.

Although Australia's spelling conventions derive traditionally from the British, the technological presence of America means this is an area of rapidly growing American influence. Another email (10 September 2011) queried *enquiry* versus *inquiry:*

> Is one just American? If so, why do the yanks do that??? Can't they get their own language to mess with?

The prominence of spelling in people's lives has intensified the widespread perception of an American infiltration of the language. Burridge and Peters (2020) document a well-established complaint tradition against American English (AmE) infiltration at various levels of language, and once again by all age groups. As they describe:

> Highly visible lexical incursions such as *trash, math* and *aluminum* are viewed as forming the thin end of a very undesirable wedge that will see the decline of Australian values and way of life. Furthermore, opposition to AmE usage shows no age watershed—all ages voice their "irrits" [feelings of extreme irritation] at AmE influence, with "loss of Australian identity" being a familiar refrain in the millennials' commentary. (Burridge and Peters 2020: 222)

Adding fuel to anti-American sentiments is the fact that many of the Americanisms in the cross hairs of complainants today coincide with people's general linguistic bugbears—they are loathed because they might represent youth slang (*bro, chill out*), irritating redundancies (*gainfully employed, off of*), jarring workplace jargon (*going forward, game changer*), trendy noun conversions to verbs (*to impact, to beverage*) and so on. However, named Americanisms are often not even American English, and misconceptions of this nature have been around since the disapproving media commentary began.[3]

3 As documented by historian Damousi (2010), disparaging commentary around American influence became apparent when American cultural products had well and truly embedded themselves and become a way of life in Australia. It seems to have taken off with the 'talkies' (talking films) of the 1920s.

As mentioned earlier, linguists do a lot of raining on people's parades—busting cherished ideas about how language works. And clearly people who hold these cherished ideas can grow hostile, especially if the issue involves punctuation or spelling. When in 2008 sociolinguist Janet Holmes presented arguments in *The Dominion Post* for dumping the possessive apostrophe, the backlash was vicious. In a piece entitled "Dumbing down of academia reaches a new low", she was described as "someone completely off the planet" (Coddington 2008). This has certainly been my experience whenever I dare to suggest changes to apostrophes or hyphens. Let me quote from "Potatoes and Apostrophes", which appeared in a British web magazine called *The Friday Thing*:

> Burridge is so desperate to duplicate the success of Lynne Truss that she would claim that the letter Q should be replaced with a swastika if she thought it'd pull in a few more readers. She may yet do it. […].

Describing my "attack on the English language" as "shameless self-promotion", the writer even suggested that a new verb be added to the *Oxford English Dictionary*:

> 'to burridge', meaning to disseminate potentially provocative but wholly insincere opinions throughout the media in an effort to attract attention and, ideally, personal wealth.

In Burridge (2010b), I described how the ABC even engaged the services of the Carlton police over two particularly nasty emails (received 13 & 19 July 2008). Here is an extract from the two (errors and punctuation original):

> I hope that you die (pleasantly) before me: so that I can <u>piss</u> on your grave […] I hope, for your sake, that we never meet in person. Words cannot express my opinion of your actions/opinions. If they were in a less tolerant society, I would fear for your well-being.

When I explained the subject matter of these emails to the police officer (the issue was etymological), his response was telling: "What would it be like if you spoke about something that really mattered?"

Forms of language, and the alleged misuse of these forms, have come to stand for values and practices that people are fearful of losing. This perhaps explains why speakers can react so viscerally when they encounter their linguistic bugbears—so often described as getting up their nose, getting under their skin, getting on their nerves or wick, turning their stomach, sticking in their throat, making their hair curl, their flesh creep, their blood run cold. To quote from just some of the emails I have received: “I know our language is always a work in progress but these are the things that get under my skin”; “Everyone around me always says ‘the data is’ and that does something to my neckhairs”; “The pronunciation *haitch* makes me feel like I’m covered in fire ants”.

I have always felt it would be interesting to measure the emotional impact of people’s pet peeves by using a technique like electrodermal monitoring, a kind of polygraph testing. Culturally sensitive expressions, such as swear-words and childhood commands, elicit strong physiological responses because young children pick up the emotive components of the words early in the acquisition process (see Allan and Burridge 2006: 244–247). Many of these linguistic pinpricks would also have been established at a young age (“Don’t say *haitch*!”) and, like other potent expressions learned early in life, would presumably trigger stronger skin conductance responses than neutral stimuli. Truthiness is what you feel in your gut—and, in the case of irritating words, phrases and grammatical constructions, many other parts of the anatomy too. Even without confirmation from a polygraph test, the emotional impact of linguistic bugbears is clear. It is hardly surprising that it is so difficult to desensitize people to their pinpricks and to persuade them to view language in a different way.

4 The Bitter Fruits of Truthiness

> Everyday knowledge about language and speech, or ‘folk linguistics’, incorporates a number of false beliefs that have a negative effect in a range of areas, nowhere more so than in the criminal justice system.
>
> FRASER 2018a: 586

As shown here, people frequently make negative judgments about others for using vocabulary, grammar, accents and punctuation that they regard as ‘bad English’, even castigating these offenders as ‘uneducated’, ‘ignorant’ or ‘stupid’. Individual speakers sometimes justify their concerns about language by appealing to rational explanations, such as the need for intelligibility. To quote from the first email: “You are encouraging what is happening to the English language and are contributing to its demise. You are contributing to those of us over the age of 50 needing an interpreter within the next 10 years.” But, as with any act of censoring, pronouncements on language use by arbiters of linguistic goodness are typically tied to their personal beliefs and preferences. As

Algeo and Pyles (2010) once quipped, ventriloquizing the early nineteenth century novelist, Captain Frederick Marryat: "My speech is pure; thine, wherein it differs from mine, is corrupt" (2010: 11).[4]

This behaviour is very out of place in an era where the basic human right of respect is understood to mean that people can no longer speak of or to others in terms that are considered insulting and demeaning. Yet somehow this expectation does not extend to the way people talk about the language skills of others. Cameron (2012: 12) said it all:

> Linguistic bigotry is among the last publicly expressible prejudices left to members of the western intelligentsia. Intellectuals who would find it unthinkable to sneer at a beggar or someone in a wheelchair will sneer without compunction at linguistic "solecisms."

It is no longer socially acceptable to criticize fellow human beings based on their race or their class, and yet it remains fully acceptable to criticize them on the basis of their language use, something so integral to their identity. For example, speakers would not disparage someone for being Chinese Australian, but cheerfully pass judgement on the features of Chinese English in their speech. In 'classless Australia', 'wrong' uses of grammar are frequently described as 'bogan' (i.e. vulgar).[5] Linguistic prejudices appear to be accepted without challenge; despite the profession of egalitarianism, conscious and unconscious discrimination against speakers of nonstandard dialects and low-status accents is rife. Consider the run-away success of the Instagram account Celeb Spellcheck (@celeb_spellcheck), an anonymous page that publicly mocked Australian influencers for their bad spelling and grammar (e.g. "I feel I am becoming inpatient I actually sit back and question it"). "Lighthearted fun", claimed the creators of the page, and the 142,000 followers appeared to agree (the account was closed April 2021 – it seems its success made it no longer sustainable).

Real problems arise when people's misconceptions about language use go on to inform decisions that shape the life chances of others, affecting their employment opportunities, their social mobility, their personal relationships. Sociolinguists have been exposing flaws in the methods immigration authorities use to decide whether or not those seeking asylum are genuine refugees (see Eades 2010; McNamara and Schüpbach 2019); the battle here is to ensure

4 I am grateful to Constantine Coutis for drawing my attention to the problems of this 'quote' (it was never actually uttered by Marryat).

5 As described by lexicographer Bruce Moore (2019), "the major criteria for boganhood are: a lack of culture and sophistication; boorishness and uncouthness and vulgarity."

that the findings of linguistic science are put above the dangerously inaccurate folk linguistic views that so often inform these methods. Much has been written about the misunderstandings surrounding the linguistic education of children, especially those who speak nonstandard dialects, and the repercussions of these misunderstandings go well beyond poor school performance (see Siegel 2012).

The legal setting bears particularly dreadful and bitter fruits of ignorance—as forensic linguists have shown, wrong-headed thinking about language can even end up putting the wrong person in jail. Let me report on one experience I have had giving expert evidence. I was asked by the legal firm Clayton Utz to "opine on matters concerning metaphoric statements"—for the purpose of defending their client in the case The Medical Board of Australia v Dr David Roberts. Here is the case in a nutshell.

In a hastily written note (based on a dictaphone recording), a pediatrician suggested to the parents of twin boys (diagnosed with Attention Deficit Hyperactivity Disorder) that they should beat them to within an inch of their lives ("… I recommend to your husband that he beat (physically) each and any of you our sons [sic] who swear and offend his wife (that is Mother) … to within an inch of his life").

The doctor didn't deny writing the note but did deny any intention on his part for the words to be taken literally. He argued that he was speaking metaphorically to motivate the father to "take an active role in defending his wife's honour", and he hoped that the "humour" would help to ease the tensions. My job in all this was to provide a linguistic account of the expression *beat to within an inch of his life* and so in my report (of around five pages) I focused on two kindred figures of speech—metaphor and hyperbole.

I showed how the phrase *beat to within an inch of his life* was one of thousands of English speech formulas structured by a metaphor, and how hearers/readers are constantly required to interpret figurative language of this nature. I gave the example of the ARGUMENT IS WAR metaphor—the fact that in English the ordinary way of talking about 'having an argument' is to use words such as *shoot down, strategy, wipe out*, etc. The expressions draw on a metaphor that speakers of English are barely aware of. I also outlined Stephen Ullmann's (1964) "law of diminishing returns"—metaphors lose their vitality and become hackneyed. For centuries *within an inch of one's life* (or *within an inch of one's skin*) has appeared in fixed expressions like to *thrash/beat/flog someone within an inch of his/her life*. Hundreds of years of use have now reduced this once expressive image to a 'lexical zombie' (as clichés are sometimes described), and I gave actual examples from the Oxford English Dictionary such as: "The grammar class were parsed and analyzed within an inch of their lives" (1909). I also wrote about hyperbole. Our human brains respond to extremes, and our social lives abound with ways of standing out. Language is no different. Phrases like *within an inch of his life* spice up what is being said or written and make the language more vivid and memorable—and they have been doing so for centuries.

Of course, as I emphasized, successful use of metaphor, hyperbole, irony, sarcasm or any other creative language relies on people co-operating with each other, if communication is going to work—whether it involves everyday conversations or messages between doctors and patients. However, given the circumstances in which the doctor uttered these words, given the long relationship between the players (Dr Roberts had been their consultant pediatrician for some years), and given the long career path of the expression he used, it is hard to imagine how this phrase could have been interpreted literally.

I was not prepared for what followed when I was examined about the report. What I imagined to be a 'commonsense' understanding of language and how it works didn't seem to be in the room at all that day. Particularly striking was the lawyer's dependence on dictionary entries, as if they were things set in stone. It seemed that Macquarie Dictionary's definitions for the idiom and its parts were going to determine the fate of this doctor. I had read about what Eades (2010: 245) dubs an "ideology of literalism" (whereby judicial officers interpret utterances literally and ignore their more probable pragmatic meanings; e.g. *Could I have a lawyer?* as a request for counsel might be taken as a theoretical query about the availability of counsel). But I was still taken aback by the lawyer's literal approach to meaning and his failure to take account of contextual aspects of the interaction—the fact that so much of our language goes beyond the literal meaning and is never subject to precise definition. After all, I'd read examples of spectacular courtroom doublespeak between lawyers, who seem at times quite willing to take account of contextual (pragmatic) aspects of interaction and "read between the lines".

I had concluded my report with the statement that "no reasonable person would have interpreted the metaphor (*to be beaten to within an inch of your life*) literally". The State Administrative Tribunal accepted that statement but went on to conclude that the doctor's note "could nonetheless be understood as a recommendation to the parents that they must discipline their children by way of corporal punishment."[6] Dr Roberts did not appeal.

6 The full decision is available at the Australasian Legal Information Institute: http://www.austlii.edu.au/cgi-bin/sinodisp/au/cases/wa/WASAT/2014/76.html?stem=0&synonyms=0&query=roberts.

> Around the world and in our own backyard, criminal justice institutions are blighted by cases of inappropriate decisions made by legal professionals who lack an understanding of how language works.
>
> GEORGINA HEYDON 2017

As described earlier, there is no straightforward unveiling of the truth about language here. Former federal court judge Peter Gray (2010) describes the fundamental ignorance on the part of most lawyers that there even exists a profession concerned with the study of language, and he goes on to portray the general legal distrust of those providing linguistic evidence (evidence that might well be seen as not involving any real expertise but "something a lawyer could just as easily command"; 2012: 597). As forensic linguist Georgina Heydon (2016) recounts, her evidence is routinely misrepresented or discounted, and on the basis of sometimes gross misconceptions about language and speech. For example, in an authorship attribution case, the judge declared that "any two educated people, writing a letter with essentially the same intention, would use punctuation in exactly the same way—that is, the correct way"; the judge concluded that how educated people express themselves really doesn't differ greatly, and he described the structured syntactic analysis in Heydon's report as "junk science of the very worst kind." It is hard to imagine the professional opinions of medical practitioners, physicists and engineers being challenged to the same degree. In his account of why linguistic evidence is rejected in court, Roger Shuy put the problem this way.

> Our analyses, reports, and testimony have to teach a great deal before we can even begin our analyses. Then the paradox is that if we make our analyses clear and simple, it can look like anyone can do it and that our involvement at trial isn't really necessary.
>
> SHUY 2007: 9

However, it gets even worse, as forensic phonetician Helen Fraser has described. Deemed common knowledge, forms of linguistic evidence are frequently not even subject to expert evaluation but are handled as "a matter for the jury", or worse are given to non-linguists professing expertise (see Fraser 2014, 2018a for examples). Fraser has exposed major problems relating to the translation of material from languages other than English, transcription of indistinct English, attribution of utterances to speakers, and 'enhancement' of poor-quality audio (Fraser 2018b).

5 The Dangerous Zone of the Unknown Knowns

> There are known knowns. There are things we know we know. We also know there are known unknowns. That is to say, we know there are some things we do not know. But there are also unknown unknowns, the ones we don't know we don't know.
>
> US Secretary of Defense DONALD RUMSFELD, 12 February 2002

Those working in the interdisciplinary field called 'Ignorance Studies' point out that certain areas of not-knowing can present considerable difficulties for the 'would-be removalists' (those who 'unmake ignorance'). As Smithson (2015: 387) writes, "[p]eople have vested interests in unknowns, and reasons for not knowing, not wanting to know, and/or not wanting others to know". And while sometimes it can be matter of removing the blinders and opening people's eyes to the truth (for example, that smoking really can cause lung cancer), "[i]t is very difficult to unmake ignorance that is neither accessible to conscious inspection nor desired to undo" (2015: 396). As described earlier, language issues can be about preserving power and privilege, traditional values and stereotypes and these make for powerful barriers to any 'unmaking'.[7]

Cognitive psychologists Cook and Lewandowsky research decision-making processes, focusing on why people embrace beliefs that conflict with scientific evidence. In their 2011 handbook on debunking misinformation, they point out that not only do facts often fail to dissuade a person from their pre-existing beliefs, they might even make things worse by inadvertently reinforcing the very myths that experts are seeking to overturn (something they dub "backfire effects").

> Several cognitive processes can cause people to unconsciously process information in a biased way. For those who are strongly fixed in their views, being confronted with counter-arguments can cause their views to be strengthened.
>
> 2011: 4

As they explain, the most potent backfire effects occur when the evidence threatens someone's sense of cultural identity and social position (what Smithson dubs "social-stereotype ignorance"; 2015, p. 395). So, if linguistic facts alone don't do the trick, how do we go about giving these facts a fighting chance?

7 See also Proctor and Schiebinger (2012) on the unmaking of ignorance.

It is clear that linguistic findings must inform any debate involving language, but if linguists are to be successful in removing the blinders and in changing the 'common knowledge' that people have about language, then they need to properly understand and take seriously what assumptions speakers hold and what concerns they have about the well-being of their language. Only then are they in a position of 'framing' (or tailoring) the message in a way that makes it more palatable and less threatening to the worldviews of individuals. Linguists must be careful when they start raining on people's parades.

Descriptivism has of course been a cornerstone of modern linguistics since the nineteenth century—a staple of every introductory linguistic course, students are taught to avoid anything that might smack of subjectivity and opinion. This oversimplified prescription-description binary has done little to better educate an underinformed or even misinformed public. Description and prescription have been pitted squarely against each other—in one camp are the linguistic experts who refuse to address the concerns of language users, and in the other camp are the language users who show no interest in listening to linguistic experts. Clearly, both camps view language very differently. For the wider community, language is more like an art form: something to be cherished, revered and preserved at all costs. For linguists, it is a natural, though of course social, phenomenon, something that evolves and adapts and can be studied objectively. But this objectivity also requires considering the subjective stance of the wider community—studying the way people like to intervene in language is crucial to a proper understanding of what human language is.

In an effort to embrace the scientific approach and to eschew anything that smacks of prescription, linguists have overlooked the fact that the prescriptive-descriptive divide is patently fuzzy. Many linguistic activities have a normative purpose (and not just the usual suspects like language policy and language planning), and the idea that language descriptions can be objective and value-neutral is a convenient fiction. By their nature, these descriptions are normative because they must match the consensus norms of contemporary speakers (see Milroy 1992). Joseph (2020), examining prescriptivism through the lens of the 'is-ought distinction' of Scottish philosopher David Hume, illustrates how 'is' statements about language (i.e. 'what is'—the observation of norms carried out by linguists) always shade into 'ought' statements (i.e. 'what ought to be'—the enforcement of norms carried out by prescriptivists). By removing the polarizing prescription-description distinction, linguists will be living up to their descriptive ideals. They will also be in a better position to engage more fruitfully with the wider community.[8]

8 See papers in Chapman and Rawlins (2020), and also Cameron (2012) and Curzan (2014) which make this same point.

Better educating the general public on language is also important. Modern pedagogy in the English language classroom has left the general public with a limited knowledge of complex aspects of the English language (in particular grammar). When educators moved away from explicit awareness of language, no attention was paid to grammar or to the forms of language—children were provided with a rich linguistic environment and were just expected to 'pick up' grammatical knowledge through use. And as a consequence, many English speakers today have been left without much of a clue about how their language works. (Ironically those who have studied other languages have slightly more of a clue.) Many people probably know more about stem cell research than they do about basic parts of speech (or, as Ronald Wardhaugh once complained, "[m]any educated people know more about space and time, uncertainty, and quantum effects than they do about nouns and verbs"; Wardhaugh 1999: 182). But there are signs that things are changing.

'Language awareness' (or 'knowledge about language') has gradually been creeping back into the school curriculum with the reappearance of language strands in English curricula (e.g. The Australian Curriculum: English Foundation to Year 10), and even the introduction of school level courses in linguistics (VCE English Language in Victoria; O-level English language in the UK); there are also success stories such as the UK Linguistics Olympiad (UKLO) and the Australian Computational and Linguistics Olympiad (OZCLO).[9] And the time is right. The profession of egalitarianism mentioned earlier has seen the introduction of "a new educational paradigm of language study", as Crystal (2006b: 408) describes it—a fresh pragmatic approach that respects variation and change. Crystal even predicts that respect for the nonstandard will spell an end to purism, a new linguistic tolerance ("eternal vigilance" being replaced by "eternal tolerance"; 2006b: 410). From what I have described here, however, eternal tolerance still doesn't seem much in evidence, even among younger speakers who have grown up with variation and change as facts of linguistic life. But it might simply be that, as Crystal has suggested, new attitudes and practices take time.[10]

Let me finish here on a positive note by mentioning some linguists whose work has been making a very real impact. Insights from Diana Eades' socio-

9 Richard (Dick) Hudson has done much to promote linguistics in language education; see details on his website https://dickhudson.com/education/.

10 Crystal (2006a: 197) even compares people's relationship with the standard language to the traumatic bonding known as Stockholm syndrome—harassed and intimated by their captor (the standard) for so long, they express positive feelings to the point of defending it. And so prescription endures!

linguistic research are now influencing courtroom processes and helping to achieve fairer judicial outcomes, for example, in the evaluation of witness accounts and the communication of rights, such as the right to silence. The speech science research of Helen Fraser has led to collaboration between the law, law enforcement and linguistics, resulting in a successful call for the reform of legal practices around the use of covert recordings as evidence in Australian criminal trials. Interdisciplinary research by Ingrid Piller is being used to inform policy and public discourse in such contexts as migration, citizenship testing, second language learning and public health communication. Joseph Lo Bianco's research on the capacity for language to resolve conflicts has facilitated dialogue between opposing factions and created new language and education policies in countries that have been embroiled in decades of conflict (e.g. Thailand and Myanmar). Notable also is the work of Sasha Aikhenvald on health and well-being, most recently addressing the language challenges around the Covid-19 pandemic.[11] These are examples of important linguistic research that have resulted in demonstrable improvements to the lives of people.

At the start of this section, I quoted Donald Rumsfeld's famous piece of wisdom distinguishing various kinds of knowing and not knowing—the known knowns, known unknowns and unknown unknowns. What this wisdom doesn't cover, however, are the things that fall within the really dangerous domain of ignorance, namely the unknown knowns, those things we think we know but we don't. The examples I've been discussing here show that even highly educated people like university lecturers and judges continue to accept false beliefs as reliable information about how language and speech works, and this can have tragic consequences. People's lives are affected by language in so many ways, and there is still plenty of work to be done to show the community at large that "the pointy-headed abstruse strudel of academic linguistics" does have practical and important applications beyond that mythical "ivory tower". I hope that what I have presented here is a further step towards a better and more constructive public discourse on linguistic issues, where language users, most especially educators, politicians, lawyers and those in the media, put well-researched principles of linguistics above what can be dangerously inaccurate

11 See for example, Eades (2018); Fraser's account of the Research Hub for Language in Forensic Evidence https://arts.unimelb.edu.au/school-of-languages-and-linguistics/our-research/research-centres-hubs-and-units/research-hub-for-language-in-forensic-evidence; Piller's sociolinguistics portal *Language on the Move* https://www.languageonthemove.com/; Lo Bianco (2019); and for a snapshot of Aikhenvald's work, see *The languages of well-being: A view from the Pacific* https://youtu.be/7cONMs0s54M.

views about how people speak, or should speak. Let us finally move language issues out of the "proud halls of truthiness" (Colbert's phrase).

References

Aikhenvald, Alexandra (2020). The languages of well-being: A view from the Pacific. Symposium on Interdisciplinary perspectives on language, health and well-being. https://drive.google.com/drive/folders/14SZCOOvuesH_1UHNzLabHNXV8mgoprnf?usp=sharing.

Algeo, John and Thomas Pyles (2010). *The Origins and Development of the English Language*. Wadsworth: Cengage Learning.

Allan, Keith and Kate Burridge (2006). *Forbidden Words: Taboo and the Censoring of Language*. Cambridge: Cambridge University Press.

Burridge, Kate (2010a). Gift of the Gob: Morsels of English Language History. Sydney: Harper Collins.

Burridge, Kate (2010b). Linguistic Cleanliness is Next to Godliness: Taboo and purism. *English Today: The international review of the English language* 26 (2): 3–13. Cambridge: Cambridge University Press.

Burridge, Kate and Margaret Florey (2002). 'Yeah-no He's a Good Kid': A Discourse Analysis of Yeah-no in Australian English. *Australian Journal of Linguistics* 22 (2): 149–171.

Burridge, Kate and Pam Peters (2020). English in Australia: Extraterritorial influences. In Sarah Buschfeld and Alexander Kautzsch (eds), *Modelling World Englishes: A Joint Approach to Postcolonial and Non-Postcolonial Englishes*, 202–227.

Burridge, Kate and Cammie McBride (2018). *Haitch or aitch? How a humble letter was held hostage by historical haughtiness* https://theconversation.com/haitch-or-aitch-how-a-humble-letter-was-held-hostage-by-historical-haughtiness-97184 (accessed 24 February 2021).

Butler, Sue (2014). *The Aitch Factor*. Australia: MacMillan.

Cameron, Deborah (2012). *Verbal Hygiene*. London: Routledge.

Campbell, David (2004). Too much speech-junk? Yeah- no! Opinion piece, *The Age*, 19 June 2004. https://www.theage.com.au/national/too-much-speech-junk-yeah-no-20040619-gdy2ga.html (accessed 24 February 2021).

Chapman, Don and Jacob D. Rawlins (2020). *Language Prescription: Values, Ideologies and Identity*. London: Multilingual Matters.

Chin, Stephen B. and David B. Pisoni (1997). *Alcohol and Speech*. San Diego: Academic Press.

Coddington, Deborah (2008). Dumbing down of academia reaches a new low. *NZ Herald*. https://www.nzherald.co.nz/nz/education/ideborah-coddingtoni-dumbing

-down-of-academia-reaches-a-new-low/OYUYV2S6ZUFP5INHA3VQ4OAXFQ/ (accessed 24 February 2021).

Cook, John and Stephan Lewandowsky (2011). *The Debunking Handbook*. St. Lucia, Australia: University of Queensland. http://sks.to/debunk (accessed 24 February 2021).

Crystal, David (2015). On a one-word reaction to reports about drunken Aussie accents. *DCBlog*. 30 October 2015. http://david-crystal.blogspot.com/2015/10/on-one-word-reaction-to-reports-about.html (accessed 24 February 2021).

Crystal, David (2006a). The Fight for English: How the Language Pundits, Ate, Shot and Left. Oxford: Oxford University Press.

Crystal, David (2006b). Into the Twenty-First Century. In Lynda Mugglestone (ed.), *The Oxford History of English*, 394–414. Oxford: Oxford University Press.

Curzan, Anne (2014). *Fixing English: Prescriptivism and Language History*. Cambridge: Cambridge University Press.

Cutler, Anne and Caroline G. Henton (2004). There's many a slip 'twixt the cup and the lip. *On speech and language: Studies in honor of Sieg Nooteboom*, 37–45. Utrecht, The Netherlands: Netherlands Graduate School of Linguistics.

Damousi, Joy (2010). *Colonial voices: A cultural history of English in Australia*. Cambridge: Cambridge University Press.

Eades, Diana (2010). *Sociolinguistics and the Legal Process*. Bristol: Multilingual Matters.

Eades, Diana (2018). Communicating the right to silence to Aboriginal suspects: Lessons from Western Australia v Gibson. *Journal of Judicial Administration* 28: 4–21.

Enfield, Nick J. (2018). The 'aitch' or 'haitch' debate has a dark side. *Sydney Morning Herald* opinion piece; https://www.smh.com.au/national/the-aitch-or-haitch-debate-has-a-dark-side-20180519-p4zgco.html (accessed 26 February 2021).

Flood, Philip (2008). *Steady Hands Needed: Reflections on the Role of the Secretary of Foreign Affairs and Trade in Australia 1979–1999*. Canberra: ANU Press. http://press-files.anu.edu.au/downloads/press/p46371/pdf/flood.pdf (accessed 24 February 2021).

Fraser, Helen (2014). Transcription of indistinct forensic recordings. *Language and Law/Linguagem E Direito* 1 (2): 5–21.

Fraser, Helen (2018a). Forensic Transcription: How Confident False Beliefs about Language and Speech Threaten the Right to a Fair Trial in Australia. *Australian Journal of Linguistics* 38 (4): 586–606.

Fraser, Helen (2018b). Thirty Years Is Long Enough: It Is Time to Create a Process That Ensures Covert Recordings Used as Evidence in Court Are Interpreted Reliably. *Journal of Judicial Administration* 27 (3): 95–104.

Frenkel, Dean 2015. Australia, we need to talk about the way we speak. Opinion piece, *The Age*, 25 October 2015. https://www.theage.com.au/opinion/the-fourth-r-missing-from-australian-education-20151025-gkhv8k.html (accessed 24 February 2021).

Gray, Peter, R.A. (2010). The future for forensic linguists in the courtroom: Cross-cultural communication. In Alison Johnson and Malcolm Coulthard, *The Routledge Handbook of Forensic Linguistics*, 591–601. London: Taylor and Francis.

Heigl, Barbara (2011). [s] Under the Influence of Alcohol. In *Working Papers in Linguistics* 8. https://www.gmu.edu/org/lingclub/WP/wp.php?Vol=8 (accessed 24 February 2021).

Heydon, Georgina (2016). How to ensure language and speech evidence is used appropriately in court. Paper presented to the Annual Conference of the Australian Linguistics Society.

Heydon, Georgina. (2017). *Ignorance is not Bliss: A Global Frictions Lecture*. Royal Melbourne Institute of Technology, 10 December 2017 (accessed 27 February 2018). https://www.youtube.com/watch?v=r7JrH9aSkXU (accessed 26 February 2021).

Hickey, Raymond (2004). The development and diffusion of Irish English. In Raymond Hickey (ed.), *Legacies of colonial English: studies in transported dialects*, 82–120. Cambridge: Cambridge University Press.

Hirst, John (2004). The Distinctiveness of Australian Democracy. *Papers on Parliament No. 42*. The Senate Occasional Lecture Series, Canberra. https://www.aph.gov.au/sitecore/content/Home/About_Parliament/Senate/Powers_practice_n_procedures/pops/pop42/hirst (accessed 26 February 2021).

Holmes, Janet (2008). That redundant punctuational paraphernalia. *The Dominion Post*, 4 April 2008. https://www.pressreader.com/new-zealand/the-dominion-post/20080604/282084862551183 (accessed 24 February 2021).

Hudson, Richard (2004). Why education needs linguistics (and vice versa). *Journal of Linguistics* 40: 105–130.

Joseph, John E. (2020). Is/ought: Hume's guillotine, linguistics and standards of language. In Don Chapman and Jacob D. Rawlins (eds.), 15–31.

Labov, William (1993). The unobservability of structure and its linguistic consequences. Paper presented at *NWAV 22*, University of Ottawa.

Lester, Leland and Royal Skousen (1974). The Phonology of Drunkeness. Papers from the parasession on natural phonology, 233–239.

Lingyun, Lai (2016). How do sticklers react to linguistic findings? *Bridging the Unbridgeable Blogpost* https://bridgingtheunbridgeable.com/2016/06/14/how-do-sticklers-react-to-linguistic-findings/ (accessed 24 February 2021).

Lo Bianco, Joseph (2019). Uncompromising Talk, Linguistic Grievance, and Language Policy: Thailand's Deep South Conflict Zone. In Michael Kelly, Hilary Footitt and Myriam Salama-Carr (eds.), *The Palgrave Handbook of Languages and Conflict*, 295–330. Springer International Publishing.

Lukač, Morana (2018). Grassroots prescriptivism: An analysis of individual speakers' efforts at maintaining the standard language ideology. *English Today* (Special issue: Prescriptivism) 34 (4): 5–12.

McEnroe, Colin (1992). *Words*. 13 January 1992 https://www.washingtonpost.com/archive/lifestyle/1992/01/13/words/a582015f-1e5b-4b2b-b31d-e150767993db/ (accessed 24 February 2021]).

McNamara, Tim and Doris Schüpbach (2019). Quality assurance in LADO: Issues of validity. In P.L. Patrick, M.S. Schmid and K. Zwaan (eds.), *Language Analysis for the Determination of Origin: Current Perspectives and New Directions*, 253–271. Cham, Switzerland: Springer.

Milroy, James (1992). Linguistic Variation and Change: On the Historical Sociolinguistics of English. Oxford, UK & Cambridge, USA: Blackwell.

Moore, Bruce (2019). A new twist in the elusive quest for the origins of the word 'bogan' leads to Melbourne's Xavier College. *The Conversation* https://theconversation.com/a-new-twist-in-the-elusive-quest-for-the-origins-of-the-word-bogan-leads-to-melbournes-xavier-college-113755 (accessed 28 February 2021).

Musgrave, Simon and Kate Burridge (to appear). Irish Influence on Australian English. In Raymond Hickey (ed.), *Oxford Handbook of Irish English*. Oxford: Oxford University Press.

Piller, Ingrid, Jie Zhang and Jia Li (2020). Linguistic diversity in a time of crisis: Language challenges of the COVID-19 pandemic. *Multilingua* 39 (5). https://www.degruyter.com/view/journals/mult/39/5/mult.39.issue-5.xml (accessed 24 February 2021).

Proctor, Robert N. and Londa Schiebinger (eds.) (2012). *Agnotology: The making and unmaking of ignorance*. Stanford: Stanford University Press.

Severin, Alyssa A. (2013). Vigilance or Tolerance? Contemporary attitudes to English language usage. Honours thesis, Monash University.

Severin, Alyssa A. and Kate Burridge (2020). What do "little Aussie sticklers" value most. In Don Chapman and Jacob D. Rawlins (eds.), 194–211.

Shaw, Julia (2016). The real reason that we don't trust experts anymore. *The Independent*, 8 July 2016. http://www.independent.co.uk/voices/the-real-reason-that-we-don-t-trust-experts-a7126536.html (accessed 24 February 2021).

Sheppard, Jill, Ian McAllister and Toni Makkai (2018). *Australian Values Study, 2018*. Social Research Centre and Australian National University. https://www.srcentre.com.au/user/pages/07.ausvalues/Australian%20Values%20Survey%202018%20-%20web.pdf (accessed 26 February 2021).

Shuy, Roger W. (2007). A Dozen Reasons Why Linguistic Expertise is Rejected in Court. http://www.rogershuy.com/pdf/A%20dozen%20reasons%20why%20ling.op.pdf (accessed 24 February 2021).

Siegel, Jeff (2012). *Second Dialect Acquisition*. Cambridge: Cambridge University Press.

Smithson, Michael (2015). Afterword: Ignorance studies: Interdisciplinary, multidisciplinary, and transdisciplinary. In Matthias Gross and Linsey McGoey (eds.), *Routledge International Handbook of Ignorance Studies*, 385–399. London: Routledge.

Stockwell, Robert and Donka Minkova (2001). *English Words: History and Structure*. Cambridge: Cambridge University Press.

Truss, Lynne (2004). *Eats, Shoots and Leaves: The Zero Tolerance Approach to Punctuation.* Harmondsworth: Penguin.
Ullmann, Stephen (1964). *Semantics: An Introduction to the Science of Meaning.* Oxford: Blackwell.
Wardhaugh, Ronald (1999). *Proper English: Myths and Misunderstandings about Language.* Malden, MA: Blackwell.

CHAPTER 3

At the Heart of the Murui

Katarzyna I. Wojtylak

I wholeheartedly thank the Murui for making me see the world differently.

And Alexandra Aikhenvald,
for believing in me.

1 Preamble

Murui (also referred to as Bue) is a Witotoan language spoken by some 2,000 people in southern Colombia and northern Peru (Wojtylak 2020a). Together with other varieties (Mɨnɨka, Mɨka, and Nɨpode), it forms a dialect continuum called Murui-Muina (see among others Agga Calderón 'Kaziya Buinaima', Wojtylak and Echeverri 2019; Echeverri, Fagua Rincón and Wojtylak forthcoming).

The Murui people traditionally inhabited the northwestern region of the Amazon Basin between the middle sections of the Caquetá and Putumayo Rivers in Colombia and Peru. Today, some pockets of the Murui are also located outside of their ancestral territories (e.g., along the banks of the Ampiyacú and Napo Rivers in Peru; numerous families also reside in cities, such as Bogotá and La Chorrera in Colombia, and Iquitos in Peru). For their survival in the Caquetá-Putumayo region, the Murui-Muina depend on gathering, fishing, hunting, and slash-and-burn agriculture (Echeverri 1997: 30).

The belief system of the Murui of today is characterized by religious syncretism, whereby various elements of Catholicism are incorporated into the originally animistic worldview. Numerous taboos still exist, including those concerning one's behavior, such as talking to spirits at night and hunting avoidance speech registers (Wojtylak 2015, 2019). Traditionally, name taboos (those against speaking real names of the others) were commonly practised. A person's name was identified as a part of their soul. Following Whiffen (1915: 153),

© KATARZYNA I. WOJTYLAK, 2022 | DOI:10.1163/9789004510395_004

should one person come into possession of the name of another, they would be able to gravely harm them. Therefore, real names were kept secret, and their substitutes, such as kin terms or indirect forms, were employed in ordinary life.

This paper analyses how the expression of 'heart', the *komekɨ*, is understood in Murui. After a brief typological profile of the language (§ 2), I discuss the real meaning behind *komekɨ* (§ 3). In § 4, I offer concluding remarks.

2 The Essence of What is Murui

Murui has a relatively simple system of six vowels and sixteen consonants. The consonantal phonemes include six stops: /p/ (orthographically represented as p), /b/ (b), /t/ (t), /d/ (d), /k/ (k), and /g/ (g); four fricatives: /ɸ/ (f), /β/ (v), /h/ (j), and /θ/ (z); two affricates: /c/ (ch) and /ɟ/ (y); three nasals: /n/ (n), /ɲ/ (ñ), and /m/ (m); and a flap /ɾ/ (r). The vowel inventory is small and is similar to that of other languages of northwest Amazonia (Aikhenvald 2012: 99–127). All the vowels—/i/ (i), /ɛ/ (e), /a/ (a), /ɔ/ (o), /u/ (u), and /ɨ/ (ɨ)—have long counterparts that are restricted to word-initial syllables only.

In terms of its structure, Murui is nominative-accusative, and mainly head marking. Words are polymorphemic and each morpheme corresponds to a single lexical meaning; the language has only suffixes (unlike other Witotoan languages, such as Ocaina and Nonuya; see Echeverri, Fagua Rincón and Wojtylak forthcoming). Grammatical relations are expressed through cross-referencing on the verb (with one cross-referencing position, the subject S/A) and a system of case marking. The case marker goes on to the last constituent of an NP. The typical clause structure is predicate final (SV/AOV). An illustrative example of cross-referencing and case marking is given in (1):

(1) [*kaɨ*$_{R}$ *kaɨma-tai-ya-kɨnuaɨ*$_{D}$]$_{NP:O}$ *oo-mo*$_{O:ADDRESSEE}$
1PL happy-BECOME E.NMLZ-CLF:NEWS.PL 2SG-LOC
yo-i-aka-dɨ-kaɨ$_{PRED}$
tell-EMPH-DES-LK-1PL
'We want to tell you our stories of joy.'

Murui has three open word classes: nouns, verbs, and adjectives, as well as ten closed word classes: adverbs, quantifiers/intensifiers, pronouns, demonstratives, interrogative words, number words, connectives, adpositions, and interjections. There is also a small closed class of adjectives containing a handful of forms (e.g., Dixon 1982), including *aiyo-* 'big' and *komo-* 'new'. Almost all the members of open and closed word classes can take predicative marking when they function as heads of intransitive predicates.[1] This is shown in (2), where the question word *buu* heads an intransitive predicate (cf., the same predicate marking—the 'linker' (glossed as LK) followed by person marking—in the transitive verb *yoiakadikai* 'we want to tell' in (1) above).

(2) *buu-di-omiko?*$_{PRED}$
who-LK-2DU.M
'Who are you (two males)?'

While the Murui verb has an extensive array of suffixes (terminative, reiterative, durative, high intensity, semelfactive, remote habitual, customary, general habitual, rapid action, body movement, reported, and two epistemic modality markers: certainty and uncertainty), the Murui noun is 'less' complex in terms of its structure. Nouns allow up to three suffix positions that follow the root:

- classifiers (up to three classifier positions),
- number (collective, kinship plural, plural; singular is generally unmarked),
- case (topical subject S/A, topical non-S/A subject, dative/locative, ablative, instrumental, translative, privative).

The three structural positions can be filled simultaneously, and are marked only once per clause. An example of a noun with all positions filled is given in (3) (classifiers are in small caps, number markers are in italics, and case is shown in bold).

(3)

*ono-BE-KUIRO-*ai-***na***	*kue-mo*$_{O:RECIPIENT}$	*ine!*$_{PRED}$
hand-CLF:LEAF-CLF:PEEL-PL-N.S/A.TOP	1SG-LOC	give.IMP

'Give me the hands!'

Murui has two types of nouns, bound and free. While bound nouns are obligatorily followed by classifiers, free nouns can either occur on their own or be followed by classifiers to further specify the semantics of a noun. 'Hands' in (3) above is an example of a bound noun: the noun root *ono-* 'hand' obligatorily occurs with the classifiers *-be* 'plain and thin objects' and *-kuiro* 'peel, skin, rind'. Note that in other contexts, *ono-* can also occur with other classifiers; this results in different readings, e.g., *ono-kobe* (with classifier *-kobe* 'small, round, leaf-like') is understood as '(hand's) nail' (Wojtylak 2016: 399).

1 The Murui predicative marking consists of the 'linker' (LK) followed by person marking (Wojtylak 2020a: 97–98).

Murui classifiers have a singularizing function (i.e., with non-human referents number marking is often omitted in discourse). The system consists of over 120 bound morphemes. Their semantics include feminine/masculine, as well as size, form, interioricity, and quantification (Wojtylak 2020a: 160–195). The classifiers occur in various morphosyntactic environments (this is a so-called 'multiple classifier system', in accordance with Aikhenvald 2000: 204–240). In addition to nouns, we find classifiers on closed word classes (i.e., demonstratives, pronouns, quantifiers, and interrogative and number words) as well as on verbs and adjectives in nominalizing functions (Wojtylak 2018). For instance, the question word *buu* in (2) above can be followed by a general classifier *-e*; that is, the word *bue* (which is also an alternative name for the Murui language) means 'what'. For more details on Murui grammar, see Wojtylak (2020a) and references therein. I now turn to discussing what lies at the heart of this paper—the Murui *komekɨ*.

3 The Murui Heart

In all Murui-Muina varieties, the word *komekɨ* simply means 'heart'. But how simple is it really? *Komekɨ* is derived from the nominal root *kome* for 'person', as illustrated in (4). In its plural form, *kominɨ* means 'human, indigenous people' (as opposed to *riaɨ* 'cannibals, flesh eaters; white man; the Carijona people')[2], as in (5).[3]

(4)	*kome*$_{S}$	*jai*	*nai-e*$_{O}$	*du-t-e*$_{PRED}$
	person	already	ANA.SP-CLF:G	chew.coca-LK-3

'One (lit. person) already chews that [the coca].'

(5)	*Elger*	*mai*	[*kaɨ*	*kominɨ*]$_{NP:O}$	*maijɨ-ta!*$_{PRED}$
	Elger	LET	1PL	people.CLF:DR.GR	work-CAUS

'Elger, let's make our people work!'

2 The Carijona are the traditional enemies of the Witotoan groups (Wojtylak 2020a: 17).

3 *Kominɨ* has an unusual archaic plural form (i.e., it is not the expected **kome-ni*). It is derived by animate classifier *-nɨ* 'human group' that occurs on nouns and the number word 'one', e.g., *Gɨdonɨ* 'the *Gɨdonɨ* clan', *Nogonɨ* 'the *Nogonɨ* clan', *kominɨ Murui* 'the Murui people', *danɨ* 'alone (as a group)' (Wojtylak 2020a: 179). The noun *kominɨ* cannot be possessed by individuals (that is, *'my people'). *Kominɨ* becomes 'possessible' when it has plural referents and is expressed in relation to a group, i.e., *kaɨ kominɨ* 'our (Murui-Muina) people', (*kaɨ*) *kominɨ uai* '(our Murui-Muina) language' (Wojtylak 2021: 223–227).

To derive *komekɨ*, *kome* 'person' takes the classifier *-kɨ*.[4] There are three types of homophonous classifiers in Murui:

1. *-kɨ* (CLF:CLUSTER) denotes objects with 'cluster-like' semantics, e.g., *onokɨ* 'hand (with all fingers, cluster-like shaped)', *jiyakɨ* 'base (of plant, spreading in cluster-like in form)', *urukɨ* 'children (stemming from one source)', *ruakɨ* 'set of ritual songs (cf. nominalized verb *rua* 'singing')' (Wojtylak 2020a: 165).
2. *-kɨ* (CLF:ROUND) is used for 'round, ovalish shape of smaller-sized objects (usually fruits)', e.g., *jagaikɨ* 'fruit of *jagairai* plant'; *jimekɨ* 'fruit of jimena peach palm' (Wojtylak 2020a: 166).
3. *-kɨ* (CLF:ESSENCE) refers to the 'essence, core' of nominal referents whose meanings are abstract, e.g., *mamekɨ* 'name' (cf. verbal root *mame-* 'to name'; see the naming taboo discussed in § 1), *maɨrikɨ* 'strength' (related to the verb *maiji-* 'to work'), *ɨniakɨ* 'sleep'[5] (cf. from the nominalized verb *ɨnɨa* 'sleeping'), as well as *raaɨkɨ* 'fire' and *jafaikɨ* 'breath, air, the Great Spirit'[6] (Wojtylak 2020a: 164).

The first instance of *-kɨ* with 'cluster-like' semantics is unlikely to derive *komekɨ* 'heart'. The latter two—the classifiers-*kɨ* for 'round' and *-kɨ* for 'essence, core'—are however equally fitting.[7] I propose in this chapter that the noun *kome* 'person' is in fact versatile: when followed by the classifier *-kɨ*, *komekɨ* can refer to either 'heart (as a body organ)' or the 'essence, core of a person'. I now turn to discussing both instances of the Murui 'heart'.

3.1 *Heart as Body Organ*

The conventional meaning of *komekɨ* is that of a muscular organ, which pumps blood through the blood vessels of the circulatory system. This is shown in (6) and (7). (6) is an excerpt from a conversation about preparation of tapir meat

4 Diachronically, the noun *kome* might be related to the adjective *komo-* 'new' (e.g., *komokɨno* 'news' (lit new stories)) which can also be used adverbially as a free form *komo* 'newly, recently' (Wojtylak 2020a: 103–104). There are two consanguineous kinship terms for cross-nephew and niece in Murui: *komo-ma* 'son of brother's sister' (*-ma* CLF.DR:M) and *komo-ño* (*-ño* CLF.DR:F) 'daughter of brother's sister' (Minor and Minor 1980: 81–82; Wojtylak 2020a: 24). *Komoma* and *komoño* literally mean 'new (man)' and 'new (woman)'.

5 In the Murui mythology, the hero Jitoma tricked the anaconda Agaro and made him fall asleep by using *ɨniakɨ* (see Agga Calderón 'Kaziya Buinaima', Wojtylak and Echeverri 2019: 62, 77).

6 The derivation of *raaɨkɨ* and *jafaikɨ* is not entirely transparent; they do contain the classifier *-kɨ* with the meaning of 'essence, core' (Juan Alvaro Echeverri, pers.comm.).

7 I partly diverge here from my previous analyses of *komekɨ* which I solely glossed as 'heart-CLF:ROUND' (e.g., Wojtylak 2020a).

for cooking. (7) is taken from a story about hunting. The semantics of *-ki* in both examples are clearly those of the heart as a body organ, 'round, ovalish' in shape.

(6) [*bai-e kome-ki-na*]$_{NP:O}$ *ri-ñe-di-kai*$_{PRED}$
that-CLF:G heart-CLF:ROUND-N.S/A.TOP eat.meat-NEG-LK-1PL
'We don't eat its heart.'

(7) *jaziki-mo*$_{LOC}$ *kome*$_{S}$ *rao-fi-re-d-e*$_{PRED}$ *raua*$_{PRED}$ [*nai-e*
forest-LOC person hunt-CUST-ATT-LK-3 hunt.E.NMLZ ANA-CLF:G
kome-ki-na]$_{NP:O}$ *o-t-e*$_{PRED}$
heart-CLF:ROUND-N.S/A.TOP get-LK-3
'He used to go hunting. (He) hunted. He got [animals'] hearts.'

The meaning of *komeki* as body organ can be pluralized (for instance, when one kills three peccaries and extracts three hearts from the animals). Such instances of *komeki* can also become the S NP argument of passivized verbs; as the S NP, *komeki* is always coreferential with S/A marking on verbs (see § 3.2).

I now turn these to instances of *komeki* that cannot be interpreted as referring to a body part. Murui everyday discourse provides an abundance of such examples. But what do they mean?

3.2 *Heart as One's Essence, Core*

Consider (8) below, where *komeki* co-occurs with a verb of THINKING *faka-* meaning 'to think, contemplate, try, count, experience, interpret, incise, provoke'.[8]

(8) [*kue kome-ki*]$_{NP:S}$ *uru-ai-mo*$_{OBLIQUE}$ *faka-di-kue*$_{PRED}$
1SG heart-CLF:ESSENCE child-PL-LOC think-LK-3
'I think of children (lit. I contemplate my heart in children).'

Consider also the following example, with a similar interpretation:

(9) [*kue kome-ki*]$_{NP:S}$ *naga-no-mo* *faka-d-e*$_{PRED}$
1SG heart-CLF:ESSENCE all.both.QUANT-CLF:PLACE-LOC think-LK-3
'I think of many things (lit. my heart weights in many places).'

8 Other examples of verbs that can occur with *komeki* are: *jonete* 'to put', as in *komekimo jonete* 'to remember (lit. put into heart)'; *uiñote*, as in *komekido uiñote* 'to remember (lit. to know by

The reading of *komekɨ* in (8)-(9) is not just as a body part term; here 'heart' refers to one's mind; it focuses on some person, thing, and/or state (cf. Dixon 2010: 32). (8) and (9) differ in their coreferentiality: in (8), *komekɨ* is coreferential with the 1st person S/A marker on the verb.[9] This expresses a strong emotion in the mind of the Murui. In (9), the S NP 'my heart' shows the usual 3rd person agreement; the emotion of the speaker towards the statement is weak.[10]

It is precisely the emotive contexts where *komekɨ* is understood as 'one's essence, core'. These emotive expressions represent mental processes one experiences in one's mind and thought (similar to those of thinking above). They can be of anger, joy, and sadness, as in (10)–(12):

(10) *kome-kɨ*$_{S}$ *rɨɨ-tai-d-e*$_{PRED}$
heart-CLF:ESSENCE be.hard-BECOME-LK-3
'(He) became angry (lit. his heart/mind became hard).'

(11) [*Rata*$_{R}$ *kome-kɨ*$_{D}$]$_{NP:S}$ *kaɨma-re-d-e*$_{PRED}$
Rata heart-CLF:ESSENCE be.joyful-ATT-LK-3
'Rata is happy (lit. the heart/mind of Rata is rejoiced).'

(12) *jaa navuida gurua*$_{A}$ [*kome kome-kɨ*]$_{O}$
soon evening thunder.E.NMLZ person heart-CLF:ESSENCE
zuu-re-ta-d-e$_{PRED}$
sad-ATT-CAUS-LK-3
'The thunder in the evening makes one's heart/mind sad.'

Unlike the instances of *komekɨ* presented in (6) and (7) in § 3.1, *komekɨ* 'essence, core' cannot be pluralized. In this, it resembles a handful of other Murui nouns that change their meanings depending on the number marking they take. Perhaps the most notable example of such a semantic change is *uai* 'voice, word,

---

heart)', and *uuide* 'cover', as in *komekɨ dajemo uide* 'to worry (lit. the heart covers in mold)'. Similarly to faka-, these verbs relate to the domain of thinking if they co-occur with *komekɨ*.

9 This is similar in Tariana, an Arawak language spoken to the north. In Tariana, the word 'heart, soul' agrees with the 1st person (Aikhenvald 2003: 500–501).

10 The instances of *komekɨ* occurring with *faka-* 'to think', shown in (8) but not (9), might also be analyzed as compound verbs of sorts (based on their resemblance to constructions with *abɨ* 'body', which today are lexicalized) (Petersen de Piñeros 1998: 35–37; Wojtylak 2020b: 176). Synchronically, only a handful of verbs show traces of such compounding. More study is needed to determine the exact nature of such compound verbs.

language'. When pluralized, *uai-yai* (word-PL) means 'voices (e.g., of people or animals)' and extends to cover 'languages'; with the collective marker, *uai-niai* (word-COLL) means 'words (e.g., spoken, written down)'.

4 The Murui Heart

The linguistic analysis of *komeki* meaning 'heart' in Murui, an indigenous language spoken in the northwestern Amazon, offers a unique window into the worldview of the Murui people. The word for 'heart' is constructed in two different ways: as a physical organ of a particular shape and as the seat of the conceptualization of interiority. This two-fold division is reflected in the language on the structural level: unlike the 'heart (essence, core)', the 'heart (body organ)' can be pluralized and function as the subject of a passivized verb. It is coreferential with subject/number marking on verb; on the other hand, the coreferentiality of 'heart (essence, core)' is emotion dependent.

Komeki, which inherently contains the notion of *kome* 'person' in itself, offers two levels of understanding of what 'heart' is. On the one hand, there is the actual heart, an internal body organ that pumps blood, has a shape, and serves specific bodily functions. This *komeki* relates to the natural world, which contains similarly shaped objects identified by the classifier *-ki*, meaning round objects, such as fruit. On the other hand, there is the conceptual heart that is a person's essence and core, perhaps better understood as a person's mind and thought. It relates to other contexts in which the individuum operates, and it is in that very heart where human emotions and feelings reside. Once evoked, they reveal themselves in thoughts, through the instance of *-ki* 'essence, core'. That second heart belongs to the realm of the spiritual world, hidden from those who are uninitiated into the Murui culture. The same *-ki*, that of essence rather than of shape, is found on other culturally important words in Murui, such as *jafai-ki* '(secret) breath, air, Great Spirit', *mame-ki* '(sacred) name', and *raai-ki* '(secret) fire'.

This chapter shows that the integration of natural environment and individual emotional life offers fascinating perspectives into how we can conceive of the world, as an entangled living place in which humans are connected to other beings, for example through the shape of the heart.

Acknowledgements

Many thanks to Juan Alvaro Echeverri for discussion and anonymous reviewers for their stimulating comments on an earlier draft. Special thanks to my darling Conor D. Holmes for smiling, while proofreading and editing this text early in the morning, on an investing day.

Abbreviations

1	1st person	KIN	kinship (plural)
2	2nd person	LK	linker
3	3rd person	LOC	locative
A	subject of transitive verb	M	masculine
ANA	anaphoric	N	noun
ATT	attributive	N.S/A	non-S/A subject
CAUS	causative	NEG	negative
CLF	classifier	NMLZ	nominalization
COLL	collective	NP	noun phrase
CUST	customary	O	object of transitive verb
D	possessed	PL	plural
DES	desiderative	PLACE	place
DR	derivational	PR	'pronominal'
DU	dual	PRED	predicate
DUR	durative	QUANT	quantifier *-ga*
E (in gloss)	event nominalizer	R	possessor
EMPH	emphatic	S	subject of intransitive verb
F	feminine	SG	singular
FUT	future	SP (in gloss)	specific
G	generic (classifier)	TOP	topical
GR	group	VCS	verbless clause subject
IMP	imperative	VCC	verbless clause complement

References

Agga Calderón 'Kaziya Buinaima', L., Katarzyna I. Wojtylak and Juan Alvaro Echeverri (2019). Murui: Naie jiyakɨno. El lugar de origen. The place of origin. In Kristine Stenzel and Bruna Franchetto (eds.), *Special issue Línguas indígenas: Artes da palavra / Indigenous Languages: verbal arts*, 15 (1): 50– 87.

Aikhenvald, Alexandra Y. (2000). *Classifiers: A typology of noun categorization devices.* Oxford: Oxford University Press.

Aikhenvald, Alexandra Y. (2003). *A Grammar of Tariana, from Northwest Amazonia.* Cambridge: Cambridge University Press.

Aikhenvald, Alexandra Y. (2012). *The languages of the Amazon.* Oxford: Oxford University Press.

Dixon, R.M.W. (1982). *Where Have All the Adjectives Gone? and other essays in semantics and syntax.* Berlin: Mouton

Dixon, R.M.W. (2010). *Basic Linguistic Theory: Methodology* (Vol. 1). Oxford: Oxford University Press.

Echeverri, Juan Alvaro (1997). The people of the center of the world. A study in culture, history and orality in the Colombian Amazon. (PhD dissertation), New School for Social Research, New York.

Echeverri, Juan Alvaro, Doris Fagua Rincón and Katarzyna I. Wojtylak (forthcoming). The Witotoan language family. In Patience Epps and Lev Michael (eds.), *International Handbook of Amazonian languages.* Berlin: De Gruyter Mouton.

Minor, Eugene and Dorothy de Minor (1980). Sistema Huitoto de parentesco. *Articulos en Linguistica y Campos Afines* 8: 67–91.

Petersen de Piñeros, Gabriele (1998). De cuerpo y alma en uitoto: una aproximación a la reflexividad. *Forma y Función* 11 (Sept): 29–40.

Whiffen, Thomas (1915). The North-West Amazon: Notes of some months spent among cannibal tribes. London: Constable and Company.

Wojtylak, Katarzyna I. (2015). Fruits for Animals: Hunting Avoidance Speech Style in Murui (Witoto, Northwest Amazonia). *Proceedings of the 41st Annual Meeting of the Berkeley Linguistic Society. University of California at Berkeley*, 545–561. doi:10.20354/B4414110007.

Wojtylak, Katarzyna I. (2016). Classifiers as derivational markers in Murui (Northwest Amazonia). In Lívia Körtvélyessy, Pavol Štekauer and Salvador Valera (eds.), *Word-Formation Across Languages*, 393–425. London/Newcastle-upon-Tyne: Cambridge Scholars Publishing.

Wojtylak, Katarzyna I. (2018). Nominalizations in Murui (Witotoan). *Nominalization: A view from North West Amazonia* 71 (1): 19–45. doi:10.1515/stuf-2018–0002.

Wojtylak, Katarzyna I. (2019). Talking to the spirits: A jungle-at-night register of the Murui people from Northwest Amazon. In Alexandra Y. Aikhenvald and Anne Storch (eds.), *The Mouth: critical studies on language, culture and society* 4: 78–90.

Wojtylak, Katarzyna I. (2020a). *A grammar of Murui (Bue), a Witotoan language from Northwest Amazonia.* Leiden: Brill. doi.org/10.1163/9789004432673.

Wojtylak, Katarzyna I. (2020b). Multifaceted body parts in Murui: A case study from Northwest Amazonia. In Iwona Kraska-Szlenk (ed.), *Body Part Terms in Conceptual-*

ization and Language Usage, 170–190. Amsterdam: John Benjamins. doi.org/10.1075/clscc.12.c08woj.

Wojtylak, Katarzyna I. 2021. Links between language and society among the Murui of Northwest Amazonia. In Alexandra Y. Aikhenvald, R.M.W. Dixon and Nerida Jarkey (eds.), *Integration of language and society: A cross-linguistic typology*. Oxford: Oxford University Press, 215–234.

CHAPTER 4

While We Are Not yet Dead: Themes of Love and Loss in a Kandozi-Chapra Drinking Song

Simon E. Overall

1 Introduction

In the Kandozi community of Caspacocha, a woman sings as she serves *masato* (manioc beer) to a male family member, tipping the beverage into his mouth from a bowl held in her hand:

(1) Drink, little brother
I'll serve you masato
drink for a moment
some other day I won't serve you [masato]
(kandozi_chapra109)[1]

This is a traditional song form among the Kandozi and Chapra people, sung by women at drinking parties as they circulate serving *masato* to the male guests. The bittersweet lyrics reflect on the fleeting nature of good times and the inevitability of death, and they include frequent references to birds—symbols *par excellence* of the familial bonds that are embodied in the sharing of *masato* and the dance parties that form both the theme and the context of these songs.

References to birds, as well as other fauna and flora, are recurrent throughout the Kandozi-Chapra oral tradition, and they play important symbolic roles in the oral traditions of other Amazonian cultures too. Similarly, the song tradition itself has analogues in many other groups.

This chapter discusses the song traditions of the Kandozi and Chapra people, centred on an analysis of the recorded song from which the extract in (1) is taken. In the first instance, then, this is a descriptive work: there has been very little analysis of the Kandozi-Chapra musical tradition in the literature,

1 This example is taken from the song that is fully transcribed and glossed in (16) below. Examples are cited with the filename of the recording deposited in the ELAR archive, and a time code in the form mm:ss if relevant.

© SIMON E. OVERALL, 2022 | DOI:10.1163/9789004510395_005

and there is an urgent need to record these songs. On the basis of the description, the chapter also discusses in detail the symbolism in the songs, focusing on the role of birds. As this song is part of a larger body of Kandozi-Chapra oral tradition, which in turn is located in the Amazonian areal context, the analysis also addresses the connections that link the song to its social and cultural context, highlighting the importance of a broad and detailed understanding of discourse and culture to linguistic analysis (cf. Sherzer 1987; Jakobson 1968).

The chapter is structured as follows. The remainder of this section gives a brief overview of the Kandozi and Chapra people and their language. Section 2 describes the areal context, and the history of intercultural contacts. Section 3 centres on an analysis of a recorded song, and Section 4 discusses the cultural context in more detail. Section 5 concludes with some implications and directions for future study.

1.1 *Kandozi and Chapra Language and Society*

The Kandozi and Chapra are two politically distinct ethnic groups of the upper Peruvian Amazon. They speak mutually intelligible varieties of what is linguistically a single language, but which are recognised within the modern Peruvian state as distinct languages (a third variety is spoken in Kandozi communities on the Huitoyacu River). The language, which I call Kandozi-Chapra (ISO 639-3: cbu; Glottocode: cand1248) following the practice of SIL analysts, is not known to be related to any other linguistic group.

The Kandozi live along the Chapuli River and other watercourses that drain into Lake Rimachi (*Musa Karusha* in Kandozi), and along the Huitoyacu River and other affluents of the Pastaza River. The Chapra people live west of the Kandozi, on the Pushaga River and other tributaries of the Morona River. Data from a census taken in 2007 give a total combined ethnic Kandozi-Chapra population of 3,255 (Valladares 2009: 12), although the current figure is likely to be higher. Geographically this area is lowland Amazon basin, with elevations of around 100–200 m, and includes extensive wetlands surrounding Lake Rimachi.

1.2 *Grammar Overview*

Kandozi-Chapra shares a number of grammatical features with other languages of the eastern Andean piedmont (Wise 2011). It has nominative-accusative alignment, a rich set of case markers for core and peripheral arguments, and the morphology is agglutinating and entirely suffixing/encliticising apart from a set of causative prefixes on verbs (see Payne 1990), and a third person possessor prefix on nouns that is transparently derived from a preposed third person singular pronoun (see the possession paradigm in Table 4.1).

TABLE 4.1 Possession paradigm for *tumuuz* 'dog'

	SG	PL
1	tumúuzi-r=i dog-PSSD=1SG	tumúuzi-ri=ni dog-PSSD=1PL
2	tumúuzi-ri=sh dog-PSSD=2SG	tumúuzi-ri=s dog-PSSD=2PL
3	wa-túmzi-ri=Ø 3-dog-PSSD=3SG	wa-túmzi-ri=naya 3-dog-PSSD=3PL

The grammar shows a mixture of head and dependent marking. Possession is head marking, with suffixes/enclitics and one prefix marking the possessum, and the possessor unmarked (or omitted entirely). Table 4.1 illustrates the possession paradigm for the noun *tumuuz* 'dog', marked with the suffix *-ri* indicating its possessed status (this does not appear with all nouns), and with prefixes and enclitics marking the person and number of the possessor.

Grammatical relations are primarily dependent marking, with case markers encliticised to the NP, and there is also subject (S/A) agreement on the verb. Example (2) illustrates an unmarked nominative subject (S) *tsumpich* 'rat', and (3) illustrates nominative subject (A) and accusative marked object (O) pronouns. (4) illustrates the full form of the accusative enclitic *=atsi* marking an object. Table 4.2 shows the basic set of verbal subject markers.

(2) *tsumpich kusa-raŋk-i=ya*
rat arrive-PST-3=EMPH
'a rat arrived' (kc2013_002-1 01:19)

(3) *sii nuw=a mpiza-k-s=a*
2PL 1SG=ACC forget-FGR-2PL=EMPH
'you have forgotten me' (kandozi_chapra015 02:41)

(4) *wapuss=atsi waa-ŋki taa-ch-sh=a*
3.masato=ACC drink-IMP say-INCOMPL-2SG=EMPH
'you will say: "drink her masato!"' (line 7 of the song in [16])

The verbal person markers are optionally followed by a mood enclitic, one of 'emphatic', 'potential', 'interrogative', and 'negative'. There is some allomorphy of both person and mood markers, giving rise to distinct constructions; for

TABLE 4.2 Verbal subject markers

	SG	PL
1	-i	-ini
2	-ish	-is
3	-u	-ana
impersonal	-ich	

example, 3sg has the allomorph *-i* when followed by emphatic or potential mood, making it homophonous with 1sg, but the mood markers also have distinct allomorphs conditioned by person, so *-i=na* (-1sg=EMPH) and *-i=ma* (-1SG=POT) are distinguished from *-i=ya* (-3sg=EMPH) and *-i=pa* (-3SG=POT).

Example (5) illustrates the dative case *=ama*, which is required for complements of some verbs such as the recipient of *pana-* 'give', and also encodes obliques; examples (6) and (7) illustrate the spatial cases superessive and allative, respectively. Note in (7) that the possessor enclitic follows case marking and the adverbial enclitic *=tam(ta)* 'also'. Locative case marked with *=shu* is illustrated in line 4 of the song in (16).

(5) *ashi-ma=tamta wa-zaranchi=**ama** pana-tar-i=tamta*
do-DUR=also 3-husband.PSSD=**DAT** give-HAB-3=also
'Then they give (it) to their husband.' (kc2013_006-3 02:10)

(6) *yasinu=**mun** kar-ee-r-u*
tree=**SUPE** go.up-INCH-BGR-CVB.3
'She went up a tree.' (kc2013_001-1 01:26)

(7) *nu=shat paŋki=**p**=tamt=i kanaapu-raŋk-i=na*
1SG=TOP house.PSSD=**ALL**=also=1SG go.back-PST-1SG=EMPH
'I went back to my house too.' (kc2013_034-1 03:28)

In clauses marked with the potential mood enclitic, which includes prohibitive clauses, there is a different treatment of speech act participants from that shown in Table 4.2. Only one argument is marked, but it can be interpreted as subject or object depending on the context—compare (8) and (9). Presumably this marking pattern is hierarchical, but such examples are infrequent in recorded texts and more data is required to fully understand the motivating factors.

(8) *imuri, punii-r-**inch**=pa*
deep be.afraid-BGR-**2SG**=POT
'It [the river] is deep, don't be afraid!' (kc2013_009-1 17:53)

(9) *shi=ama kapussi=a yas-ch-**inch**=pa*
2SG=DAT masato=ACC serve-INCOMPL-**2SG**=POT
'I'll serve you masato.' (line 2 of the song in [16])

The verbal morphology is complex, and is mostly aspectual with just one tense marker *-raŋk* 'past'. Example (10) shows a small selection of verb forms: the speech verbs appear in a very common form for narratives, with past tense marker, person, and the 'emphatic' enclitic (the term 'emphatic' is adopted from Cox (1957); the function of this marker seems to be akin to that of a declarative marker). Within the speech report in (10a), the verb is in the imperative form; in (10b) the verb combines incompletive aspect *-ch* and potential mood *=ma*, giving a future reading; there is no dedicated future tense marker. This verb also includes the adverbial enclitic *=tam(ta)* 'also' between the person and mood markers.

(10) a. *"kanusa-ŋki" ta-raŋk-i=na*
rest-IMP say-PST-1SG=EMPH

b. *"nu=sha kanus-ch-i=tam=ma" ta-raŋk-i=na*
1SG=TOP rest-INCOMPL-1SG=also=POT say-PST-1SG=EMPH
'"Have a rest", I said, "I will also rest" I said.' (kc2013_034-1 03:36)

The negative verbal enclitic (example 11) is part of the paradigm of mood markers and is replaced by a preverbal particle *nta* in clauses in which the mood marking slot is unavailable, whether because it is already filled or because the clause is non-verbal (as in example 12). In fact, the particle negator is far more frequent in texts, where most verbs are marked with the 'emphatic' enclitic. The suffixed negator seems to be an archaism, and it is noteworthy that it appears in three out of five negated clauses in the song in (16). Perhaps this is an effect of the song genre—this is an empirical question that can be answered when more texts are transcribed and analysed.

(11) *nu katuŋk-k-ee=**zi** kayupchi=atsi*
1SG eat-FGR-1SG=**NEG** fish=ACC
'I don't eat fish.' (elicited)

TABLE 4.3 Kandozi-Chapra consonants

	Bilabial	Alveolar[a]	Palatal	Retroflex	Velar	Glottal
stop	p	t			k	ʔ
fricative		s	ʃ ⟨sh⟩	ʂ ⟨z⟩		h
affricate		t͡s ⟨ts⟩	t͡ʃ ⟨ch⟩	t͡ʂ ⟨x⟩		
nasal	m	n			ŋ[b]	
glide	w		j ⟨y⟩			
tap		ɾ ⟨r⟩				

a Detailed phonetic data are lacking, but /t/ and /n/ are most likely articulated as lamino-alveolar and /s/, /t͡s/, and /ɾ/ as apico-alveolar. The specifics do not affect the analysis presented here.

b As the velar nasal only appears preceding the velar stop /k/, it is best analysed as an allophone of the alveolar nasal /n/ (see Overall forthcoming).

(12) *aan* *nta* *kuraka*
DEM.DST NEG chief
'he is not the chief' (elicited)

Subordination involves a single converbal form, marked with *-u*, which allows two clauses to be linked grammatically while leaving the semantic nature of their relationship to be inferred from context (see Haspelmath 1995 for a cross-linguistic characterisation of converbs). There is no switch-reference marking, unlike in the neighbouring Chicham languages.

A number of noun phrase enclitics mark information structural status and some adverbial meanings, of which the most frequently encountered are the following:

=tam(ta)	'also' (exemplified in line 5 of [16])
=sha(t)	'topic' (exemplified in line 21 of [16])
=ta	'exhaustive focus' (exemplified in line 12 of [16])
=ri(ta)	'intensifier' (exemplified in line 6 of [16])[2]

1.3 *Phonology and Orthographic Conventions*

Tables 4.3 and 4.4 show the inventories of consonants and vowels, respectively; the graphs that differ from IPA are included in angle brackets.

2 The label 'intensifier' is adapted from Tuggy (1966).

TABLE 4.4 Kandozi-Chapra vowels

	Front		Back	
	Short	Long	Short	Long
high	i	iː ⟨ii⟩	u	uː ⟨uu⟩
mid	e ~ eː ~ ye ⟨e(e)⟩		o ~ oː ~ wo ⟨o(o)⟩	
low			ɑ ⟨a⟩	ɑː ⟨aa⟩

Phonology is complicated by vowel elision, and reduction of the sequences /ia/ and /ua/ to [eː] and [oː] respectively. These are primarily word-internal processes, but some common collocations allow them to apply across word boundaries. An example from line 18 of (16) is shown in (13), where the word *aantar*, which consists of the irregular verb stem *at-/ta-/tu-/an-* 'say' combined with the habitual suffix *-tar*, is followed by the light verb *ashi-*. These are treated as a single phonological word, allowing /aantar/ to be reduced to /aantr/; the cluster /ntr/ would not normally be possible in word-final position.

(13) aantrashtrinaya
aantar *ash-tr-i=na-ya*
say.HAB do-HAB-1SG=EMPH-EP

Example (14) illustrates the coalescence of the sequence /ia/ to [e], when they are brought together at a morpheme boundary. In example (15), from another recorded song, the same process applies across the word boundary, as shown in the transcribed form given by a native speaker consultant.

(14) *wiizanchem*
w-izanchi=am
3-wife.PSSD=DAT
'for his wife' (kc2013_18-1 08:58)

(15) *kanup* *eshik*
kanu=pi ashi-k
canoe=ALL do-FGR
'getting into the canoe …' (kandozi_chapra009 00:28)

In this paper, transcription follows the official orthography, with a few adjustments to avoid ambiguity, following the system used in Overall (forthcoming). Note that morphemes are cited in their full phonemic form, while examples give surface forms. So for example the dative case enclitic *=ama* appears as *=am* in example (14), where its final vowel is elided.

2 The Areal Context

The western margin of the Amazon basin near the modern-day border between Ecuador and Peru is ethnically and linguistically diverse, but the indigenous cultures of the area also show notable similarities, due to a long history of contact and mutual influence. In particular, there are many cultural and linguistic overlaps between Kandozi-Chapra and Chicham (formerly known as Jivaroan). The geographical area in question is centred on the two axes of the Marañon River and its left-bank tributary the Pastaza River. Other major tributaries to the Marañon include the Santiago and Morona Rivers on the left bank and the Cahuapanas and Nieva Rivers on the right bank.

This area is home to speakers of Chicham languages: Wampis (or Huambisa), spoken on the Santiago and Morona Rivers and in close contact with Chapra communities; and Achuar, spoken on the upper Pastaza and Huitoyacu and in contact with Kandozi communities. Pastaza Kichwa (Quechuan) is also spoken in that area. Another isolate, Urarina, is spoken to the east and the Kawapanan language Shawi is spoken on the right bank tributaries of the Marañón. Of these, only Kichwa has linguistic relatives outside of the area, and its relatively recent presence is the result of Andean colonisation combined with language shift among originally Chicham speaking populations, possibly due to the use of Quechua as a *lingua franca* by early missionaries. Michael (2014) reports that Omagua and Kokama were used as pre-Columbian contact languages in the region, and colonial records attest to other languages that were lost during the era of missions and the rubber boom, especially in the upper Marañón valley near the mouth of the Urubamba River to the west of the modern Chicham speaking area (Adelaar and Muysken 2004: 405). A relative (or ancestor) of modern Kandozi-Chapra was apparently spoken in the Chinchipe River valley, well to the west of the current location (see Overall forthcoming, for more details).

The history of population movements and interethnic contacts in this part of the Amazon basin remains largely unknown. The modern Kandozi-Chapra zone and the area to the east was at least nominally under the control of the Mainas Mission, which was founded in the mid-17th century, and the social upheaval that resulted from European incursions, and especially the effects of the rubber boom in the late 19th and early 20th centuries, have had a deep and lasting impact on social structures. It is likely that some modern ethnic groups have been formed from refugees fleeing disease or conflict (see Whitten 2011 on the mission origins of Canelos Kichwa beginning in the 16th century; see also Wasserstrom 2014; Livi-Bacci 2016). Interethnic warfare was frequent until the early 20th century and often involved the kidnapping of women from different ethnic groups. The notable practice of head shrinking among Chapras is said to have been adopted from their Wampis (Chicham) neighbours (Tariri 1965), and headhunting itself was stimulated by trade with colonists (Ferguson 1990). Interethnic marriages must also have been a feature during times of peace, and the considerable number of traditional personal names shared between Kandozi-Chapra and Chicham societies is testament to a strong tradition of ethnically mixed families.

All of this social upheaval and ethnic mixing has had demonstrable linguistic and cultural effects. Shared discourse practices, including ritual language, are fundamental to an understanding of linguistic contact in the Amazonian context (Beier et al. 2002; Basso 2011; Epps 2015). It is an established tradition that Shamanic training is undertaken among the cultural and linguistic 'other', thereby forming a vector for transferring lexical material between cultures, and the use of esoteric language, including words from other languages, is widespread in shamanic and other mystical songs (Gnerre 2009; Mihas 2019; Overall 2019). The tradition of oblique reference via metaphor and allusion, and the importance of animal imagery in these discourse genres, is consistent with Epps' (2015) observation that flora and fauna terminology is disproportionately represented (relative to other parts of the world) in Amazonian loanword repertoires—a phenomenon that Epps also explicitly links to shamanic discourse of the type described by Dean (1994) for Urarina:

> The phonocentric power of Urarina myth is evoked through a naming of the lived world, a verbal *referencing* of the rainforest system as in the specific case of the serial listing of the creation of the fish, birds, serpents and vermin.
>
> DEAN 1994: 23

Ayahuasca shamanism, a central part of many western Amazonian cultures, may be largely a product of postcolonial social upheaval (Townsley 1993; Gow 1994), and ayahuasca use itself may be relatively recent (Brabec de Mori 2011b: 24; Gow 1994).

Among shared mythological themes there is some evidence of Christian influence. A central myth of the Kandozi and Chapra people includes a figure who is persecuted by envious tribespeople, killed and buried, only to rise Christ-like and then warn a Noah-like figure of an impending flood. These are clearly reminiscent of some of the more striking elements of biblical narrative and quite likely share an origin in contact with Christian missionaries. Whether this comes from the *reducciones* of the Mainas mission or more recent SIL activity remains to be determined. Strikingly similar themes appear in stories reported for Urarina (Dean 1994), Shawi (Ochoa Siguas 1992), and Shipibo (Roe 1982: 49–51).

Turning to song traditions, 'magic' songs are described for neighbouring groups: the *anɨn* of the Chicham-speaking groups (Overall 2019 and references cited therein), Urarina *baau* curing songs (Walker 2010, 2013), and *icaros* used by Kichwa shamans (Brabec de Mori 2002). The Kandozi-Chapra tradition includes comparable songs (Surrallés 2009), but no distinction is made between these and the drinking songs intended for public performance. All are labelled *yaseeshi*, a nominalisation derived from the verb *yási-* 'sing'.[3] This contrasts with neighbouring groups such as the Chicham and Urarina, whose flirtatious drinking songs form a separate named genre.

Two major vectors that are likely to have been relevant to the spread of shared song traditions are the shamanic practice of visiting different linguistic groups to study; and love songs such as the Chicham *anɨn*, which often relate to the theme of a woman adapting to married life in her new husband's household in a new community (Mader 2004; Overall 2019).

3 Singing and Dancing Together

Drinking alcoholic brews, singing and dancing together, are of course fundamental features of human societies around the world. In the eastern Andean piedmont, societies are traditionally rather scattered, so drinking parties are important occasions at which extended family members can come together and socialise. These events provide opportunities to begin or end romantic partnerships and trysts, and may be highly emotionally charged. At Matsigenka drinking parties, "Women sometimes dance frenetically as they sing songs of pure venom about treacherous husbands and their lovers. At other times, women rock slowly in dance lines with children as they sing lullaby-like melod-

3 Note that the verb *yasí-* with different stress position means 'serve (masato)'. Surrallés (2007: 323) takes these to be a single polysemous verb, ignoring the difference in stress placement; I prefer to reserve judgement on the question of relatedness.

ies that speak of the sadness of a world that takes away so many newborns and other loved ones" (Shepard 2002: 216). Among the Urarina, "Songs sung during manioc beer drinking parties refer to birds in order to express or symbolize particular emotions, especially joy and sorrow" (Walker 2010: 7).

Drinking songs are part of the discursive context within Kandozi-Chapra culture that includes other genres of verbal art, including songs of romantic love, men's hunting and battle songs, ritual greetings, and traditional stories. References to flora and fauna are characteristic of all of these genres.

The song that forms the focus of this paper is given in (16) below. The song was recorded in April 2017 in the Kandozi community of Caspacocha, sung by Chela Kamarampi. The lyrics are vague and allusive at a number of points, and some material has been added in square brackets following the suggestion of Gerardo Mando, who assisted with the translation. Epenthetic syllables that have been inserted to preserve scansion are glossed EP.

(16) Kandozi drinking song (kandozi_chapra109)

1 *waawa* *wa-ŋki*
younger.brother.VOC drink-IMP
'Drink, little brother'

2 *shi=ama* *kapussi=a* *yas-ch-inch=pa*
2SG=DAT masato=ACC serve-INCOMPL-2SG=POT
'I'll serve you masato'

3 *naatumarita* *wa-ŋki-ya*
now drink-IMP-EP
'drink for a moment'

4 *minu=shu* *zaari* *nu* *shiy=ama* *yaas-ch-ee=zi-na*
other=LOC day 1SG 2SG=DAT serve-INCOMPL-1SG=NEG-EP
'some other day I won't serve you [masato]'

5 *tsiipaa-k-u-ri=na* *shan=tam*
die-FGR-CVB-1SG=EMPH 2SG.EMPH=also
'when I die, you indeed …'

6 *puuta=ri-na* *mutrur-mash* *zaari-na* *yas-k-u-ri*
tomorrow=INTENS-EP near-SIMIL sun-EP serve-FGR-CVB-1SG
'in the morning, at first light, I'll serve [masato]'

7	*wapuss=atsi*	*waa-ŋki*	*taa-ch-sh=a*
	3.masato=ACC	drink-IMP	say-INCOMPL-2SG=EMPH

'you will say "drink her [i.e. the singer's] masato"'

8	*maya=maa*	*naatumta*	*kanuŋkasi=sha*
	why=DAT	now	youth=TOP

'because you're young now'

9	*tamare*	*tsipaa-ch-ish*
	how	die-INCOMPL-2SG

'how could you die?'

10	*shiy=ama=ri*	*taa-ch-sh=a-ya*	*naatu*
	2SG=DAT=INTENS	live-INCOMPL-2SG=EMPH-EP	now

'you alone will live now'

11	*mariita-t=ma*	*amp=rita-wa*
	give.food-THEN=POT.1SG	there=INTENS-EP

'I'll go and serve food over there'

12	*ichiŋkaru=am=ta=cha*
	all=DAT=EXH.FOC=COP

'for everyone'

13	*tputsi-ri=ats=i*	*kasa-tar-ee=zi*
	people-PSSD=ACC=1SG	abandon-HAB-1SG=NEG

'I don't abandon my people'

14	*mantar-mashi*	*ichiŋkaru=cha*
	caracara-SIMIL	all=COP

'like the caracara bird, [that attracts] everybody'

15	*marcha-k-u-ri*	*ta-tar-i=na*
	go.in.group-FGR-CVB-1SG	live-HAB-1SG=EMPH

'going in a group [like the caracara], that's how I live'

16	*iwaaz=cha*	*zaata-ta-ranch-u-ya*
	outside=COP	shine-THEN-PST.COMPL-CVB.3-EP

'out where the sun shines'

17 *maarcha-k-u-ri* *ktaaoo*
go.in.group-FGR-CVB-1SG IDEO
'I go as part of a group, [singing] "ktaaoo"'

18 *antar* *ashi-tar-i=na-ya*
say.HAB do-HAB-1SG=EMPH-EP
'that's what I say'

19 *kumpartut-ri=ats=i* *kasa-tr-ee=zi-naa*
cacique-PSSD=ACC=1SG abandon-HAB-1SG=NEG-EP
'I don't leave my cacique bird'

20 *mancheeru-r=pata=ri* *ta-ch-i=na*
oropendola-PSSD=COMIT=1SG live-INCOMPL-1SG=EMPH
ipun-tr-i=na-ya
be.together-HAB-1SG=EMPH-EP
'I live together with my oropendola bird'

21 *pshkur=mun=shat* *waziu-ee-u-ri* *ta-tr-i=na-ya*
dead.tree=SUPE=TOP perch-INCH-CVB-1SG live-HAB-1SG=EMPH-EP
'I perch on a dead tree'

22 *mancheer-mashi-ya* *chew* *ipun-tra-shina*
oropendola-SIMIL-EP IDEO be.together-HAB-AM
'I live together like an oropendola, calling "chew"'

23 *iwaa=sh=cha* *mparni* *tiuu* *tiuu* *tiuu*
which=LOC=COP light.rain IDEO IDEO IDEO
ashi-sh-tr-u *anu=sh=cha*
do-REDUP-HAB-COP.3 DEM=LOC=COP
'there where the light rain goes "tiuu tiuu tiuu"'

24 *tiuu* *aantar*
IDEO say.HAB.3
'saying "tiuu"'

25 *aash-tr-i=na-yawa* *shiy=a*
do-HAB-1SG=EMPH-EP 2sg=ACC
'I say to you'

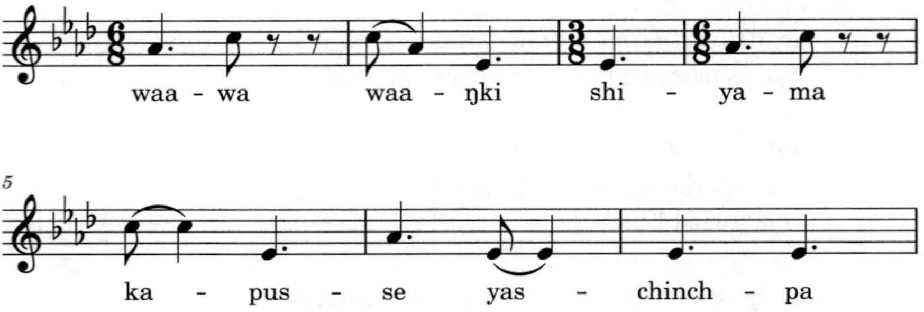

FIGURE 4.1 Transcription of lines 1 and 2 of (16)

26 *psiichna=mun=cha nta kasaa-tr-i kumpartut-maashi*
tree.sp=SUPE=COP NEG abandon-HAB-1SG cacique-SIMIL
'sitting in a big psiichna tree, like a cacique I don't leave [you]'

27 *semeechna=mun=cha nta kasaa-tr-i aaya*
tree.sp=SUPE=COP NEG abandon-HAB-1SG EP
'sitting in a big psiichna tree, I don't leave [you]'

28 *kumpartut-maashi-ya pur-mash=cha*
cacique-SIMIL-EP feather-SIMIL=COP
'cacique-like, well-feathered'

29 *zaata-t-ranch-u aanu=sh=cha kumpartutu*
shine-THEN-PST.COMPL-CVB.3 DEM=LOC=COP cacique
aantar
say.HAB.3
'when the sun rises, I sit there to sing like a cacique'

30 *ashtrashnaayaa naatu* [*kapuss=i iwatsa-ŋki*]
do.HAB.1SG.EMPH now masato.PSSD=1SG finish.up-IMP
'and now [finish up my masato]'

Musically, the song is performed at about 80 bpm (*andante moderato*) and the melody uses three notes forming a major chord (Figure 4.1). The lines resolve to the fifth below the tonic, and this note is repeated a variable number of times (as in bars 3 and 7). There is little melodic variation within the song, and no musically defined sections.

There do not appear to be any opaque words (unlike in other songs described below; cf. Surrallés 2007: 374 on words that uniquely appear in a shamanic song). As noted above, a possible archaism is the frequency of the negative enclitic, apparently more than in everyday speech. In particular, compare line 19 with lines 26 and 27, where the same verb is negated with the enclitic and the particle. Otherwise the language is not distinguished from normal speech apart from the epenthetic syllables.

The singer begins with an exhortation to drink, and highlights her role in serving the masato. She then meditates on her inevitable death and intimates that the addressee should value her while she is alive, a common theme in such songs. Another Kandozi woman, in the nearby community Nueva Yarina, introduces a similar song saying:

(17) *naatu=m shii=am yas-ee-k-i na kchit-par-ani*
now=DAT 2SG=DAT sing-INCH-FGR-1SG now alive-DUB-1PL
kchit=pata=tin ntatu=rita tsipaa-r-ini
alive=COMIT=PL NEG=INTENS die-BGR-1PL
'now I'll sing for you, we're alive now, we're alive and haven't died yet' (kandozi_chapra106)

Surrallés (2007) records a similar drinking song in Spanish translation, sung in 1993 by a woman visiting her brother's house:

Hermano, hermano mío, toma mi masato aunque no esté demasiado fuerte.
Hermano, hermano mío, no conocemos el momento de nuestra muerte; cuando mueras, me acordaré que a ti te ofrecí bebida, a ti hermano mío,
así me acordaré de ti cuando estés muerto …

[Brother, my brother, drink my masato even though it's not too strong.
Brother, my brother, we don't know the moment of our death; when you die, I'll remember that I served you drink, to you my brother,
that's how I'll remember you when you're dead …]

SURRALLÉS 2007: 324

In line 11, there is a thematic shift as the singer refers to serving food 'over there' (*amp=rita-wa* there=INTENS-EP). The shift is signalled grammatically by a change in the aspect markers: the first section of the song is characterised by verbs with the incompletive aspect marker, giving a reading of future time, while the verbs following line 11 are characterised by habitual aspect marking,

TABLE 4.5 Birds referred to in the song (16)

Kandozi-Chapra	Spanish	English	Linnaean
mantar	atatau	red-throated caracara	*Ibycter americanus*
kumpartut	paucar	yellow-rumped cacique	*Cacicus cela*
mancheer	piapia	oropendola	*Psarocolius sp.*, likely *decumanus* or *angustifrons*

as the singer describes her participation in family life by comparing herself to three bird species, listed in Table 4.5.[4]

All three species are gregarious and noisy birds that are conspicuous in the canopy and at the forest's edge near clearings and rivers (Ridgely and Greenfield 2001: 101). The singer makes reference to the birds' habit of foraging in groups and singing together, 'out where the sun shines'—that is, not in the depth of the forest. The icterid family (cacique and oropendola) make woven hanging nests in shared colonies in large trees, often near human settlements (Ridgely and Greenfield 2001: 694, 699–700).

These three bird species are analogues of humanity, due to three important properties: (i) they frequent clearings, riverbanks, and forest edges rather than the deep forest interior, the realm of human culture rather than wild nature; (ii) they live in 'villages' (nesting colonies) and 'work' (forage) in groups; and (iii) they 'talk' amongst themselves and sing together—birdsong is an obvious link to human singing (Uzendoski et al. 2005: 660). The birds offer "alternative somatic perspectives of the human condition" (Uzendoski et al. 2005: 657), and the cultural tradition invokes a central metaphor mapping the birds' lifestyle to a model of appropriate human social behaviour. The singer can claim similarity to the birds because she lives properly—she forms part of her social group and sings and dances together with them.

A ceremonial greeting dialogue recorded in English translation by Surrallés (2003) describes living properly in similar terms: "As you are still alive, you have

4 In keeping with a widespread Amazonian association between birds and souls (Walker 2010: 3), this can be read as an allusion to a kind of afterlife as a bird. Of note here is the fact that death is not necessarily permanent in Kandozi-Chapra oral tradition (cf. Surrallés 2007: 294), underscored by the apparently derivationally related lexemes *tsipáa-* 'die' and *tsíipa-* 'disappear'—death is disappearance, and may be followed by reappearance.

come to visit me … I cannot abandon my house" (Surrallés 2003: 781), showing that these are fundamental cultural values.

The icterids' habit of living together in colonies comprising more than one species provides a clear link to an allegorical device that is frequently encountered in myths, whereby different bird and animal species are people, with each species representing a particular physical or behavioural trait.[5] Kandozi elder Akumpari Kamarampi described the process of young men learning hunting magic (archived as kandozi_chapra103). They go into the forest as a group, with an older man as their teacher. There, under the influence of tobacco (*Nicotiana rustica*) they learn the songs which allow them to attract and kill prey (similar to the Chicham *anin* which work on the basis of attraction; Codjia 2017). Hunting songs refer to the same three bird species as the song in (16), and add a fourth species which is also found in their company, a toucan (*Ramphastos sp.*). These four bird species are compared to a group of young men, hanging around together trying to attract girls.

The addition of the toucan is noteworthy. The toucan contrasts with the other birds mentioned as it is a desired game bird, hunted for its coloured feathers which are important materials for making feathered crowns, an essential marker of a man's social status. The toucan is also an important symbol of romantic love and male attractiveness for neighbouring Chicham and Urarina people (Overall 2019; Taylor and Chau 1983; Descola 1996; Walker 2010). It is no accident, then, that the toucan with its highly masculine connotations should appear in a hunting song, but is absent from a song that centres on a woman's social role.

Another bird that does not feature in the woman's song in (16) is the parrot, despite their central role in Kandozi-Chapra culture. Parrots are important as the first wives of humanity in Kandozi-Chapra myth,[6] and as symbols of romantic love and conjugal harmony in Chicham magic songs (Overall 2019). So parrots symbolise conjugal love, while the song in (16) invokes symbols of familial love and group membership.

Summarising, I have shown that the analysed song refers to three bird species: caracara, cacique, and oropendola. These birds and others such as toucans and parrots reappear in other songs and discursive contexts.[7] Once we take into account the connotations of the different bird species, we find that there is

5 This is comparable to the lyrics of Huaorani traditional drinking songs, which compare the guests to different species of birds feasting on fruit from a single tree (Rival 2002: 134).

6 The name *Kandozi* itself refers to the yellow-crowned Amazon parrot *Amazona ochrocephala* (Surrallés 2007: 315).

7 In Airo-Pai (Secoya) tradition, men are compared to oropendolas—in part because of their

a clear explanation for the absence of toucans and parrots from the woman's drinking song, because their associations with masculinity and romantic love are quite distinct from the values of community and familial love symbolised by the birds in the song.

4 Magic and the Everyday

Certain binaries that may be taken for granted in Western thought are not so straightforwardly applicable to Amazonian societies:

> For the anthropologist to engage with Amazonian views of sociality, a good many boundaries of Western social thought must as a matter of course be disrupted, as for instance is particularly the case with respect to some of the major dualisms of Enlightenment thought: the contrast between civil society and the domestic, society and the individual, reason and emotions, mind and body, subject and object, art and work.
>
> OVERING and PASSES 2000: 8

To this list one might reasonably add the boundary between 'magic' ritual and everyday life.[8] While Kandozi-Chapra tradition does include songs that have magical effects as their central function, there is no clear distinction between these and the drinking songs. Brabec de Mori (2011a) describes a similar overlap in Shipibo song styles:

> In Shipibo terminology and understanding, there is no clear distinction between magical and non-magical songs ... Songs performed at drinking parties or for courtship, for instance, also carry a certain degree of magical power [...].
>
> BRABEC DE MORI 2011a: 172

More broadly, we must be mindful of the cultural context within which these examples of verbal art are embedded. Menezes Bastos (2006) cautions against

woven nests, since weaving is a masculine occupation—and women are compared to green parrots (*Amazona sp.*), which symbolise parental care (Belaunde 1994: 96, 2001: 81–99).

8 Cf. Shepard (2018) on the use of plant medicines breaking down the mind/body duality, and note that the shamanic use of plant medicines also breaks down the distinction between 'magic' and 'medicine'.

treating any piece of music in isolation, noting that musical performances in lowland Amazonia tend to be organised into larger cycles: “Tudo faz parecer, então, que peças isoladas de música não parecem fazer muito sentido.” [So everything makes it seem that isolated pieces of music do not seem to make much sense] (Menezes Bastos 2006: 8).[9] This same caution should apply equally to oral tradition more generally, which forms a network of interlocking cross-references within the culture. So the songs are not to be treated in isolation, and cannot be separated from their context and functions, in particular from their links to mythological tradition and magic ritual. Both of these contexts are heavily associated with fauna imagery.

Tapir and deer feature in more clearly magical songs sung by a female elder of the Chapra community of Unanchay. She introduces one song as follows:

(18) a. *zitamin atar=cha yas-ee-k-u sirutma sirutma*
ancestor say.HAB=COP sing-INCH-FGR-CVB.3 long.ago long.ago
ta-raŋk-ana zitamin yas-ee-k-u wa-zaarnchi=am
say-PST-3PL ancestor sing-INCH-FGR-CVB.3 3-husband.PSSD=DAT
‘the ancestors used to sing, long ago the ancestors would sing to their husband’

b. *maa-ka-t-u naa-tr-u wayuch=tam*
sleep-THERE-FGR-CVB.3 go-HAB-CVB.3 brother.of.female=also
maa-ka-t-u naa-tr-u aanu=a
sleep-THERE-FGR-CVB.3 go-HAB-CVB.3 DEM.DST=ACC
yas-ee-k-u atar=cha
sing-INCH-FGR-CVB.3 say.HAB=COP
‘when he goes hunting, also her brother when he goes hunting, they’d sing’[10]

c. *pamara yas-ee-k-u atra-sha na mazna-ŋk-tsa*
tapir sing-INCH-FGR-CVB.3 say.HAB-SECOND now listen-IMP-PL
‘they’d sing about the tapir; now listen’ (kandozi_chapra009)

9 While I have tried to illustrate precisely this embedding of performances in their cultural context throughout this paper, I acknowledge the irony of restricting myself here to the detailed analysis of a single song.

10 The phrasing *maakatu naatru* literally means ‘when he goes to sleep there’, an avoidance term referring to going hunting overnight.

The singer makes it clear that these songs function by affecting the emotional state of another person and influencing their decisions (similar to the *anin* of Chicham speakers), in this case ensuring that loved ones would return quickly and safely from hunting trips. Note that while the consultant who worked on transcribing this recording was able to identify some words in the song, he could not offer a translation or an exegesis. A similarly opaque song recorded in the Chapra community Unión Indígena by a male elder was described as being sung by warriors before attacking an enemy group. It invokes *maaka* 'snake (in general)' and *tumuuz* 'jaguar/dog,' because (as the singer describes it in a Spanish-language commentary on the recording) if the enemy warriors are startled by seeing a snake or a jaguar, they are distracted and unable to take aim and defend themselves. Finally, the hunting songs mentioned in § 3 were described as having magical effects, improving the hunter's chances of success, but the consultants I worked with claimed to have stopped singing these songs when they converted to Christianity in the 1960s, breaking the chain of transmission.

It remains an open question whether the difficulty of interpretation is a feature of the more clearly magical songs that distinguishes them from other song types, or whether it is an artefact arising from a breakdown of transmission between generations. Further research on these and other inscrutable songs remains a goal for future fieldwork.

A further point to note about the song tradition concerns the relationship between the music and the words. In a number of Amazonian societies, including Kandozi-Chapra, songs may be hummed, whistled, or performed on an instrument such as a flute, without diminishing the relevance or power of the verbal content that the 'singer' intends (cf. Brabec de Mori 2018: 79; Surrallés 2007: 322–323). Surrallés (2003) makes a similar observation in the context of a distinct discourse genre, the ceremonial greeting dialogue. He notes that the semantic content of the dialogue is far less important than the performance itself and the associated eye contact, and explicitly likens this dialogue to song: "those taking part in the ceremony engage in what is really a form of musical interpretation" (Surrallés 2003: 786). All of this is part of a widespread cultural practice that Brabec de Mori (2011a) describes as specifically linking song to animal symbols:

> There is some evidence that before the rubber boom (ca. 1870–1920), songs and theatrical performance were the most important aspects of curing rituals. At that time, such rituals may have included many processes which are rare these days. It appears, for example, that possession by or transformation into animals played a much higher role, and vocal

> music was the preferred mode of communication with these animals. Singing was also the only possibility for the animals or spirits who took possession of the performer to express themselves or to transmit their message to the human listeners.
>
> BRABEC DE MORI 2011a: 171

Returning to the song in (16), we can see a clear point of difference from shamanic singing in which the shaman is possessed by or transforms into a non-human—the singer of (16) explicitly marks her comparison to birds as a simile, using the similative suffix *-mashi*, e.g. *mantar-mashi* (caracara-SIMIL) 'like a caracara'. While I have no recordings of shamanic discourse to compare, Surrallés (2007: 373) gives a shamanic song recorded in 1994, which is sung from the point of view of the anaconda (e.g. 'I am in the swamps'). Not only is the similative suffix not used, but the singer does not even explicitly describe himself as an anaconda—the perspective of the anaconda is simply assumed.

Although these examples suggest that there may be two genres of songs, roughly one inscrutable/magic/secret type and one transparent/profane/publicly performed type, the boundary is not at all clear-cut. A song recorded in the Chapra community of Unanchay in April 2016 sits in an intermediate position. In the recording (archived as kandozi_chapra014), a male singer performs a warrior's song in which he compares himself to the *mawaazi* bird (most likely *Trogon violaceus* or *Trogon viridis*). This bird comes down from the treetops in very sunny weather, then sits and sings in the shade. The bird's song is interpreted as boastfully saying it cannot be shot, but always dodges blowdarts, and in the same way the warrior dodges bullets. The singing is accompanied by a distinctive dance miming the dodging.[11] In the recording, the singer first performed the song on the flute, then followed up with a version with sung lyrics. It was not clear whether this song was intended to have the effect of improving the warrior's skills, as was the case with the 'snake and jaguar' song described above.

To summarise, then, there appears to be no clear boundary between 'magic' and 'profane' genres of Kandozi-Chapra song, but there is a wide range of variation among the attested song types. The lyrics may be couched in everyday language, or they may be quite opaque. The song may have an explicit purpose

11 The trogon birds normally live in the canopy but are quite unafraid of humans when they are in the lower forest, and typically sit still until they spot an insect or are startled, then they fly very quickly to another perch (Ridgely and Greenfield 2001: 299–302).

such as bringing loved ones home or improving a warrior's odds of surviving a battle, or it may exist solely in the performed context, as is the case with the drinking songs. And there are various ways in which the song's musical and lyrical content may be linked to performative elements such as dance, serving masato, or playing an instrument. Again, the only clear conclusion to be drawn is that this rich and endangered tradition requires urgent documentary work if we hope to gain a deeper understanding of it.

5 Implications, Directions, and Open Questions

The cultural functions of verbal art are varied. An important one is imparting the values required to lead a morally right life; Cruikshank (1998: 43–44) cites Tagish storyteller Angela Sidney saying "I've tried to live my life right, just like a story," and within the Kandozi-Chapra contact area Walker (2013) describes the Urarina concept of *temerequiin* 'standing-leaned-together', used in the context of ayahuasca chants "both as a description of how real people do live and as a moral injunction concerning how they should live" (Walker 2013: 3).

Scalise Sugiyama (2001) shows how not only social but also ecological knowledge can be encoded in traditional stories, through a combination of metaphorical and literal references. A number of traditional stories in Kandozi-Chapra and neighbouring cultures make reference to the consequences of overexploitation of natural resources, for example. The theme of the birds referred to in the song in (16) is of living properly, fulfilling social obligations; and explicit references to correct social roles in Kandozi-Chapra songs and greeting rituals show that such knowledge is transferred directly as well as metaphorically in these genres.

More examples of verbal art of all genres will also allow us to build up a bigger picture of the details of connotations of the various flora and fauna. Detailed knowledge of this type can help to shed light on rhetorical effects like those described by Adelaar (2004) for Quechua song texts, which involve parallel constructions using semantically related pairs of words. Consider the pair *tuku* 'owl' and *waychaw* 'flycatcher' in (19)—these are related because "their call is interpreted as an ill omen" (Adelaar 2004: 64), so their appearance in this poetic construction is only fully interpretable when the shared connotations are taken into account. Prieto Mendoza (2019) describes similar effects for Kakataibo, a Panoan language spoken in the southern part of the Andean piedmont.

(19) *ripu-na-y* *urqu-pi* ***tuku**-lla* *waqa-n* *pasa-na-y*
depart-NMLZ-PSSD.1 hill-LOC owl-LIM cry-3SG leave-NMLZ-PSSD.1
qasa-pi ***waychaw**-lla* *waqa-n*
snowy.mountain-LOC flycatcher-LIM cry-3SG
'The owl sings on the hill where I depart / The flycatcher sings in the snow-capped mountain where I am leaving' (Adelaar 2004: 64; glosses adapted from Prieto Mendoza 2019: 388)

Positioning the songs described in this paper in the wider context of Kandozi-Chapra oral tradition, and taking into account overlapping imagery with myth and ritual dialogue, allows us to understand some of the subtle connotations involved in the symbolic use of birds, and offers an explanation for the appearance of particular birds in particular contexts.

The birds in the song in (16) are symbolic of human sociality, due to their preference for forest-edge habitats near human settlements, their communal nesting habit reminiscent of human settlements, and their constant vocalisation reminiscent of human speech and song. We can draw a distinction between caracara, cacique, and oropendola, representing familial love and social values, and other birds—toucans with connotations of masculinity, and parrots with connotations of romantic love and marriage. Further research will be able to support or falsify this distinction, which makes an empirical prediction regarding the lyrical content of women's drinking party songs.

The most urgent challenge for future research is to document this endangered tradition as richly as possible. Only then can we deepen our understanding of the interwoven symbols and discourse genres, and their functions.

Acknowledgements

I gratefully acknowledge all the consultants and others who helped me with language and logistics during the research that led to this paper, especially the performers and those who helped with transcription, translation, and elucidation. Fieldwork planned for 2020 was cancelled due to the COVID-19 pandemic, which necessitated continuing the discussions in virtual form. This was no easy feat given that the majority of Kandozi and Chapra speakers live well out of the reach of internet or mobile phone coverage, and I thank Sandra Mando Totarica for her willingness to help with the Chapra texts discussed in this paper.

The seeds of the analysis presented here were planted while I was a Postdoctoral Research Fellow at James Cook University's Language and Culture Research Centre, under the supervision of Sasha Aikhenvald and Bob Dixon.

Sasha was also the primary supervisor of my PhD at La Trobe University, and it is impossible to express the depth of my appreciation for the fundamental role that she has played in my academic development. Her breadth and depth of knowledge combined with her encouraging and exacting supervision style were instrumental in my training as a linguist, for which I am truly grateful.

Additional fieldwork funding came from ELDP grant SG0471. Recordings are deposited in the ELAR archive https://www.elararchive.org/dk0416/

Abbreviations

The following abbreviations are used in glosses:

ACC	accusative
ALL	allative
AM	associated motion
BGR	backgrounded
COMIT	comitative
COMPL	completive
COP	copula
CVB	converb
DAT	dative
DEM	demonstrative
DST	distal
DUB	dubitative
DUR	durative
EMPH	emphatic
EP	epenthetic
EXH.FOC	exhaustive focus
FGR	foregrounded
HAB	habitual
IDEO	ideophone
IMP	imperative
INCH	inchoative
INCOMPL	incompletive
INTENS	intensifier
LIM	limitative
LOC	locative
NEG	negative
NMLZ	nominaliser
PL	plural
POT	potential
PSSD	possessed
PST	past
REDUP	reduplication
SECOND	second
SG	singular
SIL	Summer Institute of Linguistics
SIMIL	similative
SUPE	superessive
THEN	then
TOP	topic
VOC	vocative

References

Adelaar, Willem (2004). Linguistic peculiarities of Quechua song texts. In Guillermo Delgado & John M. Schechter (eds.), *Quechua Verbal Artistry: The Inscription of Andean Voices*, 61–75. Aachen: Shaker Verlag.

Adelaar, Willem and Pieter Muysken (2004). *The Languages of the Andes*. Cambridge: Cambridge University Press.

Basso, Ellen B. (2011). Amazonian Ritual Communication in Relation to Multilingual Social Networks. In Alf Hornborg and Jonathan D. Hill (eds.), *Ethnicity in ancient Amazonia: reconstructing past identities from archaeology, linguistics, and ethnohistory*, 155–171. University Press of Colorado.

Beier, Christine, Lev Michael and Joel Sherzer (2002). Discourse forms and processes in indigenous lowland South America: An areal-typological perspective. *Annual Review of Anthropology* 31: 121–145.

Belaunde, Luisa E. (1994). Parrots and oropendolas: the aesthetics of gender relations among the Airo-Pai of the Peruvian Amazon. *Journal de la Société des Américanistes* 80 (1): 95–111.

Belaunde, Luisa E. (2001). *Viviendo Bien: Genero y Fertilidad entre los Airo-Pai de la Amazonia Peruana*. Lima: CAAAP.

Brabec de Mori, Bernd (2002). Ikaro: Medizinische Gesänge im Peruanischen Regenwald. MPhil thesis, Vienna University.

Brabec de Mori, Bernd (2011a). The Magic of Song, the Invention of Tradition, and the Structuring of Time among the Shipibo (Peruvian Amazon). In Gerda Lechleitner and Christian Liebl (eds.), *Jahrbuch des Phonogrammarchivs der Österreichischen Akademie der Wissenschaften* [*Yearbook of the Phonogrammarchiv at the Austrian Academy of Sciences*], Vol. 2, 169–192.

Brabec de Mori, Bernd (2011b). Tracing Hallucinations: Contributing to a Critical Ethnohistory of Ayahuasca Usage in the Peruvian Amazon. In Hendrik Jungaberle and Beatriz C. Labate (eds.), *The Internationalization of Ayahuasca*, 23–47. Zürich: LIT–Verlag.

Brabec de Mori, Bernd (2018). "The Inka's Song Emanates from my Tongue:" Learning and Performing Shipibo Curing Songs. In Fabrice Lengronne (ed.), *La música y los pueblos indígenas*, 73–107. Montevideo, Uruguay: Centro Nacional de Documentación Musical Lauro Ayestará.

Codjia, Paul (2017). Comment attirer le gibier?: Pratique du jeûne et récitation de chants magiques dans les activités cynégétiques wampis (jivaro). *Journal De La Société Des Américanistes* 103 (2): 81–110.

Cox, Doris (1957). Candoshi verb inflection. *International Journal of American Linguistics* 23 (3): 129–140.

Cruikshank, Julie (1998). *The Social Life of Stories: Narrative and Knowledge in the Yukon Territory*. Vancouver: UBC Press.

Dean, Bartholomew (1994). The Poetics of Creation: Urarina Cosmogony and Historical Consciousness. *Latin American Indian Literatures Journal* 10: 22–45.

Descola, Philippe (trans. Janet Lloyd) (1996). *The Spears of Twilight: Life and Death in the Amazon Jungle*. London: Harper Collins.

Epps, Patience (2015). The dynamics of linguistic diversity: Language contact and language maintenance in Amazonia. Slides from a talk presented at 18th Annual Workshop on American Indigenous Languages, UCSB, May 8 2015.

Ferguson, R. Brian (1990). Blood of the Leviathan: Western contact and warfare in Amazonia. *American Ethnologist* 17: 237–257.

Gnerre, Maurizio (2009). "While I Sing I Am Sitting in a Real Airplane:" Innovative contents in Shuar and Achuar ritual communication. In Gunter Senft and Ellen B. Basso (eds.), *Ritual Communication*, 293–316. Oxford: Berg.

Gow, Peter (1994). River People: Shamanism and History in Western Amazonia. In Nicholas Thomas and Caroline Humphrey (eds.), *Shamanism, History, and the State*, 90–113. Ann Arbor: University of Michigan Press.

Haspelmath, Martin (1995). The converb as a cross-linguistically valid category. In Martin Haspelmath and Ekkehard König (eds.) *Converbs in cross-linguistic perspective: Structure and meaning of adverbial verb forms*, 1–56. Berlin: Mouton de Gruyter.

Jakobson, Roman (1968). Poetry of Grammar and Grammar of Poetry. *Lingua* 21: 597–609.

Livi-Bacci, Massimo (2016). The Depopulation of Upper Amazonia in Colonial Times. *Revista de Indias* 76 (267): 419–448.

Mader, Elke (2004). Un discurso mágico del amor. Significado y acción en los hechizos shuar (anent). In María Susana Cipolletti (ed.), *Los mundos de abajo y los mundos de arriba. Individuo y sociedad en las tierras bajas, en los Andes y más allá*, 51–80. Quito: Abya Yala.

Menezes Bastos, Rafael José de (2006). Música nas Terras Baixas da America do Sul: Estado da Arte (Segunda Parte). *Antropologia em Primeira Mão* 89: 5–20.

Michael, Lev (2014). On the Pre-Columbian origin of Proto-Omagua-Kokama. *Journal of Language Contact* 7 (2): 309–344.

Mihas, Elena (2019). Documenting ritual songs: Best practices for preserving the ambiguity of Alto Perené (Arawak) shamanic *pantsantsi* 'singing'. *Language Documentation & Conservation* 13: 197–230.

Ochoa Siguas, Nancy (1992). El mito del diluvio y la creación de la división sexual entre los kanpopiyapi de la Amazonia peruana. *Journal de la Société des Américanistes* 78 (2): 163–180.

Overall, Simon E. (2019). Parrots, peccaries, and people. *International Journal of Language and Culture* 6 (1): 148–174. https://doi.org/10.1075/ijolc.00020.ove

Overall, Simon E. (forthcoming). Kandozi-Chapra. In Patience Epps and Lev Michael (eds.), *International Handbook of Amazonian Languages*. Mouton de Gruyter.

Overing, Joanna and Alan Passes (2000). Introduction: Conviviality and the opening up of Amazonian anthropology. In Joanna Overing and Alan Passes (eds.), *The Anthropology of Love and Anger: the Aesthetics of Conviviality in Native Amazonia*, 1–30. London and New York: Routledge.

Payne, David L. (1990). Some widespread grammatical forms in South American languages. In David Payne (ed.), *Amazonian Linguistics*, 75–87. Dallas: University of Texas Press.

Prieto Mendoza, Alejandro (2019). Semantic Parallelism in Traditional Kakataibo Chants. *Open Linguistics* 5 (1): 383–404. https://doi.org/10.1515/opli-2019-0021

Ridgely, Robert S. and Paul J. Greenfield (2001). *The Birds of Ecuador, vol. 2: Field Guide*. Cornell University Press.

Rival, Laura (2002). *Trekking Through History: The Huaorani of Amazonian Ecuador*. New York: Columbia University Press.

Roe, Peter (1982). *The Cosmic Zygote: Cosmology in the Amazon Basin*. New Brunswick, New Jersey: Rutgers University Press.

Scalise Sugiyama, Michelle (2001). Food, Foragers, and Folklore: The Role of Narrative in Human Subsistence. *Evolution and Human Behavior* 22 (4): 221–240. https://doi.org/10.1016/S1090-5138(01)00063-0

Shepard, Glenn H. (2002). Three Days for Weeping: Dreams, Emotions, and Death in the Peruvian Amazon. *Medical Anthropology Quarterly* 16 (2): 200–229.

Shepard, Glenn H. (2018). Spirit bodies, plant teachers, and messenger molecules in Amazonian shamanism. In Dennis McKenna (ed.), *Ethnopharmacologic search for psychoactive drugs*, vol. II: *50 years of research (1967–2017)*, 70–81. Santa Fe: Synergetic Press.

Sherzer, Joel (1987). A Discourse-Centered Approach to Language and Culture. *American Anthropologist* 89 (2): 295–309.

Surrallés, Alexandre (2003). Face to Face: Meaning, Feeling and Perception in Amazonian Welcoming Ceremonies. *The Journal of the Royal Anthropological Institute* 9 (4): 775–791.

Surrallés, Alexandre (2007). Los Candoshi. In Fernando Santos Granero and Frederica Barclay Rey de Castro (eds.), *Guía Etnográfica de la Alta Amazonía*, vol. 6, 244–380. Lima, Peru: Smithsonian Tropical Research Institute / Institut Français d'Etudes Andines.

Surrallés, Alexandre (2009) (trans. Rosa Álvarez). *En el corazón del sentido: Percepción, afectividad y acción en los candoshi* (*Alta Amazonía*) [translation of *Au coeur du sens: perception, affectivité, action chez les Candoshi* (2003)]. Lima: Instituto Francés de Estudios Andinos.

Tariri, with Ethel E. Wallis (1965). *Tariri: My Story. From Jungle Killer to Christian Missionary*. New York, Evanston and London: Harper & Row.

Taylor, Anne-Christine and Ernesto Chau (1983). Jivaroan magical songs: Achuar *anent* of connubial love. *Amerindia* 8: 87–127.

Townsley, Graham (1993). Song Paths. The ways and means of Yaminahua Shamanic Knowledge. *L'Homme* 126–128: 449–468.

Tuggy, John (1966). *Vocabulario Candoshi de Loreto*. Lima, Peru: SIL.

Uzendoski, Michael A., Mark Hertica, and Edith Calapucha Tapuy (2005). The Phenomenology of Perspectivism: Aesthetics, Sound, and Power in Women's Songs from Amazonian Ecuador. *Current Anthropology* 46 (4): 656–662.

Valladares Alcántara, María Isabel, ed. (2009). *Resumen Ejecutivo: Resultados definitivos de las comunidades indígenas*. Lima, Peru: Dirección Nacional de Censos y Encuestas—Instituto Nacional de Estadística e Informática. https://www.inei.gob.pe/media/MenuRecursivo/publicaciones_digitales/Est/Lib0789/Libro.pdf (accessed 15 March 2019).

Walker, Harry (2010). Soulful Voices: Birds, Language and Prophecy in Amazonia. *Tipití: Journal of the Society for the Anthropology of Lowland South America*, 8 (1), Article 1.

Walker, Harry (2013). *Under a Watchful Eye: Self, Power, and Intimacy in Amazonia*. Berkeley/Los Angeles: University of California Press.

Wasserstrom, Robert (2014). Surviving the Rubber Boom: Cofán and Siona Society in the Colombia-Ecuador Borderlands (1875–1955). *Ethnohistory* 61 (3): 525–548.

Whitten, Norman E., Jr. (2011). Ethnogenesis and Interculturality in the "Forest of Canelos": The Wild and the Tame Revisited. In Alf Hornborg and Jonathan D. Hill (eds.), *Ethnicity in ancient Amazonia: Reconstructing past identities from archaeology, linguistics and ethnohistory*, 321–334. University Press of Colorado.

Wise, Mary Ruth (2011). Rastros desconcertantes de contactos entre idiomas y culturas a lo largo de los contrafuertes orientales de los Andes del Perú. In Willem F.H. Adelaar, Pilar Valenzuela Bismarck and Roberto Zariquiey Biondi (eds.), *Estudios sobre lenguas Andinas y Amazónicas: Homenaje a Rodolfo Cerrón-Palomino*, 305–326. Lima: Fondo Editorial, PUCP.

CHAPTER 5

Research, Rituals and Reciprocity: The Promises of Hospitality in Fieldwork

Rosita Henry and Michael Wood

1 Introduction

Attempting to become embedded in a natural speech community lies at the very heart of Alexandra Aikhenvald's research endeavour. Throughout her distinguished career she has advocated for 'immersion fieldwork' as "… the backbone of an empirically-based science of linguistics" (Aikhenvald 2007: 3). For Aikhenvald, firsthand documentation in the field "is essential for our understanding of human languages, their structural properties and their genetic relationships" (2007: 3). In this paper we reflect on the nature of the relationships between field researchers and the speech communities that host us, focusing particularly on practices of hospitality and the promises, obligations and expectations that are entailed.[1]

Young (2020: 5) provides us with a working definition of hospitality as follows:

> Hospitality is […] a set of practices for establishing social relations between hosts and visitors […] if we think of hospitality as a formal system for establishing a set of relations meant to negotiate encounter, it emerges as a kind of practical pidgin language for the negotiation of alterity.

Yet hospitality is not simply the transformation of alterity into sociality. It is also a practical language for the assertion of identity (sameness), and, at its best, the practice of mutual care and 'love' (Aikhenvald 2013). Like gift-giving, it "involves reciprocity, a tension between spontaneity and calculation, generosity and parasitism, friendship and enmity, improvisation and rule; like the gift, hospitality encompasses distant agents, it embeds social transactions in materiality and raises complex questions relating to economy and time" (Candea and da Col 2012: S1–S2).

1 Part of the fieldwork on which our reflections are based, especially our focus on life-cycle exchanges linked to hospitality as a form of care-giving, was funded by the Australian Research Council (ARC) project DP140100178.

© ROSITA HENRY AND MICHAEL WOOD, 2022 | DOI:10.1163/9789004510395_006

2 Hospitality: The Political Economy of the Stranger Guest

The hospitality that was granted to us as anthropologists among the Kumula and the Penambi Wia respectively, and that is granted to researchers in many different fieldwork contexts, has long been understood to be structured by cultural imaginaries of the stranger and the host. In some Melanesian contexts, for example, effective and dangerous power is typically thought to be a property of an external 'other'. Such an 'other' in colonial times could take the form of the European, who was in fact the local ruler and representative of the sovereign. Europeans could also stand for forms of vitality derived from outside of the local world (Candea and da Col 2012: S7) and were understood as capable of redefining relationships with the dead and redefining inequalities in the global distribution of wealth and technology. Hospitality to the stranger emerged primarily on the horizon of an anticipated future and an ability to provisionally and partially incorporate the stranger within existing 'socio-cultural geographies' (Frieze 2009: 52). Yet such hospitality never fully assimilates the stranger into the self.

There is often a persisting sense of a partial or incomplete relationality between researcher and host that can amplify into a non-relationship. Hospitality in research is not just organised by mutual sharing of value but also by the negative contours of sociality (Shryock 2019; Serres 2007). Such negative contours involve the creation of a world without exchange where consumption can occur without sharing, where nothing we possess is given to another, where one can accumulate without adequate reciprocity or indeed any reciprocity. Such a world of taking without giving is ultimately defined by theft—of cultural heritage, of intellectual property, of anything. This is a world defined by inadequate recognition, or by the complete substitution of self by an intrusive other who comes to speak for you and who seemingly never stops speaking for you or about you. This is a world of accumulation rather than transaction. In PNG the stranger, such as a visiting European researcher, can be understood as a hoarder, as defining a site of vast accumulation without any capacity to share, give or transact. This kind of subject also informs post-colonial critiques of colonial knowledge production as appropriation, ceaseless accumulation and even destruction. This subject is no longer a guest, but an exploitative, deceptive other. At best such a researcher-guest is considered a parasite (Serres 2007) who is sincerely engaged in recording, securing and partially consuming local forms of social, linguistic and cultural expression.

On the other hand, the critique of the researcher in PNG as a knowledge extractor is balanced by PNG understandings of relations with Europeans as opening up 'roads' and other possibilities of extraction of valuable things from the Europeans without return. Such narratives imply that Papua New Guineans could potentially be equivalently parasitic on strange researchers. The two extractive economies are not necessarily morally equivalent—the foreign researcher currently contains more oppressive characteristics than any PNG extractor. Nonetheless both outline some of the current liveliness of negative hospitality involved in fieldwork by strangers.

It is within such an ecology of alien power and ambiguous possibility that the anthropologist or the linguist arrives as a guest and begins work. Gaining access to the field and acceptance within a community generally requires a key member of that community to be willing to take responsibility for the researcher. Fieldwork, especially in remote regions, often places a researcher in a position in which they must rely on the hospitality of members of the community, and where they become dependent on the cultural, political and environmental knowledge of their hosts to facilitate research access to others in the community or to ensure their safety in the field.

The relationship between researcher and research participant has received much attention in the literature, especially since the reflexive turn in anthropology and moves for greater collaboration between researchers and their hosts (Glowczewski et al. 2013; Modan 2016; Rice 2011; Schwartz and Lederman 2011; Yamada 2007). What we write may be an ethnography, a grammar or a dictionary or a work that addresses debates from within our respective disciplines, but if we are to succeed in our endeavours we must, as Jane Hill proposes, "incorporate a cultural and ethnographic understanding of language into the very foundations of our research" (2006: 113). This echoes Aikhenvald's commitment to 'immersion fieldwork'.

3 Immersion Fieldwork and Reciprocity

In the face of increasing language endangerment and the threat of language extinction, Aikhenvald has strongly advocated for recording languages as spoken naturally within their social and cultural contexts. This, she argues, can only be done through 'immersion fieldwork', which she defines as "observing the language as it is used, becoming a member of a community, and often being adopted into the kinship system" (Aikhenvald 2015: 21).

Dobrin and Schwartz (2016: 254) argue that linguistic fieldwork requires that "linguists and community representatives work together as equal partners to design and establish project goals that will serve both academic and community needs". Such research aims to create accessible and useful material for community members. What is ultimately promised by this mutual engagement is that the hospitality of the research participants is reciprocated by the researcher with valued language material. However, the language material valued by the research participants may not be the same as that valued by the researcher. For example, Aikhenvald (2013: 178–179) lists, in order of merit, the outcomes of her research work that are valued by academia (such as monographs and papers on typological topics, language contact and language change) in comparison with the outcomes that are valued by her Tariana research participants (such as dictionaries and text collections). She notes:

> [...] academia tends to discard what the Tariana value. As a result, the more I succeed academically, the more unfulfilled debt I feel with respect to what I ought to do for the remaining Tariana speakers, my Tariana family. There is never enough.

In some contexts, value may not be ascribed by research participants to the existing language at all, nor to any materials produced about it. Rather, what might be valued is new forms of expression and access to the language, knowledge and institutions of the powerful; gaining access to a text in English may be more useful to community members than having it written in a heritage language few understand (Dobrin and Schwartz 2016: 255–256).

Immersion fieldwork enables researchers to grasp the culturally specific values that often inform local expectations of research outcomes. It allows researchers to engage with members of speech communities "in ways that resonate with their cultural values, even though these may be implicit or counterintuitive from the researcher's point of view" (Dobrin and Schwartz 2016: 256). It is only by attuning ourselves to what constitutes adequate reciprocity for our research participants that we can begin to understand what good relationships might look like from their perspective (Dobrin and Schwartz 2016: 160). However, reciprocity, certainly in the PNG contexts in which we have worked, does not just privilege the host's perspective but typically involves a continuous series of 'promissory prestations' (Dapuez 2013) that continually redefine the hospitable actors, their perspectives on each other and their value to each other.

4 Hospitality as Promissory Gift

How does the stranger become someone you care for? We think this is achieved through what we call here hospitality. We argue that hospitality enables the incorporation of the researcher into social relationships, without the eradication of difference, by drawing host and guest into promissory relations of possibility. Such promises can involve long-term relationships of care between the researcher and particular members of the host community. An initial act of hospitality can open up the possibility of an open-ended series of transactions. However, as Dapuez (2016) notes:

> […] to ensure that they continue through time, promises and engagements need to be particularly and timely fulfilled. Just as gifts can sometimes work as instruments for producing engagement, gifts also realize a vow in an object with the aim of promising an even larger or meaningful object. After the movement of a minor gift that realizes the vow in an object, engagement is actualized. In these cases, the given gift does not close any reciprocity circuit […] but the given object refers to a promise already made, becoming a promissory gift.

In other words, the aim of hospitality and the series of transactions it initiates is to allow the relationship and its imagined possibilities to continue into an indefinitely defined future, even if expectations sometimes remain unfulfilled.

To make good on promises in the particular and timely fashion expected can be difficult. Aikhenvald (2015: 23) reflects on this in relation to her own fieldwork as follows:

> Being integrated into the Tariana community of Santa Rosa in northwest Amazonia, and into the Manambu community at Avatip in New Guinea, has never been easy for me. The 'adopted' family ties impose moral and financial obligations, and may even hamper further research.

Anthropologists, linguists and other field researchers often make promises to research participants and they make promises to us. Promises have complex properties and are not necessarily always kept by either side. This may be due to misunderstandings about whether a promise was made in the first place or to different ideas about the moral status of particular promises—whether it is actually necessary to 'make good' on them.

There are often multiple culturally specific understandings of a promise in play in these contexts. Such understandings are also reflected in Smith's (1997: 154) account of promising, which in her terms is a moral institution that

> […] gives agents the power to control the moral status of their future actions. By making a promise to do A an agent makes A obligatory for

> him, and thus typically changes its moral status [...] Some promises convert an otherwise morally neutral act to an obligatory one, while others merely render more obligatory an act that was already morally required.

In terms of our own cultural values, as researchers, breaking a promise has negative moral value. On the surface of things, at least trying to uphold a promise is something that we take for granted as being crucial for creating and maintaining good relations with others. Yet, much like many politicians, we sometimes do not 'make good' on our promises.[2] In the context of fieldwork we might prevaricate by making promises that we know are expected of us or that we feel obliged by our hosts to make, even though we are not certain we can keep them. In other words, we might take risks in making promises in the hope of being able to make good on them later, but not being sure that we can. There are also promises we might make and then subsequently regret, say if we discover that fulfilling the promise might cause more harm than good. Or we might say we will do something without meaning it to be a binding promise, but it is interpreted as such by our hosts, and vice versa.

In addition, the speech act of promising in other cultural contexts can take a different form to Anglo-European performances of promises (Rosaldo 1982: 216). In egalitarian societies, where promises cannot easily be enforced, a hospitable openness to a visitor might be an effective way to engage with the potential powers contained in that stranger. Offering hospitality to a stranger reflects a kind of hopefulness about a future state that cannot yet be fully understood or fully realised. The promise of what such hospitality might return is indefinite and ambiguous and there is no clear time of fulfilment. In PNG, promises are often a fundamental part of an economy of future revelation.

Drawing on our fieldwork experiences in PNG, we reflect below on some long-term relationships we developed with particular research participants that centred on both promises that involved binding obligation and promises involving possibilities that may be revealed. In our discussion we outline some of the temporal and spatial complexities of 'making good' on promissory obligations and more diffuse expectations. We position these promises as something realised in our long-term interactions with our research participants. We emphasise daily interactions, as it is in such interactions that both hospitality and promises are publicly generated, displayed and critically evaluated. It is in food sharing, mobilising resources for life cycle payments and feasts

2 For example, a recent media headline: 'Will Papua New Guinea's New Leader Make Good on His Reform Promises?' (Kabuni 2019).

and other mundane transactions that hospitality and promises of reciprocity are realised. Promises are now also routinely defined by formal contracts that can facilitate often unequal access to the status, wages, land and wealth that emerge from such state authorised promises. The promises of the contract and market and the promises of the gift co-exist, sometimes productively and sometimes in destructive tension with each other, and both crucially define the nature of research and its social relationships.

5 The Gift of Hospitality: Penambi Wia Promises

Perhaps it is unusual, but it can happen that a friendship precedes fieldwork. This was the case with Rosita Henry's fieldwork among the Penambi Wia in the Western Highlands of PNG. In fact, the friendship in question began while she was still at high school. A Penambi Wia girl, Maggie Leahy (Maggie Wilson after marriage) had attended the same boarding school in Australia with Rosita. Maggie was a fluent speaker of Temboka, which belongs to a linguistic continuum that includes Melpa, spoken by the people living north of Mt. Hagen township, and the language known as Ku Waru (as documented by Merlan and Rumsey 1991), spoken in the Western Nebilyer Valley, Western Highlands Province of Papua New Guinea. The speakers themselves call their way of speaking *tok ples* (in Tok Pisin) or *mbo ung* (lit. seedling/cutting talk) in their *tok ples*. The metaphor of planting, growth and fertility is cosmologically and ontologically important for peoples of the Western Highlands, who refer to themselves as *mbo*—planted beings (seedlings, cuttings or offshoots). This is important for comprehending the promise of hospitality, as understood among Penambi Wia people. Penambi Wia think of themselves as offshoots grown from the work invested in them by others. In turn, their relationships with others have to be cultivated and fertilised by their own labour, including acts of hospitality.

Maggie and Rosita maintained the friendship they had begun during their schooldays for over 40 years, until Maggie passed away in 2009, but the relationship they forged has lasted well beyond her death. When Rosita went to PNG to conduct field research for a postdoctoral project, Maggie became more than a friend extending hospitality to another friend, but an invaluable cultural guide and source of insights into the political complexities of social relations in the Highlands of PNG. In other words, Maggie became what some researchers call a 'key informant'. The friends began to plan to work together as research partners on a project exploring problems of gender relations and women's political empowerment. Although Maggie's death interrupted these plans, the promises that Maggie and Rosita made to one another continue to be fulfilled after Maggie's death and will possibly do so after Rosita passes away through the strong relationships that have been created among their children.

Since travelling from Australia to attend Maggie's funeral in 2009, Rosita has been a regular guest of Maggie's family and her lineage—the Wia Ulgamp Komp—while conducting field research to complete Maggie's life story (Wilson 2019). During one field trip, Rosita brought her daughter, Roselani, then a medical student, to do a placement at the nearby hospital in Mt Hagen. Several years later, Rosita also invited her younger sister Rosemarie to help her with an ethnographic field school run in collaboration with Maggie's daughter, Bernadine. The field school was itself a highly structured reflexive enactment of a ritual of hospitality (Pitt Rivers 2012) providing the students with the knowledge and organisational infrastructure relevant to being a good guest/visiting researcher who ideally can move across, and articulate between, multiple differences in culture, language and power.

The field school was held once a year for 4 years, until the Covid-19 pandemic prohibited travel. For Rosita, the field school presented a means to meet the promise of the hospitality that the Penambi Wia had extended to her in the past. Field school funds enabled the student group to appropriately recompense members of the host village for their hospitality, their time and their knowledge. Both this small contribution to the local economy and access to a wider social universe was appreciated by our hosts. The students were incorporated as guests via the hospitality rituals of the host community. In turn, the host community was incorporated into the staged rituals of the field school, including the welcome and farewell ceremonies and the public presentation of gifts and speeches.

The field schools drew Rosita more deeply into a promissory relationship with Maggie's kin, who continue to hope that she will return one day with another group of students and that past students will come back. Their expectations have been partly met by the fact that several students have in fact returned. Rosita's sister, Rosemarie, returned to continue her doctoral research and one of the field school students, Jack Growden, returned to do research for his honours thesis. Later, Jack established a not-for-profit organisation, called Litehaus, to supply computer technology to schools in PNG and he has returned numerous times, on occasion with other past students. The fact that Rosemarie, Jack and other students came back is significant. While Penambi Wia and their neighbours, the Kopi tribe, are used to tourists coming and going, never to be seen or heard of again, return visits hold the promise of reciprocities that flow from the growth of long-term relationships. That Rosita not only brought her own sister and daughter but also returned each year with groups of students to the village, some of whom themselves returned, is in itself the expression of the continuing promise of her friendship with Maggie.

The promise of the relationship partly found expression in the small contributions that Rosita made to bridewealth exchanges and to mortuary exchanges—what she has elsewhere called 'gifts of grief' (Henry 2012), the field school, and the completion and presentation of her research work on Maggie's memoir (Wilson 2019). However, ultimately it was Rosita's willingness to share her own kin (in a sense, to gift something of herself) that cemented her 'social ties' with Maggie's kin, including everything that lies hidden behind that dispassionate phrase—'social ties'. As Graeber (2001: 161) notes, social scientists rarely use terms such as 'surrender, forgiveness, renunciation, love, respect, dignity, redemption, salvation, redress, compassion, everything that is at the heart of relationships between people'.

Graeber (2001), in his review of the debates about Mauss's (2016) famous study of gift exchange, distinguished between 'open' and 'closed' forms of reciprocity. He noted that "reciprocity keeps no accounts, because it implies a relation of permanent mutual commitment; it becomes closed reciprocity when a balancing of accounts closes the relationship off, or at least maintains the constant possibility of doing so" (Graeber 2001: 220). Hospitality, we argue, is an expression of open reciprocity. The gift of hospitality lies in its promise—that is, the generative possibilities of the relationship that it forges.

Among Penambi Wia people and their neighbours in the Western Highlands, the generative possibilities of relationships are expressed in daily life both privately, through everyday acts of sharing, especially food, and publicly, through large scale ceremonial gift exchanges. An example of promises made privately between individuals in the context of everyday life is the practice of reciprocal food naming. Some foods commonly found as reciprocal names include: *kaimegl* 'liver', *mokh* 'leg of pig/pork', *kantemung*—a type of cucumber, *towe* and *kennge*—types of banana, *gey puk* 'sweet potato', and *mundumong* 'heart'.

In practice, two people share a piece of food and from then on call each other by the name of that food. The pair enter into a sort of relationship contract with one another. The quality of relationship that is signified by the use of these reciprocal names suggests that defining them as 'terms of endearment' is appropriate. For example, the term *kennge*—a type of banana—is also commonly used to mean 'sweetheart' (Wilson 2019: 115). No longer do the two people address one another by their proper names. From the time they make the vow, they reciprocally address one another by the name of the food they shared. During the ethnographic field school, several of the students were encouraged by their host mentors to enter into such reciprocal food-name agreements.

Andrew Strathern understands this practice by relating it to Melpa ideas about humans as *mbo* 'planted' beings and the way that 'concepts of descent, kinship and locality ... are mediated by ideas of substance created by food' (1977: 507). According to Strathern (1977: 507–508):

> [...] the sharer associates the other with himself metonymically through their act of sharing contiguous pieces of food. The metonymical act then sets up an association between them which is a metaphorical form of kinship [...]

Sharing food here is not merely a general statement that people are related through commensality. Sharing the food actually acts to *create* a relationship based on shared substance. In other words the practice is 'relationally constitutive' (Stasch 2011: 102). The food name serves as a label for the dyadic relationship created and as a description of the originating event of consuming the shared food (Stasch 2009: 82). Through this reciprocal naming, the memory and promise of the foundational event of commensality is maintained and alluded to every time the two people address one another (Stasch 2009: 82).

At the same time, this practice enables the avoidance of the use of proper names, which draw attention to persons as uniquely differentiated entities as opposed to metonymical related 'offshoots'. As with affinal relationships, where name avoidance is the rule, if one person in a food-name-sharing partnership, whether deliberately or accidentally, does not call the other by the agreed food name, but uses their proper name instead, a small fine can be demanded to restore the continuity of the relationship (Strathern 1977: 509).

Proper names, or autonyms, stress individuality and imply a distinction between 'self' and 'other' (Levi-Strauss 1966: 192). In contrast, the abrogation of the use of autonyms downplays distinctions. Through the relinquishment of their personal names in favour of the commemorative name of a shared food the parties signify a close social bond through mutual identification. At the same time, by avoiding each other's personal names, like affines do, they signal that they are mutually separate. Paradoxically, name avoidance is a way that people reciprocally make themselves both strange *and* familiar to one another. As Maggie's son, Maki, explained to Rosita, the sharing of food and its name with his adoptive mother allowed him to avoid addressing her as mum and her him as son, while enabling a mother-son relationship to be gradually nurtured:

> My mum and my nickname for each other is Punt [...] It's a kind of bean [...] It was comfortable calling her Punt because then I didn't have to call her mum, you know what I mean? It was my way of calling her mum, I suppose.

The mother-son relationship in this case was nurtured through kinship term avoidance. Name avoidance here "makes relatedness through relational restraint" (Stasch 2011: 105).

While food name vows are made privately (though not secretly) between two people, among the Penambi Wia promises also feature in large public events such as compensation payments following conflict and warfare, bridewealth and mortuary exchanges among segmentary clan groups. The material goods presented at public ceremonial events are given in exchange for something of value (such as a relationship of alliance). The gifts represent an undertaking by the segmentary groups to do, or forbear from doing, certain acts in relation to another group, but what is valued above all is the promise of the relationship itself. Promissory gifts (gifts that promise more at a later time), such as pigs, vegetable foods and sums of money, presented at such exchanges, are acceptable as the materialisation of a continuing relationship. For example, if a man who was given a big pig by an exchange partner as contribution to his son's bridewealth is not able to pay it back when called upon to do so, he may secure the promise of the relationship by, instead, contributing a smaller promissory gift.

Each of the types of exchanges described above—from the personal sharing of food names to the public ceremonial exchanges between segmentary groups—may involve explicit speech acts of promise. However, promises can also be understood without the use of a speech act. A promise can be made, for example, through actions such the presentation of a promissory gift or an act of hospitality. Whether a promise is made via a speech or any other kind of act, it can be considered by Penambi Wia to be morally binding and sanctionable.

Yet, while promises are expected to be met, the ideal is that the relationship is not closed off but continues into the future. Here we can see promise expressed as potential. A relationship that has promise is one that fosters the growth of hope, which is in itself a value. The political vagaries of social relations and the uncertainties of human existence mean that promises may never be fully realised, and dreams sometimes shattered, but the promissory acts that define hospitality aim to allow hope to flourish.

6 Kamula Hospitality Story: A Birthday Party

The promise of continuing social relationships is also highly valued among the Kamula. Like the Penambi Wia, the Kamula use reciprocal naming to mediate relationships between self and other. This story focuses on intergenerational relationships through the development of naming practices and bringing Michael's children to the 'field'. At issue is the way a promise, in this case to maintain social relationships, might be understood to be something that can be practically extended across or over time. Once when some Kamula men were talking about the fact Michael had only managed to have daughters, there was a fairly standard commiseration centred on their concern that Michael's 'bone' or male substance had not been reproduced. One man optimistically expressed the idea that Michael's daughters would have sons and those sons would continue to visit the Kamula much in the way Michael had. This was not so much a solution to Michael's lack of a son as a way of reproducing something like Michael's relationships with the Kamula, if not in the next generation then in the generation after that of his daughters. In 2021 Michael learnt that his younger daughter Eleanor was expecting a son.

These Kamula's long term perspective was not entirely surprising and reflects to some extent a Kamula orientation to the long term organisation of sociality over time. It is not uncommon for forms of reciprocity to be extended over three generations. Take, for example, marriages, which are ideally supposed to be reciprocated immediately by an exchange of spouses, usually discussed in the literature as 'sister exchange'. If an immediate exchange cannot be organised then reciprocity for a marriage can be delayed until the next generation and the flow on effects in bestowal rights and associated adoptions mean that the transaction may not be resolved until the next generation. At issue here is the salience of maintaining sociality through equivalence; in the case of Michael's daughters, the same kind of long-term sociality by the substitution of their sons for him seemed to provide a possible kind of equivalence to Michael's on-going social relationships with the Kamula.

In September 2001, Michael visited the Kamula with his youngest daughter Eleanor; he returned in December 2015 and again in January–February 2017 with his eldest daughter Patricia. On the 2015 visit Michael and Patricia stayed with Hawo Kulu and his wife, who was pregnant at the time. After they left, she gave birth and she and Hawo decided to name the child after Eleanor. This naming after Europeans was by then a common feature of Kamula naming practices. Michael has a number of namesakes among the Kamula and his mother, Patricia and Eleanor are all part of existing namesake relationships.

Among the Kamula, creating a namesake relationship involves what the Kamula call a *daiyo* relationship. Such namesake relationships are established by the intergenerational transmission of names within a named lineage or clan, including between living and dead members. A namesake relationship codes a specific history of the kin group's members. *Daiyo* relationships can also be established as a kind of reciprocity for a contribution to a husband's payment of bridewealth—a child from the marriage is named after the contributor. This suggests that a person (a child) can be understood as an extension or consequence of another's consideration and generosity. However, those in *daiyo* relationships are not supposed to completely intrude into each other's being—before *daiyo* can touch each other there should be gift transaction lest the younger namesake become ill due to the loss of his or her spirit into that of the more senior name sharer. This small ritual enacts an obligation not to encroach into each other and highlights differentiating relational otherness as part of this kind of dyadic sociality (Stasch 2009: 84). A *daiyo* relationship involves celebrating identity but simultaneously those in such a relationship need to be somewhat separate from each other. It is as if the underlying identification entailed by name sharing 'creates the need for avoidance in the first place' (Stasch 2009: 84).

Among the living, the term *daiyo* can be used by the two namesakes to directly address each other—typically on meeting they can boisterously call each other *daiyo*. The term *daiyo* effectively, in such interaction, replaces any use of the two namesakes' actual shared name. What is enacted involves the simultaneous production of both identity and a lack of identity through name avoidance. In a broader sense namesakes are both present and absent to each other and this becomes somewhat poignant when the namesake relationship is between two persons who are physically absent from each other (such as with the two Eleanors) or where the namesake relationship involves both the living and the dead. This kind of sense of loss or absence is poetically amplified in Kamula performances of rituals concerning the dead, where songs are sung in such a way that griefstruck audience members weep at their own sense of loss and compassion for the dead. Ideally there should be a namesake relationship between the audience member and the person singing the song. The effects of time and death are expressed in the ritual as a beautiful, poetically intense emotionally intrusive destabilising conjunction of the self and the deceased, mediated by the *daiyo* relationship, which creates both a remembered absence and an overwhelming cathartic presence.

In 2015 Michael and his elder daughter Patricia arrived at Wawoi Falls. Patricia, a dancer then developing a Master's thesis in dance, was hoping to learn some dances from Kamula women. In exchange for the women teaching Patricia their dances and songs each morning, Patricia taught, mainly to young Kamula, some contemporary dance moves and ran exercise and Pilates classes. Michael's primary function was to film the dances and songs the Kamula women taught Patricia and, in turn, Patricia's dance and Pilates classes. Most of these activities took place in the local church. The songs were transcribed and translated primarily by their host Hawo Kulu, who had previously worked on an SIL project that had translated the New Testament into Kamula. Gelabu Akami, who had earlier named his daughter Patricia, also assisted in the transcription and translation.

A return trip in early 2017, to further pursue issues raised during Patricia's and Michael's earlier visit, corresponded with Patricia's birthday. Their hosts, Hawo, his wife and other family members and friends, decided that they would hold a birthday feast for Patricia and for their daughter Eleanor, whose birthday was roughly the same as Patricia's. When the cooked food was ready to be blessed and eaten Patricia was asked to sit on the bench where the food was displayed. Hawo's wife sat next to Patricia with Eleanor on her lap. In a sense this highly staged celebration of hospitality merged two families into one via the physical proximity of Eleanor and Patricia, while also celebrating the differences between the two. As a celebration of the inter-generational sociality of two different, but similar families, the birthday party indexed what Hawo later described in a letter to Michael as our "precious time together". It was the realisation of the promise of long term intercultural sociality—of keeping one's word, a certain steadfastness in the maintaining and developing of relationships (Ricoeur 2004: 165)—here calibrated into the simultaneity of two birthdays. It was also about the promise of a future sociality as if it were already present in the birthday party, because such a future could be based on similar kinds of long-term relationships and reciprocities.

The promise of Michael's future relationship also rested on past reciprocities and forms of political engagement. Michael's most obvious reciprocities involved routine payments to research participants, either in cash or sometimes by the presentation of clothes and other goods bought in Australia. Michael also organised visits by a couple of students from James Cook University interested in studying topics of interest to the Kamula, but after their initial visit neither committed to developing a long term relationship with the Kamula.

Michael has also intervened in Kamula and national debates concerning logging and the carbon trade and has helped organise funding for the construction of a guest house that was supposed to create an alternative flow of income to that provided by logging. It failed to do this and some supporters of logging started to accuse Michael of stealing from this project. Since neither the guest house nor logging really succeeded as effective development projects these debates faded away as interest shifted to discoveries of orphaned gas fields in and around Kamula and Doso lands, but our conflicts may resume in the near future. Such long-term relationships are complex and shifting, but always interesting and fulfilling.

7 Conclusion

The gift-like constructions of hospitality that we, following Candea and da Col (2012), have positioned as the basis of our fieldwork and the social relations of information gathering and data acquisition, emphasise reciprocity and exchange and the possibility of subtle combinations of difference with similarity or identity. We have explored aspects of fieldwork through specific relationships of long-term, inter-generational hospitality. The concept of hospitality, like the gift, runs the risk of becoming vacuous when it is extended to any social relation, any exchange or reciprocating sociality. Thus, we have chosen to focus here on some rituals of incorporation that feature in the practice of hospitality.

We have looked at the way hospitality can be anchored in daily interactions that emphasise histories of social relationships based on name sharing and inter-generational transactions. Such transactions enabled us to highlight the role of the promise of relationships over the long term in the context of field research. We narrowly focused attention on rituals of hospitality that incorporate the outsider into the inside via the "creation of bonds analogous to the adoption of new kinship ties" (da Col 2019: 20) as a way that might avoid some of the pitfalls of generalising hospitality to 'sociality' or the 'gift'.

The hospitable events we have reviewed were highly reflexive staged events, involving complex dynamics of presence and absence, similarity and difference, in which the promise of hospitality was defined across time, across barriers and periods of separation. We highlighted two elements of the promise—first, as involving obligation and an explicit and timely outcome, and, second, as a horizon of possibilities. We focused on both these notions of promise as found in everyday naming relationships between researcher and researched.

The Penambi Wia relationships based on naming involve both obligatory and possible aspects of promise. These relationships index the nurturant capacities of food sharing as a fundamental basis for on-going sociality between researchers and their hosts. These sharers of food are forbidden to harm the relationship (and each other) by drawing attention to the other by calling them by their proper name rather than by their relational name linked to the food shared. In the case of the Kamula, name sharing indexes the generative capacities involved in the literal and figurative reproduction of the lives and identities of other persons. Among the Kamula, as presented here in one highly limited but deliberately chosen example, the emphasis is more on the incorporation of the other into another person—a person-person transformation, rather than the substitution of a thing (food, wealth) for a person as emerges in the Penambi Wia examples. Understood in these general terms the small dyadic relationships we have presented as rituals of incorporation are our host's definition and expression of some of the essential qualities of hospitality—intimacy, generosity, care, convivial commensality and affection.

Yet such understandings of hospitality only involve a small subset of the relationships that inform any fieldwork. It is the case that the promises of long-term field work are often suspended between the ongoing demands of binding promises and the 'work of time', which unravels and reweaves one's obligations and capacities in often unexpected and unfulfilling ways. As a result, complete fulfilment of any promise can be difficult to realise (Adams 1988; Hammett, Jackson and Vickers 2019).

There is also an 'evaluative volatility' (Stasch 2016: 15) in claims about research relationships. Some claims suggest research has a capacity to create an internationally significant good (as with the Australian government's funding of field schools); others argue that any research by outsiders is neo-colonial knowledge extraction, typically without adequate reciprocity or any local utility or relevance. While research ethics demands reciprocity as an 'unambiguously desirable' feature of the research relationship, and reciprocity is expected by and from our research participants, what is actually expected can remain undefined. Tensions between researcher and research participants are always possible as hopes remain unfulfilled. Indeed, expectations can change over time and what at one time was considered appropriate recompense may later be considered inadequate (Aikhenvald 2013). Researchers may even be the subject of threats to their lives and property. Yet such threats, like promises, reflect hopes. Negative critiques of fieldwork relations are often about expectations not being fulfilled in a timely manner and can involve attempts to pressure, even coerce, researchers into conforming to these expectations.

We argue that hospitality between researchers and research participants is never fully defined by such tensions, as our case studies of inter-generational host-guest relationships reveal. It is our hosts as much as us who define the hospitality of our mutual relationship and its promise. What hospitality promises can only ever be partially achieved and in this sense is always somewhat frustrating, but these frustrations do not define the totality of the relationship. Moreover, as with any social relationship, any apparent final 'resolution' of a specific issue has the capacity to generate further problems. Given our example of reciprocal naming, we researchers have yet to name any of our own family members with proper names derived from PNG. However, we have begun to enmesh our families and histories in the social worlds of our hosts. It is from immersion in such a flow of interactions that hospitable fieldwork emerges, with both its promises and its problems.

References

Adams, Jacqueline (1998). The wrongs of reciprocity: Fieldwork among Chilean working-class women. *Journal of Contemporary Ethnography* 27 (2): 219–241.

Aikhenvald, Alexandra (2007). Linguistic fieldwork: setting the scene. *STUF—Sprachtypologie und Universalienforschung* 60 (1): 3–11.

Aikhenvald, Alexandra (2013). A story of love and debt: the give and the take of linguistic fieldwork. *The Asia Pacific Journal of Anthropology* 14: 172–182.

Aikhenvald, Alexandra (2015). *The Art of Grammar: A Practical Guide*. Oxford University Press.

Candea, Matei and Giovanni da Col (2012). The return to hospitality. *Journal of the Royal Anthropological Institute* 18 (S1): S1–S19.

Da Col, Giovanni (2019). The H-factor of anthropology: Hoarding, hosting, hospitality. *L'Homme* 231–232 (3–4): 13–40.

Dapuez, Andrés Francisco (2013). Promissory Prestations. PhD thesis, John Hopkins University.

Dobrin, Lise and Saul Schwartz (2016). Collaboration or participant observation? Rethinking models of 'linguistic social work'. *Language Documentation and Conservation* 10: 153–277

Frieze, Heidrun (2009). The limits of hospitality. In Mustafa Dikeç, Nigel Clark and Clive Barnett (eds.), Extending Hospitality: Giving Space, Taking Time. *Paragraph* 32 (1): 51–68.

Glowczewski, Barbara, Rosita Henry and Ton Otto (2013). Relations and products: Dilemmas of reciprocity in fieldwork. *The Asia Pacific Journal of Anthropology* 14 (2): 113–125.

Graeber, David (2001). *Toward an Anthropological Theory of Value: The False Coin of Our Own Dreams*. New York: Palgrave Macmillan.

Hammett, Daniel, Lucy Jackson and Daniel Vickers (2019). The ethics of (not) giving back. *Area* 51 (2): 380–386.

Henry, Rosita (2012). Gifts of grief: performative ethnography and the revelatory potential of emotion. *Qualitative Research* 12 (5): 528–539.

Hill, Jane (2006). The ethnography of language and language documentation. In Jost

Gippert, Nikolaus P. Himmelmann and Ulrike Mosel (eds.), *Essentials of language documentation*, 113–128. Berlin: Mouton de Gruyter.
Kabuni, Michael (2019). Will Papua New Guinea's New Leader Make Good on His Reform Promises? *World Politics Review*
https://www.researchgate.net/publication/334376944_Will_Papua_New_Guinea's_New_Leader_Make_Good_on_His_Reform_Promises
Levi-Strauss, Claude (1966). *The Savage Mind*. London: Weidenfeld and Nicolson Ltd.
Mauss, Marcel (2016 [1925]). *The Gift. Expanded Edition*. Chicago: Hau Books.
Merlan, Francesca and Alan Rumsey (1991). *Ku Waru: Language and Segmentary Politics in the Western Nebilyer Valley, Papua New Guinea*. Cambridge: Cambridge University Press.
Modan, Gabriella (2016). Writing the relationship: Ethnographer-informant interactions in the new media era. *Journal of Linguistic Anthropology* 26 (1): 98–107.
Pitt-Rivers, Julian A. (2012 [1977]). The law of hospitality. *Hau: Journal of Ethnographic Theory* 2 (1): 501–517.
Rice, Keren (2011). Documentary linguistics and community relations. *Language Documentation & Conservation* 5: 187–207.
Ricouer, Paul (2004). *Memory, History, Forgetting*. Chicago: University of Chicago Press.
Rosaldo, Michelle Z. (1982). The things we do with words: Ilongot speech acts and speech act theory in philosophy. *Language in Society* 11: 203–237.
Schwartz, Saul and Rena Lederman (2011). Collaborative methods: A comparison of subfield styles. *Reviews in Anthropology* 40 (1): 53–77.
Searle, John (1979). *Expression and Meaning: Studies in the Theory of Speech Acts*. Cambridge: Cambridge University Press.
Serres, Michel (2007 [1980]). *The Parasite*. Translated by Lawrence R. Schehr. Minneapolis: University of Minnesota Press.
Shryock, Andrew (2019). Keeping to oneself: Hospitality and the magical hoard in the Balga of Jordan. *History and Anthropology* 30 (5): 546–562.
Slotta, James (2015). The perlocutionary is political: Listening as self-determination in a Papua New Guinean polity. *Language in Society* 44: 525–552.
Smith, Holly M. (1997). A paradox of promising. *The Philosophical Review* 106 (2): 153–196.
Stasch, Rupert (2009). *Society of Others: Kinship and Mourning in a West Papuan Place*. Berkeley: University of California Press.
Stasch, Rupert (2011). Word avoidance as a relation-making act: A paradigm for analysis of name utterance taboos. *Anthropological Quarterly* 84 (1): 101–120.
Stasch, Rupert (2016). Dramas of otherness. "First Contact" Tourism in New Guinea. *Hau: Journal of Ethnographic Theory* 6 (3): 7–27.
Strathern, Andrew J. (1977). Melpa food-names as an expression of ideas on identity and substance. *The Journal of the Polynesian Society* 86 (4): 503–511.

Wilson, Maggie (2019). *A True Child of Papua New Guinea: Memoir of a Life in Two Worlds*. Edited and with additions by Rosita Henry. Jefferson, North Carolina: McFarland Press.

Yamada, Racquel-María (2007). Collaborative linguistic fieldwork: Practical application of the empowerment model. *Language Documentation and Conservation* 1 (2): 257–282.

Young, Adrien (2020). Putting anthropology in its (hospitable) place: Harry Shapiro's fieldwork on Pitcairn Island, 1934–1935. *History and Anthropology* 1–21. DOI: 10.1080/02757206.2020.1762591.

CHAPTER 6

Zande Politeness Strategies and Their Verbal Expressions

Helma Pasch

1 Introduction

Politeness is expressed primarily by linguistic behaviour, which shows considerable variation in different cultures. It shows in the way that, in social interaction, speakers take into consideration their interlocuters' emotions and needs when communicating information and their own emotions and attitudes. Research on linguistic politeness emerged as a subdiscipline of anthropological linguistics that began in the 1970s and its importance since then has continually increased.

Robin Lakoff, whom Eelen (2001: 2) calls "the mother of modern politeness theory", was the first scholar to investigate politeness from a pragmatic perspective, as influenced by the conditions in specific social situations. She complements Grice's maxims[1] for communication with the principle of politeness, comparing the notion of politeness with the maxims in terms of "rules", and she outlines three valid norms in her perception of what is polite: Rule 1: "Don't impose"; Rule 2: "Give options"; Rule 3 "Make A feel good—be friendly" (Lakoff 1973: 298).

Politeness theory was developed by Penelope Brown and Stephen C. Levinson (1987). On the basis of Goffman's concept of 'face', i.e., "the positive social value a person effectively claims for himself by the line others assume he has taken during a particular contact" (Goffman 1967: 5), they posit two competing faces. Positive face is the need to be appreciated, and negative face is the need to be free to decide and act and not to be imposed upon. The two faces are the basis of two styles of politeness: positive politeness, which expresses solidar-

1 Culpeper (2011: 397) observes that all studies on politeness have been influenced by Grice's Cooperative Principle (Grice 1975, 1989). It must, however, be observed that Grice's topic of research is not politeness but the features which make conversation successful. "Be polite" is one of a number of maxims which are normally observed by participants in conversations (Grice 1975: 47).

© HELMA PASCH, 2022 | DOI:10.1163/9789004510395_007

ity with the counterpart, and negative politeness, which aims at minimizing imposition on him or her by avoiding face-threatening acts (FTAs).

On the basis of comparative research, Brown and Levinson claim that linguistic politeness follows universal principles. Among these are: 1) people are normally more polite towards to social superiors; 2) among people of the same social level, they are normally more polite towards persons they do not know; and 3) the more an imposition conforms to social norms and values, the more likely people are to respond to it. This means that the degree of politeness that people invest depends on a number of different sociological parameters. This applies to hierarchical politeness as well as to symmetrical politeness.

The universality of face and of politeness patterns have been challenged by Matsumoto (1988) and Ide (1990) with the argument that negative face, with the need not to impose on the counterpart, reflects Western individualism more than Eastern norms and values. Pizziconi (2003) attempts to demonstrate that Japanese politeness strategies are not inconsistent with Brown and Levinson's politeness theory.

With regard to the African continent, politeness is still understudied. A restricted number of studies on politeness strategies deal with widely spoken languages like Swahili (Yahya-Othman 1994, 2005), Lingala and Swahili as spoken in Kisangani (Nassenstein 2018) and Zulu (de Kadt 1998), but African vernaculars have not yet been investigated with regard to politeness.

The aim of the present paper is to outline and analyze the politeness strategies of the Azande, their linguistic expressions and proverbial definitions and behaviour rules, and how politeness is learned. These strategies were observed in the Zande Empire (19th century and first decades of the 20th century) and they are still practised in rural areas of Zande speaking territory, which covers the triangle Central African Republic (CAR), Democratic Republic of Congo (DRC) and South Sudan (SS). Most of these rules are also practised in urban centres like Kisangani, Isiro (DRC), Bangassou, Bangui (both CAR) and Juba (SS), and among refugees. The investigation is based on the evaluation of historical texts, from which politeness can be learned about, on the blog of a Zande from South Sudan, on discussions with Zande language consultants in Kisangani (DRC), with a speaker from Rafai (CAR) and on correspondence with a speaker from Sudan and on his blog *Worondimo* (Waanzi s.d.).

This chapter is organized as follows. Section 2 presents some general features of Zande politeness and the use of silence. In two subsections upward and downward hierarchical politeness are analyzed. Section 3 investigates expressions of symmetrical politeness, which plays a role in daily life, and does so increasingly among displaced Zande. Conclusions are drawn in Section 4.

2 Zande Politeness

Evans-Pritchard (1957: 61) states that among early travelers in the "Heart of Africa",[2] Zande princes were renowned for their politeness and their tactful manners, which, according to the descriptions, were comparable to those of the aristocrats in Europe and in other parts of the world. It is likely that these descriptions refer more to their display of tact and etiquette than to social behaviour towards their subjects. In fact, Schweinfurth (1874: 21), one of the first travelers in the area, mentions their "majestic deportment and gesture", but he also describes the Zande chieftains as fairly rude towards their enemies and even towards their subjects. According to him, "defiant imperious bearing" is the sole feature constituting their "outward dignity", since they disdain pomp and showiness.

It is astonishing that the politeness of commoners never attracted the attention of travelers and anthropologists. Even in comprehensive descriptions of the language (Lagae 1921, Gore 1926), expressions of politeness do not play a role; there are no entries for the terms 'polite' and 'politeness' in the dictionaries (Lagae and Vanden Plas 1922, 1925, Gore and Gore 1952), and they are also not found in the online dictionary *Glosbe*.

Irrespective of clan affiliation, Zande people are nowadays quite generally known among the neighbouring ethnic groups for their politeness. This holds true not only with regard to rural areas, but also to urban centres like Kisangani, Kinshasa (DRC), Bangassou and Bangui (CAR), where many Zande have gone because of better job opportunities, or to Aru, Gulu and Kampala (Uganda), where many Zande from Sudan have gone to seek asylum. Zande people are aware of their noticeably polite behaviour, which a speaker of Zande in Kisangani describes in example (1).

(1)	*irisɘ*	*fwo*	*auro*	*wa*	*a-zande*	*te*[3]
	politeness	at.place.of	foreigners	like	PL-Z.	NEG

'the politeness of other people is not like that of the Azande'

When asked for the criteria of this politeness, non-Zande describe Zande as friendly, well-behaved and correct people, who pay their rent on time and do

2 *The Heart of Africa* (Schweinfurth 1874) is the title of one of the first travelogues to give ethnological, historical, linguistic, geographical and botanical information on the Zande territory. It covers the area in which Zande territory is located.

3 Faustin Dusa made this statement to me in Kisangani in May 2020.

not destroy other people's property, don't steal, and do not sell all their produce, such as three bags of rice, to only one person, but make sure that several customers can be served. In discussions they often apply negative politeness strategies in order to avoid open conflicts. They do not quarrel and avoid arguing and creating fights. An alleged typical strategy to prevent conflict is not to give counter-arguments but to remain silent in situations where they do not agree with what has been said. Such silence allows them to keep their own face, and does not actively threaten the face of their counterparts, but when they do not convey their thoughts and their opinions, their counterparts cannot know how things stand. As a consequence, Zande people also have the reputation of being difficult.

Silence is in fact an ambiguous form of communication which can express positive or negative politeness, which can be "cold or companionable" (Lakoff 1990: 47) and which can be polite or impolite. In cases where it indicates respect for the negative face needs of the interlocuter it is a manifestation of negative politeness (Tannen 1985: 98). In situations where talk is expected, however, silence may be used to establish or maintain distance, and it is not considered a polite reaction (Sifianou 1995: 106, 107). No matter how a given refusal of communication and silence is judged by a Zande himself, their non-Zande interlocuters do not appreciate being left in the dark. When the first speaker in a discussion expects an interlocutor to give some statement or explanation and the latter refuses to do so, the first speaker may know or feel that such silence expresses disagreement. Unfortunately, there is no good way for the first speaker to react and he/she must recognize that, with that silence, the interlocutor gains control over the situation, at least to some degree. In short, it is not an action, i.e., an utterance or its content, that makes the interlocutor's behaviour impolite, but its demonstrative omission (Kaul de Marlangeon 2012: 82–83). It is, however, important to note that, acording to their own estimation, Zande do not normally remain silent when a solution to conflict is sought, but they consider it important to actively participate in the discussion. This is expressed by the proverb *sungu pati pai nae nga garagaha te* 'she who sits around a case won't hesitate to comment' (Waanzi, pers. comm. 05.05.2021).

Another strategy of conflict avoidance lies in the endeavour to solve problems independently, without bothering others and asking for help, and even in difficult situations a Zande does not beg for money (Landi, pers. comm. Sep. 2020). In order to keep face he will accept any type of job in order to survive. This attitude is found in rural areas and urban centres, and also abroad, i.e., wherever Azande have gone to make their living. It is expressed in the following proverb (example 2).

(2)

zande	*a-kpi-nga*	*be*	*gomoro*	*te*
Z.	PERF-die-NEG	because.of	hunger	NEG

'A Zande does not die of hunger.'

Such a survival strategy is basically a type of non-linguistic politeness, but silence, i.e., the withholding of a linguistic (re-)action, again plays a role. Since Zande society is hierarchical, many politeness rules reflect this situation. We must distinguish between upward politeness, i.e., the obligation to show respect for social superiors, and downward politeness, which aims to treat subordinate people in fair manner or to be generous to them. Both types of politeness strengthen the hierarchical structures of the society.

2.1 *Upward Politeness*

When Zande men are asked about politeness, they tend to talk first about the rules of obedience and service behaviour that women have to fulfil towards their husbands, children towards their parents, and commoners towards a prince or a chief. Compliance is mandatory, and face plays far less a role than is the case in the well-known requests for a glass of water in Western societies, which are discussed in several studies on face-threatening and face-saving acts.

To be polite towards higher ranking persons, in particular the princes, some of whom have maintained prestige and influence until today, means to show respect and obedience. The term *irisɔ*, a nominalization of the verb *irisa* (*i*) 'to be polite, to honour, to favour, to esteem', is the causative extension of the verb *irã* (*i*) 'to be honourable, to be honoured, to be favoured'. This latter verb indicates that it is the natural right of superiors, inherent in their status, to be honoured and obeyed by their subordinates.

(3)

irisɔ	*na-yugɔ*	*gu*	*ra-ka*	*na*	*manga*	*pai*
politeness	PROG-teach	DEF	sleep-PLUR	PREP	make	thing

rengbe	*Zande*	*ka*	*du*	*na*	*ni*	*koyo*	*du*	*kura-ni*
obligatory	Z.	SUB	COP	PREP	ANAPH	towards	COP	other-ANAPH

ni
ANAPH

'Politeness teaches life and the matters which are obligatory for a Zande to follow them towards another person.'[4]

4 The literal translation is: 'Politeness teaches living and doing things (which are) compulsory for a Zande to be with them towards where the other one is.'

As shown above, the basic meaning of *irisɔ* is 'respect', but this respect is not a mere subjugation philosophy; rather, it includes the right of the subalterns to be treated in a fair and lawful way and to enjoy some generosity and hospitality from the respected person. It is astonishing that today *irisɔ* is given as equivalent for 'politeness' which may result from a development which has taken place during the last 50 years. The comprehensive dictionaries by Lagae and Vanden Plas (1922, 1925) and Gore and Gore (1952) have no entries for 'polite', 'friendly' or 'politeness', 'friendliness', and here 'honour, respect' is given as the equivalent of *irisɔ*. 'To be friendly' is expressed, if at all, by the verb *ngba* (see example 5), which is normally used to qualify actions or things as 'good, nice, beautiful, agreeable or useful'.

According to what Zande men told me in Kisangani, these rules apply in the rural areas where society is still strongly hierarchically organized, but they have lost their function in urban centres, where the rules for peaceful cohabitation are the same for all ethnic groups. According to my observations, however, urban politeness rules do not differ much from those in the home territories and many typically Zande types of behaviour can be observed in the towns.

In whatever reading, the term *irisɔ* is not frequently used and its use is mainly restricted to discussions about the concept of respect or politeness (examples 1 and 3), not to its application. When talking about (dis-)respectful or (im-)polite behaviour the term is not used, but rather the respective actions are referred to. An example is provided by Gangura, a protagonist in one of Evans-Pritchard's stories (1963), who is upset about Mbitiyo's disrespectful reaction to his installation, in such a way that in the end he orders that the latter's hands to be cut off as a punishment. In his accusation he does not speak about lack of *irisɔ*, but about Mbitiyo's shaking his fist at him (example 4).

(4)	*Mbitiyo,*	*gu*	*pa*	*mo*	*a-zanzia*	*be-ro*	*ti-ni*	*fe-re*
	M.	DEF	matter	2SG1	PERF-shake	hand-2SG2	at-ANAPH	for-1SG2

'Mbitiyo, it is because you shook your fist at me …'

I had a comparable experience with some language consultants in Bangassou and in Kisangani, who used *irisɔ* as an equivalent of 'politeness'. Whenever they came to see me, I served them water from the fridge, which they enjoyed as a luxurious drink. It must be noted that at the mission station where I stayed in Bangassou, and at the university guesthouse in Kisangani, cold water is available for residents, while local visitors are normally given water from the tap, which is lukewarm. When expressing their gratitude (example 5), they did not speak of *irisɔ*, but more specifically of what I had done for them. I had the impression that they considered my sharing the cold water not only an act of mercy, but also as a symbol of respect for them, as their knowledge was indispensable to me and they therefore deserved to enjoy cold water as well. It was perhaps also a way of overcoming the complicated hierarchical situation.

(5) *Si*	*ngba* /	*Tambuahe*	*mo*	*fu*	*zezere*	*ime*	*fu-rani*	*dedede*
INAN1	nice	thanks	2SG1	give	cool	water	for-1PL2	always

'It is nice / Thank you that you always give us cool water.'

In Zande society the status of women is lower than that of men. Within their families, women have to show respect and obedience to their husbands and parents-in-law, and children have to respect and obey their parents, in particular the father, and they must not call them by their names. In the village, the wife will address her husband as *ba-ira-kporo* ('big-owner-home') 'great head of household', *gi ba-kumba* ('my great-husband') 'my responsible' or *kumba mi* ('man 1SG1') 'my husband', and a husband will address his wife *dia-re* ('wife-1SG2') 'my wife'. It must be noted that the form 'my wife' is an inalienable construction, which indicates inherent possession, hence a low degree of control[5] by the woman. The form 'my husband', *gi bakumba*, is an alienable possessive construction, which indicates a distance between possessor and possessed and which implies a high degree of control by the possessed. The second form, *kumba mi*, is an example of a rare possessive construction with a pronoun of series 1. It is found only with a small list of designations of male persons who rank higher than the possessor; it indicates a similar distance between possessor and possessed to that of *gi bakumba* and the same low degree of control by the possessor i.e. the wife.

If a woman is not happy with some behaviour or decision of her husband, she may tell him in a low voice inside the house, but she must not complain in a loud voice[6] or nag or lament outside the house. In rural areas, if the husband does not comply with her request, she may go to the local chief and ask him to intervene, ready to submit herself unconditionally to his judgement. There she will wait at some distance from the chief and after being told to announce

5 The question of control in Zande possessive constructions was investigated for the first time in Pasch and Mbolifouye (2011). There are two series of pronouns: the pronouns of Series 1, which have the feature +CONTROL, are used primarily in subject position, and the pronouns of Series 2, which have the feature -CONTROL, serve primarily as object pronouns.

6 When I told my language consultants about a young Zande woman, a successful trader, who used to defend her interests with a strong voice, their amused reaction was that she would never find a husband, at least not a Zande.

her matter she will say *gi gbia, mi ye fo-ro ni* 'my chief, I bring it [my matter] for you' or *mi ye na gi ngbanga* 'I come with my (legal) case'. She may approach the chief only when he invites her to do so, *mo gbisi* 'come close', and she squats at his side, but she does not greet him or shake hands with him and while talking to him she does not look into his eyes. She may only begin to voice her request after the chief has invited her with the words *mi na-gia-ro* 'I am listening to you'. When she has finished, she expresses her highly respectful submission to his decision (example 6).

(6) *mi ni-ye ka kusa-ha ku bangiri gbia ko*
1SG1 X-come SUB make.appear-INAN2 DIR eye chief 3M
zi-re
seize-1SG2
'I came to outline it before the chief who may seize me [i.e., put me into prison].'

When she has ended, he confirms that he has listened and sends her home (example 7), i.e., he responds to her respectful request by indicating that he will take care of the matter, but not whether he will react to her expectations. He may help her or not, and again, she has no control over what is going to happen.

(7) *mi na-gia-ha, mo ga fwo gudé*
1SG1 PROG-hear-INAN2 2SG1 go.home at.place.of child
'I heard it, you may go home to your children.'

In urban centres there is no institution like the chief whom a woman can consult because of marital problems.

The chief is not the only person who must not be called by his name; this rule applies to all persons of the older generation who are addressed by their genealogical status: *tita* 'grandfather', (*b*)*uba* or *baba* 'father', *nina* or *nana* 'mother', *ando* 'uncle' and *deliba* 'aunt'. A widow must not pronounce the name of her late husband lest she might become uncontrollably obese and at times lose control of her speech. Such effects, of which nobody knows when and to what degree they will materialize, are not imposed by a person as a punishment for misbehaviour. This indicates that non-respect of the avoidance rule is not only a case of impoliteness, but also of breaking a taboo.[7] Mentioning the name

7 The relationship between politeness and taboo is discussed in Pasch and Gumekpala (in press).

is, however, not a taboo breach for the brothers and the adult sons, though they may mention the name only when it is unavoidable, not otherwise. These avoidance rules differ clearly from in-law avoidance rules in Southern Africa, as among the Hlonipha (Finlayson 1982), or those of the Kambaata in Ethiopia (Treis 2005), insofar as names of male and female relatives must be avoided by both men and women. It is, however, true that stricter compliance is expected from women than from men, which reflects the lower social status of women.

In order to address a single person, speakers of Zande distinguish a T-form (*mo*) (also used as 2nd singular subject pronoun) and a V-form, *oni*, (also used as 2nd plural pronoun) to express solidarity and power in a non-reciprocal way (cf. Brown and Gilman 1960). The reciprocal use of the V-form to indicate social distance, as is the case in several European languages, is not known. The V-form is used towards people of higher status, like school teachers and university professors. Workers, who in rural areas may be borrowed from prison, are addressed by everybody with the T-form. These workers, for their part, address their employer with *oni*.

Within the household, the head of the family will use the T-pronoun *mo* to address his wife, the younger brother, the children and even his girlfriend, while all of the latter address him with the V-pronoun; they also use this pronoun to address the older brother of the father and the male in-laws. Even the wife and children of a prisoner address the head of their family as *oni*. In case of dispute, a wife may turn to the pronoun *mo*, but children will not easily do so because this counts as highly undisciplined behaviour. In case they do use it, if this happens within the family and inside the house they are scolded. If they do it outside, the parents may utter a curse: *mo nabihe na ni* 'they will make this same experience'. While all people address the chief with the pronoun *oni*, in particular when asking for assistance in case of some problem, even commoners may happen to turn to the pronoun *mo* when they have a conflict with the chief himself.

Other formalized morphological and lexical expressions of politeness are the equivalents for 'thank you', *tambuahe* (example 5) or *tambuapai*, which are frequently used, and the far less frequent *nga-* of reverence, which is suffixed to the verb. It was used by my language consultants in Kisangani in the request below (example 8) but only after I had asked about polite ways of asking for water, and about the way a woman would ask for water.

(8) *ka mo fu-nga ime fe-re*
SUB 2SG1 give-REV water for-me
'Please give me water.'

Men normally do not see any good reason for making use of the *-nga* of reverence, since it is normally women who provide water to drink. Only when I enquired about a woman's way of asking for water did they produce this expression. Before, they had asked for water the way they did it at home, just saying *ime!* 'water!' or *ime ka bira!* 'water to drink!', and on request they confirmed several times that this is the polite way to ask for something to drink. Towards women men do not use the *-nga* of reverence.

2.1 *Downward Politeness*

Hierarchical politeness is not always upward-oriented, but it may also be oriented downwards. But while the first is characterized by strict rules which lower ranking persons have to obey in order to meet the expectations of their superiors, lest they may be punished, the second is characterized by a sympathetic attitude and the benevolent treatment of subordinate persons. It is not obligatory but voluntary and is motivated by the wish to gain the sympathy of the subalterns and strengthen authority.

For the princes in the Zande Empire, hospitality towards visitors played an important role and many princes had visitors most of the time. Prince Gbudwe, in particular, was renowned for his hospitality because he gave food several times per day to his visitors and occasionally peanuts as snacks in between. In the story "The attempted slaying of Mongbi" (Evans-Pritchard 1962), this regular serving of food is mentioned twice. The second mention is shown in example (9).

(9) *Rago ki ta gira kina boro ngbawiso Gbudue ki*
place SEQ SIMUL shine just person early.morning Gb. SEQ
kuru ngbanga yo fuo a-boro, ka ko a-fu-nga
appear court there towards PL-person SUB 3M PERF-give-NEG
liae fu-yo mbata ya.
food for-3PL before NEG
'Very early next morning Gbudwe came into court to the men there (in order to talk to them first), before he would send out food to them.'

In the Zande Empire, where princes could also expect hospitality from the population, there were always some princes who took their chance to exploit people, taking away their goods or even women. Such a way of ruling was perceived as ill-treatment by the subjects, who might feel motivated to move to the territory of another prince (example 10) in order to live in peace and see their personal interests respected.

(10) *ka si du wa Gangura na-manga-re ni gbegbere*
SUB INAN1 be like G. PROG-make-1SG2 MANNER bad
pai, mi ki ga sa kina Bafuka, ka ko a-manga-re
matter 1SG1 SEQ go towards just B. SUB 3M PERF-make-1SG2
ni gbegbere pai, mi ki ga sa na kura gbia
MANNER bad matter 1SG1 SEQ go towards PREP other prince
berewe.
again.
'If Gangura treats me ill I will go to live in Bafuka's country. If he (Bafuka) treats me ill, I will go and live in the country of yet another prince.' (Evans-Pritchard 1963)

Waiving such privileges, which would make the population suffer, was a strategy to gain their sympathy and confidence, and for the princes it was an effective means to improve their reputation and gain face. In the stories documented by Evans-Pritchard, people refer to such waivers when praising the positive qualities of a prince (example 11), who respects the rights of his subjects to their wives and to their material goods.

(11) *Ani ani-wari gani buda ki fu-he na akoro ni*
1PL1 PAST-brew our beer SEQ give-INAN2 with pot be
wene-he fu Ndukpo, ko ana-dia nga pere te, ko
good-INAN2 for N. 3M PAST-seize NEG pot NEG 3M
ani-gasi gani pere buda a-gasa.
PAST-return our pot beer PERF-return
'When we brewed our beer and gave it in our best pots to Ndukpo, he did not keep [take] the pots, he always returned the beer-pots.' (Evans-Pritchard 1963)

Gbudwe, the highest-ranking prince of the Zande, who was famous for his caring and supporting attitude towards his subjects, knew about some princes who ill-treated their subjects. In some situations he offered to help the subjects against these princes (example 12). He did so after the installation of Gangura as successor to Ndukpo when he realized that people were afraid of their new prince (Evans-Pritchard 1963).

(12) *ko ta manga-roni gbegbere, bakumba a-boro kina dagba-roni*
3M yet make-2PL2 bad elder PL-person just between-2PL2
no ka ye ki kuru ko-yo du u ni
here SUB come SEQ appear DIR-there be LOG.SG1 ANAPH

'Should he do you ill, the elders among you should come and appear before me.'

Most princes were hospitable to their daily visitors, and occasionally they would also generously support certain subjects with material goods, such as spears with which to pay the bride price; sometimes they gave them wives or administrative positions (example 13).

(13) *mbiko gine, Maotadi, wa mi ni-za-ha ta na Ndukpo*
because why M. like 1SG1 X-stop-INAN2 travel with N.
gbe ko a-fu gimi kporo fe-re, ko ki fu gimi a-de
very 3M PERF-give my village for-me 3M SEQ give my PL-woman
ue
two
'For that, Moatadi, when I stopped the many travels with Ndukpo, he gave me my village [as administrative post] and then he gave me two wives.' (Evans-Pritchard 1963)

Nowadays, with the economic situation of the princes getting more and more difficult, such generosity can hardly be practised.

Within the Zande community, downward politeness is practised both within families and beyond. With regard to children and young people it is done primarily by giving blessing (*maku*) in order to make sure that they will be successful in life. People are, of course, aware that without hard work, patience and gifts, success in life is not possible, but they are convinced that blessings will make success greater because they are a powerful and 'important cultural factor'. Blessings are not given without reason, but as a kind of reward when a child has voluntarily carried out a certain job (*sunge*) for an elderly person, like fetching water or running errands. In order to get blessings, children and young people pay attention to when and where they can help elderly people or do some *sunge maku* 'work for blessings', or they give an elder some *makawa* 'first fruits', which may consist of, e.g., the first fruits from the garden, the first catch in hunting or fishing, or the first salary (Waanzi s.d.).

Both sides, the children and the elderly people, who participate in the exchange of voluntary help for blessings, maintain their own face and that of their counterparts, and they create a situation which is not only free from conflict, but which is friendly and allows them to make each other feel good (cf. Lakoff 1973: 298). The children, by voluntarily helping the elders, create situations where conflicts are prevented, i.e., their behaviour is anticipatory conflict avoidance which exempts the elders from giving orders. When receiving a blessing from an elder, a child will kneel in front of that person, put hands into the hands of the elder, and avoid looking into his or her eyes.

It is important to know that Gore and Gore (1952) give *irisɘ* also as equivalent of 'blessing', while the reverse is not the case. Considering the fact that the primary meaning of the term is 'respect', it becomes clear that children and young people, when they voluntarily fulfil their duties, deserve respect from the older people, which is given in the form of blessings. This is a kind of compensation, just as the subjects of the princes in Zande Empire could expect hospitality and generosity as compensation for their respect.

3 Symmetrical Politeness

While Azande are very much aware of hierarchical politeness, in particular upward politeness, symmetrical politeness is hardly ever treated as an issue, although it is extremely important for a peaceful life and for survival in difficult situations. It is characterized by fairness, honesty, trustworthiness and reliability towards other persons of equal or different social rank, by solidarity and helpfulness.

The obligation to support others in case of need is part of the requirement to be helpful, which must not only be obeyed by the princes, but by everybody. The consequences of compliance or non-compliance with this rule are outlined in several of the stories documented by Evans-Pritchard, from which children learn how to behave well and show empathy for others (Pasch and Gumekpala in press).

Hospitality towards travelers is a major feature of helpfulness. To give a visitor and even travelers water to drink is an act of politeness which is highly appreciated. This has been shown above in example (5), where fresh water was shared, and it is a topic in many stories. For some people, offering water to drink is a self-evident obligation and people do not normally boast of being hospitable. However, when Gangura was installed as a prince, people were afraid of him and in order to soothe him they declared how generous they had been to the predecessor (example 14), which implied that he could expect the same service.

(14) *gbia ta kura ani ki zi kina kondo*
king SIMUL appear 1SG1 SEQ seize just hen
'as soon as the prince appeared we caught a fowl'

The extreme opposite of hospitality is the habit of preparing food only for oneself and eating it all alone, which is considered shockingly impolite and stingy. For a real person to do so is inconceivable, and people know about such behaviour from a fantastic story about a cannibal (example 15) (Evans-Pritchard 1965).

(15)

ki	*ni-pasi-e*	*rogo*	*ga-ni*	*akoro*	*ni sa ni.*	*kura*	*boro*
SEQ	X-cook-INAN2	inside	POSS-ANAPH	pot	all.alone	other	person

a-zada-nga-ha	*wa*	*sa*	*te,*	*ga-ni*	*ba-we*	
PERF-touch-NEG-INAN2	like	one	NEG	POSS-ANAPH	place-fire	

a-kia	*ni sa ni*	*pangba*	*rago*	*yo*
PERF-be.apart	all.alone	beside	place	there

'And he then cooked it in his pot by himself. Another man would not touch it at all. His fireplace was by itself on one side.'

The man's behaviour is unheard of to the degree that at the end of the story people sit around the place and stare at him; they even ask him questions about his practice of preparing and consuming human flesh by himself. This reaction in itself is highly impolite, since nobody should stand close to a person in order to observe the other. Even if someone does something as repulsive and shameful as practising cannibalism, nobody should do something as face threatening as asking explanations for such a practice, lest the questioner also loses face. Some of the onlookers in the story even openly mock the man-eater, which is a further impolite act. It is acceptable to amuse people with stories about preventable difficult situations, like somebody's suffering from scabies, which he got simply because he was too tired to maintain normal bodily hygiene. It is, however, grossly impolite to mock a person who actually suffers from scabies or any other disease (Pasch and Gumekpala, in press).

Even more than in the normal Zande villages, a spirit of hospitality is required with regard to those Zande who have been displaced as a result of political unrest in South Sudan, CAR and DRC. This hospitality helps them to find refuge in the host communities among their relatives, i.e., members of the same clan. Among Zande, wherever they are on earth, it is quite normal when encountering people to ask them about their clan affiliation, hence is almost impossible that 'you go past your relatives [without knowing it]', *mo andu ka susa gumero* (Waanzi s.d.).

Although genuine clan members are the first to be supported, it is not only members of the same clans who help each other, but help is also offered to people from different clans if they are in need, as is expressed by the following proverb (example 16). They, and any refugee may even be integrated into the clan of the helper.

(16) *boro* *ga-mo* *ni* *nga* *gu* *ni* *nadusio-ro*
person POSS-2SG1 ANAPH COP DEF ANAPH PROG-overtake-2SG2
rago *kerepai*
time disaster
'Yours is the one who comes to take care of you when you're in disaster'

4 Conclusion

The Zande language has only a small inventory of lexical and morphological items to express politeness. The first is the use of the 2nd plural pronoun as an indicator of respect when addressing a single higher ranking person. The second is the suffix *-nga*, which makes requests less imperative and indicates reverence towards the interlocutor. The third is the use of *tambuahe* or *tambuapai* to express gratitude. The latter two are not very frequently used, because overuse of expressions of politeness is counterproductive since it gives the impression of hypocrisy. Although Zande agree that conflicts should be solved in discussion and that they should give their opinion, they do not like to repeat arguments or participate in a discussion that risks being futile. Therefore, more often than non-Zande, they tend to remain silent.

Politeness rules help to reduce friction in personal interaction, but in Zande society this is only a basic function, which in itself serves to stabilize and maintain existing hierarchical structures.

Brown and Levinson's research on the theory of politeness is based, among other things, on requests which are face threatening acts for the hearer, who might refuse to comply. In the strongly hierarchical society of the Zande, where most orders are given by higher ranking persons (usually men) to lower ranking persons (often women, children), obedience is normally obligatory and refusal will be sanctioned. Therefore, face plays far less of a role than in Western societies. The persons who give commands have the natural right to do so. This explains why a man who makes a one-word order for water, *ime!*, will not consider this impolite. Several men told me that women are accustomed to being given this type of order, and several women told me that they are comfortable with a situation where such orders are given. It must, in fact, be noted that in a family where all orders by the men are given in the imperative, there may be a friendly atmosphere. Furthermore, presents like new, fashionable loincloths are welcome compensations for the situation of difference in status between men and women.

When a woman goes to the chief to ask for help in marital problems, the request is at least as much a recognition of his competence as a face threatening act. What is more face threatening in this situation for the woman herself is the fact that she takes family problems to the outside which should stay inside the house.

The politeness strategies of rural Zande and town folk are fairly similar. In both contexts, status, age and gender determine the rules of politeness. It is likewise only few features which makes Zande behaviour look so much more polite than that of other groups. First, they never raise their voice, especially not women; second, they don't argue, and when they stick to their position they tend to keep silent rather than defending it. This silence is often considered difficult by non-Zande. who deplore that they cannot know where they stand.

Abbreviations

ANAPH	anaphor	PREP	preposition
COP	copula	PROG	progressive
DEF	definite	REV	reverential
DEM	demonstrative	SEQ	sequential
DIR	direction	SIMUL	simultaneous
NEG	negation	SUB	subordinator
PAST	(distant) past	CAR	Central African Republic
PL	plural	DRC	Democratic Republic of Congo
PLUR	pluractional	SS	South Sudan
POSS	possessive		

Pronouns

1SG1	1st singular series 1	INAN2	inanimate series2
1SG2	1st singular series 2	1PL1	1st plural series 1
2SG1	2nd singular series 1	1PL2	1st plural series 2
2SG2	2nd singular series 2	2PL1	2nd plural series 2
3M	3rd singular masculine	3PL	3rd plural
INAN1	inanimate series1		

References

Brown, Penelope and Stephen C. Levinson (1978). Universals in language usage: politeness phenomena. In Esther N. Goody (ed.), *Questions and Politeness*, 56–289. Cambridge: Cambridge University Press.

Brown, Penelope and Stephen C. Levinson (1987). *Politeness. Some Universals in Language Usage*. Cambridge: Cambridge University Press.

Brown, Roger and Albert Gilman (1960). The pronouns of power and solidarity. In T.A. Sebeok (ed.), *Style in Language*, 253–276. Cambridge: MIT Press.

Culpeper, Jonathan (2011). Politeness and impoliteness. In Karin Aijmer and Gisle Andersen (eds.), *Sociopragmatics, Volume 5 of Handbooks of Pragmatics*, 391–436. Berlin: Mouton de Gruyter.

de Kadt, Elizabeth (1998). The concept of face and its applicability to the Zulu language. *Journal of Pragmatics* 29 (2): 173–191.

Eelen, Gino (2001). *A Critique of Politeness Theory, vol. 1*. New York and Manchester: Routledge and St Jerome Publishing.

Evans-Pritchard, Edward E. (1957). Zande Kings and Princes. *Anthropological Quarterly* 30: 61–90.

Evans-Pritchard, Edward E. (1958). The Ethnic Composition of the Azande of Central Africa. *Anthropological Quarterly* 31 (4): 95–118.

Evans-Pritchard, Edward E. (1960). The organization of a Zande kingdom. *Cahiers d'Études Africaines* 4: 5–37.

Evans-Pritchard E.E. (1962). The attempted slaying of Mongbi. In *Some Zande Texts—part 1. Kush. Journal of the Sudan National Board for Antiquities and Museums* [Khartoum] 10: 289–314.

Evans-Pritchard, Edward E. (1963). Installation of Gangura and mutilation of a noble (Kuagbiaru). In *Some Zande texts—part 2. Journal of the Sudan National Board for Antiquities and Museums* [Khartoum] 11: 273–301.

Evans-Pritchard, Edward E. (1965). Cannibalism: A Zande text. *Africa* 26: 73–74.

Evans-Pritchard, Edward E. (1976). *Witchcraft, Oracles and Magic among the Azande*. Oxford: Clarendon Press.

Finlayson, Ruth (1982). Hlonipha—The women's language of avoidance among the Xhosa. *South African Journal of African Languages* 2 (1): 35–60.

Glosbe (s.d.). The English-Zande dictionary, https://glosbe.com/en/zne (accessed 05.05.2021).

Goffman, Erving (1967). Interaction ritual: essays on face-to-face interaction. Chicago: Aldine.

Gore, Canon E.C. (1926). *A Zande grammar*. London: Sheldon Press.

Gore, Canon E.C. and Mrs. E.C. Gore. ([1931]1952). *Zande and English Dictionary*. London: The Sheldon Press.

Grice, H. Paul. (1975). Logic and conversation. In R. Wright, P. Cole and J. Morgan (eds.), *Syntax and Semantics 3: Speech Acts*, 41–58. New York, London: Academic Press.

Grice, H. Paul (1989). *Studies in the way of words*. Cambridge, Mass. and London: Harvard University Press.

Gumekpala, Faustin Dusa and Helma Pasch (in press). Quelques chansons Pazande. *Cahiers du centre de recherche en langues et cultures africaines*. Kisangani: Centre de Recherches.

Ide, Sachiko (1990). How and why do women speak more politely in Japanese? In S. Ide and N. McGloin (eds.), *Aspects of Japanese women's language*, 63–79. Tokyo: Kuroshio.

Kaul de Marlangeon, Silvia (2012). A typology of verbal impoliteness behaviour for the English and Spanish cultures. *Revista Espanola de Linguistica Aplicada* 25: 69–92.

Lagae, C.R. (1921). La langue des Azande, vol. 1: Grammaire, exercices, légendes. Ghent: Editions Dominicaines VERITAS.

Lagae, C.R. and V.H. Vanden Plas (1922). *La langue des Azande, vol. 2. Dictionnaire français-zande*. Ghent: Editions Dominicaines VERITAS.

Lagae, C.R. and V.H. Vanden Plas (1925). *La langue des Azande, vol. 3. Dictionnaire zande-français*. Ghent: Editions Dominicaines VERITAS.

Lakoff, Robin T. (1973). The logic of politeness: or minding your p's and q's. *Papers from the 9th Regional Meeting of the Linguistic Society of Chicago*, 292–305.

Lakoff, Robin T. (1990). *Talking Power: The Politics of Language*. New York: Basic Books.

Matsumoto, Yoshiko (1988). Reexamination of the universality of face: Politeness phenomena in Japanese. *Journal of Pragmatics* 12 (4): 403–426.

Nassenstein, Nico (2018). Politeness in Kisangani Swahili: speakers' pragmatic strategies at the fringes of the Kiswahili speaking world. *Afrikanistik-Aegyptologie-Online*, https://www.afrikanistik-aegyptologie-online.de/archiv/2018/4654 (accessed 04.03.2021).

Pasch, Helma and Faustin Dusa Gumekpala (in press). On politeness and taboo in Zande. In Andrea Hollington, Alice Mitchell and Nico Nassenstein (eds.), *Anthropological Linguistics: Perspectives from Africa*. Amsterdam and Philadelphia: John Benjamins.

Pasch, Helma and François Mbolifouye (2011). I am Subordinate to Gbudwe, but your sovereign. Using a subject pronoun in object position in order to claim power. *Afrikanistik-Aegptologie-Online*, https://www.afrikanistik-aegyptologie-online.de/archiv/2011/2907 (accessed 04.03.2021).

Pizziconi, Barbara (2003). Re-examining politeness, face and the Japanese language. *Journal of Pragmatics* 35 (10–11): 1471–1506.

Schweinfurth, Georg (1874). *The Heart of Africa. Three Year's Travels and Adventures in the Unexplored Regions of Central Africa from 1868–1871*. New York: Harper & Brothers, Publishers.

Sifianou, Maria (1995). Do we need to be silent to be extremely polite? Silence and FTAs. *International Journal of Applied Linguistics* 5 (1): 95–110.

Tannen, Deborah (1985). Silence: anything but. In Deborah Tannen and Muriel Saville-Troike (eds.), *Perspectives on silence*, 93–111. Norwood, NJ: Ablex Publishing Corporation.

Treis, Yvonne (2005). Avoiding their names, avoiding their eyes: How Kambaata women respect their in-laws. *Anthropological Linguistics* 47 (3): 292–320.

Waanzi, Isaac Hillary (s.d.). Zande perception on kin: What binds humans together, https://invisiblechildren.com/blog/2021/02/10/zande-perception-on-kin-isaac-waanzi/ (accessed 01.07.2021).

Waanzi, Isaac Hillary (s.d.). Worondimo. essays on culture and tradition of South Sudanese Zande (Blog), https://worondimo.wordpress.com/ (accessed 04.05.2021).

Yahya-Othman, Saida (1994). Covering one's social back: politeness among the Swahili. *Text* 14 (1): 141–161

Yahya-Othman, Saida (2005). Aren't you going to greet me? Impoliteness in Swahili greetings. *Text* 15 (2): 209–227.

CHAPTER 7

Sensual Language: Three Stories

Anne Storch

To Sasha, with admiration.

∵

1 *Pùc*

> What do you do when your world starts to fall apart? I go for a walk, and if I'm really lucky, I find mushrooms. Mushrooms pull me back into my senses, not just—like flowers—through their riotous colors and smells but because they pop up unexpectedly, reminding me of the good fortune of just happening to be there. Then I know that there are still pleasures amidst the terrors of indeterminacy.

This is how Anna Lowenhaupt Tsing begins her text on *The Mushroom at the End of the World* (2015: 1), a tale of ruination and of survival in the midst of ruins. The ruins, in this case, are the remains of industrialized forests. Yet there is life and pleasure in these exploited environments, namely as wondrous, unexpected sights and smells. Sensory experience is connected to mirativity and to amazement in order to be endowed with meaning here. It is the unexpected smell and sight that puts us on the path which leads to truth and revelation. However, there is a curious twist in that it is the smell of rotten and musty matter that appears to indexicalize just the opposite, if not the outcome of decay: the possibility of something new.

In Khartoum, one of the lesser-visited historical collections is kept in the Museum of Ethnography. At the time I was learning Luwo, a Western Nilotic language of South Sudan, the museum still offered an exhibition that included artifacts from the area where Luwo is mostly spoken, namely Bahr el-Ghazal. After the secession, the museum was slightly remodeled, and now basically shows objects from central and northern Sudan, even though an explanatory map placed at the entrance still offers an overview of the placement of ethnic groups in colonial fashion and picturing the former borders of the country. But back then, the dioramic representations of cattle camps and homesteads

© ANNE STORCH, 2022 | DOI:10.1163/9789004510395_008

with life-sized plaster figures of their imaginary inhabitants that were on display in the museum offered one of the few possibilities to discuss the meanings of certain language practices, such as proverbs, colour terminology and so on, while violent conflict made trips to Bahr el-Ghazal improbable. In the musty air of the museum with its shady halls, a particular scent was perceptible: that of moist clay, perhaps, or of reddish soil. While the dry environment of Khartoum did not offer much olfactory diversity, this brought some sense of life to the memories on which the tales and explanations of my Luwo teacher Pierina relied. In Luwo, there was a word for a smell, she said, of freshly dug-out roots: *pùc*. She said it was a bit like the smell in the museum, which I remember as mouldy rather than rooty.

The museum, which before its opening in 1956 had been a British army club, is located in an area that remains shaped by colonial urban planning. Two streets down, there is a road sign that says شارع الزبير باشا / al-ZIBER BASHA STREET. Still close to the museum and its collections of indigenous material culture, this street continues to be named after a wealthy merchant and slave trader, who in 1873 had become the governor of Bahr el-Ghazal under Ottoman rule. The tension between the *pùc*-infested dioramas and the inscription of al-Zubayr Pasha into the urban space surrounding them generates a dialectics in storytelling that insists that the unexpected detail and the whole arise out of each other. Like the mushrooms in the ruined industrialized forest, the mouldy smell is the actual wonder which powerfully and in meaningful ways puts the exhibited objects, their labels, the street name outside and the rectangular order of the space through which we walk into connection. What root is it that has been dug out?

Al-Zubayr Pasha's toponymic legacy sits right in the midst of colonially administered ethnographic spaces. The map in the museum not only gave its beholders an idea of where the various groups such as Dinka, Nuer and Shilluk were to be located, it also offered a particular kind of order. Hardly any of the ethnonyms displayed on it (and on most other such maps, for that matter) had much to do with how people would refer to themselves, and how they would explain their relationships with others. The Luwo were referred to as جور 'Jur', a pejorative name that persists not only in maps but also in scholarly literature. A bit to the left, there was an indication of another obscure ethnonym, فرتيت 'Fertit', which denotes any group other than Dinka, Luwo or Zande. Just between these two ethnic terms there was a dot that represented a place called ديم الزبير 'Deim Zubayr'. On the map, other place names and ethnic designations abounded, all of them arranged as if they had little connection with one another.

Deim Zubayr literally translates as 'camp of Zubayr.' It was a centre of the slave trade in the second half of the nineteenth century, consisting of buildings fortified with enclosures referred to as *zaribah* (زريبة) 'cattle pens', and kilometres of entrenched space where enslaved people were kept. Zachary Berman's (2017) study on slavery and the empire in nineteenth-century Sudan suggests, together with earlier work such as Ahmad Sikainga's contributions to the social history of work in southern Sudan (1991, 1996), that this part of the world was by then fully integrated into capitalist networks of trade and power. Zubayr's camp existed not prior to the world falling apart, but was created after that had already happened. The vastness of Bahr el-Ghazal had been transformed into a site for the exploitation of luxury goods such as ostrich feathers and ivory for northern markets, as well as of massive slavery in order to sustain the lifestyles of Ottoman (and other) elites and to supply the labour on the plantations where coffee, spices and tea were produced for growing global markets (Lenski and Cameron 2018). Ottoman and Arab merchants and political players such as Zubayr Pasha acted out of similar interests and sustained similar imperial power configurations to other contemporary colonialists and slavers, operating in global networks.

Inscribed into landscapes crossed in urban walks, as well as in memory-making while gazing at a map, are not only historical slave trade routes and those who operated them, but also the contemporary effect the slave trade and its colonial context continue to have on the inhabitants of these landscapes. Pierina said she was angry every time she saw the street sign: it humiliated the citizens, who now lived in a country that honoured the slavers, violating the dignity of those whose ancestors had been captured and sold. The roots for which people had dug in Bahr el-Ghazal—had they not been eaten out of desperation after farming and keeping livestock had become impossible in those days of war and slave raiding? *Pùc* did not trigger Proustian memories of childhood roots, but also anger and, contradictorily, resignation. As we walked down al-Ziber Basha Street, leaving behind us *inter alia* a former British club and a beached gunboat, we passed the Acropole Hotel, founded by a Greek-Alexandrine family in the days of Anglo-Egyptian Sudan. Besides Arabic, Turkish and English, Greek, too, had made its imprint on the imperial map. And while it is common to observe this and to know that the bottle of بزيانوس *Pasgianos* for refreshment has something to do with a colonial Sudanese Greek soda producer, it is less common to observe and to know that the languages that participate in this multilingual display of literacy overshadow different multilingualisms and different literacies. *Pùc* is the smell of a recently dug-out root, mushroom-like smelling, like mouldy pages in a book that enshrines language in a certain form, such as Giur[1] in a mission school, and the colonial languages in a selection of used books on display on a sidewalk.

1 Santandrea's 1946 grammar of Luwo uses Giur as the Italian form of Jur in order to refer to the language.

But this smell does not erase the terrors of indeterminacy. Looking back at his travels in the 1880s, the Russian natural scientist and traveler Wilhelm Junker (1891) also wrote about the extreme diversity of people living along the rivers he intended to explore. He attributed the pervasive cultural mobility and multilingualism he was able to observe to the impact of slavery and displacement, rather than to a social strategy that helped people to face these experiences of uprooting. While slavery and colonial rule must have left traumatic memories, people still struggled to create strategies to resist and retain their sovereignty. To create relatively xenophile social environments and to theorize language as shared, hospitable and open were replies to the violent duress which formed part of imperialism in Bahr el-Ghazal. Family histories shared in Luwo often emphasize the role of adopted family members and of the inclusion of refugees in a household (Storch 2014: 271–273). To become a member of a diverse and multilingual community involved learning Luwo, but did not involve giving up one's previously acquired linguistic repertoire. Similar perspectives on multilingualism as hospitable practice are found in other West Nilotic communities close to Luwo, such as Belanda Bor (Heyking 2013) and Chopi (Storch 2015, Storch and Mietzner 2021). Such linguistic indeterminacy poses serious problems to linguistic positivism, but also offers the possibility of something new.

By recovering and reclaiming theory from the south, such as the inclusive multilingualism and local linguistic thought manifest in performative and ritual language practice, new ways of knowledge production are created. In Juba, the Likikiri Collective have set out to invite people to storytelling:

> The term *likikiri* means "stories" in Bari, a language spoken across several communities in South Sudan. *Likikiri* are part of a broader South Sudanese oral tradition, historically a vehicle for the intergenerational transmission of social and cultural information and values.[2]

By framing language as shared—"across several communities"—and as something that is mobile and mobilizes at the same time, it turns into a hospitable and liberating tool. Likikiri claim that this could not only be helpful for educative purposes, but that it could also enhance peace building activities.

In Cairo in 1912, one year prior to al-Zubayr Pasha's demise, May Ziadeh published a short text on the arts. Its first lines are as follows:

2 http://www.likikiri.org/about/.

> [...] Imagination is a lost guest roving the earth; it is the strongest cultural force. Its movement never ceases throughout our lives. Rather, like the heart, it is constantly at work; its work is continuous, in sleep or in walking. It preserves all memories of the past and all impressions conveyed by the senses—sights, sounds, melodies, scents, and other stimuli—and the commingling of these memories and impressions forms the roots of the arts. Then come conception and innovation, which work to expand those roots, multiply their branches, and fulfill their potential.
>
> ZIADEH 2018 [1912]: 45–46

2 *Kúr*

Pierina's full name is Pierina Akeelo Nyabut Zubayr. In Luwo, like in several other Western Nilotic languages, *nyíŋ* does not inflect for number and denotes a plural concept, 'names'. This reflects the actual naming practices, which involve an accumulation of names as a person grows into his or her various social roles. But the practice of carrying various names not only helps to construe identity, it also indexes the meaning of various historical experiences. Hence, as a consequence of missionary activities after the arrival of the Comboni Fathers, an Italian congregation based in Verona, in Wau in 1904, baptismal names of Italian origin are frequent in many communities of Bahr el-Ghazal and beyond. Names given after birth also include epithets that indicate when, where or how a person was born, and under what general circumstances. In the case of *Ákeelo* this is the birth of a child after twins; the prefix *á-* denotes a girl, while the masculine form would be *Úkeelo*. Names that are acquired later in life include status names (such as bull names), names given in ritual joking relationships, and names that refer to the paternal family (in Pierina's case, this is *Nyàbút* 'daughter of But'). The last name, *Zubayr* (in Luwo, which has no fricatives, it actually is *Jìbɛɛr*), is her grandfather's name, which is used as a family name in an attempt to match European naming practices.

In an essay on names and naming as the very core of language and linguistic epistemology in his community, the Kenyan philosopher Frederick Ochieng'-Odhiambo (2013) describes the difficulties of creating a form of one's names that would match the requirements of a passport or identity card. The names one bears are all meaningful and part of a person's connectedness to family, society, the region one hails from or lives in, historical entanglement and current positioning, as well as self-perception; they are therefore essential parts of one's existence. Names given out of context, such as European names, are colonial outfall and harmful, he argues: "The [Kenyan] Luo customs and practices require that a name be a signifier; a name has to express something about the person called by it" (Ochieng'-Odhiambo 2013: 57). With regards to the slaver's name she bears, Pierina has a slightly different point of view. Such names too may bear complex meanings, particularly if they are introduced to others through storytelling.

> I am Akeelo, daughter of But. I asked Anne whether I told her how and why my grandfather was actually given the name Zubayr. Well, the father of my grandfather's name was Akol. Akol's wife was called Abwolo. This Zubayr now was capturing people, it was known that he caught people. It was one day that Zubayr came to our village Boo and detected my [great]grandfather Akol together with his wife Abwolo in the house. All people run away, but Abwolo has stomach pains. Then comes Zubayr and says: 'What do you do here? All people flee!'—'I, how can I flee, with my wife being in labour! This is why I remain near my wife. Whatever will kill us then kills us. And if we live, we live.' Zubayr feels sorry deep inside and says to his soldiers: 'This I say! You should not catch them!'—He looks sad at his wife.

At this point, Pierina's story takes an exquisite turn. Zubayr is not only compassionate, he also delivers the material proof for the unexpectable development in the relationship between the young couple and himself:

ù-yood=é	*cábùùne*	*ù-cùb=é*	*ŋɔ́*	*yír*	*àkɔ́ɔ́l*	*kéé*	*yín*
IPFV-find=3SG	soap	IPFV-give=3SG	O:3SG	PREP	Akol	speak	2SG

néé	*cí=í*	*ù-nywɔ̂lɔ̀*	*ù- nywɔ́l=é*	*ké*	*nyìdhɔɔk*
if	wife=POSS.2SG	IPFV-deliver:AP	IPFV-deliver=3SG	CONJ	boy

ké	*nyíŋ=é*	*jìbɛɛr*	*ènéé*	*à-nywɔ́l*	*ké*	*nyááków*
CONJ	name=POSS.3SG	Zubayr	if	PFV-deliver:TR	PREP	girl

à-ké-càk	*nyíŋ=é*	*ké*	*nyíŋ*	*miy=á*	*jeenàb*
PFV-DUR-call	name=POSS.3SG	PREP	name	mother=POSS.1SG	Zaynab

'and he took some soap and gave it to Akol and said: "you, if your wife delivers, and delivers a son then his name will be Zubayr if she delivers a girl then she will be called by the name of my mother, Zaynab."'

Abwolo then gave birth to a boy, who was named Zubayr. Pierina continues by telling the story of her grandfather Zubayr's life, which was spent under the threat of slavery and displacement until he was an adult. But it is this short passage of the story where she creates the framework within which she wants it to be situated. Not a story about binary oppositions between well-defined groups of players in this tale about the possibilities of life in a ruined world, but about encounters between different people and the sovereignty individuals can claim in these encounters.

Soap, which here is referred to as *cábùùne*, from Arabic صابون, Italian *sapone* and Swahili *sabuni*, is a particular type of gift. Even though it can be conceived as a simple offering to the poor, such as when homeless people in the streets of Khartoum were given soap by missionaries and members of various NGOs at the time when Pierina told her grandfather's story, it has a different meaning here. The smell word that expresses the scent of soap is *kúr* 'nice smell', which is also used in order to describe the aroma of perfume and incense. The latter is بخور *bakhūr* in Arabic, which sounds slightly similar to the Luwo smell term. Aromatic substances such as soap and perfume oil, in the context of festive occasions, such as marriage, childbirth and so on, are gifts that indexicalize hospitality and aesthetics that permeate social life in various ways. In her *Ethnography of Fragrance*, Dinah Jung (2011) describes how perfume, aromatic plants and incense were used in Adan and Laḥj in southern Yemen. The fine art of perfumery, based on religious ethics of cleanliness and purity as it is practised in East Africa, including the Sudan, was strongly influenced by Adani aromatics and olfactory rituals, through trade networks across the Red Sea and the Indian Ocean. Perfumes and other precious fragrant substances were not only used as cultural finery and to purify the home, Jung explains, but also to create sacred olfactory spaces, by perfuming the walls of mosques and prayer rooms, and by offering fragrant gifts as gifts and blessings to guests. Thus, when Zubayr spares Akol and Abwolo from enslavement and offers his name for their child, he does something that, following Pierina's interpretation, we can only understand as a performance of hospitality and benediction (*baraka*). The embodied language practice at work in encounters with strangers gets structured as a grammar of fragrance, and is theorized as a normative form of social interaction:

> Instead of being an issue of *jamāl* (beauty), Muslim theoreticians reflected upon perfumes in the context of discussing the matters of *ṭahāra* (purity), *adab* (courtesy, refinement), and *ẓarf* (elegance); and perfumery production has traditionally been part of pharmacy (*ṣaydala*), and often been explained in the so-called *adab* literature and its encyclopaedias.
>
> JUNG 2011: 206

This theoretical approach involves the use of a large terminology related to fragrance and aroma, as Jung (2011: 209– 227) illustrates. Like the large smell terminology in Luwo, these lexemes do not exclusively refer to olfactory experiences, but to the contexts in which these experiences are culturally and socially meaningful, and to practices that require specialized discursive techniques. Hence, they do much more than what Floyd, Majid and San Roque (2018: 178) claim that smell terms basically do, namely "refer to events of perceiving and emitting odors [or] refer to the qualities of odors." From a Sudanese perspective, Pierina's story offers a mooring of local language theory to shared knowledge about social processes. The term *kúr* is directly related to *bakhūr* in terms of the cultural meaning it conveys about aromatics and the practices and rituals attached to them. It expresses ideas about language as embodied social behaviour and fine art, as well as the spiritual connectedness of different people, the living and the dead, the individual and the world. In this respect, smell terminologies and proper names are theorized in rather similar ways: as language about the invisible bonds between the Self and Others.

In her painting *Preparation of Incense*, the Sudanese artist Kamala Ishaq presents her vision of a *zar* ceremony, a spirit possession ritual that has both healing purposes and works as a form of transmission of difficult knowledge (Kenyon 2012). We get to see a group of women, perhaps possessed by the Zar spirits, perhaps spirits themselves, whose faces express suffering and pain (L'Roubi 2018: 13). Around them there are the aromatic herbs and flowers that form part of the fine art of perfumery.

3 *Bʎdh*

Kamala Ishaq was one of the artists who published a text called 'The Crystalist Manifesto' in the *al-Ayyam* newspaper in Khartoum on January 21, 1976. The other authors were Hisham Abdallah, Hashim Ibrahim, Muhammad Hamid Shaddad and Naiyla Al Tayib—artists of the Khartoum School, one of the modernist movements in African arts of the twentieth century. The Manifesto was a statement about the categories present in and made conceivable through the arts, namely number, time, knowledge, space, shape, community and language. The goal of the Crystalists was to recover transparency and connection between people and between the Self and the world. In order to achieve this, they set out to create a new language—in terms of art and philosophy, but also in a poetic as well as a linguistic sense. In her commentary on the text, Anneka Lenssen (2018) writes that "the Crystalists sought to find an aesthetic and critical language that would emphasise the notions of pleasure and knowledge in order to permanently abolish differences and boundaries." This endows the art of *adab* with different meanings, by using its idea not as a means to affirm social order, but to critique it. The shared historical experiences of violence and ruination are addressed as difficult heritage, which results in the conservation of boundaries and segregation, rather than in new possibilities of open and hospitable encountering. This is particularly meaningful for a deeper understanding of the language of odour, such as in Luwo, and its connection to spiritual concepts.

Writing about Zar in central Sudan, Susan Kenyon observes that historical processes of domination, such as the succession of the Funj sultanate by the Ottoman Empire, which was itself replaced by the Mahdiyya and then the British colonialists, are often narrated as a seemingly endless series of disruptions and catastrophes (Kenyon 2012). Memories may combine references to different historical uprooting events and sites of disruption and be correlated with various present-day experiences. In central Sudanese Zar, the spirits are conceptualized as winds (similar to Zar in Zanzibar and elsewhere; Declich 2018), and in the ways in which they are endowed with certain qualities, smells and functions, these winds resemble smells: a whiff of perfume or of uprootedness. Thinking about the connections between the spirits or winds and memory, Kenyon (2012: 20) concludes:

> The categories of spirits, though grounded in a specific historical moment, do not refer to single periods of the Sudanese past but rather incorporate different levels of memory and the past, stretching into the present. This is what several writers referred to as "palimpsest memories," describing similar processes elsewhere in Africa in which events from different historical moments are compressed into a single memory.

To create a language that resists segregation and overcomes boundaries would not only mean creating a language that could also be used outside the Zar, turning a form of spirit language into an everyday language, but also creating a form of expression that would do justice to "palimpsest memories". By not forcing the remembering subject and society into the trauma of order and quantity ("Quantity is corrupt!", wrote the Crystalists; see Abdallah et al. 2018 [1976]: 396), but by offering new possibilities of seeing the same event from different perspectives, justice is done to stories about the world falling apart. Like the kaleidoscopic view of the world when seen through a crystal, the fragmented nature of reality becomes conceivable. Sharing memories, language and art in such an environment is still based on hospitality—the Crystalists emphasized the connection between pleasure and knowledge—but is a form of hospitable sharing and encountering that allows for fragmentation and palimpsest memories. In Crystalist thought about language, this is brought in a critical way into a relationship with western, academic language theory:

> Language, in its current state, being extremely close to objects, demonstrates its own corruption. The only way out of this is to dissolve language and turn it into a transparent crystal that moves in all directions: between the name, the subject, the thought, and their components; between the word and its components; and between the letter and its components. We expect this to happen in such a way that the fundamental opposition in language becomes an opposition between the crystal of meaning and the crystal of vocalization, which is a first and necessary step. We should mention here that the science of semiotics, [Claude] Shannon's information theory, the methods for measuring quantitative possibilities of all information contained in a vocalization, the methods of measuring the information contained within one letter of the alphabet, and all associated mathematical laws—are nothing but dry academic methodologies as far as the problem of language is concerned. They are all based on the corrupt notion of quantity, and so do not rise to the level of the crisis.
>
> ABDALLAH et al. 2018 [1976]: 396

Transparency as the most prominent property of the crystal here encodes, in a metaphoric way, an understanding that fragmentation already excludes the notion of boundaries. And without boundaries, there remains nothing to be quantified. In Luwo, transparency as an olfactory concept translates into *bʌ́dh* 'neutral, breath'. What remains when there is nothing on which a boundary could be fixed is one's breath, air, a whiff, but nothing more, and yet the ultimate sign of life.

Language as it is conceptualized and theorized in and through storytelling, the arts and in memory-making, is open and hospitable—an offer rather than a received gift. The particular notion of smells, among other sensory language, and the ways in which language, courtesy, memory and knowledge are presented as intertwined with the senses suggests that there indeed is the possibility of looking at language anew, as the Crystalists have suggested. One possibility in doing this is to consider social activity and cultural ideas as being inscribed and embedded in various ways in linguistic form. Olfactory terms in Luwo—as well as in other languages such as Chopi—refer not simply to the sensory quality of a given object, but to the idea that perception can be shared. Tasting a meal together, being together in a hospitable place, where fragrance encodes safety, learning about the other's memories and sharing them as stories—these are fundamental experiences of community and encountering, which in some African language theories and philosophies are crucial. Without the possibility of sharing language as sensory practice and expression, there would be no art of encountering the other, of sharing space and experience. In a disruptive and ruinous reality, sensual language as *adab* and as hospitable practice offers a powerful means to resist as the world falls apart and to reconstruct community.

This meaning, enshrined in smell terminologies and the ways in which they can be used, distinguishes sensual language from (other) epistemic language, such as evidentials in Luwo (Storch 2014: 161–162). While in olfactory language categories blur—semantically, structurally, pragmatically—evidentials work as order, by indicating the difference between first-hand and second-hand knowledge, memory not as a palimpsest but as based on either bearing witness or listening to storytelling.

In her work on evidentials, Alexandra Aikhenvald (2004) has shown precisely this. Even though in many languages nonvisual evidentials can cover a wide range of perception modalities and may even refer to smell as the metaphorical extension of a given form or construction, "no language has a special evidential to cover smell, taste, or feeling […]" (Aikhenvald 2004: 367). Smells tend to refer to more fragmented knowledge, to the world and the memories of it on the verge of everything falling apart. They categorize lifeworlds according to long-internalized knowledge (see Appendix), and not so much according to information the source of which can still be unambiguously named. But by being able to metaphorically encode fragmentation and infinite transparency through their powerfully imaginative meanings, smell words can also express the possibility of healing that which falls apart.

Acknowledgements

I remain deeply grateful to Pierina Akeelo Zubayr, Joseph Wol Modesto and the Luwo Group for so generously sharing knowledge about Luwo with me. I also owe much gratitude to them, together with Al-Amin Abu-Manga and his family, and to Leoma Gilley, for offering outstanding hospitality to me. I wish to thank Bob Dixon for a brilliant idea. And I want to express my very deep gratitude to Sasha Aikhenvald for many inspiring conversations and for her intellectual generosity.

Appendix

Luwo Odours (excerpt from a paper presented by Joseph Modesto for the Luwo Team at the Consultant Seminar, Tuesday 13 Nov. 2001, Omdurman)

Cäú	'fish before being cooked'
Kúr	'nice smell, incense'
Tïú	'non-castrated he-goat'
Cér	'smell of urine'
Lêm	'smell of honey'
Wàj	'fermented flour'
Pèèd	'rotten meat'
Kèèj	'smoke which brings tears to one's eyes'
Ngïr	'smell of termites'
Kód	'smell of pounded sesame'
Ngweedh	'roasted meat'
Puj	'a recently dug out root'
Cùng	'smell of snake'
Yùng	'smell of dirt'

Importance of Tastes and Odours for Luwo

a) The Luwo environment has many things with different odours and tastes. This makes it important to give distinction to each odour and taste.

b) The Luwo have a sense of self-esteem which causes them to be selective about things to eat. Some of these are not eaten because of tastes or smell especially among women.

c) Mocking songs are composed comparing a person to a bad taste or smell and in this way they are effective.

d) Certain smells associated with dangerous fierce animals may cause the feeling of danger to a person. E.g. Smell of "raw" (millet) is associated with leopard. Smell of "telaango" (black ants) is associated with snake. Smell of non-castrated he-goat is associated with lion.

e) In hunting the hunters follow the wind so that the animals can't smell them and run away.

Abbreviations

1, 2, 3	1, 2, 3 person
AP	antipassive
CONJ	conjunction
DUR	durative
IPFV	imperfective
O	object
PFV	perfective
POSS	possessive
PREP	preposition
SG	singular
TR	transitive

References

Abdallah, Hassan, Hashim Ibrahim, Kamala I. Ishaq, Muhammad Hamid Shaddad and Naiyla al-Tayib (2018 [1976]). The Crystalist Manifesto. In Anneka Lenssen, Sarah Rogers and Nada Shabout (eds.), *Modern Art in the Arab World*. Primary Documents, 393–401. New York: MOMA.

Aikhenvald, Alexandra Y. (2004). *Evidentiality*. Oxford: Oxford University Press.

Berman, Zachary S. (2017). *Owing and Owning: Zubayr Pasha, Slavery, and Empire in Nineteenth-Century Sudan*. New York: CUNY Academic Works. https://academicworks.cuny.edu/gc_etds/1779 (accessed 23.11.2020).

Declich, Francesca (ed.) (2018). *Translocal Connections across the Indian Ocean*. Leiden: Brill.

Floyd, Simon, Asifa Majid and Lila San Roque (2018). Smell Is Coded in Grammar and Frequent in Discourse: Cha'palaa Olfactory Language in Cross-Linguistic Perspective. *Journal of Linguistic Anthropology* 28 (2): 175–196.

Heyking, Beatrix von (2013). *A Grammar of Belanda Bor*. Cologne: Köppe.

Jung, Dinah (2011). *An Ethnography of Fragrance: The Perfumery Arts of 'Adan*. Leiden: Brill.

Junker, Wilhelm (1891). *Travels in Africa during the Years 1879–1883*. London: Chapman.

Kenyon, Susan M. (2012). *Spirits and Slaves in Central Sudan*. New York: Palgrave Macmillan.

L'Roubi, Roubi (2018). *Forests and Spirits*. London: Saatchi.

Lenski, Noel and Catherine M. Cameron, eds. (2018). *What is a Slave Society?* Cambridge: Cambridge University Press.

Lenssen, Anneka (2018). "We painted the crystal, we thought about the crystal"—The

Crystalist Manifesto (Khartoum, 1976) in context. *Post, Notes on Art in a Global Context*. https://post.moma.org/we-painted-the-crystal-we-thought-about-the-crystal-the-crystalist-manifesto-khartoum-1976-in-context/ (accessed 20.11.2020).

Ochieng'-Odhiambo, Frederick (2013). What's in a name? Four levels of naming among the Luo people. In Chike Jeffers (ed.), *Listening to Ourselves*, 52–89. Albany: State University of New York Press.

Santandrea, Stefano (1946). *Grammatichetta Giur*. Verona: Missioni Africane.

Sikainga, Ahmad (1991). *The Western Bahr Al-Ghazal Under British Rule, 1898–1956*. Athens Ohio: Ohio University Center for International Studies.

Sikainga, Ahmad (1996). *Slaves into Workers: Emancipation and Labor in Colonial Sudan*. Austin: University of Texas Press.

Storch, Anne (2014). *A Grammar of Luwo. An Anthropological Approach*. Amsterdam: Benjamins.

Storch, Anne (2015). Linguistic etiquette in a frontier situation: a case study from Chopi. In Angelika Mietzner and Anne Storch (eds.), *Nilo-Saharan Languages: Description and Modelling*, 373–380. Cologne: Köppe.

Storch, Anne and Angelika Mietzner (2021). *Language and Tourism in East Africa*. Bristol: Channel View.

Tsing, Anna Lowenhaupt (2015). *The Mushroom at the End of the World*. Princeton: Princeton University Press.

Ziadeh, May (2018 [1912]). Something about art. In Anneka Lenssen, Sarah Rogers and Nada Shabout (eds.), *Modern Art in the Arab World. Primary Documents*, 45–47. New York: MOMA.

CHAPTER 8

Othering Based on Communicative (In)competence: Examples from West Africa

Felix K. Ameka

1 Introduction

A distinction between 'self' and 'other' is a human universal (Brown 1991). Kearney (1984: 41) notes that this distinction is a universal worldview category. There are linguistic reflexes of this distinction. Thus, as far as we know, there is no language on the planet that does not have an expression for an 'I' and a 'YOU'. These represent the interactional participants in communication, which is assumed to be a joint activity (Clark 1996). There are cultural constraints on the understanding of this distinction, however. For instance, how does one sequence the 'I' and the 'YOU' in coordination? In Standard Average European (SAE) languages, language users are socialised to put the 'YOU' before the 'I'. Thus, it is more appropriate to say *you and I* whereas ??*I and you* is proscribed. In many African languages, including Ewe, it is de rigeur to put the 'I' before the 'YOU': *nye klpé wò* [1SG COM 2SG] 'I and you', conforming to a kind of me-first principle. The violation of this principle sounds very odd. Dixon (2017) draws attention to the special grammar of the 1SG pronoun *I* in English. He notes that "whereas *she, he, we,* and *they* come first in a coordination—*She and John* rather than **John and she*—*I* must go last *John and I* not **I and John*" (Dixon 2017: 42). Dixon offers a socio-cultural reason for the exceptional behavior of the 1SG pronoun, namely that: "In many English-speaking societies, there is a social convention not to put oneself first." (Dixon 2017:42).[1] This explanation is consistent with our view that this is a manifestation of the distinction between the "Self" and "Other" and the anti-me-first principle as a politeness strategy in many SAE lingua-culture groups.

Moreover, there are differences in the conceptualisation of the terms of 'self' and 'other'. For instance, a distinction has been made between Asian cul-

1 Perhaps one should say in Inner circle English speaking countries founded on Anglo cultural values such as Great Britain, United States of America, Canada, Australia, and New Zealand.

© FELIX K. AMEKA, 2022 | DOI:10.1163/9789004510395_009

tures and western cultures in terms of the "interdependent conception of the self". "The interdependent construal of 'self'," Winnie Cheng (2003: 6) argues, "is more likely to pay attention to the group when forming opinions and attitudes […] and emphasize harmony and cooperation in the in-group. The other-orientation is therefore essential to an interdependent self". Triandis (1989) draws attention to three aspects of the 'self'. One aspect is the 'private self', which addresses the question: How do I think of myself? This perspective invokes characteristics such as: I am honest; I am thirsty; etc. This aspect can be paraphrased simply as:[2]

[A] I think about myself like this:

The 'public self' aspect is the generalised other's view of the self; i.e., how people think of me (see Goffman 1978). This relates to the fact that people (others) can evaluate things I do and on the basis of that think something good or bad about me. This aspect of the self can be roughly characterised in a cultural script as follows (see, e.g., Ameka and Breedveld 2004 and Goddard and Wierzbicka 2004 on cultural scripts):

[B] [when I do something like this:]
people can think something good about me
people can think something bad about me

Finally, there is the 'collective self' which relates to what members of the group I belong to now or that I identify with for the purposes of this interaction will think of me, and how that impacts on the group. Goddard and Wierzbicka (2021) show that there is variation in the semantics of the pronoun 'we', which relates partly to the nature of the group it is used to refer to. In the context of this discussion, one can think of the pronoun 'we' and its various conceptualisations as relating to different perspectives on the 'collective self'.

---

2 In making explicit the conceptual content of linguistic signs or explaining associated practices, I follow the age old lexicographical principle of using a metalanguage of Minimal English (ME) (Goddard and Wierzbicka 2018) based on the principles of the Natural Semantic Metalanguage (NSM) and of the Moscow school (e.g. Apresjan 2000). The ME metalanguage is comprised of three layers: first is a set of 65 indefinable semantic primes such as I, YOU, BODY, THIS, WANT, KNOW, THINK, SEE, SOMEONE, SOMETHING, PEOPLE and BECAUSE. The second layer consists of putative universal molecules, terms which can be defined and have equivalents across cultures, such as FATHER, MOTHER, CHILDREN, BE BORN, SKY, SUN, HANDS, MOUTH, DAY, GROUND and SLEEP. The third layer is made up of

The knowledge structure associated with this collective aspect of the 'self' can be represented as:

[C] I am part of something
some other people are part of the same thing as me
when I do something like this
people I am part of the same thing with can think something good about me
people I am part of the same thing with can think something bad about me

Similarly, the notion of the 'other' is conceptualised differently across linguacultures. For instance, Sarukkai (1997) notes that in Indian languages such as Tamil or Hindi, the notion of 'otherness' can be understood as being quantified, as the words for the concept roughly mean 'one more' or 'second'. This encapsulates a different idea of the 'other' than the notion in SAE languages. We will see below that the concept of the 'other' in some West African languages is tied to the manner of saying things with words in a way different from the way the 'self' and the 'collective self' of the group of people who use the same language do. Furthermore, the otherness is also based on the extent to which the other who may speak the language of the group understands the oblique forms of the language.

Another worldview category is that humans have a predisposition to classify and categorise things into groups based on similarity in some form or feature. In interactions we tend to identify with people who share some features with ourselves as belonging to the same group—the in-group; and to differentiate ourselves from others depending on features we identify ourselves by—the out-group. Language is intimately tied to identity and we tend to distinguish ourselves from others based on language or identify with others because we speak the same language. Indeed, we construct, establish and maintain identity through language (Edwards 2009).

As Duranti (1997: 5) observes, linguistic signs (words) are "used for the construction of cultural affinities and cultural differentiations." In interaction we tend to engage in forms of 'othering' by conceptualising people as a kind of someone who is one of us or not one of us based on various factors. One of these is whether they speak the same language like us. Another is that we

non-universal yet useful words which can be translated into most languages, such as SKIN, LEGS, GROW, HOUSE, VILLAGE, TREE and GOD (see Goddard 2018 for details on NSM methodology).

tend to form strong attitudes about others based on the way they speak. In this chapter I examine the strategies for othering in some West African communities based on the communicative competence of the other with respect to the language of the 'self'. I draw on linguistic practices of the Ewe (Kwa), Gã (Kwa), Dangme (Kwa) and Wolof (Atlantic). One strategy involves naming the 'other' based on terms relating to manner of speaking, such as speaking unintelligibly. I illustrate this from Wolof and Ewe (Section 2). The second strategy relates to negotiation in communicative practice of the degree to which the 'other' is competent in the language of the group of the 'self'. I discuss speech routines indexical of local cultural activities and other idiomatic expressions that are used to articulate the lack of communicative competence and at the same time to signal that the 'other' may have some understanding of the code (Section 3). The chapter concludes with Section 4, reflecting on the similarities in the strategies and expressions used in communicative competence based othering in West Africa.

2 Alter Ethnonyms Based on Manner of Speaking

One of the linguistic practices through which people draw boundaries around themselves and others is by identifying the other through names. In this section we discuss names of out-group people from the point of view of Ewe (Section 2.1) and from the point of view of Wolof (Section 2.2). What is striking is that they both base the alter ethnonyms on the other's manner of not speaking intelligibly.

2.1 *Ewe*

The Ewe are surrounded by several lingua-cultural groups, some of which use the Ewe language as a lingua franca or second language. Thus, to the north of them are Ghana-Togo Mountain language groups such as Avatime, Tafi, Nyagbo, Logba, Likpe, Lolobi-Akpafu, Santrokofi and Tuwuli, where Ewe is used as a lingua franca (Ring 1987; see also Ameka 2007 and 2018 and references therein on the interactions among these groups and the Ewe). Also neighbouring the Ewe speaking area are various Guang language speaking groups such as Nkonya and Anum. To the west of the Ewe are the Dangme, the Gã and the Akan and further afield are the Gur/Mabia languages and languages from other families such as Fulfulde, Hausa and Mande languages. What is interesting is that the Ewe have one term for all these people whose languages are not intelligible with Ewe, namely *fa-fia-lá-wó* [RED-V-A.NZER=PL] 'people speaking unintelligibly'; except for one group, the Akan, whom they refer to and call *blu-a-wó*

[N-DEF=PL] 'the Akans'. I will discuss each of these terms in turn and show that they both relate to manner of speaking.
Lexicographers characterise the verb *fia* as in (1):

(1) a. *fia*: to speak a foreign, unintelligible language (Westermann 1928)
    b. *fia*: parler une autre langue que la sienne propre (Adzomada 1983) ['to speak another language different from one's own' (my translation)]

While the dictionary definitions cited in (1) present the verb as an act of speaking a foreign language, which is therefore unintelligible, in fact the verb is used to talk about speaking Ewe unintelligibly, not just a foreign language, although one can construe the relationship. Consider the context in (2).

(2) One person speaks and the interlocutor feigns or shows signs of not understanding. The speaker may ask the interlocutor whether they were not being understood because they were speaking a foreign language:
    fa-fia-ḿ *me-le=a*
    RED-speak.unintelligible-PROG 1SG-be.at:PRES=Q
    'Am I speaking a strange language?' / 'Am I speaking unintelligibly?'

The term *fa-fia-lá=wó* 'people who speak strange languages' is a deverbal agentive nominalisation based on the verb *fia*. When applied to the group it can refer to a particular group of people who speak the same language, e.g. *Tafi=a=wo* 'the Tafi', but it also applies to the multilingual groups who do not identify as Ewe as a collective. This term identifies them as non-Ewe. The conceptual content of the term can be made explicit as follows:

[D] fa-fia-lá=wó
  a. People of different kinds
  b. These people live in places different from the places the Ewe think of like this: This is our home
  c. These places are not far from the places where the Ewe live
  d. These people are not like us (Ewe)
  e. They do not say things the way we (Ewe) say things
  f. When they say things it is like this:
      One can hear something
      One cannot know what they are saying

Unlike ethnonyms based on identity, such as Fulbe (Breedveld 1999), which can be used both in reference and address, the term *fa-fia-lá=wó* 'speakers of strange languages' can be used to refer to people but it is not used to address them. This seems to be a feature of the alter ethnonyms based on manner of speaking. Some components in [D] give clues as to why the term is not applied to the Akan. First of all, as we shall see below, some of the Akan live among the Ewe, hence components (b) and (c) do not apply to them. That is, they live in places the Ewe think of as home and they live in places where the Ewe live. Moreover, it appears that because some of the Ewe, especially the northern Ewe dialect speakers in places such as Peki, are bilingual in Ewe and Akan and hence some of them can understand what the Akan are saying. Thus Akan is not unintelligible to them. Hence component (e) is not applicable. It is the case that even though Ewe is used as a second language in several of the Ghana-Togo Mountain (GTM) language communities, the nature of the contact is an asymmetrical one where speakers of Ewe do not speak these languages, whereas the GTM language users do speak and understand Ewe. Thus people who identify as Ewe do not understand or speak GTM and other languages of their neighbours. For this reason, the languages are unintelligible to them, whereas Akan may not be.

If the Akan are not *fa-fia-lá=wó* 'speakers of strange unintelligible languages' then what are they? How do the Ewe refer to them? The lexicographers give us some answers, as shown in (3).

(3) a. *blǔ* n. Akan (Westermann 1928)
b. *blǔ* Akan; Blu, Twi (personne ou langue) (Rongier 2015)
'person or language' (my translation)
c. *bluawó* [*blu*=DEF=PL] *le peuple Akan, les Akans* (Rongier 2015, my glosses)
'the Akan people, the Akans' (my translation)
d. *blǔgbe* [*blu*-language] ashanti, akan, twi (*langues* du Ghana) (Rongier 2015, my glosses)
'Asante, Akan, Twi, languages of Ghana' (my translation)
e. *blǔme* [*blu*-containing.region.of] *pays Akan* (Rongier 2015, my glosses)
'Akan country' (my translation)

As the entries from the dictionaries show, the term for the Akan is *blǔ=a=wó*. The derivatives provided by Rongier (2015) show that this term is entrenched and that it is the basis for talking about Akan country or the Akan language. With respect to the glosses provided for *blugbe* 'Akan language', which include dialects, e.g., Twi, and sub dialects, e.g., Asante, this term could well just be glossed as 'Akan lect'. Be that as it may, one wonders whether there is any connection between *blǔ* and any verbs in the language similar to the relationship discussed above between the verb *fia* 'speak a strange language' and the alter ethnonym *fa-fia-lá=wó* 'speakers of unintelligible languages'.

We turn to the lexicographers again and find a verb *blù* with various readings, as shown in (4):

(4) a. *blù* v. to stir (water) knead (dough); to confuse, to be confused (Westermann 1928)
b. *blù* v. *gronder* 'to scold' (Adzomada 1983: 162)
c. *blù* v.2. *gronder, crier, rugir* 'to scold, scream, roar' (Rongier 2015)
3. eblouir 'dazzle' (my translations)

The readings suggested by Rongier (2015) reproduced in (4c) provide the clearest clues to the manner of speaking interpretation of the verb. He further provides a collocation which makes explicit the manner of speaking feature of the verb, as shown in (5). The phrase in (5) could also be interpreted as 'shout at someone'.

(5) *blu ɖé … ta* [Verb ALL … head]
gronder (un enfant), injurier, faire de reproaches à, invectiver
'to scold (a child), to curse, to reproach, to curse' (my translation)

In example (6) the verb is used to characterise a manner of speaking of Amuzu, whose utterance is compared to the roaring of a lion. The context of the story makes it clear that Amuzu spoke very angrily to his interlocutors.

(6) *Amuzu blu abé dzata-tsú ené …*
NAME V SEMBL lion-male SEMBL
'Amuzu roared (spoke angrily) like a male lion' (Nyaku 1980: 20; glosses and translation mine)

Apart from an emotional colouring in the manner of speaking usage, the verb can be used to describe a loud noise or thud, such as, for example, the noise of gun shot in example (7):

(7) *kásía, kpigim! tú blu ɖé wó títína*
at.once IDEO gun V ALL 3PL middle
'Just then kpigim; a gun sounded in their (= animals') midst'
(Bureau of Ghana Languages: Ɖe Modzaka 3: 20)

Similarly the noise of thunder is also described as such, as in (8).

(8) *dzíŋgɔli le bu-blu-ḿ*
sky be.at:PRES RED-roar-PROG
'The sky is roaring', i.e. it is thundering.

My claim is that the noun *Blǔ* for Akan is derived from the verb *blu* by high tone suffixation yielding a rising tone on the word (see Ameka 1999 and Ofori 2002 on nominalisation in Ewe), based on various perceptions of the Akan people and language by the Ewe. The stereotypes about the Akan include that they are loud and when they are speaking it is as if they are angry and shouting (see e.g. Aikhenvald 2003 on ethnic stereotypes). From this perspective, it can be argued that the term *Blǔ* is based on the manner of speaking reading of the verb *blù* 'yell, roar, speak in anger with a thud'.

Another reading of the verb *blu* as 'mix, stir', as noted in Westermann's entry, could also have contributed to the emergence and entrenchment of the ethnonym *Blǔ* for the Akan. Historically, it has been observed that between 1700 and 1874, the Akwamu nation, an Akan group, was one of the strongest in the southern sections of present-day Ghana (Ansre 1997: 3) and they exercised hegemony over a part of the Ewe country that was referred to as Krepi. Apart from the Akwamu expansion in the 18th century, "wars of state formation amongst the Akan west of the Volta between 1670s and 1730s inundated the Ewe of southeastern Ghana with refugees" (Akyeampong 2001: 39). With these interactions, the Akan may have been perceived as people mixing with the Ewe in those times. This mixing of peoples has had linguistic and cultural consequences. One of these is that the Ewe dialect of Peki, a place that was the seat of government of Krepi and headed by the chief of Peki, has several distinctive features on all levels of linguistic structure, phonology, lexicon and syntax, which can be explained as the result of change brought about due to contact with Akan (see Ofori 1988). These newcomers into Ewe country seem to have learned the Ewe language. It appears that, as second language learners, it was observed that they had good linguistic competence; however, they did not fully grasp the 'deep' idioms and aphorisms of the language. In other words they were not fully communicatively or pragmatically competent in the language (see Thomas 1983 on pragma-linguistic competence, and Hymes 1987 and Saville-Troike 2003 on communicative competence). This gave rise to the saying in (9). The message of this traditional saying is that no matter how much you may have mastered a language, in this case Ewe, as a second language learner, there are aspects of the language that you cannot grasp, including its semantic style.

(9) *Blŭ se ve mé-se adágáná o*
Akan hear Ewe NEG-hear idiom NEG
'An Akan that understands Ewe does not understand Ewe idioms and aphorisms.' (a saying)

A strategy that the Ewe use in making a distinction between themselves as 'self' and others around with whom they interact is to describe them in terms of aspects of their manner of speaking. Given their specific interactions with the Akan, they single them out based on the perception of them as loud. The more or less imperfect grasp of the semantic style or the encoding idioms of Ewe by the Akan has generated the saying in (9). There is no distinction among the other groups who speak languages that are unintelligible to the Ewe and, given the asymmetric nature of contact with these people, their languages remain incomprehensible to the Ewe speaking people. In the next section, I discuss the strategy of othering based on communicative competence as it can be gleaned from Wolof, an Atlantic language of the Senegambia and beyond.

2.2 *Wolof*

Wolof has a speech act verb *lakk* 'speak' with various derivatives and interpretations. One can derive an agentive nominal from it as shown in (10).

(10) *làkk-kat*
V:speak-AGENT
'speaker'

This agentive form is used to refer to someone who speaks a language different from Wolof. Thus, a multilingual speaker who has Wolof as one of the languages in their repertoire can be referred to as a *lakk-at*. I think this has led to an associated meaning of a speaker of a foreign language, as many Wolof dictionaries indicate, as outlined in (11):

(11) Dictionary definitions of *lakk*
a. Fal et al. (1990)

làkk v.	parler (une langue étrangère) 'speak (a foreign language)'	*Bambara lay làkk*. Il parle bambara. 'He speaks Bambara'

làkk w-, n.	langue 'language'	*Nit kooku dégg na làkk yu.* Cette personne comprend beaucoup de langues. 'This person understands a lot of languages'
làkkkat Ø		

b. Diouf (2003)

làkk 1 v.t.	parler (une langue) 'speak a language'	*Man nga làkk bambara?* Sais-tu parler bambara? 'Can you speak Bambara?' (my translation)
làkk w-	langue; dialecte 'language; dialect' 'It is a language that I like' (my translation)	*Làkk wu ma neex la.* C' est une langue qui me plait.
làkkkat Ø		

c. Munro and Gaye (1991)

làkk	1. To speak a language other than ordinary conversational Wolof; to speak unintelligibly 2. To speak a language. *Dafay làkk Àngale.* He is speaking English. 3. Language. *Yan làkk lë dégg?* Which languages does he speak?
làkkkat	speaker of a tonal African language

The various paraphrases from the dictionaries, whether they are Wolof-French or Wolof-English, agree on the verb meaning as 'speak a language' and Fal et al. (1990) add optionally 'a foreign language'. Although the dictionaries recognise the derivative of *làkkkat*, it is only Munro and Gaye that give an elaboration. It is interesting that they phrase it as a speaker of a tonal African language. The implication here is that there is a distinction between a speaker of Wolof and a speaker of other African languages. It is not clear to me why they indicate tonal language, as the speaker of a language like Fulfulde (or Pulaar), which is not a tonal language can also be a *làkkkat*. It is not inconceivable that, like in the Ewe case, the term *làkkkat* as an ethnonym applies to someone who speaks an unintelligible language, a language I as a speaker of Wolof do not understand.

Mc Laughlin (2017) interprets *làkkkat* as a speaker of a language that is or has been in contact with Wolof; or a member of an ethnic group that is or has been in contact with Wolof. She suggests that a prototypical *làkkkat* is a Bambara, an idea which resonates with the entry of Fal et al. (1990) as speaking a foreign language. From the point of view of othering, which is based on interactions, in contact situations of the kind that occurred between Atlantic languages and Mande languages and specifically between Wolof and Bambara, it makes sense to have a way of designating the 'other' as speaking a language different from that of our group. In the next section, we discuss the language of negotiating othering in social interaction in some of the lingua-cultures.

3 Speech Routines for Practising 'Othering'

As observed earlier, we use language and linguistic signs to enact 'othering' in social interaction. In this section we discuss linguistic routines, conventionalised expressions tied to particular communicative situations, that language users of Gã, Dangme and Ewe employ to negotiate 'otherness' based on communicative competence in everyday discourse. A common interactional situation that arises is where there would be two or more members of a lingua-culture group and a third person whose affiliation with the group may not be known to some participants in the communicative situation. There is a routine strategy with its accompanying linguistic expressions to, as it were, warn the other members of the competence of the participant in question so that the interactants should know how to use language. The expressions all relate to the linguistic and communicative competence of the 'other'. What is interesting is that there are recurrent tropes of bodies of water and of references to local products that are emblematic of the group or area. This suggests a conceptual pattern that is shared across the languages in the speech and cultural area.

3.1 *Gã*

Kropp Dakubu (1997: 11) reports that there is a well-known Gã expression which is "deliberately indirect and richly ambiguous" which is deployed in asserting group membership and at the same time ascertains the Gã communicative competence of a member of the group. The expression, as cited by Dakubu from Ankrah (1966: 36), is given in (12).

(12) Ekɔɔle yaa ŋshɔŋ
E=kɔɔle ya-a ŋshɔŋ
3SG=Korle go-HAB sea
Lit. 'His/her Korle goes to the sea.'

The expression in (12) is used to indicate that someone who you may not think understands the current discussion does understand what is being said. In other words, they speak and are competent in Gã. It is used as "a warning from one Gã to another in the presence of a third (the referent of ***e*** 'his/her') who is not Gã" (Kropp Dakubu 1997: 12). A variant of this expression, a saying, is in (13).

(13) *Kɔɔle* *ŋya* *ŋshɔŋ*
Korle.lagoon PROG-go sea
'Korle is going to the sea'

Zimmermann (1858: 158) notes that the saying in (13) is used to warn people not to reveal secrets. If one is not aware of the linguistic competence of the 'other' they may say things that were not intended for them to understand, hence the use of such a saying to warn the group members. As Kropp Dakubu (1997) explains, there is a symbolism of 'them and us' at work. She suggests that the key to understanding the symbolism is in the opposition between Korle, the lagoon, and the sea. The opposition between the sea and the lagoon represents the 'us vs. them' dichotomy: the sea is associated with being Gã. The characteristic occupation of traditional Gã is sea fishing. And the Gã being linked with the sea is in opposition to inland people and the rivers that are inland. When someone's Korle goes to the sea it means the inland bodies (of water) have moved to the Gã domain and hence have acquired Gã-ness (even though an 'other'). In terms of language, it means they have also acquired Gã and hence secrets expressed in Gã may be understood. This is the sense in which othering is manifested based on communicative competence. In the next subsection, expressions from Dangme, a sister language to Gã, together with which they form a genetic subgroup in the Kwa family, is discussed. Other tropes are employed in Dangme but for the same purpose of othering.

3.2 *Dangme*

The expressions in (14) are used in Dangme to advise an interlocutor that a third (another) participant is communicatively competent and can interpret the code, i.e. the language that is being used, just like the Gã expressions in (12) and (13). The Dangme expressions use different symbolisms and tropes to articulate this idea.

(14) a. *Kofí* *bà* *gbù-ú*
NAME leaf perforate-HAB
Lit. 'Kofi's leaf is perforated'
'Kofi understands the language.'

b. *Kofi* *ye-e* *ngo*
NAME eat-HAB salt
Lit. 'Kofi eats the salt'
'Kofi understands the language.'

Example (14a) is taken from Caesar (2017: 5) who explains the VP *ba gbuu* as 'understands a specific language under discussion'. How does one get from the literal meaning to the interpretation? A first step is to understand the metonymy, where the leaf is a stand-in for the ear. A native speaker of Dangme, Prosper Akortia, explains the symbolism as follows:

> The leaf symbolises the ear drum. It is assumed that one cannot perceive speech waves if the ear drum is not perforated, literally speaking. If someone is unable to understand the language you speak it means that although the waves get to the ear drum (leaf), they are not able to enter it since it is not perforated.
>
> Prosper Akortia, personal email 19.09.2017

The perforation of the ear is being compared to the competence of the 'other' and if there is someone else, a Dangme in-group member, in the communicative situation who may not suspect this, that person is thus advised using a metonymic trope.

The expression in (14b) is frequently used in the Ada dialect where a regular activity is salt mining. As such, salt is emblematic of the place. One can understand that someone who is a group member will be someone who eats salt. Thus, if another has knowledge of linguistic habits of the place, they are said to 'eat' salt. This then warns the other interactants that they have to be careful about what they say. Interestingly, a parallel expression exists in Ewe, as we shall see in the next sub-section.

3.3 *Ewe*

In Ewe the main way in which the othering with respect to communicative competence is typically presented is in the form of a question to the members of the group about a third party whose status with respect to the community is not clear. In parts of Ewe country, salt mining is a main occupation and like the Dangme expression, one can ask whether the person eats the local salt, which stands for whether they speak Ewe, as in (15a). Similarly, one can also ask whether the person drinks the water, where water stands again for the language, Ewe, as in (15b).

(15) a. *É-ɖu-ɔ* *dze-ɛ=a* Inland Ewe
3SG-eat-HAB salt-DEF=Q
Lit. 'Does he or she eat the salt?' i.e. 'Does he or she understand/speak Ewe?'

b. *É-no-ɔ* *tsi-ɛ=a* Inland Ewe
3SG-drink-HAB water-DEF=Q
Lit. 'Does he drink the water?'
i.e. 'Does he understand/speak Ewe?'

In Ewe, the indication that someone is communicatively competent is to use local bodies of water to stand for the language. The Volta River, called *Amu*, is on the western border of Ewe country. It is emblematic of the Ewe and it is used as a source of drinking water in parts of Ewe land (16a). This explains why one can warn an interlocutor that the third party understands the Ewe language by indicating that they drink *Amu* (16a), therefore they cannot say things that an Ewe can understand. Similarly, the names of local streams can be used to stand for local Ewe dialects in places. For instance, in Anfoega there is a stream called *Dzibi* and if one wants to give warning that an 'other' is competent in the local Anfoega dialect, one can say that the third party drinks the River Dzibi, as illustrated in (16b).

(16) a. *É-no-ɔ* *Amu=ɔ* Inland Ewe
3SG-drink-HAB Volta=DEF
Lit. 'S/He drinks the Volta.'
i.e. 'S/he speaks/understands Ewe'

b. *É-no-ɔ* *Dzibi=ɛ=a* Anfoe dialect
3SG-drink-HAB NAME-DEF=Q
Lit. 'Does s/he drink the Dzibi?'
i.e. 'Does s/he understand the Anfoe dialect?'

In Ewe, affinity with other local symbols is also used to evaluate the extent to which an 'other' may be communicatively competent and participate fully in the current discussion and in understanding the idioms and aphorisms of the language.

4 Concluding Remarks

In this chapter I have explored the ways in which some communities of practice in West Africa identify the members of the in-group and out-group based on communicative competence. Two main strategies were surveyed. One is the use of ethnonyms based on manners of speaking as well as intelligibility. This helps manifest a distinction between 'people who say things in a way I can know what they are saying' vs. 'people who say things in a way I cannot know what they are saying'; 'I say things like you say them' vs. 'this person does not say things like I say them'.

A second strategy draws on using local symbols that are metonymically used to stand for the identifying properties of the lingua-culture. Thus, the Gã represent the 'us vs. them' distinction as an opposition between the sea and the lagoon that flows into it, where Gã-ness is represented by the sea, and the lagoon represents people of the interior who move into Gã territory. The Dangme and the Ewe connect their respective languages to cultural activities involving salt mining. The Ewe also use local bodies of water such as the Volta to ascertain the communicative competence-based group membership of participants in a social interaction.

The 'self' and 'other' opposition is a worldview category but its articulation varies from one culture to the next. I hope to have shown that even though there is cultural and linguistic variation in its manifestation, there is an underlying conceptual pattern. Furthermore, the case studies from West Africa show that there may be shared areal patterns. There is the need for further investigation into how people and groups identify themselves in social interaction based on communicative competence.

Abbreviations

ALL	allative
DEF	definiteness
HAB	habitual
IDEO	ideophone
NEG	negative
PRES	present
PROG	progressive
Q	question
RED	reduplicative
SEMBL	semblative
SG	singular
PL	plural
1	first person
2	second person
3	third person

References

Adzomada, Kofi (1983). *Dictionaire ewe-français*. Lome HAHO

Aikhenvald, Alexandra Y. (2003). Multilingualism and ethnic stereotypes: the Tariana of northwest Amazonia. *Language in Society* 32: 1–21.

Akyeampong, Emmanuel Kwaku (2001). *Between the Sea and the Lagoon: An Eco-Social History of the Anlo of Southeastern Ghana, c. 1850 to Recent Times*. Athens: Ohio University Press /Oxford: James Curry

Ameka, Felix K. (1999). The typology and semantics of complex nominal duplication in Ewe. *Anthropological linguistics* 41 (1): 75–106.

Ameka, Felix K. (2017). Grammars in contact in the Volta Basin (West Africa): On contact induced grammatical change in Likpe. In Alexandra Y. Aikhenvald and R.M.W. Dixon (eds.), *Grammars in Contact: A Cross-Linguistic Typology*, 114–142. Oxford: Oxford University Press.

Ameka, Felix K. (2018). Ghana-Togo-Mountain Languages: a socio-cultural, a typological or a genetic grouping? *Afrika und Übersee* 92 (2015/2016): 1–12.

Ameka, Felix K. and Anneke Breedveld (2004). Areal cultural scripts for social interaction in West African communities. *Intercultural Pragmatics* 1 (2): 167–187.

Ankrah, E.A. Nee-Adjabeng (1966). *Agwaseŋ Wiemɔi kɛ Aba Komei*. Accra: Bureau of Ghana Languages

Ansre, Gilbert (1997). *A history of the Evangelical Presbyterian Church*. Ho: EP Church Book Depot

Apresjan, Jurij (2000). *Systematic lexicography*. Oxford: Oxford University Press

Breedveld, Anneke (1999). Prototypes and ethnic categorisation: On the terms pullo and fulbe in Maasina (Mali). In Victor Azarya, Anneke Breedveld, Mirjam de Bruijn and Han van Dijk (eds.), *Pastoralists under pressure? Fulbe societies confronting change in West Africa*, 69–90. Leiden: Brill.

Brown, Donald E. (1991). *Human universals*. New York: McGraw Hill Inc.

Bureau of Ghana Languages (1993). *Ɖe modzaka 3* [Entertain yourself] Accra: Bureau of Ghana Languages.

Caesar, Regina (2017). Word formation in Dangme. Paper presented at the 47th Colloquium of African Languages and Linguistics, Leiden University (August).

Cheng, Winnie (2003). *Intercultural Conversation*. Amsterdam: John Benjamins

Clark, Herbert (1996). *Using language*. Cambridge: Cambridge University Press

Diouf, Jean Léopold. (2003). *Dictionnaire wolof-français et français-wolof*. Paris: Kartha laEditions,

Dixon, R.M.W. (2017). The grammar of English pronouns. *Lingua* 200: 33–44. https://doi.org/10.1016/j.lingua.2017.08.002

Duranti, Alessandro (1997). *Linguistic anthropology*. Cambridge: Cambridge University Press.

Edwards, John (2009). *Language and identity: An introduction*. Cambridge: Cambridge University Press.

Fal, Arame, Rosine Santos and Jean L. Doneux (1990). *Dictionnaire wolof-français suivi d'un index français wolof*. Paris: édition Kartala

Goddard, Cliff (2018). *Ten lectures on Natural Semantic Metalanguage: Exploring language, thought and culture using simple translatable words*. Leiden: Brill.

Goddard, Cliff and Anna Wierzbicka (2004). Cultural scripts: What are they and what are they good for? *Intercultural Pragmatics* 1 (2): 153–166.

Goddard, Cliff and Anna Wierzbicka (2018). Minimal English and How It Can Add to Global English. In Cliff Goddard (ed.), *Minimal English for a Global World Improved Communication Using Fewer Words*, 5–27. Cham: Palgrave MacMillan.

Goddard, Cliff and Anna Wierzbicka (2021). "We": conceptual semantics, linguistic typology and social cognition. *Language Sciences* 83: 101327.

Goffman, Erving (1978). *The presentation of self in everyday life*. London: Harmondsworth.

Hymes, Dell (1987). Communicative competence. In Ulrich Ammon, Norbert Dittmar and Klaus J. Mattheier (eds.), *Sociolinguistics: An international handbook of the science of language and society*, 219–229. Berlin: Walter de Gruyter.

Joseph, John (2004). *Language and identity: National, ethnic, religious*. Springer.

Kearney, Michael (1984). *World view*. Novato, CA: Chandler & Sharp.

Kropp Dakubu, Mary Esther (1997). *Korle meets the sea. A sociolinguistic history of Accra*. Oxford: Oxford University Press.

Mc Laughlin, Fiona (2017). Sociolinguistics in language documentation. A Plenary Lecture given at the 2017 Summer School on Language Documentation: Theory and Methods, University of Education, Winneba July 2017.

Munro, Pamela and Dieynaba Gaye (1997). *Ay baati wolof: A Wolof dictionary*. Department of Linguistics, University of California, Los Angeles.

Nyaku, Kofi (1980). *Amedzro etɔlia* [The third stranger]. Accra: Bureau of Ghana Languages.

Ofori, Kafui (1988). Some peculiarities of the Pekigbe dialect of Ewe. Diploma in Ghanaian Languages Long Essay, Language Centre, University of Ghana, Legon.

Ofori, Kafui (2002). Nominalisation in Ewe. In Felix K. Ameka and E. Kweku Osam (eds.), *New directions in Ghanaian linguistics*, 173–200. Accra: Black Mask.

Ring, Andrew J. (1981). *Ewe as a Second Language: A Sociolinguistic Survey of Ghana's Central Volta Region*. Legon: Institute of African Studies.

Rongier, Jacques (2015). *Dictionaire ewe-français*. Paris: L'Harmattan.

Saville-Troike, Muriel (2003). *The ethnography of communication: An introduction*. 3rd edition. Malden: Blackwell.

Sarukkai, Sundar (1997). The 'Other' in Anthropology and Philosophy. *Economic and Political Weekly* 32 (24): 1406–1409. www.jstor.org/stable/4405512 (accessed 22 May 2021).

Thomas, Jenny (1983). Cross-cultural pragmatic failure. *Applied linguistics* 4 (2): 91–112.

Triandis, Harry C. (1989). The self and social behavior in differing cultural contexts. *Psychological Review* 96 (3): 506–520.

Westermann, Dietrich (1928). *Ewefiala or Ewe-English Dictionary*. Berlin: Dietrich Riemer [Nendeln: Kraus reprint 1973].

Zimmermann, Johann (1858). *A grammatical sketch of the Akra-or Ga-language*. Vol. 2. Basel Missionary Society, shared by West African communities.

CHAPTER 9

On Politeness and the Expression of Socially Valued Behaviour in Tarma Quechua Verbs

Willem F.H. Adelaar

1 Introduction

Politeness and hierarchical differences in society are seldom reflected in the lexicon or in the morpho-syntactic structure of Quechuan languages.[1] As a consequence, Quechua discourse may be perceived as straightforward and unvarnished. Quechua speakers appear to be aware of this as they often mention the absence of euphemisms and stylistic embellishment as distinctive traits of their culture. This does not mean, however, that Quechua speakers are insensitive to issues of politeness and socially valued behaviour in language use. As observed by Aikhenvald (2010: 105, 158–159; 2012: 190), some South American languages use delayed imperatives as a means to express politeness. Such usage is also found in Quechuan languages, in which future tense forms may be interpreted as delayed imperatives suggesting a reduced urgency and thereby an overtone of politeness. In addition, Weber (1989: 132) points out, in connection with Huallaga Quechua, that the verbal derivational affix *-yku-* (historically a directional marker denoting inward motion) can be used as an indication of politeness in imperative constructions. Nevertheless, most Quechuan languages do not have dedicated verbal affixes that unambiguously refer to a notion of politeness. The observed politeness effect is often indirect and bound to imperative contexts. In many cases the utterances at issue are open to other interpretations as well.

As members of strictly organized rural communities, Quechua speakers occasionally do feel the need to emphasize that their actions are in accordance with the rules and expectations that hold these communities together. For instance, conversations must not be interrupted or terminated without

1 Quechuan languages are spoken today by more than 7,000,000 inhabitants of the South American countries Argentina, Bolivia, Brazil, Chile, Colombia, Ecuador, and Peru. The data discussed in this chapter are all from Peru, which has the largest Quechua-speaking population (ca. 4,000,000). They were mostly collected in 1971 and 1974.

© WILLEM F.H. ADELAAR, 2022 | DOI:10.1163/9789004510395_010

the explicit consent of a speech partner. In Andean Spanish such consent is obtained through phrases such as *con (su) permiso* 'with (your) permission', to which the addressed person may respond with *siga no más* 'just go ahead!' With their high dependence on morphology, Quechuan languages use morphological rather than lexical resources for the purpose of obtaining social consent. Morphological markers, however, are rarely used to this end alone. They normally have well-defined semantic or syntactic functions which can be extended to the societal applications in question.

The following pages deal with the occurrence of the directional affixes *-rgu-* (< **-rku-*) 'upward motion' and *-y(g)u-* (< **-yku-*) 'inward motion', focussing on their derived use as markers of socially valued behaviour and politeness in Tarma Quechua. Tarma Quechua belongs to the Quechua I subdivision of the Quechuan language family, also known as Central Peruvian Quechua.[2] Tarma Quechua is spoken by a declining number of speakers in villages situated in the western and southern surroundings of the provincial capital of Tarma in the Peruvian department of Junín.[3] It is part of a dialect complex known as North Junín Quechua or Yaru (Chirinos 2001).

2 Historical Background and Context

As established and reconstructed by Parker (1973: 22–23), the Quechuan language family, at an earlier stage of its development, featured a set of four verbal derivational affixes referring to direction: **-rku-* UP, **-rpu-* DOWN, **-rqu-* OUT, and **-yku-* IN.[4] These four reconstructed directional affixes can still be found throughout Quechua I in sets of verb roots consisting of lexicalized combinations of a non-productive root element with a directional affix, notably in

2 The division into two main branches of the Quechuan family was established by Parker (1963) and Torero (1964); cf. Adelaar (2013) for an assessment of its continued validity. The denominations Quechua I and II were introduced by Torero.

3 A salient phonological characteristic of Tarma Quechua is that velar and labial stops in word-internal position, unless preceded by a nasal consonant, have become voiced before a vowel. A notable exception (among several others) is that the consonant in the element *-ku-*, denoting 'reflexive' and related meanings has remained unvoiced. This exception holds both for *-ku-* itself and for its derivatives *-baku-, -ba:ku-, -naku-, -ra:ku-*, etc.

4 In Quechua I and in southern Peruvian Quechua II all word-internal verbal affixes with a canonical form ending in *-u-* have allomorphs ending in *-a-* (for instance, *-yka-* instead of *-yku-*). These allomorphs occur before a specific set of other verb-internal affixes, such as *-či-* 'causative', *-mu-* 'cislocative', and *-pu-* 'beneficiary'. In Quechua I this rule of vowel lowering also extends to non-adjacent affixes when an intervening affix is affected.

ya.rku- 'go up', *ya.rpu-* 'go down', *ya.rqu-* 'go out', and *ya.y(k)u-* 'go in'. There are also a few isolated cases of defective roots combining with only one or two of the directional affixes, for instance, *ša.rku-* 'rise', 'stand up' and *ša.y(k)u-* 'halt', 'stand still' (but cf. *šaya-*, *-ša:ku-* 'stand').

In all the Quechuan daughter languages, directional affixes have undergone radical semantic changes due to their tendency to develop into grammatical markers denoting aspect, tense, or modality. As a result, the original directional affixes for IN and OUT are still productive from a formal point of view but have obtained new, non-directional meanings throughout the Quechuan family. By contrast, the 'vertical' directional affixes for UP and DOWN (Hintz 2011: 188) have been preserved with their original directional meanings in Quechua I, but are no longer in use as productive affixes in Quechua II.[5]

It should be noted that the two directional affixes for UP and DOWN are not exclusively found with motion verbs. They can also be attached to bases that do not refer to a change of location, as, for instance, in *ana-rbu-* 'look down' and *ana-rgu-* 'look up'. In other cases a previous motion to a lower or higher place may be implied, as in *punu-rbu-* 'sleep in a lower place' from *punu-* 'sleep'.

The non-directional semantics of the original directional affixes for IN, OUT, and UP which have been attested in Quechua I are notoriously elusive, as is clearly visible in the linguistic literature dedicated to the verbal morphology of the different dialectal varieties. Fairly elaborate treatments of the directional affixes and their non-directional derivations can be found in Cerrón-Palomino (1976) for Huanca Quechua; Hintz (2011) for South Conchucos Quechua; Parker (1973) for Ancash Quechua; Sayk (1974) for Junín Quechua (closely related to Tarma Quechua); and Weber (1989) for Huallaga Quechua.

3 Aspectual Interpretation of the Non-directional Use of Directional Markers

In the Northern Junín varieties of Quechua I, as well as in the highly conservative Pacaraos variety formerly spoken in the Upper Chancay valley on the Pacific slopes of the Andes, the directional affix **-rqu-* 'outward motion' has developed into a straightforward perfective aspect marker *-r(q)u-* (*-ru-* in Tarma Quechua and most of northern Junín). The semantics of this highly frequent

5 For a more detailed account of historical developments affecting the directional affixes in Quechua I, see Adelaar (2006) and Hintz (2011).

aspect marker are typically those of a perfective aspect category as defined in the literature, including such semantic components as punctual, completive, and resultative (see Comrie 1976). In Tarma /North Junín Quechua this perfective aspect marker has come to function in a system of binary opposition with the equally ubiquitous progressive aspect marker *-yka(:)-* (*-ya(:)-* in Tarma Quechua). The two are mutually exclusive and occupy the same slot in the order of affixes.

One might assume that this state of affairs would leave little room for two more ex-directional affixes to occupy part of such a closely knit aspectual system, but this is not necessarily the case. In his study of aspectual frontiers in South Conchucos Quechua, Hintz (2011: 27–32) provides an insightful overview of the aspectual features, most of them related to perfective or completive meaning, which appear to unite all the ex-directional affixes in transformation (even including the semantically conservative 'downward motion' affix *-rpu-*). In the following paragraph we will explore how different meaning components interact in the case of the 'upward motion' affix *-rgu-* and its non-directional derivatives in Tarma Quechua.

4 Non-directional Derivatives of the 'Upward Motion' Affix *-rgu-* in Tarma Quechua: Consecutiveness and Social Act

In addition to the inherited 'upward motion' interpretation, two more semantically distinct applications of the affix *-rgu-* (< **-rku-*) can be found in Tarma Quechua. One of them, a wide-spread formation throughout Quechua I, is limited to subordinate verbs in hierarchically complex sentences. It consists of a subordinate verb containing the affix *-rgu-* in what is normally the so-called 'same subjects' (SS) form used in a switch-reference relationship with a superordinate verb. Occasionally, examples of the 'different subjects' (DS) form have also been attested in similar constructions in Quechua I varieties (Weber 1989: 127). In the SS form, the highly frequent ending *-rgu-r* (*-rku-r* in most of Quechua I, *-lku-l* in the Huanca varieties of southern Junín) is formally composed of the upward motion marker *-rgu-* and the Quechua I 'same subjects' subordinate (adverbial) marker *-r*.[6] Semantically, this combination indicates that an action expressed by the subordinate verb immediately precedes the event expressed by the main verb in time. It can be translated into English approximately as 'immediately after doing so', 'having done so', etc.

6 Note that the suffix sequence in question can be interrupted by other affixes, because the

The function of this 'sequential' application of *-rgu-* is clearly aspectual. It occupies the same affix order slot as the perfective aspect marker *-ru-* and cannot be combined with it. The semantic difference between the two options resides in the fact that the interpretation of sequential *-rgu-* is more explicitly temporal than that of *-ru-*. There can be no doubt that the sequential application of *-rgu-* justifies its classification as separate from the directional affix *-rgu-* (cf. Adelaar 1977: 131–132). It can easily be combined with the same marker *-rgu-* in its upward motion function, as in (1):

(1) *kačạ-rgu-**rgu**-r*
let.go-UP-SEQ-SS.SUB
'after letting it [the balloon] go upward'[7]

The second non-directional application of the affix *-rgu-* is a lot more complex and elusive than the preceding one, as can be inferred from the numerous different and often conflicting interpretations that are found in the literature. Among the authors who sought to unify these semantic interpretations under a single heading, Parker (1973: 23–26; 1976: 126) opted for 'action without resistance' in Ancash-Huailas Quechua, whereas Hintz (2011: 30, 132) refers to 'mutual consent' in South Conchucos Quechua. The semantic interpretation that emerges for non-directional, non-sequential *-rgu-* in Tarma Quechua (and in neighbouring San Pedro de Cajas Quechua) is that of a socially motivated activity which seeks to harmonize the interests of an addressee with those of the speaker and the community. This interpretation, to which we have referred as 'social act' (Adelaar 1977: 145), appears to be close to the notion of mutual consent as defined by Hintz. It also comes close to a general notion of politeness as expressed in many of the world's cultures.[8]

---

order of affixes in the Quechua verb has to be respected. Hence sequences such as *-rga-či-r* in *muyu-rga-či-r* 'after having turned into …' or *-rga-mu-r* in *ša-rga-mu-r* 'having come here'.

7 The following glosses and abbreviations are used in this chapter: 1, 2, 3 first, second, third person; A actor; ABL ablative case; ACC accusative case; ASS assertive [evidential]; CISL cislocative ('hither'); CONC concessive; DOWN downward motion; DS different subjects; FUT future [tense]; IMPER imperative [mood]; IN inward motion; INCL inclusive (first + second person); NEG negation; NMLZ nominalizer; OUT outward motion; P patient; PLUR plural, pluractional; POINT direction pointed at; POSS possessor; PRES present [tense]; PROGR progressive [aspect]; REFL reflexive; RESTR restrictive ('just', 'only'); SEQ sequential [aspect]; SOC social act; Sp. Spanish; SPEC special care; SS same subjects; STAT stat(iv)e; SUB subordinator; UP upward motion; VBLZ verbalizer.

8 Weber (1989: 124, 154) mentions two examples in which Huallaga Quechua *-rku-* indicates politeness in imperatives.

All in all, it should be observed that *-rgu-* in its social act interpretation is not frequently found in narrative texts, so a field researcher remains highly dependent on elicitation for the collection of critical examples. Some straightforward examples, for which a directional interpretation is excluded, are presented below.

The first example (2) is a classic invitation to drink according to the customary habits of the community.

(2) *upya-[ku-]**rgu**-šun*
drink-[REFL-]SOC-1A.INCL.IMPER
'Let us have a drink together [if it appeals to you]!'

The following examples (3a–c) are based on the verb *mali-* 'try', 'taste', taking into account that tasting local food is seen as a sign of respect for the community's traditional habits.

(3) a. *mali-ku-**rgu**-y*
try-REFL-SOC-2A.IMPER
'Try a bit of this [we are sure you will like it, and it will please us if you do]'

b. *mali-ku-**rgu**-nki*
try-REFL-SOC-2A.FUT
'You will have to try this [we would not want you to miss it]'

c. *mali-ka-**rga**-:ri-čun* *kay* *miku.y-ta*[9]
try-REFL-SOC-PLUR-3A.IMPER this food-ACC
'Let them taste this food [they really should try it]!'

Example (4) illustrates a combination of *-rgu-* 'upward motion' and *-rgu-* 'social act'. Such combinations of formally identical affixes are considered to be perfectly grammatical, although they do not occur often.

(4) *kaça-rgu-**rgu**-šax*
let.go-UP-SOC-1A.FUT
'I shall release it [the balloon], with your permission.'

9 The plural marker *-:ri-* is one of the affixes that trigger vowel lowering from *-u-* to *-a-* in Tarma and North Junín Quechua (cf. footnote 4).

Example (5) illustrates an action in the interest of one's fellow villagers. Note that the affix *-rgu-* in its 'social act' function is combined with the progressive aspect marker *-ya(:)-*, which excludes the possibility of a perfective aspect interpretation in this case.

(5) *marga-n-pita* *rima-**rgu**-ya-n*
village-3POSS-ABL speak-SOC-PROGR-3A.PRES
'He is speaking about his village [on behalf of his people].'

The following example (6) is from San Pedro de Cajas Quechua. This Quechua dialect differs from Tarma Quechua, *inter alia*, by the absence of voicing, although it has essentially the same morphology.

(6) *ka-**rku**-y*
be-SOC-2A.IMPER
'Please stay [you are welcome with us]!'

5 Non-directional Derivative of the 'Inward Motion' Affix *-y(g)u-* in Tarma Quechua: Special Care

The derivational affix *-y(g)u-* (< **-yku-*), which was reconstructed as a directional affix of inward motion for an earlier stage of the language, is occasionally used in Tarma Quechua in utterances referring to a direction. This direction is usually pointed out by the speaker and has no particular relationship with inward motion. A possible example is (7):

(7) *xita.ra-**yu**-y*[10]
lie.down-POINT-2A.IMPER
'Lie down over there!'

However, the most frequent application associated with *-y(g)u-* in Tarma Quechua is not directional. It refers to activities that can be performed in a short

10 We use the symbol *x* for the velar fricative sound resulting from the merger of glottal/velar *h* and uvular *q* in Tarma Quechua. Most Quechuan varieties in Northern Junín retain this distinction.
The verb base *xita.ra(:)-* is a lexicalized combination of *xita-* 'throw' with the affix *-ra(:)-* denoting state or condition; cf. Andean Spanish *estar echado* 'to lie'.

period of time and without much waste of energy, but with special care and attention.[11] A suitable English translation could be 'for a while', 'for a moment'. It is often used in requests in which the speaker asks an addressee to perform a task that should not take much time, but which is nevertheless important to the speaker. Since such requests are usually made in the speaker's interest, they imply a certain amount of politeness, especially in imperative constructions, as suggested by our use of 'please' in the translation of examples (8), (9), and (10).

(8) *rixi-ya-mu-y*
know-SPEC-CISL-2A.IMPER
'Please go and make his acquaintance!'

(9) *šuya-[ra-]ya-ma-y*
wait-[STAT-]SPEC-1P-2A.IMPER
'Please wait for me for a little while!'

(10) *riya-yu-y*
wake.up-SPEC-2A.IMPER
'Please wake him up for a moment!'

The following examples (11) and (12) illustrate possible uses of *-y(g)u-* in non-imperative contexts.

(11) *mana-m rima-yu-na-ču*
not-ASS speak-SPEC-FUT.NMLZ-NEG
'He is not to be spoken to [be careful not to address him!].'

(12) *rirga-yu-ya-n*
look-SPEC-PROGR-3A.PRES
'He is having a look at what there is [for instance, when inspecting merchandise].'

11 The notion of 'impact' that has been associated with this affix in the literature on other Quechuan varieties (e.g. Weber 1989: 134) does not seem to apply to Tarma Quechua.

6 Verbal Plural Marking as a Criterion for the Distinction between Homophonous Categories

Like most Quechuan languages belonging to the southern part of Quechua I, Tarma Quechua has more than one way to express plural of actor, and occasionally plural of patient, in a verb form. If a verb contains no aspect markers, no affix *-ku-*, nor one of its derivatives ending in *-ku-*, plural can be indicated by means of the affix *-ba:ku-*.[12]

By contrast, the perfective aspect marker *-ru-*, a reflex of the reconstructed directional marker **-rqu-* for outward motion, requires a plural marker *-:ri-*, which also triggers the lowering of a preceding vowel *-u-* to *-a-* within a chain of verbal affixes. Hence, the pluractional equivalent of the perfective aspect marker *-ru-* is *-ra:ri-*. Note that the plural marker *-:ri-* is also the only possible option in combinations with sequential *-rgu-*.

The other directional and ex-directional affixes obligatorily take the plural marker *-:ri-*, under the same conditions, whenever they are preceded by the affix *-ku-* or one of its derivatives ending in *-ku-* (cf. example (3c)). By contrast, when these affixes are not preceded by *-ku-*, both types of plural marking are theoretically possible.

There is, however, a tendency, if not an obligation, for real directionals to take the *-ba:ku-* plural and for ex-directionals with non-directional meanings to take the *-:ri-* plural. This same tendency was registered by Sayk (1974: 50) for the Junín area. These two options are illustrated in (13, 14).

(13) *ana-**rga**-ba:ku-y*
look-UP-PLUR-2A.IMPER
'Look upward [plural]!'

(14) *mali-**rga**-:ri-y* *mamala-guna* *učuk=učuk-la-ta-si*
taste-SOC-PLUR-2A.IMPER lady-PLUR a.little²-RESTR-ACC-CONC
'Please taste it ladies, even just a little bit!'

Example (15) from San Pedro de Cajas is remarkable because it features a combination of both *-rku-* 'social act' and *-yu-* 'special care' with the plural marker *-:ri-*. The affixes are preceded by *-ku-*, which in this case is not the reflexive marker but a verbalizer. This has no consequence for the obligatory selection of *-:ri-* as a plural marker.

12 Obviously, the affix *-ba:ku-* itself contains an element *-ku-*, but this fact is no longer relevant for a synchronic analysis of the language.

(15) *lunči-ka-**rka-ya**-:ri-la-y*
afternoon.tea(Sp.*lonche*)-VBLZ-SOC-SPEC-PLUR-RESTR-2A.IMPER
'Just enjoy your [customary] afternoon tea [for a moment]!'

7 Conclusion

In spite of the absence of verbal affixes denoting politeness in earlier stages of development of the Quechua language group, a modern dialect variety such as Tarma Quechua has proven able to exploit the ongoing transformation of the inherited directional markers in order to create space for a grammatical expression of politeness and socially motivated conduct. Both the original markers denoting upward and inward motion are now used to express a certain amount of politeness. The question of whether or not the suffix *-rgu-* in its social act interpretation should be considered as synchronically separate from its directional ancestor can be answered positively on the basis of their tendency to associate with different plural markers. Although both social act *-rgu-* and special care *-y(g)u-* have acquired features akin to perfective aspect and the ability to replace the perfective aspect marker *-ru-* in specific constructions, they are not part of the aspect system themselves, because they can also occur in environments that are not compatible with perfective aspect.

References

Adelaar, Willem F.H. (1977). *Tarma Quechua. Grammar, Texts, Dictionary.* Lisse: Peter de Ridder Press.

Adelaar, Willem F.H. (2006). The vicissitudes of directional affixes in Tarma (Northern Junín) Quechua. In Grażyna J. Rowicka and Eithne B. Carlin (eds.), *What's in a verb? Studies in the verbal morphology of the languages of the Americas*, 121–141. Occasional Series 5. Utrecht: LOT Netherlands Graduate School of Linguistics.

Adelaar, Willem F.H. (2013). Quechua I y Quechua II: En defensa de una distinción establecida. *Revista Brasileira de Linguística Antropológica* 5 (1): 45–66.

Aikhenvald, Alexandra Y. (2010). *Imperatives and Commands.* Oxford: Oxford University Press.

Aikhenvald, Alexandra Y. (2012). *The Languages of the Amazon.* Oxford & New York: Oxford University Press.

Cerrón-Palomino, Rodolfo Marcial (1976). *Gramática Quechua Junín-Huanca.* Lima: Ministerio de Educación & Instituto de Estudios Peruanos.

Chirinos Rivera, Andrés (2001). *Atlas Lingüístico del Perú.* Cusco-Lima: Ministerio de Educación & Centro Bartolomé de Las Casas.

Comrie, Bernard (1976). *Aspect.* Cambridge, New York & Melbourne: Cambridge University Press.

Hintz, Daniel J. (2011). Crossing Aspectual Frontiers. Emergence, Evolution, and Interwoven Semantic Domains in South Conchucos Quechua Discourse. Linguistics Volume 146. Berkeley, Los Angeles & London: University of California Press.

Parker, Gary John (1963). La clasificación genética de los dialectos quechuas. *Revista del Museo Nacional* 32: 241–252.

Parker, Gary John (1973). *Derivación verbal en el Quechua de Ancash.* Documento de Trabajo No. 25. Lima: Universidad Nacional Mayor de San Marcos, Centro de Investigación de Lingüística Aplicada.

Parker, Gary John (1976). *Gramática Quechua Ancash-Huailas.* Lima: Ministerio de Educación & Instituto de Estudios Peruanos.

Sayk Cruz, Elfriede (1974). *Derivación verbal en el Quechua del norte del departamento de Junín.* Documento de Trabajo No. 28. Lima: Universidad Nacional Mayor de San Marcos, Centro de Investigación de Lingüística Aplicada.

Torero Fernández de Córdova, Alfredo A. (1964). Los dialectos quechuas. *Anales Científicos de la Universidad Agraria* 2 (4): 446–478.

Weber, David John (1989). *A Grammar of Huallaga (Huánuco) Quechua.* Linguistics Volume 112. Berkeley, Los Angeles & London: University of California Press.

PART 2

How to Imbue Words with Power

CHAPTER 10

The Power of Kin Terms in White Hmong: Reinforcing Rights and Duties and Redefining Identity

Nerida Jarkey

1 Introduction

This study discusses kinship terms in White Hmong (Hmong-Mien [Miao-Yao]), a minority language spoken in Southeast Asia in the mountains of northern Vietnam, Laos, Thailand, and Myanmar. The language is also spoken in southern China (the source of Hmong migration to Southeast Asia in the nineteenth century) as well as in widely dispersed diasporic communities around the world. Hmong society is generally considered highly egalitarian, with no formal system of governance beyond the village head. The primary social structures are the patrilineal clan and lineage.

The extent of integration of Hmong communities with the majority society in the countries in which they live, as well as the extent of their involvement in market-based economic activities, varies considerably according to factors such as degree of remoteness from larger centres and national and local policies. Even those still living a fairly traditional lifestyle in Laos and Thailand, who are the focus of this study, generally have increasing connection to and influence from the nation state, particularly through improving access to schooling, transport, and technology. The picture of traditional practices presented in this chapter is by no means intended to suggest that a uniform lifestyle and experience is shared by all White Hmong people in Laos and Thailand, but rather to contextualize the understandings presented here of the kin-term system and of the ways in which this system relates to and reinforces traditional rights, duties, and power relationships in Hmong society.

In the high altitudes in which Hmong people traditionally dwell, numerous factors combine to make life particularly precarious. Access to water is limited, and soils are less fertile than in the valleys, often allowing for little more than subsistence farming, with supplementation through some hunting and gathering. Slash-and-burn agricultural practices result in the frequent need to relocate due to soil exhaustion, meaning that larger village units must be

© NERIDA JARKEY, 2022 | DOI:10.1163/9789004510395_011

broken up. Hmong peoples also have a long history of dislocation and relocation in the context of political pressures and competition for resources from other groups.

In this context, it is not surprising that a clear system of mutual support through the extended family, the lineage, and even through less closely related clan members is often crucial to survival. Furthermore, it is these groups that are responsible for passing on skills and knowledge, both practical and spiritual, to the younger generations. For these reasons, relocation is most often along clan lines, or to join others of the same clan.

In many societies of Southeast Asia, particularly in those associated with the national languages (which tend to be most widely spoken in the fertile lowlands), social power is related to political, religious, and age-based hierarchies. Such systems of power are linguistically recognized, reinforced, and to some extent also constructed by elaborate honorific systems. Another common linguistic feature that relates to hierarchical structures of social power in many Southeast Asian languages is the use of open-class systems for person reference, rather than closed-class pronoun systems. These open-class systems have an especially important role, through both interlocutor reference and vocative address, in showing deference to the addressee. In this function they draw extensively on both the literal and fictive use of kin terms.

Along with some of the other minority languages in Southeast Asia, however, White Hmong has no system of honorifics and has closed-class, grammatical personal pronouns (Müller and Weymuth 2017: 409–410). The White Hmong pronoun system has singular, dual, and plural forms for all persons, with no gender distinctions, nor any alternants to express deference. First and second person pronouns, rather than open-class person-reference terms, are consistently used for interlocutor reference.

When it comes to vocative address, however, as well as to third-person reference, White Hmong draws on an extensive system of kin terms that reflect consanguineal and affinal kin relationships. While respect for elders is a core Hmong value, the kin-term system does not work to show deference to age *per se* but is most elaborate and most sensitive to differences in generation and age in the case of relationships that involve rights and duties within the patrilineal clan. The system also extends to the fictive use of kin terms for vocative address in non-blood/non-marital relationships, e.g. *me tub* 'dear son', *nus* 'brother (of unmarried female)', *txiv ntxawm* 'uncle (younger brother of father)', *niag yawg* 'ol' grandad'. In these contexts, it can serve to express deference (Moua 2003: 4–5), not only asymmetrically, such as when showing respect to an older person, but also symmetrically (Goffman 1956: 478), such as when indicating familiarity and closeness or making a stranger feel welcome.

This chapter focuses on the literal rather than the fictive use of kin terms and demonstrates that, in this use, their function is not *primarily* to express deference, either asymmetrically to acknowledge and construct social hierarchy, nor symmetrically to express appreciation of a social equal. Rather, in their literal use, particularly in their extremely frequent use for vocative address, kin terms function to reinforce understandings of the *type* of relationship between interactants, and consequently of expectations concerning rights and duties within that relationship. As Enfield (2013: 6) explains (making reference to Linton (1936: 113–131)),

> Types of relationship [...] define types of social statuses and identities that will be defining components of higher-level social structures, ultimately definitive of what we might call societies. ... [Relationship types] are "statuses," defined originally by Linton as sets of rights and duties with respect to specific others. A constantly demanding feature of social life is the management of *changes* of status.

White Hmong kinship terms work powerfully for social purposes in two main ways: first to reinforce key social rights and duties within the patrilineal clan and second to reflect changes in the social identity of a woman as she enters her husband's clan through marriage. The most empowering social rights and responsibilities that are reinforced through the kin-term system relate to the male within the patrilineal clan, particularly in relation to the tradition of the levirate. The most disempowering ways in which the kin-term system works relate to the change in a woman's social statuses and identities upon marriage. This disempowerment is represented both in the terms others use for her and in those she uses for others. Not only does she lose her own identity almost entirely when entering her new clan but she also loses distinctions in the kin terms she is expected to use for her natal family members, who now join the class of her affinal kin.

Following this Introduction, the chapter first illustrates the use of kin terms in vocative address (§ 2), claiming that this frequent reminder of the *type* of relationship between interactants works to consistently reinforce the social expectations each holds of the other. The chapter then critically examines the common assumption and ideology of thoroughgoing egalitarianism in Hmong society, noting the areas of society in which this assumption holds true (for males, at least)—spiritual practices and politics—along with those in which it clearly does not—gender relations (§ 3). The analysis of kin terms presented in Section 4 addresses first the terms used by the male ego, unmarried (§ 4.1 and § 4.2) and married (§ 4.3), and then those used by the female ego, unmarried (§ 4.4) and married (§ 4.5). These sections serve to show that *distinctions* between kinship terms relate to *distinctions* in the rights and duties that one has in relation to kin of that type, while the *loss* of such *distinctions* signals significant loss of specific rights and duties between kin. The evidence given for this claim, along with the discussion concerning how the kin-term system works in both empowering and disempowering ways, is summed up in the Conclusion (§ 5).

2 Kin Terms Used for Vocative Address

Speakers of White Hmong draw on the kin term system very frequently for use in vocative address. Between family members, this serves as a clear strategy for mutually reinforcing their relationship and all that it entails. Vang (2016: 125–126) observes:

> Addressing an immediate family member inappropriately, without properly mentioning their cultural and familial status, is considered impolite and insulting.

In examples (1)–(3), we can see how kin terms are used for vocative address, alongside the use of personal pronouns for interlocutor reference. Kin terms are in bold.

(1) *Nyob.zoo os, **Niam.tais.** Kuv nco~nco koj os.*[1]
hello IP maternal.aunt/grandmother 1SG REDUP~miss 2SG IP
'Hello there, **Aunty**! I miss you so much!'

(2) a. *Nom Npis ... thiaj nug Soob Lwj tias koj muaj kev-tu-siab*
N.N. and.then ask S.L. COMP 2SG have sadness
*dab.tsi **Txiv.ntxawm?***
what **younger.paternal.uncle**
'And then No Npi asked Shong Lue, "What's the matter with you, **Uncle?**"'

1 In the orthography used here, consonants at the end of a syllable represent the tone (with one tone represented by the lack of a final consonant).

b. *Soob Lwj tau teb tias* ***Me-tub*** *luag tso kuv los*
S.L. PERV answer COMP little-son others send 1SG come
cev lus thiab cawm nej Hmoob no ...
pass.on word and save 2PL Hmong here
'Shong Lue answered, "**My dear son**, I was sent to come to pass on a message and to save all you Hmong here ..."' (Vang, Yang, and Smalley 1990: 77)

Examples (1–2a) illustrate the use of vocative kin terms for older relatives, while (2b) shows that they are also used for younger relatives. In all of these cases, interlocutor reference is accomplished by personal pronouns, while kin terms are used only for address. These examples also show that vocative kin terms can appear either sentence finally (1–2a) or sentence initially (2b). They can also appear twice, both before and after the sentence, as in (3).

(3) *Nws ... los hais rau leej txiv tias,* ***Txiv****, xib.hwb ua luaj*
3SG come say to CL father COMP Dad teacher do greatly
diam es yuav ciaj los yuav tuag na, ***Txiv****?*
so.much and.so IRREAL live or IRREAL die IP Dad
'He came (and) said to his father, '**Dad**, (my) teacher is (scolding me) too much, so will (I) live or will (I) die, **Dad**?'' (Johnson 1985: 464, paragraph 20).

While all these examples involve bare kin terms, many can also be used with a given name, for example, *Niam hlob Pov* 'Aunty Po' (wife of father's older brother Po). In this case, as a married woman is the addressee, the personal name used is not that of the woman herself but of her husband (§ 3).

Morrow (2012) notes a similar but more limited use of kin terms in Japanese, explaining it as a 'relational strategy' that works as part of a broader strategy to refer to "a shared understanding of social roles ... and the proper behavior associated with that role" (270). By 'role' here, Morrow is talking about a *type* of relationship, and thus 'statuses' in the sense of Linton (1936), that is, "sets of rights and duties with respect to specific others" (Enfield 2013: 6). The extremely high frequency of the use of this relational strategy in White Hmong thus works powerfully to constantly remind interactants of their rights and duties with respect to one another.

3 White Hmong Society: Egalitarian or Hierarchical?

Hmong society has often been characterized as highly egalitarian (Lemoine 2012: 1; Michaud 2012: 1854; Tapp 2010: 64, 84). Tapp (2010: 64) claims:

> The traditional social system has been correctly thought of as egalitarian since there were no hereditary positions [...] Hmong society may be seen as egalitarian also, I would like to say, in spirit. The attitudes of humility and deference, or arrogance and pretension, necessitated in the hierarchically organized status-conscious societies of the Vietnamese, Burmese, Thai, Laotian or even Chinese, have always been disapproved of by Hmong who are brought up not to defer to others unless it is on account of their combination of seniority with some talent or wisdom [...].

As we shall see, this spirit of egalitarianism does not extend to gender relationships in many areas of Hmong society, starting from the level of the family. However, along with many scholarly accounts, Hmong ideology pays little attention to hierarchical structures within the family, nor to the issue of gender at all, and focuses on the portrayal of equality in both spiritual and political life.

Traditional Hmong spiritual beliefs and practices involve animism, shamanism, veneration of ancestral spirits within the lineage, and geomancy. Within a local clan group, a shaman (usually male but sometimes female) is responsible for communication with tutelary (guardian) spirits (*neeb*), for purposes such as calling the soul to return to the body in cases of serious illness. The shaman is respected for his or her skills and more generally for wise counsel and advice in times of trouble, but holds little actual authority. Ritual leadership tends to be distributed among males in a local clan group according to knowledge and ability: one might be more capable when it comes to knowing the appropriate ritual for a particular situation, while another might have expertise in performing the ritual itself (Gary Lee, personal communication). When it comes to the perpetuation of the lineage, women are central, not only through bearing its future members but also by bringing into the world the bodies through which the souls (*plig*) of the ancestors can be reincarnated (Lemoine 1972: 169; Symonds 2004: 163–164).[2] Within each household, however, the male head is

2 Hmong believe that each person has multiple souls—at least three main souls (or parts of souls) and possibly many more (see Lee and Tapp 2010: 36). Beliefs amongst at least some Hmong in Laos and Thailand have been influenced by Buddhism, so not all have a clear belief

responsible for attending to the needs of household spirits and venerating the ancestors (*dab*). These rituals, so crucial in the ongoing prosperity of the lineage, are the exclusive domain of men (Lee 1994–1995).

In the political sphere, as Tapp (2010: 64) notes, Hmong have no custom of hereditary leadership, nor any formal system of governance beyond the village head. This is an appointed or elected position, often though not always assumed by a lineage or ritual leader (Lee and Tapp 2010: 199). A village head does not make decisions independently, but on the basis of consultation, primarily with male elders. Furthermore, the role is not a particularly stable one, with villages often breaking up and reforming when the number of families grows beyond a sustainable number or when swiddens become depleted of nutrients. The instability in the role of village head is reflected in the Hmong proverb:

(4) *Hla dej yuav hle khau. Tsiv teb tsaws chaw*
cross water IRREAL remove shoe(s) move field set.aside place
yuav hle hau.
IRREAL remove leader
'(When you) cross a river (you) take off (your) shoes. (When you) move to a new place (you) change (your) leader.'

The primary social structures in Hmong society are, first, the patrilineal (and generally patrilocal) clan (*xeem*) and, within that, the sub-clan (*ib tug dab qhuas* 'one ceremonial household') and the lineage (*ib cuab kwv tij* 'a family of brothers'). The sub-clan are those clan members who share key spiritual and ritual practices, while the lineage consists of males who share a known ancestor (along with their wives and unmarried daughters) who may share further spiritual practices, rituals, and taboos beyond those common to the sub-clan (Lee 1994–1995; Lee and Tapp 2010: 194–195).[3] No clan is considered superior or inferior to any other and bonds between clans are reinforced through marriage ties involving a strict rule of clan exogamy. In this way, although temporary alliances or enmities between certain clans may occur, on a larger scale, a sense of equality between all clans is a core value of Hmong society.[4]

that rebirth is in the form of a Hmong person within the same clan, nor even necessarily as a human being (Gary Lee, personal communication).

3 Adopted children are also included amongst clan members (Lee 2015: 38).

4 Symonds (2004: xxiii–iv, 21) explains a belief held among the Hmong she worked with in northern Thailand: when a female ancestor's soul is reborn, it is ideally in the body of a male

While the Hmong egalitarian ideology relates, to at least some extent, to the lived experience of many men, it has little relevance to that of women in most aspects of their lives. The female child, as only a temporary member of her natal clan, will leave the clan upon marriage. For this reason, consanguineal female kin are referred to as *ntxhais qhua* 'guest daughters/daughters of another clan' (Vang 2016: 118), well translated by Lee (1994–1995) as 'other people's women'. The term for consanguineal males on the other hand, is *tub cag* 'root sons', as they are the foundational and life-long members of the clan.

Although only temporary clan members, daughters are very much valued. The bride-price they will bring at the time of their marriage will help the family to pay the bride-price needed for sons to marry and thus to produce future members of the lineage (Symonds 2004: 107); furthermore, daughters will themselves become the key points of contact with other clans. Ongoing connections, particularly through New Year visits between brothers and sisters (Symonds 2004: 33), will be maintained when possible and may eventually result in the ideal (though by no means required) marriage of the siblings' own offspring: cross-cousin marriage. The only essential duty to her natal clan that a sister must perform is to be present (or to be represented) at the funeral of a brother that predeceases her, to ensure his safe passage to the land of darkness. A living brother will perform a similar role at her own funeral (Symonds 2004: 32). It is this role that siblings of different genders have at the end of life that is crucial, rather than any mutual support they may exchange during their lifetimes.

In traditional communities, a Hmong girl is usually married in her mid-teens (Symonds 2004: 95), maximizing her chance of producing as many children as possible. Except in some cases of remarriage through the levirate (see § 4.3), she is nearly always younger than her husband. Just as the soul of a child is called into the body on the third day after birth, so the soul of a new wife/daughter-in-law (*nyab*) is summoned into her new household three days after her arrival, with a *hu plig* 'soul-calling ceremony'. She is thus symbolically 'reborn' into her new lineage (Yang 1999: 286), completely relinquishing her connection to her natal household spirits and taking on those of her husband's family. This con-

child of the same clan, and so as one who will be a stable clan member throughout life. A male ancestor's soul, on the other hand, is ideally reborn in the body of a female child. Thus, due to the practice of exogamy and through the process of reincarnation in the body of a child of the opposite gender to that of one's previous life, one's soul can move between different clans; one's natal clan in one life is not necessarily the same as the clan in which one will die in the next life. For those Hmong who share this belief, it clearly reinforces the notion of equality between all clans.

nection to the household spirits of her husband's family will continue even if he dies or the couple divorce (unless she remarries outside his clan), and will include the rituals performed at the time of the woman's own death (Lee 1986). It is at this time, when a married woman dies, that she becomes one with her husband as a clan ancestor and thus, at last, a full clan member.

It will be a life-long process for her to gain that status. As a newly-wed she retains her own clan name. However, as Lemoine (2012: 6–7) explains,

> [...] she will not use her [personal] name and former clan identity in her [new] parents' house—except with her husband. Other people will only address her as "wife of so and so": that is, her husband's personal name. All these changes show eminently that she has lost her past identity to be reborn in another family and hereafter belongs to a different lineage in a different clan.

The newly married couple will nearly always live patrilocally, most often in the husband's parents' house, perhaps until two or three children are born or the house becomes overcrowded as other brothers marry (Lee and Tapp 2010: 192–193). The daughter-in-law encounters a number of prohibitions within her new household, symbolizing her low status and the fact that, although she 'belongs' to her new clan, she is still very much in a liminal state. Customs may differ between clans, sub-clans, and lineages. For example, in some cases she is not permitted to go up to the food-storage platform (*nthab*), due to its proximity to the central house post, a site of particular importance in relation to household spirits. Particular taboos also apply to a daughter-in-law's interactions with her husband's father. In many clans she may not enter her father-in-law's sleeping area, nor may he enter hers (Lee and Tapp 2010: 133, 206), and in the Vaj clan they may not eat at the same table (Symonds 2004: 33). As the newest member of the household and the one with the lowest status, she must learn the ways of the family and prove her worth to her mother-in-law (Symonds 2004: 72–73). She is expected to rise first, before dawn, to build the fire, feed the animals, and begin the cooking and cleaning, before going out with the other able-bodied family members to work in the fields all day.

A woman's status begins to improve with the birth of her first child, and subsequently with each child she brings into the lineage. In this way she proves not only her productive but more importantly her reproductive worth to the clan. For a month after the birth of each child the couple's roles are temporarily reversed, with the husband caring for his wife, especially by providing and preparing the highly valued food of chicken for her to eat (Symonds 2004: 81–83, 167–168).

At the arrival of the first child, the increased standing of both the woman and her husband as parents is acknowledged through the practice of teknonymy; they can now be addressed as 'so-and-so's mother/father' that is, using the first child's personal name (whether male or female). Vang (2016: 122) reports that this is a particularly common form of address between married women, though it seems not to be much used between married men. A married man will later receive an additional personal name of his own, usually after the birth of several children (Symonds 2004: 39–40). It is bestowed by his in-laws in a ceremony called *tis npe laus* 'giving a name of maturity', acknowledging his stature as both a father and a household head.

A woman's loss of personal identity upon marriage is reflected not only in the terms others use for her but also in the change in terms she is now expected to use for most of her natal family members. Now that she belongs to a different clan, she speaks from the perspective of her husband and children, rather than from her own perspective. This is because her duties are now towards her husband's family, lineage, and clan.

These changes in the kin terms a woman uses for her natal family will be thoroughly explored in Sections 4.4 and 4.5. First, in Sections 4.1–4.3, we will turn our attention to the kin terms used by the male ego, terms that remain stable across his life.

4 Empowerment and Disempowerment through White Hmong Kinship Terms

Age differences between kin of the same generation, as well as across generations, are highly salient in some cases in Hmong society; in these cases, information about age in relation to ego (older or younger; same generation or different) is incorporated within the kin terms used. However, these differences are by no means a part of the meaning of all kin terms. As the analysis below will reveal, kin terms that do incorporate information about age and generational differences tend to be those that are used for kin who have the most significant rights and responsibilities in relation to the male ego, the stable members of the lineage in general, and brothers and uncles in particular. Affinal kin, on the other hand, or females within the lineage who will become affinal kin as they marry into another clan, bear far fewer significant rights and duties in relation to the male ego. This is reflected in the kin terms used for them, which not only tend to lack age distinctions between kin of the same generation, but which even fail to distinguish between kin of different generations in some cases. The system is one, therefore, that reinforces the power of the lineage, especially that

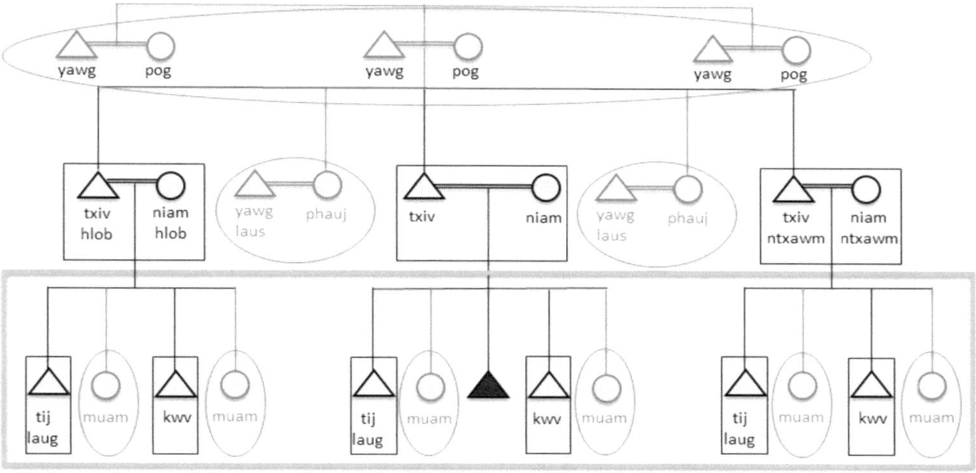

FIGURE 10.1 Unmarried male ego—his own and ascending generations

of the males within it. However, it disempowers women, both within their natal clan, which they are bound to leave upon marriage, and within their husband's clan, in which they lose much of their personal identity as they take on the roles of wife and mother.

4.1 *The Unmarried Male—His Own and Ascending Generations*

We will begin by looking at kin terms in the unmarried male ego's own generation, his fathers' generation, and his grandfather's generation, which are shown in Figure 10.1. In all figures, dark rectangles highlight kin terms that are distinguished according to age within a generation; light ovals represent those that are not. Older full siblings appear to the left of ego, and younger to the right.[5] In Figure 10.1, all (classificatory) siblings in ego's generation are referred to by the collective term *nus muag* 'siblings' (lit. brothers (of unmarried female) [and] sisters (of male)) (enclosed in the large grey rectangle).[6]

As Figure 10.1 shows, terms for those in the male ego's grandfather's generation are differentiated only by gender. The same term, *yawg*, is used for grandfather, grandfather's older brother, and grandfather's younger brother.

5 This right-to-left ordering only applies to children of the same parents. Paternal parallel cousins (Figure 10.1) and paternal half-brothers (Figure 10.2) do not necessarily appear in order of age in relation to ego.

6 See Figure 10.3 regarding the term *nus* meaning '(classificatory) brother of unmarried female ego'.

Likewise, the same term, *pog*, is used consistently for the wife of *yawg*: for grandmother and for the wives of all grandfather's brothers.

The lack of terminological distinction according to birth order between members of this generation does not mean that they bear no responsibilities towards ego, nor that they have no rights in relation to him. In fact, obligations between these kin are extremely important. For example, *pog* '(classificatory) grandmother' is likely to have significant caring responsibilities for ego while he is too young to contribute to work in the fields, and both she and *yawg* '(classificatory) grandfather' have the right to expect ego to perform the ceremonies necessary to ensure their well-being in the afterlife (§3). What this lack of distinction in kin terms does mean is that these rights and responsibilities do not vary in any way depending on the age of kin in this generation relative to one another, nor depending on whether their relationship to ego is lineal (in the strict sense of involving direct descent) or collateral.

In ego's own generation and in his father's, some kin terms are distinguished according to age while others are not. Amongst consanguineal kin, while all (classificatory) brothers (including male paternal parallel cousins) are differentiated according to their age in relation to ego, and all paternal uncles are differentiated according to their age in relation to ego's father, this does not apply to (classificatory) sisters (which include female paternal parallel cousins) nor to paternal aunts. These female kin—*muam* 'sister of male ego (older or younger)' and *phauj* 'paternal aunt (older or younger than father)'—have no specific rights or responsibilities that vary according to their age in relation to ego. In fact, women born into a clan (unlike those who marry into it) are considered only temporary clan members (§3). After their marriage, the most important duties remaining for sisters and brothers to perform for each other occur not during their lifetime but at the time of their death (see §3).

It is important to notice that age differentiation is, in some kin terms but not others, indeed, a factor of ongoing clan membership, and not strictly of gender. This is evident from the terms used for women who marry into the lineage, and thus become ongoing clan members. The kin terms that ego uses for these women reflect not their own age difference in relation to ego's father but that of their husbands: *niam hlob* 'wife of father's older brother' versus *niam ntxawm* 'wife of father's younger brother' (Figure 10.1). This differentiation, however, does not apply to the husbands of *ntxhais qhua* 'guest daughters / daughters of another clan'. As shown in Figure 10.1, the husband of *phauj* 'paternal aunt' is *yawg laus*, regardless of his wife's age in relation to ego's father. The future husband of *muam* '(classificatory) sister of male ego' will be *yawm yij* (not shown), again with no distinction according to the age of *muam* in relation to ego.[7] As members of another clan, just like their wives, these male kin have no specific rights or responsibilities at all in relation to ego during his lifetime.

It is certainly possible to indicate age difference, if needed to disambiguate between any kin identified by the same term as one another. For example, when making third-person reference, the terms *muam hlob* 'older sister', *muam nrab* 'middle sister', and *muam yau* 'younger sister' can be used, along with the pet name (*muam*) *ntxawm* (Heimbach 1979: 210), often used by brothers for their youngest sister. However, these are noun phrases, composed of a noun followed by an adjective, and should not be confused with kin terms. The use of a personal name appended to the kin term is also a common way to distinguish between kin identified by the same term, either in reference or in address (§ 2).

4.2 *The Unmarried Male—His Own and Ascending Generations ~ Stable Clan and the* kwv tij

As noted (§ 4.1), (classificatory) siblings in ego's generation are referred to by the term *nus muag* 'siblings' (enclosed in the large grey rectangle in Figure 10.1). When it comes to specific rights and responsibilities within Hmong society, however, the concept of the *kwv tij* 'brothers' is far more significant than that of *nus muag* 'siblings'. This term is a combination of *kwv* 'younger brother' and *tij*, the first component of *tij laug* 'older brother'. Figure 10.2 shows the *kwv tij* of an unmarried male ego within the large black rectangle.[8]

As paternal parallel cousins are classified as siblings, all male cousins of this type belong to ego's *kwv tij*, along with his brothers. All sons of the same father are also members of one *kwv tij*, even if they have different mothers (as in Figure 10.2, in which ego's father has three wives). The *kwv tij* is the base from which the ongoing lineage is formed.

4.3 *The Married Male Ego—His Own, Ascending, and Descending Generations ~ Age-Related Rights and Responsibilities*

The kin terms that are clearly and consistently differentiated by age according to birth order within a generation are those that refer to members of a male ego's own *kwv tij* and of his father's *kwv tij*, along with their wives. Figure 10.3

7 See Ratliff (1992: 136–163) on the morphotonemic variation that sometimes occurs between kin terms depending on whether the connection is via a male ('g' tone) or a female relative ('m' tone), as in *yawg laus* 'paternal aunt's husband' and *yawm yij* 'sister's husband'.

8 The term *kwv tij* is also used in a more general sense to refer to males within a sub-clan or lineage.

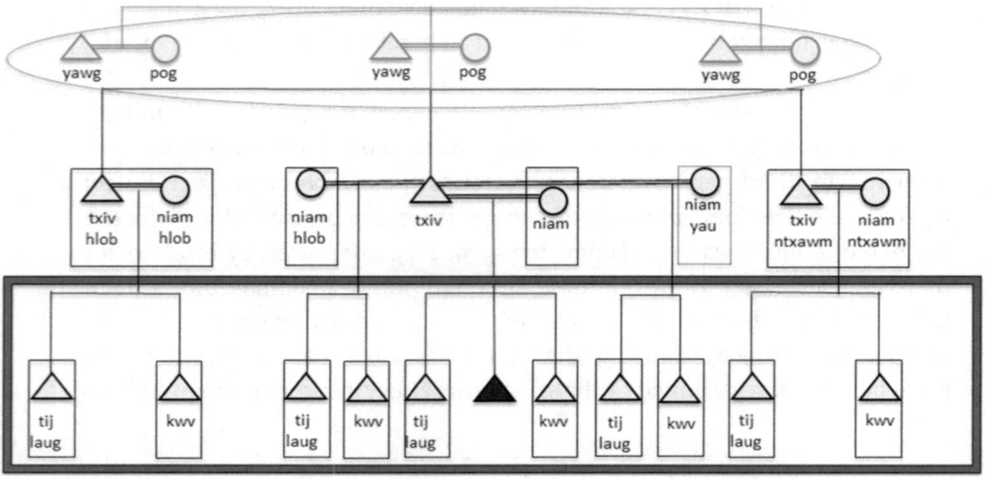

FIGURE 10.2 Unmarried male ego—his own and ascending generations ~ Stable clan and the *kwv tij*

shows that these age distinctions are confined to the kin terms used within these two generations; they occur neither in the generation above, nor in those below.

The kin in his own and his father's *kwv tij* are precisely the ones with whom the male ego has the highest level of mutual rights and responsibilities. The reasons for age differentiation between these kin terms are clear: some of ego's rights and responsibilities in relation to these kin vary according to their age in relation either to him or to his father.

The most significant of these age-related rights and responsibilities concerns the tradition of the levirate. If a man dies while his children are still minors, the care of his children, and preferably of his widow as well, should be assumed by his extended family. Even if the widow wishes to go elsewhere, for example to remarry someone from another clan, she would be expected to leave her children (at least her sons) behind in the care of her husband's family. The ideal situation is if one of the *kwv* '(classificatory) younger brothers' within the *kwv tij* marries the widow of the '(classificatory) older brother' who has passed away. This practice would ensure that her labour, her ability to care for her children, and her future reproductive capacity stays within the clan. Lee (1986) points out that this role is strictly reserved for a 'younger brother'; no other male related to the deceased man can marry the widow.

The practice of the levirate clearly has potential consequences for ego if a death occurs within his father's *kwv tij* or within his own. If ego's own father were to die, then a *txiv ntxawm* 'junior father (classificatory paternal uncle, younger than father)' would be most likely to take the responsibility of marry-

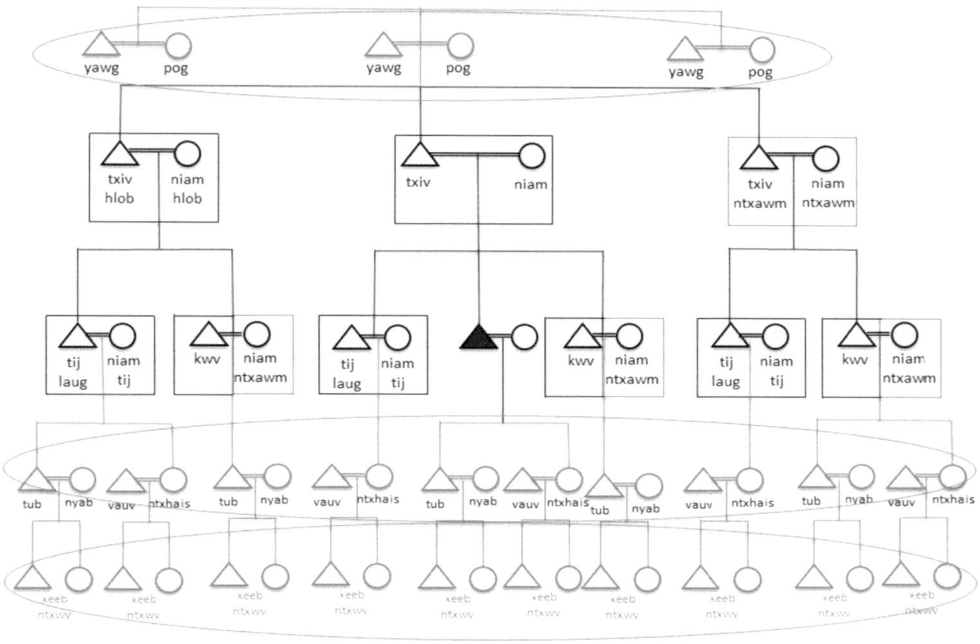

FIGURE 10.3 Married male ego—his own, ascending, and descending generations

ing ego's mother.[9] In the event of the death of ego's *txiv hlob* 'older father (classificatory paternal uncle, older than father)', his wife, *niam hlob* 'older mother (aunt)', may become an additional wife to ego's father.

When it comes to the male ego's own generation, Figure 10.3 shows that he also has distinct kin terms for the wives of his older and younger (classificatory) brothers. The wife of ego's older brother (*tij laug*) is *niam tij* (a potential wife through the levirate, if his older brother dies), and that of ego's younger brother (*kws*) is *niam ntxawm* 'junior mother/woman' (a potential mother to his own children if he himself dies and his younger brother marries his wife).[10]

9 It may be for this reason that the term *txiv* 'father' (used in some communities as a general fictive kin term for men of roughly one's father's generation) is used very commonly to show affection to 'junior father' (uncle who is, indeed, a potential father). This term does not seem to be used for *txiv hlob* 'older father' (uncle who is not a potential father); in this case the abbreviated term of address is *hlob* 'older (one)' (Lee 1986), which shows appropriate respect to his status as older than ego's father.

10 The term *niam ntxawm* 'lit: junior mother/woman' is used for both wife of younger (classificatory) brother and wife of father's younger (classificatory) brother (Figure 10.3). This

The tradition of the levirate may also have some relevance to the terminology within ego's own *nus muag* 'siblings', whereby paternal parallel cousins are all referred to as 'brothers' and 'sisters'. In addition to the sense of close connection felt between these same-generation kin, any of these cousins may well come to share a father (formerly *txiv ntxawm*) or a mother (formerly *niam hlob*) with ego.

As discussed above in relation to Figure 10.1 (also shown in Figure 10.3), the terms for ego's paternal grandparent's generation—*yawg* 'paternal grandfather' and *pog* 'paternal grandmother'—apply to all members of grandfather's *kwv tij* and their wives, regardless of age in relation to grandfather. Likewise, as shown in Figure 10.3, neither the kin terms for ego's children and their spouses, nor for ego's grandchildren, are distinguished according to birth order. While ego does have certain important rights and responsibilities in relation to members of each of these generations, these do not differ according to their age in relation to others in their generation.

4.4 *The Unmarried Female Ego—Her Own and Ascending Generations*

An unmarried female ego, shown in Figure 10.4, uses the same terms as her brothers (§ 4.1) for relatives in her grandfather's generation, with no distinction according to age. Likewise, she uses the same terms as do her brothers for her father's generation: terms that distinguish between father's older and younger brothers (and their wives), but not between father's older and younger sisters (and their husbands). For the unmarried female ego, just as for her brothers, the custom of the levirate means that these age distinctions between kin terms in her father's generation are highly salient.

When it comes to kin terms within her own generation, however, the terms used by an unmarried female ego differ significantly from those used by an unmarried male. While a male ego distinguishes his older and younger brothers by completely different terms (*tij laug* and *kwv* respectively), an unmarried female ego refers to all her brothers as *nus*. She can, of course, add optional adjectives to distinguish older—*nus hlob* 'older brother'—from younger—*nus yau* 'younger brother'—but these are used only to disambiguate; they are not part of the kin term. Her brothers will have no specific responsibilities towards her that vary according to their age in relation to her. As she will leave her natal clan upon marriage, neither do these brothers have any specific rights or responsibilities in relation to her future family.

---

reflects the role of both these kin as potential second mothers: for oneself in the case of wife of *txiv ntxawm* 'father's younger brother' and for one's children in the case of wife of *kwv* 'younger brother'.

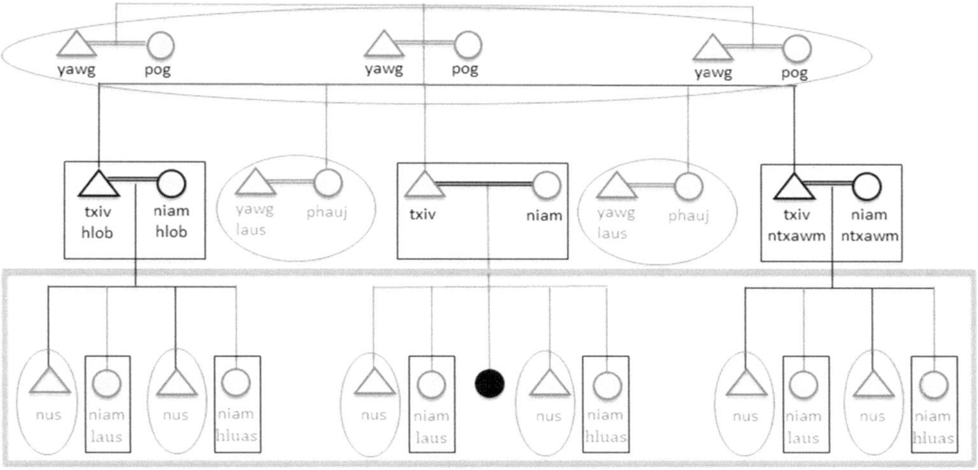

FIGURE 10.4 The unmarried female ego—her own and ascending generations

For her sisters, on the other hand, the age distinction is a part of the kin term that an unmarried female ego uses: *niam laus* 'senior (classificatory) sister' and *niam hluas* 'younger (classificatory) sister'. The reason here seems to relate to the important role older sisters play, along with mothers and grandmothers, in socializing younger sisters to grow up to be good Hmong women (Symonds 2004: 45). From a very young age, any girl with younger siblings is not only charged with considerable responsibility for their care, but is also expected to help to train her younger sisters in good manners and appropriate demeanour, as well as in practical skills like housework, cooking, and embroidery.

4.5 *The Married Female Ego—Affinal Kin*

When a woman marries and joins her husband's clan (in all but clan name), the terms she uses for her natal family members change completely. In virtually all contexts she now refers to and addresses her natal family members from the perspective of her husband and/or her children. Three kinds of distinction are now lost: first, between the women's natal kin and affinal kin (her natal clan members now merging into the class of her affinal kin); second, between her natal kin of different ages within the same generation; and third, between her natal kin of different generations. In Figure 10.5, where alternative terms exist, terms used from the perspective of one's children are given in shaded ovals.

The change from natal to affinal kin terms results in new kin terms even for the married female ego's own parents. Although she may still call her mother and father *niam* 'mother' and *txiv* 'father' if she ever visits them alone, it is now her husband's parents whom she most consistently calls *niam* 'mother' and

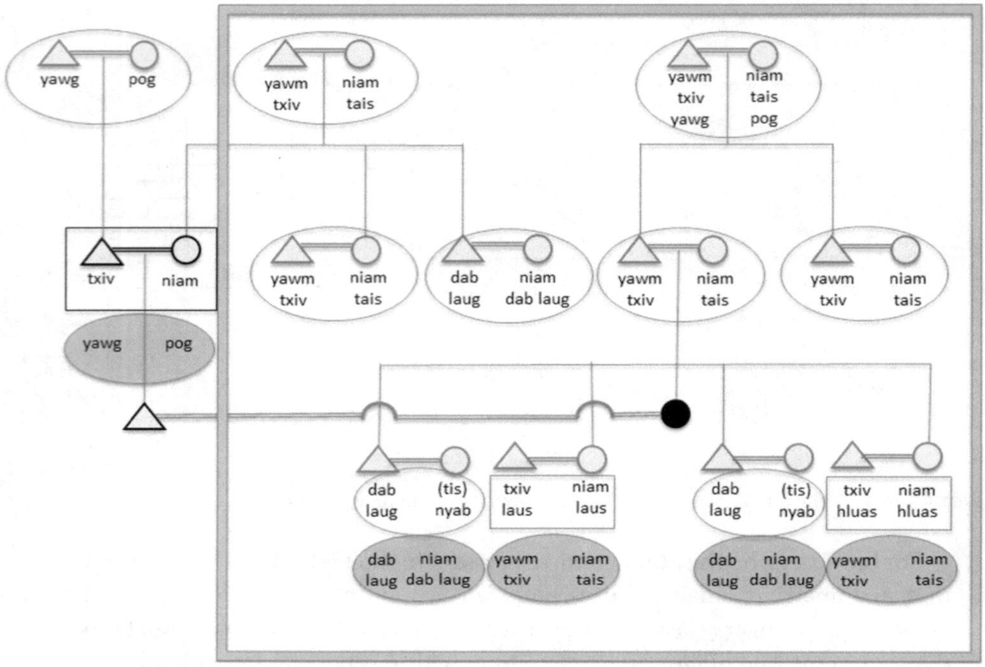

FIGURE 10.5 Married female ego—affinal kin

txiv 'father' (or *pog* 'paternal grandmother' and *yawg* 'paternal grandfather' in the presence of her children). In nearly all contexts the terms she uses for her own parents are those that her husband and her children use for them: *niam tais* '(affinal) woman (mother-in-law / maternal grandmother / maternal aunt)' and *yawm txiv* '(affinal) man (father-in-law / maternal grandfather / maternal uncle)'. These are, of course, identical to the terms that her husband (and now she too) uses for her husband's maternal grandmother and grandfather (as well as for his maternal aunts and their husbands). The kin terms for the married woman's natal family thus merge with those of her husband's mother's natal family to become part of her husband's, and thus her own, *neej tsa* 'affinal kin' (shown in the large grey rectangle in Figure 10.5).

The age distinction that the female ego made before her marriage between her father's brothers, along with their wives—*txiv hlob* 'older paternal uncle' and *niam hlob* 'older paternal uncle's wife' on the one hand, versus *txiv ntxawm* 'younger paternal uncle' and *niam ntxawm* 'younger paternal uncle's wife' on the other (see Figure 10.4)—is now lost. Her paternal uncles and their wives are all called by the same kin terms as her own father and mother—*niam tais* and *yawm txiv*—regardless of their age in relation to her father. The age distinction between her natal kin of this generation is no longer relevant to her; a death within her father's generation will be potentially relevant only to her unmarried (classificatory) brothers and sisters (see § 4.3 regarding the levirate).

In the case of kin terms used for her natal sisters, the married female ego (and her husband) may vary somewhat, perhaps being more inclined to use the terms the woman used before her marriage in some cases. For example, Lee (1986) reports that a man can use the term *niam laus* 'senior sister' and *niam hluas* 'younger sister' (see § 4.4) for his wife's sisters, indicating that she can continue to use these terms herself, even after her marriage. However, both husband and wife tend to adopt the perspective of their children, and more often call the wife's sisters *niam tais* '(affinal) woman (mother-in-law / maternal grandmother / maternal aunt)' and *yawm txiv* '(affinal) man (father-in-law / maternal grandfather / maternal uncle)'. Both the distinction in age between her sisters and the distinction in generation between her mother and her sisters, as well as between her father and her sister's husbands, is lost in these kin terms. Of course, as in all cases, disambiguation is a simple matter if needed. For example, she may call her mother *niam tais laus* 'senior affinal woman' and will often call her sisters *niam tais* + name to ensure clarity. The basic kin terms, however, register difference in neither age nor generation.

The term of reference used for the brothers of a female ego changes from *nus* '(classificatory) brother of unmarried female ego' to *dab laug* '(classificatory) affinal uncle'. Both the married woman and her husband use this term, from the perspective of their children. While no distinction in age in relation to ego is lost in this case (as there was no such distinction prior to ego's marriage (see Figure 10.4)), generational distinction is lost, the same term being used for husband's mother's brothers. The female ego may refer to the wives of her brothers from her parent's perspective, as (*tis*) *nyab* 'affinal daughter-in-law', or from the perspective of her children, simply as *niam dab laug* 'affinal uncle's wife'.

Thus, in the affinal kin terms that the married female ego adopts for her natal family members, there tends to be a loss of distinction in age within a generation (her own and her father's) and a loss of distinction across generations, as well as the loss of distinction between terms for her own natal family and her husband's other affinal kin (his mother's natal family). The female ego in Figure 10.5, for example, will use the terms *niam tais* '(affinal) woman' and *yawm txiv* '(affinal) man' for her own parents, her husband's mother's sisters and their husbands, and his maternal grandparents, as well as for her sisters and their husbands when speaking from the perspective of her children. Of course, there are always ways to disambiguate if reference is unclear, but these kin terms themselves do not distinguish between age or generations in the ways that lineal kin terms do. This loss of distinction across multiple parameters clearly relates to the fact that these kin are members of neither her husband's clan nor his lineage, and so have few specific rights or responsibilities in the life of the married female ego's husband and, thus, nor in her own.

5 Conclusion

This chapter has discussed the ways in which social power in White Hmong communities in Laos and Thailand is represented and reinforced through the kin-term system of the language. Given the significant differences between the nature of social power in these communities and that in many of the more widely known societies of Southeast Asia, it is not surprising that we find significant differences, too, in the ways in which power is encoded in language systems. In a society with such a strong ideology of egalitarianism, with no use of honorifics or interlocutor-reference systems as strategies to show deference, the power differential between White Hmong men and women has sometimes been ignored. It is, however, an undeniable reality for women living a traditional lifestyle. Through a close analysis of the system of White Hmong kin terms we have seen how this linguistic system reflects and reinforces the power imbalance between men and women.

In the case of the male ego, first, terms that clearly delineate between kin of different generations consistently occur only for clan members; these distinctions are not made when addressing or referring to affinal kin, who are, by definition, outside the clan. Second, kin terms that distinguish birth order *within a generation* are highly restricted, occurring only in ego's generation and that of his father. Amongst the male ego's consanguineal kin, the distinction occurs only for males ((classificatory) uncles and brothers). Female consanguineal kin ((classificatory) aunts and sisters), who begin their life as clan members but are bound to marry outside the clan, are not distinguished by age (although females who marry *into* the clan in these generations *are* distinguished according to the age of their husbands in relation to ego and ego's father). This elaboration of distinctions between kin terms within a generation thus occurs only in the case of kin relationships that involve the most extensive rights and duties, those that are most relevant to the maintenance and perpetuation of the lineage through the tradition of the levirate. On the other hand, the lack of attention by the male ego to age difference amongst affinal kin (whether within a generation or across generations) relates to the fact that affinal kin have few specific rights or duties related to their age or generation with respect to him.

In the case of the female ego, many terminological distinctions are lost when she marries and has children. First, she no longer distinguishes between her natal kin and affinal kin, her own family of origin now merging into the class of her husband's affinal kin and thus her own. As a result, she loses distinctions between her natal kin of different ages *within the same generation* (the terms for all her father's brothers and their wives merging with those for her own parents). Through the common practice of addressing others from the perspective of her children, she also no longer tends to use distinct terms for her natal kin *across generations*. Distinctions that were crucial within her family of origin are now lost to her. Perhaps most significantly, a woman's own personal identity is also lost upon marriage: she becomes (simply another) *nyab* 'daughter-in-law' to her husband's parents and is addressed by many others using compounds involving her husband's relationship to the speaker, her husband's given name, or that of her first child. Her only ongoing, specific duty to her family of origin is to her brothers; this concerns not their well-being in this life but their safe passage to the next.

The analysis has shown that *distinctions* between kinship terms in White Hmong relate to *distinctions* in the rights and duties that one has in relation to kin of that type. The sites where these distinctions are most elaborate relate to the empowerment of men in ensuring the prosperity of the lineage, particularly through the tradition of the levirate. The sites where they are least elaborate relate to the disempowerment of women. This is particularly relevant upon her marriage, when she undergoes a complete loss of her personal identity, and a reconfiguration as a wife and mother whose primary role is to produce and reproduce to support the lineage of her husband. Over the course of her life, she journeys from 'guest daughter' and sister to daughter-in-law, wife, and mother, and finally to mother-in-law. Throughout that journey the real sites of her power lie in birth and in death.

Acknowledgements

To Sasha Aikenvald, I owe an enormous debt of gratitude. Her mentorship and encouragement ever since I have known her has meant more to me than I can possibly say. Sasha's deep understanding of the importance of kinship in all its forms has inspired my own interest in this topic. The understanding of Hmong kinship presented in this chapter has benefitted greatly from discussions with Thaiv Thoj (Luang Prabang Province, Laos) and from the outstanding and invaluable knowledge and scholarship of Gary Yia Lee. All errors are my own. This research was initially presented at the *Workshop on Language and*

Social Hierarchy in Southeast Asia held at the University of Sydney, 21–22 June 2019, supported by a grant from the Sydney Southeast Asia Centre. I would like to thank all participants at this event, particularly Dwi Noverini Djenar, Luke Fleming, and Jack Sidnell. My work on this chapter was supported by an Australia Research Council Discovery Project Grant, *The integration of language and society* (DP170100918).

Abbreviations

Abbreviations used in glosses:

CL	classifier
COMP	complementizer
INTENS	intensifier
IP	illocutionary particle
IRREAL	irrealis
PERV	perfective
PL	plural
REDUP	reduplication
SG	singular

References

Enfield, Nick J. (2013). *Relationship thinking: Agency, enchrony, and human sociality*. New York: Oxford University Press.

Goffman, Erving (1956). The nature of deference and demeanor. *American Anthropologist* 56: 473–502.

Heimbach, Ernest E. (1979). *White Hmong—English Dictionary*. Revised edition. Ithaca, NY: Cornell University Southeast Asia Program.

Johnson, Charles, ed. (1985). *Dab neeg Hmoob: Myths, legends and folk tales from the Hmong of Laos*. St Paul, MN: Linguistics Department, Macalester College.

Lee, Gary Yia (1986). White Hmong kinship: Terminology and structure. In Brenda Johns and David Strecker (eds.), *The Hmong world*, 12–32. New Haven, CT: Council on Southeast Asia Studies.

Lee, Gary Yia (1994–1995). The religious presentation of social relationships: Hmong world view and social structure. *Lao Studies Review* 2: 44–60.

Lee, Gary Yia and Nicholas Tapp (2010). *Culture and customs of the Hmong*. Santa Barbara, CA: Greenwood.

Lee, Mai Na M. (2015). *Dreams of the Hmong kingdom: The quest for legitimation in French Indochina*. Madison, WI: University of Wisconsin Press.

Lemoine, Jacques (1972). *Un village Hmong Vert du Haut Laos*. Paris: Centre National de Recherche Scientifique.

Lemoine, Jacques (2012). Commentary: Gender based violence among the (H)mong. *Hmong Studies Journal* 13: 1–27.

Linton, Ralph (1936). *The study of man: An introduction*. New York: D. Appleton-Century Co.

Michaud, Jean (2012). Hmong infrapolitics: A view from Vietnam. *Ethnic and Racial Studies* 35: 1853–1873.

Morrow, Phillip R. (2012). Online advice in Japanese: Giving advice in an internet discussion forum. In Holger Limberg and Miriam A. Locher (eds.), *Advice in discourse*, 255–280. Amsterdam: John Benjamins.

Moua, Teng (2003). The Hmong culture: Kinship, marriage and family systems. Masters Research Paper, University of Wisconsin-Stout.

Müller, André and Rachel Weymuth (2017). How society shapes language: Personal pronouns in the Greater Burma Zone. *Asiatische Studien-Études Asiatiques* 71: 409–432.

Ratliff, Martha (1992). *Meaningful tone: A study of tonal morphology in compounds, form classes, and expressive phrases in White Hmong*. DeKalb, IL: Northern Illinois University, Center for Southeast Asian Studies.

Symonds, Patricia V. (2004). *Calling in the soul: Gender and the cycle of life in a Hmong village*. Seattle: University of Washington Press.

Tapp, Nicholas (2010). *The impossibility of self: An essay on the Hmong diaspora*. Berlin: LIT Verlag.

Vang, Christopher Thao (2016). *Hmong refugees in the New World: Culture, community and opportunity*. Jefferson, NC: McFarland & Company.

Vang, Chia Koua, Gnia Yee Yang and William A. Smalley (1990). *The life of Shong Lue Yang: Hmong 'Mother of Writing'*. Minneapolis, MN: Center for Urban and Regional Affairs, University of Minnesota.

Yang, Kao-Ly (1999). Naître et grandir: Les processus de socialisation de l'enfant en milieu Hmong. PhD dissertation, University of Aix-Marseille I.

CHAPTER 11

Imbuing Words with Power in Ersu

Sihong Zhang

1 Introduction

Ersu is a Qiangic language of the Tibeto-Burman language stock in the Sino-Tibetan language family, spoken in the southwestern part of Sichuan Province, China. The language has three dialects—the western dialect, Lizu; the central dialect, Tosu; and the eastern dialect, Ersu proper. The names of the three dialects are consistent with the local people's auto denominations. This chapter focuses on how to imbue words with power in the eastern dialect, Ersu, a language with about 12,000 speakers distributed in Ganluo and Yuexi counties of Liangshan Yi Autonomous Prefecture, and Hanyuan and Shimian counties of Ya'an Municipality, Sichuan Province (Zhang 2016:29). Although the language was once quite under documented (e.g., Sun 1982; Liu 1983), recent years have seen quite a few studies (e.g., Yu 2012; Chirkova 2017; Chirkova et al. 2015; Chikova and Wang 2017; Zhang 2014a, b; Zhang 2016; Zhang and Wang 2017; Zhang and Yu 2017; Zhang et al. 2018; Wang et al. 2020; etc.). Among them, Zhang's monograph (2016), *A Reference Grammar of Ersu, A Tibeto-Burman Language of China*, the production of which was based on the author's PhD thesis finished under the supervision of Alexandra (Sasha) Aikhenvald, was remarked on as a model grammar for a Tibeto-Burman language and was thought to have filled an important lacuna in the descriptive literature of linguistic typology.

As suggested by Aikhenvald (2010:38), commands and directives are cross-linguistically common, and every language has a way of urging someone to do something. In Ersu, there are four major grammatical strategies to imbue words with power to ask or require an addressee to follow or believe what a speaker says. They are: to use imperatives (§ 2); to employ causatives (§ 3); to empower words with a persuasive sentence-final particle *mǎ* (§ 4); and to use tag interrogatives (§ 5). This chapter offers a brief description of these strategies in Ersu and then gives a summary of how words are imbued with power in the language (§ 6).

© SIHONG ZHANG, 2022 | DOI:10.1163/9789004510395_012

2 Imperatives Used as a Strategy to Imbue Words with Power

The imperative, as a linguistic category, is tightly associated with command in real world, but it is semantically pliable and versatile since it cannot only denote commands, but also express entreaties, requests, wishes, suggestions, instructions, invitations, principles, life mottos, etc. (Aikhenvald 2010: 1–2; Aikhenvald 2017: 23). An imperative is thus the most commonly seen and the most frequently used grammatical category to imbue words with power in utterances where an addressee is commanded or instructed to act. This section first discusses canonical imperatives in Ersu (§ 2.1), then moves on to the negation of imperatives, namely, the prohibitive (§ 2.2), and finally focuses on the relationship between imperatives and other grammatical categories (§ 2.3).

2.1 *Canonical Imperatives*

Canonical imperatives, which are second person imperatives, are viewed as the prototypical commands (Aikhenvald 2010: 18–48). Although they can be expressed with a variety of means (Aikhenvald 2010: 18), the bare root, or stem, of the verb is the mostly commonly found canonical imperative forms in many of the world's languages (Aikhenvald 2017: 5). However, a canonical imperative form in Ersu is generally realised through a verb root taking a directional prefix. There are nine directional prefixes encoding different directions in Ersu: *də-* 'UPWARD-'; *nə-* 'DOWNWARD-'; *khə-* 'INWARD-'; *ŋə-* 'OUTWARD-'; *thə-* 'AWAY-'; *khua-* 'LEFTWARD-/AWAY FROM THE SPEAKER'; *ŋua-* 'RIGHTWARD-/TOWARD THE SPEAKER'; *dʑi-* 'UPWARD-'; and *ȵi-* 'DOWNWARD-' (Zhang 2016:297–305); however, in imperatives, a directional prefix is grammaticalised to function as an imperative marker and does not necessarily have any reference to directions, as shown in (1):

(1) *ŋə-dzɿ!*
OUTWARD-eat
'Eat!'

We can see from (1) that the directional prefix *ŋə-* 'OUTWARD-' prototypically encodes the direction of 'outward'. However, it does not have any semantic connections with the direction that it denotes in this context.

Ersu does not formally distinguish between second person singular and second person plural imperatives. The subject of an imperative is always the second person(s), which may or may not be overtly expressed. If it is not overtly expressed, this indicates that a speaker's manner of speaking is much stronger, which makes the imperative mood function like an order. If it is overtly expressed, it indicates that a speaker's manner of speaking is more mild, which makes the imperative mood function unlike an order, but more like a common request or demand. Additionally, if people call someone by name in this context, a speaker's manner of speaking is the same as when the subject is overtly expressed. For example:

(2) a. *nə-zì!*
DOWNWARD-sit
'Sit down!'

b. *nə nə-zì.*
2SG DOWNWARD-sit
'You sit down.'

c. *amu nə-zì.*
PN:amu DOWNWARD-sit
'Amu, sit down.'

(3) a. *kha-ma=tshua!*
INWARD-sleep=IMMI
'Go to bed immediately!'

b. *nə kha-ma=tshua!*
2SG INWARD-sleep=IMMI
'You go to bed immediately.'

c. *amu kha-ma=tshua.*
PN:amu INWARD-sleep=IMMI
'Amu, go to bed immediately.'

All of the forms in (2) and (3) are acceptable to native speakers. However, if a speaker uses (a), it implies that they strongly urge a listener to do what is said. Therefore, both (2a) and (3a) function as a strong order. However, (b) and (c) are used to imply that a speaker requests (but does not order) a listener to do what is said. From this perspective, both (2b–c) and (3b–c) function as common demands or requests. In addition, (3) illustrates the use of the immediate aspect imperative. It means that a command is to be performed immediately.

Commands to third person(s) and first person(s) are not attested. (4) and (5) below seem, on the surface, to be commands to a third person and a first person respectively. However, in fact they function as requests to the second person, that is, to the addressee, asking permission from the addressee to allow a third person or a first person to do something. In this context, the verb always takes a causative suffix *-su* '-CAUS'. Examples (4) and (5) are given here, and we will further discuss this in § 3:

(4) *tha=và kha-ma-su.*
3SG.PRT=ACC INWARD-sleep-CAUS
'Let him go to sleep.'

(5) *a=và si tʂʅ ǿi-su.*
1SG.SLF=ACC wood cut go.NPST-CAUS
'Let us go to cut firewood.'

2.2 *Prohibitives*

The negation of imperatives, that is, the prohibitive, is used in the context when an addressee is commanded not to do something. Ersu has two distinctive negative markers: *ma-* 'NEG-' and *tha-* 'PHTV-'. The former is only used to negate declaratives, while the latter is only used to negate imperatives. Consequently, we define the former as a "negative marker", and the latter as a "prohibitive marker". The two overt markers are mutually exclusive, as example (6c) indicates, and are therefore quite effective in differentiating a declarative from an imperative, as shown in (7) and (8), respectively:

(6) a. *da-ma-khatho.*
UPWARD-NEG-tell
'not tell'

b. *da-tha-khatho.*
UPWARD-PHTV-tell
'Do not tell.'

*c. *da-ma-tha-khatho.*
UPWARD-NEG-PHTV-tell
'Do not not tell.'

(7) *ja-ʂə tə phu na=và tha-ma-ndo =á.*
APFX-long one CL:a.period.of.time 2SG=ACC AWAY-NEG-see
'(We) haven't seen you for a long period of time.'

(8) *nə=nɛ̀, jò=Ǿì ʂʅ̀=nɛ̀, ŋa-tha-dzɿ.*
2SG=TOP 1SG.OTR=GEN flesh=TOP OUTWARD-PHTV-eat
'You must not eat my flesh.'

We can observe from (6b) and (8) above that the prohibitive in Ersu is realised through the insertion of the prohibitive marker *tha-* 'PHTV-' between a directional prefix and a verbal root. Since, in canonical imperative forms, the co-occurrence of directional prefix and verbal root is almost obligatory, as described in § 2.1, the prohibitive marker *tha-* 'PHTV-'is accordingly often inserted between a directional prefix and a verbal root, forming the structure [DIR+PHTV+V]. This is also one of the seldom attested co-occurrences of prefixes in Ersu. Example (9) below is given to further illustrate this.

(9) *sɛ̀-wo ja-bu*
breath-CL:generic,non-sticklike APFX-big
ŋa-tha-Ǿi-su
OUTWARD-PHTV-go.NPST-CAUS
'(You) must not breathe heavily.' Lit: Do not let breath go out big.

2.3 *Imperative and Other Grammatical Categories*

This section discusses the relationship between imperatives and other grammatical categories, including directionality (§ 2.3.1) and aspect (§ 2.3.2).

2.3.1 Imperatives and Directional Prefixes

As mentioned above, a canonical imperative form can be formed through a verb root taking a directional prefix in Ersu. One exception is that in an asymmetrical serial verb construction (SVC) consisting of a major verb and a minor verb, more specifically, *la* 'come' or *Ǿi* 'go.NPST', if the minor verb is grammaticalised to denote a movement or an action toward (*la* 'come') or away (*Ǿi* 'go.NPST') from deictic centre, the major verb which is used in imperatives does not co-occur with a directional prefix. However, the negative form of an SVC imperative is still realized by the major verb taking a directional prefix. For example:

(10) a. *nə la, ʂada ntsha la=gə.*
2SG come basket make come=PROS
'You come to make a basket.'

b. *nə la, ʂ̨ada da-tha-ntsha la=gə.*
2SG come basket UPWARD=PHTV-make come=PROS
'You mustn't come to make a basket.'

(11) a. *dzɿ ǿi!*
eat go
'Go to eat!'

b. *ŋa-tha-dzɿ ǿi!*
OUTWARD=PHTV-eat go
'Don't go to eat!'

2.3.2 Imperatives and Aspectual Markers

Ersu has quite a complex aspectual system, consisting of 11 aspectual markers. Specifically speaking, these are the markers that denote perfective, perfect, experiential, delimitative, state-changing, habitual, progressive, prospective, imminent, continuous, and repetitive (Zhang 2016: 348–370). Among them, prospective aspect and imminent aspect can be used in the imperative context. This might be because both aspects denote that an event occurs subsequent to a given time, in other words, an event that has not happened when an addresser gives an instruction or a command and will happen in future time following their instructions or demands.

When the prospective aspect co-occurs with the imperative, it is formally unmarked and thus the prospective marker *=gə* '=PROS' is not used. This is often used in the situation when the addressee is commanded to perform an action in the future. For example:

(12) a. *a suɲo pu tʂ̨ɿ ǿi=gə.*
1SG.SLF tomorrow potato plant go:NPST=PROS
'I will go to plant potatoes tomorrow.'

b. *nə suɲo pu tʂ̨ɿ ǿi.*
2SG tomorrow potato plant go:NPST
'You should go to plant potatoes tomorrow'

c. *nə suɲo pu tʂ̨ɿ ǿi=gə.*
3SG.PRT tomorrow potato plant go:NPST=PROS
'He will go to plant potatoes tomorrow.'

As can be seen from (12a) and (12c), the prospective marker is used in the context of first and third person statements. However, it is not used in the second person imperative, as shown in (12b). This implies that the addressee is commanded to perform an action in a later period of time, that is, 'tomorrow' in this example.

Similar to prospective marking as described above, the marking of imminent aspect also shows person distinction. First person is marked with *=gə=tshuá* '=PROS=IMMI'. Second person is marked with *=tshuá* '=IMMI' and is only used in the imperative mood, which means that an addressee is commanded to perform an action as soon as possible. Third person is marked with *=gá* '=IMMI'. The marking of first person imminent aspect is obviously the combination of a prospective aspectual marker *=gə* '=PROS' and an imminent marker *=tshuá* '=IMMI'. For example:

(13) a. *a* *gamɛ* *tshɛ=gə=tshuá.*
1SG.SLF clothes wash=PROS=IMMI
'I will wash clothes immediately.'

b. *nə* *gamɛ* *nə-tshɛ=tshuá.*
2SG clothes DOWNWARD-wash=IMMI
'You should wash clothes immediately.'

c. *thə* *gamɛ* *□tshɛ=gá.*
3SG.PRT clothes wash=IMMI
'He is going to wash clothes immediately.'

3 Causatives Used as a Strategy to Imbue Words with Power

The causative construction in languages is a way to increase valency—to change intransitivity into transitivity. Its formation mechanisms involve morphological processes, two verbs in one predicate, periphrastic causatives, etc. (Dixon 2012: 239–250). In Ersu, the formation of causatives is realised through morphological process including devoicing (§ 3.1) and suffixation (§ 3.2). Causatives in Ersu can imbue words with power to let or make a referent involved in a speech do something. A "referent" in a causative context might refer to both speech act participants (first person and second person) and non-speech act participants (third person participants). This is unlike an imperative context in which only the first and second person are involved, especially the second person.

3.1 *Causatives Formed through Devoicing*

Consonants in Ersu are comparatively stable in most morpho-phonological contexts. However, there are three pairs of consonants in verbs that are found to be devoiced in the language. They share the same properties: a causative can be realized by changing the voiced initial consonant of a verb into a voiceless one. This must be a vestigial transitivity-changing alternation pattern inherited from Proto-Sino-Tibetan languages (Handel 2012). The three pairs of verbs are given in (14).

(14)	dzɿ	'eat'	tsɿ	'let/make ... eat'
	ʐʅ̀	'put on'	ʂʅ̀	'let/make ... to put on'
	guɑ	'take off'	kuɑ	'let/make ... to take off'

Examples in a clausal context are given in (15) below to show how a causative can be used to imbue words with power in Ersu:

(15) a. *nə gamɛ tha-guá.*
2SG clothes AWAY-take.off.PFV
'You took off clothes.'

b. *nə thə jadʐə wo=và gamɛ*
2SG DEM:this child CL:generic,non-sticklike-ACC clothes
tha-kuá.
away-let.take.off.PFV
'You let the child take off clothes.'

As (15b) shows, the initial voiced consonant /g/ of *guá* 'take off.PFV' changes into the initial voiceless consonant /k/ of *kuá* 'let ... take off.PFV'. In this situation, the valency of the intransitive verb *guá* 'take off.PFV' has increased and it has become a transitive verb *kuá* 'let ... take off.PFV', taking an O argument, *jadʐə* 'child'. In this way, *guá* 'take off.PFV' is imbued with power to push the referent, that is, the child to act as demanded.

3.2 *Causatives Formed through Suffixation*

While causatives formed through devoicing are not productive, the causative marker *-su* '-CAUS' suffixed to a verb or an adjective to form a causative construction with the meaning of 'let/make ... do/be ...' is comparatively quite productive in the language. In this context, only intransitive verbs can be causativised. More specifically, the causative mainly functions to increase the valency of an intransitive verb, an existential verb, a copula or an adjective, thus attributing a causative reading to those intransitive words. Examples are given in (16).

(16)

thə-so	'AWAY-die'
thə-so-su	'AWAY-die-CAUS:make ... die'
thə-pu	'AWAY-become'
thə-pu-su	'AWAY-become-CAUS:MAKE ... become'
dzo	'ext'
dzo-su	'EXT-CAUS:make ... have'
jɑ-li	'good'
jɑ-li-su	'APFX-good-CAUS:make ... good'
jɑ-ntho	'sharp'
jɑ-ntho-su	'APFX-sharp-CAUS:make ... sharp'

(17) below shows how *-su* '-CAUS' contributes to changing the valency of an intransitive verb and imbuing it with power in Ersu:

(17) a. *thə* *thə=kə* *nə-zɿ=á*
3SG.PRT (S) DEM:this=RLN.LOC:in<here DOWNWARD-sit (V)=PFV
'She/He sat here.'

b. *thə* *thi* *a-pa=và* *si* *psɿ* *tə*
3SG.PRT (A) 3SG.PRT.GEN KPFX-father(O)=ACC wood flat IDFT
nə-zɿ-su=á
DOWNWARD-sit(V)-CAUS=PFV
'She/He let their father sit on a wooden bench.'

(17) indicates that the verb *nə-zɿ* 'DOWNWARD-sit' is intransitive and takes only one S core argument *thə* '3SG.PRT' in (17a). However, when it is followed by a suffix *-su* '-CAUS' denoting causative, the verb becomes transitive and takes two core arguments: the A argument *thə*'3SG.PRT' and the O argument *thi a-pa* '3SG.PRT.GEN KPFX-father:their father'. In addition, the referent *thi a-pa* '3SG.PRT.GEN KPFX-father:their father' that the O argument refers to was made to do as demanded by the referent *thə* '3SG.PRT' that the A argument denotes.

(18) below shows how *-su* '-CAUS' contributes to changing the valency of the copula *thə-pu* 'AWAY-become' in Ersu:

(18) a. *thə=nɛ̀...* *nbò* *də-əɹ* *tə* *nbò*
[3SG.PRT]$_{CS}$=TOP [horse APFX-white IDFT RPT:horse]$_{CC}$
thə-pu=á
[AWAY-become]$_{COP}$=PFV
'He (the toad) became a white horse.'

b. *sìzà=nɛ̀,* *tha=và* *nbò* *də-əɹ* *tə* *nbò*
god (A)=TOP 3SG.PRT=ACC (O) horse APFX-white IDFT RPT: horse
thə-pu-su=á
AWAY-become-CAUS(V)=PFV
'The god made him (the toad) become a white horse.'

As can be seen, in (18a), *thə-pu* 'AWAY-become' is a copula that takes a copula subject, *thə* '3SG.PRT' and a copula complement, *nbòdə-əɹtənbò* 'horse UPWARD-white IDFTRPT:horse→a white horse'. However, when the copula takes a causative *-su* '-CAUS' (18b), it has the features of a transitive verb. It takes an A argument, *sìzà* 'god', and an O argument, *tha* '3SG.PRT'. What is more, the causative marker *-su* '-CAUS' empowers the word *thə-pu* 'AWAY-become' with the meaning that makes the third person referent, "the toad" here, act as demanded.

(19) below shows how *-su* '-CAUS' contributes to the valency changing and imbuing with power of an adjective in Ersu:

(19) *tsho=gə* *xa=nɛ̀* *nə* *do+ku* *na+ku*
shoot=PROS time=TOP:when 2SG (A) eye+?hole:eye ear+?hole:ear (O)
ja-ntho-su
APFX-sharp-CAUS (V)
'When you are shooting, you should make your eyes and ears sharp.'

(19) indicates that when the adjective *ja-ntho* 'APFX-sharp' takes a causative suffix *-su* '-CAUS', then the [adjective-causative] construction functions like a transitive verb, taking two core arguments: the A argument *nə* '2SG' and theO argument *do+ku na+*ku 'eyes and ears'. Furthermore, the adjective *ja-ntho* 'APFX-sharp' is imbued with power to make the referents "eyes and ears" act as required.

(20) below shows how *-su* '-CAUS' contributes to the valency changing and imbuing with power of an existential verb in Ersu.

(20) *xuafu* *na-pa* *thə=Ǿikə* *tʂʅ=kə*
apple two-CL:roundish, fist-like 3SG.PRT=AGT cabinet=RLN.LOC:in
na-kua *dzo-su=á*
DOWNWARD-place EXT-CAUS=PFV
'She placed the two apples in the cabinet (and) put (them) there.'

4 Persuasive Sentence-Final Marker Used as a Strategy to Imbue Words with Power

In Ersu, a speaker often uses a clause-final marker *mă*to make imperatives sound either more polite, more intimate, friendlier, or more persuasive. We thus define it as a requestive marker. This is especially used by an elder to a younger person, or by a person with a higher social status to a person with a comparatively lower one, when one hopes an addressee will perform as one says. For example:

(21) *nə thi tʂ̻aŋa=nɛ̀, da-tha-ʒu=à=mă.*
2SG DEM:this later=TOP UPWARD-PHTV-feed=PAUS=RQT
'From now on, you had better not keep (dogs).'

(21) shows that *mă*is used in a prohibitive context. The example is extracted from a traditional folktale about a rabbit and an orphan. The rabbit is in fact a god with the image of an old gentleman. (21) is the reported speech of what the rabbit said to the orphan. He asked the orphan, his adopted son in the story, not to feed dogs because dogs always chased him, a rabbit and he could not visit the orphan's family.

(22) below shows that *mă* is also used in an imperative context. The example is extracted from a folktale about the adventure of two sisters. It is reported speech from the two girls' father. He gave each of the two girls one ball of thread and one horse. He requested them to go to the top of a mountain and throw off the ball of thread and just let it roll down. He then asked them to go and live in the place where the ball of thread stopped rolling. (22) is what he said to his two girls.

(22) *nə=dzi nə-wo=nɛ̀, zà*
2SG=DL two-CL:generic,non-sticklike=TOP go
thə=kə, zɿ̀=mă.
DEM:this=RLN.LOC:in<here go:NPST=RQT
'You two, go here, go.'

5 Tag Interrogatives Used as a Strategy to Imbue Words with Power

In Ersu, there are two copulas: one is *thə-pu* 'AWAY-become' as shown in (19) above, and the other is *zɿ* 'COP:general', which is much more generally used in the language. *zɿ* 'COP:general' often takes either the negative marker *ma-*

'NEG-' or the interrogative markers *a*=and =*ɛ̀*, forming the constructions *ma-zɿ=a* and *a=zɿ=ɛ̀*. The two structures show no differences in either semantics or pragmatics. Either of the two functions as a "question tag" following a declarative statement, with a meaning similar to 'isn't it?' or 'right?' In this context, the speaker aims to push the addressee to believe what s/he said. For example:

(23) *'ban̥i=sù* *ma-dzo'=dʑà.* *ma-zɿ=a?*
take care of=NMLZ NEG-EXT=EVID:quotative NEG-COP:general=ITRG
'(She said like this): "there was no one who cared about her." Right?' Lit: Care person not have. Not be?

(24) *tʂaŋa nə-tshɿ* *khə-tsɿ=à=nɛ̀,* *dʑo* *la,*
later two-ten:twenty INWARD-increase=PFV=PAUS return come
dʑi. *a=zɿ=ɛ̀?*
consequently ITRG=COP:general=ITRG
'He later came back when he was approximately 20 years old. Right?' Lit: Later, increased to 20, come back. Be?

Both (23) and (24) are extracted from a narrative story about the speaker's parents' previous experiences. Although the two tag questions are used in the two examples above, the speaker did not pause and wait for an answer in her speech. In (24), she used *ma-zɿ=a* to make her audience believe what she said by highlighting the hardship that her mother suffered. In (25), *a=zɿ=ɛ̀* is used to imply that, on one hand, she was not quite sure what she was describing, while, on the other hand, she wanted to persuade both herself and the audience of the accuracy of her description. Later elicitation shows that the two tag interrogatives can be used interchangeably, which means that the two have no semantic and pragmatic differences.

Furthermore, if a speaker uses either of the two structures in daily conversations, one might expect confirmation from others. The answer to a question like this is either *zɿ=tə/zɿ=dǒ* 'COP:general=DES/COP: general =PART:affirmative' (similar to English 'yes'), as in (26), or *ma-z =tə/ ma-zɿ=dǒ* 'NEG-COP:general=DES/NEG-COP:general=PART:affirmative' (similar to English 'no'), as in (25).

(25) A: *nə=nɛ̀,* *za+pu*
[2SG]VCS=TOP [hundred+manage:king
tə-wo, *ma-zɿ=a?*
one-CL:generic,non-sticklike]VCC NEG-COP:general=ITRG
'You (are) the king. Right?'

B: *zɿ=tə/zɿ=dŏ.*
COP:general=DES/COP:general=PART:affirmative
'Yes.'

(26) A: *nə* *hailong=zì* *a-ma.*
[2SG]VCS [PN. MC:person name=GEN:family KPFX-mother]VCC
a=zɿ=ὲ?
ITRG-COP:be=ITRG
'You (are) Hailong's mother. Right?'

B: *ma-zɿ=tə*
NEG-COP:general=DES

/ma-zɿ=dŏ.
/NEG-COP:general=PART:affirmative
'No.'

Besides *ma-zɿ=a* and *a=zɿ=ὲ, adà* is another form of tag interrogative in Ersu. This is especially used in a situation when the speaker knows some fact that is inconsistent with what the listener has previously described or promised. The speaker does not really expect an answer from the addressee, but imbues this tag with power to urge the addressee to confirm their previous description or not to break their previous promises. Consequently, this tag form is more rhetorical than interrogative. For example:

(27) *"ni* *gamɛ* *tshu* *ta* *tsha=nὲ,* *tɕiǾi* *ndənda*
2SG.GEN clothes such one CL:paper-like=TOP always really.RDUP
jakhua=tə."=dʑa. *adà?*
APFX-big=DES=EVID:quotative ITRG
'People say: "Your clothes are always really magnificent." Are you sure?'

6 Summary

Ersu has multiple ways to imbue words with power to order, command, request or invite a referent to do as required. Imperatives are the most common means used. Imperatives in the language are realised through a verb root taking a directional prefix, which is grammaticalised to denote the imperative. This is unlike most of the languages in the world, in which a bare verbal root or stem can be used to function as an imperative. The negative form of an imperative structure requires the insertion of a prohibitive marker *tha* 'PHTV' between a directional prefix and a verb root, forming the structure [DIR+PHTV+V]. Ersu has 11 aspectual markers. Among them, only imminent and prospective markers can be used in the imperative mood. Causatives are also often employed to imbue words with power to make a referent act as required or demanded. Unlike imperatives, which give commands to a second person referent, causatives encode an order or command given to an addressee to make a third person referent do something. When persons who are senior in age or social status command junior ones to do something, they might use the clause-final requestive marker *mǎ* to make their words sound more polite, intimate, friendlier, or persuasive. Consequently, the requestive marker *mǎ* is quite frequently used in an imperative context. Ersu has three tag interrogatives, the constructions *ma-zɿ=a* and *a=zɿ=ɛ̀* and the tag marker *adà*. They are used in contexts where a speaker imbues their words with power to make the addressee believe what they say or to ask for confirmation from their audiences. As described above, Ersu imbues words with power in ways which not only share common characteristics with other languages of the world, but also have their own typological particularities.

Abbreviations

*	wrong or unacceptable examples
?	semantically unknown or uncertain morphemes or words
:	lexical meaning. For example: *Pɳo-ma*'day-SFX.FEM:sun'
<	lexical meaning that derives from affixation, cliticisation or compounding
+	compound boundary
-	affix boundary
=	clitic boundary and relator noun boundary
1	first person
2	second person
3	third person
ACC	accusative
AGT	agentive
APFX	adjective prefix
CAUS	causative
CL	numeral classifier
COP	copula
DEM	demonstrative
DES	descriptive
EVID	evidential
EXT	existential verb
GEN	genitive
IMMI	imminent
IDFT	indefinite
ITRG	interrogative
KPFX	kinship prefix
LOC	locative
NEG	negative
NMLZ	nominaliser
NPST	non-past
OTR	other speaker
PAUS	pausal marker

PFV	perfective	RDUP	reduplication
PHTV	prohibitive	RLN	relator noun
PN	proper noun	RQT	requestive
PART	particle	SG	single
PRT	present speaker	SLF	self speaker
PROS	prospective	TOP	topic

Tonal marking: All tones for Ersu transcribed in this paper are given in isolation without considering that tonal variations often occur in reality. High level tones are formally unmarked. Other tones are marked with diacritic signs as follows: mid level: ˋ, middle rising: ˊ, falling rising: ˇ.

References

Aikhenvald, Alexandra Y. (2010). *Imperatives and Commands*. Oxford: Oxford University Press.

Aikhenvald, Alexandra Y. (2017). *Commands*. Oxford: Oxford University Press.

Dixon, R.M.W. (2012). *Basic Linguistic Theory*, Vol. 3. Oxford: Oxford University Press.

Chirkova, Katia (2017). Lizu (Ersu). In Randy J. LaPolla and Graham Thurgood (eds.), *The Sino-Tibetan Languages* (2nd edition), 823–839. New York: Routledge.

Chirkova, Katia, Dehe Wang, Yiya Chen, Angélique Amelot and Tanja Kocjančič Antolík (2015). Ersu. *Journal of the International Phonetic Association* 45 (2): 187–211.

Chirkova, Katia and Dehe Wang (2017). Verbal Aspect in Ersu. *Language and Linguistics* 18 (3): 355–382.

Handel, Zev (2012). Valence-changing prefixes and voicing alternation in Old Chinese and Proto-Sino-Tibetan: Reconstructing *s- and *N-prefixes. *Language and Linguistics* 13 (1): 61–81.

Liu, Huiqiang. (1983). The sketch of Ersu langauge. In Shaoming Li and Junbo Liu (eds.), *Studies on the Ersu Tibetan*, 1–16. Beijing: The Ethnic Publishing House.

Sun, Hongkai. (1982). A sketch of Ersu (Tosu). *Linguistic Study* 2 (3): 241–264.

Wang, Dehe, Ke Wang, Xuan Wang, Katia Chirkova, Tao Gu (2020). *A Collection of Ersu Vocabulary*. Hefei: Anhui University Press.

Yu, Dominic (2012). Proto-Ersuic. PhD thesis, University of California, Berkeley.

Zhang, Sihong (2014a). Numeral classifiers in Ersu. *Language and Linguistics* 15 (6): 883–915.

Zhang, Sihong (2014b). The expression of knowledge in Ersu. In Alexandra Y. Aikhenvald and R.M.W. Dixon (eds.), *The Grammar of Knowledge: A Cross-linguistic Typology*, 132–147. Oxford: Oxford University Press.

Zhang, Sihong (2016). *A Reference Grammar in Ersu, A Tibetan-Burman Language of China*. Munich: Lincom Europa.

Zhang, Sihong and Xuan Wang (2017). A study of verb-based reduplication in Yuexi Ersu. *Journal of Minzu University of China* (Philosophy and Social Sciences Edition) 44 (2): 163–169.

Zhang, Sihong, Hongkai Sun and Dehe Wang (2018). Adjectives as a separate word class in Ersu. *Studies on Languages and Linguistics* 38 (1): 101–117.

Zhang, Sihong and Cheng linYu (2017). Existential and possessive verbs in Ersu and their typological significance. *Minority Languages of China* 3: 54–67.

CHAPTER 12

Commands, Curses, Blessings and Invocations among the Iraqw of Tanzania

Maarten Mous

1 Introduction

The Iraqw live in Northern Tanzania on the high plateau between Lake Eyasi and Lake Manyara. They speak a Cushitic language in a country in which the national and dominant language is Swahili (Bantu) and in which most people speak a Bantu language. They are sedentary farmers and keep cattle. The area where Iraqw is spoken is linguistically extremely diverse. In addition to Bantu speaking neighbours (Mbugwe, Nyihanzu, Nyiramba), the Iraqw are and have been in close contact with the Nilotic Datooga cattle people for a long period (Kießling 1998). Another neighbouring group are the Hadza, a hunter-gatherer population who speak an unclassified language. The languages and modes of subsistence may be very different between these groups, but the cultural contact has been intense over the last centuries and for most groups in the wider area cursing and blessing are important cultural practices; see Mitchell (2020) for the Datooga and Bender Shetler (1998: 325, 404–405, 464, 506–507, 524) for several groups in the area to the north in the Serengeti plains.

The anthropological literature on the Iraqw discusses the societal functions of curses at length (Hagborg 2001; Lawi 2000; Rekdal 1999; Snyder 2005; Thornton 1980). Mous (2021) discusses how their culture is reflected in their language and in particular how 'togetherness' is one of the key concepts that is entrenched in their language. In this article I concentrate on blessing and cursing, which likewise derive their power and importance through the cohesion of the community.

Before discussing cursing and blessing, I briefly discuss imperatives. Aikhenvald (2020: 53) has shown that "curses, bad wishes, and maledictions […] are often phrased as if they were commands. They appear in an imperative form, as if telling the addressee what to do and where to go, to their detriment." Iraqw curses, however, make little use of imperatives. This is because curses are often voiced in the absence of the intended victim and are addressed to God in order to have an effect on a specified person and his/her lineage. Blessing, on the other hand, is done in the presence of the intended target and blessings do

© MAARTEN MOUS, 2022 | DOI:10.1163/9789004510395_013

contain imperatives. Imperatives are typically addressee oriented and do not have a subject. This is also what is encoded in Iraqw imperatives, which are quite rich in their inflection. This is presented in the next section. Section 3 deals with curses and Section 4 with blessings. Section 5 addresses a third category, here termed invocations, which, like curses, operate through the power of God and also gain power from their joint expression by the audience; they are not aimed at an individual but rather at the community as a whole. They can be either benevolent or malevolent in terms of content of expression, but are always beneficial to the community.

2 Imperatives

Iraqw imperative sentences are independent clauses that contain an imperative verb form; unlike all other clauses, they do not contain a separate inflectional complex, which is present in all other types of clauses (termed selector) (Mous 2005, 2015). The imperative verb is clause final and, unlike other inflected verb forms, is not marked for tense or for person of subject. Imperatives are inflected for the following categories: number of addressee, direction to speaker (or on behalf of, or to the benefit of the speaker), and transitivity, resulting in eight different forms of the imperative (1). In non-imperative clauses, transitivity is apparent from the presence of objects or object pronouns in the selector. See Mous (1993) for more information.

(1) Imperative forms

Dóosl	'dig!'
dooslé'	'dig! (to many)'
doosleek	'dig it!'
dooslaak	'dig it! (to many)'
dooslang	'dig for me!'
dooslaré'	'dig for me! (to many)'
huwang	'bring it to me!'
huware'	'bring it to me! (to many)'

Negative imperatives, or prohibitives, are different in that they do need an additional selector, an inflectional complex which is preceded by the prohibitive marker *ma-*; the verb form distinguishes only number of addressee (2). This prohibitive prefix indicates the negative element; the imperative form itself is marked by the suffix *-aar* which indicated direction towards the speaker or the deictic centre in proto West-Rift, as is still the case in Iraqw *dooslaré'* 'dig for me (to many)'; however, the formative got reinterpreted in pre-Iraqw in the prohibitive imperative forms (Kießling 1990: 400–401). Transitivity is no longer marked in the verb form of prohibitives but objects are represented or referred to by an object pronoun in the selector, as in non-imperative clauses (3). Direction towards the speaker is not indicated in the verb but again the addition of the selector makes it possible to mark this on the selector (4). In the negative imperative forms, only a singular or plural addressee is distinguished.

For subjects other than second person, the prefix *m-* and the dependent 'to be' with the background suffix *-wa* is used for prohibitions, while the verb is inflected for subject (5). There is homophony in the selector *i*: in (5) it marks third person subject while in (6) with a transitive verb it can only be interpreted as 1SG object. In sum, imperative verb forms do not express subject but indicate singular or plural addressee, specify direction towards speaker, and transitivity either in the selector, for prohibitive imperatives, or on the imperative verb form itself for affirmative imperatives.

(2)	ma dooslaar	'don't dig'
	ma dooslara'	'don't dig (to many)'

(3) *mi-ti* *taahh-aar*
PROH-O1PL beat-IMP
'Don't beat us!'

(4) *kurmo* *mu-ngu* *huw-aar*
hoe.M PROH-O3:HITH:O.M bring-IMP
'Don't bring me the hoe!'

(5) *garma* *m-i-wa* *axwées*
boy PROH-3-BGND talk:3M
'the boy should not talk!'

(6) *hee* *m-i-wa* *tlees*
man PROH-O1SG-BGND waken:3M
'nobody should waken me!'

The following suffixes can be analysed in these imperatives, as shown in Table 12.1.

All imperative verb forms with an object have low tone. This low tone can be seen as a marker for the presence of an object and thus as a separate morpheme. The forms *-ang* and *-are'* are considered to consist of two morphemes

TABLE 12.1 Imperative morphemes

Suffix	Meaning	Gloss
-é'	plural addressee	IMP.PL
-eek	there is an object	IMP.TR.SG
-aak	idem and plural addressee	IMP.TR.PL
-áng	towards the speaker	IMP.HITH.SG
-aré'	idem and plural addressee	IMP.HITH.PL
-ang	towards the speaker and there is an object	IMP.HITH.SG:TR
-are'	idem and plural addressee	IMP.HITH.PL:TR
-aar	negative imperative	IMP for NEG
-ara'	idem and plural addressee	IMP.PL for NEG

-áng IMP.HITH.SG and low tone. The suffix *-ara'* consists of *-aar* plus the plural marker *-a'*. The plural marker *-a'* is used in the plural second and third person present tense indicative verb forms. The suffix *-aré'* seems to be a fusion of *-aar* and *-é'*; however, the subjunctive suffix *-é'*. Kießling (2002: 398–402) discusses the historical developments of imperatives in Southern Cushitic. He shows that proto-West-Rift Southern Cushitic already made the same distinctions in imperatives but used different suffixes due to re-interpretation after various processes of loss of the final vowel.

There are some irregular imperative forms. The stem *qwal* only occurs in the imperative forms *qwaláng* 'come here', *qwalasaré'*, idem to many, *qwalasé'* 'come on, let's go'. The form *xawee(k)* also means 'come here', from the verb *xaw* 'to come', but has the suffix *-eek*, although there is no object. The forms *xawé'* and *xawaré'* also mean 'come' (to many). There are no forms *xáw* or *xawaak*. There is an additional form *xawaas*, also meaning 'come here!' A suffix *-as*, which is no longer productive, can be recognised in *xaw-aas*, *qwal-as-é'*.

The form *aré'*, literally 'look!' (said to many) from the verb *ar* 'to see' is also used in speaking to a single person to express that you have something for him/her. Alternative forms are *areengw* and *areengwaay*. When presenting someone with something one says *hanoo(s)*, related to *haniis* 'to give'. There are fixed expressions containing imperatives, for example *ii'ari qaasaak*, literally 'put it in the ears', meaning 'listen!' (said to many) and used when starting a narration.

3 Cursing

A curse is a very serious matter in Iraqw culture. Various anthropologists have written extensively on the role of cursing in Iraqw society, (Hagborg 2001; Kamera 1986; Rekdal 1999; Snyder 2005; Thornton 1980). The Iraqw word *lo'o* (f) refers to a solemn wish for frightful things to happen to an opponent who has wronged the curser. It is God who will make this happen, but only if there is a valid ground for the curse. The word *lo'o* is only used for such a serious event and is not used more loosely for 'bad language', similar to what Mitchell (2020) states for the Datooga word 'to swear'; hence *lo'o* does not have the wide range of usage of the English term 'curse', as Ameka (2020) explains. From the noun *lo'o* a verb may be derived by a causative verbalizer resulting in *lu'uus* (v) 'to curse'. For example, in the story about Amsi, she is told to curse her mother using a subjunctive (7) (Wada 1976: story 31). There is an alternative verb in Iraqw, */oosl*, that has 'curse' as a translation equivalent (e.g. in Berger and Kießling 1988), but that is only used for the non-solemn sense, and has 'insult' as its meaning in Mous et al. (2002: 80).

(7) *Amsí, iyoo-r-óg na lu'us-e!*
Amsi mother-F-2SG.POSS HORT curse:CAUS-SBJ
'Amsi, curse your mother!' [ulaani mama yako!]

Another verb for cursing is *alwahaam* (v) 'curse, complain, swear'. This word is less specifically used to refer to a ritual curse. The break-up of the word is to be drinking together; *al-* is a comitative pre-verb, *wah* is the verb 'to drink', and the suffix *-aam*, underlyingly *-iim*, is an imperfective marker indicating durative aspect. Yet another word for a curse is */untsaa* (p) 'curse', a noun derived from a defunct verb */uunts* 'to curse', a form that is still present in the derived verb *hara/uunts* (v) 'treat unjustly, oppress'. The preverb *hara-* indicates an action done simultaneously (Kießling 1990: 73). This word is seldom used and I have no details on how it differs from *lo'o* semantically. As far as I know there is no separate verb or noun for the looser usage bad language against someone, but an example of a swear word is *tsarar'eét* 'get lost!' (Mous et al. 2002: 107); one can also swear at someone by calling him a hyena.

Administering the curse is referred to as 'cutting' (*tsatiit*) the curse or 'bringing' (*huuw*) the curse, as in (10) below. Receiving a curse is referred to as 'eating' (*/ayma*) the curse; the same is also true for neighbouring Nilotic Datooga in *qwaak habeawooda*, literally meaning 's/he ate an oath/curse' (Mitchell 2020: 80).

The curse is always aimed at someone but often not addressed to that person, as the adversary is commonly not present when the curse is uttered. As a consequence, imperatives are seldom used in curses in Iraqw, although this is a common feature cross-linguistically (Aikhenvald 2020: 53).

The curse is a deliberate act that is formally invoked (Lawi 2000: 136). The purpose of a curse is the well-being of the community. It corrects improper social behaviour, as is explained by Rekdal (1999: 38), who adds that it differs in that respect from witchcraft (*da/ari*) which is exclusively evil in intent. Hagborg (2001: 111–118) distinguishes three types of curses. The most severe one is called *lo'ór /ayma* 'curse of eating', which is decided upon in a meeting; *lo'ór afa* 'curse of mouth' can be pronounced by any individual any time; and finally there is *lo'ór muuna* 'curse of the heart', which is unconscious and uncontrollable, and not actually pronounced. Major breaches of social norms are termed *iringeé(t)* 'sin', a loan from Datooga. Such sins include disobeying one's mother or other ladies of her age (Lawi 2000: 135). *Iringeet* also refers to a serious crime affecting the family (e.g. incest, beating of parents) and may result in effects that are similar to a curse. Both curses and 'sins' typically result in not bearing offspring and in skin diseases. Leprosy, *tiqtír tsatmit*, literally 'illness of being cut' (Mous et al. 2002: 101), is considered a typical punishment (8). A cultural text about the marriage rules (Wada 1976: story 42) reports that breaking these rules brings about a curse which has the effect of having no children.

(8) *iringeét g-w-a /ág*
sin.F O3-O.M-PRF eat:3F
'He has leprosy', lit.: the sin ate him.

Lawi (2000: 98–99) argues, in a similar vein, that people who do not adhere to the norm are ritually condemned in the poetic prayer *slufay*, in particular in the following lines (9).

(9) Lines of *slufay* condemning wrong-doers (spelling slightly adapted)

Hee muk waa tlaakw	A wicked person amongst us
Nee aten mawa al ki/aán	Let him not unite with us again
Kar bar aakoo	If it is an old man
Hula'rós lo ir awhiin	May his fire place go silent
Kwisyángw da/atén kar lo' ngir aal	Let it be infested with the red fleas
Kar bar masomoo	If a young man
/A/ewós /uwaa ngi dahhir	Let the cry of his demise come from the west

Bar dasír niina	If an unmarried girl
Sagós xwa'aro nguwa xufit	May the crows drink [water] from her skull
Bar /ameenír niina	If a young woman
Mahángw xwayla lo' gar gaas	May she be killed by the arrow of labour [pains]
Kar bar am 'aar uur	If an old woman
Umtór na/aá nangós ngir gexeér	Let her leave behind the pleasure of caring for her children's children

The deliberate act of cursing can be either an individual act or a communal one. Thornton (1980: 149) views the curse as a tool of the elders who represent the neighbourhood, *aya*. They decide on a curse in their responsibility for correct ritual observances, safeguarding the fertility of land, and providing rain. He remarks that pronouncing an individual curse may be punished with fines or exile. Individual curses are not excluded, though, and are quite common. In fact, even curses decided in a meeting are pronounced by an individual. This is clear in a text (Wada 1976: story 40) explaining how marriage within the family got cursed. It is crucial that the curse was decided upon at a meeting, and one person was specified to pronounce the curse, using the verbs *huuw* 'bring' and *tsaat* 'cut' (10). In another text (Wada 1976: story 31), the wife pleads that it wasn't she who had spoken the curse and that she should be spared, again confirming that the actual pronouncing of the curse is an individual matter.

(10) *Aluuwo daxta kwasleema lo'o ka-na huúw, nee*
later now meeting curse O3:IMPS:O.F-PAST bring:3M and
lo'o-daá-dá' heé g-a huúw a aakó
curse:F-DEM4-DEM4 person:M:CON O3-O.F bring:3M COP G.father
xwayla-r-ós aa tsatit,
children-F-3SG.POSS 3PRF cut:IMPFV:3M
'Now, later, at a meeting a curse was pronounced and the one to pronounce that curse was the father of his children who cut the curse.'

In terms of speech act, as Agyekum (2004: 317) points out, one has to integrate the sociocultural context rather than approach the speech act only from a personalistic perspective. Even though the actual curse is performed by an individual, it is within the community and its beliefs and cohesion that the curse can be effective; moreover, the effect goes far beyond the individual and can only be lifted in a communal act.

Snyder (2005: 114–121) explains how curses are useful in court cases when there is no other evidence. In such cases, the curse comes to function as an oath. She recounts a case involving different interpretations of which individual was referred to by a name that was mentioned by a diviner. Before the court, the diviner was forced to pronounce "Oh Looaa, if it is not true that I divined that Qamara, the grandson of Qamara and not Qamara the first wife of Baran, was responsible for Basso's mother's illness, then let me not see the harvest of the coming year. If it is true that Basso did not pronounce the name of Qamara, grandson of Baran, as the source of his mother's illness, let me not eat the harvest of the coming year." And likewise, the client: "Oh Looaa, hear what I am saying. Take me before this year's harvest if truly I said that Qamara, the grandson of Baran was a witch". This double curse within the context of the traditional court functions as an oath.

To utter a curse is to call upon God, *Looaa*, to deliver justice upon an offender (Snyder 2005: 114). The Iraqw perceive *Looaa* (f) 'sun' as a female deity. In putting a curse on somebody, she is directly addressed with *ayir'eé* 'my mother' (Lawi 2000: 129).

There is no specific precise formula that needs to be used in curses. Curses often use the subjunctive for an optative expression. They seldom contain imperatives. It is common for the curser to be standing on a termite mound, or near a stream of spring with his cloth upside-down, covering his head with a cloth (Thornton 1980: 178; Snyder 2005: 114, 116; Yoneyama 1970: 95).

A specific way of cursing land is to bury *tlaraangw* in the soil; this refers to a charm consisting of soil mixed with the bones of a cat or dog, and the remains of a hoe (Mous et al. 2002: 103).

The curser may openly inform his victim but often the curse will only become apparent when its effects are felt. What exactly will occur to the opponent is sometimes specified and sometimes is not. A typical curse statement in which it is specified is *do'ós i qwaar* 'his house will be lost', which Thornton (1980: 33) reports as a typical curse by elders after wrong doing against a 'house', a family. The effect of a curse is often only noted after a long period of time when the victim realizes that his or her family is having more than usual misfortune (Snyder 2005: 114; Lawi 2000: 136). The effect can affect the next generations. Bender Shetler (1998: 325) reports on the intergenerational effects of curses among the Nata (Bantu, Mara region of Tanzania). Typical consequences are sudden death, not having (male) children, diseases, particularly skin diseases and leprosy, insanity (Yoneyama 1970), death of livestock and diseases of livestock. A cow disease that is considered to be caused by a curse is *tiqtír qulhháy* 'illness of pimples'; the cow dies suddenly and is not to be touched (Mous et al. 2002: 88).

In tales, curses occasionally occur. In the story of Simbooya, he searches for messengers that can find his parents. The first candidate, the crow, produces an unsatisfactory message, *xwaá-xwaá*, and is cursed by Simbooya, who pronounces *let the milk that you have just drunk kill you* (Hhao to appear).

Not only people but also land can be cursed. Wilderness or uncultivated land is perceived as dangerous. When people plead for dangers and diseases to go away, they wish them to go to such faraway places. Moreover, the most severe punishment in traditional justice is to be expelled from the community and to disappear to such areas. One of these areas, that was known to be cursed by the famous prophet Nade Bee/a, was the Mount Harar area. However, during the course of the Iraqw expansion, this area came to be inhabited by Iraqw, and the curse on Harar had to be removed. Both Rekdal (1999: 147–148, 228–233) and Lawi (2000) recount the removal of this curse by the Tuua Masay, a famous leader in the 1950s. In the prayer-poem *slufay*, this mountain, the curse and its removal is mentioned (Lawi 2000: 119):

(11) *Dirkaa* *handaay*
place:F:INDF.F there
'There is a place'

Didaa *Harár*
place:F:DEM4:CON Harar
'That place is Harar'

Dirqá' *aáng* *a* *lo'o*
place-F-DEM3 past COP curse
'The place we cursed long ago'

Lo'odá *amór* *hhó'*
curse:F-DEM4:CON place:F:CON nice:F
'May that curse be turned around and made good'

Just as Nade Bee/a cursed Harar, the prophet Khambageu, among the Bantu Nata of Mara region in Tanzania, cursed the village of Tinaga, leading to its destruction by the Maasai (Bender Shetler 1998: 464).

Curses are so central in Iraqw society that some of them are known by a name. A very famous one is the curse of Mount Harar discussed above. Curses are often named after the family or clan to which they are directed. In one story, Cat refers to a curse before it jumps over the spears in order to give extra weight to her claim (12). Jumping over spears is an ordeal undertaken in order to determine innocence or guilt. Cat shouts:

(12) *Lo'ór* *doó* *Tsuntsi!* *Lo'ór* *doó* *Tsuntsi!*
curse:F:CON house:M:CON Tsuntsi curse:F:CON house:M:CON Tsuntsi
Lo'ór *doó* *Tsuntsi!* *Aayí* *aga*
curse:F:CON house:M:CON Tsuntsi mother O.F-PRF
kwatitiiká, *sákw!*
touch-PRED:PAST-NEG IDEO.jump
'Curse of the house of Tsuntsi, curse of the house of Tsuntsi, curse of the house of Tsuntsi, I did not touch mother, *sákw* (sound of jumping over the spears).' (Wada 1976: story 18).

There is a specific verb meaning 'to lift a curse', *amohhu'uum* (v) 'relieve a curse, repent, ask for forgiveness, be converted, return to where one belongs' (Mous et al. 2002: 14). The verb contains the preverb *amo-*, meaning 'place', and the verb *hhu'uum* as a no longer existing base for reduplicated *hhu'u'uum* 'to repent'. Kamera (1986) contains a detailed account of the ritual to lift a curse. The lifting of a curse is an elaborate event that is carefully prepared and can easily take a whole day. Both families involved have to agree to the ritual and both must be present, as well as an extensive audience to witness the reconciliation. It is thus crucial that the family of the curser reconciles with the family of the opponent, who are expected to admit their guilt in public. In the present day it is not uncommon for Christian pastors to play a role in the traditional ritual of lifting the curse, as is evident in one of the recordings in my files, by my research companion Basilisa Hhao; Hagborg (2001: 114) also reports on the complications of organising a ceremony to lift a curse as one of the parties had become Pentecostal; this issue was resolved by including the pastor. The ceremonies crucially include a meal that is shared. Yoneyama (1970) reports that an ox is sacrificed to *Looaa* and that beer, often enhanced by honey, is provided for the elders. Honey is an important element to cool danger (Lawi 2000: 109).

4 Blessing

In opposition to cursing, there is blessing. But blessing differs fundamentally from cursing in modality of speech act. Blessing is not necessarily directed at a person. People can be blessed, but the blessed object need not be human; often a house is blessed (13). Moreover, there is more agency and control assumed in the blesser compared to the curser. While the curser leaves it up to God, this is not explicitly evoked in blessing, although, of course, ultimately all is still in the powers of *Looaa*. It is often older men who bless, and in that sense blessing is a way to show presumed higher power, similar to what Kratz (1989: 637–638) reports for the Nilotic Akiek hunter-gatherers in Kenya. One way of blessing is to spit, on the person's forehead or hand, with or without a blessing spoken. The verb *tsuuq* 'to spit' also means 'to bless' and even 'to bewitch'; and its nominalization *tsunqaa* (p) is not only 'saliva (as blessing)' but also 'gifts (even in the form of money) to newly-weds'.

(13) *aakoo i doó bafiít*
G.father 3 house:M:CON bless:IMPFV:3M
'Father blessed the house.'

A more specific verb is *baaf* (v) 'spit out liquid as blessing, bless'. This verb is used in standard expressions such as *buurár baafa* /beer:F:CON blessing/ 'first beer of the newly harvested millet'. A different word for blessing is */ami* (f) 'blessing'. An example of a formulaic spoken blessing is (14), with the verb in an archaic subjunctive form.

(14) *do'ók i hats-i*
house-M:2SG.POSS 3 fill-SBJ:3M
'Let your house be filled.'

A common item used in blessing is *barsi* (f) 'some leaves/grass as symbol of peace or blessing'. Such a bunch of fresh green grass is used in several situations. Lawi (2000: 130) reports that it used to be customary for the Iraqw to greet the sun/God in the early morning, spitting out a bit of the *barsi* grass in the direction of the sun. It is also used when one visits someone for a serious request for help (financial or otherwise). Such a request is preceded and given weight by placing *barsi* under the roof above the door, referred to as *barsi kwahha* 'throwing barsi' (15a or b) (Mous et al. 2002: 20). Snyder (2005: 157) confirms that "when *barsi* is used, a request should not be denied".

(15) a. *barsirí oh-eek*
barsi-F-DEM1 catch-IMP.TR.SG
'Accept the *barsi*, help me.'

b. *tam barsi huw-eek na'as*
even barsi bring-IMP.TR.SG please/thanks
'Please help me.'

In conflict situations, throwing *barsi* into the quarrelling group (Lawi 2000: 68) or approaching a group of people with *barsi* in the hand are all expressions of seeking peace. *Barsi* is dipped into the beer while reciting a *slufay* prayer-poem (Beck and Mous 2014; viewable at Mous et al 2018).

5 Invocations

Mitchell (2020) needs a category separate from blessings and curses for Datooga, for which she uses the term *invocations*. Although Iraqw does not have a separate term in the lexicon for this category I feel it is of use too, specifically for the strong wishes that abound in the poem-prayer *slufay* (literally 'blessing'), both in the *slufay* proper and in its introduction *fiiro* (literally 'asking, praying'); see Beck and Mous (2014). These are strong wishes, both positive and negative. In the *fiiro*, the introduction to the *slufay*, the current situation of the community is discussed and thieves are wished to be expelled and sent far away, while people who are ill are wished to recover and get up. When the main performer utters these invocations he speaks faster and faster and louder and louder while the community ululates in accordance, waving their hands in the air or pointing them to the ground; this can be watched in Mous et al (2018). The participation of the audience in unity empowers these invocations (Rekdal 1999: 194).

The *slufay* can be viewed as consisting of invocations aiming at the well-being of the community. The audience acknowledges each line, with *haya* 'indeed' uttered in unison and providing the rhythm for the performance but also adding power to the words to make these invocations happen. Many of these invocations contain archaic subjunctive forms expressing wishes. A typical example is (16) from Lawi (2000: 98). The standard last lines of the *slufay* strengthen the eternity and universality of the invocations by naming a series of sets of two items that are always together.

(16) *Puupuhhaay tii sla'a~sla-i*
neighbours REC like~IMPFV-SBJ:3M
'Let our neighbourhood remain in harmony.'

Até kahi tii ya/aan
1PL say:SBJ:3M REC agree
'Let our conversations end in agreement.'

Tii sla'a~sla'-an-e'
REC like~IMPFV-1PL-SBJ
'Let us love one another.'

Bar ma'ay nee danu'
COND water and honey
'Like water and honey'

Eea nee saga
ear and head
'The ear and head'

Tlawu nee danda
cloth and back
'Clothes and the body'

Afa nee dawa
mouth and hand
'The mouth and the hand'

Yaae nee ya/ati
foot and sandal
'The foot and the sandal'

Uhumo nee waqaasi
pole and beam
'The pole and the beam'

Nu/ú nee nu/ú
thing and thing
'The sex organ and the sex organ'

6 Summary and Conclusion

Iraqw curses are not uttered in the presence of the opponent and rather speak to *looaa* 'God'; hence, they tend not to contain imperatives. Cursing is a serious matter and is unacceptable and punishable if done lightly. The word referring to 'curse' cannot be used loosely; there are different words for 'insult', etc. Curses can have an effect over generations and can be lifted in a communal ritual requiring acceptance of the lifting by the parties concerned, in the presence of neighbours. Curses get to be known in the community and can even be named. Apart from persons, land and areas can also be cursed, as can cattle. A specific result of a curse is skin disease, including leprosy; other effects include death and infertility. Curses are important in Iraqw society and are mentioned in their verbal art. Similar but different to a curse is what I have termed invocation. These invocations, for good or bad, are common in the *fiiro*, the introduction to the most prominent specimen of Iraqw verbal art, the *slufay*. They are uttered in unison by all present. Blessings are common too in the *slufay*. Blessings and invocations are different from curses in that they are uttered in the presence of the intended receiver. This entails a different setting in which the speech act functions. Rather than a personal message to *looaa* 'God' in inner speech, blessings and invocations are public and, in fact, a speech act that is conducted by the group of people present, in unison. As a consequence, there is no inhibition on using imperatives in blessings, or on optatives expressed in a subjunctive verb form in invocations. Both moods are appropriate in a speech act addressed to all those implied as actors in the speech act. The expression of control and coercion in these imperatives is one of the community in unison or of a representative of the community for the community and not of an individual over another individual. Imperatives are absent in curses because of the nature of the speech act of the curse (inner speech) and the fact that it is directed towards *looaa* 'God'. Any suggestion of control over or even coercing God which the use of an imperative would entail is unimaginable. The imperative category is quite rich in inflection in Iraqw; it is marked not only for number of addressee but also for transitivity and for speaker direction. The usage and absence thereof of certain verb forms such as imperatives in certain genres can only be comprehended in a holistic analysis of these genres, their nature in terms of speech act constellation, and their function in society.

Orthography

The Iraqw orthography is used in this paper: / is a voiced pharyngeal fricative with creaky voice, *hh* is a voiceless pharyngeal fricative, ' is a glottal stop (not written but present word-initially and between different vowels; thus, *ai* is in fact *a'i*), *sl* is a voiceless lateral fricative, *tl* and *ts* are ejective affricates, the former with lateral release, and *ng* is a velar nasal word-initially and word-finally and is followed by a voiced velar stop between vowels. Double vowels are long; (high) tone is only marked on the second vowel symbol. Low tone is left unmarked.

Abbreviations

1/2	first or second person	IMPFV	imperfective
1,2,3	first, second, third person	INDF	indefinite
BGND	background	M	masculine
CON	construct case	P	plural gender
CAUS	causative	NEG	negative
COND	conditional	O	object
COP	copula	PRES	present
DEM	demonstrative (numbers refer to degree of distance)	PRF	perfect
		PL	plural
DEP	dependent (clause)	POSS	possessive
DIR	directional	PRED	predicative
F	feminine	PROH	prohibitive
HITH	hither	REC	reciprocal
HORT	hortative	SG	singular
IMP	imperative	SBJ	subjunctive
IMPS	impersonal	TR	transitive

References

Agyekum, Kofi (2004). Ntam 'reminiscential oath' taboo in Akan. *Language in Society* 33: 317–342.

Aikhenvald, Alexandra Y. (2010). *Imperatives and Commands*. Oxford: Oxford University Press.

Aikhenvald, Alexandra Y. (2017). Imperatives and commands: a cross-linguistic view. In Alexandra Y. Aikhenvald and R.M.W. Dixon (eds.), *Commands: A cross-linguistic typology*, 1–45. Oxford: Oxford University Pres.

Aikhenvald, Alexandra Y. (2020). "Damn your eyes!" (Not really): Imperative imprecatives, and curses as commands. In Nico Nassenstein and Anne Storch (eds.), *Swearing and Cursing Contexts and Practices in a Critical Linguistic Perspective*, 53–78. (Language and Social Life, 22.) Berlin: De Gruyter Mouton. https://doi.org/10.1515/9781501511202-003

Ameka, Felix (2020). "I sh.t in your mouth": Areal invectives in the Lower Volta Basin (West Africa). In Nico Nassenstein and Anne Storch (eds.), *Swearing and Cursing Contexts and Practices in a Critical Linguistic Perspective*, 121–144. (Language and Social Life, 22.) Berlin: De Gruyter Mouton. https://doi.org/10.1515/9781501511202-006

Beck, Rose-Marie and Maarten Mous (2014). Iraqw slufay and the power of voice. In

Hannelore Vogele, Uta Reuster-Jahn, Raimund Kastenholz and Lutz Diegner (eds.), *From the Tana River to Lake Chad, Research in African Oratures and Literatures. In memoriam Thomas Geider*, 357–371. Cologne: Rüdiger Köppe.

Bender Shetler, Jan (1998). The Landscapes of Memory: A History of Social Identity in the Western Serengeti, Tanzania. PhD thesis, University of Florida.

Berger, Paul and Roland Kießling (1988). *Iraqw texts*. Cologne: Rüdiger Köppe.

Hagborg, Lars (2001). Silence: Disputes on the ground and in the mind among the Iraqw in Karatu District, Tanzania. PhD thesis, Uppsala University.

Hhao, Basilisa (to appear). Aama Irmí na hadithi nyingine za Kiiraqw.

Kamera, W.D. (1986). Loo Ammohhuuma An Iraqw Reconciliation Rite. *Anthropos* 81: 137–149.

Kießling, Roland (1990). Preverbal position as a cradle of grammatical innovation in Iraqw. *Afrikanistische Arbeitspapiere* 21: 67–86.

Kießling, Roland (1998). Reconstructing the Sociohistorical Background of the Iraqw Language. *Afrika und Übersee* 81 (2): 167–225.

Kießling, Roland (2002). Die Rekonstruktion der südkuschitischen Sprachen (West-Rift). Von den systemlinguistischen Manifestationen zum Gesellschaflichen Rahmen des Sprachwandels. Cologne: Rüdiger Köppe.

Kratz, Corinne A. (1989). Genres of power: A comparative analysis of Okiek blessings, curses and oaths. *Man* 24 (4): 636–656.

Lawi, Y.Q. (2000). May the spider web blind witches and wild animals: Local knowledge and the political ecology of natural resource use in the Iraqwland, Northern Tanzania, 1900–1985. PhD thesis, Boston University.

Mitchell, Alice (2020). "Oh, bald father!": Kinship and swearing among Datooga of Tanzania. In Nico Nassenstein and Anne Storch (eds.), *Swearing and Cursing Contexts and Practices in a Critical Linguistic Perspective*, 79–102. (Language and Social Life, 22.) Berlin: De Gruyter Mouton. https://doi.org/10.1515/9781501511202-004

Mous, Maarten (1993). *A Grammar of Iraqw*. Hamburg: Helmut Buske.

Mous, Maarten (2005). Selectors in Cushitic. In F.K. Erhard Voeltz (ed.), *Studies in African Linguistic Typology*, 303–325. Amsterdam: John Benjamins.

Mous, Maarten (2015). Copulas in Iraqw, a Cushitic language from Tanzania. *Lingue e Linguaggio* 14 (2): 179–196 (Special issue on "Copulas" edited by Ekaterina Golovko and Maria Mazzoli). https://www.rivisteweb.it/doi/10.1418/81747

Mous, Maarten (2021). The Iraqw society reflected in their language. In Alexandra Aikhenvald, R.M.W. Dixon and Nerida Jarkey (eds.), *The integration of language and society: a cross-linguistic typology*. Oxford: OUP.

Mous, Maarten, Sandra Bleeker and Amy Catling (2018). *Iraqw Oral Literature* (*Verba Africana* 6). http://verbafricana.org/iraqw/ (accessed 29.03.2021).

Mous, Maarten, Martha Qorro and Roland Kießling (2002). *An Iraqw—English Dictionary*. Cologne: Rüdiger Köppe.

Rekdal, Ole-Bjorn (1999). The invention by tradition: Creativity and change among the Iraqw of northern Tanzania. PhD thesis, University of Bergen. http://hdl.handle.net/11250/2481840

Snyder, Katherine A. (2005). The Iraqw of Tanzania: Negotiating Rural Development. (Westview Case Studies in Anthropology). Cambridge, MA: Westview Press.

Thornton, Robert J. (1980). *Space, time, and culture among the Iraqw of Tanzania.* New York: Academic Press.

Wada, Shohei (1976). *Hadithi za mapokeo ya Wairaqw. Iraqw folktales in Tanzania.* (*African language and ethnography* 5.) Tokyo: ILCAA.

Yoneyama, Toshinao (1970). Some basic notions among the Iraqw of Northern Tanzania. *Kyoto University African Studies* 5: 81–100.

CHAPTER 13

Directive Speech Acts: Imperatives and Hortatives in Northern Amis (Austronesian)

Isabelle Bril

1 Introduction

Imperative, prohibitive, hortative/optative moods have some common points: they project the speaker's urge or wish to have some prospective state of affairs be performed, though with distinct illocutionary force and illocutionary mood. Canonical imperatives and their negative prohibitive counterpart express commands about desired states of affairs, usually addressed with varying force to second person singular or plural addressees who are viewed as being potential performers in control of the situation (Searle 1969, Aikhenvald 2010, van der Auwera et al. 2013). Hortatives are also directive speech acts, generally aimed at first person plural inclusive addressees, possibly self-addressed with first singular pronouns, or which may concern third person singular or plural actors (e.g., let him/them do it); in the latter case, the addressees are distinct from the actors. On the other hand, optatives express some wish about a desired state of affairs without any implied command.

In Amis,[1] imperatives, prohibitives, hortatives/optatives are expressed by dedicated morphemes which cumulate voice and mood features, for instance imperative Actor Voice (AV) or imperative Undergoer Voice (UV). Canonical imperatives and prohibitives have second person singular or plural addressees, but imperatives in UV and LV (Locative Voice) may occur with first person plural inclusive addressees, expressing more commissive speech acts than standard

1 Amis is an Austronesian language spoken along the eastern coast of Taiwan; it has four main dialects (northern, central, coastal and southern (Tsuchida 1988)) with significant differences in phonology, lexicon and morphosyntax. Northern Amis (N. Amis) is the focus of this analysis; it is spoken in various locations around the city of Hualien. Unless otherwise indicated, all examples originate from my corpus, recorded and collected over a period of approximately 14 months of fieldwork. My analyses are based on this corpus which mainly contains spontaneous oral productions (i.e., narratives of various types, procedural texts), with additional elicitations in order to check paradigms and obtain missing data. I extend my gratitude to all Amis consultants and friends for their patient and precious collaboration.

© ISABELLE BRIL, 2022 | DOI:10.1163/9789004510395_014

hortatives. Hortative and optative speech acts share the same morphological exponents, with contextual readings; hortatives are directive, while optatives are not.

The discussion unfolds as follows: Section 2 discusses the voice and mood morphology in indicative and non-indicative moods; Section 3 presents the voice system and argument structure; Section 4 presents the rationale underlying voice selection in the imperative mood, and the distribution of imperative forms according to types of stems and types of constructions, including reciprocal and cleft constructions; Section 5 discusses the semantic range of imperatives; the prohibitive mood is presented in Section 6 and the hortative/optative mood forms and their negative counterparts in Section 7; Section 8 shows that morphemes used in imperative and hortative speech acts intersect with modalised declarative speech acts; Section 9 discusses some diachronic sources and evolutions of voice and mood morphology; Section 10 concludes.

2 The Voice and Mood Morphology in Indicative and Non-indicative Moods

In Amis, imperative, prohibitive, hortative/optative speech acts are marked by way of affixes cumulating voice and mood features within its symmetrical voice system.[2]

As shown by Table 13.1, all voice affixes in the indicative mood, i.e., Actor voice *mi-* (AV), Non-Actor voice *ma-* (NAV) (including *mu-* and the ⟨*um*⟩[3] infix), Undergoer voices *ma-* and *-en* (UV) and Locative voice *-an* (LV) have their counterparts in the hortative/optative, imperative and prohibitive moods.

The hortative/optative mood selects the indicative Actor Voice (AV) *mi-* or Non-Actor Voice (NAV) *ma-* which is prefixed to finite verb stems and suffixed by *-a*, while the imperative and prohibitive moods select non-finite verb stems (e.g., *pi-…-i* for AV *mi-* stems, and *ka-* for NAV *ma-* stems, ⟨*um*⟩ stems and *mu-* stems). The non-finite *pi-* and *ka-* stems also occur on verb stems dependent on negative auxiliaries like *caay*, or modality auxiliaries (like 'want, refuse', etc.) and in some subordinate clauses. UV *ma-* and LV *-an* are marked by distinct suffixes in the hortative/optative and imperative moods, while UV *-en* remains formally identical in all these moods. Finally, the negative indicative construc-

2 For reasons of space, the voice system and its alternations in indicative mood is not presented here, this can be read in Bril (2016, 2017, forthcoming 2022).

3 The infix ⟨*um*⟩ is written ⟨*em*⟩ [əm] in Northern Amis.

TABLE 13.1 Voice and mood morphemes in Northern Amis

	AV	NAV	⟨UM⟩	MU-	UV	UV	LV
Indicative	mi-	ma-	⟨em⟩	mu-	ma-	–en	–an
Hortative	mi-...-a	ma-...-a	⟨em⟩...-a	mu-...-a	–a(w)	–en	–ay
Imperative	pi-...-i	ka-	ka⟨em⟩	ka-mu-	–a	–en	–i
Prohibitive	aka pi-	aka ka-	aka ka⟨em⟩	aka ka-mu-	aka stem-i	aka stem-i	aka stem-i
Negative indicative	caay pi-	caay ka-	caay ka⟨em⟩	caay ka-mu-	caay (ka)-stem-i	caay stem-i	caay stem-i

tion with the auxiliary *caay* and the prohibitive construction with the auxiliary *aka* have the same form in all UV and LV verb stems, i.e., they are marked by the suffix *-i*.

Though imperatives and prohibitives are morphologically distinct from hortatives, UV and LV imperative morphemes may occur with first person plural inclusive addressees, thus reaching into the hortative domain and expressing more commissive[4] speech acts than standard hortatives. Imperative morphemes may also express greetings (e.g., have a nice day!); on the other hand, canonical wishes are either expressed by hortative/optative voice morphemes or by optative verbs/auxiliaries meaning 'wish'. The cline of directivity is shown in Table 13.2.

Another characteristic feature is that some of these morphological exponents also occur in declarative speech acts and express modalities, as discussed in Section 8.

4 i.e., committing the speaker to having the action performed.

TABLE 13.2 The cline of directivity in Amis

+ **directive**	>		**non-directive**
2nd person addressee	1st person addressees		all persons
canonical imperatives	commissive hortatives with **imperative** UV & LV morphemes	canonical hortatives (hortative/optative morphology)	optatives (hortative/optative morphology)
aka prohibitives	**aka** commissive hortatives or avertive hortatives	gentle negative hortatives with future ***a caay*** stems	

3 The Voice System and Argument Structure

Each voice selects a nominative subject as its preferred syntactic argument (Dixon 1979), and one of two patterns of case-marking, i.e., antipassive-likes and ergative, encoding the roles of A, S and P[5] arguments. In the antipassive-like construction, the nominative subject is case-marked by *k-* and the oblique patient/theme by *t-*; in the ergative construction, the Undergoer subject (or arguments treated as such) is marked by nominative *k-*, while Agents are marked by genitive *n-*. The semantics of the voice affix and the thematic role of the subject must match, e.g., AV *mi-* selects an Actor subject, while UV *ma-* and UV *-en* select an Undergoer subject.

As shown in Table 13.3, restricted to indicative, hortative and imperative moods, the various voices are distributed within the overarching bipartite antipassive-like and ergative argument structures. Negative indicative and prohibitive moods have the same pattern.

AV *mi-* and NAV *ma-* voices (plus the two residual ⟨*um*⟩ and *mu-* voice affixes) have the same antipassive-like encoding with *k-* and *t-* case-marking. All other voices, UV *ma-*, UV *-en*, and LV *-an*, have ergative encoding with *k-* and *n-* case-marking.

The nominative subject (S) of AV and NAV is thus marked differently from the genitive Agent of other voices which have a Patient subject, i.e., UV *ma-*, UV *-en* and LV *-an*. S and P are thus marked as nominative, A (agent) is genitive, and T (theme/patient) is oblique.

5 In typological terms, S stands for the argument of an intransitive verb or a low transitive verb; A stands for the Agent of a transitive verbs; and P for the Patient/ Undergoer of a transitive verb (or applicative arguments treated as P) (Comrie 1978, 2005; Dixon 1979).

TABLE 13.3 Argument structure in indicative, hortative and imperative moods

VOICE	SEMANTIC ROLE OF *k*- nominative SUBJECT	ARGUMENT STRUCTURE	VALENCY
AV *mi-* HORT *mi-...-a* IMP *pi-...-i*	*k*- Actor	ANTIPASSIVE-LIKE S NOM; *k*- T (OBL theme) *t*-	1 or 2 arguments
⟨*um*⟩ HORT ⟨*um*⟩..-*a* IMP *ka*-⟨*um*⟩	*k*-±Actor, experiencer		mostly 1
mu- HORT *mu-...-a* IMP *ka- mu-*	*k*-non-actor, experiencer		1
NAV *ma-* HORT *ma-...-a* IMP *ka-*	*k*- non-actor, experiencer, seat of properties		1 or 2
UV *ma-* HORT *-aw* IMP *-a*	*k*- patient, fully affected	ERGATIVE P NOM; *k*- A GEN agent *n*-	2
UV *-en* HORT & IMP *-en*	*k*- patient, ± fully affected		1 or 2
LV *-an* HORT *-ay* IMP *-i*	*k*- patient, superficially affected & location		1 or 2

The same bipartite argument structure applies to all non-indicative moods; all non-UV and non-LV constructions have the actor or the experiencer as nominative subject; all UV and LV constructions have a nominative Undergoer.

Imperative AV and NAV stems have a second person subject encoding the addressee, while UV and LV imperatives have a Patient subject and a non-subject second person addressee marked as a genitive Agent. As with indicative mood constructions, imperatives thus evidence S and P pivots, a pattern found in various other Austronesian-Oceanic languages such as Bunun (Formosan), Maori and Hawaiian, in which "the Agents of imperatives in Austronesian languages are typically non-subjects" (Starosta, Pawley and Reid 1982 [2009]: 305). So, in Amis, directive moods and imperatives in particular do not evidence any privileged nominative-accusative alignment, but reflect its split alignment system.

3.1 *Elision of Addressees*

The addressees of imperatives (i.e., the nominative S of AV and NAV voices, or the genitive A of UV and LV voices) can be left unexpressed, unless some emphasis is intended. However, their omission is not a distinctive feature of imperatives, unlike in French where second person pronouns are banned in imperatives, e.g., *fais-le!* 'do it!' in contrast with the jussive indicative *tu le fais!* Nor is there any distinction in word order between indicative and non-indicative moods in Amis.

Since referential arguments are most generally dropped in all moods, the elision of the addressee as in (1, 2) is not a compelling test with respect to alignment; elision of the S or A addressee is as frequent and follows discourse and referential triggers.

(1) a. *Pi-'ala-i* *(k-isu)* *t-u* *qelun!*
NFIN-take-IMP.AV NOM-2SG OBL-NM chair
'Take the chair!'

b. *Ala-en* *k-u* *qelun!*
take-IMP.UV NOM-NM chair
'Take the chair!'

(2) *Tengil-i(=isu)* *k-u* *tangic* *n-iyam.*
listen-IMP.LV(=GEN.2SG) NOM-NM cry POSS-1PL.EXCL
'Listen to our weeping!' (polite entreaty to deity)

4 Imperative Mood: The Rationale Underlying Voice Alternations

In the indicative mood, voice alternations are driven by multivariate features, such as (i) verb classes (i.e. denoting activities for AV *mi-* vs. states for NAV *ma-* stems), (ii) telicity, and (iii) degree of patient affectedness and definiteness (Bril forthcoming 2022). In imperative or prohibitive moods, voice alternations express a cline of politeness (with Actor Voice at the lower end, Locative Voice at some intermediate point and Undergoer Voice at the highest point). This is summarised below.

UV >	LV >	AV, NAV
+ polite deities, aged persons	intermediate	- polite children, equals, inferiors

In the indicative, declarative mood, voice alternations do not correlate with politeness; politeness is expressed by attenuative markers or by prosody at sentence level.

In the imperative mood, the more direct, thus less polite, AV imperatives with an Actor subject are addressed to children and equals, while the polite, less direct LV or UV imperatives with patient subjects are addressed to elderly and respected people.

Example (3a) is an AV imperative form with an Actor subject (*k-isu*, possibly elided), an oblique patient and an oblique instrument; (3b) is a gentle order or an invitation expressed in the imperative Locative Voice, and (3c) is a polite imperative with the UV *-en* form. Both UV and LV imperatives have a Patient subject and a non-subject addressee, the genitive Agent, which is optionally expressed (as in (2) above).

(3) a. ***Pi-sulsul-i*** *(k-isu)* *t-ina* *titi* *t-u* *aul!*
NFIN-pierce-IMP.AV NOM-2SG OBL-DEICT meat OBL-NM skewer
'Pierce the meat with the skewer!' (order)

b. *Sulsul-i* *k-ina* *titi* *t-u* *aul!*
pierce-IMP.LV NOM-DEICT meat OBL-NM skewer
'Pierce the meat with the skewer!' (gentle order)

c. *Sulsul-en* *k-ina* *titi* *t-u* *aul!*
pierce-IMP.LV NOM-DEICT meat OBL-NM skewer
'(please) Pierce the meat with the skewer!' (polite command)

4.1 *Distribution of Imperative Forms According to Types of Stems*

Imperatives occur with all types of verb stems. In the declarative sentence in (4), the root *tuku* 'be quiet, motionless, stop' is an ⟨UM⟩ stem, whose argument structure is the same as NAV, and is thus marked by *ka-* in the imperative, as in (4b); its UV imperative form is shown in (4c); the addressees are elided in (4b, c).

(4) a. *T⟨em⟩uku k-u ayam i dipung.*
⟨UM⟩stop NOM-NM bird LOC nest
'The bird is quiet in the nest.'

b. *Ka-t⟨em⟩uku!*
NFIN.IMP-⟨UM⟩stop
'Stop! / Be quiet!' (order to equals)

c. *Tuku-^{w}-a!*
stop-^{EP}-IMP.UV
'Stop!'/'Be quiet!' (lit. let it be stopped) (polite command to respected person)

NAV *ma-* intransitive verbs like *ma-butiq* 'sleep' or *ma-bekac* 'run' have *ka-* imperative forms, e.g., *ka-butiq!* 'go to sleep!', *ka-bekac!* 'run!', or polite UV imperatives, *bekac-en!*[6] 'hurry up!'. The LV imperative also occurs in gentle commands, as in (5).

(5) *Kadat-i=tu! baba-i k-u saba*
come-IMP.LV=PFV carry-IMP.LV NOM-NM younger.sibling
'Come here and carry your younger brother!' (Arikakai.021, Ogawa)

Imperatives are not restricted to active verbs; all types of verb stems, including stative verbs, occur in the imperative mood. Some stative verbs have no voice markers, but are marked by *ka-* in the imperative mood; one such case is Ø-*lipahak* 'happy': Ø-*lipahak k-aku* 'I'm happy' > *ka-lipahak* 'rejoice!'.

Various types of predicates may occur in the imperative mood, e.g., numerals (6), locatives (7) and time words in predicate function. Restrictions only bear on their morphological exponent, restricted to UV *-en* in the case of numerals.

(6) *Cacay-en k-u buhcal-ay a 'ayam!*
one-IMP.UV NOM-NM white-MODF LNK hen
'(take) one white hen!' (lit. let it be one the white hen)

6 UV *-en* is hosted by all types of verbs, i.e., stative, (in)transitive, whose PSA is a patient or an experiencer.

(7) *Ka-itini=tu* *k-isu!*
NFIN.IMP-here=PFV NOM-2SG
'Stay around here!' (Mulecep ci Sawa.004)[7]

Predicative pronouns in the imperative construction are marked by *ka-*; compare (8a) with the self-addressed hortative in the Locative voice in (b).

(8) a. *Ka-amu=tu!*
NFIN.IMP-2PL=PFV
'Let it be you now!' (i.e., it's your turn)

b. *Aku-ʷ-ay=tu!*
1SG-EP-HORT.LV=PFV
'Let it be me!' (let it be my turn to do it!) (Lalagawan.049)

Ditransitive verb stems may choose either the theme/object (T) or the beneficiary (G) as the nominative subject of imperative UV constructions, as in (9a, b):

(9) a. *Pabeli-en* *k-u* *waneng* *itakuwan!*
give-IMP.UV NOM-NM sugar OBL.1SG
'Give the sugar to me!'

b. *Pabeli-en* *k-aku* *t-u* *waneng!*
give-IMP.UV NOM-1SG OBL-NM sugar
'Give me the sugar!' (let me be given the sugar)

Example (c) is a gentler LV *-i* imperative taking the beneficiary as subject.

c. *Pabeli-i* *t-u* *cudad* *k-u* *mi-cudad-ay!*
give-IMP.LV OBL-NM book NOM-NM AV-learn-NMZ
'Give the student a book!'

4.2 *Imperatives in Other Constructions*

Reciprocal and collective constructions are based on NAV *ma-* stems and thus marked by *ka-* in the imperative mood. They also pattern after NAV constructions, with nominative reciprocal Actors and oblique Themes/Patients. Com-

7 These reference the title and line of the story in Toolbox.

pare the reciprocal construction marked by *Ca-* reduplication as *ma-Ca-* in the indicative mood (10a) with the imperative in (10b).

(10) a. *Ma-pa-pabeli k-uhni t-u ni-tamaq-an.*
NAV-Ca-give NOM-3PL OBL-NM PFV.NMZ-hunt.game-OBL
'They gave each other some hunted game.'

b. *Ka-pa-pabeli k-amu t-u ni-tamaq-an!*
IMP.NAV-Ca-give NOM-2PL OBL-NM PFV.NMZ-hunt.game-OBL
'Give each other the hunted game!'

The examples in (11) illustrate the indicative inchoative morpheme *mal(a)-* and its imperative form *kal(a)-*, which also pattern after NAV constructions.

(11) a. *Mal-kakawa k-uhni t-u lusid.*
INCH.NAV-tidy.up NOM-3PL OBL-NM belongings
'They started tidying up (their) things.'

b. *Kal-kakawa k-amu t-u lusid.*
IMP.INCH.NAV-tidy.up NOM-2PL OBL-NM belongings
'Start tidying up your belongings!'

4.3 *Imperatives in Clefted Constructions*

Clefted constructions occur in indicative and non-indicative moods. In such constructions, the clefted NP is predicative and contains the new information, while the presupposition is expressed by a subordinate clause, either a relative clause or a complement clause. If the clefted predicative NP is a core argument, it triggers a headless relative clause marked by the nominative marker *k-u* as in (12); if the clefted NP is a non-core argument or an adjunct, it triggers an [*a* COMP] clause, as in (13b).

Clefted NPs are predicative and may host the perfective clitic *=tu*. In the imperative mood, clefted NPs pattern after stative stems and are marked by *ka-* as in (12, 13).

(12) [*Ka-u daqulaw=tu*] *k-u ni-sa-qunuc!*
NFIN.IMP-NM ivory.wood=PFV NOM-NM PFV.NMZ-INST-carrying.pole
'Let your carrying-pole be made of ivory wood!' (lit. let it be ivory wood that's used as carrying-pole) (u patay ni Calaw Ilikic.071)

Compare the indicative clause in (13a) with the imperative in (13b), in which a non-core oblique argument marked by the locative *i* is clefted with an *a* COMP clause and a finite verb stem.

(13) a.

A	*mi-palita*	*i*	*c(i)*	*ina-an*	*n-i*	*Dihang!*
FUT	AV-ask	LOC	PM	mother-OBL	GEN-PM	Dihang

'(s)he will ask Dihang's mother.'

b.

[Ka-i	*c(i)*	*ina-an*	*n-i*	*Dihang]*	*a*	*mi-palita!*
NFIN.IMP-LOC	PM	mother-OBL	GEN-PM	Dihang	COMP	AV-ask

'Ask Dihang's MOTHER! (lit. let it be Dihang's mother whom he'll ask)
ka-i c(i) ina-an is pronounced [kaj ɕinaʔan]

Clefted locative nominal predicates also occur in the imperative mood, sometimes triggering complex verb constructions with *a* COMP clauses, as in (14a, b). Compare these with the respective indicative constructions.

(14) a.

Ka-i	*sapad*	*a*	*k⟨em⟩an!*
NFIN.IMP-LOC	table	COMP	⟨UM⟩eat

'(sit) AT THE TABLE to eat.'

vs.

K⟨em⟩an	*cira*	*i*	*sapad.*
⟨UM⟩eat	NOM.3SG	LOC	table

'He eats at the table.'

b.

Ka-i	*likul*	*a*	*t⟨em⟩ireng!*
NFIN.IMP-LOC	back	COMP	⟨UM⟩stand

'Stand BEHIND!'

vs.

T⟨em⟩ireng	*cira*	*i*	*likul.*
⟨UM⟩stand	NOM.3SG	LOC	back

'He stands behind.'

5 Imperatives: Semantic Range

The voice alternations in the imperative mood (AV/NAV, UV, LV) have been shown to correlate with politeness and respect, with intermediate LV imperative forms. This section focuses on the semantics of imperatives and hortatives.

As already mentioned, although there are dedicated forms for imperative and hortative moods, some imperative forms occur with first person plural inclusive addressees, thus reaching into the hortative domain, expressing a more directive type of exhortation than canonical hortatives.

5.1 *UV Imperative* -en*: Imperative and Hortative Usages*

UV *-en* has two specific properties; it occurs in all moods, indicative, imperative and hortative/optative, and the addressee (i.e., the genitive agent) must be human and in control of the event. On the other hand, UV *ma-* is restricted to the indicative mood and has distinct forms in the imperative (*-a*) and the hortative (*-aw*).

Since UV *-en* is not a dedicated marker of imperative mood, its indicative and imperative usages are distinguished by prosody and context. Without context and prosody, example (15) may have indicative and imperative readings.

(15) *Lalu-(e)n(=tu) k-u panay (!)*
soak-IMP.UV(=PFV) NOM-NM rice
'Soak the rice!' (or:) 'The rice is soaked.'

UV *-en* has a wide range of meanings. Some contexts favour the imperative reading, like (16), which is uttered as a series of instructions delivered by a deity to a follower, in this case, to take his gall and put it into the sea to make it blue and salty.

(16) *Ala-en k-u besi numaku!*
take-IMP.UV NOM-NM gall GEN.1SG
'Take my gall!' (lit. let my gall be taken) (Maciwciw.086)

UV *-en* also occurs with first person plural addressees, thus with hortative reading as in (17). In (18), due to the future/prospective marker *a*, the reading of UV *-en* may be hortative or declarative depending on context and prosody; the declarative reading implies some strong commitment to the projected action.

(17) *Tangic-en=ita!*
cry-IMP.UV=GEN.1PL.INCL
'Let's implore (him)!' (prayer)

(18) *A bulaw-en=tu=ita k-ira Arikakay* (*!*)
FUT chase-IMP.UV=PFV=GEN.1PL.INCL NOM-NM Arikakay
'Let's chase this Arikakay away!' (Or:) 'We shall chase this Arikakay away.' (Arikakai.064, Ogawa)

5.2 *UV Imperative -a, Imperative and Hortative Usages*

Declarative UV *ma-* has an imperative form *-a* and a hortative form *-aw*. Imperative UV *-a* expresses polite invitations, permissions and commands.

(19) *Kaen-a k-ina buting!*
eat-IMP.UV NOM-DEICT fish
'Eat that fish!' (polite invitation, allowing to eat)

As with UV *-en*, UV imperative *-a* may occur with first person plural inclusive pronouns and a commissive hortative reading (20).

(20) *Sangaq-a=ita=may k-u tataak-ay a*
make-IMP.UV=GEN.1PL.INCL=ATTEN NOM-NM big-MODF LNK
pa-pulul-an.
Ca-cage-LOC
'Let's make a big cage!' (U tumay.030)

5.3 *LV Imperative -i, Imperative and Hortative Usages*

With LV *-an*, whose imperative form is *-i*, the nominative subject is a location or a superficially affected patient. LV *-i* imperatives, as in (21, 22), express gentle, polite commands concerning actions on non-fully affected patients.

(21) *Kalat-i k-u tangila numaku haw!*
bite-IMP.LV NOM-NM ear GEN.1SG DISC
'Seize my ear (between your teeth)!' (Maciwciw.066)

(22) *Tada absaq k-ina kabi, tungal-i aca t-u cila!*
too bland NOM-NM soup add-IMP.LV again OBL-NM salt
'This soup has no taste—add some more salt!'

The LV imperative *-i* also occurs with first person inclusive plural addressees and a commissive hortative reading, as in (23a); compare with the imperative UV *-en* in (23b).

(23) a. *Palal-**i**=tu=ita* *k-u* *wawa!*
awaken-IMP.**LV**=PFV=GEN.1PL.INCL NOM-NM child
'Let's wake up the children!'

b. *Palal-**en**=tu* *k-u* *wawa!*
give-IMP.**UV**=PFV NOM-NM child
'Wake up the children!'

The hortative reading of imperatives with first person plural inclusive pronouns, be they UV *-en*, UV *-a* or LV *-i*, are more commissive than a standard hortative, but less commanding than a standard imperative.

There are semantic differences between imperatives in UV *-en* and LV *-i*. While UV *-en* imperatives must have human addressees in control of the projected event, those in LV *-i* are neutral for animacy and control.

(24) *"Pacuk-en* *k-ira* *babuy!"* *—"hay!"* *sa-an* *k-u* *selal.*
kill-IMP.UV NOM-DEICT pig agreed say-LV NOM-NM age.group
'"Kill that pig!"—"All right!" the age group said.' (kalalaisan nu Ciwidian. 197)

5.4 *The Semantic Range of Imperative Voices*

Imperative forms often express other types of speech acts than commands (Aikhenvald 2012: 234), such as imprecations, admonitions, entreaties, invitations and phatic speech acts with illocutionary force. Example (25a) with an AV imperative is an admonitive, cautionary speech act addressed to equals or children; (25b) is a polite imperative in LV *-i*, calling for the addressee's attention and taking *cidal* 'sun' as its subject.

(25) a. *Pi-araw-i!*
NFIN-look-IMP.**AV**
'Watch out!'

b. *Melaw-i* *saw* *k-u* *cidal!*
watch-IMP.**LV** DISC NOM-NM sun
'Look at the sun!' (phatic, attracting attention)

Some imperative or prohibitive forms are supplicative pleas, as in (26) with LV *-i*.

(26) a. *Padang-i k-aku!*
help-IMP.LV NOM-1SG
'Help me (please)!'

b. *Aka'a patay-i k-aku!*
PROH.LENGTH kill-IMP.LV NOM-1SG
'*Don't* kill me!'

Some imperatives serve as guidance instructions; context and prosody allowing, they may also have a deontic declarative reading, as in (27b).

(27) a. *Icuwa k-u lumaq=isu?*
where NOM-NM house=GEN.2SG
'Where's your house?'

b. *Lakuit-en k-iya ciris tala i lumaq=aku.*
cross-IMP.UV NOM-DEICT river go LOC house=GEN.1SG
'Cross this river to go to my house.' (or:) 'You must/need to cross this river to go to my house.'

Cautionary commands such as the following with the LV *-i* imperative may be given assertive force by means of additional discourse markers, like *saw*, e.g., *melaw-i saw!* 'do watch out!' (Kakunas.044), or may be softened with attenuative *may*, as in *melaw-i may!* '(go) see!' (Masababainayay.013).

Phatic speech acts, such as greetings, blessings, curses, warnings, pleas and requests, can be expressed by imperative constructions. The imperative form *ka-lipahak* expresses a greeting (28), while the imperative LV *-i* in (29) expresses a plea.

(28) *Ka-lipahak t-u baluh-ay a mihca-an!*
NFIN.IMP-happy OBL-NM new-MODF LNK year-OBL
'Happy new year!' (lit. enjoy the new year)

(29) *Tengil-i=isu k-u tangic n-iyam.*
listen-IMP.LV=GEN.2S NOM-NM cry POSS-1PL.EXCL
'Listen to our weeping!' (polite entreaty to deity)

Thus, in some of their usage, imperative forms express illocutionary force and they express the speaker's commitment when used with first person plural addressees.

Phatic speech acts are also commonly expressed with the verb *han* 'do so' in complex verb constructions, e.g., *tuku han!* 'keep still!', possibly hosting the perfective clitic =*tu*; e.g., *na'un han=tu!* 'do be careful!'. Constructions with *han* pattern after UV verbs, as shown in (30a, c), i.e., with a patient subject. Compare these with the imperative LV form in (30b), which also denotes a strong entreaty aiming at getting the addressee to act according to the speaker's wishes.

(30) a. *Padang han=tu k-aku!*
help do.so=PFV NOM-1SG
'Do help me!'

b. *Padang-i k-aku!*
help-IMP.LV NOM-1SG
'Help me!' (Raraq.042)

c. *Ka'en han=tu n-amu k-ira dungec!*
eat do.so=PFV GEN-2PL NOM-DEICT rattan.heart
'Do eat your rattan hearts!' (kalalaisan nu Ciwidian.158)

6 Prohibitive, Negative Injunctions with *aka*

Prohibitive or negative injunctions and exhortations are marked by the auxiliary *aka* and a non-finite verb stem also displaying some voice alternation (AV, NAV, UV, LV). Just as in the imperative mood, voice alternations in the prohibitive mood denote a cline of politeness.

With AV and NAV, the auxiliary *aka* commands the dependent, non-finite *pi-* stems (for AV *mi-*) and *ka-* (for NAV *ma-* stems, as in (31a)); in the case of ⟨*um*⟩ and *mu-* stems, *ka-* appears in addition to the ⟨*um*⟩ and *mu-* forms, e.g., *aka ka-t⟨em⟩angic* 'don't cry!', and (31b). *Aka* can be made emphatic by lengthening to *aka'a*, as in (31b); it may host the perfective clitic =*tu* as in (32). Compare the declarative construction *ma-cinglaw k-uhni* 'they make noise, be noisy' with the prohibitive (31a).

(31) a. *Aka* *ka-cinglaw* *k-amu* *'amin!*
PROH NFIN.NAV-noisy NOM-2PL all
'Don't be noisy all of you!'

b. *Aka'a* *ka-mu-ciriw* *k-u* *rakat!*
PROH.LENGTH NFIN-MU-err NOM-NM walk
'Don't take the wrong way!' (lit. don't let your walk err)

(32) *Aka=tu* *ka-sa-suwal* *k-amu* *'amin!*
PROH=PFV NFIN-Ca-speak NOM-2PL all
'Don't chatter away with each other all of you!'

The prohibitive forms of UV *ma-*, UV *-en* and LV *-an* stems are neutralised as the prohibitive *aka* stem *-i*, as shown in (33b).

(33) a. *Pa-cumud-en* *k-u* *sapad!*
CAUS-enter-IMP.UV NOM-NM table
'Bring the table in!'

b. *Aka'a* *pa-cumud-i* *k-u* *sapad!*
PROH.LENGTH CAUS-enter-IMP.LV NOM-NM table
'Don't bring the table in!'

As with imperatives, prohibitive constructions may have commissive-hortative use, as shown by the following excerpt from a narrative about the rituals of age groups and coming of age. Examples (34a–b) allow a prohibitive reading or a commissive-hortative reading, due to the first person plural possessive *numita* in (34a), which may also be unexpressed, as in (34b).

(34) a. *Aka'a* *haw* *ka-pawan* *t-uinian* *u* *tada* *tu'as*
PROH.LENGTH DISC NFIN-forget OBL-DEICT NM true ancestor
n-umita.
GEN-1PL.INCL
'Don't forget these genuine rituals of our ancestors!' (or:) 'Do let's not forget these genuine rituals of our ancestors!' (Age groups.285)

b. *Aka'a* *pa-lasawad-i!*
PROH.LENGTH CAUS-abandon-IMP.LV
'Don't abandon them!' (or:)
'Do let's not abandon them!' (lit. let them not be abandoned) (Age groups.286)

7 Hortative/Optative

By contrast with imperative AV and NAV stems, hortative/optative AV and NAV stems are based on finite, indicative stems together with the suffix *-a*, thus occurring as AV *mi-…-a* stems, NAV *ma-…-a* stems, ⟨*em*⟩*…-a* stems and *mu-…-a* stems. UV *ma-* and LV *-an* hortative stems have distinct forms, hortative UV *-a*(*w*) and LV *-ay* respectively.

The canonical hortative voice is restricted to first person singular or first person plural inclusive or exclusive pronouns, which occur as nominative subjects in AV and NAV constructions and as genitive agents in UV and LV constructions.

Hortative mood generally correlates with clusivity, i.e., including the speaker in the projected state of affairs or as a self-addressed injunction.

7.1 *The Rationale Behind Voice Alternations in Hortative Mood*

AV and NAV hortative forms with first person plural inclusive subject pronouns tend to aim at the immediate achievement of the speech act, and thus tend to be more directly performative, the central relationship being between the Actor and the action, as in (35a–c), while UV and LV hortatives with Patient subjects tend to urge for some desired potential course of action with varying degrees of immediacy and illocutionary force.

(35) a. *M-aruq-a* *k-ita!* (vs. imperative *ka-maruq!* 'sit down!')
NAV-sit-HORT NOM-1PL.INCL
'Let's sit!'

b. *Ma-keru*[8]*-w-a* *hen* *k-ita!*
NAV-dance-EP-HORT still NOM-1PL.INCL
'Let's dance!'

c. *Mi-kilim-a* *saw* *k-ita* *t-u* *saka-ramud.*
AV-search-HORT DISC NOM-1PL.INCL OBL-NM PURP-marry
'Do let's find someone to marry.' (u patay ni Calaw Ilikic.084)

In UV and LV voices, the hortative/optative morphemes are UV *-aw* and LV *-ay*. In (36), the first hortative form is an AV *mi-…-a* (*mi-taneng-a*); the second is a UV hortative *-aw* (*cekeruh-aw*). The AV hortative *mi-taneng-a*, with a first per-

8 *Keru* 'dance' is a *ma-* stem (not a **mi-* stem).

son plural inclusive Actor subject, urges for the immediate performance of the action, while the UV hortative *cekeruh-aw*, with a Patient subject and genitive agent, suggests some potential course of action, possibly expecting some agreement, as in 'let's … shall we?'.

(36) *Mi-taneng-a k-ita t-u kilmel,*
AV-try-HORT NOM-1PL.INCL OBL-NM power
'Let's measure up our power,

cekeruh-aw=ita k-u bekeloh!
push-HORT.UV=GEN.1PL.INCL NOM-NM rock
how about us pushing a rock!' (Masababainayay.073)

In contrast with imperatives, voice alternations in the hortative mood do not correlate with politeness, as shown in (36), in which the two clauses have the same addressees. Rather, as in indicative voice constructions, they select the Actor (in AV) or Patient (in UV, LV) as the salient subject, and this has semantic undertones: AV hortatives tend to be more performative, while UV hortatives are more indirect, potential and suggestive speech acts.

7.2 *Hortatives vs. Imperatives*

All UV and LV constructions, irrespective of mood, have an Undergoer subject and a genitive agent, as shown in (37). Compare the UV *-aw* hortative (37a), which denotes a polite invitation, with the UV *-a* imperative (37b) used with the first person inclusive plural pronoun, which constitutes a more commissive hortative.

(37) a. *Ka'en-aw=(num)ita*[9] *k-u sinabel!*
eat-HORT.UV=GEN.1PL.INCL NOM-NM dish
'Let's eat the dish!' (shall we?)

b. *Ka'en-a=(num)ita k-u sinabel!*
eat-IMP.UV=GEN.1PL.INCL NOM-NM dish
'Let's eat the dish!'

9 The form *numita* is considered more correct, but in common language, speakers use the short form *=ita*.

7.3 *Hortative/Optative* UV *-aw*

Hortative/optative UV *-aw* urges for some desired and potential course of action, possibly expecting agreement from the addressee. Some of these hortatives may be self-addressed, as in (38).

(38) *Nanum-aw=aku!*
drink.water-HORT.UV=GEN.1SG
'Let me drink it!' (lit. let it be drunk by me)

(39) *Sa-lipahak-aw numita!*
do-happy-HORT.UV GEN.1PL.INCL
'Let's enjoy it!' (lit. let it be enjoyed by us)

In (40), the UV hortative *-aw* has a second person addressee subject (*k-isu*) and a first person singular agent utterer and controller of the help extended.

(40) *Padang-aw=tu (num)aku (kisu) a mi-ala!*
help-HORT.UV=PFV GEN.1SG 2SG COMP AV-take
'Let me help (you) take it back!' (lit. let you be helped by me) (Tatakulaq atu Hungti.040)

In the following excerpt, *ingir-i* in (41a) is an LV imperative, followed in (41b) by a self-exhortation with the UV hortative *tengil-aw*, in which the unexpressed patient subject is the object sitting in the pot, and the utterer/experiencer is the first person genitive agent.

(41) a. *Ingir-i k-u tangila n-umisu pasayra i dangah*
lean-IMP.LV NOM-NM ear GEN-2SG toward LOC pot
a mi-tengil!
COMP AV-listen
'Lean your ear towards the pot to listen!' (U nipiketun ni Hayan.0079)

b. *Damay, tengil-aw n-umaku!*
all.right listen-HORT.UV GEN-1SG
'All right, let me listen!' (lit. let it be heard by me) (U nipiketun ni Hayan.0081)

Vocative *-aw*: On nouns, *-aw* is also a vocative marker, e.g., *ama-aw!* 'o father!', *Dungi-aw*! 'o Dungi!'.

7.4 *Hortative* LV *-ay*

LV *-ay* is the hortative counterpart of the indicative LV *-an* construction. Hortative LV *-ay* is used to soften demands or make suggestions like "how about …?", "let's … shall we?". As with indicative LV *-an*, the subject is a location or a superficially affected patient, for instance with perception verbs, or verbs of attempt like 'try'. The genitive agent addressee can be expressed, as in (42a), or not, as in (b), depending on referentiality or saliency.

(42) a. *Anu ma-haen, kilim-ay=tu=niyam!*
if NAV-be.so search-HORT.LV=PFV=GEN.1PL.EXCL
'If that's so, let's look for it!' (lit. let it be looked by us) (kalalaisan nu Ciwidian.031)

b. *Melaw-ay aca ma k-u liyut n-ina pala!*
see-HORT.LV again DISC NOM-NM surrounding GEN-DEICT area
'Let's look again around this area.' (lit. let the surroundings be looked at (by us)) (u patay ni Calaw Ilikic.054) (*ma* is an attenuative, persuasive marker)

LV *-ay* has hortative and optative readings, possibly self-addressed as in (43a, b), or as a way of announcing one's intentions and getting approval, as in (44).

(43) a. *"Melaw-ay=aku k-ira wawa!" sa=tu k-u*
see-HORT.LV=GEN.1SG NOM-DEICT child say=PFV NOM-NM
ina.
mother
'"Let me have a look at that child!" the mother said.'

b. *Cucu-ʷ-ay hen aca k-ira wawa!*
breast.feed-ʷ-HORT.LV still again NOM-DEICT child
'Let (me) feed this child once again.' (or:) '(I'm) going to breast-feed this child once again!' (Ogawa, Arakakai.015)

(44) *Hay! taneng-ay numaku!*
yes try-HORT.LV GEN.1SG
'Yes! let me try!' (kalalaisan nu Ciwidian.125)

7.5 *Negative Hortative*

Negative exhortation or invitation is marked by the negative indicative mood auxiliary *caay* and the future marker *a*, as in (45a). Context and prosody allowing, example (45a) may read as a negative hortative or as a negative declarative clause; compare it with the prohibitive *aka* in (45b).

(45) a. *A caay k-ita pi-cumud i lalabu n-u*
FUT NEG NOM-1PL.INCL NFIN-enter LOC inside GEN-NM
lumaq (*!*)
house
'Let's not enter the house!' (or:) 'We won't enter the house.'

b. *Aka'a pi-cumud i lalabu n-u lumaq!*
PROH.LENGTH NFIN-enter LOC inside GEN-NM house
'Don't enter the house!'

Just as UV and LV imperatives may express commissive hortative speech acts with first person pronouns, so may prohibitive *aka*, as shown in (46c), which is a commissive, emphatic exhortation. The hortative context is set by the first person plural inclusive *=ita* in (46a), *a tala-cuwa-en=ita?* 'where shall we go?'. In (46b), the pronoun is elided since it is referential and retrievable, but it may be expressed for emphasis, as in (46b').

(46) a. *Suwal sa ci Tipus "A tala-cuwa-en=ita a mi-limek?"*
say do PM Tipus FUT go-where-UV=1PL.INCL COMP AV-hide
'Tipus says: "Where are we going to hide?"' (Mi-laliw.014)

b. *"Mi-limek-a i sasa n-u ka-ka-butiq-an."*
AV-hide-HORT LOC under GEN-NM Ca-NFIN-sleep-LOC
'Let's hide under the bed!' (Mi-laliw.015)

b'. *"Mi-limek-a k-ita i sasa"...*
AV-hide-HORT NOM-1PL.INCL LOC under
'Let's hide under (the bed)!'

c. *"Aka'a ka-i-sasa n-u ka-ka-butiq-an*
PROH.LENGTH NFIN-LOC-under GEN-NM Ca-NFIN-sleep-LOC
a mi-limek! tada puqner!"
COMP AV-hide too short
'Don't let's hide under the bed, it's too short!' (Mi-laliw.016–017) (lit. let it not be under the bed that (we) hide!)

In the context of (46c), with the speaker involved in the event, the reading is that of a negative commissive exhortation, not a prohibitive. The negative commissive hortative is similarly marked by the auxiliary *aka* and the hortative suffix *-aw* in (47).

(47) *Aka-aw* *ka-pawan!*
PROH-HORT.UV NFIN-forget
'Let's not forget!' (Age groups.285)

8 Directive Mood vs. Modalised Declarative Propositions

As shown in Table 13.4, some of the morphemes expressing imperative and hortative moods also occur in modalised declarative contexts, expressing deontic, permissive modalities for the former, and admonitive, apprehensive, avertive modalities and epistemic and potential modalities for the latter.

8.1 *Hortatives vs. Modalised Declarative Constructions*

The hortative voice alternations, AV *mi-...-a*, NAV *ma-...-a*, *mu-...-a*, UV *-a(w)*, UV *-en* and LV *-ay*, may occur in modalised declarative constructions, only differing in the type of pronouns and the illocutionary force.

In their hortative/optative use, as in modalised declarative contexts, these morphemes express uncertainty, potential, epistemic modality, and other specific meanings.

8.1.1 AV or NAV Hortative and Modalised Declarative Constructions

Hortatives in AV or NAV forms are based on indicative/finite verb stems; these same forms also occur in modalised declarative contexts, with non-first person plural addressees, with admonitive, apprehensive or avertive shades of meanings, or with epistemic, potential meanings. In (48), *mu-ciriw-a* is a speech act aiming at averting some malefactive event.

(48) *Pi-sinanut-i!* *mu-ciriw-a* *k-u* *rakat=isu!*
NFIN-pay.attention-IMP.AV NAV-err-POT NOM-NM walk-GEN.1SG
'Pay attention! you might take the wrong way!' (or:)
'Pay attention! you might get lost.' (lit. your walk might err)

Negative avertive and deontic modalities are marked by *aka* together with the non-finite hortative/optative suffix *-a*, as in (49).

(49) *Aka'a* *ka-ramud-a* *t-ina* *tamdaw.*
PROH.LENGTH NFIN-marry-OPT OBL-DEICT person
'You shouldn't marry this person!' (Cabay aku.00017)

TABLE 13.4 Voice and mood morphemes in directive vs. modalised declarative contexts

	AV	**NAV**	**⟨UM⟩**	**MU-**	**UV**	**UV**	**LV**
Indicative forms	*mi-*	*ma-*	*⟨em⟩*	*mu-*	*ma-*	*-en*	*-an*
Hortative forms **& modalised declarative** contexts:	*mi-...-a*	*ma-...-a*	*⟨em⟩...-a*	*mu-...-a*	*-a(w)*	*-en*	*-ay*
	-----	-----	---------	-------	-------	------	-----
—avertive	x	x	x	x			-
—admonitive	x	x	x	x	x	x	x
—apprehensive	x	x	x	x	x		x
—epistemic	x	x	x	x	x		x
—potential	x	x	x	x	x		x
							x
Imperative forms & **deontic declarative** contexts					*-a*	*-en*	*-i*

8.1.2 UV *-aw* in Hortative and Modalised Declarative Contexts

UV *-aw* occurs both in the hortative mood and in modalised declarative contexts, such as (50), with an apprehensive, avertive reading, also expressing uncertainty and epistemic modality.

(50) *Patay-aw k-amu anu awa k-u lisin!*
die-EPIST.UV NOM-2PL if NEG.EXS NOM-NM ritual
'You might be dead if there are no rites!'

8.1.3 LV *-ay* in Hortative and Modalised Declarative Contexts

LV *-ay* may have either hortative, deontic or epistemic readings varying with context, prosody and illocutionary force, as in (51).

(51) *Risar-ay hen k-ira tumay* (*!*)
reduce-HORT.LV still NOM-DEICT bear
'Let's reduce these bears in numbers!' (or:)
'These bears should be reduced in number' (U tumay.029)

The verb *laliw-ay* in (52) has an avertive, timerative reading; its subject *k-isu* denotes a superficially affected patient.

(52) *Bekac-en, laliw-ay n-u kisya k-isu.*
run-IMP.UV leave-MOD.LV GEN-NM train NOM-2SG
'Run! or you will miss the train!' (lit. run or you will be left by the train)

8.2 *Imperatives vs. Modalised Declarative Constructions*

UV *-en* with a second person plural addressee has a polite imperative reading or a deontic, prescriptive reading, as in (53), varying with prosody and illocutionary force.

(53) *Ulah-en=namu k-u ina n-amu (!)*
speak-IMP.UV=GEN.2PL NOM-NM mother GEN-2PL
'Love your mother!' (or:) 'You must love your mother!' (U lisin.055)

Contexts like (54) favour an optative reading or a deontic, prescriptive reading, varying in the same features.

(54) *Suwal-en k-u suwal n-u Pangcah (!)*
speak-IMP.UV NOM-NM language GEN-NM Amis
'Let the Amis language be spoken!' (or:) 'The Amis language must be spoken.'

In (55), UV *-a* has a phatic and deontic meaning.

(55) *Suwal-a han k-isu.*
speak-IMP.UV do.so NOM-2SG
'Do allow (me) to tell you!' (lit. let you be told (by me)) (Luke 22: 33)

Imperative LV *-i* also occurs in declarative contexts like (56) with deontic meaning.

(56) *Yu ma-tiya, tengil-i k-u suwal n-u*
when NAV-be.thus listen-DEONT.LV NOM-NM speech GEN-NM
ma-tu'as-ay
NAV-old-NMZ
'At that time, the words of the old people must be listened to!' (wawa nu Ciwidian.083)

Emphatic commands and strong deontic modality referring to rules are marked by the double negative expression *aka kanca'*, containing the negative adverb *kanca'*. The expression *aka kanca'* in (57) favours a deontic, prescriptive reading because of its non-specific or impersonal, elided addressees. Since there is no potential performer or controller to perform the directive speech act, an imperative reading is disfavoured.

(57) a. *Aka kanca' pi-tengil t-u suwal n-u*
PROH NEG.ADV NFIN-hear OBL-NM speech GEN-NM
ma-tu'as-ay!
NAV-be.old-NMZ
'One must listen to the words of the old people!'

b. *Aka kanca' ka-tayni i pi-lisin-an!*
PROH NEG.ADV NFIN-come LOC NFIN-celebrate-NMZ
'One must absolutely come to the festival!'

The other expression with *caay kanca'* (meaning approximately 'no doubt not') also has deontic meaning.

(58) *Caay kanca' pulul-i!*
NEG NEG.ADV prison-DEONT.LV
'For sure (you) must be sent to prison!' (Malasang Ciyaw.077)

The functions of the voice affixes in imperative, hortative speech acts and in modalised declarative propositions lead to the question of their origin.

9 Some Diachronic Considerations on Mood Morphology

Imperative forms in Amis roughly reflect the Proto-Austronesian (PAN) system reconstructed by Wolff (1973: 73) as shown in Table 13.5.

Table 13.6 shows the reconstructed PAN affixes in independent/ indicative moods and in dependent/non-indicative moods, based on Wolff (1973), Starosta, Pawley and Reid [SPR] (1982), Ross (2009) and Blust and Chen (2017). The main divergence between their analyses lies in the function of some of these voice affixes; UV *-en and LV *-an are reconstructed as indicative by Wolff (1973), but Ross (2009) analyses them as nominalisers which were reanalysed as indicative voice markers at a later stage, while Blust and Chen (2017) state that they had both functions originally.

TABLE 13.5 The Proto-Austronesian and the Amis systems compared

PAN	indicative	imperative	AMIS	indicative	hortative	imperative
AV	*⟨um⟩	Ø	AV	*⟨em⟩√*	*⟨em⟩√-a*	*ka-⟨em⟩√*
UV	*-en	*-a	UV	*√-en*	*√-en*	*√-en*
				ma-√	*√-a(w)*	*√-a*
LV	*-an	*-i	LV	*√-an*	*√-ay*	*√-i*

TABLE 13.6 Reconstructed PAN indicative and non-indicative voice forms

	AV	UV	LV
Indicative (Wolff 1973)	*⟨um⟩	*√–en	*√–an
Nominalisers (Ross 2009)		*√–en	*√–an
Dependent, subjunctive (Wolff 1973)		*√-a	*√-(a)i
(Ross 2009)	*⟨um⟩	*√-a	*√-i
Optative, hortative (Ross 2009, Blust and Chen 2017)	*⟨um⟩-√-a	*√-a-w	*√-a-y
Imperative (Ross 2009)	*√	*√-u/-i (?)	*√-i
(Blust and Chen 2017)		*√-u/-i	

In N. Amis indicative mood, the voice affixes are fairly conservative; the ⟨*um*⟩ forms are now residual and are replaced by AV *mi-* and NAV *ma-*. UV *ma-* is also innovated in N. Amis and exists side by side with UV *-en*. The hortative and imperative forms are fairly conservative: imperative UV *-a* and LV *-i* appear to originate from the reconstructed dependent, subjunctive forms. It is cross-linguistically common for imperatives to be marked by non-finite forms, infinitives or subjunctives. On the other hand, AV *pi-…-i* and NAV *ka-* imperatives are innovated in Amis.

Starosta, Pawley and Reid [SPR] (1982) also believe that Patient-subject imperatives were a feature of the ergative proto-language and point out that traces of this system are found in Seediq (Formosan) and Amis, marked by reflexes of the original derivational suffixes *-i and *-a. SPR (1982 [2009]: 324) cite Dahl (1973: 120) on the use of an imperative-optative AV affix *-a* in Malagasy, and point out that PAN *-*a* is found in many languages with optative and subjunctive meanings.

10 Conclusion

With respect to their range of usage, canonical imperatives and prohibitives have second person addressees; in N. Amis, they also occur with first person addressees as more commissive hortatives than the dedicated and canonical hortative constructions. Voice alternations in imperative and prohibitive constructions express degrees of politeness.

Hortative/optative constructions are restricted to first person addressees, which may be elided if contextually referential. Voice alternations in hortative/optative constructions have different readings: AV and NAV hortative constructions, with subject addressees, aim at the immediate performance of the action, while UV and LV hortatives, with patient subjects and non-subject addressees, are less direct and aim at more potential actions.

It is also noteworthy that some of the morphemes expressing imperative and hortative speech acts also occur in modalised declarative contexts with deontic and permissive modalities as the declarative counterpart of imperatives, while admonitive, avertive and apprehensive modalities, as well as epistemic and potential modalities, are the declarative counterpart of hortatives.

Acknowledgements

This is a contribution in honour of Alexandra Aikhenvald's inspiring work on the topic of imperatives, among so many others.

This research is supported by the LACITO-CNRS and financed by the research strand 3 "Typology and dynamics of linguistic systems" of the Labex EFL (Empirical Foundations of Linguistics) (Investissements d'Avenir, ANR-10-LABX-0083/CGI). It is part of IdEx Paris University (ANR-18-IDEX-0001).

Abbreviations

ABILT	abilitative	CAUS	causative
ATTEN	attenuative	COLL	collective
AV	actor voice	COMP	complementiser
CA.RDP	Ca-reduplication	COS	change of state

CV	conveyance voice	MOD	modality
DEICT	deictic	MODF	modifier
DEONT	deontic	NAV	non-actor voice
DISC	discourse	NEG	negation
EP	epenthetic	NFIN	non-finite
EPIST	epistemic	NOM	nominative
EXCL	exclusive	NM	noun marker
EXS	existential	NMZ	nominaliser
FUT	future	OBL	oblique
GEN	genitive	PM	personal marker
HORT	hortative	POT	potential
IMP	imperative	PFV	perfective
IMP.NAV	imperative non-actor voice	PM	person marker
INCH	inchoative	POSS	possessive
INCL	inclusive	PREP	preposition
INST	instrumental	PROH	prohibitive
IRR	irrealis	PURP	purpose
LENGTH	lengthening	RDP	reduplication
LNK	linker	TIMER	timerative
LOC	locative	TPC	topic
LV	locative voice	UV	undergoer voice

References

Aikhenvald, Alexandra (2010). *Imperatives and commands*. (Oxford Studies in Typology & Linguistic Theory). Oxford: O.U.P.

Blust, Robert and Victoria Chen (2017). The pitfalls of negative evidence: 'Nuclear Austronesian', 'Ergative Austronesian', and their progeny. *Language and Linguistics* 18 (4): 577–621.

Bril, Isabelle (2016). Information Structure in Northern Amis (Formosan): a morpho-syntactic analysis. *Oceanic linguistics* 55 (2): 451–481.

Bril, Isabelle (2017). Roots and stems: lexical and functional flexibility in Amis and Nêlêmwa. In Eva van Lier (ed.), *Studies in Language. Special issue on lexical flexibility in Oceanic languages*, 41 (1): 358–407.

Bril, Isabelle (forthcoming 2022). Lexical restrictions on grammatical relations in voice constructions (Northern Amis). In Eva van Lier and Maria Messerschmidt (Eds.) Lexical restrictions on grammatical relations in voice and valency constructions. STUF Language Typology and Universals, 75:1, 21–73.

Comrie, Bernard (1978). Ergativity. In Winfred P. Lehmann (ed.), *Syntactic typology: Studies in the phenomenology of language*, 329–394. Austin: University of Texas Press.

Comrie, Bernard (2005). Alignment of case marking. In Martin Haspelmath, Matthew S. Dryer, David Gil and Bernard Comrie (eds.), *The World Atlas of Language Structures*, 398–405. Oxford: Oxford University Press.

Dahl, Otto Christian (1973). *Proto-Austronesian*. (Scandinavian Institute of Asian Studies Monograph Series, No. 15.) Lund: Studentlitteratur.

Dixon, R.M.W. (1979). Ergativity. *Language* 55: 59–138.

Ross, Malcolm (2009). Proto Austronesian verbal morphology: a reappraisal. In Alexander Adelaar and Andrew Pawley (eds.), *Austronesian Historical Linguistics and Culture History: A Festschrift for Robert Blust*, 295–326. Canberra: Pacific Linguistics.

Searle, John R. (1969). *Speech Acts. An Essay in the Philosophy of Language*. Cambridge: Cambridge University Press.

Starosta, Stanley, Andrew Pawley and Lawrence A. Reid (1982 [2009]). The evolution of focus in Austronesian. *Papers from the Third International Conference on Austronesian Linguistics*, Vol. 2, 145–170. Canberra: Pacific Linguistics.

Tsuchida, Shigeru (1988). Amis. In Kamei Takashi, Rokuro Kono and Eiichi Chino (eds.), *The Encyclopedia of Linguistics, Vol. 1: Languages of the World, Part One*, 447–449. Tokyo: Sanseido.

van der Auwera, Johan, Nina Dobrushina and Valentin Goussev (2013). Imperative-Hortative Systems. In Matthew S. Dryer and Martin Haspelmath (eds.), *The World Atlas of Language Structures Online*. Leipzig: Max Planck Institute for Evolutionary Anthropology. http://wals.info/chapter/72 (accessed on 28.12.2020).

Wolff, John U. (1973). Verbal inflection in Proto-Austronesian. In Andrew B. Gonzalez (ed.), *Parangal kay Cecilio Lopez: Essays in Honor of Cecilio Lopez on His Seventy-fifth Birthday*. (Special Monograph Issue No. 4), 71–91. Quezon City: Linguistic Society of the Philippines.

CHAPTER 14

The Healing Words of the Ayoreo

Luca Ciucci

1 Introduction[1]

The present paper offers a linguistic perspective on the so-called *sarode*, magic formulas traditionally used by the Ayoreo with the main purpose of curing diseases. After introducing the Ayoreo and their culture (Section 1.1), the taboo associated with *sarode* and their relationship with the Ayoreo cosmovision are addressed (Section 2). Some of these ritual formulas are analyzed (Section 3) and their role in present-day Ayoreo society is discussed (Section 4). Magic formulas never constituted a closed corpus, but new ones were created over time, adapting to changes and innovations in Ayoreo mythology. Section 5 shows the origin of a new healing formula inspired by the epidemics that occurred after contact with the Jesuits in the 18th century. Conclusions are in Section 6.

1.1 *The Ayoreo Language and People*

Ayoreo is spoken by about 4,500 people in a vast area of the northern Chaco divided between Bolivia and Paraguay. It belongs to the Zamucoan family, along with Old Zamuco† and Chamacoco. Although their ancestors interacted with the Jesuits in the 18th century, the Ayoreo began regular contact with Western culture in 1947. Since then, almost all Ayoreo have gradually abandoned their traditional way of life, although small Ayoreo groups are still isolated in the forest. The Ayoreo language, although endangered, is still in vigorous use; at the same time, many elements of the Ayoreo culture are being lost. Although here I mostly refer to the traditional culture and use the present tense, many assertions no longer apply to the current lifestyle of the Ayoreo (excluding those who live in isolation). The traditional Ayoreo cosmovision is possibly very similar to

1 Data are reported in the Ayoreo orthography (see Bertinetto 2014 and Ciucci 2016 for details). The reference work for Ayoreo lexicography is Higham et al. (2000). Zamucoan nouns and adjectives distinguish a predicate, an argument and an indeterminate form (see Bertinetto et al. 2019 for details). In Ayoreo, nouns are usually cited in argument form. The form is not indicated in the glosses of feminine nouns and adjectives whose predicate and argument form coincide. In addition, Zamucoan nouns inflect for possessor (also indicated in the glosses).

© LUCA CIUCCI, 2022 | DOI:10.1163/9789004510395_015

that of the Old Zamuco-speaking people (Ciucci 2019), who, after evangelization by the Jesuits, mostly merged with the Chiquitano (previously known as Chiquito) living in the missions, and gradually lost their identity; also for this reason, Old Zamuco is extinct. By contrast, the Chamacoco cosmovision differs sharply from the Ayoreo one, possibly owing to the cultural influence exerted by other indigenous populations on the Chamacoco (Cordeu 1989–1992). Not all 18th-century Zamucoan peoples spoke Old Zamuco: the Jesuits identified several 'dialects', and present-day Ayoreo is descended from the varieties spoken by those groups who decided to maintain their traditional way of life, often after having spent some time in the missions.

2 *Sarode:* The Healing Words of the Ayoreo

In traditional Ayoreo medicine, there are two main possibilities to cure diseases: (i) the use of ritual or magic formulas/songs, called *sarode* (M.PL.AF),[2] and (ii) the intervention of a shaman (Sebag 1965a,b). In what follows, I only focus on *sarode*, chants whose main function is to perform a healing. Indeed, *sarode* represent a merging between language and traditional medicine. By contrast, herbal remedies play a limited role in Ayoreo medicine, which only employs a few medicinal plants (Schmeda-Hirschmann 1993, Otaegui 2014: 86). Although most *sarode* are curing songs/chants, some of them perform other functions: for instance, there are *sarode* for the rain (Pia 2018: 83) and *sarode* that serve to do someone damage. In the latter case, they are sung on something connected to the person one wants to harm; the kind of damage depends on each chant, and some *sarode* are even used to kill people (Idoyaga Molina 2000: 121–129).

The connection between language and traditional medicine is based on the belief that certain stories or formulas exert power on reality: it is not the person who pronounces some words, or the spirits listening to them, but the words themselves that have magic power (Otaegui 2014). This explains the use of *sarode*, but also the secrecy characterizing some Ayoreo oral texts. Indeed, Ayoreo myths cannot be recounted entirely, because the act of telling myths, independently of the narrator's intention, can have magic consequences, often nefarious for the listener, the narrator and their community (see, for examples, Bórmida 2005, I: 106, Idoyaga Molina 2000: 69–98, Otaegui 2014: 81–82 and Pia 2016: 41). For this reason, even though there are collections of Ayoreo myths (Fischer-

2 The singular is *sari* (M.SG.AF).

mann 1988, Wilbert and Simoneau 1989, Bórmida 2005 and Pia 2014–2018), it is hard for anthropologists to document them.

Myths are often incomplete, because telling them involves risks, and asking the Ayoreo for mythological narratives can destroy the relationship of trust with the investigator;[3] similar considerations apply to *sarode*. Furthermore, most Ayoreo have abandoned those aspects of their traditional culture that are deemed contrary to the new Christian belief: *sarode* are thus dangerous, considering the enormous power of *Dupade* (M.SG.AF), the Christian God (Ciucci and Pia 2019). Ethnographers who want to collect myths and *sarode* are often seen as tricksters and in Paraguay are called *abujadie* (lit. 'the beards') (Bessire 2011).

In Ayoreo mythology, almost all non-human entities (natural phenomena, plants, animals, traditional objects, states of mind, etc.) result from the transformation of an Ayoreo who, for various reasons, decided to turn into the given entity.

(1) *Eram-i taninga-i, ijnoque por-idie,*
world-M.SG.AF beginning-M.SG.AF 3.NEG.EXIST tree-F.PL.AF
ijnoque cuchis-ode, gusu ayore-ode iji eram-i.
3.NEG.EXIST animal-M.PL.AF only person-M.PL.AF ADP world-M.SG.AF
Ayore-ode ch-ijnoningase=re aja por-idie
person-M.PL.AF 3-change_completely=3.RFL ADP tree-F.PL.AF
je_aja cuchis-ode.
along_with animal-M.PL.AF
'At the beginning of the world, there were no trees, no animals, (there were) only the Ayoreo (lit. 'the people') in the world. The people changed completely into trees and animals' (Bertinetto et al. 2010: 115).

The Ayoreo grammar has significantly affected the Ayoreo mythology. Indeed, Ayoreo distinguishes between masculine and feminine gender, and the grammatical gender of nouns determines the social gender of the person who transforms him or herself into the noun's referent.[4]

For instance, *dequeyutiguei* (M.SG.AF) 'smallpox' is a masculine noun. Before turning into a sickness, smallpox used to be a powerful Ayoreo leader (Fischer-

3 The late Gabriella Erica Pia was able to collect many myths and *sarode* after her adoption by the *Etacõri* clan (Pia 2014: 48, 54–56).

4 This and other aspects of the interaction between language and Ayoreo myths, including their taboo nature, are dealt with in more detail in Ciucci (2019, 2021).

mann 1988: § 7.1). Only men can be leaders, and smallpox is represented as a man, because the noun is masculine (see Aikhenvald [2016: 120–135] for other examples of gender as a source of poetic metaphor). Other diseases also originated from the metamorphosis of a human.

In myths, the Ayoreo character very often decides to turn into a non-human entity because of a conflict with the rest of the community. However, before the metamorphosis, the person is asked to leave something useful for the other Ayoreo, which is usually a magic song (Pia 2014: 50–51). In each *sari* (M.SG.AF), the singular of *sarode* (M.PL.AF), the protagonist of the myth speaks in the first person. The magic effect obtained through the formula is often connected with some quality of the mythological character or the non-human entity they turn into (see examples in Section 3).

Sarode are sometimes called *ujñarone* (3.M.PL.AF) in the literature (e.g. Sebag 1965a,b), while Otaegui (2014: 61–62) considers the *ujñarone* a particular type of *sarode*. The word *ujñari* (3.M.SG.AF), *ujñarone* (3.M.PL.AF) properly means 'breath' and refers to the whole healing process, which involves both the recitation of a *sari* and the act of blowing on the sick person; according to Pia (2014: 50–51), the concept of *ujñarone* also includes the myth from which the *sari* originates.

Each *sari* has its specific function, which is generally to heal a particular disease. The definition of disease or illness is very wide in the Ayoreo culture: it applies when someone is unable to perform their role and obligation in society (e.g. is unable to hunt) or when there is a lack of well-being or enjoyment, which occurs, for instance, if one is afraid, depressed or exhausted (Fischermann 1988, Otaegui 2014: 221–223). If someone is unlucky in love, they are also considered sick (Pia, pers. comm.), and there is even a *sari* for bad dreams (Pia 2014: 83). Generally, each Ayoreo who has turned into a non-human entity has left a *sari*. While not everybody is allowed to listen to a myth, everyone (not necessarily a shaman) can listen to a *sari* and use it to cure a disease. However, there is a caveat. Magic formulas can only be pronounced when they are needed. Otherwise, there could be adverse consequences for the person who performs the chant and for their community. For the same reason, the *sari* used must be the appropriate one for a given disease. In addition, if the *sari* is not recited in the right way, it has the opposite effect, so that not everybody dares to learn and recite *sarode*, and those who can perform them are held in high estimation (Pia 2014: 52, 81–82). The correct recitation of the *sari* does not "depend on the exact replication of formulaic words, but rather, on the ability of the chosen words and performance to evoke the desired effects" and correctly refer to the related myth and its protagonist (Bessire 2011: 272). In this sense, Ayoreo curing songs do not exclude some creativity by the healer. The formula can thus vary, while the tonality is the same in all *sarode*. For this reason, there can be different versions of the same *sari* (see an example in Bessire 2011). *Sarode* can vary considerably in length, depending on the place and time in which they were collected (Dasso 2019). According to Pia (2014, 2016: 40), there are hundreds of *sarode*, but owing to cultural change and the already mentioned taboos, there are nowadays only a few people who know these formulas and the corresponding myths. Documenting *sarode* is thus extremely difficult, and some people pretend not to be able to repeat a *sari*, even though it is often a short formula (Pia 2014: 50–51).

3 Collecting and Analyzing *Sarode*

The use of *sarode* shows the importance of language in the Ayoreo cosmovision, but this has inauspicious consequences for the field linguist, because it is hard, if possible at all, to analyze *sarode* during fieldwork. Since working with a native speaker is a requisite for a good-quality transcription (Dixon 2010: 322), a linguist cannot provide a reliable transcription of these texts. While a linguist is not required to share the vision of the community where they work, they should respect the local beliefs both for ethical reasons and to be trusted. Since a linguist collects texts for language documentation, and the kind of text plays a secondary role, one should avoid asking informants to narrate something which would make them feel uncomfortable. For instance, one of my Ayoreo informants, Vicente, had a particular talent for telling stories. Even though I did not ask him for myths, because I knew their taboo nature, he spontaneously recounted myths, restricting the narration to fragments of stories that he felt allowed to share with me. Since I was aware of the prohibition, and out of respect, I did not ask him for more information. By contrast, an anthropologist such as Pia spent many years living with the Ayoreo, thus gaining the trust that allowed her to collect myths and *sarode*. In particular, she visited remote communities, looking for older people (often shamans) who might have learned *sarode*. The danger of disregarding taboos is much diminished for older people, who are destined to die relatively soon (Ciucci and Pia 2019). Sebag (1965b: 95) mentions an old Ayoreo who did not care about dying and wanted to teach all of the *sarode* he knew to the other men of his group. He took two nights to do this, and at the end got sick and died.

The interested reader can find transcriptions of *sarode* in the original language in Fischermann (1988), Bessire (2011) or Pia (2014, 2015, 2016, 2018). Bórmida 2005 [1973–1979], Renshaw (2006) and Dasso (2019), among others, provide translations of *sarode*.

In examples (2–4) are three *sarode* from Pia's Ayoreo anthropological dictionary. Since no linguist was present when the *sarode* were collected, there is a problem concerning the overall quality of the texts.[5] The *sarode* in (2–4) do not present particular textual issues. I have followed Pia's transcription (including the accents), but I have added linguistic glosses and have partly changed the translation to make it more literal.[6]

The first is the *sari* of *carujnaguejna* (Pia 2016: 40), a local tree (*Peltogyne confertiflora*). She was a woman who bled while pregnant. She healed herself and, despite some problems, gave birth to a child. She left the following *sari*, which, along with her story, serves to help women during childbirth (2).

(2) *Carujnanguejna tu yu éee, Carujnanguejna tu yu éee,*
tree_name.F.SG COP 1SG eee tree_name.F.SG COP 1SG eee
Carujnanguejna tu yu éee, y-iyo-de que ch-odajá,
tree_name.F.SG COP 1SG eee 1SG-blood-M.PL.AF[7] NEG 3-stop
mu ajé y-iqueta yu,
but 3.inside 1SG-heal 1SG
e ch-o_jnaqué éee, e ch-o_jnaque éee, e
already 3-stop eeee already 3-stop eeee already
ch-o_jnaque éee.
3-stop eeee
'I am the *carujnanguejna* eee, I am the *carujnanguejna* eee, I am the *carujnanguejna* eee, my bleeding does not stop, but it is inside, I heal myself, it already stops eee, it already stops eee, it already stops, eee.'

The following *sari* (from Pia 2016: 46) is particularly dangerous. It is used when someone has been cursed, so that the malediction goes back to the person who first pronounced it. It was left by *Iriria*, the brushland tinamou, a type of bird (*Nothoprocta cinerascens*). When *Iriria* was an Ayoreo, she was a female shaman who cursed people, causing their death.

---

5 I was the linguistics editor of the Ayoreo texts in Pia's anthropological dictionary. Although I could correct obvious linguistic mistakes in myths and *sarode* (Ciucci 2014), there were sometimes passages whose correctness was uncertain, but it was not possible to check them with native speakers since these texts are taboo. Similar considerations apply to the other authors who have transcribed *sarode*.

6 Depending on the author, there are different criteria concerning orthographic accents (see Higham et al. 2000, Bertinetto 2014 and Ciucci 2014 for more details).

7 Menstruation is a taboo in Ayoreo, so that there is no specific word, and the plural of 'blood' is used to refer to it (Ciucci and Pia 2019).

(3) *Iriri-á tu yu éee, Iriri-á tu yu éee,*
tinamou-F.SG.AF COP 1SG eee tinamou-F.SG.AF COP 1SG eee
Iriri-á tu yu éee,
tinamou-F.SG.AF COP 1SG eee
cuchabe tu yu éee, cuchabe tu yu éee, cuchabe tu yu éee.
big.F.SG COP 1SG eee big.F.SG COP 1SG eee big.F.SG COP 1SG eee
Y-o_jnipe éeee, jnipe éeee, jnipe éeee,
1SG-be_in_trance eeee in_trance eeee in_trance eeee
[jnipe (IDEO) 'sound of the fire with tremulous flame']
y-o_seré éee, y-o_seré éee, y-o_seré éee.
1SG-faint eee 1SG-faint eee 1SG-faint eee
[seré (IDEO) 'sound of calm, tranquillity']
'I am the brushland tinamou eee, I am the tinamou eee, I am the tinamou eee, I am big eee, I am big eee, I am big eee. I am in trance eeee, (I am) in trance eeee, (I am) in trance eeee, I faint eee, I faint eee, I faint eee.'

The silk floss tree used to be an Ayoreo woman who healed very rapidly when she was wounded. Before turning into a tree, she left the *sari* in (4), which is useful if someone cuts themselves (Bertinetto et al. 2010: 121–122, Pia 2014: 87–88).

(4) *Cucó uyú éee! Cucó uyú éee!*
silk_floss_tree.F.SG 1SG eee silk_floss_tree.F.SG 1SG eee
'I am the silk floss tree, eee! I am the silk floss tree, eee!'

udé sar-i, udé sar-i, y-isiome.
this.M.SG formula-M.SG.AF this.M.SG formula-M.SG.AF 1SG-give
'This magic formula, this magic formula, I give.'

Cucó uyú éee! Que oré ch-aquesu yu,
silk_floss_tree.F.SG 1SG eee NEG 3PL 3-cut 1SG
'I am the silk floss tree! They do not wound me,'

ore ch-ijnó, nanique, yu, ñ-ijungoró,
3PL 3-hit_with_an_axe long_ago 1SG 1SG-neck.F.SG
'they hit me long ago, at my neck,'

yojoá, yojoá, yojoá, pac, pac, pac
IDEO IDEO IDEO IDEO IDEO IDEO
[*yojoá* 'sound of sliced wood'; *pac* 'sound of the blow of an ax']

y-aquesu yu y-aró-i, ch-uchengari ucha-de
1SG-cut 1SG 1SG-skin-M.SG.AF 3-open pulp-M.PL.AF
'I cut my skin, the pulp opens.'

Cucó uyú éee! Cucó uyú éee!
silk_floss_tree.F.SG 1SG eee silk_floss_tree.F.SG 1SG eee
'I am the silk floss tree eee! I am the silk floss tree, eee!'

Cucó uyú éee! Y-isiome udé sar-i,
silk_floss_tree.F.SG 1SG eee 1SG-give this.M.SG formula-M.SG.AF
'I am the silk floss tree eee! I give this magic formula,'

ee y-o_tac, ee y-o_tac, ee y-o_tac,
already 1SG-heal already 1SG-heal already 1SG-heal
[*tac* (IDEO) 'sound of wound that heals, of ground that dries up']
'I already heal my wound, I already heal my wound, I already heal my wound'

chicrí chicrí chicrí e suru éee, e
IDEO IDEO IDEO already 3.close eee already
[*chicrí* 'sound of the wound that heals']
'(the wound) is already closing,'

suru éee, e suru éee.
3.close eee already 3.close eee
'is already closing, is already closing.'

The structure of all *sarode* is very similar: the protagonist presents themselves and their power; in longer *sarode*, more details of the story are referred to. *Sarode* offer interesting data on ideophones, because they contain and usually end with sound-symbolic words, which are the climax and "express through the sound the therapeutic or preventive action and are a symbol of the healing and regenerative efficacy of the word and its ritualized use" (Idoyaga Molina 2000: 137, my translation). Although some authors talk about onomatopoeias, they are better referred to as ideophones, because not all of them are proper onomatopoeias (Bertinetto 2014). Ayoreo, like the other Zamucoan languages, is very rich in ideophones; they often follow the verb 'to be like, look like' (*yo* in the first person singular, *cho* in the third person) with which they form a verbal periphrasis. In (2–4), I have glossed each verbal periphrasis as a whole, but I have also reported, whenever possible, the meaning of the ideophones as indicated by Pia.

The use of *sarode* is very simple and was described by Sebag (1965b: 95) and Pia (2016: 52–53). When someone is sick, people can look for someone who knows *sarode*, or a shaman (they can also be the same person). An expert in *sarode* who is not a shaman is usually preferred, since shamans are feared because they are more powerful (Pia 2016: 52). Pia (2016: 37–55) distinguishes three types of non-shamans who are knowledgeable in *sarode* (5): the *igasitai* is at the highest level, the *sarode irajasõri* at the lowest. The *igasitai* knows more *sarode* than the others, including the most dangerous ones, and in some cases can even be a better healer than a shaman. Shamans and *sarode* experts can be either men or women.

(5) a. *sarode igasitai* (M.SG.AF), *sarode igasite* (F.SG) or simply *igasitai* (M.SG.AF), *igasite* (F.SG) < *sarode* + *igasitai* (M.SG.AF), *igasite* (F.SG) 'intelligent, wise'
b. *sarode irajatai* (M.SG.AF), *sarode irajate* (F.SG) < *sarode* + *irajatai* (M.SG.AF), *irajate* (F.SG) 'knowledgeable'
c. *sarode irajasõri* (M.SG.AF), *sarode irajato* (F.SG) < *sarode* + *irajasõri* (3.M.SG.AF), *irajato* (F.SG) 'who knows, understands'

Any expert in *sarode* has to smoke tobacco in a pipe and inhale it ten or twenty times before performing the healing. According to Fischermann (1988: § 7.4), only those who know *sarode* can smoke a pipe. Then, for about 10–15 minutes, the *sarode* expert blows on several parts of the body of the sick person and sings the specific *sari* for the disease. The *sari* is repeated several times; at the end, the healer blows upwards. There can be some variants of this technique; for instance, the healer can hesitate to blow on a child who is afraid or, out of shame, on the stomach of a woman. In this case, he blows on a glass of water that the woman then drinks or that is then used to massage the sick child (Sebag 1965b: 95). The healer cannot charge anything, but the family of the sick must offer them something appropriate to the importance of the 'service' received. An expert in *sarode* receives less important gifts than a shaman, who is more powerful (Pia 2016: 52–53). The effectiveness of *sarode* has never been investigated from a scientific point of view. Renshaw (2006) hypothesizes that healing chants might strengthen the patient's immune system owing to suggestion. If the person is not healed, the next step is to try with a shaman, who is more 'specialized' in curing than someone who only knows *sarode*. Shamans are the most knowledgeable people in traditional medicine and can choose to use *sarode*. Indeed, some of them began as experts in *sarode* (Pia 2016: 51). Shamans have a different healing technique that only they can perform, which is reserved for the most severe cases, but it does not involve language and is not addressed here (see Sebag 1965a,b).

4 *Sarode* in a Changing Culture

The Ayoreo culture changed very fast after contact. Today the few remaining shamans are very old, and nobody wants to become a shaman, owing to the influence of evangelical and Catholic missionaries. Some parts of the traditional knowledge are disappearing, including *sarode*. Today the Ayoreo want to turn to modern medicine, but their communities are in remote areas with limited access to healthcare, apart from the community in Santa Cruz de la Sierra (Bolivia). In addition, Western medicine is often out of reach, because it is too expensive for the modest means of the average Ayoreo.

Modern medicine has not completely replaced traditional practices, and *sarode* are still considered useful to cure someone. The persistent taboo concerning *sarode* provides indirect evidence for this. However, today *sarode* are rarely used in Paraguay (Renshaw 2006: 259). The Ayoreo do not question the effectiveness of their magic formulas, but missionaries associated traditional healing practices with the devil, thus causing them to be abandoned (Bessire 2011). Otaegui (2014: 86–109), who has investigated the Ayoreo community of Jesudi, in the Paraguayan Chaco, describes the co-existence of traditional and modern medicine. As he notes, both are scarce, which makes a complementary use of the two even necessary. On the one hand, today only a few people know *sarode*; on the other, the Jesudi community only has sporadic access to medical treatment and medicine. *Sarode* and modern medicine are seen as equivalent. In addition, new elements from the Christian religion integrate traditional beliefs and are beginning to play a role in the healing process.

Some Ayoreo still consider modern medicine as not wholly effective and as being unable to explain the cause of illness (Otaegui 2014: 94). Several authors point out that in the perception of the Ayoreo, there were fewer diseases when they lived in the forest, and indeed, many diseases, such as flu and smallpox, resulted from contact with the non-Ayoreo. As is well-known, populations who have lived a long period of isolation are particularly vulnerable to common diseases, and contact with Western people can lead to the deaths of many indigenous people. This happened in the 20th century, when the Western world tried to establish regular contact with the Ayoreo: many of them died as soon as they went to live in the evangelical and Catholic missions (see some dramatic stories in Bartolomé 2000: 106–107, 120–121). Even before some of the groups moved to the missions, the emergence of new diseases led to the killing of shamans, who were considered the culprits of illnesses they could not cure (Bartolomé 2000: 284–285, Bessire 2014: 74). At the same time, epidemics allowed missionaries to use modern medicine to convince the Ayoreo of the power of their new religion as opposed to traditional Ayoreo beliefs (Bessire 2011: 278–279). The lack of immunological memory remains an issue that in the future might affect the uncontacted Ayoreo groups, whose habitat is threatened by deforestation.[8]

5 Epidemics and the Origin of a *Sari*

Contact-related epidemics affected Zamucoan populations even before the 20th century. In 1724, the Jesuits founded the mission of *San Ignacio de Zamucos* to evangelize the Zamucoan tribes. A substantial group of ancestors of the present-day Ayoreo lived for some time with the Jesuits (Fischermann 1993), before escaping back into the woods and living in isolation. Epidemics were frequent in the missions and also affected Zamucoan people (Combès 2009: 83). In 1736–1737, there was a terrible epidemic of smallpox in San Ignacio de Zamucos; consequently, the power relations between the different Zamucoan groups changed and internal conflict arose, ultimately leading to the abandonment of the mission in 1745 (Combès 2009: 56, 83). This also had consequences for the Jesuits' linguistic policy and for the decline of Old Zamuco, now extinct. Indeed, San Ignacio de Zamucos was the only mission where Old Zamuco was the language of evangelization. For this reason, the Jesuit father Ignace Chomé wrote a dictionary and a grammar of the language (both extremely useful for present-day linguistic studies). In all other missions of south-eastern Bolivia, the official language was Chiquitano, and people speaking other indigenous languages were supposed to learn it. When San Ignacio was abandoned, most people speaking Old Zamuco and its dialects moved to the neighboring missions, where they were gradually assimilated and shifted to Chiquitano, which until a few decades ago was widely spoken owing to the cultural heritage of the missions.

The diseases caused by contact with the Jesuits have remained in the oral memory of the Ayoreo. Fischermann (1988) reports several stories that are set at the time of the Jesuits. One of them is about *dequeyutiguei* (M.SG.AF) 'smallpox', which killed most of the inhabitants of San Ignacio de Zamucos (Fischermann 1988: myth number 65), and indeed the epidemic of 1736–1737 claimed the lives of 400 people, leaving only 130 families in the mission (Combès 2009:

8 See the campaign of Survival International at https://www.survivalinternational.org/tribes/ayoreo.

83). The Old Zamuco dictionary by Ignace Chomé was written in San Ignacio de Zamucos between 1738 and 1739, so that a number of examples and expressions referred to the recent epidemic. Chomé used the generic expressions *ducoz yugoritie* 'mortal disease' (6a) or *ducoz datetie* (lit. 'the big disease'), translated in Spanish as *peste*, which in South America designates an infectious disease or smallpox (6b–c). These data come from the upcoming critical edition of Chomé's dictionary (Ciucci, forthcoming).

(6) a. *iré amiño'hi yidaire ome ducoz yugoritie* 'those who remained after the mortal disease in my village'
b. *ducoz datetie chuena ayaquiogaizodde* 'the infectious disease/smallpox (lit. the big disease) consumed all of our ancestors'
c. *ducoz datetie chuena yiguiosoddoe nez* 'the infectious disease/smallpox killed all of my relatives'

In the dictionary, there is also a more specific expression for 'smallpox', *ducoz tarataue* (7). *Ducoz* is the generic term for 'disease', while *tarataue* means 'rotten', so that smallpox is literally the 'rotten disease' (7). This is different from the Ayoreo term *dequeyutiguei* (M.SG.AF) 'smallpox'.[9] A 'linguistic trace' of the smallpox epidemic is the lemmatization of the specific term for the pockmarks left by smallpox. The entry is reported in (8).[10]

(7) *ducoz tarataue* (M.SG.PF), *ducoz taratautie* (M.SG.AF), plural *ducoz tarataucho* (M.PL.PF), *ducoz tarataugoddoe* (M.PL.AF) 'disease, infectious disease of smallpox'

(8) *eddiciguit* (3.M.SG.PF), *eddiciguitie* (3.M.SG.AF), plural *eddiciguicho* (3.M.PL.PF), *eddichiguidoddoe* (3.M.PL.AF) 'pockmarks left by smallpox on the face', possessive *yeddiciguit* (1SG.M.SG.PF), *eddiciguit* (2SG/3.M.SG.PF), plural *ayeddiciguicho* (1PL/2PL.M.SG.PF); *eddiciguidoddoe unahâpuz* 'he is pretty marked by smallpox'; *eddiciguitac* 'distinguished by smallpox in the face'.

9 *Dequeyutiguei* comes from *eyutiguei* (M.SG.AF) 'weariness, fatigue, tiredness, emptiness, destruction' (Higham et al. 2000: 309). This noun is unpossessable, yet *dequeyutiguei* (M.SG.AF) 'smallpox' has the prefix *dequ-*, normally used for the unspecified possessor of possessed nouns. The derivation of *dequeyutiguei* from *eyutiguei* indicates that the former was recently adapted for 'smallpox' and that its mythological explanation (see Section 2) is also an innovation.

10 The English translation and the glosses between parentheses are mine.

The Old Zamuco dictionary also provides examples showing how the Jesuits explained and justified epidemics and other diseases to the Zamucoan people (9).

(9) a. *Tupâde chiguina ducozitie, amati chagüetie a güaque ati añeño ayayutigo, ega tirogore ayutigo* 'When God sends you disease or hunger, subject your will to his will'
b. *ducadoddoe Tupâde chiguina ducozoddoe a, amati chagüetie a yoc, ega yinucoi om* 'Sometimes God sends us diseases or hunger so that we remind ourselves of him'
c. *naco ducozitie dihi ayitonoriga o* 'Hopefully you will learn a lesson with the disease', 'Hopefully the disease will teach you a lesson.'

The present-day Ayoreo descend from Zamucoan groups who did not go to live or did not remain with the Jesuits, who had taught them about *Dupade* (M.SG.AF) 'God'. Examples such as (9) explain why, in the Ayoreo culture, the name of God, *Dupade*, was a linguistic taboo before the recent evangelization. *Dupade* is traditionally seen as "a powerful and terrible divinity such that no shaman can cope with him, hence pronouncing his name can be dangerous" (Ciucci and Pia 2019: 36).

This also contributes to explaining the formation of a new *sari*, that of the *cojñoque eduguejnai* (M.SG.AF) lit. 'foreign leader' or 'leader of the foreigners'. This figure can be identified with the Jesuit missionary leading the mission of San Ignacio de Zamucos. Unlike the other *sarode*, this is an exception, because it is not a *sari* left by a mythical Ayoreo who turned into a non-human entity. In addition, it reflects how the indigenous people who did not want to live in the missions saw the Jesuits. There is only one version of this *sari*, transcribed by Fischermann (1988: § 9.3, *sari* 1) and reported in (10) (my translation).

(10) I am a disgusting foreigner full of diseases / I am a particularly harmful foreigner, whom nobody understands, and full of diseases / I am a disgusting foreigner full of grave diseases / I will punish my people (servants) / I will destroy my people / I am a powerful chief of the foreigners, full of grave diseases / I will have big diseases / but I have powerful magic formulas and my powerful magic formulas will destroy me / my powerful magic formulas will come back against myself / I am a foreigner whom nobody can understand, full of diseases / I am a foreigner whom nobody can understand, full of big diseases / I bring many diseases / I am a powerful leader of the foreigners, full of diseases / I am the owner of

> many things / I am the boss of the foreigners, a chief and owner of many things / I am someone who goes through the forest / I will go through the world / I am the owner of many things / but I have many big diseases / I am someone who goes through the forest [noise of a foreigner who moves].

This *sari* is employed to heal those who have contracted a disease brought by the white people. It also shows that epidemics and other diseases that occurred at the time of the Jesuits left a deep trace in the memory of the Ayoreo. Some northern Ayoreo groups still know San Ignacio de Zamucos as *Guidai toi* (lit. the 'dead village'), because of the many people who died there (Fischermann 1988: §1.1.2).

This example shows that *sarode* never constituted a closed corpus, but that new *sarode* have continuously been created. As seen in Section 2, *sarode* refer to the content of myths, and indeed Fischermann (1988, 1993) documents stories set in San Ignacio de Zamucos (such as the one mentioned above about smallpox). Even in the 20th century, new stories inspired by Christianism and new *sarode* emerged (Bessire 2011: 276–277) before the Christian belief started to replace traditional healing practices.

6 Conclusions

In traditional Ayoreo culture, the word itself can exert a magic power. This explains the use of magic formulas or songs, the so-called *sarode*. They are mainly used for healing purposes and represent the intersection between language and traditional medicine (Section 2). Since *sarode* are taboo, it is difficult for the researcher to document them. The healing ritual in which they are sung is very simple and can be performed by anybody who knows the appropriate formula for a given disease (Section 3). Nowadays, fewer and fewer people know *sarode*. Although they are rarely employed, they can still co-exist with modern medicine, which is often unavailable (Section 4). At the same time, contact with Western people resulted in the transmission of previously unknown diseases. The epidemics that occurred in the 18th century in the Jesuit missions inspired a new *sari* to heal 'white people's diseases' (§5). Such an issue was never forgotten by the Ayoreo, and re-emerged when they were recontacted after 1947. Indeed, when the Ayoreo began to sedentarize, many people died because of diseases transmitted by outsiders.

There is an impressive and touching story reported by Barrios et al. (1992: 54–57) which shows that, during their first contacts with outsiders in the 20th century, the Ayoreo were aware of the health risks involved. In 1971, the Ayoreo group of the Garaigosode from Paraguay left their traditional way of life, and consequently many older people died. As narrated by Manene, a young Ayoreo at that time, the elder knew that they would die, but they felt that, at that point in time, it was necessary to break their isolation to ensure the long-term survival of the group; thus, they decided to sacrifice themselves for the sake of their children. The Ayoreo are descended from Zamucoan groups who met the Jesuits in the 18th century but chose to maintain their traditional way of life. The fear of diseases was one reason for this choice and contributes to explaining the subsequent hostility of the Ayoreo towards outsiders until the second half of the 20th century (Bartolomé 2000: 121). The lack of antibodies against diseases that are common in the Western world is a matter of most serious concern for the future of the uncontacted Ayoreo, for whom *sarode* are possibly still the most practiced healing technique.

Acknowledgements

I owe a debt of gratitude towards Gabriella Erica Pia † for her precious observations while I was writing the first version of this paper. Thanks are also due to Alexandra Y. Aikhenvald, Pier Marco Bertinetto, R.M.W. Dixon, Brigitta Flick and Anne Storch.

Abbreviations

1, 2, 3	first, second, third person	M	masculine
ADP	adposition	NEG	negative
AF	argument form	PF	predicative form
COP	copula	PL	plural
EXIST	existential	RFL	reflexive
F	feminine	SG	singular
IDEO	ideophone		

References

Aikhenvald, Alexandra Y. (2016). *How gender shapes the world.* Oxford: Oxford University Press.

Barrios, Armindo, Domingo Bulfe and Eustacia Bogado (eds.) (1992). *Beyori ga yicatecacori. Ayoreo-español.* Asunción: Don Bosco.

Bartolomé, Miguel Alberto (2000). *El encuentro de la Gente y los Insensatos. La sedentarización de los cazadores* Ayoreo *en el Paraguay*. Ciudad de México: Instituto Indigenísta Interamericano / CEADUC.

Bertinetto, Pier Marco (2014 [2009]). Ayoreo. In Mily Crevels and Pieter Muysken (eds.), *Lenguas de Bolivia, Tomo 3: Oriente*, 369–413. La Paz: Plural Editores.

Bertinetto, Pier Marco, Luca Ciucci and Gabriella Enrica Pia (2010). Inquadramento storico, etnografico e linguistico degli Ayoreo del Chaco. In R. Ajello, P. Berrettoni, F. Fanciullo, G. Marotta and F. Motta (eds.), *Quae omnia bella devoratis. Studi in memoria di Edoardo Vineis*, 109–146. Pisa: Edizioni ETS.

Bertinetto, Pier Marco, Luca Ciucci and Margherita Farina (2019). Two types of morphologically expressed non-verbal predication. *Studies in Language* 43, 1: 120–194.

Bessire, Lucas (2011). *Ujnarone chosite*: Ritual poesis, curing chants and becoming Ayoreo in the Gran Chaco. *Journal de la Société des Américanistes* 97, 1: 259–289.

Bórmida, Marcelo (2005 [1973–1979]). Ergon y mito. Una hermenéutica de la cultura material de los Ayoreo del Chaco Boreal (2 vols). *Archivos del Departamento de Antropología Cultural* 3, 1–2. Buenos Aires: CIAFIC Ediciones.

Ciucci, Luca (2014). Introducción lingüística al Diccionario antropológico ayoreo. In Gabriella Erica Pia (ed.), *Ensayo introductivo al Diccionario antropológico ayoreo*, 7–14. Pisa: Laboratorio di Linguistica della Scuola Normale Superiore.

Ciucci, Luca (2016). *Inflectional morphology in the Zamucoan languages*. Asunción: CEADUC.

Ciucci, Luca (2019). A culture of secrecy: The hidden narratives of the Ayoreo. In Anne Storch, Andrea Hollington, Nico Nassenstein and Alexandra Y. Aikhenvald (eds.), *Creativity in language: Secret codes and special styles.* A special issue of the *International Journal of Language and Culture* 6, 1: 175–194.

Ciucci, Luca (2021). How grammar and culture interact in Zamucoan. In Alexandra Y. Aikhenvald, R.W.M. Dixon and Nerida Jarkey (eds.), *The integration of language and society: A cross-linguistic typology*. Oxford: Oxford University Press. 235–287.

Ciucci, Luca (ed.) (forthcoming). *Ignace Chomé: Vocabulario de la lengua zamuca—Edición crítica y comentario lingüístico.* Madrid / Frankfurt: Iberoamericana Vervuert Verlag.

Ciucci, Luca and Gabriella Erica Pia (2019). Linguistic taboos in Ayoreo. *The Mouth* 4: 31–54.

Combès, Isabelle (2009). *Zamucos*. Cochabamba: Instituto de Misionerología.

Cordeu, Edgardo J. (1989–1992). Aishnuwéhrta. Las ideas de deidad en la religiosidad chamacoco. *Suplemento Antropológico* 24, 1–27, 2.

Dasso, María Cristina (2019). Los sarode ayoreo en el tiempo. Formas y valores en el contacto intercultural. *América Crítica* 3, 1: 43–93.

Dixon, R.M.W. (2010). *Basic Linguistic Theory*. Vol. 1., *Methodology*. Oxford: Oxford University Press.

Fischermann, Bernd (1988). *Zur Weltsicht der Ayoréode Ostboliviens*. PhD thesis, Rheinische Friedrich-Wilhelm-Universität, Bonn [Spanish translation: *La Cosmovisión de los Ayoréode del Chaco Boreal*, manuscript].

Fischermann, Bernd (1993). Viviendo con los Pai. Las experiencias ayoreode con los Jesuitas. In Juan Carlos Ruiz (ed.), *Las misiones de ayer para los días de mañana*, 127–139. Santa Cruz: Editorial El País.

Higham, Alice, Maxine Morarie and Greta Paul (2000). *Ayoré-English dictionary*. Sanford, FL.: New Tribes Mission. Three vols.

Idoyaga Molina, Anatilde (2000). *Shamanismo, brujería y poder en América Latina*. Buenos Aires: CAEA-CONICET.

Otaegui, Alfonso (2014). *Les chants de nostalgie et de tristesse ayoreo du Chaco Boreal paraguayen* (*une ethnographie des liens coupés*). PhD thesis, École de Hautes Études en Sciences Sociales, Paris.

Pia, Gabriella Erica (2014). *Diccionario antropológico ayoreo. Parte primera: Ensayo introductivo*. Pisa: Laboratorio di Linguistica della Scuola Normale Superiore.

Pia, Gabriella Erica (2015). *Diccionario antropológico ayoreo. Parte segunda: Abalanzarse—Achuma*. Pisa: Laboratorio di Linguistica della Scuola Normale Superiore.

Pia, Gabriella Erica (2016). *Diccionario antropológico ayoreo. Parte tercera: Adecuado—Adulto casado*. Pisa: Laboratorio di Linguistica della Scuola Normale Superiore.

Pia, Gabriella Erica (2018). *Diccionario antropológico ayoreo. Parte cuarta: Aéreo—Agujero*. Pisa: Laboratorio di Linguistica della Scuola Normale Superiore.

Renshaw, John (2006). 'The effectiveness of Symbols' revisited: Ayoreo curing songs, *Tipití: Journal of the Society for the Anthropology of Lowland South America* 4, 1: 247–269.

Schmeda-Hirschmann, Guillermo (1993). Magic and medicinal plants of the Ayoreos of the Chaco Boreal (Paraguay). *Journal of Ethnopharmacology* 39: 105–111.

Sebag, Lucien (1965a). Le chamanisme Ayoreo (I). *L'Homme* 5, 1: 5–32.

Sebag, Lucien (1965b). Le chamanisme Ayoreo (II). *L'Homme* 5, 2: 92–122.

Wilbert, Johannes and Karin Simoneau (eds.) (1989). *Folk Literature of the Ayoreo Indians*. Los Angeles: UCLA, Latin American Centre Publications.

PART 3

How to Keep Languages Strong

CHAPTER 15

Kumatharo, Mother of the Tariana, Mother of the World

Jovino Brito

Note by Bob Dixon

In 1991 when Sasha Aikhenvald commenced fieldwork among the Tariana of north-west Amazonia she was absorbed into the classificatory kinship system. The late Graciliano Brito adopted her as his younger sister, and she became older sister to Jovino (Tariana name Kuda). Sasha was accorded the Tariana name Kumatharo, and I was called Serewhali.

I called Jovino, by What'sApp, telling him that Anne Storch and I were putting together a book which celebrated Sasha's achievements, and inviting him to contribute. I spoke in Portuguese and Jovino responded in Tariana. By the use of Sasha's fine dictionary and grammar of Tariana, I was able to translate Jovino's message into English.

Bom dia, Serewhali.

Good morning, Serewhali.

Nhua-naka hĩ Kuda kuite pi-sa-do i-we-ri Kumatharo i-we-ri.

Here I am, Kuda, your spouse's younger brother, Kumatharo's younger brother.

Hĩ pi-sa-do duha duhpani-nipe kalisi hanipa-mha wa-na alia-mha.

We have a lot to tell about your spouse's work.

Hĩ kuite nu-phe-ri hĩ Graciliano kepitanite-nhina di-keta-nhi, walikasu-nuku di-keta du-na. Du-ine di-sape, 'hĩ wa-sape-nipe-nuku nu-bueta-de' du-a-hyume.

© JOVINO BRITO, 2022 | DOI:10.1163/9789004510395_016

This older brother of mine, Graciliano, met her a long time ago, met he. He talked to her after she had said 'I will learn our language'.

Hĩ wa-na wa-kesi-do kayu, nu-phe-ru kayu nu-de-naka nuhua du-na, hĩ Kumatharo-nuku. Kayumaka duha wa-na hanipa du-ni du-waketa-na.

She is like a female blood relative of ours, like my older sister. I have her, this Kumatharo. So she has helped us a lot.

Hĩ pasi hĩ Talia-seni nha na-yarupe, na-sape-nipe-nuku nha na-mayẽta-kayami-nuku, hi livru-pe-nuku duha du-ni, hĩ kasina-pe-nuku du-ni.

As they, the Tariana, were forgetting their language, their speech, she made these books, she made these ABC*-books.*

Hĩ du-ni-ka-nuku pasi hanupe hĩ Talia-seni kwaka nayarupe-nuku na-mayẽta-nipe nawada na-nu-na.

As she did this, many Tariana came to remember their language.

Diha-nuku-naka revilita...revitalização-nuku kepitana-peri-nuku wha wa-sape-naka ikasu-piaka-nuku. Hi na ičiri i-pitana kwe-peri, hĩ heku-da i-pitana, kuphe i-pitana, thuyme-nuku nha na-sape-naka ikasu-pia-ka-nuku, na-dana na-ni-naka.

Because of this—what is called revitalização (revitalization)—we now speak (the language). They are now saying all the names of animals, names of fruit, names of fishes, all of them, they can write them.

Kayumaka hĩ kuite-nuku hĩ Kumatharo-nuku Kumatharo wa:-naka, wa-phe-ru wa:-ka wha du-na.

So we call Kumatharo as Kumatharo (that is, we have given her a Tariana name), we call her our older sister.

Talia pheri-či ha-do kayu alite-naka duhua. Wha hanipa wa-na duha du-ni du-waketa-naka, duha hĩ Kumatharo wa-na.

She is like the mother of the first-born Tariana. She has helped us a lot, this Kumatharo.

Hanipa wha puwhi wa-wa-naka du-ine wha whameta-li-se wa-kale-se-nuku. Nuhua ne ma-mayẽ-kade-naka du-na. Ne hanupe pa:pe duna hĩ audio-se nu-sape nu-ni-ka.

We are very happy about her in our feelings, in our heart. I am not forgetting her. I talk to her a lot via audio.

Nu-phe-ru kayu-naka nhua nhupa nu-de-naka du-na. Hĩ pasi hanupe nu-awada-naka du-na, kweka kweka duha manukade kasina-nuku, du-a, na: na-sape-naka.

I honour her as an older sister. I think about her a lot, why why is she not coming, say (others).

Hanipa wha whepa wa-de wa-ni-naka du-na duha Kumatharo-nuku. Hi-naka pi-na nu-kalite-naka. Wa-na wa-phe-ru kayu-naka,

We respect/honour her a lot, Kumatharo. This is what I am telling you. She is like an older sister for us.

Pa:-hipe-se, pa:-ehkwapi-se duha alia-ke-nuku, wha wa-wada-naka du-na.

With her being in a different country, in a different world, we think about her.

Yuwapika wa-ine hĩ wa-kesi-do kayu-na duha duhpani duhya du-nu. Wyaka-se du-nu, wa-na duhpa du-de du-ni-na. Hi-naka pi-na nu-kalite-naka.

She has been with us like our female relative, working with us. She came from afar, she respected us. This is what I am telling you.

Kapa livro-nuku, Serewhali, hi-kayu pia pierita, Iri, Iri-ne, Iri-ne hado, Iri-ne hado Kumatharo pi-a- pi-erita ne-nuku, kapa do livro-nuku. Irine hado Kumatharo, ehkwapi hado ehkwapi hado pi-a pi-erita.

Serewhali, write like this on the cover of the book: Tariana, mother of the Tariana, mother of the Tariana Kumatharo, write there, on the cover of the book. 'Mother of the Tariana, Kumatharo, mother of the world, mother of the world', you write.

CHAPTER 16

Appreciation of Alexandra Aikhenvald

James Sesu Laki

Alexandra, commonly known as Sasha, is a professional linguist who made friends and regarded them as part of her family where ever she went. Hence the relations she created with my late wife, Pauline Yuaneg Luma-Laki, in Melbourne in 1995. That sisterly relationship, a younger sister to Pauline was so good that she, Pauline gave one of her many names, Ngyamamairatauk to Sasha, which practically meant the 'High Spirited woman that glows', In Manambw language, *Ngyama*—glowing; *maira*—high spirited; *tauk*—woman.

Where ever she went in the Manambw world she was a glowing figure, especially with her skin colour some call it white but not so in Manambw Community. She has empathy, kindness, embracing, and outreaching in the Manambw way as well, or the greetings by various accolades that Manambw do to each other without calling names, as this was more respectful then a name. Sasha understood these accolades because they appeared to be standard amongst every clan in the tribe, once she knew the clan system. Name can be called but only another, which may be middle or one of many. Ngyamamairatauk was a middle name common to the Manambw community for Sasha.

She was well regarded and highly respected that some prohibited men-only issues and discussions were easily facilitated by the men folks for her.

She still has a place in almost everyone's heart, more so because she also understood the Manambw culture and referred to me as her Maam, being a husband of her big sister. She was a mother too to our Children and Pauline also became a big mother to Michael, Sasha's only son. Her legacy lives in our Manambw Community with many of our nephews, nieces, brothers and sisters, and many more cousins. She will never be missed in Manambw. She has also created a Mother daughter relations with Yuamali, one of our nieces that she worked with for the Manambw and Yalaku language. She will be well embraced by many of our relatives if she ever went back to the Manambw Community of the Upper Sepik Area (USA) in East Sepik, Papua New Guinea.

As for me I was personally intrigued by the quick nature in which Sasha could muster a language and regard her as one of unique linguist, a professional who has time for everybody. I have been privileged to have known her and highly respect her, wuna ngyamus, Ngyamamairatauk, Kul Yamban, Yambunai Ngyaur.

© JAMES SESU LAKI, 2022 | DOI:10.1163/9789004510395_017

CHAPTER 17

Nungon Near Future Tense in Child and Child-Directed Nungon Speech: A Case Study

Hannah Sarvasy

1 Introduction: The Poly-functional Nungon Near Future Tense

One of the milestones of child linguistic and cognitive development is the ability to articulate hypothetical situations and events: either those set in a general non-past time, or those which could have occurred in the past, but did not (on hypothetical situations, see Kuczaj and Daly 1979 and Kuczaj 1981; on counterfactuals, see Harris et al. 1996). But the timing of production may relate in intricate ways to both cognition and language-particular grammatical features, such as the characteristics of verb forms used in describing hypothetical situations (Gathercole 2006).

In the Papuan language Nungon (1,000 speakers, Morobe Province, Papua New Guinea), hypothetical events set in a general future (non-present, non-past) time can be described using the near future tense inflection (Sarvasy 2016, 2017). Nungon is an agglutinating language with some fusion; the language makes much use of clause chains (see Sarvasy 2015, 2017, 2020, 2021), where multiple clauses with under-specified verbal predicates, lacking tense or mood, are followed by a single clause with a fully-specified verbal predicate, replete with tense or mood marking, and obligatory marking of subject person/number. The near future tense inflection is one of five Nungon tense inflections; Nungon verbs can also inflect for two imperatives (immediate and delayed), counterfactual modality, or take a variety of under-specified forms that often lack subject person/number marking. When Nungon speakers talk of non-negated future occurrences set in particular time frames, the applications of the two future tenses are strictly delineated, except in the murky realm between 'tonight' and 'tomorrow morning.' That is, the near future tense is obligatorily used for anything anticipated to occur in the period between 'now' and the end of 'today', while the remote future tense must be used for anything anticipated to occur 'tomorrow' or beyond. (As discussed in Sarvasy 2017: 264–265, the decision by someone waking in the middle of the night as to whether events expected in the early morning should be couched in the near or remote future tense may hinge on how much sleep the person expects to get

© HANNAH SARVASY, 2022 | DOI:10.1163/9789004510395_018

before waking to those events.) Thus, for describing future events with known timing, the time frame for application of the near future tense is much more limited (less than twenty-four hours from the present moment) than that for the remote future tense (potentially, years into the future). Example (1) shows a verb inflected for near future tense that describes an action that is imminent: a father here tells his child (aged 3;1) that once she has eaten, the two of them will leave that location. Following the conventions established in Sarvasy (2015), the clauses in clause chains that have under-inflected verbal predicates ('medial' clauses) are enclosed in single curly brackets, and clauses with fully-specified verbal predicates ('final' clauses) are enclosed in double curly brackets.

(1) *{Na-i-ya},* *urop* *{{**ongo-rangka-mok**}}.*
eat-DS.2SG-MV enough go-NF.DU-1DU
'You having eaten, then **we two will go.**' (TO father, 3;1, 35:16)

Example (2) shows a verb inflected for remote future tense that describes an action that is projected to take place the following day, spoken by the mother of the child addressed in (1)—here aged 3;2:

(2) *Dedi* *{gogo* *maa* *y-i-ya}* *wo-rok* *keembok*
daddy PRO.FOC speech say-DS.2SG-MV DIST-SEMBL tomorrow
bisiget *wo-rok* *{numa* *i-m-un-a}* *{to-nga}*
biscuit DIST-SEMBL who 3SG.-give-DS.3SG-MV SG.O.take-MV.SS
*{{**e-i-k-ma**}},* *I.* *mak-no.*
come-IRR-3SG-RF I. mother-3SG.POSS
'(If) you speak, then tomorrow who giving Daddy a biscuit, taking it along, **he will come**—I.'s mother.' (TO mother, 3;2, 2143844)

Under negation, the distinction between the two tenses blurs, with an inflection called the irrealis, which is morphologically almost identical to the remote future, used to state that events will *not* occur in any future time, near or remote. In my nine months of fieldwork on Nungon (and subsequent years of re-examination of Nungon texts and my field notes) before embarking on child acquisition studies, the near future was never attested directly negated. Instead, the denial that an event would occur between the time of the speech event and the end of that day was always expressed in the same way as a denial that an event would occur in the next week or the next year: with the negated irrealis. This is shown in (3):

(3) *Nog-u* *naga=ha* *ho-ng* ***na-wangka-t***}}, {{*gok*
PRO.1SG-TOP PRO.1SG.EMPH=BEN cook-DEP eat-NF.SG-1SG PRO.2SG
ma=na-i-rok}}.
NEG=eat-IRR-2SG
'As for me, **I will** cook and **eat** (it) for myself; **you won't eat** (it).' (Father to TO, 3;0, 10:04)

Here, TO's father teases TO (age 3;0) that he will eat something by himself, and that she won't get any. He uses the near future tense for the non-negated instance of 'eat' (*na-wangka-t*), but the negated irrealis for the negated instance of 'eat' (*ma=na-i-rok*); the two eating events are set in the same, hodiernal, time frame.

Put another way, one could say that the distinction between the two Nungon future tenses is neutralized under negation (as per Aikhenvald and Dixon 1998).

Given all this, it might seem paradoxical that, of the two future tenses, it is the more-constrained near future, not the remote future—nor the remote future-linked irrealis—that is used to refer to a general future time that is not confined to the period immediately following the speech act. Example (4) comes from a procedural text, dictated to me, that described the process of house construction. The text was mostly framed in the near future tense, even though the different component sub-processes themselves would generally take more than one day to complete.

(4) {{*Doo* ***yemo-nangka-ng***}}.
bamboo.sp weave-NF.PL-2/3PL
'**They will weave** the floors.'

The near future tense in its general future sense also often occurs in the apodosis of conditional statements (discussed in Sarvasy 2017: 266–268). Then, the event described by the near future verb can sometimes be interpreted as possibly occurring in the hodiernal period, as in (5), but sometimes this is impossible, as with the examples in Sarvasy (2017: 266– 268). In those examples, the near future is used to describe conditional events that would be highly unlikely to occur on the day of the speech acts, including one in a written letter that, if it eventuated, could only occur from several days to a week or more after the addressee could be expected to receive the letter.

(5) {*Hat-no* *wep* *m-i-ya*} {*mö-un-a*} *wo* {{*papa*
hat-3SG.POSS 3SG.O.touch do-DS.2G-MV fall-DS.3SG-MV DIST papa
ge-engka-k}}.
2SG.O-beat-NF.SG-3SG
'You touching his hat, it falling, then Papa **will beat you.**' (TO's mother, 3;2, 3:28) [Here, the first two clauses of the clause chain function as the protasis of a conditional.]

In sum, the Nungon near future has two main functions: first, to describe strictly hodiernal events—events projected to occur between the speech act and the end of 'today'—and second, to describe events set in a general future time. Why is the near future used for this second function, and not the remote future, or the irrealis? In fact, the situation in Nungon is paralleled by at least two Bantu languages with multiple future tenses: in Logoori (Sarvasy 2016) and Kikuyu (Johnson 1977: 19), it is the near future tense (that closest to the speech act) that can alternatively indicate a general or potential future (Sarvasy 2016). It is possible that the Nungon, Logoori and Kikuyu near future tenses are able to moonlight as general future tenses precisely because each is the closest future tense to the present moment, for each language. If the present time shifts to a hypothetical 'present', the near future will be the tense that is closest to that present, without additional connotations of removal in time, while the remote future (and the other future tenses in Logoori and Kikuyu) must still be interpreted as removed by at least one day from that hypothetical present tense, hence bringing further relative-temporal 'baggage' to the job.

This chapter investigates parent and child uses of the Nungon near future inflection in a small sub-set of the 175-hour Nungon Child Speech Corpus (NCSC; Sarvasy 2018), comprising about 5.5 hours of parent-child interaction. This sub-set, with five transcripts from the child NN and one from the child TO, is the only sub-set at present in which all morphemes are fully coded and searchable using the program CLAN (MacWhinney 2000). This case study explores parent and child uses of the near future tense to describe general future and hodiernal future occurrences. Beyond this, the near future is also a vehicle for threats and promises of rewards as the parents play-threaten and cajole their children into speaking for the recorder. As it turns out, these pragmatic functions represent just over half of all parental uses of the near future tense in the sample. Clearly, threatened punishments or promised rewards loom large in the repertoire of parental discussion of near future events. Unsurprisingly, the children themselves do not promise rewards to their parents in these recording sessions, and, at least in this sample, threaten much less.

2 Background on Child Acquisition of Nungon Tense Inflections

This exposition of language development for children learning Nungon as a first language draws on a portion of the data from the first 110 hours of the NCSC, for which detailed information on verb inflections is available. This portion is: 15 months of transcribed recording sessions with the child TO and her parents (child aged 2;1–3;3), six months of transcribed recording sessions with the child NN and his mother (child aged 2;10–3;3), and 13 months of transcribed recording sessions with the child AB and his parents (child aged 1;1–2;1).

The most detailed developmental description for any of the Nungon-speaking children is available for TO (presented in Sarvasy 2019, 2020). TO's recording period spanned her very early speech production stage, from age 2;1 through to about 2;6, in which she produced relatively few verbs, and continued through to an advanced state, from age 3;1 to 3;3, when she produced complex sentences productively and was accomplished at sparring verbally with her father. In between, TO went through a stage (2;7 through 3;0) when she often relied on the nominalized form of verbs to stand in for a verb inflected for tense and subject person/number, which I called the 'root nominal' stage (Sarvasy 2019).

The near future tense inflection was the last tense inflection to be produced by the child TO, several months after she already productively used all four other tense inflections, the two imperative inflections, and various other non-finite verb forms (Sarvasy 2019).

Sarvasy (2019: 13–15) showed that while TO's production of the near future tense lagged behind her production of, for instance, the near past and the remote future, this does not clearly stem from frequencies in her parents' speech. On the contrary: over a 15-month period, TO's parents consistently produced more near future verb tokens than either near past or remote future tokens in hour-long recording sessions. TO's own delayed use of the near future tense could stem from: a) sampling methods that missed her scattered productions, b) the morpho-phonological complexity of the near future inflection, compared with other inflections, c) limitations on discourse content for young children, or d) the bi-functionality of the near future inflection, and its application to general, as well as hodiernal, future events.

3 Children's Use of the Near Future Tense in Child-Parent Interactions

Overall, there are three main contexts in the child-parent interactions recorded in the NCSC in which the children themselves use the near future tense, described below.

3.1 *Immediate Context*

They sometimes use the near future tense to discuss the activities in which they and their parents are involved during the recording session, such as looking at pictures in a book. Then, the near future often implicitly expresses their desire, along with the desired action. Nungon has a form called the imminent aspect that encodes desire, or imminence, or both (Sarvasy 2017: 333–336). But it may be the case that use of the near future tense instead of the imminent aspect makes for a more forceful statement of desire: 'I *will*' rather than 'I wish to.' An example of this use is in (6):

(6) {{*ngo-rok* ***y-aa-wangka-t***}}.
PROX-SEMBL 3NSG.O-see-NF.SG-1SG
'**I'll look at** these **ones.**' (NN, 3;0, line 1578)

The recording context, in which parents seek to elicit *maa* 'speech' or *hat* 'story' from their children, also makes for child utterances featuring the verb *yo-* 'say' in the near future, as in (7):

(7) {{*ök ök hat imbange* ***yo-wangka-t***}}.
IJ IJ story wonderful say-NF.SG-1SG
'Yes, yes, **I will tell** a wonderful story.' (NN, 3;2, line 1490)

3.2 *Hypothetical Events with Plausible Hodiernal Time Frames*

A second context in which children use the near future tense in these recording sessions involves joint parent-child descriptions of hypothetical sequences of actions and movements that *could* take place within the hodiernal period, although generally do not seem to be necessarily planned in advance of the recording session. Parents most often lead children through description of these with prompting questions, asking children whether they will go bathe in a particular waterfall later that day, and if so, with whom they will go, and if they pick fruit or catch fish, who will eat them, etc. The children then supply the details, as in (8), in response to the parental questioning.

(8) {*Au* *S.=ha* *i-mo-nga*} {{***to-wangka-t***}}.
other S.=BEN 3SG.O-give-MV.SS do-NF.SG-1SG
'**I will** also **do** giving (sweet potatoes) to S.' (NN, 3;1, line 5607)

Discussion of hypothetical events like these in the near future is more frequent than in the remote future, across the parent-child pairs. Hypothetical stories framed in the remote future do occur in the sessions, but tend to cluster around known planned events, such as TO's father's scheduled return by plane from the city of Lae, or events that hinge on a particular person's eventual return to the region, such as 'Hannah giving you a biscuit' (which could not occur on the same day as a recording session when I was not present in the village).

3.3 *Threats*

Here, the children reproduce the near future 'I'll/he'll beat you' threats oft-issued by their parents, and threaten them back, often with more gusto and imagination than their parents. TO and her mother engage in several bouts of threat one-upmanship, usually triggered by an uncooperative behavior by TO and the mother's play-threatening response, in the near future: 'I'll beat you'; 'You won't get any breastmilk'; 'I'll go far away and leave you here.' In one case, TO (age 3;2) threatens to cut her mother on an existing wound on her leg, in (9):

(9) {{*Eer-a=dek* *wee-ya=dek* *hai-ng*
leg-2SG.POSS=LOC wound-2SG.POSS=LOC cut-DEP
ga-mo-wangka-t}}.
2SG.O-give-NF.SG-1SG
'**I will** cut your leg on your wound **for you**.' (TO, 3;2, 2212747)

The threats may be triggered by a parent's threat that another adult will beat the child. For instance, at 3;3, TO's father warns TO not to touch the digital sound recorder, or else her uncle, who was overseeing the recordings, would beat her. This sets off a blustering story, built action by action, from TO, about what she would do to avoid her uncle's beating. She would run to Yawan village, she says, bang her uncle on the leg with a stick, and he would cry. The scaffolding from her father here takes a different form than for many of the non-blustering near future stories in (3.2) above; here, rather than ask content questions, the father simply echoes TO's previous utterance, and then she builds up the tall tale even more: she will tell her older brother to beat the uncle; she will hit the uncle with a rock, etc. An excerpt is in (10):

(10) *nn* {*böörong=ko* *w-e-ya*} {{*irom* *amba*
IJ rock=FOC 3SG.O.beat-DS.1SG-MV free huge
ur-engka-k}}=*ma.*
cry-NF.SG-3SG=SUB
'Yeah, I having beaten him with a rock, **he'll** just **cry** a huge amount.' (TO, 3;3, 40:35)

When the time frame is left unspecified through a temporal adverb, both the neutral hypothetical events of use 3.2 and the threatening events of use 3.3 could be seen as verging on general future uses. But there is little evidence of unambiguous general future functions of the near future used by TO or NN in the smaller 5.5-hour sub-set of transcriptions, which includes just one transcript from TO (at 2;3) and five from NN (at 2;11, 3;0, 3;1, 3;2, and 3;3). The children also do not display, for understandable reasons, the 'cajoling' function of the near future tense, which is found in their parents' speech.

4 Parents' Use of the Near Future Tense

In the small 5.5-hour sample, the parents did not clearly exhibit instances of the general future use of the near future tense. Instead, parental near future tokens could perhaps best be divided into three pragmatic functions: threatening ('I will beat you'; 's/he will die'), cajoling ('she'll give you a biscuit …'), or simply discussing the future without either of those pragmatic functions.

Threatening by parents is similar to the threats used by children, in that (in these recording sessions, at least!) the threat often has a comical over-reach to it. At one point, TO's mother warns her, comically, that a chicken will beat TO if she does not speak for the recorder:

(11) *Hup* {*maa* *ma=y-i-ya*} *wo* {{*hup* *og-ese*
chicken speech NEG=say-DS.2G-MV DIST chicken same.level-DEIC
wo ***ge-engka-k***}}.
DIST 2SG.O-beat-NF.SG-3SG
'The chicken, you not saying speech, then the chicken over there, **it will beat you**.' (Mother to TO, 3;1, 30:27)

Threats often also take the form of asides to bystanders, as in the first clause of (12):

(12) {{*Urop* ***we-engka-r-a***}}, {{ {{***om-engka-rok***}}, *ya-a-t*}}.
enough 3SG.O.beat-NF.SG-1SG-ATT die-NF.SG-2SG say-PRES-1SG
'That's it, **I'll beat him**, I say: **you're going to die**!' (Mother to NN, 3;0, line 1565)

In example (12), the second clause is also a threat, directed at the child himself.

Parents often try to cajole the children into talking with promises of the treats they will be given if they do speak. Sometimes, these treats are framed in the remote future, when they hinge on a particular person's arrival into the region, but more often, they use the near future, as in (13):

(13) {*Maa yo-ng=dup t-i-ya*} *wo* {{*hup modow-o*
speech say-DEP=COMPL do-DS.2G-MV DIST chicken egg-3SG.POSS
ga-m-angka-t}}.
2SG.O-give-NF.SG-1SG
'You having said speech completely, then **I will give you** a chicken's egg.' (Mother to TO, 3;2, 1765303)

The Nungon expression *i-no-ng yuu-* '3SG.O-say-DEP 3SG.O.roll,' 'lie to,' is used to describe such empty promises, which—like the threats—must be understood by both parent and child to be facetious.

As with the children (uses A and B above), parents also use the near future to discuss both imminent actions within the recording session (as in example 14), and plausible hypothetical actions that could occur later that day (as in example 15).

(14) {{*Moi* ***to-wangka-k***}}.
bad do-NF.SG-3SG
'**It will** spoil.' (Mother to TO, 3;2, line 358)

(15) *Nn oro* {{*öön* ***möng-nangka-mong***}} *ha?*
IJ well farm.plot plant-NF.PL-1PL QUES
'Yeah, okay, **will we plant** a farm plot?' (Mother to NN, 3;1, line 7175)

The distributions of the pragmatically motivated threats and promises, and the other, more descriptive, uses of the near future by parents and children are in Table 17.1. (Here, "TO 2;3" refers to TO's own usage in the transcript from when she was two years and three months, while "TO mother 2;3" refers to TO's mother's use in that same transcript.)

TABLE 17.1 Near future verb tokens in child and adult speech in the 5.5-hour sample

	THREAT	CAJOLE	HODIERNAL NF	Total verbs	% NF of total verbs
TO 2;3	0	0	0	78	0.00%
TO mother 2;3	7	3	8	737	2.44%
NN 2;11	1	0	3	312	1.28%
NN 3;0	1	0	8	293	3.07%
NN 3;1	0	0	27	597	4.52%
NN 3;2	0	0	9	442	2.04%
NN 3;3	0	0	12	389	3.08%
NN mother 2;11	9	11	15	1185	2.95%
NN mother 3;0	13	22	5	1352	2.96%
NN mother 3;1	10	16	47	1245	5.86%
NN mother 3;2	7	1	23	920	3.37%
NN mother 3;3	10	3	15	589	4.75%

Table 17.1 shows that parental threats and cajoling, taken together, are close to, equal to or greater than non-pragmatically charged hodiernal uses of the near future in four of the six transcripts. Further, from age 3;0, NN's percentages of total verbs that are inflected for the near future appear similar to the two adults' percentages. (TO's first use of the near future occurred at age 2;11; Sarvasy 2019).

One could infer from Table 17.1 that a very high proportion of near future tense tokens addressed to children by adults occur in either threats or cajoling promises—and that this might affect children's acquisition of the form, and their own use of it. It is true that NN himself, and TO (in transcripts not included in Table 17.1 counts), apparently relish using the near future to threaten adults back (as in examples 9 and 10). There is no evidence of their cajoling their parents in these transcripts. But it is important to note that the high incidence of threats and cajoling in these transcripts were usually directly linked to the artificial recording context, in which the children were being asked to speak over and over again, and threatened or cajoled if they hesitated. It is unclear how intensively children of 2;1–3;3 are asked to perform in this way outside the research study, but my impression is that it would be infrequent, and definitely not extend for one hour at a time, as the recording sessions did. Some of the threatening in the sessions related to the children's desires to touch items that did not belong to them, such as the recorder, and these contexts are indeed plentiful outside the recording context.

No strong statement about why TO was so slow to produce the near future tense—months after she produced all the other tenses—can be made based on the near future tense functions presented here. Certainly, there is no evidence that the near future tense's applicability to both hodiernal future events and general future events features large in speech directed to children. These new data could imply, however, that if the near future is associated with pragmatic 'adult' acts like threatening and cajoling, then a certain maturity would be necessary to use it. Examination of later transcripts shows that by age 3;2, both TO and NN are clearly comfortable employing the near future for both neutral hodiernal possible events and a range of creative threats.

5 Conclusion

Examination of the functions of the Nungon near future tense in a small sample of child-parent conversational transcripts showed that the near future tense has strongly pragmatic functions, the frequency of which often matches those of less-pragmatically charged descriptions of hodiernal events and actions. Prominent among these is verbal sparring, in which children retort to parents' playful threats by describing the hypothetical ways they will fight back, or run away, if they are beaten: this sort of playfully aggressive exchange is similar to 'teasing' routines attested for adult-child interactions in diverse cultures (Briggs 1971; Brown 2002; Miller 1986; Paugh 2012; Schieffelin 1986, *inter alia*). Nungon-speaking parents, but not children, also use the near future to promise rewards for desired behaviors. Both threats and promises are understood to be conditional apodoses, and hinge on the child's following the parent's direction. Other uses of the near future, in contrast, simply build a narrative about plausible, hypothetical events for later that day. In this sample, there were no clear uses of the near future to describe events framed in a general, non-hodiernal future time. Unlike what Rumsey (2013) described for parent-child interactions in the Papuan language Ku Waru, 'deceit' does not seem to play a major role in the Nungon corpus, hence is not generally related to patterns of use of the near future tense in framing hypothetical statements by Nungon-speaking children. While this study does not yield clear answers to the puzzle of why the Nungon near future tense is the last to be produced by children, it contributes new information on the extent to which the near future in child-directed Nungon speech may be associated with adult-like behaviors (threatening and cajoling) that could require some maturity to master and reproduce.

Abbreviations and Conventions

{}	medial clause boundaries	NEG	negator
{{}}	final clause boundaries	NF	near future
1SG, 2DU	person/number	NSG	non-singular
ATT	attention	O	object
BEN	benefactive	PL	plural
COMPL	completive	POSS	possessive
DEIC	deictic	PRO	pronoun
DEP	dependent	PROX	proximal
DIST	distal	QUES	polar question
DS	different-subject	RF	remote future
EMPH	emphatic	SEMBL	semblance
FOC	focus	SG	singular
IJ	interjection	SS	same-subject
IRR	irrealis	SUB	subordinator
LOC	locative	TOP	topic
MV	medial verb		

References

Aikhenvald, Alexandra Y. and R.M.W. Dixon (1998). Dependencies between grammatical systems. *Language* 74 (1): 56–80.

Briggs, Jean L. (1971). *Never in anger: Portrait of an Eskimo family*. Cambridge: Harvard University Press.

Brown, Penelope (2002). Everyone has to lie in Tzeltal. In Shoshana Blum-Kulka and Catherine E. Snow (eds.), *Talking to adults*, 241–275. Mahwah: Erlbaum.

Gathercole, Virgina C.M. (2006). Introduction to the Special Issue: Language-specific influences on acquisition and cognition. *First Language* 26(1): 5–17.

Harris, Paul L., Tim German and Patrick Mills (1996). Children's use of counterfactual thinking in causal reasoning. *Cognition* 61: 233–259.

Johnson, Marion R. (1977). A semantic analysis of Kikuyu tense and aspect. PhD dissertation, Ohio State University.

Kuczaj, Stan A. (1981). Factors influencing children's use of hypothetical reference. *Journal of Child Language* 8: 131–137.

Kuczaj, Stan A. and Mary J. Daly (1979). The development of hypothetical reference in the speech of young children. *Journal of Child Language* 6: 563–579.

MacWhinney, Brian (2000). *The CHILDES Project: Tools for analyzing talk*. 3rd edition. Mahwah, NJ: Lawrence Erlbaum Associates.

Miller, Peggy (1986). Teasing as language socialization and verbal play in a white working-class community. In Bambi B. Schiffelin and Elinor Ochs (eds.), *Language Socialization across Cultures*, 199–212. Cambridge: Cambridge University Press.
Paugh, Amy L. (2012). *Playing with language: Children and change in a Caribbean village*. New York: Berghahn Books.
Rumsey, Alan (2013). Intersubjectivity, deception and the 'opacity of other minds': Perspectives from Highland New Guinea and beyond. *Language and Communication* 33: 326–343.
Sarvasy, Hannah S. (2015). Breaking the clause chains: non-canonical medial clauses in Nungon. *Studies in Language* 39 (3): 664–696.
Sarvasy, Hannah S. (2016). The future in Logoori oral texts. In Doris L. Payne, Sara Pachiarotti and Mokaya Bosire (eds.), *Diversity in African Languages: Selected Papers from the 46th Annual Conference on African Linguistics*, 201–218. Berlin: Language Science Press.
Sarvasy, Hannah S. (2017). *A Grammar of Nungon: A Papuan Language of Northeast New Guinea*. Leiden: Brill.
Sarvasy, Hannah S. (2018). Nungon. In *CHILDES*. https://childes.talkbank.org/access/Other/Nungon/Sarvasy.html
Sarvasy, Hannah S. (2019). The root nominal stage: a case study of early Nungon verbs. *Journal of Child Language* 46 (6): 1073–1101.
Sarvasy, Hannah S. (2020). Acquisition of clause chains in Nungon. *Frontiers in Psychology* 11: 1456. doi: 10.3389/fpsyg.2020.01456.
Sarvasy, Hannah S. (2021). Quantifying clause chains in Nungon texts. *Studies in Language*. https://doi.org/10.1075/sl.19058.sar.
Schieffelin, Bambi B. (1986). Teasing and shaming in Kaluli children's interactions. In Bambi B. Schiffelin and Elinor Ochs (eds.), *Language Socialization across Cultures*, 165–181. Cambridge: Cambridge University Press.

CHAPTER 18

Ngiä dm bloyag dand: Coconut Stories from Southern New Guinea

Dineke Schokkin

1 Dedication

This chapter is dedicated to the people in the two communities in Papua New Guinea I have spent time with: the Paluai speakers of Baluan Island, and the Idi speakers of Dimsisi village. As so many researchers have observed before me, I feel it is quite an understatement to say that fieldwork, with all its elation and heartbreak, changed me forever. Sasha lives and breathes fieldwork, and I will always be grateful to have had the honour of being her student.

More than about what it means to be a linguist, fieldwork is about what it means to be a human. More vividly than the breakthroughs in figuring out a particularly tough intricacy in a TAM system, I remember the kids on Baluan, running down the hill on late afternoons, shrieking with laughter, to bomb-dive into the ocean. I remember my adoptive mum poking up the fire and putting the kettle on when I was sick, just so I could wash with hot water for once. I remember the tears I couldn't stop when the Dimsisi women came and hugged me, themselves crying, when I showed them pictures of my 1-year-old who had stayed behind in Australia. To be a part of people's lives like that has been the biggest privilege of all, and I hope that in return some of their voices can be heard throughout this chapter.

2 Prologue

An ordinary day during the dry season in September 2014. In Zeri, a garden place on the banks of the Mai Kusa River in the territory of Nen-speaking Bimadbn, a hole is being dug by a few of the village women. Our party of researchers has just arrived by dinghy from Daru earlier that day. After taking care of our most immediate needs, mainly getting out of our seawater-soaked boots, hanging gear out to dry and putting up our mosquito netting for the night, we are invited to partake in a little ceremonial activity that has a lot of meaning throughout the region. To commemorate our arrival, the newbies in

© DINEKE SCHOKKIN, 2022 | DOI:10.1163/9789004510395_019

our team are going to plant a coconut each. As a white person, I am deemed too frail to dig the hole myself and fill it, so pretty much all I do is hold onto the sizeable sprout already emerging from the coconut while others do the work, basically the way things are done when it is a little kid planting the coconut tree.

A few weeks later, after we have settled into our field site in Dimsisi village, my husband and I visit Bimadbn to catch up with the rest of the team. We have started work on documenting the Idi language spoken in Dimsisi, and one of the aims of the visit is to start setting up a plan and workflow to collect sociolinguistic interviews, ultimately to provide data on language variation for our ARC Laureate project *The Wellsprings of Linguistic Diversity*. The idea is that by choosing an engaging and culturally important topic in our various field sites, we will get at speakers' most informal speech registers, as per Labov (1972), and so we plan on gathering 'coconut interviews' in which people share a story about an important coconut they planted. We make a skeleton list of questions to ask, and then set about training a few local consultants as interviewers. This has one very practical reason, namely that after only a few weeks' exposure we ourselves haven't become near conversant yet in the incredibly morphologically complex language, and one methodological one: we hope that by having a peer conversation, the interviewees are less likely to accommodate to us and the unfamiliarity of the situation by using a more formal register.

We then take off to practise on a few coconut trees near the village. Dry grass and coconut fronds make their typical rustling background noise while we are standing underneath a palm, a sound that will bring me back to these days every time I listen to the recordings afterwards. Bystanders are getting stubborn branches out of the way with their machetes, and making sure there are no sightings of the feared Papuan black snake. Both the interviewers and interviewees take to the exercise as if it is second nature to them. They question each other about their important coconut trees and life stories, sometimes seamlessly switching language with each conversational turn: the speaker asks a question in Nen, and the addressee answers in Idi.

Back in Dimsisi, we train our own team of Idi assistants, and collect an incredible number of coconut stories during the remainder of that field trip and the following ones. Interviewers are given free rein when it comes to asking follow-up questions, leading to a large range of topics being discussed in relation to the coconut. It is these stories that are distilled in this chapter.[1]

1 Evans (2020) contains an account of coconut stories collected in Bimadbn village, and raises many themes similar to the ones featuring prominently in this chapter.

3 Landscape

Idi (Pahoturi River family) and Nen (Yam family) are two unrelated languages spoken in the southernmost part of New Guinea Island. Most languages of the region are scarcely documented, although the degree of coverage is improving in recent years (see Evans 2012, Evans et al. 2017 for introductions and overviews). There also exist relatively few anthropological resources detailing cultural practices, with Ayres (1983) and Williams (1936) the most important ethnographic works—both of these, however, mainly focus on groups further west, speaking Yam languages, and do not cover the Pahoturi River area in much detail.

In the entire southern New Guinea area, as in many other places in the Pacific, coconut trees (*Cocos nucifera*) and their products saturate every aspect of life. While yams are considered the crop with the highest status, connected with a variety of customary activities (as documented in Williams [1936] and more recently in Döhler [2018]), coconuts are important in many ways too, and there is a huge extent of indigenous knowledge with respect to their cultivation and integration into cultural practices, which is the topic of the current chapter.

The southern New Guinea area is a flat, alluvial plain, consisting of savannah with interspersed rainforest. A few large tidal rivers meander through it, and it is bordered on the northern side by the vast Fly River. Nothing in this landscape is very permanent. There are very few clear landmarks such as large hills. Each wet season, the rivers overflow their banks, flooding large swathes of land, making orientation difficult and confining people to their villages. True stones are very rare and were used in precolonial times to perform rain magic. In this day and age, the only 'stone' available is *tgl kp*, chunks broken off anthills, with which ground ovens are lined. Groups used to live (and still are living) an itinerant lifestyle, often spending months on end at their garden places deep in the bush, away from the main villages. These gardens are made by slash-and-burn cultivation of patches of rainforest. They are very fertile, but once abandoned after a few years' use, nature is quick to reclaim the land. The same is true for the bush material houses, which are quickly absorbed by the forest once they fall into disuse.

In this ever-changing landscape, the coconut is the only long-lasting witness of human intervention or indeed mere presence, dependent as it is on humans for its spread inland (Chan and Elevitch 2006). Because the trees are typically planted near villages, they can serve as literal landmarks. After a long trek through the savannah and bush, especially on a hot day, the sight of the tops of coconut trees is certainly greeted with relief by everyone.

(1) Ngiä gänduä ibäny yralo ada may thmnggawa, la bngnamo, ada gta meydu dand.[2]

ngi=ä	*gänduä*	*ibäny*	*y-r-alo*	*ada*	*may*
coconut=CORE	DEM	plant	3SGO-PRES.NSG.AUX-3NSGA	thus	place

thmngg-awa	*la*	*b-ngnam-o*	*ada*	*gta*	*meydu*
garden-ALL	man	FUT-recognize-3NSGA	thus	this	village

da=nd
INT.DEM=SG.COP

'Coconuts are planted so that people know that there is a village.' (20150808_DIM_CI_M17_1 # 27).

The southern New Guinea cultures don't erect statues or build cathedrals to leave their mark on their environment; rather, they plant coconut trees as a reminder of a specific time or event or to mark a particular place. On our bush walks, we passed the site of an abandoned village or hamlet several times. Nothing would remind you of the fact that people once lived here, except the planted coconut trees gently swaying in the breeze, now grown very thin and tall.

4 Reasons

Often, but not always, coconut trees are planted to mark a particular occasion. One woman told the story of how she planted a coconut tree as a child, together with her mother, on the day a family member died. Some coconuts were planted as a celebration of finishing high school. Many coconuts were planted to mark Papua New Guinea becoming independent from Australia in 1975, and at the turn of the century in 2000. The latter time period more or less coincided with the exodus of several clans back to their tribal lands and the founding of new settlements there, and trees were also planted to mark this change. There are also several cases in which a coconut that someone had brought from further away was planted as a reminder of their trip.

Many people stated that their main reason for planting coconut trees is to provide sustenance for their children, and also their children's children and fur-

2 Abbreviations in glosses follow the Leipzig Glossing Rules, with the following additions: ATTR = attributive; AUG = augment; CORE = core argument; EXT = extension; INT = intermediate; LNK = linker; NOM.PRT = nominal particle; PERL = perlative; PRES = present progressive; REC = recent past; RED = reduplicant.

ther generations. In Idi, the concept of reason or purpose is expressed with the noun *mit*, which also means 'base of a tree' or *wénd*, also meaning 'meat'. The future generations can eat and drink the coconuts from their own trees, and don't have to be dependent on other people's goodwill or charity. At the same time, the trees serve as a memorial for them to remember their family members and ancestors by.

(2) Gta ngiä ngn yibänyin glä, bo krkräyäbli dä.
gta ngi=ä ngn y-i-bäny-in glä
this coconut=CORE 1SG.NOM 3SGO-REC-plant.NPL-1|3SGA FOC
bo krkr-äyäbli dä
1SG.POSS small.ones-NSG.BEN INT.DEM
'I planted this coconut for my small ones.' (070915_DIM_CI_M25 # 8–9).

(3) Gänduä ne glabay rmbrmb bogeo, bo gakr kdhkdha bom soyam bandeo, bngnonggmndmo ada, "Yayabänä ngi ibänyäthä gd."
gänduä ne glabay rmb~rmb b-o-g-eo bo
to.here if later RED~big FUT-INTR-PFV.NPL.AUX 1SG.POSS
gakr kdh~kdh=a bom soyam
children RED~small=CORE 1SG.ACC remember
b-a-nd-eo b-ngnongg-mnd-mo ada
FUT-AUG-IPFV.NPL.AUX-3NSGA FUT-think-EXT-3NSGA thus
yaya=bänä ngi ibäny-äthä gd
father=SG.POSS coconut plant-ABL this
'Later when they will have grown big, my children will remember me, and will be thinking "Father planted this coconut."' (20150907_DIM_CI_M24 # 29–30).

5 Sustenance

Coconuts form an indispensable staple in an area where diets are often lacking in proteins and other important nutrients, and where many have no reliable access to clean drinking water. Garden foods, such as a variety of yams, taro and tapioca, are made into a stew, cooked over the fire, with the addition of grated dry coconut and coconut cream. When visitors pass through the village, the first thing offered as a sign of hospitality and welcome is a drinking coconut. A few children are sent up into a tree to cut down a bunch of green coconuts:

(4) Thbäd lablä dä gl baklyäo ngathong, gta da gl bamndeo.
thbäd *la-blä* *gl* *b-a-klyä-o* *ngathong* *gta*
stranger man-SG.BEN FUT FUT-AUG-climb-3NSGA first this
da *gl* *b-a-mnd-eo*
INT.DEM FUT FUT-AUG-feed-3NSGA
'They will climb [the coconut tree] for a visitor, and give them [a coconut to drink].' (20141024_IBL_CI_M07 # 92).

This is customarily followed by some light foods like ripe bananas and some tobacco. There are also many special dishes containing coconut that are prepared only on special occasions when there is a *tre* 'feast'. One such dish is *qély*, a mixture of sliced yam or taro mixed with coconut, which is wrapped in banana or coconut leaves and cooked in a ground oven. Another is formed by various kinds of *pinipini*, or sago pancakes mixed with coconut.

6 Building and Crafting

The coconut trees are not only important for food, but for a multitude of other purposes. Occasionally, the flesh of dry coconuts is scraped and boiled in order to produce oil, used for hair and skin care. Palm fronds are used as a first layer of ground cover, to protect the sleeping mats woven from pandanus leaves that are rolled out on top. The side stalks of the palm fronds are used to make brooms, and from the leaves, various types of baskets are woven. The coconut husks, and the dry shells that remain after the nuts have been scraped free of flesh, called *ḡad*, are used to start lighting the fire. The stalks from dry fronds can be burned to produce a special type of ashes called *päg*, which is eaten together with particular ant species. Dry coconuts in particular are also a source of income, as any surplus of them (or of their products, like oil) can be sold to other villagers. A somewhat controversial use of the coconut is to produce palm wine, or *tubä*. For this, several notches are made in the top part of a coconut palm where the flower was attached, and a bamboo container is hung onto the stem to catch the liquid coming out. When this liquid is left to ferment it turns into an alcoholic drink. Some people disapprove of this, saying it is not a traditional way to use coconuts, while others appear to be more agnostic.

(5) Ngimä yau dzin bi nganggas dand, yau obo wéndä gd rmb mg da ngi.
ngi-mä *yau* *dzin* *bi* *nganggas* *da=nd* *yau*
coconut-LOC NEG one NOM.PRT make INT.DEM=SG.COP NEG
obo *wénd=ä* *gd* *rmb* *mg* *da* *ngi*
3SG.POSS reason=CORE this big real INT.DEM coconut

'There is not one particular thing made out of the coconut, but it has a lot of purposes, it is very important.' (20150810_DIM_CI_M20 # 10–11).

7 Life and Death

In traditional lore, the coconut is connected to fertility. It is said that when a man eats lots of coconuts, he will father many children.

(6) Mn ḡédith story dand, ngiä ne noto, gädä gl nanggaso.
mn ḡéd-ith story da=nd ngi=ä ne
just before-ABL INT.DEM=SG.COP coconut=CORE if
n-ot-o gäd=ä gl n-a-nggas-o
FUT.2SG-eat.NPL-1|2SGA child=CORE FUT FUT.2SG-AUG-make-1|2SGA
'There is an old story: if you eat coconuts, then you will conceive (many) children.' (20150816_BIR_CI_M35 # 153–154).

Conversely, burying the placenta and umbilical cord beneath a planted coconut after a birth is a traditional ceremony with the aim of preventing further births from happening.

When someone dies, nuts from a coconut tree planted by this person are off limits for a certain time period. This is called *qar* in Idi, often translated as 'law'. The coconuts are not harvested, but people wait until they start dropping by themselves and producing shoots; they are then collected and tied together. A bundle of grass is tied in a knot and attached to the tree to indicate that the coconut tree is under *qar*. When someone steals the nuts, this leads to retributions, such as a pig destroying their garden. It is up to the relatives to decide how long the *qar* will last. The sequence below describes how the ban will be lifted: there will be a ceremony and the coconuts with shoots from the dead person's tree are given out to family members to be planted. This is taken from a single interview, with a number of intervening utterances removed for the sake of brevity.

(7) Obo mokoa dzin bi gn o ewli qak…
obo moko=a dzin bi gn o ewli qak
3SG.POSS love=CORE one NOM.PRT year or how.many moon
'It is up to them [the relatives], if they want to wait one year or some months …'

(8) Gl doawa ä oba nnggpa ne ämibi bogen…
gl do-awa ä oba nggp=a ne ämibi
FUT given.location-ALL LNK 3NSG.POSS mind=CORE if alright
b-o-g-en
FUT-INTR-PRES.NPL.AUX-FUT.3SGA
'Until their mind will be at ease.'

(9) Gl ako bo bwmämo oba kulummä, yeka botändmo.
gl ako bo b-wmä-m-o oba kulum-mä
FUT again 3.NOM FUT-gather-PLA-3NSGA 3NSG.POSS group-LOC
yeka b-o-tänd-m-o
speech FUT-INTR-discuss-PLA-3NSGA
'(Then) they will gather together and talk about it within their group.'

(10) Wota bbdégo.
wot=a b-bdég-o
garden.food=CORE FUT-cook-3NSGA
'They will cook food.'

(11) Bambetanendemo oba kulum may gpe.
b-a-mbeta-ne-nde-m-o oba kulum may
FUT-AUG-pass.on-PLO-DUR-PLA-3NSGA 3NSG.POSS group place
gp-e
inside-PERL
'They will pass them on [the coconuts from the tree, with shoots] among the group [to be planted].'

(12) Gl ako bi wotang gta yénmändä bgäya.
gl ako bi wot-ang gta yénmä-ndä
FUT again 1NSG.EXC.NOM garden.food-ATTR this later-INSTR
b-gä-ya
FUT-3SGO.PFV.AUX-1|2NSGA
'After that, we will once again eat [nuts from] this [coconut].'

(13) Obana ne gta qara dzémi bi bläkia.
obana ne gta qar=a dzémi bi
3SG.POSS if this ban=CORE already 1NSG.EXC.NOM
b-läk-ia
FUT-destroy-1|2NSGA
'In that way, we will destroy the taboo on his coconut.' (20150925_BIM_CI_F25 # 111–121)

8 Time

Coconuts also mark the passing of time. As was mentioned previously, planting coconuts is strongly connected with the idea of providing nourishment for future generations, not only in the form of the single tree from which the nuts are eaten, but also in the form of new suckers it will create, which will be distributed further among the family group. As the coconut trees multiply and prosper, so will the people who depend on them for their livelihood. Linguistically, it is noteworthy that in this context, we see a high incidence of verb roots specified for pluractionality and/or plural objects.

(14) Gl bambetandeo dédrä ne buspelndin, gl btrindimu.
gl *b-a-mbeta-nd-eo* *dédr=ä* *ne*
FUT FUT-AUG-pass.on-DUR-3NSGA dry=CORE if
b-u-spel-nd-in *gl*
FUT-INTR-drop.PL-DUR-3SGA.FUT FUT
b-tri-ndi-m-u
FUT-collect.PL-DUR-PLA-3NSGA
'[My children] will pass on the dry ones when they are falling, they will collect them.'

(15) Gl bo ako gta dédrä bokomendemo, bibänändimu kokoanga da.
gl *bo* *ako* *gta* *dédr=ä* *b-o-kome-nde-m-o*
FUT 3.NOM again this dry=CORE FUT-AUG-carry.PL-DUR-PLA-3NSGA
b-ibänä-ndi-m-u *koko-ang=a* *da*
FUT-plant.PL-DUR-PLA-3nsgA shoot-ATTR=CORE INT.DEM
'They will carry the dry ones and plant the ones that have a shoot.'

(16) Gta yba nganggas dand.
gta *yba* *nganggas* *da=nd*
this 1NSG.INC.POSS make INT.DEM=SG.COP
'This is our way of doing things.'

(17) Gl gaytha dä bomblonden ako ngiä.
gl *gaytha* *dä* *b-o-mblo-nd-en* *ako*
FUT from.here INT.DEM FUT-AUG-reproduce-DUR again
ngi=ä
coconut=CORE
'Out of it will grow many coconuts.'

(18) Ngiä yau gänduä bi da wotawa.
ngi=ä *yau* *gänduä* *bi* *da* *wot-awa*
coconut=CORE NEG to.here NOM.PRT INT.DEM eat-ALL
'Coconuts are not only for eating.'

(19) Ngiä di dm bloyag dand.
ngi=ä *di* *dm* *bloy-ag* *da=nd*
coconut=CORE INT.DEM sucker reproduce-ATTR INT.DEM=SG.COP
'The coconut is also producing new suckers.' (20150810_DIM_CI_M26 # 46–50).

When a coconut tree comes to the end of its life cycle, there are a few tell-tale signs that it will probably die soon. Older coconut trees grow extremely tall and thin, and at some point stop bearing fruit. People will still honour the ancestors that planted them, and refer to these long palms as "our grannies' trees". The top shoot will get very small and the leaves will start to wilt.

(20) Thämä ne wau bogen, wéthä ako ketket mg bonden…
thäm=ä *ne* *wau* *b-o-g-en* *wéth=ä*
leaf=CORE if ripe FUT-INTR-PFV.NPL.AUX-3sgA.FUT top.shoot=CORE
ako *ketket* *mg* *b-o-nd-en*
again very.small real FUT-INTR-IPFV.NPL.AUX-3SGA.FUT
'When the leaves will have wilted, the top shoot is becoming very small …'

(21) Bokapamn gl oboobo.
b-o-kapam-n *gl* *obo~obo*
FUT-INTR-break-3sgA.FUT FUT RED~3SG.POSS
'It will break by itself.'

(22) Bulä kdhkdh bogen, da wathkän.
bul=ä *kdh~kdh* *b-o-g-en*
frond.stem=CORE RED~small FUT-INTR-PFV.NPL.AUX-3sgA.FUT
da *w-a-thkä-n*
INT.DEM INTR-AUG-break-3sgA.FUT
'The frond stems will get very small and then they will break.' (20150810_DIM_CI_M18 # 70–72)

When asked how long a tree they have planted will last, people indicate that any coconuts they planted during their lifetime are likely to outlive them.

(23) Dhob gna gl bren, doawe pthe ne bogen.
dhob gn=a gl b-r-en do-awe
some year=CORE FUT FUT-go-3SGA.FUT given.location-ALL
pthe ne b-o-g-en
tall.coconut if FUT-INTR-PFV.NPL-AUX-3SGA.FUT
'Some years will go by, and if/when the coconut grows very tall …'

(24) Bo kämä, ngn nma qédl balo o ngiä nma gl gäbin bi bonden.
bo kämä ngn nma qédl b-a-l-o o
1SG.POSS ignorance 1SG.NOM might dead FUT-AUG-go-1|2sg.FUT or
ngi=ä nma gl gäbin bi
coconut=CORE might will stand still
b-o-nd-en
FUT-INTR-IPFV.NPL.AUX-3sgA.FUT
'I don't know, I might die (first) or the coconut might still be standing.' (20140929_BIM_CI_F25 # 40–41).

9 Epilogue

In this chapter, Idi speakers' own reflections on the meaning and uses of coconuts for them have been given centre stage, in order to illustrate the great importance this crop has for the communities in this region. Coconuts play a role in pretty much every aspect of life: as food, as building and crafting material and for personal care. Even more important is their symbolic role as commemorative signs, in both space and time. The planted coconuts provide a visible connection between the people who planted them and the places these people inhabited, including when these places have since been left behind. Similarly, the coconut trees connect Idi speakers' past, present and future. The previous generations' coconuts, while not themselves productive anymore, provided the suckers from which the present-day trees have grown. They, in turn, will provide suckers that, when planted, make sure the next generations are provided for. Across time, generations of people and generations of coconut trees are joined together in an intricate web of offshoots and offspring, mutually interdependent.

Within the *Wellsprings* project, we set out to introduce a methodology from a different field of linguistics, (an adapted version of) the sociolinguistic interview (Labov 1972), into the field of language documentation and description. Besides an array of linguistic variables to study, the materials we collected supplied us with much more than we could have dreamed of: a unique glimpse into the vast wealth of knowledge the Idi community possesses with respect to the cultivation of the coconut, and how this is integrated into their culture and society. Having Idi speakers take the lead in structuring the interviews turned out to be a crucial factor in this. If I, as an outsider, had tried to put a bigger stamp on the scope of data collection myself, we would not have accomplished these same rich results. This highlights the importance of collaboration with indigenous communities within language documentation projects, in order to support these communities in keeping their languages and cultures strong. While this is not always easy to do (as academics we all know the pressures to secure jobs, bring in grant money and work on our impact factors), I have attempted to show that at times it is better to take a back seat when it comes to carrying out our research.

Acknowledgements

The fieldwork on which this study is based was funded by the Australian Research Council (Grant # FL130100111). My sincerest thanks to the Idi speech community, in particular Puli Ämädu, Simon Bagi, Birke Eka, Carls Gana, Kaune Gana, Masa Gegera, Kmonde Gigu, Magham Greh, Judy James, Qandro Kaeko, Titi Masa, Pastor Deba Masro, Paul Mikuku and Bess Purge, and my partner in everything, Tobias Maletz, for all their hard work in gathering these great stories. Thanks are also due to my colleagues in the Wellsprings project and other linguists working in the southern New Guinea area for the numerous valuable conversations.

Appendix: List of Vocabulary Related to Coconut Trees, Their Parts and Their Uses

bébgä	coconut type, red/yellow nuts
bkal	coconut palm with rolled-up leaves
blg	coconut type
bul	coconut frond stem
dm	sucker
dmang	grove
dhn	knock down (one fruit or coconut)
dh	knock down (one bunch of fruits or coconuts)
dhe	knock down (many fruits or coconuts)
(ngi) dédr	dry coconut

dzange	coconut type with sweet, chewable nuts
gogo	coconut type, green nuts
gulymgulym	oil or cream from *kmth* (spongy inside of a ripe coconut)
ḡad	shell
ibäny	plant (one)
ibänän	plant (many)
käbädu	sago pancake, like *pinipini* but fried first
kämtkämt	coconut type, small nuts
kängg	sucker
kmth	spongy inside of a ripe coconut
koko	shoot
kp	fruit, nut
krkrmb	soft shell of a young coconut
kukup	husk a coconut
nurly	soft meat inside a young coconut
ngi	coconut
qéd	coconut meat that is a bit firmer
qrap	stalk of a coconut frond
qth	spoon from a coconut shell
soke	flower stump, with which coconuts are attached to the tree; palm wine is made from this part
päg	ashes made from burned coconut shells
pal ngi	coconut type, yellow/orange nuts
pinipini	sago pancake with coconut
pth	tree trunk
pthe	very tall coconut tree
qély	yam cake
qéth speléngg	basket type, made from broad coconut leaves
suängg	baby basket made from coconut leaves
täktäk	dish with scraped coconut
tan	broom, made from coconut leaves
tawadz	tie dry coconuts together by cutting out a bit of husk and tying them with it
tikép	very small unripe coconut
(*ngi*) *tm*	drinking coconut
trmb	coconut flower
tubä	palm wine
thäk	half-ripe coconut
thäm	leaf, frond
thämthämäng	basket type, made from split coconut leaves

thkl	mix of yam and coconut cream
thupä	dry coconut, without water inside
wanymang	stage of coconut growth
wéth	top shoot of a coconut palm
wuriwuri	coconut scraper (bench)
wuthwuth	becoming small, of the top shoot of a coconut palm
yéd	coconut cream; juice, sap (from which palm wine is made)

References

Ayres, Mary C. (1983). This side, that side: Locality and exogamous group definition in Morehead area, Southwestern Papua. PhD thesis, University of Chicago.

Chan, Edward and Craig R. Elevitch (2006). *Cocos nucifera* (coconut). Digitised chapter from *Traditional trees of Pacific Islands*, available from https://agroforestry.org/free-publications/traditional-tree-profiles (accessed 22.10.2020).

Döhler, Christian (2018). *A grammar of Komnzo*. Berlin: Language Science Press.

Evans, Nicholas (2012). Even more diverse than we thought: the multiplicity of Trans-Fly languages. In Nicholas Evans and Marian Klamer (eds.), *Melanesian Languages on the Edge of Asia: Challenges for the 21st Century. Language Documentation and Conservation* Special Publication 5, 109–149.

Evans, Nicholas (2020). One thousand and one coconuts: Growing memories in Southern New Guinea. *The Contemporary Pacific* 32 (1): 72–96.

Evans, Nicholas, Wayan Arka, Matthew Carroll, Yun Jung Choi, Christian Döhler, Volker Gast, Eri Kashima, Emil Mittag, Bruno Olsson, Kyla Quinn, Dineke Schokkin, Philip Tama, Charlotte van Tongeren and Jeff Siegel (2017). *The languages of Southern New Guinea*. In Bill Palmer (ed.), *The Languages and Linguistics of New Guinea: A Comprehensive Guide*, 641–774. Berlin: Walter de Gruyter.

Labov, William (1972). Some Principles of Linguistic Methodology. *Language in Society* 1 (1): 97–120.

Williams, F.E. (1936). *Papuans of the Trans-Fly*. Oxford: Clarendon.

CHAPTER 19

Code Copying and the Strength of Languages

Lars Johanson and Éva Á. Csató

1 Introduction

This chapter deals with the stability—in terms of strength and weakness—of indigenous languages. It focuses on Turkic, with its incredibly manifold language contacts. Moving beyond ahistorical universalism, the linguistic study of contact languages should now direct its attention to the specific historical circumstances under which codes have arisen, changed, and vanished. Key determinative factors are whether copied items are 'taken over' or 'carried over', if their codes are superstrata, substrata, or adstrata, and whether they appear as primary codes or secondary codes.

As befits a publication in honor of a linguist who has made eminent contributions to the documentation, description, and analysis of less-studied languages, both theoretically and in fieldwork, this paper will also contribute to the complex discussion about how linguists and their discipline can help speech communities to adopt successful strategies for maintaining and revitalizing their languages. Infelicitous strategies can mislead the speaker communities and even contribute to generational language shift. Learning new varieties always implies inequality and power imbalances. Relationships between weak purified and high-copying varieties will illustrate the problems. We will argue that the acquisition of code-copying strategies may facilitate the maintenance of communication skills in lesser used or endangered codes.

2 Code Copying

The framework applied is the Code-Copying Model (Johanson 2002a, 2021), a coherent conceptual basis for describing complex matters of contact-induced copying. It defines a framework of relationships and describes them in an approach based on adequate sets of concepts.

The term 'code' is used for a language or its varieties. Code copying is not identical with 'code switching', which refers to alternation between languages in one and the same stretch of discourse.

Copying occurs from a source (model) code to a target (basic) code. Two types are known:

© LARS JOHANSON AND ÉVA Á. CSATÓ, 2022 | DOI:10.1163/9789004510395_020

– ‘Take-over copying’ occurs when speakers of a primary code (L1) take over copies from a secondary code (L2). The secondary code is the source code and the primary code is the target code.
– ‘Carry-over copying’ occurs when speakers of a primary code (L1) carry over copies from this code into their own variety of a secondary code (L2). The primary code is the source code, and the secondary code is the target code.

Copies can be different with respect to what is copied:
– ‘Global copying’ is used as a metaphoric image for copying an entire (global) linguistic item with its material side, semantics, combinability, and frequency of use.
– ‘Selective copying’ is used for separate properties: materials, semantics, combinability, and frequency of use. See examples below.

The motivation for copying is to increase the functionality of a variety, i.e. to accommodate it to the communicative needs of speakers. Both take-over and carry-over copying can strengthen varieties and support their maintenance. They can keep varieties strong and contribute to their retention. Copying can make varieties more viable, through shared lexical items and typological patterns. No language has become extinct because of intensive copying (Johanson 2002b).

Copying concerns lexicon, morphology, phonology, and syntax. It is often difficult to distinguish the results of carry-over and take-over copying, but certain typical differences are found. It is well-known that loosely structured lexicon is easily copiable. Nouns are more easily copiable than verbs, when provided with inflections. Function words are less copiable. Heavy lexical copying leads to major changes. With increasing proficiency in a foreign language, speakers may gradually also take over bound morphology. Derivational morphology is relatively copiable, whereas inflectional morphology is obviously not.

3 Types of Copying

The roles of affinity and genealogical relatedness of the codes in contact have an impact on code copying, code shift, and resulting substrata. They affect the acquisition, development, shift, survival, attrition, death, and revival of codes. Originals and copies always differ. Copies are adapted to the recipient system with respect to material, semantic, combinatory, and frequential properties, and they undergo further development there. They are inserted into the morphosyntactic frame of the target code, which changes gradually. The results vary:

- The copy may be added to the target code as a new element.
- The copy may replace a corresponding element of the target code.
- A corresponding element of the target code may be retained, but assume a modified function.

Copying is determined by the degree to which the primary and secondary codes are acquired. Its nature and extent may vary, according to the stages in the processes of acquisition.

Speakers are by definition originally more proficient in their primary code than in the secondary code. But this may change in the course of their acquisition of a secondary code. A speaker may even become more proficient in the latter.

Carry-over copying can occur because of imperfect learning of the secondary code. This is not necessarily the case, however, since creative power may also be involved. The inferiority decreases as learners become more proficient in the secondary code, but it may still continue to be operative.

Code shift means that speakers for reasons of a social nature abandon their code in favor of the other code. The typical scenarios are population movement and migration caused by unstable political or social settings. Shift may be preceded by carry-over influence. The result may live on as a substratum in a surviving successor code. The abandoned code has then become an underlying stratum.

Local codes are spoken in a given territory. Speakers of another code may immigrate, bringing their primary code with them. If the incoming code is socially stronger, the local code may end up as a substratum. It becomes a code that has lower status or prestige than the supplanting code.

Carry-over copying generally does not affect the vocabulary. Speakers of the primary code want to be understood by speakers of the dominant code. They do not carry over unfamiliar lexemes. Contentive elements generally determine the intelligibility between codes, though not when semantic equivalents of primary-code lexemes are—or are assumed to be—lacking in the secondary code. These lexemes denote specific cultural or natural phenomena. Place names, for instance, are mostly carried over in their intact shapes.

Carry-over copying leads to phonetic influence. When learning a secondary code, speakers easily carry over features of their own sound system. In their pronunciation of secondary code words, they resort to the closest sounds in their primary code. Articulatory habits are stable, since they are motoric, occurring through the innervation of muscles. This leads to innovative modes of pronunciation, so-called 'accents', which are hard to correct and get rid of. Compare the predictable pronunciations of English words in different languages around the world.

Carry-over copying does not necessarily decrease when speakers reach higher degrees of proficiency in the secondary code. The articulatory features of the source codes are frequently not acquired even by speakers with a high degree of proficiency in other respects.

Grammatical structures can be carried over to some extent. This occurs especially when speakers are less aware of differences between the codes. It mostly leads to reduction of the inflectional systems. Verb systems may be remodeled through unconscious carry-over and reduction of aspect-mood-tense features. The employment of English perfects instead of preterites is a well-known example.

Inflectional morphemes of the primary code are carried over in a few cases. The Romani variety described by Birgit Igla (1996) is an example of unique carry-over influence, since it contains carried over Turkish inflected verb forms.

Knowledge about substratum effects in attested contact situations may help us understand unattested prehistorical situations. The task of linguists is to improve the methods for determining the effects of substratum interference in reconstructed languages by:

- refining the concepts and methods for determining substratum interference on the basis of recently attested or historically attested language shift situations,
- applying the refined concepts and methods to specific case studies of language shift in linguistic prehistory,
- and finally applying the available methods to specific case studies of language shift in linguistic prehistory.

Adstratum codes are in contact with each other without higher or lower prestige. Their contact involves mutual copying between codes of about equal rank. Spanish and Portuguese have an Arabic adstratum. French and Dutch in Belgium are adstrata with roughly the same status. Superstratal carry-over is found in Gaulish and Basque elements in Western Romance. Gaulish has disappeared, but remnants of its vocabulary survive in French words and placenames. An Irish substratum is found in English, where carry-over has led to shifts and substratum influence. Remnants of the North Germanic Norn language are found in the Scots dialects of the Shetland and Orkney Islands. The Germanic substratum hypothesis is an attempt to explain the distinctive nature of Germanic in the Indo-European family. Germanic, in its earliest form, may have been influenced by a non-Indo-European language. Roughly a third of Proto-Germanic lexical items have come from a non-Indo-European substratum. In controversial hypotheses on the creation of Indo-European protolanguages in northern Europe, it has been argued that the pre-Germanic substratum was of Uralic origin. Other researchers argue that the proto-Germans encountered a non-Indo-European speaking people and just copied many features from their language.

4 Turkic Examples of Carry-Over Copying

Local non-Turkic codes have been abandoned in favor of intrusive immigrant Turkic codes, but have caused substrata of carry-over copying. Carry-over of lexical elements has been limited, but there are changes in grammatical structures, and even inflectional morphemes have been carried over. The major effects of carry-over copying are found in the phonology, i.e. sound changes due to inherited articulation habits. Codes of Turkicized groups represent the results of efforts to pronounce Turkic sounds. Though nearly all Turkic languages show systematic sound correspondences within their genealogical family, carry-over copying has led to irregularities in some cases. Minority groups rarely copy over lexicon, which, as mentioned above, would not be understood by the majority. If the model codes are unrelated to Turkic codes, phonology becomes discrepant. Umlaut is certainly not an attractive feature to take over, but can be carried over; see the Uyghur case below. Minority groups shifting to Turkic displayed their own characteristic pronunciation habits. On the pronunciation of Turkish by minorities in Turkey, see Kowalski (1934: 993).

Non-substratic Turkic languages mainly display results of take-over influence. Kazakh represents a normal Turkic type, without recognizable substrata, but with lexical copies from Mongolic and other languages.

It is impossible to determine the degree of bilingualism and plurilingualism in older speaker communities. Multiple model languages may have resulted in homogeneity. Codes may be subject to limited or extensive copying, determined by social circumstances and attitudes: differences can be observed in the extent and degree of copying. Turkic communities have always been ready to mix socially with other groups, and nomadic groups have had great freedom to modify their codes.

In the Russian-dominated area, Russian achieved dominance as the common language of administration, education, and media. Smaller languages were exposed to enormous influence from Russian and had low chances of survival.

Take-over copying is an intense form of contact. Languages that were more stable were weakly affected, and those that were less stable were strongly affected.

4.1 *Uyghur*

Genealogically unrelated situations will be treated first. Speakers of East Old Turkic once migrated from South Siberia to Eastern Turkestan, present-day Xinjiang. The incoming speakers of East Old Turkic encountered resident groups of speakers of non-Turkic languages such as Tokharian and Soghdian. These eventually acquired the incoming elements as an L2 code, and carried over phonological L1 features to it. The Turkic lexicon, which was widely known in the region, was copied in large part, along with phonological features. The carried-over features were preserved as a substratum when the non-Turkic groups shifted to Turkic. Uyghur was thus subject to carry-over copying from Indo-European. Populations carried over phonetic features to their brand of Turkic. Large non-Turkic groups shifted to Turkic. After these non-Turkic shifts to Turkic, these non-Turkic features were preserved as a substratum. Uyghur displays many features that are lacking or uncommon in other Turkic languages. Certain vowel changes and other phonological irregularities can be interpreted as Indo-European substratum phenomena. Modern Uyghur shows traces of bidirectional copying: both take-over and carry-over copying. Uyghur displays features that are lacking in other Turkic languages, especially phonological idiosyncrasies in the vowel system, such as umlaut in Uyghur *beliḳ* 'fish' < **balïḳ*.

4.2 *Uzbek*

The case of Uzbek, which was influenced by Persian, is comparable. Speakers of East Old Turkic, including the Karakhanid variety, migrated to Transoxiana, the land between the Oxus and Amu Darya Rivers, where they took over numerous elements from the Iranian codes spoken by large resident populations. The resident Iranian-speaking population eventually acquired the incoming Turkic code as an L2 code, carrying over phonological L1 features to it. After they had shifted to Turkic, the features were preserved as a substratum. The result is a Persian-influenced vowel system. The vowel inventory underwent centralizations that affected the phonemic distinctions /ä/ vs. /a/, /ö/ vs. /o/, /ü/ vs. /u/, and /i/ vs. /ï/. The phoneme /å/, which corresponds to /a/ in most Turkic languages, is realized as a slightly labialized back vowel [ɒ]. Considerable syntactic features were also carried over to this brand of Turkic.

In the case of Uzbek and Azeri, large non-Turkic populations carried over both phonetic and syntactic features to their brand of Turkic, and this brand became predominant.

4.3 *Azeri*

A small number of Seljuk speakers of an Oghuz Turkic that was influenced by the unrelated language Persian migrated into the Transcaucasian area. Although Turkic was introduced by a small elite group, it gradually supplanted a number of regional languages. Numerous resident speakers of Iranian and Caucasian languages acquired this incoming code as an L2 variety and carried over some phonological L1 features to it. After the shift to Turkic, some of their primary-code features were preserved as a substratum. Azeri was mildly influenced by Persian, which had already been influenced and simplified through intensive contact with Turkic.

4.4 *Chuvash*

Speakers of Oghur Turkic migrated into the Volga-Kama area around the end of the 8th century. Resident speakers of Finnic languages, e.g. Mari, acquired it as an L2 code and carried over phonological features from their L1 to their own brand of Oghur Turkic. The resulting phonology in Chuvash is confusing because the languages were genealogically unrelated. Chuvash displays numerous irregular and complicated sound changes, especially among the vowels, whose correspondences with Common Turkic vowels are amazingly unsystematic. The development of Chuvash was complicated by a series of sound changes and replacements; however, it remained typologically similar to other Turkic languages in syntax and lexicon. After the Finnic groups had shifted to Turkic, phonological features of their varieties were preserved as a substratum. The influence was so strong that Chuvash was incorrectly considered a Finno-Ugric language by earlier scholars. The language is, however, clearly Turkic in lexicon and grammar (Johanson 2000). It was just subject to phonological carry-over copying from Finnic model codes. Chuvash is an example of profound phonological carry-over copying.

4.5 *Yakut*

The speakers of the ancestor of Yakut once migrated northward from South Siberia. They first took over lexical and other elements from Mongolic on the shores of Lake Baikal. Advancing further north, they encountered resident speakers of Tungusic. These acquired the Turkic language as an L2 code, carrying over to it syntactic, morphological, and phonological features from their L1. When the Tungusic groups shifted to Turkic, features of their own language were preserved as a substratum. Incoming speakers of Yakut brought their Turkic language to a region whose Tungusic speakers acquired it as an L2 variety.

Yakut did not undergo carry-over copying of Tungusic phonology of the sort that caused confusion in Chuvash. Tungusic lexical loans are rare in Turkic. Few Tungusic lexemes were carried over to standard Yakut, as is typical of a substratum situation. Standard Yakut does have a few loans belonging to the domains of husbandry and everyday life, e.g. *ǰiä* 'house'. Non-standard Yakut dialects have some hundred words copied from Tungusic. Dolgan, a north Siberian relative, displays numerous Evenki loans.

There are almost no carry-over copies of Tungusic derivational morphemes. Yakut has not copied any derivational suffixes from Tungusic, but the derivational system is strongly influenced by take-over copying from Mongolic.

Interestingly enough, there is Tungusic influence on the inflectional system, which is hardly to be expected between genealogically unrelated languages (Johanson 2014). The Yakut imperfect is formed according to the pattern aorist stem + copula 'was', e.g. *Bar-ar ä-tị-m* 'I went', which corresponds to the norm in Turkic. A second imperfect has the pattern aorist stem + person-number agreement marker of the possessive type, e.g. 1SG *Bar-ar-ịm* 'I went'. The latter imperfect lacks a preterite marker, which is highly remarkable for Turkic, but can be explained as a Tungusic copy.

Yakut converbs provided with subject person-number agreement markers represent one interesting case. Evenki possesses converbs provided with personal markers, part of a switch-reference system of marking different-subject constructions. Speakers of Evenki have partly carried over this feature to Yakut, changing the combinatory properties of Yakut converbs with respect to personal markers. However, while Evenki uses suffixes of a possessive type, Yakut uses suffixes of a pronominal type. The switch-reference system has not been carried over, leading to claims that Evenki influence has not played any role in the development of person-marked converbs in Yakut (Pakendorf 2007: 7–14). Considered from the point of view of the code-copying framework, however, providing converbs with person markers is surely a combinatory copy carried over from the Evenki substratum. The possessive suffixes were replaced by suffixes of the pronominal kind, which were already common in the system. Though this development represents an innovation, it was not independent, but the result of contact influence. Speakers of Evenki carried over these forms as selective copies and adapted them to the receiving system of Yakut.

4.6 *Effects of Copying*

Effects of copying depend on the degree of affinity between the participant codes. The question is whether affinity can be defined as genealogical relatedness. The Uyghur substratum consists of genealogically unrelated Indo-European languages. The Uzbek and Azeri substrata consist of genealogically unrelated Persian varieties. The Chuvash substratum consists of genealogically unrelated Finnic, close to present-day Mari. The Yakut substratum is Tungusic, a language possibly related to Turkic. The influence of the non-related languages has led to phonological anomalies, and in the case of Chuvash even to a confusing phonology. The Tungusic influence on Yakut has not led to phonological irregularities. Carry-over copying in inflectional systems seems to be extremely rare between unrelated languages, but Yakut undoubtedly shows traces of a Tungusic substratum in its inflectional system. These states of affairs might be seen as arguments in favor of the genealogical relatedness of the languages.

Karachay-Balkar, spoken in the Caucasus area, is affected by lexical take-over copying and displays a relatively normal Turkic morphology and syntax. Some dialects, however, exhibit a Caucasian phonological substratum involving, for instance, ejective consonants. Karachay-Balkar has strong ejectives *p', t', k', ḳ', č'* beyond the prime syllable, and glottalic egressive consonants, e.g. *ärtʰ-t'ä* 'in the morning'.

These observations can be compared with other data. Some South Siberian varieties exhibit words of Yeniseic origin as a result of substratum influence, Slavic substrata are found in Balkan Turkish, and some South Siberian varieties exhibit Yeniseic phonological substratum influence. Greek substrata are found in several Turkic varieties, for instance in the Black Sea dialects of Trabzon and Rize, and probably also in Galician Karaim. The Romani variety spoken in the Athenian suburb Ajia Varvara, described by Birgit Igla (1996), is an example of unique carry-over influence, where Turkish inflected verb forms were carried over to a Romani code. Before settling in Greece, this Gypsy group had lived in Turkey as bilingual speakers of Romani and Turkish. Their Romani code includes copies of verbs carried over from Turkish with preserved inflectional aspectual and personal markers in the present and past tense paradigms, e.g. *Calus-ur-um* 'I work', copied from *Čalïš-ïr-ïm*.

4.7 *Turkic Examples of Take-Over Copying*

Take-over copying typically occurs in asymmetrical contact situations when speakers of a dominated language take over copies from a dominant language. The examples chosen here to illustrate this type of copying are Turkic varieties spoken in eastern parts of Europe, Gagauz in the Balkans, and Karaim in the Baltic area. Gagauz and Karaim are both high-copying languages that have undergone profound typological change as a result of frame-changing take-over copying.

Global copying has influenced the lexical stock of both languages. For instance, kinship terms, typically denoting non-core family relations, are frequent: Lithuanian Karaim *dvoyunarodnïy* 'cousin', *semya* 'family name'. A number of Gagauz kinship terms are copied from Bulgarian, like *batü* 'older brother', *kaku* 'older sister', *lelü* 'aunt', *unuka* 'grandchild' (Csató and Menz 2018). Phonetically and morphologically these global copies have been accommodated to the frame of the copying languages. The copied lexical elements serve as genuine Turkic nominal stems when taking inflectional suffixes such as case, possessive, and plural. Thus, speakers use and learn them in their inflected forms, such as *semya-m* 'my family name'. Also, copied Karaim verbs such as *vïzvat' et'-* 'to call', 'to send for' are naturally used and learned in an inflected form, such as *Vïzvat' et'-t'ị-m skora-nï* 'I called for an ambulance'. This contributes to the astonishing stability of the inherited Turkic morphology in both languages.

Global copies of phrases have also served as initiators of syntactic changes; i.e. non-Turkic syntactic patterns have been copied through copied phrases. Successive copying of combinational patterns has changed the original Turkic syntactic frame, resulting in a syntactic type that is accommodated to the typology of the dominating languages. This serves the communicative needs of the speakers by establishing correspondences between L2 and L1 structures, e.g. Russian 'когда ребенок рождается' [when child be.born- PRES-3SG] vs. *ńečik bir ulan tuv-a-t* [when a child be.born-PRES-3SG] 'when a child is born'.

Selectional copies, for instance of phonetic and phonological features, have also had an impact on the original phonological system. An example is the palatalization of consonants in Turkic languages dominated by Slavic languages. The underlying Turkic principle of sound harmony is maintained, but the realization of the sounds is accommodated to Slavic phonology.

Frequential copying has resulted in more frequent use of variants that correspond to structures found in L2. For example, the possessive construction of the locative type *M'än'-d'ä bart uŋlu yüv* [I-LOC existent big house], cf. Russian 'У меня большой дом' [by I-GEN big house] 'I have a big house', has become relatively frequent in Karaim at the expense of the typically more frequent genitive structure.

Copying the semantic features of L2 elements onto L1 items is an easy way of extending the functionality of the native vocabulary. The Turkic verbs *ket-* and *bar-*, which were originally near synonyms, reflect in Karaim the semantic difference between Russian 'идти' 'to go (on foot)' and 'ехать' 'to travel', 'to go (by train, car, etc.)'. Thus, this selective copying has introduced a semantic differentiation between two native L1 items. The semantic distinctions in the two languages as used by the bilingual speakers have therefore become isomorphic.

5 The Complex Task of Linguists and the Role of Copying

Linguists document and reconstruct data in diachronically and typologically coherent ways. They "are generally concerned with one particular language and speak of the 'language community' as their primary target (sometimes adopting a puristic approach that aims to document the 'true' language, untainted by loans and language mixing)" (Austin and Sallabank 2014). This attitude of wishing to keep the linguistic data free from contact influences may be reflected in the efforts of speaker communities to purify their variety. If a language is endangered, however, this may also threaten the language's survival (Csató 1998).

As mentioned, copying is a strategy to make a strongly dominated language fit to serve the communicative needs of the speakers. Speakers have native intuition concerning how to insert copies of elements of the dominating code into their basic code. Verbs are copied in different ways in different languages. Karaim speakers, for instance, copy infinitive forms of Slavic verbs and add semantically empty light verbs that serve as native stems able to take inflectional suffixes, e.g. *Zvont' et'-ä-m* [call.do-PRES.1SG] 'I make a phone call'; Swedish speakers add inflectional suffixes directly to copied English verb stems, e.g. 'Jag jogg-ar' [I jog-PRES] 'I jog'; and Hungarian speakers add derivational suffixes to the copied verb stems, e.g. 'Jogg-ol-ok' [jog-DER-PRES1SG]. The accommodation processes are also governed by rules included in the native language competence. Thus, for instance, in the Swedish example, the consonant *g* is long because of Swedish phonotactic principles. Copying is learned by the speakers of a community that already has a high-copying variety. When copying is banned, the acquisition of copying strategies breaks down. This leaves the speakers with the choice either to find a native word, which can be impossible, or to switch to the dominating code entirely.

Linguists may have negative experiences with high-copying languages. As Aikhenvald (2020: 254) formulates it, it has been empirically observed that:

> [t]he impact of the increasingly dominant language onto an endangered language tends to involve a massive influx of non-native forms from the dominant language; a high amount of structural diffusion; reinforcement of forms and patterns shared with the dominant language; and the loss of forms or patterns absent from the dominant language. Language endangerment and impending language shift may result in dialect leveling, and creating new mixed, or 'blended' languages.

This is undoubtedly a correct observation. It does not, however, imply that copying processes themselves lead to obsolescence. As Johanson (2002b) argues, structural changes in a language do not lead to 'structuritis', i.e. endangerment. Speakers shift to the dominating language when the primary code ceases to have a communicative function. The world is full of examples of successful high-copying varieties, which can be both large and small languages such as English and Gagauz.

It seems evident that linguistic descriptions should pay attention to the genuine native grammar of a variety. Mosel, who has published several guidelines for documentary linguistics and linguistic assistance in revitalization, mentions "purification by the replacement of loan words" as the first task in editing recorded texts (Mosel 2012: 114). In a later publication (2014: 141–142) Mosel modifies this recommendation concerning creating texts for the communities:

> when speech communities want their language to become a written language and the means of instruction in primary schools, it certainly belongs to the responsibilities of linguists to help them create it by keeping the uniqueness of their language, but also avoiding a rigid purism that would put off younger speakers.

In fact, normativeness or purism, i.e. preserving the uniqueness of a language, often negatively affects maintenance and revitalization efforts. Purists advocate the avoidance of loans or the upholding of a regularity that cannot be implemented in reality.

A grammar of Karaim has been published, for example, in which each sentence has a typically Turkic verb-final word order. This is extremely strange for speakers who apply a typologically dominant AVO order (Csató and Johanson 2020). Such experiences demotivate people to express themselves in the recommended varieties. A purist attitude stigmatizes a spoken copying variety as inferior or wrong. If a precontact state of the language is selected as an aim, this reduces the chances of language retention. The aim of revitalization must be to reinforce the use of the variety that, to some extent, is in use or at least remembered.

The difference between strongly and weakly normed languages is important. An obstacle to learning and using a certain variety of a language should not be imposed. It is common for people in the world to speak several varieties of a language. The fact is often overlooked that even minority and endangered languages have several varieties. Depending on the given communicative situation, Turkish speakers in Germany may use a high-copying or low-copying variety of Turkish. As emphasized in several lectures by Stephen Wurm, it is the communicative functionality of a language that keeps it alive. High-copying varieties are instrumental in motivating young bilingual Turkish speakers to use Turkish when communicating with their bilingual peers. In situations where the other participant, e.g. the grandmother, is a monolingual Turkish speaker, they use a low-copying variety (Johanson 1991). The acquisition of competence in a high-copying variety can pave the way for the acquisition of a low-copying variety. For instance, if a Russian-speaking Karaim learns to say *Tuvχan k'ün'ün'b'ä pozdravlat' et'äb'iz'* 'We congratulate you on your birthday', building a sentence by using full Karaim morphology and one lexical copy, then the replacing of the Russian verb *pozdravlat'* with a Karaim word will be a trivial matter.

The complexity of multilingual skills is often viewed in an over-simplistic way, since it is poorly understood. This is a concern of linguists engaged in safeguarding endangered languages. This chapter calls attention to the importance of understanding the role that code copying can play in language maintenance.

References

Aikhenvald, Alexandra Y. (2020). Language Contact and Endangered Languages. In Anthony P. Grant (ed.), *The Oxford Handbook of Language Contact*, 241–260. Oxford: Oxford University Press.

Austin, Peter K. and Julia Sallabank (2014). Introduction. In Peter K. Austin and Julia Sallabank (eds.), *Endangered Languages: Beliefs and Ideologies in Language Documentation and Revitalization*, 1–25. British Academy Scholarship Online.

Csató, Éva Á. (1998). Should Karaim be 'purer' than other European languages? *Studia Turcologica Cracoviensia* 5: 81–89.

Csató, Éva Á. and Lars Johanson (2020). The Northwestern Turkic (Kipchak) languages. In Martine Robbeets and Alexander Savelyev (eds.), *The Oxford Guide to the Transeurasian Languages*, 370–391. Oxford: Oxford University Press.

Csató, Éva Á. and Astrid Menz (2018). On the linguistic distances between Gagauz and Karaim. *Turkic Languages* 21: 43–62.

Igla, Birgit (1996). *Das Romani von Ajia Varvara: Descriptive und historische-vergleichende Darstellung eines Zigeunerdialektes* [The Romany of Ajia Varvara: Descriptive and historical-comparative treatment of a Gypsy dialect]. Wiesbaden: Harrassowitz.

Johanson, Lars (1975). Gesprochenes Türkisch als Forschungsobjekt [Spoken Turkish as research object]. *Materialia Turcica* 1: 1–8.

Johanson, Lars (1988). Zur Entwicklung türkeitürkischer Varietäten in Nordwesteuropa [On the development of Turkish varieties in north-western Europe]. *Turkish in North-West Europe Newsletter* 1 (1): 3–8.

Johanson, Lars (1991). Zur Sprachentwicklung der "Turcia Germanica" [On the language development of the "Turcia Germanica"]. In Ingeborg Baldauf, Klaus Kreiser and Semih Tezcan (eds.), *Türkische Sprachen und Literaturen. Materialien der ersten deutschen Turkologen-Konferenz Bamberg, 3.–6. Juli 1987*, 199–212. Wiesbaden: Harrassowitz.

Johanson, Lars (2000). Linguistic convergence in the Volga area. In Dicky Gilbers, John A. Nerbonne and Jos Schaeken (eds.), *Languages in Contact* (Studies in Slavic and General Linguistics 28), 165–178. Amsterdam, Atlanta: Rodopi.

Johanson, Lars (2002a). *Structural Factors in Turkic Language Contacts*. London: Curzon.

Johanson, Lars (2002b). Do languages die of 'structuritis'? The role of code-copying in language endangerment. *Italian Journal of Linguistics* 14: 249–270.

Johanson, Lars (2013). Isomorphic processes: Grammaticalization and copying of grammatical elements. In Martine Robbeets and Hubert Cuyckens (eds.), *Shared Grammaticalization. With Special Focus on the Transeurasian Langugages*, 101–109. Amsterdam & Philadelphia: John Benjamins Publishing Company.

Johanson, Lars (2014). A Yakut copy of a Tungusic viewpoint aspect paradigm. In Martine Robbeets and Walter Bisang (eds.), *Paradigm Change in the Transeurasian Languages and Beyond*, 235–242. Amsterdam, Philadelphia: John Benjamins Publishing Company.

Johanson, Lars (2021). *Turkic*. Cambridge Language Surveys. Cambridge: Cambridge University Press.

Kowalski, Tadeusz (1934). Osmanisch-türkische Dialekte [Ottoman Turkish dialects]. In *Enzyklopaedie des Islam* 4, 991–1010. Leiden: Brill.

Mosel, Ulrike (2012). Creating educational materials in language documentation projects: creating innovative resources for linguistic research. In Frank Seifart, Geoffrey Haig, Nikolaus P. Himmelmann, Dagmar Jung, Anna Margetts and Paul Trilsbeek (eds.), *Potentials of Language Documentation: Methods, Analyses, and Utilization*, 111–117. Honolulu: University of Hawaai'i Press.

Mosel, Ulrike (2014). Corpus linguistic and documentary approaches in writing a grammar of a previously undescribed language. In Toshihide Nakayama and Keren Rice (eds.), *The Art and Practice of Grammar Writing*, 135–157. Honolulu: University of Hawai'i Press.

Pakendorf, Brigitte (2007). *Contact in the Prehistory of the Sakha (Yakuts): Linguistic and Genetic Perspectives*. Leiden: Leiden University.

Pakendorf, Brigitte (2014). Paradigm copying in Tungusic: The Lamunkhin dialect of Ėven and beyond. In Martine Robbeets and Walter Bisang (eds.), *Paradigm Change. In the Transeurasian Languages and Beyond* (Studies in Language Companion Series 161), 287–310. Amsterdam, Philadelphia: John Benjamins Publishing Company.

Robbeets, Martine (2012). Shared verb morphology in the Transeurasian languages: Copy or cognate? In Lars Johanson and Martine Robbeets (eds.), *Copies Versus Cognates in Bound Morphology*, 427–446. Brill: Leiden, Boston.

CHAPTER 20

Blurring the Lines at InField/CoLang: Examining Inclusion and Impacts

Carol Genetti and Carlos M. Nash

1 Introduction

The Institute for Collaborative Language Research (CoLang, initially InField, Institute for Field Linguistics and Language Documentation) is a biennial summer institute that began in 2008.[1] The goal of the Institute is to bring together practicing linguists, students of linguistics, and Indigenous members of endangered language speech communities from around the world for shared teaching and learning about language documentation and revitalization.[2] The Institute begins with two weeks of co-taught workshops and auxiliary activities, followed by a three- or four-week practicum, loosely based on a traditional course in linguistic field methods. There have now been seven instantiations of the Institute, each occurring on even-numbered years and alternating with the Linguistic Society of America's (LSA) summer institute. The planned 2020 Institute at the University of Montana was canceled due to the pandemic; it will be offered there in 2022. CoLang did run a 3-day web series in June of 2020. This included curated sessions and Q&A, and significantly focused on impacts of the pandemic.

From its inception, the Institute was designed to be collaborative and inclusive of all voices, and to honor and recognize the expertise that each participant brings to the conversation. As the Institute has evolved, a central focus has been on shaping the Institute to be inclusive of 'community language experts', a

1 InField/CoLang has been supported by multiple grants to the hosting universities by the Documenting Endangered Languages Program at the National Science Foundation (BCS-0724221 [2008], BCS-0924846 [2010], BCS-1065469 [2012], BCS-1263939 [2014], BCS-1500841 [2016], BCS-1664464 [2018], and BCS-1836574 [2020]), in addition to generous support from the hosting universities and other institute-specific funding agencies. Since 2015, it has also been by sponsored by the Linguistic Society of America, which provides invaluable administrative support and funding.

2 We correct here the characterization of InField/CoLang as "targeting US graduate students" in Seifart et al. (2018); this oversimplifies both the audience and the goals of the Institute.

© CAROL GENETTI AND CARLOS M. NASH, 2022 | DOI:10.1163/9789004510395_021 term we use to refer to members of speech communities whose languages are endangered or sleeping, and who are actively engaged in the documentation and/or revitalization of those languages.[3] This inclusion is intended not only to be realized in numerical terms with regard to overall participation levels, but in driving the curriculum so it is reflective of the needs, interests, and knowledge systems of these experts.

A central question, since the instantiation of the Institute, has been how to provide an inclusive experience and sense of belonging for community language experts, especially those who identify as Indigenous, Native American, or First Nations. Universities have not traditionally provided a climate of inclusion and belonging for Indigenous students, and can be intimidating for potential participants.[4] For people from outside academia, the support of the National Science Foundation and LSA can exacerbate the sense of alienation. This in part reflects the history of colonialist, exploitative, and even unethical research practices carried out in these communities in the name of science (for discussion see Medicine 1998; Brayboy and Deyhle 2000; Davis and Keemer 2002; Penfield et al. 2008; James et al. 2013, Pacheco et al. 2013; Leonard 2018).[5]

Many documentary linguists have consciously worked to understand this history and positionality, to critically examine the relationship between linguists and Indigenous communities, and, like researchers in other fields, to promote ideologies and practices that empower members of Indigenous communities as research partners. This has been especially true in the years since the Institute was founded. Evidence for this includes:

- An increase in the literature on this relationship and on the ethics of linguistic research (Holton 2009; Dorian 2010; Dobrin and Berson 2011; Rice 2012; Aikhenvald 2013; Genetti and Siemens 2013; Czaykowska-Higgins 2018; Good 2018; Singer 2018)
- The promotion of collaborative models of linguistic research in articles and research guides (Penfield et al. 2008; Czaykowska-Higgins 2009; Glenn 2009; Leonard and Haynes 2010; Guérin and Lacrampe 2010; Chelliah and deReuse

3 Various terms are used to refer to this group, including (community) language activists and Indigenous participants. Not every community language expert identifies with the term 'activist' or 'Indigenous', although many (perhaps most) do so.

4 This is an ongoing issue; a First Nations participant at the Tuttle and Taff (2017) ICLDC presentation stated: "There is no such thing as a University for First Nations people that is a safe place." The idea of the Institute as a 'pop-up university' (to cite Tuttle and Taff) was viewed by another Indigenous participant in the audience as a mitigating factor.

5 This is especially—but by no means exclusively—true in the area of public health (Medicine 1998; Davis and Keemer 2002; James et al. 2013; Pacheco et al 2013).

2011: 141–145; Crippen and Robinson 2013 and responses to it; Cruz and Woodbury 2014; Yamada 2014; Sapién 2018)
- Incorporation of Native American presenters in the Annual Meetings of the LSA[6]
- Intentional inclusion of content relevant to Indigenous populations in the biennial International Conference on Language Documentation and Conservation (ICLDC), including making "Focus on Relationships" (between academics and communities) the theme of 2021

In addition, this time period has seen a number of Native American graduate students who have become visible in leading discussions about race and Indigeneity in linguistics, including calling for the decolonization of linguistics (Leonard 2017, 2018) and the establishment of Natives4Linguistics.[7]

InField/CoLang has been integral to these changes, both catalyzing and reflecting broader conversations in the field about Indigenous inclusion. Each set of organizers has had to approach this question within the physical, social, and institutional contexts of their home universities. In addition, Indigenous inclusion has been central to the work of the Advisory Circle that provides broader oversight of the Institute.

In this chapter we trace the history of the Institute with a focus on the intentional blending of community-based and academic participants. Following a brief overview of InField/CoLang (§2), we discuss how inclusion has been embedded as a core value of the Institute (§3) and is central to the Advisory Circle (§4). We use interview data to trace how each Institute's organizing team approached how best to serve the blended audience (§5). We then explore the impacts that the Institute has had on individual participants and on communities through four in-depth participant interviews and one descriptive study (Yamada 2014) (§6). We conclude (§7) that each Institute was intentionally shaped to be inclusive of a blended audience, but note that blending audiences is always challenging. However, the Institute ethos of inclusion and collaboration, as mutually reinforcing dimensions of interaction, provided participants with a supportive environment in which to work through and navigate tensions, and to develop and model problem-solving skills. Overall, the Institute

6 For example, the 2012 meeting included a panel primarily made up of Native Americans that directly addressed interactions between linguists and Native American communities. The 2018 meeting saw the inclusion of the first Natives4Lingusitics symposium.

7 This group seeks to "improve the field of Linguistics by broadening the participation of Native Americans within Linguistics: 1) by directly bringing Native Americans to the Linguistic Society of America annual meetings, and 2) by developing and promoting strategies to better integrate Native American needs and values about language into linguistic science" https://natives4linguistics.wordpress.com/ (accessed 23.02.2021).

TABLE 20.1 InField/CoLang Institutes

Year	Host institution	Primary organizer(s)
2008	University of California, Santa Barbara	Carol Genetti, Rebekka Siemens
2010	University of Oregon	Spike Gildea
2012	University of Kansas	Arienne Dwyer, Carlos Nash
2014	University of Texas, Arlington	Colleen Fitzgerald
2016	University of Alaska, Fairbanks	Siri Tuttle, Alice Taff, Lawrence Kaplan
2018	University of Florida	George Aaron Broadwell
2020	Canceled	
2022	University of Montana	Mizuki Miyashita, Susan Penfield

has reinforced calls for community-based research paradigms, and provides a biennial opportunity to try out innovative practices.

2 InField/CoLang History

The idea for a summer institute on language documentation and revitalization was first presented by Carol Genetti at a conference entitled "Language Documentation: Theory, Practice, and Values," held at Harvard University in conjunction with the LSA Summer Linguistic Institute in 2005. At the end of the presentation, Genetti circulated a questionnaire to participants to gauge interest in the idea and received an enthusiastic and positive response. She created an Organizing Committee and applied for funding from the NSF's Documenting Endangered Languages Program.[8,9]

The core structure of the Institute is two weeks of workshops followed by an intensive 'practicum'. There have been six completed instantiations of the Institute, shown in Table 20.1, with the seventh deferred until 2022.

For the initial Institute, workshop topics were in part selected by the Organizing Committee and in part through an open call for proposals. The workshops fell into five different categories:

8 The Organizing Committee consisted of Arienne Dwyer, Margaret Florey, Spike Gildea, Matthew Gordon, Marianne Mithun, Susan Penfield, Kenneth Rehg, and Keren Rice. Peter Austin, Jost Gippert, and Nicholas Thieberger served as External Consultants.

9 NSF Division of Behavioral and Cognitive Sciences, award 0724221.

- Broad overviews taught as plenaries (Steps in Language Documentation ('Steps') and Models of Language Documentation and Revitalization ('Models'))
- Workshops aimed at enhancing technological skills (audio and video recording, data management and archiving, specialized software (ELAN, Toolbox, building wikis))
- Workshops focused on particular facets of language documentation and revitalization (orthography development, lexicography)
- Courses on linguistics (Linguistics for Language Activists, Phonetics)
- Meta-level courses on societal aspects of engaging in this work (Language Activism, Life in the Field, Problematizing the Field Experience, Grant Writing)

Over the six instantiations of the Institute, some of these elements have remained fairly constant (Steps and Models, audio and video recording, data management and archiving, Language Activism, Grant Writing), but—as discussed further below—each Institute has also shaped the curriculum in unique ways, including workshops related to Indigenous knowledge systems and other topics responsive to interests of community language experts.

The practicum was designed to provide a hands-on collaborative research experience that put into practice the skillsets taught in the workshops. Each practicum was led by a professor of linguistics working with one or more speakers of an endangered language.

While the practica are roughly modeled on a traditional field methods class, they differ from this in a number of important ways: the class is intensive, the research is explicitly collaborative, the participants do not have shared training in linguistics, and the needs and interests of the speakers emergently shape the goals and outcomes of the class. It is both a challenging and highly rewarding experience.

The list of practica offered across Institutes is provided in Table 20.2.

3 Creating Inclusion for a Blended Audience

The audience for the Institute includes language experts from Indigenous communities, linguists, students of linguistics, native speakers, latent speakers, heritage speakers, and all combinations thereof. Because language endangerment is a global phenomenon, the Institute has an international scope. Hearing stories about endangered language communities and the projects of people leading language revitalization efforts from across the world highlights the global nature of language endangerment. This can be especially true

TABLE 20.2 Practicum courses across Institutes

Year	Languages	Linguists	Speakers
2008	Ekegusii [guz[a]]	Carol Genetti	Kennedy Bosiré, Gladys Machogu
2008	Kwak'wala [kwk]	Patricia Shaw	Beverly Lagis, Daisy Sewid-Smith, Mikael Willie, Laura Ann Cranmer, and Deanna Nicolson
2008	Mende [men]	Tucker Childs	Momoh Taziff Koroma
2010	Northern Paiute [pao]	Tim Thornes	Ruth Lewis
2010	Uyghur [uig]	Arienne Dwyer	Reziwan Aili, Abuduwaili Ayifu, Mayila Yake
2010	Wapishana [wap]	Sergio Meira	Adrian Gomes
2012	Amazigh (Berber) [ber]	Yamina El Kirat El Allame	Abdessamad Ait Dada, Mustapha Ouzir
2012	Cherokee [chr]	Brad Montgomery-Anderson	Harry Oosahwee
2012	Uda [uda]	Eno-Abasi Urua	Prince Chris Abasi Eyo, Barrister Mfon Ibok Asanaenyi
2014	Alabama [akz]	Colleen Fitzgerald	Jonelle Battise
2014	Apoala Mixtec [mip]	Christian DiCanio	José Carlos Jímenez Hernández
2014	Innu Cree [moe]	Monica Macaulay	Gaëlle Mollen, Uapukun Mestokosho
2014	Ngambai [sba]	Amanda Miller	Priscille Mekoulnodji Ndjerareou
2016	Han Athabascan (Dene) [haa]	Willem De Reuse	Ruth Ridley, Ethel Beck, Bertha Ulvi, Percy Henry
2016	Miyako (Ryukyuan) [mvi]	Toshihide Nakayama, Yoshi Ono	Hiroyuki Nakama
2016	Unangam Tunuu [ale]	Anna Berge, Moses Dirks	Moses Dirks; also demonstrated use of archival data
2018	Timucua [tjm]	George Aaron Broadwell	Sleeping language; relied on archival data
2018	Macuiltianguis Zapotec [zaa]	John Foreman, Margarita Fore-man	Margarita Foreman, Filemón Pérez Ruiz
2018	Nyangbo (Tutrugbu) [nyb]	James Essegbey, Felix Ameka, Adam McCollum	Judith Glover
2018	Choctaw [cho]	Jack Martin, Jason Lewis[b]	Abrianna Tubby, DeLaura Saunders

a Codes in square brackets are ISO 639-3: 2007 identifiers for languages.
b Jason Lewis is a data specialist for the Tribal Language program at Mississippi Band of Choctaw Indians; he served as a technical advisor and data specialist for the course.

for non-academic participants, who may not be as familiar with the statistics on language endangerment or accustomed to thinking in global terms. Finding that they are part of an international movement can be inspiring, as can the opportunity to build supportive networks with people doing similar work.

There were several reasons for explicitly including Indigenous members of endangered language speech communities in the target audience. First, providing community leaders in language revitalization efforts with opportunities to increase their skills and knowledge enhances the likelihood of their success. Community language experts become empowered through training (Genetti and Siemens 2013). Second, linguists and community language experts typically have aligned goals; bringing these populations together promotes communication and greater understanding that will make achieving those goals more likely. Third, providing linguists with the opportunity to listen to community language experts broadens their perspectives on their work and on the materials that they are producing. It can help them reflect on how they can make those materials relevant to the community and serve the needs of language conservation and revitalization. Finally, the inclusion of community language experts was seen as an opportunity to shift the relationship between linguists and Indigenous communities, i.e., to 'blur the lines' between traditionally distinct groups embedded in an unequal power relationship and to create parity and partnership.

Broad inclusivity in the target audience results in remarkable diversity in the participants: cultural diversity, linguistic diversity, educational diversity, gender diversity, national diversity, racial diversity, religious diversity, and a whole span of ages from infants accompanying their parents to elders. The challenge, then, is to create a suite of offerings that will advance all groups, deepen understanding, and foster collaboration. Central to this is the core ideology of InField/CoLang: everyone has something to learn and everyone has something to teach. This simple idea puts all participants on the same level, allows all voices to be heard and honored, and implicitly construes any individual's specific expertise as a product of their own history, without judgement or imputing of value.

This ideology is explicitly stated during the first plenary at the beginning of every Institute. The ideology is then instantiated in a number of ways:

- All workshops are co-taught (where possible by teams combining linguists and community language experts), so that they model cooperation and building of bridges
- Workshops involve hands-on collaborative classwork and discussion in breakout groups
- Small group projects encourage participation
- Research in the practicum is conducted collaboratively
- Models talks are plenaries that explicitly recognize the expertise of community-based participants
- Individual stories are welcomed and valued in workshops and evening activities
- Space is created for individual accomplishments (such as materials produced for language revitalization) to be shared and honored

Recognizing each individual's expertise helps to foster the spirit of collaboration and communication that can help groups establish and achieve shared goals. The immersive collaborative environment provided by the Institute helps participants gain communication and other skills and build their confidence in using the collaborative framework in their own work. Collaboration and inclusion are mutually reinforcing: inclusion makes for productive collaboration and engaging people as full partners in collaborative work means they are included and valued.

Of course, collaboration is always challenging, especially when working with diverse constituencies. Realizing the ideals of equality and inclusivity is especially difficult when there is distrust left in the wake of a centuries-old history of betrayal, and high-stakes issues to address, such as questions of ownership and alignment of goals. In addition, people from different cultures bring different sets of stereotypes and implicit biases that shape their assumptions and interpretations in different ways, resulting in culturally-based misunderstandings. Working through this complexity both develops interactional problem solving skills and models them for others. These problems are actively aided by the ideology that frames all participants as teachers and learners, which fosters active listening and openness to change. We return to this point below.

4 InField/CoLang Charter and Advisory Circle

Every instantiation of InField has benefited from the engagement of a body of external advisors. For the first two Institutes, these advisory groups were ad hoc. To ensure the long-term sustainability of the Institute, a formal Charter was drawn up, including the creation of an Advisory Circle of rotating membership that would steward the Institute over time. The CoLang/InField Institute Charter was approved during CoLang 2012.

The Charter explicitly lists inclusion and collaboration as core Institute values. The principles guiding the Institute are laid out as:

- Collaborative learning, in which all are contributors with participants and instructors teaching and learning together
- Collaborative teaching, with multidisciplinary, indigenous, and non-indigenous expertise
- Collaborative research, with participation at every level by those community members whose languages are at stake
- Inclusivity, with international orientation and encouraging of participants from all backgrounds

- Accessibility, by removing barriers to language documentation and creating accessible resources
- Outreach, using networks to reach academic and community linguists to foster synergistic training events and the dissemination of the products of language documentation
- Advocacy, to support language initiatives and language minority communities around the world

The Advisory Circle is also explicitly inclusive. It is constituted of 12 to 15 people, with representation from the following groups (recognizing that some individuals may fill multiple categories):

- At least three Institute organizers: the organizer(s) of the previous two Institutes, and the organizer(s) of the upcoming Institute
- At least four community linguists (i.e., language experts)
- At least two students
- At least two international participants

As members rotate out, other participants are invited to serve, based, in part, on "demonstrated commitment to the ideals of the institute (inclusivity, collaboration, and the desire to work with others to help preserve the world's linguistic diversity)."

The explicit embedding of the principles of collaboration and inclusivity in the guiding documents and the requirement that Advisory Circle members have demonstrated commitment to these values have ensured that these core principles have remained central. We now demonstrate this by examining each instantiation of the Institute in turn.

5 Evolution of InField/CoLang

While many aspects of InField/CoLang have remained constant over time, the Institute has a degree of flexibility which allows it to be adapted based on the host institutions' strengths, needs, and available resources. In order to determine the innovations implemented by each organizing team, we combined information gathered from extant and archived websites with direct interviews with the primary organizers.[10] Here we particularly focus on how each Institute was shaped to enhance inclusion and effective collaboration.

10 All co-directors received an invitation to participate in an interview session. Of those who agreed to participate, there was at least one co-director from each Institute. We acknowledge and thank the following for their critical contributions to this study: Aaron

5.1 *InField 2008: University of California, Santa Barbara*

The 2008 InField offered 18 different workshops, 14 of which were co-taught. Participants were allowed to participate in any of the workshops. However, the organizers and advising committee were sensitive to the fact that participants would have differing levels of linguistic training, degrees of sociocultural awareness, needs, and interests. Therefore, the organizers provided three 'workshop tracks', each totaling 60 hours of instruction, to help guide participants in their course selections.[11] The tracks were developed with three kinds of audience in mind: language activists, individuals who would continue to the four-week field training, and individuals who would only participate in the two-week instructional workshops. There was considerable overlap across the three tracks; however, there were a few courses that made each track unique (e.g., "Language Resources and the Community" for language activists, and "Field Phonetics" for those participating in the field training section). Although the tracks were initially designed to ensure that all participants had clear curricula and to facilitate their navigation of the complex offerings, some felt that the effect was to separate the community language experts from the linguists, creating barriers to inclusion. The tracks were discontinued at subsequent Institutes.

A number of workshops initiated in 2008 have been consistently offered at most or all Institutes. Especially notable is Models of Language Documentation and Revitalization, a plenary session that features a different language community each day. Presenters are community language experts, sometimes in partnership with a linguist. The workshop is designed to showcase the variety of approaches to language documentation and revitalization taken by communities across the globe, and especially the relationship between the model being used and the context of the community (historical, degree of endangerment, societal and cultural factors, access to technology, etc.). In addition, Models spotlights the work of community language experts so that it is salient within the Institute, recognized, and honored. Some Models presenters have described the experience as validating, both at the Institute and within their home communities. This workshop has been central to realizing the Institute's goal of inclusion.

Broadwell, Colleen Fitzgerald, Spike Gildea, Lawrence Kaplan, Mizuki Miyashita, Susan Penfield, Madeleine Shek, Alice Taff, and Siri Tuttle. Any errors of representation are our own.

11 This followed a recommendation made by reviewers of the NSF grant proposal.

5.2 *InField 2010: University of Oregon*

The 2010 InField in Eugene, Oregon expanded course offerings to 29 workshops. A few were completely redeveloped from 2008 to keep up with new technology and practices (e.g., "Web and Wikis for Language Documentation" became "Principles and Multimedia Tools for Sustainable Language Documentation" and "Introduction to Toolbox" became "FLEx"). Some technology courses were subdivided into beginning and advanced levels (e.g., "Audio Recording 1 & 2", "ELAN 1 & 2"). Nine workshops were new additions (e.g., "Transcription", "Blurring the Lines", "Ethnobiology"). The revised course offerings allowed participants to select courses that were more closely aligned to their skillsets and interests.

Of particular note with regard to blended audiences was the introduction of "Blurring the Lines", a workshop that explicitly addresses collaborations between linguists and community partners and how those collaborations can be structured so that each partner has their needs met. It addresses issues such as ownership of project results, defining shared goals, and recognizing varying cultural expectations. The workshop is taught from the vantage point of personal experience, with group discussion of example situations. Since its instantiation in 2010, "Blurring the Lines" has become an Institute staple.

In addition to the revised courses, the 2010 Institute sought other ways to increase the participation of community language experts. First, the organizers tapped community language experts who attended 2008 to be co-instructors in 2010 (e.g., community language experts Kennedy Bosiré and Daryn McKenny presented Models talks and were workshop instructors). Second, the organizers coordinated with the Northwest Indian Language Institute (NILI), which held an integrated summer session with InField 2010. This served to increase the overall percentage of language experts with representatives from communities across the Pacific Northwest, profiling NILI's work for a broader audience. Third, organizers hosted the 17th Stabilizing Indigenous Languages Symposium (SILS) the weekend before InField2010, allowing for overlap and shared sessions. Finally, the Institute hosted a group of Indigenous scholars from Suriname, who had been working with a graduate student in Linguistics at the University of Oregon. The InField curriculum included a special class on Cariban languages tailored to this group. In addition, one of their members co-taught a workshop, and the group presented a Models talk. We return to the impact of InField on these Kari'jna participants below.

5.3 *CoLang 2012: University of Kansas*

Following Oregon's lead, the 2012 CoLang in Lawrence, Kansas aimed to continue the participation of Native American scholars by partnering with the

Siouan and Caddoan Languages Conference and reaching out to connections at Haskell Indian Nations University, which is located approximately two miles southeast of the University of Kansas main campus. The Institute added six new workshops (e.g., "Map-making", "Dissemination", and "XML").

2012 also brought a permanent change to the language associated with and used within the Institute. The co-organizers solicited advice from the newly formed Advisory Circle and individuals who participated in 2008 and 2010 regarding a name change from 'InField' to 'CoLang'. The rationale for the name change was to distance the Institute from colonial references, especially when it aims to support the documentation efforts of Indigenous scholars, who do not view their communities as a 'field' to be researched. The notions of 'field' and 'fieldwork' directly implicate a scientific paradigm that some Institute participants found alienating and that served to reinforce traditional academic hierarchies. With the word 'collaborative' in the title, the new name explicitly invoked the Institute's core values. Other vocabulary changes followed suit: the workshop "Life in the Field" was renamed "Life in the Community" and the four-week field methods session was renamed the "Language Practicum". Again, the leveling of traditional hierarchies was a goal of this change.

5.4 *CoLang 2014: University of Texas at Arlington*

The 2014 CoLang expanded the workshop offerings to 57. This increase was made possible by reducing the timing of the traditional workshops from five 90-minutes sessions to four. This allowed for the addition of 21 two-hour workshops on a wide variety of topics. A number of these were specifically tailored for Indigenous participants (e.g., "Language and Wellness", "Indigenous Language Revitalization", "Master-Apprentice Adult Immersion", "Cherokee Immersion Demonstration"). The Institute also provided a unique opportunity to attend office hours with the Archive of the Indigenous Languages of Latin America (AILLA), the Sam Noble Oklahoma Museum of Natural History, and the NSF Documenting Endangered Language program, thus further removing barriers for those who traditionally had little access to these institutions.

The 2014 Institute also emphasized raising the awareness of the general public and of institutional administrators regarding language endangerment. CoLang 2014 created 11 events that were open and free to the public, including a screening of Brian McDermott's documentary *Heenetiineyoo3eihiiho'* (*Language Healers*) and *Star Wars IV: A New Hope*, dubbed into Navajo with English subtitles.

5.5 *2016: University of Alaska, Fairbanks*

The 2016 CoLang in Fairbanks, Alaska contracted the six-week timeframe to five weeks by overlapping the first week of the practicum session with the second week of instructional workshops. This was done specifically with an eye to Alaska Native participation: given that the Institute occurs during the summer when many potential local participants were engaged with seasonal fishing and other community responsibilities, the organizers reasoned that a six-week program would be too long a commitment for many. In the five-week framework, participants received similar content and activities to those in the six-week structure. There were several new workshops, e.g., "Cultural Impact in Community Linguistics", "Documentation of Orature", and "Documenting the Language of Landscape".

Prior iterations of the Institute actively sought repeat participants. However, the co-organizers of CoLang 2016 wanted to ensure broader reach, especially among local Native communities. To have more control over the participant blend, they instituted an application process, screened potential participants, and advised them on participation.

5.6 *2018: University of Florida*

Similar to the 2016 CoLang, the 2018 co-organizers opted for a five-week structure; the two-week workshops occurred in late June and the three-week practica were in July. Of the three languages offered during the practica, one was a 'sleeping' language, Timucua. The intention of including Timucua was to (1) recognize and honor the memory of the previous Indigenous communities of northern Florida, (2) encourage discussion on the effects of colonialism (such as wars, plagues, and forced relocation) on Indigenous populations, and (3) explore the possibilities of working with archival materials. The 2018 Institute also included a mini-practicum on Choctaw. The co-organizers wanted to include a traditional Indigenous language of Florida, even though no speakers of the original languages remain. They therefore reached out to a nearby Choctaw community in Mississippi, as historically the Choctaw territory extended into Florida. The co-organizers also incorporated more 'free time' into the programming, so as to allow more time to complete collaborative projects and to build relationships. Therefore, the co-organizers intentionally reduced the number of activities that had been previously scheduled, including the plenary Models talks.

5.7 *2020 and 2022: University of Montana*

The 2020 CoLang was unfortunately delayed due to the COVID-19 pandemic, but will be offered in Missoula in 2022. The Montana organizers have taken further steps toward increasing the participation of and collaboration with North American and international community language experts. They were especially inspired to do so by two events at the 2018 Annual Meeting of the LSA: the "Sharing Our Views" symposium, and the initial presentation of the Natives4Linguistics project. Furthermore, co-organizer Mizuki Miyashita participated in the Natives4Linguistics symposium at the 2019 LSA Annual Meeting, where she presented on the multilateral collaboration that underscores CoLang 2020. Further inspiration comes from co-organizers' work on a project called CLPP (Collaborative Language Planning Project) which aims to enhance communication amongst language activists, scholars, and researchers from Indigenous and non-Indigenous communities in Montana.

To instantiate deeper collaboration with local Native American communities, the 2020 Institute was to be the first CoLang to be co-hosted by a Tribal College or University (TCU).[12] This resulted from considerable outreach aimed at the seven TCUs surrounding the University of Montana. An especially important relationship was with Richard Littlebear, President of Chief Dull Knife College, who was slated to serve as Co-Organizer for the 2020 Institute. Details for 2022 have yet to be announced.

Another intentional change was made by the Montana organizers to further the collaborative ethos of the Institute: replacement of the terms 'teacher' and 'instructor' with 'facilitator'. All Montana workshops will be co-facilitated by a team that includes at least one Indigenous scholar or activist.

Besides fostering collaborative opportunities, the co-organizers made a concerted effort to highlight Indigenous voices and perspectives in the planning and execution of the Institute. This has led to the broadening of workshop offerings, including topics such as "Health Benefits from Indigenous Language Use", "Animating Traditional Stories as Pedagogical Tools", and "Interacting with Children to Support Language Use".

5.8 *Summary*

To summarize, the programming of the Institute has evolved in four ways. First, there has been an increase in the number of workshops and a diversification of the topics offered. The number of workshops focused on core linguistic topics typically encountered in the traditional field methods course has remained stable; however, courses focused on technology, application, and community language work have grown considerably (see Table 20.3).

---

12 In the United States, the Higher Education Act of 1965 defined a number of minority-serving institutions, including TCUs, which are able to receive enhanced federal funding. TCUs are controlled by American Indian tribes within the US borders.

TABLE 20.3 Workshops offered at the Institutes

	2008	2010	2012	2014	2016	2018	2020[a]
Core Linguistic Topics	7 (39%)	8 (28%)	9 (20%)	7 (13%)	7 (23%)	6 (14%)	6 (14%)
Technology, Application, and Community Language Work	11 (61%)	21 (72%)	37 (80%)	49 (88%)	24 (77%)	36 (86%)	38 (86%)
Total	18	29	46	56	31	42	44

a Proposed courses.

Second, the Institute has modified its general timeline to accommodate the personal, community, or career responsibilities of participants, especially those of community language experts. Third, co-organizers have engaged current or prior participants as advisors regarding the language used within the Institute, promoting inclusion. Fourth, organizers are actively creating new networks by engaging local institutions, scholars, and community language experts.

This brief survey of the evolution of the Institute has demonstrated that each set of Institute Organizers intentionally worked to shape the Institute to better advance 'blurring the lines' and promote effective collaborative partnerships. Many of the changes reflected the institutional settings of the host universities (e.g., NILI for Oregon, TCUs for Montana, the focus on archival material in Florida, where no Indigenous communities remain, the Alaska decision to reduce the length of the Institute). All of the changes were motivated by the commitment to further inclusion and collaboration, the core values of the Institute. To better understand how experiencing these values has impacted particular participants, we turn now to case studies.

6 Impacts on Individuals and Communities

Section 3 above outlined the ideological motivations for blending audiences and emphasizing inclusion and collaboration. The question remains as to the impacts of these ideologies and the blending of audiences on Institute participants. To begin to address this complex question, we conducted interviews with four Institute participants.[13] In addition, impacts on the Kari'nja community from Suriname are taken from Yamada (2014).

6.1 *Adrienne Tsikewa*

Adrienne Tsikewa is a CoLang participant and long-time member of the Advisory Circle who identifies as both a community language expert/activist and as a graduate student in linguistics. She is currently pursuing a doctoral degree at University of California, Santa Barbara, but she first learned about the Institute as early as 2012 when she was enrolled in a master's program in Native American Languages and Linguistics at the University of Arizona. She was especially motivated to attend the Institute to engage with the practicum, since a similar course was not available in her program at the time. She attended the 2014 CoLang, where she was a student assistant, a position which provided her with access to the local organizers and instructors, in addition to other participants. She was able to get direct feedback on her projects, including a community-based survey that she was then designing and later implemented in her home community. She also found that attendance helped her to establish critical networks of supporters, in both academic and community circles, that continue to be important.

Since 2014, she has continued her engagement by serving on the Advisory Circle, first as a community representative, then as a student member, and now as a co-convener. She indicated that participation in the Advisory Circle was synergistic with her progress as a doctoral student and career objectives: "It's all connected to what I do focus on, in terms of working with Natives4Linguistics, [having] more Indigenous representation within the linguistics field, and having more voice in these things." She stated that visibility can be a significant factor in advancing the participation of community language experts and Indigenous community members: "[As discussed] in Natives4Linguistics, they have to see others working in this field ... and to be able to network and find peer-support."

Regarding the intersection of her identity as a Native scholar and as a member of an academic institution, Adrienne describes her role in the Institute as being in a position of advocating for both perspectives, but with the emphasis

13 Recommendations to interview former or current Institute participants occurred during the interviews with co-directors. We acknowledge and thank the following for their insightful contributions: Kennedy Bosiré, Jean-Luc Pierite, Daisy Rosenblum, and Adrienne Tsikewa.

on those of Native communities. As she has pursued higher education in the United States, she has repeatedly felt that she was put into a position of needing to educate people about Native perspectives. The Institute is no exception to this. She stated that a number of community-based participants have felt slighted by people from academic institutions both in their previous and personal experiences and at CoLang, and that interactions have at times been fraught or painful. She wonders whether sensitivity and/or cultural training for instructors should be required. Her visibility as a member of the Advisory Circle means that people come to her to discuss problematic interactions and she struggles with how to articulate these and resolve them in a manner that does not reflect negatively on her, especially given her status as a graduate student. She recognizes the need to be collegial and professional regarding communicating these issues to the Advisory Circle, but there is also a need to be forward and persistent in ensuring that all are aware of these problems and are willing to examine them.

6.2 *Jean-Luc Pierite*

Jean-Luc Pierite is a community language expert and activist and President of the North American Indian Center of Boston. Like Adrienne, he participated in his first CoLang in 2014. He was encouraged to attend the Institute by a friend who was serving on the tribal council for the Choctaw-Apache Tribe (Zwolle, Louisiana) and by another community member who was familiar with his family's work in the language and cultural revitalization of Tunica-Biloxi. He also served on the Advisory Circle, as a member and then as co-convenor.

In addressing the question of blended audience, Jean-Luc stated the importance of including community-based participants in both the programming of the Institute and in the Advisory Circle:

> I felt that there was a real value in bringing together academics and community members who could really benefit from this democratization of access to tools and processes, but don't necessarily have access to institutionalized education. […]

It absolutely matters what the makeup of the Advisory Circle is. […] It really matters having community members who center the needs of communities through the perspective that has been cultivated through their own work but then understand the unique community CoLang has cultivated […]

Another theme throughout Jean-Luc's interview was the value he placed on his participation in CoLang:

> There was a value [to the information] I brought back to my community, in terms of language documentation and revitalization efforts. For my own job with the Fab Foundation (MIT), being able to talk about the democratization and access to education, in terms of digital technology and community-based research ethics. Those were things that I brought into my own career.

Jean-Luc cites tensions between community members and students at CoLang, but describes the important networks that the Institute fostered as being supportive in navigating these issues:

> One of the things that I remember most fondly about the whole experience was the opportunity to find affinity groups, whether we were all community language activists or queer community members, and finding a way to support each other as we try to navigate these tensions between community members and students, whether they're undergrad or graduate, who are very passionate about linguistics, but perhaps not always the best when it comes to actually working with communities [...] [finding ways] to come together.

Prior to CoLang Jean-Luc had observed tensions between academic linguists and community-based experts whose careers are centered in language and cultural revitalization work. CoLang was, by contrast, a supportive environment for navigating such tensions when they arose.

He also discussed the importance of including Indigenous representatives in the Advisory Circle as resources to support community members as they navigate conflicts that arise:

> I think it matters that we have community members in leadership to be able to carry forward those values and goals and to be able to have an [Advisory Circle] that is able to respond and conceive of those needs and priorities in the instance if [issues] come up.

6.3 *Daisy Rosenblum*

Years before beginning the first year of her doctoral program in 2007, Daisy Rosenblum, who does not identify as Indigenous, had already worked with Kwak'wala archival materials. She had expressed interest in continuing that line of work; however, her advisors had recommended that she should work with speakers. Her opportunity to work with Kwak'wala speakers became possible when the InField organizers arranged to have Kwak'wala as one of the three practica languages to be offered at the 2008 Institute:

> It was really life-changing, transformational in so many ways. [...] It was like picking up the thread of something that had brought me to linguistics, that had brought me into graduate studies, [...] and I was able, for the first time, to work with speakers, which I never expected I'd be able to do. And then also connect with language teachers, learners, and people within multiple Kwak'wala communities.

The elders who served as speakers for the course were not the only Kwak'wala speakers present; there were also community members who were invested in the language and in working with language survivance. She describes the practicum as highlighting the relational experience and connection, which goes beyond the topics of language documentation and field methods. As the summer institute wound down, there were group discussions on how to continue the work and collaborations they had just begun: "Deanna Nicolson, Mike Willie, Laura Cranmer, and Pewi Alfred ... were interested in that collaboration." Eventually, she and Mikael Willie would apply for a grant which allowed her to visit Fort Rupert (in British Columbia, Canada) in 2009. For six weeks they and other community members worked together on various language projects. The experience proved to be foundational to her continued work on Kwak'wala: "Not just working with speakers, but also with community members and having those relationships ... be something that was initiated at InField and [still] continues." Daisy wrote her doctoral dissertation on Kwak'wala and obtained a faculty position at the University of British Columbia; their collaborative work continues.

A number of other significant outcomes can be traced back to participation at the Institute:

- Mikael Willie, who currently works in Aboriginal tourism, continues to foster language revitalization efforts by collaborating with a business partner who is starting a lodge focused on language revitalization
- Deanna Nicolson has recently become a language revitalization coordinator
- Pewi Alfred is active in developing Kwak'wala language learning materials
- Laura Cranmer completed a PhD

Rosenblum concluded the interview by discussing the 'ripple effect' that InField has had on the Kwak'wala community:

> [Some of their collaboration] preceded InField, but there were many things they got from InField that have carried on. When you look at these ripples, the "ripple effect", the layers of impact spread out because you got all of these new generations of people that have access to that work and doing that work.

6.4 *The Konomerume Kari'nja of Suriname*

Yamada (2014) provides an extensive history of her collaboration with the Konomerume Kari'nja of Suriname, which she worked with following a Community Partnership Model (Yamada 2010) for some years prior to their attendance at InField. Her work had included training individuals on aspects of language documentation, but they all felt that they would benefit from a broader training experience. In the end, a nine-person team attended InField 2010, with the goals of building their own capacity, sharing with others, and supporting their continued work on language documentation.

In addition to the NILI offerings and regular InField workshops, the organizers provided a special course for the group on Kari'jna and Cariban linguistics. The group also presented a Models talk, and Chief Mandé, the group's leader, both co-taught "Blurring the Lines" and attended the language practicum course on Wapishana, a language spoken in Guyana and unrelated to Kari'nja. The summary of impacts provided below is drawn from Yamada (2014).

All community members who attended InField said it had a positive impact on their teaching, learning, and ability to advocate for the language. They noted increased confidence and they found inspiration by learning together with members of other communities from across the globe. Yamada noted that "knowing one is not alone mitigates the ongoing, often thankless day-to-day struggle of language work. All participants expressed gratitude for the interactions with other language activists and the friendships they forged" (2014: 340).

Since returning to Suriname, the group has continued to document their own and other varieties of Kari'nja. In addition, they have widened the scope and impact of their language work. Some examples of this include:

- Training teachers in the community in computer skills, language teaching methods, and materials development (2014: 332)
- Sharing their knowledge with two other Kari'nja communities (2014: 338)
- Creating two language nests, inspired by the Māori that they met at InField (2014: 339)
- Drafting a press release submitted to a local newspaper (2014: 339)
- Successfully arguing for recognition of their Kari'jna variety by local governmental organizations, which allowed the development and adoption of a Kari'njya math curriculum

Yamada notes "that the Konomerume team was empowered to participate actively in decisions that affect them is a direct result of a newfound confidence that was developed and nurtured through the training they received at NILI/InField (2014: 340)."

These positive impacts amply demonstrate that the inclusion of community language experts in training activities can result in increased capacity and efficacy to bring about positive change. As Yamada notes, "training for speech community members can blur the lines between (academic and speech) communities as speech community members take on roles and responsibilities that have traditionally been the sole purview of outsider academics" (Yamada 2014: 329). Their inclusion as equals in an international institute provided validation of their work and its importance, seen both through their own eyes and through those of the broader society.

6.5 *Kennedy Bosiré of the Ekegusii*

As early as 2002, Kennedy Bosiré wanted to document the Abagusii culture. "The idea was to be able to pass on to my children what my father had taught me …" A few years into his endeavor, he turned his attention to creating an Ekegusii dictionary. Trained as a mechanical engineer, he realized that there was much he needed to learn about language description and lexicography; therefore, he began to solicit aid from Kenyan scholars and universities. Unfortunately, there were few responses. He eventually encountered the announcement for InField in Santa Barbara. Kennedy, together with his colleague Gladys Machogu, attended the two weeks of workshops, then served as a language consultant for one of the four week field methods courses.

Kennedy's participation in the Institute had many impacts: on his own understanding of language, on the development of the Ekegusii dictionary, and even more broadly on language attitudes in many Kenyan communities. The workshops on recording and data management, along with special tutoring on Lexique Pro, helped to advance the initial word list into a dictionary that would later be published online (Genetti and Siemens 2013: 68).

The intensive engagement with the language during the field methods course was transformational. Kennedy and Gladys's roles were not limited to those of language consultants; having clear goals for their language work and wanting to learn more about language description, they became active collaborators with the other course participants (Genetti and Siemens 2013: 71). The course taught them a number of important features of Ekegusii linguistics that were pivotal in the development of the dictionary: phonemic vowel length, the lack of orthographic representation of lower-mid vowels, tone and tone spreading, and nominal class prefixes (Nash 2017: 175–181). "Attending InField 2008 [with] all the rigorous programming we had, the wonderful instructor of Ekegusii, and the wonderful participants, that was wonderful exposure."

When the dictionary was published and launched in 2014, there were numerous promotions in national media outlets. The Cabinet Secretary for Education,

Fred Matiang'i, attended the dictionary launch and provided acknowledgement and praise for its completion. The publication of the Ekegusii dictionary has encouraged many other Indigenous communities in Kenya to begin their own dictionary projects. Kennedy has received many invitations to speak and work with other communities who are encountering difficulties in producing their dictionaries. Another significant impact is the Kenyan government's recognition of the importance of protecting Indigenous property, including language.

Kennedy's participation in the linguistics field continued after InField 2008. He attended each Institute through to 2016. He served as an international representative on the Institute's Advisory Circle from 2014 to 2016. Although he maintains a full-time career in Mombasa and there are nearly 800 km between Mombasa and Kisii, where Ekegusii is primarily spoken, he remains optimistic for future Ekegusii projects, such as the development of an Abagusii cultural learning center.

The production and publication of the Ekegusii dictionary is a clear example of how the Institute provided capacity-building opportunities for community language experts. Not only did Kennedy and Gladys gain important skills necessary to fully develop the dictionary, but they also gained a supportive network of academics: "We got a lot of support from you. The moral support we got from you, the material support we got from you, improved the quality of the work we were doing."

7 Conclusions

The case studies presented above show that InField/CoLang has had significant impacts on the individuals interviewed, their careers, and their language projects. The blending of audiences and putting all participants on an equal footing is humbling to some and empowering to others, creating openness and encouraging active listening that allows for shifts in perspective. These intangible results, combined with the tangible outcomes of the explicit curriculum and skills development, make for an impactful experience.

A full survey of all participants is beyond the scope of the current study, but we would hypothesize that such a survey would demonstrate that the Institute significantly impacted the development of many participants. We recognize that as non-Indigenous participants ourselves, our own perspectives are limited to observations based on conversations, evaluations, interviews, and academic literature. A future study, written or co-authored by community language experts shaping the study and questions, is likely to provide different insights.

In tracing the development of the Institute across the years, this article has demonstrated a consistent commitment to shaping the Institute for non-academic participants. Many of the changes reflected the institutional setting of the host university. All of the changes were motivated by the commitment to further inclusion and collaboration, the core values of the Institute.

The paper also found that collaboration and inclusion are mutually reinforcing: inclusion makes for productive collaboration and engaging people as full partners in collaborative work means they are included and valued. The Institute, through capacity-building, collaboration, and inclusion, increased participants' confidence as they found inspiration by learning together with members of other communities from across the globe.

However, collaboration and integration are always challenging, especially when working with diverse populations who don't fully understand each other's cultural framing and who are bound by stereotypes and biases, as all humans are. As noted in the literature on collaboration in community-based linguistic research (Rice 2006, Penfield et al. 2008; Czaykowksa-Higgins 2009), collaboration requires negotiating goals, methods, ownership, and other complex facets of the project, while establishing trust and mutual respect. The *ex situ* and time-bound nature of the Institute provides participants with a lower-stakes training ground and a set of new relationships to practice the interactional skills needed for collaborative research. When interactional issues at CoLang do arise, there is a supportive environment within which to navigate them. Cranmer, Smith, and Shaw (2009), reporting lessons learned from the Kwak'wala practicum in the 2008 InField, echo this point. The strategies they employed to negotiate difference across class participants included: maintaining open, respectful, and constructive communication; defining a communal purpose; and building a knowledge collective.

Finally, we conclude that InField/CoLang, in providing an inclusive and collaborative model of linguistic research, has reinforced the community-based research paradigms promoted in recent literature (cited above). As it develops dynamically over time, it functions both as a biennial reflection of trends in endangered language work and a site for creating and sharing innovations in inclusive and collaborative research and teaching in support of language documentation and revitalization.

References

Aikhenvald, Alexandra Y. (2013). A Story of Love and Debt: The Give and the Take of Linguistic Fieldwork. *The Asia Pacific Journal of Anthropology* 14 (2): 172–182. DOI: 10.1080/14442213.2013.769118

Brayboy, Bryan and D. Deyhle (2000). Insider–outsider: Researchers in American Indian Communities. *Theory into Practice* 39 (3): 163–169.

Chelliah, Shobhana L. and Willem J. De Reuse (2011). *Handbook of Descriptive Linguistic Fieldwork*. Dordrecht: Springer.

CoLang (2012). *CoLang* 2012. The Wayback Machine. https://web.archive.org/web/20120512021506/https://idrh.ku.edu/colang2012 (accessed 22.2.2020).

CoLang (2014). *CoLang* 2014: Institute on Collaborative Language Research. The Wayback Machine. https://web.archive.org/web/20191106124222/http://www.uta.edu/faculty/cmfitz/swnal/projects/CoLang/ (accessed 22.09.2020).

CoLang (2016). *CoLang* 2016. University of Alaska. https://www.alaska.edu/colang2016/ (accessed 22.09.2020).

CoLang (2018). *CoLang* 2018. University of Florida. https://colang.lin.ufl.edu/ (accessed 22.09.2020).

CoLang (2020). *CoLang* 2020. University of Montana. http://hs.umt.edu/colang/colang2020/default.php (accessed 22.09.2020).

Cranmer, Laura, Juliane Smith and Patricia Shaw (2009). Reconciling difference and building trust: International collaboration in Indigenous language revitalization. Paper presented at the 2nd International Conference on Language Documentation and Conservation, University of Hawai'i.

Crippen, James A. and Laura C. Robinson (2013). In Defense of the Lone Wolf: Collaboration in Language Documentation. *Language Documentation & Conservation* 7: 123–135.

Cruz, Emiliana and Anthony C. Woodbury (2014). Collaboration in the Context of Teaching, Scholarship, and Language Revitalization: Experience from the Chatino Language Documentation Project. *Language Documentation & Conservation* 8: 262–286.

Czaykowska-Higgins, Eva (2009). Research models, community engagement, and linguistic fieldwork: Reflections on working within Canadian indigenous communities. *Language Documentation and Conservation* 3: 15–50.

Czaykowska-Higgins, Ewa (2018). Reflections on ethics: Re-humanizing linguistics, building relationships across difference. In Bradley McDonnell, Andrea L. Berez-Kroeker and Gary Holton (eds.), *Reflections on Language Documentation 20 Years after Himmelmann 1998. Language Documentation & Conservation Special Publication* No. 15: 110–112. Honolulu: University of Hawai'i Press. http://hdl.handle.net/10125/24813

Davis, Jamie D. and Kelly Keemer (2002). A Brief History of and Future Considerations for Research in American Indian and Alaska Native Communities. In: *Work Group on American Indian Research and Program Evaluation Methodology* (AIRPEM), *Symposium on Research and Evaluation Methodology: Lifespan Issues Related to American Indians/Alaska Natives with Disabilities.*

Dobrin, Lise M. and Joshua Berson (2011). Speakers and language documentation. In Peter K. Austin and Julia Salabank (eds.), *The Cambridge handbook of endangered languages*, 187–211. Cambridge: Cambridge University Press.

Dorian, Nancy C. (2010). Documentation and responsibility. *Language and Communication* 30: 179–185.

Genetti, Carol and Rebekka Siemens (2013). Training as Empowering Social Action: An Ethical Response to Language Endangerment. In Elena Mihas, Bernard Perley, Gabriel Rey-Doval and Kathleen Wheatley (eds.), *Responses to Language Endangerment. In Honor of Mickey Noonan. New Directions in Language Endangerment and Language Documentation*, 59–77. Amsterdam & Philadephia: John Benjamins Publishing Company.

Glenn, Akiemi (2009). Five Dimensions of Collaboration: Toward a Critical Theory of Coordination and Interoperability in Language Documentation. *Language Documentation & Conservation* 3 (2): 149–160. http://hdl.handle.net/10125/4437

Good, Jeff (2018). Ethics in Language Documentation and Revitalization. In Kenneth L. Rehg and Lyle Campbell (eds.), *The Oxford Handbook of Endangered Languages.* Oxford: Oxford University Press. DOI: 10.1093/oxfordhb/9780190610029.013.21

Guérin, Valérie and Sébastien Lacrampe (2010). Trust Me, I am a Linguist! Building Partnership in the Field. *Language Documentation & Conservation* 4: 22–33. http://hdl.handle.net/10125/4465

Holton, Gary (2009). Relatively Ethical: A Comparison of Linguistic Research Paradigms in Alaska and Indonesia. *Language Documentation & Conservation* 3 (2): 161–175. http://hdl.handle.net/10125/4424

InField (2008). *Infield: Institute on Field Linguistics and Language Documentation.* UC Santa Barbara. http://infield.faculty.linguistics.ucsb.edu/ (accessed 22.09.2020).

InField (2009). *Infield 2010: Institute on Field Linguistics and Language Documentation.* The Wayback Machine. https://web.archive.org/web/20100622002214/http://logos.uoregon.edu/infield2010/home/index.php (accessed 22.09.2020).

James, Rosalina, Kathleen McGlone West and Teresa M. Madrid (2013). Launching Native Health Leaders: Reducing Mistrust of Research Through Student Peer Mentorship. *American Journal of Public Health* 103 (12): 2215–2219.

Leonard, Wesley (2017). Producing Language Reclamation by Decolonising 'Language'. In Wesley Y. Leonard and Haley De Korne (eds.), *Language Documentation and Description* 14: 15–36. London: EL Publishing.

Leonard, Wesley (2018). Reflections on (De)Colonialism in Language Documentation.

In Bradley McDonnell, Andrea L. Berez-Kroeker and Gary Holton (eds.), *Reflections on Language Documentation 20 Years after Himmelmann 1998. Language Documentation & Conservation Special Publication* No. 15, 55–65.

Leonard, Wesley Y. and Erin Haynes (2010). Making 'collaboration' collaborative: An examination of perspectives that frame linguistic field research. *Language Documentation & Conservation* 4: 268–293.

Lewis, Diane (1973). Anthropology and Colonialism. *Current Anthropology* 14 (5): 581–602. http://www.jstor.org/stable/2741037

Medicine, Bea (1998). American Indians and Anthropologists: Issues of History, Empowerment, and Application. *Human Organization* 57 (3): 253–257. https://www.jstor.org/stable/44127270

Nash, Carlos (2017). Documenting Ekegusii: How Empowering Research Fulfills Community and Academic Goals. In Jason Kandybowicz and Harold Torrence (eds.), *Africa's Endangered Languages*, 165–186. Oxford: Oxford University Press.

Pacheco, Christina M., Sean M. Daley, Travis Brown, Melissa Felippi, K. Allen Greiner, and Christine M. Daley (2013). Moving Forward: Breaking the Cycle of Mistrust between American Indians and Researchers. *American Journal of Public Health* 103 (12): 2152–2159. doi:10.2105/AJPH.2013.301480

Penfield, Susan, Angelina Serratos, Benjamin V. Tucker, Amelia Flores, Gilford Harper, Johnny Hill Jr. and Nora Vasquez (2008). Community Collaborations: Best Practices for North American Indigenous Language Documentation. In Nancy Dorian (ed.), *Small Languages and Small Communities 59: Special Issue of the International Journal of Sociology of Language*, 187–202. Berlin: Mouton de Gruyter.

Rice, Keren (2006). Ethical issues in linguistic fieldwork: An overview. *Journal of Academic Ethics* 4: 123–155.

Rice, Keren (2012). Ethical Issues in Linguistics Fieldwork. In Nicholas Thieberger (ed.), *The Oxford Handbook of Linguistic Fieldwork*, 407–429. Oxford: Oxford University Press.

Sapién, Racquel-María (2018). Design and Implementation of Collaborative Language Documentation Projects. In Kenneth L. Rehg and Lyle Campbell (eds.), *The Oxford Handbook of Endangered Languages*, 203–224. Oxford: Oxford University Press. DOI: 10.1093/oxfordhb/9780190610029.013.12

Seifart, Frank, Nicholas Evans, Harald Hammarström and Stephen C. Levinson. 2018. Language documentation 25 years on. *Language* 94 (4): e324–e345. https://www.linguisticsociety.org/sites/default/files/e05_94.4Seifart_0.pdf

Singer, Ruth (2018). Reflections on Linguistic Fieldwork in Australia. In Bradley McDonnell, Andrea L. Berez-Kroeker and Gary Holton (eds.), *Reflections on Language Documentation 20 Years after Himmelmann 1998. Language Documentation & Conservation Special Publication* no. 15: 267–275. Honolulu: University of Hawai'i Press. http://hdl.handle.net/10125/24828

Smith, Juliane, Laura Cranmer and Patricia Shaw (2011). Reconciling Difference and Building Trust: International Collaboration in Indigenous Language Revitalization. Paper presented at the 2nd International Conference on Language Documentation and Conservation, University of Hawai'i. http://hdl.handle.net/10125/5033

Tuttle, Siri and Alice Taff (2017). CoLang: Disciplinary Change and the Pop-Up University. Paper presented at the 5th International Conference on Language Documentation and Conservation, the University of Hawaii. Link to MP3: https://scholarspace.manoa.hawaii.edu/handle/10125/41975 (accessed 23.02.2021).

Yamada, Raquel-María (2010). Speech Community-Based Documentation, Description, and Revitalization: Kari'nja of Konomerume. PhD Dissertation, University of Oregon.

Yamada, Racquel-María (2014). Training in the Community-Collaborative Context: A Case Study. *Language Documentation & Conservation* 8: 326–344. http:/hdl.handle.net/10125/24611

CHAPTER 21

Working with the Last Guardians of a Language

R.M.W. Dixon

1 Introduction

The purpose of linguistics is to investigate the nature of human language. There are different ways of approaching this task. One may pull a hypothesis out of one's head, draw deductions from it, and check these by cursory scrutiny of a handful of convenient languages. Or the investigation can be undertaken from the opposite direction, exposing the integrated nature of a representative selection of individual languages and then inductively generalising from these to a characterisation of language as a human attribute. That is the stance I espouse.

From this point of view, the basic task for linguists is to provide comprehensive accounts of individual languages, in an explicit and consistent manner. The great majority of languages are spoken by small ethnic groups living in out-of-the-way places. The linguist undertakes fieldwork (real fieldwork, not interview fieldwork sitting in a cafe in town asking for translation of sentences from some manual). This involves going to live as part of a small community where everyone uses the language. Learning to speak the language; gathering vocabulary; recording, transcribing, translating, and analysing texts; paying attention to what is said in the course of daily interaction. After a while the linguist formulates grammatical principles which appear to control the ways in which the language is used. These are checked, revised, and checked again, by generating sentences and eliciting opinions on them.

This is the *ideal script* for linguistic fieldwork. And there are—across South America, Africa, Asia, and islands in the Pacific—many languages in need of description where such conditions do prevail. In all such situations the methodology of the fieldworker is basically similar, with minor variations due to local conditions.

There are also many languages in need of description for which *the situation is not quite ideal*. For instance, only some people (perhaps just the older ones) in the community may use the language on a daily basis. Or there may be only a few fluent speakers, whose locations are scattered. In these circumstances, basically the same methodology applies as in the ideal case (save that daily interaction will be very limited).

© R.M.W. DIXON, 2022 | DOI:10.1163/9789004510395_022

But there are also a considerable number of important and interesting languages which are only remembered—often with an effort—by one or just a few people who used to speak the language many years before. Here the methodology for an ideal situation is inapplicable. One just has to do what one can, exploiting every ploy to try to find out as much as possible about the nature of the language. These are *salvage situations*.

In summary, fieldwork with living languages is generally on a regular pattern. But moribund tongues pose such diverse challenges that there is no regular template to follow. Each such language situation presents its own problems, which have to be negotiated in an appropriate manner.

This chapter describes the varying techniques I used when working in salvage situations with three Australian languages for which there were just rememberers—Mbabaram, Warrgamay, and Nyawaygi. But first it will be useful to say a little about fieldwork with living languages.

2 Foundation

Undertaking fieldwork should not be like a business transaction. There are linguists who get speakers to sign an 'ethics clearance form', agree on an hourly rate of pay, arrange for the work to be done at the linguist's place of abode rather than at the speaker's, note the exact time at which each 'informant session' begins and when it ends, pay accordingly, and ask for a signed receipt. The results of such an endeavour will be of some use, but are unlikely to reveal the inner character of the language, the way it is moulded to the lifestyle and mental outlook of its speakers. The ideal fieldwork practice is of a quite different nature.

Ideally, work on creating an insightful description of a language involves *bonds* being established between one or more expert speakers and the questing linguist. This involves mutual respect, an understanding of each other's point of view, and a personal commitment to the task in hand. A real friendship develops in which each helps the other. In return for being taught the language, the linguist may provide aid in dealing with the outside world, either on a daily basis or more widely. An extreme example of this dates from 1972 when a Labor government was elected in Australia after 23 years in opposition. I was instrumental in obtaining land rights and good housing for the Dyirbal people, who had been sharing their language with me for the past nine years.

A good field linguist must also be something of an anthropologist. Language is a manifestation of social behaviour and can only be appreciated in terms of its role in the community. Quite often—but not always—the linguist is adopted as someone's brother or daughter and thus becomes related to everyone else in the ethnic group. This gives them certain responsibilities towards various classes of kin. Agreement is reached, sometimes implicitly, on how the linguist will 'pay their way'. It may be by bringing in food or other gifts, or by money transferred in a non-obtrusive manner.

In almost every village there will be a few speakers who will naturally bond with the linguist and become their mentors. Each of the pair will be tuned in to the interests and needs of the other. Often the speaker will anticipate what the linguist is about to enquire after and volunteer it instead. Of course, things do not work out well in every case. Just occasionally, the members of a particular community may have no interest in their language being documented, or else the linguist's personality may be such that they cannot immerse themself in an unfamiliar culture.

As mentioned before, the modus operandi is in outline the same for every ideal fieldwork situation, where everyone—or almost everyone—in the community speaks the language and one or more speakers take the linguist under their wing. Of prime importance is that the language must be analysed in its own right, from the inside as it were. It is not good practice to elicit translations of sample sentences from a lingua franca. The crucial task is to get texts, of varying sorts, in the language, and then to analyse them. What one does is as follows.

(*a*) *Start using the language* yourself as soon as you can. People will be pleased with this and they will respond. Ask how to describe some action. Try and describe it yourself and solicit corrections. (Tell people that you need their feedback if you are to learn to speak the language properly. They mustn't hold back, mustn't be timorous about correcting you.)

(*b*) *Work out the basic phonology*, at least the likely system of phonemes, so that the language may be written with a fair degree of confidence.

(*c*) *Build up a vocabulary*. Body parts are straightforward. Other sets of nouns can be approached systematically. Suggest to your teacher: 'Let's do bird names tomorrow.' They will think about these overnight. For each bird, get a sentence or two—spontaneously from the speaker—describing its habits; for example, 'The black duck eats shrimps', 'The brown pigeon calls out when tree grubs are ready to be gathered and eaten'.

(*d*) Right from the beginning, *record texts* in the language. Texts of all sorts—monologues, dialogues, conversations. Legends, history, personal experiences (such as: 'the time when I had to fight off a jaguar'), procedural accounts of how to make artefacts, when to plant crops, and so on. A speaker may have mentioned some notable story or incident. Ask them if they would tell about it in detail; not now but maybe tomorrow, then they can think about it and prepare it overnight. *Transcribe each text*, with the help of either the person who recorded it or some other (perhaps younger) speaker. Play it back phrase by phrase and make sure you can pronounce it correctly before writing it down. Try and divide each word into morphemes and make sure you understand what each word and each sentence means.

(*e*) An important source is *participant observation*, when this is available. Join in on some everyday activity—it might be weaving or cooking, or just clearing away weeds from around the houses. Listen to what people say. Try to understand it. Write down in your pocket notebook new words and meanings, new bits of grammar.

(*f*) It is important to *keep up with filing*. When in the field, I try each evening to go through what has been gathered that day (from text processing, participant observation, and anything else), extracting the new material. For example, new verbs of speaking may come up each day for a while. When there is a stack of them, these will be gone through with my teachers, clarifying the full range of meaning for each and contrasting their denotations.

(*g*) Not quite from the beginning, but fairly soon, the linguist begins to *recognise grammatical patterns*—the order in which affixes follow one another, techniques for asking questions, how to address people of different social ranks. Paradigms will be constructed and their boxes gradually filled in. There may be a few gaps, for items which haven't yet turned up in texts or conversation; maybe something like '2nd person dual alienable possessive pronoun'. These can be elicited, within a suitable context.

(*h*) *Grammatical hypotheses*—for example, concerning the properties of relative clause constructions—will be developed, and checked by letting the hypothesis generate new sentences and enquiring whether they are acceptable. Corrections may be offered, the hypothesis refined, new sentences generated, to be checked in their turn.

Apart from the initial stage of building up the vocabulary, elicitation from the lingua franca (be it English, Spanish, Portuguese, Tok Pisin in New Guinea, or whatever) is not recommended. Questions or relative clauses may be used in quite different circumstances in the language of study and in the lingua franca. The order of words in sentences obtained by elicitation may faithfully mirror the order of words in the lingua franca, whereas, when one examines texts, or just listens to people talking around one, there are many other possibilities, each with its own conditioning factors.

When checking a tentative hypothesis, one employs elicitation of a quite different kind, just from within the language of study. (The lingua franca will have been used in the initial stages, but as work proceeds the language under study will increasingly be used as the meta-language.) This is roughly what goes on in an ideal or almost ideal fieldwork situation.

3 Background

I came out from England in 1963 to work on languages in the Cairns Rainforest region of north-east Queensland, The best spoken language there was Dyirbal. It was a good, but not quite ideal, fieldwork situation. There were around 100 fluent speakers (almost all of those aged over thirty). However, they did not live in one community but were scattered over a number of farms with non-indigenous owners. Dyirbal was the language of choice among the speakers and I was able to achieve a limited amount of participant observation. Otherwise, the methodology outlined above for an ideal situation was followed, with satisfactory results as I was able to record good texts from 15 speakers.

Most importantly, I established strong bonds of friendship and cooperation with, in the first place, Chloe Grant and George Watson. My grammar was published in 1972 but I continued fieldwork until 1992, linking up with half-a-dozen other knowledgeable elders. I worked on the avoidance (or 'mother-in-law') speech style, and on song language, the kinship system and a full thesaurus/dictionary across several dialects (Dixon and Koch 1996; Dixon 2015a).

Yidiñ, Dyirbal's northerly neighbour, had been more seriously impacted by the European invasion. When I started serious work on it, in 1971, there were just three fluent speakers. But we bonded at once; they became dedicated to working with me to document their language before it was too late, recording texts, explaining vocabulary, and helping to articulate the grammar. The only item missing from the methodology outlined above was participant observation. But even that was not entirely lacking. I'd put a sentence to Dick Moses. He'd accept or perhaps slightly correct it, and then say how someone else would respond. Then how the first person would continue the dialogue, and for the next two hours or so he might dictate an interactive conversation. The fieldwork was certainly not ideal, but it approached this. I was able to publish a hefty grammar of Yidiñ in 1977, and later (1991a) a volume of texts, place names, and songs.

I also undertook salvage studies of the three languages discussed in later sections. Then came time for a change. For 20 years I'd worked on five Australian languages with varying levels of vitality. A sojourn in an ideal fieldwork situation now beckoned. It was found on the Fijian island of Taveuni where I lived for six months in 1985 as a (rather unusual) member of a monolingual community of about 120 people. A few of them knew a little English for talking to outsiders, but in the village it was just the local Boumaa dialect of Fijian. I would sit at the desk in my house in the middle of the village and wonder if it was alright to say such-and-such. Two minutes later I'd hear someone who was walking by say that very sentence.

The villagers were cordial enough; they didn't mind having me there, but there was only a passing interest in what I was doing. With only one person did I establish a real bond; this was the chief's younger brother, Josefa Cookanacagi. He took me to accomplished storytellers in nearby villages, and helped with transcription and grammatical discussions. Josefa had a keen mind; he'd been thinking about language all his life and harmonised with my mission. Some of the other villagers gave me a little of their time but without commitment. What made up for this was total immersion in the language. I soon learnt to speak and understand it and participant observation was 24/7. There had been earlier works on Fijian, but with little on syntax and no account of the Boumaa dialect. My grammar was published in 1988.

Then, in 1991, I ventured into a domain which was different in every way, but even more ideal. There were all told about 150 speakers of Jarawara, and around 40 lived in the small village of Casa Nova, deep in the Amazonian rainforest. Alan Vogel, a missionary linguist with the Summer Institute of Linguistics, organised for them to build me a small hut, and all day people came to visit and talk. In contrast to Fiji, just about every person was keenly interested in my linguistic endeavours. Special bonds were established with Okomobi, the village chief, and with Mioto, who was a teenager when we began and in his late twenties by the time of my seventh and last field trip in 2003. Half-a-dozen other men were always available to assist in unravelling the intricacies of Jarawara grammar.

The physical setting was entrancing, the insects intolerable, the language challenging, and the people as welcoming as could be. I remarked to Okomobi on arrival that I knew only little Portuguese; he replied: 'It's the same with us.' Every component of the ideal fieldwork situation was in place. Ample texts of varied genres from a variety of speakers. Patient teachers as I tried to speak Jarawara. Observing the language as it was used in many situations. Insightful discussions about its structure. My grammar, published in 2004, was a substantial tome.

Those, then were the four languages which I was able to work on fully—Dyirbal, Yidiñ, the Boumaa dialect of Fijian, and Jarawara. But a linguist can't confine themself just to rich pastures. There had been other languages around Dyirbal and Yidiñ which had fallen out of use. However, they were not fully forgotten. There could be one or two people who had spoken a language in their youth and were able to remember bits of it. We can refer to them as the *last guardians* of their languages, and working with them as a *salvage study*.

4 Salvage Situations

The differences between ideal fieldwork and a salvage study are considerable. Some of the main points are as follows.

(*i*) In an ideal situation the data for grammatical analysis comes principally from recorded texts and participant observation. Using elicitation from a lingua franca is bad practice and will yield limited results. A last guardian may be able to record just a couple of short texts, but often no texts at all are obtained. There can be no input from observing language use since this doesn't happen.

In a salvage situation one generally has to carry out *bilingual elicitation*. This is, quite simply, the only thing which is possible.

Care must be taken to *check exactly what it is you are getting*. Some last guardians remember bits of several languages and tend to muddle these together. Sometimes the guardian is aware of this, and is happy to work with the linguist in trying to untangle things. If they are not, the linguist must attempt to solve the problem themself (for example, by consulting available material on nearby languages).

(*ii*) Be *relaxed* and approach the task *gently*. The guardian may be slow at remembering from long ago. Do not try to rush them.

In the ideal fieldwork situations, my teachers would sometimes be indefatigable. Okomobi and I could have been transcribing a Jarawara story for several hours. I'd feel exhausted and suggest that we should stop for the day. Okomobi would demur: 'Let's do two more pages.' This is extreme, but people are normally happy to work for a two or three hour stretch.

In most salvage situations about *an hour—or at most two hours—of questioning* is long enough. Most guardians are pretty old, and thinking back to the language of one's youth requires an effort. If you make them too tired, they may not want you to return. The secret is to stop before that point is reached, so that they will be content for you to return.

(*iii*) An ideal fieldwork situation involves hundreds of hours of interaction. The linguist records selectively. My recording would be limited to texts and portions of the language illustrating important phonological contrasts, so that they could be studied at leisure.

In contrast, one will often *record everything* in salvage work. The material is so limited and so delicate that it is wise to maintain a complete audio record.

(*iv*) Sometimes a last guardian will have a real interest in documenting as much as possible of their traditional language and will *bond* with the linguist, making the salvage enterprise congenial and maximally productive. Other times they are friendly but don't really care, so that there is *no bonding*. In that circumstance, the linguist just has to make the best of the situation.

(*v*) The salvage linguist must *employ a strategy* in order to keep the guardian interested. Some 'linguists' go through a standard word list, which is arranged alphabetically on English. The word for 'ear' is elicited, and the guardian then wants to offer 'nose' and 'mouth'. No—those come later. The next things on the list are 'earth', 'eat', 'egg'.

The questions asked should be semantically structured and adapted to the guardian's interests. Ask for 'moon', 'sun', 'stars', and 'rainbow' together. When eliciting sentences, string together a quasi-narrative. Here is a sequence of nine sentences from a Nyawaygi elicitation session: 'I ran down the hill', 'I fell down', 'I began to cry', 'That man laughed at me', 'So I got up and hit him', 'He fell down', 'I'd knocked him down', 'He just lay there', 'He was dead'.

(*vi*) *Every word* which is obtained *must be checked* on a later occasion. If a guardian does not recognise a word which they gave earlier, then that word should be omitted from the vocabulary list (or, at the least, marked with a symbol indicating that it could not be confirmed).

(*vii*) As the linguist works out as much as possible of the grammar, they can try to *generate new sentences*—as in an ideal fieldwork situation—and ask if these are correct. However, there is likely to be only limited scope for this.

Beyond these recurrent features, every salvage situation has its own special character. This relates to the personality and attitude of the guardian(s) and the techniques required to reconstitute as much as possible of the language.

5 Mbabaram

In a typical Australian language, each word has at least two syllables, is stressed on the initial syllable, begins with a single consonant, and cannot end with a stop consonant. Anthropologists Norman Tindale and Jo Birdsell (1941) reported a language that they called Barbaram which showed unusual features—monosyllabic words with a final stop such as ['kok] 'water', words commencing with a vowel and stressed on the second syllable such as [a'wa] 'mother', and words with an initial consonant cluster such as [n'ka:la] 'leg'.

When I commenced field work in 1963, a high priority was to locate a speaker of this language, which was spoken beyond the rainforest, some way inland from Cairns. Its name is actually Mbabaram. A cantankerous old lady called Lizzie Simmons, in Mount Garnet, had had an Mbabaram father. I managed to get her to offer a few words, but they were all of regular shape—*guwu* 'nose', *jina* 'foot', and a few more. It turned out that these were a mixture of Gugu-Yalanji, her mother's language, and Warungu, her late husband's language. In vain did I plead for some Mbabaram. Mrs Simmons shook her head: "No, Mbabaram too hard. Too hard for me, far too hard for you."

Then I went to visit Albert Bennett, who had had an Mbabaram mother and was now living near Petford, in traditional Mbabaram country. He wasn't impressed when I explained my mission. Albert didn't remember any Mbabaram language, but who'd want it anyway? What good was it?

He sat in the shade outside his kitchen door. I stood nearby, in the sun, and persisted. "You know what we call dog?" Albert volunteered, as a point of interest, "we call it [dok]." Hearing this, I just felt defeated. But it was actually a fact of considerable importance. A few years later, linguist Ken Hale explained that it was a regular reduction from an original form *gudaga* 'dog' (which is retained as is in Yidiñ). In Mbabaram the a in the second syllable became o when the word began with *g-* or *ŋ-* or *wu-*; thus *ŋaba-* > *bo-* 'bathe', *ganda-* > *ndo-* 'burn', among others. The initial syllable had dropped off many words (for example *bamba* > *mba* 'belly') and sometimes also the final vowel (as in *gugu* > *gug* 'water'). Thus *gudaga* > *dog* ([g] and [k] are alternative pronunciations of the single dorso-velar stop phoneme).

In earlier times, it appeared, words in Mbabaram had been of regular Australian shape. Then various changes had applied quite systematically, shortening words, raising vowels, and so on. An initial syllable with a short vowel would just be dropped; another example was *guyu* > *yu* 'fish'. But if the initial syllable included a long vowel, then it was replaced by a. Thus the original word for boomerang, *waaŋal* (which is the word in Nyawaygi), became *aŋal* in Mbabaram. Hence the unusual features which Tindale and Birdsell had commented on.

On that first afternoon, Albert Bennett thawed a little when I told him that I was collecting words for a museum down south. I squatted there in the sun and went through scores of things—body parts, animals, birds, fire and water. He remembered 28 words that day. When I went back a couple of months later his greeting was "I don't think I can help you any more." But he made room for me to sit with him on the bench in the shade and we did get to scratch together another 75 words. A further visit three weeks later yielded 50 more words and a dozen short sentences such as: 'Who is coming?', 'Where are you from?', 'I am going out to kill a kangaroo'.

Albert was about sixty and worked for the railway, keeping the line in order. He hadn't spoken Mbabaram since his mother died, twenty years or more before. He evinced no enthusiasm for the linguistic work but was indulgent towards me. There could be no bond between us, as I'd always had in ideal—or almost ideal—fieldwork situations.

I saw him on eight occasions, across 1964, 1967, 1970, and 1971 (he died the following year). Albert was never eager to resume our journey into the past, but once he got into the swing of it again, we'd have a productive hour. There had to be a gap of a least a week between visits; Albert wouldn't have welcomed me returning any sooner.

Working with him was a delicate matter. I shouldn't ask the Mbabaram correspondents for a string of English words. If Albert didn't know three in a row he'd become dispirited and want to stop. So, I'd ask one new word then a couple we'd had before, which he could supply, then another new word, a couple more familiar ones, a third new word, and so on.

In an 1899 book called *Eaglehawk and Crow* by John Mathew, I found a word list labelled "Walsh River language" which was plainly Mbabaram. After moving from London to the Australian National University in Canberra, in 1970, I lost no time before travelling north for further work on Dyirbal, and a trifle more Mbabaram. I met Albert on the track between his house and Petford, off to visit a friend. "I haven't got anything new to tell you," Albert insisted. But when I produced the old vocabulary, he did show a whiff of interest.

For an hour and a half, we sat on the sand by the side of the track with the tape recorder on the tailgate of Albert's ancient truck (all the Mbabaram was recorded). First we went through that old vocabulary. '*Yaman*, "rainbow".' "Yes, he's got that right." '*Milivir* "lighting".' Albert shook his head; that word didn't ring a bell. Then I went on to ask him lots of simple sentences: 'Bring it here!', 'You spear it!', 'Leave it there!', 'Dig it up!'

Altogether, Albert Bennett and I retrieved about 300 words of Mbabaram vocabulary. Each word was put in grammatical frames and its forms studied. *Mog* was 'man' and *aru* was 'wallaroo'. 'The man shot the wallaroo' was *mokul aru ndare*, the verb coming last (as is common in Australian languages). In this sentence, 'man' is in transitive subject function and bears the ergative suffix *-ul*. A few hundred sentences like this yielded an outline (27 pages) of the grammar. A full account is in Dixon (1991b).

This was the most difficult field situation I encountered. But it was worth persevering with, since the language was so unusual and so fascinating.

6 Warrgamay

To the south of Girramay, the most southerly dialect of Dyirbal, the Warrgamay language was spoken. There were three guardians for its two dialects. John Tooth and Lambert Cocky remembered the Warrgamay proper dialect, spoken up from Ingham around the middle Herbert River, and Norah Boyd represented the Biyay dialect, spoken at the mouth of the Herbert around Halifax and Bemerside.

John Tooth worked as stockman at Glen Ruth station, about 100 kilometres down a dirt track from Mount Garnet. Alone of the last guardians I worked with, John Tooth had taught himself to read and write; he said he'd read one complete book in his life, a western. John's command of Warrgamay—which hadn't been spoken for a couple of generations—was a trifle rusty but this was compensated for by his intelligence and interest in the project. We developed the same sort of bond that I'd had with my teachers of Dyirbal and Yidiñ.

I played a short text in Dyirbal (which he could understand), as encouragement, and John recorded two stories, a couple of minutes each—one about seeing a ghost and another about two black wallabies (dreamtime men) who had two parrots as wives, and the two eaglehawks who stole them away. That was it. All the rest came through elicitation from English. However, here there were no limits on what I could ask. Words of every type. Simple sentences to elucidate the inflected forms of each noun, adjective, and verb. Complex sentences featuring relative clauses, and more. John had an appealing way of rejecting a sentence I had concocted which was incorrect. "It doesn't rhyme," he would comment.

As mentioned earlier, some guardians know bits of several languages. In the 1960s I worked with Alf Palmer, whose mother tongue was Warungu, spoken in the hills to the west of Warrgamay and Dyirbal. Alf told me that he also knew a fair bit of Warrgamay and of the Girramay and Jirrbal dialects of Dyirbal. He said that he tended to "muddle things up a bit" and suggested that each lexeme should be given in all four varieties, as a way of "keeping them apart". In this way, we went through more than 400 vocabulary items (and some bits of grammar). Checking the Warrgamay, Girramay and Jirrbal forms with those given by speakers of these varieties, there are only a few errors in Alf Palmer's information. In the 1970s Tasaku Tsunoda worked with Alf for an MA thesis on Warungu. Alf was older and there was now no attempt to "keep things apart". Tsunoda's published grammar (2011) and dictionary (2003) includes everything that Alf Palmer gave me in Warrgamay, Jirrbal, and Girramay, all now lumped together as 'Warrongo' (see Dixon 2015b.) John Tooth also knew Girramay so we took care that every lexeme should be noted in both languages, ensuring that what he gave me really was nothing but Warrgamay.

I drove down from Mount Garnet to visit John Tooth in November 1972. He was tremendously welcoming and we did a straight six hours exploring the mysteries of Warrgamay. Then I returned the following day. John had the interest and stamina of anyone in an ideal field situation. Unlike Dyirbal, Warrgamay has a contrast between short and long vowels which we were able to study: there was *badi-* 'to hook a fish' and *baadi-* 'to cry, weep', *julu* 'buttocks' and *juulu* 'black'.

The following year John arranged for me to stay for a few nights in a spare bedroom in the stockmen's quarters. He had to attend to some duties but we carried on with Warrgamay in between. A mare gave birth and I grabbed a leg to help hold down an energetic two-hour-old foal so that a suppository could be inserted to make sure that its bowels were in working order. That same day I realised the unusual nature of verb inflection in Warrgamay. There appeared to be no tense as such, just endings showing perfect, purposive, irrealis, and so on. I went back in 1974 and 1977 and we recovered a great deal of John's heritage language.

John directed me to one other guardian, Lambert Cocky, who worked at Sheahan's cane farm, by the Herbert River, in Warrgamay territory just up from Ingham. He was about the same age as John Tooth, both born in the 1890s, but of a totally different mien. Lambert and I occupied different worlds. It was useful to check with Lambert the material I had already collected; about two hours at a time was enough, but I could return the next day. He did record just one short text, an account of a massacre by the 'native police' at the end of the nineteenth century. Sometimes I could elicit words and sentences but other times Lambert retreated into himself. I would ask about something and get no direct response but then he would start just talking in Warrgamay (all recorded) and within a few minutes the word I had asked after would be employed in a quasi-discourse. I worked with him at Sheahan's in 1972 and 1973 and then at the Eventide Home in Charters Towers in 1974, 1975, 1977, and 1980.

The Biyay dialect was remembered by Norah Boyd, who was seriously old; her son was in the old folk's home in Charters Towers (I called in to pass on his mother's greetings when there to work with Lambert Cocky). I worked with Norah, an hour or so at a time, in 1973, 1974, and 1975 (she died the following year, reputably aged 100). Norah could not give texts but was unfailingly courteous in responding to my lexical and grammatical queries, and the differences between dialects. In most Australian languages, verbs fall into two conjugational classes and two transitivity classes, which correlate but do not coincide. A notable feature of the Warrgamay proper dialect is that transitivity and conjugation classes have fallen together. And, thanks to Norah Boyd's shrewdness, I discovered that in Biyay they are still—to some extent—separate.

From these three guardians of Warrgamay, I assembled a vocabulary of about 940 words and a useful 57-page grammar sketch. See Dixon (1981).

7 Nyawaygi

On my first long field trip, from October 1963 until August 1964, I concentrated on Dyirbal but also endeavoured to record something from other languages of the region. Nyawaygi was spoken to the south of Warrgamay, below Ingham almost as far down as Rollingstone and extending to the sea. I recorded some vocabulary from each of the last two guardians—Willie Seaton, who was blind and about 70, and Long Heron, a tall man (hence his name) who was perhaps 20 years Willie's senior.

On the next field trip, in 1967, I again contacted Willie Seaton and he suggested that we get together with Heron, who knew the language far better than him. Heron's mind was still good but he was failing physically—the once upright body was now bent and his speech was slurred. How the elicitation session went was as follows. I'd ask a sentence in English, then Heron would drawl the Nyawaygi in such a way that I couldn't pick it up. But Willie Seaton could, and he'd now pronounce it clearly for the tape recorder. Sometimes Seaton could produce the translation himself; Heron might just nod or add a word or two.

The elicitation was thematic. For example: 'You go and fetch some water!', 'Take the water over to mother!', 'Give it to mother to drink!', 'She's finished the water, drunk it all up'. Another segment of our work that day was quoted under (v) in section 4. We got through around 250 sentences in about an hour, before Willie Seaton started to feel tired and asked: "About finished now, have you?"

From 1963 I'd focussed mainly on Dyirbal, finalising the grammar in 1971. My aim then was to document what I could of the other languages of the area. Serious work on Yidiñ commenced in 1971 and on Warrgamay in 1972. Then in 1973 I turned my attention again to Nyawaygi. Long Heron had died in 1970 (believed to be aged 100), leaving Willie Seaton as the sole remaining guardian.

In Dyirbal and Warrgamay every verb root has at least two syllables and there are just two conjugations. Nyawaygi is markedly different, with seven verbal conjugations, four of them consisting of just a handful of monosyllabic roots. For instance, one conjugation has the following three members: *ñaa-* 'see', *buu-* 'drink' and *wu-* 'give'. Suffixes are added to these, including the positive imperative *-ga*, creating the verb word *wu-ga* 'give!' and the perfect suffix *-gi* producing *wu-gi* 'gave'. It is fascinating to note that the verb root 'give' is *wuga-* in Dyirbal and *wugi-* in Warrgamay. Nyawaygi probably represents a more archaic stage, with monosyllabic verbal roots. The disyllabic roots in Dyirbal and Warrgamay relate to root-plus-affix (a different affix for each language) in Nyawaygi.

Willie Seaton was intelligent and interested, a pleasure to work with. He thought back to his youth for more lexemes and produced short sentences exhibiting every inflectional form for each verb, monosyllabic and disyllabic. He could not give texts so all the data was through elicitation from English. On my arrival one day, he asked how I had travelled. "Left Canberra at six o'clock, changed planes in Brisbane, picked up a vehicle in Townsville and here I am in Ingham at just after noon." Willie Seaton responded with the longest sentence he ever gave spontaneously.

mali	*gaambl-jam*	*bulbay-ma*
DON'T	do.like.that-NEGATIVE.IMPERATIVE	fall-IRREALIS

'Don't do thing like that, you might crash (lit. fall down).'

Willie Seaton and I would do an hour or so each day—for several days in a row—almost every year commencing in 1973 until 1982. He was always as glad to welcome me as I was to see him. A bond developed between us, a relationship of trust and friendship.

In salvage fieldwork it is important to check and double-check every item which has been gathered. In the case of Warrgamay, each word given by John Tooth was checked with Lambert Cocky, and vice versa. For a word given in Mbabaram, I tried to get it recognised by Albert Bennett on another occasion. Similarly, for Nyawaygi, I endeavoured to check each item with Willie Seaton on different occasions.

Willie Seaton was eager that I should get everything absolutely correct. Like most Australian languages, Nyawaygi has two contrasting '*r*' sounds—a trill, *rr*, as in Scottish English, and a continuant, *r*, similar to Standard British and Australian English. Willie knew that non-indigenous folk often have difficulty with these two consonants and he set himself to educate me. When we were discussing animals and came to *wuruwuru* 'frog', he told me not to confuse it with *wurruwurru* 'ibis'. He also pointed out a minimal pair consisting of the noun *rrubi* 'worm' and the verb *rubi* 'swallow'.

Besides its monosyllabic verbs, Nyawaygi shows several other fascinating features. For instance, it doesn't have one word for each of 'sun', 'moon', and 'thunderstorm'. Instead it has two:

jula 'hot sun (at midday)' (also 'summer time')
bujira 'less hot sun (as in the early morning)'

ngilgan 'full moon'
balanu 'new moon'

guñjunu 'the early stages of a thunderstorm'
migubara 'a thunderstorm in its full ferocity'

In all, I compiled a vocabulary of about 700 words in Nyawaygi, plus a useful sketch grammar of 53 pages. See Dixon (1983).

8 Envoi

It will be seen how different is each instance of salvage fieldwork on languages that are only—to a greater or lesser extent—remembered by one or a few elderly people. Success depends on the knowledge, resilience, application, and attitude of the last guardians. On their personality. On the social circumstances. And also, on what kind of bond can be forged between linguist and guardian.

Notes

There are a number of minor sources on the three 'salvage' languages, mostly just a handful of words, Full details are in Dixon (1991b: 352–353) for Mbabaram, Dixon (1981: 9–13, 101–106) for Warrgamay, and Dixon (1983: 435–436) for Nyawaygi.

My 1984 book *Searching for Aboriginal languages: Memoirs of a field worker* is an account of fieldwork from 1963 to 1977. Work on the three 'salvage' languages is described on the following pages:

- Mbabaram: pages 54–57, 105–107, 125–130, 145–146, 176, 207, 220–221.
- Warrgamay: pages 112–113, 180, 254–256, 276–280, 285–287, 301–302, 310–312, 317–322.
- Nyawaygi: pages 17–18, 135–136, 178, 181–182, 283–285, 303–304, 308–310, 317, 326–327.

None of the guardians I worked with had been able to pass on any of the heritage language to younger people. But today, decades after the last speakers died, there are descendants who have programmes for learning back the language, on the basis of the information I was able to record and publish.

References

Dixon, R.M.W. (1972). *The Dyirbal language of North Queensland.* Cambridge: Cambridge University Press.

Dixon, R.M.W. (1977). *A grammar of Yidiñ.* Cambridge: Cambridge University Press.

Dixon, R.M.W. (1981). Warrgamay. In R.M.W. Dixon and Barry J. Blake (eds.), *Handbook of Australian languages*, volume 2, 1–144. Canberra: ANU Press; and Amsterdam: John Benjamins.

Dixon, R.M.W. (1983). Nyawaygi. In R.M.W. Dixon and Barry J. Blake (eds.), *Handbook of Australian languages*, volume 3, 430–525. Canberra: ANU Press; and Amsterdam: John Benjamins.

Dixon, R.M.W. (1984). *Searching for Aboriginal languages: Memoirs of a field worker.* St Lucia: University of Queensland Press. Reissued by the University of Chicago Press in 1989, and by Cambridge University Press in 2010.

Dixon, R.M.W. (1988). *A grammar of Boumaa Fijian.* Chicago: University of Chicago Press.

Dixon, R.M.W. (1991a). *Words of our country: Stories, place names and vocabulary in Yidiny, the Aboriginal language of the Cairns/Yarrabah region.* St Lucia: University of Queensland Press. Reissued as an e-book in 2012.

Dixon, R.M.W. (1991b). Mbabaram. In R.M.W. Dixon and Barry J. Blake (eds.), *The Handbook of Australian languages, volume 4, The Aboriginal language of Melbourne and other grammatical sketches*, 348–402. Melbourne: Oxford University Press.

Dixon, R.M.W. (2004). *The Jarawara language of southern Amazonia.* Oxford: Oxford University Press.

Dixon, R.M.W. (2015a). *Edible gender, mother-in-law style, and other grammatical wonders: Studies in Dyirbal, Yidiñ, and Warrgamay.* Oxford: Oxford University Press.

Dixon, R.M.W. (2015b). Review of Tasaku Tsunoda, *A grammar of Warrongo. Anthropological Linguistics* 56: 219–222.

Dixon, R.M.W. and Grace Koch (1996). *Dyirbal song poetry: The oral literature of an Australian rainforest people.* St Lucia: University of Queensland Press.

Mathew, John (1899). *Eaglehawk and Crow.* London: David Nutt.

Tindale, Norman B. and Joseph B. Birdsell (1941). Tasmanoid tribes in North Queensland. *South Australian Museum Records* 7: 1–9.

Tsunoda, Tasaku (2003). *A Provisional Warrungu Dictionary.* (ICHEL Linguistic Studies Vol. 8). Tokyo: University of Tokyo.

Tsunoda, Tasaku (2011). *A Grammar of Warrongo.* Berlin: de Gruyter Mouton.

PART 4

How to Make Language Transparent

CHAPTER 22

The Particle *ba*: A Mirative Strategy in Greek

Angeliki Alvanoudi

1 Introduction

This study takes us to the world of miratives in the Balkan linguistic area, focusing on the uses of the particle *ba* in Greek. *Ba* is a small, uninflected, independent one word construction that carries a range of affective and epistemic meanings, and constitutes a pragmatic borrowing in the languages of the Balkan linguistic area.

A linguistic area (also known as Sprachbund) is defined by Aikhenvald and Dixon (2002: 11) as "a geographically delimited area including languages from two or more language families, sharing significant traits" which are common, reasonably distinctive and are not found in languages from these families spoken outside the area. Diffusion of linguistic features may include borrowing of lexical and discourse features, and system-altering changes, such as the introduction of new categories, gradual convergence and isomorphism. The Balkan linguistic area consists of Albanian, Greek, Bulgarian and Macedonian, some dialects of the Bosnian-Croatian-Serbian-Montenegrin complex, Aromanian, Romanian and Meglenoromanian, the co-territorial dialects of the Indic language Romani, and to some extent the co-territorial dialects of Judezmo and Turkic (Friedman and Joseph 2017: 55). Balkan languages share a large number of 'areal features' (also known as 'Balkanisms', Seliščev 1925) found on the levels of phonology, morphology, syntax, semantics and lexicon (described in detail by Friedman 2006, 2011; Joseph 2003, 2010; Tzitzilis forthcoming). Balkan 'areal features' include, for example, the formation of a future tense based on a reduced, often invariant, form of the verb 'want', and pragmatic borrowings, such as the vocative *vre*, the negative interrogative *ðe mu les* ('tell me' [lit. 'don't you tell me?']), and the particle *ba*.

1.1 *Ba: A Pragmatic Borrowing in the Balkan Linguistic Area*

Ba is a pragmatic borrowing in all Balkan languages displaying cross-linguistic and intra-dialectal similarities and differences (discussed in Tzitzilis forthcoming). More specifically, *ba* is used as a negative and surprise token in all Balkan languages. In Greek, Bulgarian and Albanian, *ba* is used as an independent element, whereas in Romanian *ba* is used along with the particles *da* ('yes') and *nu*

© ANGELIKI ALVANOUDI, 2022 | DOI:10.1163/9789004510395_023

('no'). In Standard Modern Greek, *ba* is deployed as a negative response token. Yet, in certain Modern Greek dialects the particle is used as a positive response token.[1] *Ba* occurs in both affirmative and negative sentences in Romanian and Bulgarian but it is only found in negative sentences in Albanian. In Greek, *ba* expresses surprise, admiration, irony, frustration, negation and disagreement. According to Tzitzilis (forthcoming), the different meanings of *ba* derive from a single pragmatic core meaning, 'counterexpectation' (see also Katsiveli 2020 for a similar approach). In line with these observations about the particle's profile, I propose that in Greek *ba* is a mirative particle that expresses a range of mirative meanings.

Mirativity is a universal semantic category that conveys new or unexpected information, with overtones of surprise (DeLancey 1997, 2001). According to Aikhenvald (2012: 437), mirative meanings across languages include: (i) sudden discovery, sudden revelation or realization; (ii) surprise; (iii) unprepared mind; (iv) counterexpectation; and (v) new information. Each of these meanings can be defined with respect to the speaker, the addressee or the main character. As DeLancey (1997: 49) observes, all languages have means to express mirativity but they differ "in the degree to which its expression is integrated into the grammar". In languages in which mirativity is grammaticalized (such as Magar, a Tibeto-Burman language of Nepal (Grunow-Hårsta 2007), or Tariana, an Arawak language from north-west Amazonia (Aikhenvald 2003)), mirative meanings can be expressed through a dedicated complex verbal construction, a special verbal affix or a special series of pronouns (Aikhenvald 2012: 438). In other languages, mirative meanings of sudden discovery or unexpected information can be expressed through lexical items, prosodic features or particles/interjections. These means are known as 'mirative strategies' (Aikhenvald 2012: 436). In Greek, the expression of mirativity is optional, that is, mirativity does not form an obligatory grammatical category with mirative and unmarked forms in paradigmatic contrast. In this paper, I demonstrate that the Greek particle *ba* is a mirative strategy that conveys a range of mirative meanings in different interactional contexts and serves to mitigate disaffiliative actions. In the next section, I explain data and method. The analysis is in Section 3 and the discussion is in Section 4.

1 To the best of my knowledge, *ba* is not used in the Greek dialects of Southern Italy or Cypriot Greek. To date, there are no studies on the uses of *ba* in Modern Greek dialects or on the etymology of *ba*.

2 Data and Method

The analysis builds on conversation-analytic informed interactional linguistics, that is, an empirical, data driven approach to the investigation of language as used in social interaction that establishes a link between the sequential analysis of naturally occurring talk-in-interaction and a linguistic analysis of the lexico-semantic, morpho-syntantic and prosodic means mobilized in sequences (Couper-Kuhlen and Selting 2018). The data examined stem from approximately 29 hours of 145 audio-recorded telephone calls and 40 audio-recorded everyday conversations among friends and relatives from the Corpus of Spoken Greek (Institute of Modern Greek Studies).[2] Data are fully transcribed following standard conversation analytic conventions (see Jefferson 2004; an abbreviated representation of transcription conventions following Couper-Kuhlen and Selting 2018: 606–607 is provided at the end of the chapter).

The study is based on a total of 43 occurrences of *ba* found in the data. *Ba* is used either as a negative token (34 occurrences), i.e. the most common function, or as a cognitive and emotional change-of-state token (9 occurrences). *Ba* is usually delivered as a distinct prosodic phrase, namely one intonational unit uttered "under a single coherent intonation contour" (Du Bois et al. 1993: 47; Chafe 1993) that signals the boundary of the intonational unit and its relationship to other units. *Ba* as a negative token is delivered with falling or non-falling intonation, whereas *ba* as a change-of-state token occurs with falling or rising intonation, is prosodically marked with higher pitch or increased loudness, and may be reiterated.

3 Analysis

3.1 *Ba: A Mirative Strategy in Greek*

The particle *ba* conveys a range of mirative meanings in Greek conversation. In initiating actions and in second/responsive position after an informing, *ba* is used as a cognitive and emotional change-of-state token that conveys sudden realization/surprise of the speaker and registers receipt of new unanticipated information.[3] Moreover, in responsive position, *ba* is used as a negative token

2 A description of the features of the corpus can be found at http://ins.web.auth.gr/index.php?option=com_content&view=article&id=626&Itemid=251&lang=en.

3 A different reading of this function is in Katsiveli (2020, initially presented at the Symposium on Pragmatic Particles in (Greek) Talk-in-Interaction). The author argues that when expres-

that expresses counterexpectation to the addressee and/or the speaker. These functions are illustrated with Excerpts (1) and (2).

Excerpt (1) comes from a telephone call between two female friends, Rena and Areti.

(1) 1 *Rena* *=Lipón.*
so
=So.

2 (.)

3 *Rena* *Se afíno.*
you.SG leave.1SG.PRS
I've got to go.

4 (.)

5 *Areti* *Símera ↑jórtaza.*
today celebrate.1SG.IMPERF
Today ↑is my name day.

6 *Rena* -> *↑Ba:. jatí ðe mu to pes?*
Ba why NEG me it say.2SG.PST
↑Ba:. Why didn't you tell me?

7 [((laughs...................................))]

8 *Areti* *[i Galín-* ((*laughs*))]
DEF.F.SG.NOM Galíni
[Galín-]

In lines 1 and 3, Rena starts a pre-closing sequence, which is suspended by Areti's announcement in line 5 ('Today ↑is my name day.'). Areti's turn is prosodically marked and presents the news as possibly counter to what the recipient might expect. In line 6, Rena responds to the news. In the first turn constructional unit (TCU henceforth), Rena uses the particle *ba* to register receipt of

sing surprise, *ba* operates as a repair initiator. I take this claim to be a misinterpretation of the work done by the particle in responsive position. A counter-example is in Excerpt 1.

the news, confirm the newsworthiness of the information and display her surprise. *Ba* is delivered as a distinct prosodic phrase, with a sharp intonation rise, high pitch and lengthening, as depicted in Figure 22.1. In the second TCU, the speaker requests an account for not having been informed earlier about the matter at issue and invites more talk on the topic. In this exchange, *ba* indicates a cognitive shift from uninformed-to-informed as well as an emotional change-of-state associated with the receipt of unanticipated news. Equivalent practices in other languages include, for example, *oh* and *ah* in English (Heritage 1984, 1998, 2002; Reber 2012), *ach, achso* and *oh* in German (Golato 2010, 2012), and *ai nii(n)* and *aa* in Finnish (Koivisto 2015a,b).

Excerpt (2) comes from a conversation among three friends, Nefeli, Antigoni and Thanos. Participants have been joking about the proper name *Tsabikas/Tsabika* that is often used on Rhodes Island. In the preceding lines, Thanos has presented a funny hypothetical scenario in which parents name their son *Tsabikas*.

(2) 1 *Nefeli* *.h Θa ton évɣaza me káti pço*
FUT him name.1SG.IMPERF with something more
.h I would give him a more

2 *anaɣno[rísimo. (étsi?)/> (ðen gzéro.)<]*
((laughing ...))
recognizable right NEG know.1SG.PRS
recogni[zable name. (Right?)/>(I don't know.)<]

3 Thanos [Θa su kane] mínisi.
((laughing...))
FUT you.SG do.3SG.IMPERF sue
[He would] sue you.

4 ((laughs))=

5 *Nefeli->* *=**Ba**. ðe nomízo.* ((*laugh*))
ba NEG think.1SG.PRS
=Ba. I don't think so.

6 *i e:*
DEF.F.PL PART
The e:h

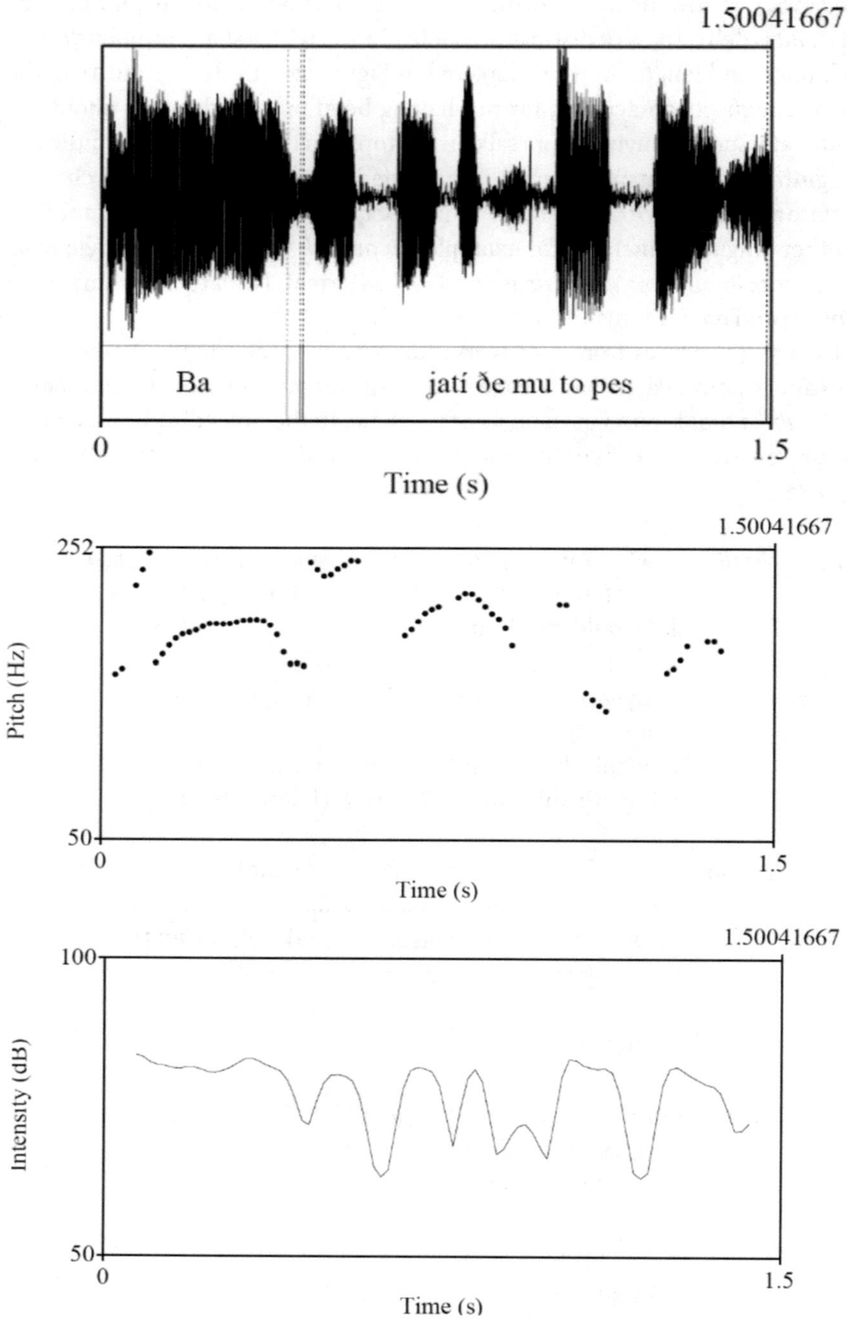

FIGURE 22.1 Waveform, pitch trace and intensity of *ba* in line 6 of (1)

7 *i* *çiʎáðes* *Tsabíces* *tis* *Róðu*
DEF.F.PL thousands Tsabikes(F) DEF.GEN Rhodes.GEN
are thousands of female residents of Rhodes called Tsabika

8 *kánun* *kampá mínisi stis manáðes tus?*
((laughing……………………………………………))
do.3PL.PRS INDEF sue to mothers their
suing their mothers?

In overlapping talk with Nefeli's response, in line 3, Thanos describes a possible future state-of-affairs using the conditional construction 'future particle *ϑa* + imperfective past verb form' that expresses a supposition. In line 5, Nefeli disconfirms Thanos' assertion. Her turn consists of two TCUs. In the first TCU, the speaker uses the particle *ba* to express her disbelief and in the second TCU, she deploys the clause *ðe nomízo* ('I don't think so') to overtly disagree with the prior speaker's assertion. Unlike the change-of-state *ba* in Excerpt (1), the negative *ba* in Excerpt (2) is relatively prosodically unmarked, as shown in Figure 22.2.

In this segment, *ba* expresses counterexpectation to the addressee, because it indicates that what the speaker is doing runs counter to what would be treated as expected behavior by the addressee, i.e. agreement/confirmation. *Ba* mitigates the strong negation that follows in the next TCU and, thus, operates as a 'soft' negative token. The relational work done by the particle *ba* in the context of disaffiliative actions is examined in the next section.

3.2 *Ba at the Service of Mitigating Disaffiliative Actions*

The Greek society has a predominant positive politeness orientation (Brown and Levinson 1987), as demonstrated by numerous studies (see e.g. Marmaridou 1987; Pavlidou 1991, 1994, 1997; Sifianou 1992a,b; Sifianou and Antonopoulou 2005; and studies in Bayraktaroğlu and Sifianou 2001). For example, in carrying out requests, Greek speakers tend to use present indicative interrogatives that express certainty, immediacy and involvement, as well as diminutives that convey affection, endearment and informality (Sifianou 1992a,b). Positive politeness strategies, such as informal address terms (first names, kin terms or diminutive forms) and particles of familiarity (such as *re*, *vre*, *more*) are common in Greek conversational arguing (Kakavá 1993, 2002). Tannen and Kakavá (1992: 31) describe such features as markers of solidarity that show the 'friendly' nature of disagreement in Greek discourse and reinforce co-participants' involvement, which is potentially threatened by disagreement. As shown in the following examples, Greek speakers use the particle *ba*

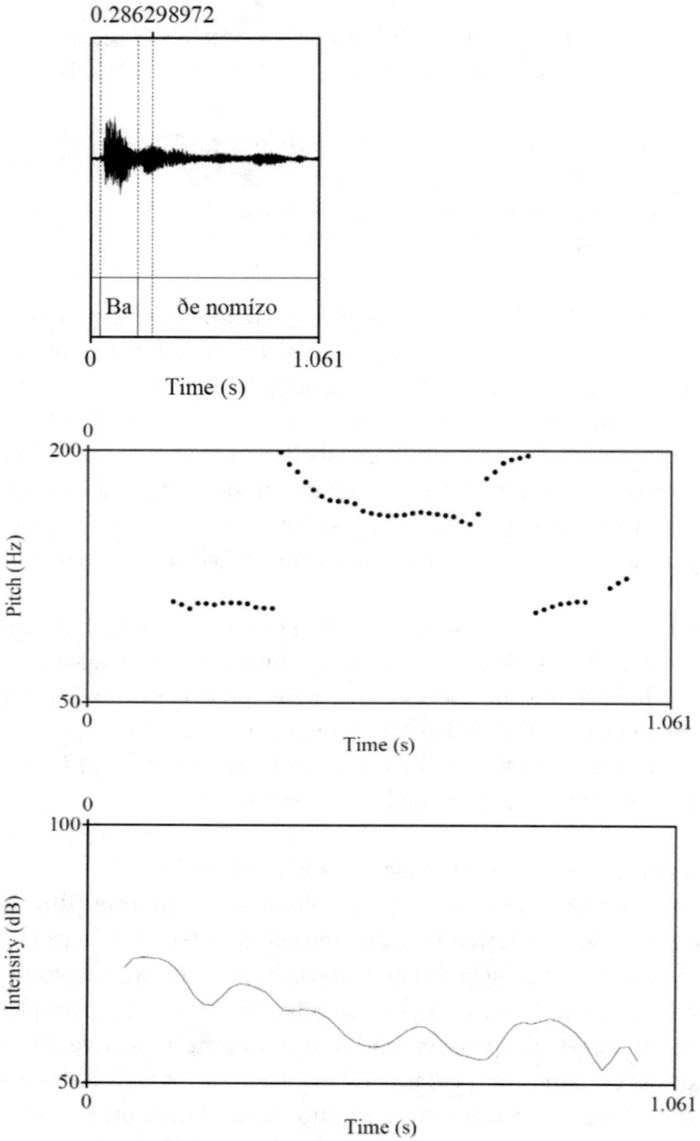

FIGURE 22.2 Waveform, pitch trace and intensity of *ba* in line 5 of (2)

as a positive politeness device to mitigate disaffiliative actions and minimize conflict in interaction.

In Excerpt (3), in lines 1–2, Amalia offers drinks to Tasos and Yannis. The offer is made via the *do you want X* syntactic format that foregrounds the recipients' need for the object being proffered (see Curl 2006 on a similar practice in English), and makes compliance conditionally relevant (Schegloff 2007: 59). In lines 3–4, recipients reject the necessity or desirability of the offer, implying that they have no need for what is offered. The turn of interest is in line 4.

(3)	1	*Amalia*	*Θes*	*na*	*pçis*	*↑káti?*	
			want.2SG.PRS	SBJV	drink.2SG.PFV	something	
			Do you want to drink ↑something?				
	2		*θélete*	*krasáci?*			
			want.2PL.PRS	wine.DIM			
			Do you want wine?				
	3	*Tasos*	*>O[:çi*	*óçι,<*	*Ama]lía*	*mu.=*	
			no	no	Amalia	my	
			>No[: no,< Ama]lia.=				
	4	*Yannis ->*	[°***Ba:.***	*(óçi.)*]			
			Ba	no			
			[°Ba:. (no.)]				
	5	*Yannis*	*=As*	*érθun*	*próta*	*i*	*ipólipi.*
			PART	come.3PL.PFV	first	DEF.M.PL.NOM	others
			=Let's wait for the others to come first.				
	6		*°vlépume.*				
			see.1PL.PRS				
			°We'll see.				
	7	*Amalia*	*M::.*				
			PART				
			M::.				

In line 3, Tasos' dispreferred response consists of the repeated particle *óçi* ('no') and the vocative *Amalía mu* that conveys social proximity among interlocutors and softens the rejection. In line 4, Yannis uses the particles *ba* and *óçι* ('no') to reject the offer. The turn initial *ba* mitigates the unexpected action of rejection that is overtly expressed in the second TCU. In lines 5–6, the speaker defers the fulfillment of the offer, and in line 7 Amalia closes down the sequence via the neutral receipt token *m::*.

In the lines preceding Excerpt (4), Yanna, Katerina and Vaso have mentioned the sudden engagement of their friend Danai. In this segment, they provide accounts for the event. The turn of interest is in line 8.

(4) 1 *Yanna* *=Áde. °ce sta ði[ká mas.]*
PART and to DEF ours
=Come on. °Same to [us.]

2 *Katerina* *[Mípos] ín éɟos?*
PART COP.3SG.PRS pregnant
Is she pregnant [by any chance?]

3 (.)

4 *Vaso* *°Ðen gzéro.*
NEG know.1SG.PRS
°I don't know.

5 (0.6)
((audible sound))

6 *Katerina* *Fadázese:?*
imagine.2SG.PRS
Would you believe: it?

7 (.)

8 *Vaso ->* ***Ba.*** *to apoklío.*
ba it rule out.1SG.PRS
Ba. I think it's impossible.

9 (.)

10 *Katerina* *Ceɣó to apoklío.*
and I it rule out.1SG.PRS
I also think it's impossible.

In line 2, Katerina puts a possible scenario on the conversational table via the polar question 'Is she pregnant by any chance?' that seeks confirmation or disconfirmation, and in line 4, Vaso delivers a non-answer ('°I don't know.'). In line 6, Katerina requests confirmation of the possible scenario via another polar question ('Would you believe: it?'), and Vaso disconfirms in line 8. Her response comes after a micropause indicating trouble and it consists of two TCUs, the particle *ba* and the clause *to apoklío* ('I think it's impossible.'), both uttered with emphasis. The turn initial *ba* indicates the speaker's disbelief and mitigates the negation that is overtly expressed via the clause *to apoklío*.

Excerpt (5) comes from the same conversation among Yanna, Katerina and Vaso.

(5) 1 *Vaso* *>Nomízo ðilaðí óti e: prin ʝíno<*
think.1SG.PRS namely that PART before become.1SG.PFV
>That is I think that e:h before<

2 *enós étus, óti >ϑimáme káрça< práɣmata.*
one year that remember.1SG.PRS certain things
age one, that >I remember certain< things.

3 (.)

4 *Vaso* [*Tóra¿ °m.*]
now PART
[Now¿ °m.]

5 *Yanna* -> [°***Ba.*** *polí*] *mikrí ísuna ʝa* [*na ϑimá*]*se.*
ba very young COP.2SG.PST to SBJV remember.2SG
[°Ba.] You were too young [to reme]mber.

6 *Vaso* [↑*Ne::.*]
yes
[↑Yes::.]

In lines 1–2, Vaso claims that she can recall memories from her early childhood and uses the verb *nomízo* ('I think') to downplay her epistemic certainty over the asserted proposition. In line 5, Yanna challenges the likelihood of the proposition. She uses the particle *ba* in the first TCU and provides an account in the second TCU ('You were too young to remember'). In line 6,

Vaso affectively aligns with Yanna's disagreement via the prosodically marked response token *ne* ('yes').

In the three segments analyzed above, *ba* occurs in dispreferred second pair parts that do not promote the accomplishment of the action launched by the first pair part and, thus, are treated as "destructive of social solidarity" (Heritage 1984: 268). Dispreferred seconds are often prefaced, elaborated, mitigated and delayed (Schegloff 2007: 64–73). In Greek conversation, speakers use the particle *ba* in turn initial position to preface and soften disagreements, disconfirmations and rejections. In these contexts, *ba* operates as a soft negative token that addresses the recipient's unfulfilled expectation, weakens the predictably unpleasant effect of the action performed (Caffi 2007: 82) and, thus, serves as a 'pro-social' device (Stivers et al. 2011) that enhances solidarity between speaker and recipient. In this sense, the use of *ba* aligns with the positive politeness orientation in Greek conversation.

4 Discussion: The Balkan 'Soul' of Greek Pragmatics

To sum up, in Greek, *ba* is a mirative strategy that indicates the 'unprepared mind' of the speaker or the addressee. More specifically, *ba* conveys (i) counter-expectation to the addressee and/or speaker, and (ii) the speaker's surprise at new unanticipated information. Mirative meaning (i) pairs with the function of the particle as a negative response token, whereas mirative meaning (ii) pairs with the function of the particle as a cognitive and emotional change-of-state token. Note that *ba* is not a typical marker of negation. The particle expresses the speaker's disbelief and doubt, and its function as a negative token derives from the mirative meaning of 'counterexpectation'.

When used as a negative token in responsive position, *ba* serves to minimize conflict in environments of disagreement. The function of *ba* as a positive politeness device may be further motivated by the Balkan profile of the particle. Ariel (1998: 223) suggests that "quite opaque form-functions correlations often hide a historically transparent, or at least motivated, form-function correlation". In the same spirit, I propose that the Balkan origin of *ba* enhances its use as a pro-social mitigating device that aligns with the positive politeness ethos in Greek and other Balkan languages (Tzitzilis forthcoming). Aikhenvald and Dixon (2002: 13–14) highlight the importance of the social landscape of linguistic areas in the study of areal diffusion. This dimension is key to our understanding of the Balkan linguistic area. Diffused discourse features in the Balkan languages correlate with social parameters such as positive politeness (for example the vocative *vre* is a Balkan areal feature that enhances solidarity among interlocutors). The study of the interactional functions of *ba* in other Balkan languages from a comparative and areal perspective (see Auer and Maschler 2016; Sidnell 2009) is a promising area for future research on pragmatic borrowing.

In *The Art of Grammar* (2015), Aikhenvald observes: "The question 'why is a language the way it is' is most fascinating. And it is most elusive." (p. 286). The study of *ba* indicates that answers to big questions can also be found in small words, like particles, that tend to be overlooked by grammars. As humble as they may be, pragmatic particles offer interesting insights into the social history of a language and unlock the 'language puzzle' in unexpected ways. The Greek *ba* provides a glimpse of the complexities of language contact in the Balkan linguistic area and reveals the Balkan 'soul' of Greek pragmatics that to date remains under-examined.

Acknowledgements

An earlier version of this paper was presented at the Symposium on Pragmatic Particles in (Greek) Talk-in-Interaction, organized by the Institute of Modern Greek Studies (Thessaloniki, 24–25 June 2019) (Alvanoudi 2020). I thank the participants of this event for their valuable feedback. Special thanks go to Prof. Christos Tzitzilis for stimulating discussions on the topic of this paper.

Abbreviations

1	first person
2	second person
3	third person
COP	copula
DEF	definite
DIM	diminutive
F	feminine
FUT	future
GEN	genitive
IMPERF	imperfect
INDEF	indefinite
M	masculine
NEG	negation
NOM	nominative
PART	particle
PFV	perfective
PL	plural
PRS	present
PST	past
SG	singular
SBJV	subjunctive

Transcription Conventions

->	line of analytic focus
[	point of onset of overlap
]	point of end of overlap
=	latching
(0.8)	silence in tenths of a second
(.)	micro-pause (less than 0.5 second)
.	falling/final intonation
?	rising intonation
,	continuing/non-final intonation
: ::	sound prolongation or stretching; the more colons, the longer the stretching
Word	red is used to indicate some form of emphasis, either by increased loudness or higher pitch (The standard transcription convention is underlining; red is used here in line with Brill Typographic Style)
°	following talk markedly quiet or soft
-	after a word or part of a word: cut-off or interruption
↑	sharp intonation rise
> <	talk between the 'more than' and 'less than' symbols is compressed or rushed
.hh	inhalation
(( ))	transcriber's description of events
(word)	uncertain transcription

References

Aikhenvald, Alexandra Y. (2003). *A Grammar of Tariana, from Northwest Amazonia*. Cambridge: Cambridge University Press.

Aikhenvald, Alexandra Y. (2012). The essence of mirativity. *Linguistic Typology* 16 (3): 435–485.

Aikhenvald, Alexandra Y. (2015). *The Art of Grammar*. Oxford: Oxford University Press.

Aikhenvald, Alexandra Y. and R.M.W. Dixon (2002). Introduction. In Alexandra Y. Aikhenvald and R.M.W. Dixon (eds.), *Areal Diffusion and Genetic Inheritance: Problems in Comparative Linguistics*, 1–26. Oxford: Oxford University Press.

Alvanoudi, Angeliki (2020). Οι λειτουργίες του μορίου μπα στην ελληνική από τη σκοπιά της Ανάλυσης Συνομιλίας [The functions of the particle ba in Greek: A conversation analytic perspective]. In Theodossia Pavlidou (ed.), *Pragmatic Particles in (Greek) Talk-in-Interaction*, 56–76. Thessaloniki: Institute of Modern Greek Studies.

Ariel, Mira (1998). Discourse markers and form-function correlations. In Andreas H. Jucker and Yael Ziv (eds.), *Discourse Markers: Descriptions and Theory*, 223–259. Amsterdam: John Benjamins.

Auer, Peter and Yael Maschler (eds.) (2016). *NU and NÅ: A Family of Discourse Markers Across the Languages of Europe and Beyond*. Berlin: Walter de Gruyter.

Bayraktaroğlu, Arın and Maria Sifianou (eds.) 2001. *Linguistic Politeness across Boundaries: The Case of Greek and Turkish*. Amsterdam: John Benjamins.

Brown, Penelope and Stephen C. Levinson (1987). *Politeness: Some Universals in Language Usage*. Cambridge: Cambridge University Press.

Caffi, Claudia (2007). *Mitigation*. London: Elsevier.

Chafe, Wallace L. (1993). Prosodic and functional units of language. In Jane A. Edwards and Martin D. Lampert (eds.), *Talking Data: Transcription and Coding in Discourse Research*, 33–43. Hillsdale, NJ: Lawrence Erlbaum.

Couper-Kuhlen, Elizabeth and Margret Selting. (2018). *Interactional Linguistics: Studying Language in Social Interaction*. Cambridge: Cambridge University Press.

Curl, Traci S. (2006). Offers of assistance: Constraints on syntactic design. *Journal of Pragmatics* 38 (8): 1257–1280.

DeLancey, Scott (1997). Mirativity: The grammatical marking of unexpected information. *Linguistic Typology* 1 (1): 33–52.

DeLancey, Scott (2001). The mirative and evidentiality. *Journal of Pragmatics* 33 (3): 369–382.

Du Bois, John W., Stephan Schuetze-Coburn, Susanna Cumming and Danae Paolino (1993). Outline of discourse transcription. In Jane A. Edwards and Martin D. Lampert (eds.), *Talking Data: Transcription and Coding in Discourse Research*, 45–89. Hillsdale, NJ: Lawrence Erlbaum.

Friedman, Victor A. (2006). The Balkans as a linguistic area. In Keith Brown (ed.), *Elsevier Encyclopedia of Language and Linguistics*, vol. 1, 657–672. Oxford: Elsevier.

Friedman, Victor A. (2011). The Balkan languages and Balkan linguistics. *Annual Review of Anthropology* 40: 275–291.

Friedman, Victor A. and Brian Joseph (2017). Reassessing Sprachbunds: A view from the Balkans. In Raymond Hickey (ed.), *The Cambridge Handbook of Areal Linguistics*, 55–87. Cambridge: Cambridge University Press.

Golato, Andrea (2010). Marking understanding versus receipting information in talk: Achso and ach in German interaction. *Discourse Studies* 12 (2): 147–176.

Golato, Andrea (2012). German oh: Marking an emotional change of state. *Research on Language and Social Interaction* 45 (3): 245–268.

Grunow-Hårsta, Karen (2007). Evidentiality and mirativity in Magar. *Linguistics of the Tibeto-Burman Area* 30 (2): 151–194.

Heritage, John (1984). A change-of-state token and aspects of its sequential placement. In J. Maxwell Atkinson and John Heritage (eds.), *Structures of Social Action: Studies in Conversation Analysis*, 299–345. Cambridge: Cambridge University Press.

Heritage, John (1998). Oh-prefaced responses to inquiry. *Language in Society* 27 (3): 291–334.

Heritage, John (2002). Oh-prefaced responses to assessments: A method of modifying agreement/disagreement. In Cecilia E. Ford, Barbara A. Fox and Sandra A. Thompson (eds.), *The Language of Turn and Sequence*, 196–224. Oxford: Oxford University Press.

Jefferson, Gail (2004). Glossary of transcript symbols with an introduction. In Gene H. Lerner (ed.), *Conversation Analysis: Studies from the First Generation*, 13–31. Amsterdam: John Benjamins.

Joseph, Brian D. (2003). The Balkan languages. In William Frawley (ed.), *International Encyclopedia of Linguistics*, 2nd edition, 194–196. Oxford: Oxford University Press.

Joseph, Brian D. (2010). Language contact in the Balkans. In Raymond Hickey (ed.), *The Handbook of Language Contact*, 618–633. Oxford: Wiley-Blackwell.

Kakavá, Christina (1993). Negotiation of Disagreement by Greeks in Conversations and Classroom Discourse. Unpublished PhD dissertation, Georgetown University, Washington, DC.

Kakavá, Christina (2002). Opposition in Modern Greek discourse: Cultural and contextual constraints. *Journal of Pragmatics* 34 (10–11): 1537–1568.

Katsiveli, Stamatina (2020). Marking the unexpected: The case of ba in Greek talk-in-interaction. *Journal of Pragmatics* 170: 55–68.

Koivisto, Aino (2015a). Displaying now-understanding: The Finnish change-of-state token aa. *Discourse Processes* 52 (2): 111–148.

Koivisto, Aino (2015b). Dealing with ambiguities in informings: Finnish aijaa as a "neutral" news receipt. *Research on Language and Social Interaction* 48 (4): 365–387.

Marmaridou, Sophia (1987). Semantic and pragmatic parameters of meaning: On the interface between contrastive text analysis and the production of translated texts. *Journal of Pragmatics* 11: 721–736.

Pavlidou, Theodossia (1991). Cooperation and the choice of linguistic means: Some evidence from the use of the subjunctive in Modern Greek. *Journal of Pragmatics* 15: 11–42.

Pavlidou, Theodossia (1994). Contrasting German-Greek politeness and the consequences. *Journal of Pragmatics* 21 (5): 487–511.

Pavlidou, Theodossia (1997). The last five turns: Preliminary remarks on closings in Greek and German telephone calls. *International Journal of the Sociology of Language* 126: 145–162.

Reber, Elisabeth (2012). *Affectivity in Interaction: Sound Objects in English*. Amsterdam: John Benjamins.

Schegloff, Emanuel A. (2007). *Sequence Organization in Interaction: A Primer in Conversation Analysis*. Cambridge: Cambridge University Press.

Seliščev, Afanasij (1925). Des traits linguistiques communs aux langues balkaniques: Un balkanisme ancien en bulgare. *Révue des Études Slaves* 5: 38–57.

Sidnell, Jack (ed.) (2009). *Conversation Analysis: Comparative Perspectives*. Cambridge: Cambridge University Press.

Sifianou, Maria (1992a). The use of diminutives in expressing politeness: Modern Greek versus English. *Journal of Pragmatics* 17: 155–173.

Sifianou, Maria (1992b). *Politeness Phenomena in England and Greece: A Cross-Cultural Perspective*. Oxford: Clarendon Press.

Sifianou, Maria and Eleni Antonopoulou (2005). Politeness in Greece: The politeness of involvement. In Leo Hickey and Miranda Stewart (eds.), *Politeness in Europe*, 263–276. Clevendon: Multingual Matters.

Stivers, Tanya, Lorenza Mondada and Jakob Steensig (2011). Knowledge, morality and affiliation in social interaction. In Tanya Stivers, Lorenza Mondada and Jakob Steensig (eds.), *The Morality of Knowledge in Conversation*, 3–24. Cambridge: Cambridge University Press.

Tannen, Deborah and Christina Kakavá (1992). Power and solidarity in Modern Greek conversation: Disagreeing to agree. *Journal of Modern Greek Studies* 10 (1): 11–34.

Tzitzilis, Christos (forthcoming). "Balkan and Anatolian Sprachbund". In Christos Tzitzilis and George Papanastasiou (eds.), *Language Contact in the Balkans and Asia Minor*. Thessaloniki: Institute of Modern Greek Studies.

CHAPTER 23

How Grammar Encodes Knowledge in Munya: Evidentiality, Egophoricity, and Mirativity

Junwei Bai

1 Introduction

1.1 *Aikhenvald's Contribution to the Study of Evidentiality*

Among the many important contributions that Aikhenvald has made to modern linguistic research, her studies in evidentiality are both groundbreaking and monumental. Her inquiry into this phenomenon started while doing fieldwork on two languages spoken in northwest Amazonia, Tariana and Tucano (Aikhenvald and Dixon 1998), was broadened by the volume she co-edited with Dixon (Aikhenvald and Dixon 2003), culminated in her seminal monograph (Aikhenvald 2004), which draws data from over 500 languages, and expanded in the ensuing collections of works for which she acted as the editor (Aikhenvald 2018b; Aikhenvald and Dixon 2014). In addition to these, she also published or co-authored numerous papers on various aspects of this topic, such as its characteristics in certain language families (Aikhenvald and Dixon 1998; Aikhenvald and LaPolla 2007) and grammaticalization (Aikhenvald 2011). Marked for their depth and scope, these works have not only significantly promoted our understanding of evidentiality but also laid a solid foundation and framework for further research.

A recent development of her exploration into this topic is the focus on the interactions and dependencies between evidentiality and other grammatical systems, as seen in Aikhenvald (2014, 2015). Of particular importance are the efforts she made to tease evidentiality apart from other connected categories and subsume them under the more encompassing notion of the grammatical encoding of knowledge. For example, in Aikhenvald (2018a), she noted the connections and differences between evidentiality and egophoricity. In Aikhenvald (2021), she reiterated the demarcations between evidentiality, egophoricity, mirativity, and modality, summarized the possible semantic links between them, and pointed out the uniqueness of evidentiality as compared to other grammatical systems for encoding knowledge.

© JUNWEI BAI, 2022 | DOI:10.1163/9789004510395_024

1.2 *About This Study*

This study is intended as a tribute to Aikhenvald's passion and dedication to linguistic research, particularly her investigation of evidentiality. It looks at the grammatical means of expressing knowledge—evidentiality, egophoricity, and mirativity—and their semantic connections, in Munya, a language which belongs to the Qiangic branch of the Tibeto-Burman family. The remainder of this chapter is organized as follows. § 1.3 presents background information and relevant linguistic features of Munya. § 2 looks at evidentiality, including the direct evidential (§ 2.1), the inferential evidential (§ 2.2), and the reported evidential (§ 2.3). There are two egophoric markers in Munya. § 3.1 discusses the one that only occurs with volitional actors and § 3.2 describes the one that can occur in all environments. The functions of the one mirative marker in Munya will be examined in depth in § 4. § 5 concludes this chapter.

1.3 *About Munya: Relevant Linguistic Features*

Munya is spoken in western Sichuan Province of China by a group of around 16,000 people who identify themselves as Tibetans. The language is traditionally believed to have an eastern dialect and a western dialect, which are separated by Mount Gongga (Sun 1983). Recent studies show that the western dialect can be further divided into a northern and a southern dialect (Bai 2021). The language data used in this study were collected during my own fieldwork between 2016 and 2018, from the northern dialect area. In the following discussion, 'Munya' will be used to refer to the northern dialect of this language, unless otherwise specified.

Munya has a fairly large inventory of consonants (44) and vowels (13). It contrasts a high tone (indicated with an acute marker in this study) and a low tone (not marked), and they form a restricted set of patterns on polysyllabic words. In terms of morpho-syntax, Munya is mildly agglutinating and fusional, with a default constituent order of SV/AOV. Many verb roots are morphologically required to take a directional prefix (there are seven such prefixes in Munya). A verb root can in addition take an interrogative prefix or a negative prefix. Person-number information of the subject is registered on verb roots through ablaut. Many grammatical functions, such as aspect, evidentiality, and egophoricity, are expressed with auxiliaries, which are phonologically independent words with a strong monosyllabic tendency. There are three aspect markers, an imperfective *pi*, a perfective *sə*, and a gnomic *ti*. Based on semantics and syntactic behavior, verbs can be broadly categorized as volitional verbs and non-volitional verbs. Volitional verbs refer to actions that are normally exercised under the control or awareness of an agent, such as *hə́* 'go', *tə́da* 'hit' and *éndzə* 'eat'. Non-volitional verbs denote actions that are uncontrollable, and generally refer to bodily experiences or internal feelings, as well as emotions, such as *ngɯtʂ̥é* 'miss (someone)', *təŋé* 'be sick' and *təkú* 'feel cold'. These two types of verbs have different requirements for the case marking of S and A, whether or not person-number inflection is indexed, and the choice of evidential and egophoric markers.

Grammatical categories pertaining to knowledge and information include evidentiality, egophoricity, mirativity, and modality.[1] There are three evidential markers in Munya, which mark how information is acquired. Two egophoric markers are used to indicate that the action is carried out consciously and intentionally, and also for information sharing. The expectation of knowledge is denoted by a mirative particle, for surprise and deferred realization on the part of the speaker. With this brief introduction, we now turn to the first grammatical category of knowledge expression—evidentiality.

2 Evidentiality

Evidentiality is generally understood to be the grammatical means of expressing information source (Aikhenvald 2004: xi). There are three evidentials in Munya—a direct evidential *ra*, an inferential evidential *sə*, which also functions as a perfective aspect marker, and a reported evidential *tə́pi*. The first two are auxiliary verbs and can take an interrogative or a negative prefix. The inferential evidential in addition marks the person-number information of the subject through vocalic change. The reported evidential, however, is a clause-final particle and seldom shows any morphological change.

2.1 *Direct Evidential*

The direct evidential marker *ra* cannot be used for future situations. When used after a dynamic verb, it denotes an accomplished event; when used after a stative verb, it signals an ongoing or past state (the interpretation depends on the context). While this evidential is most often used to indicate that the information is visually acquired (1a) (native speakers often say 'you use it because you saw such and such happened'), the source can also be auditory (1b), olfactory (1c), or simply personal experience (1d) (Bai 2019: 235–236).

1 Due to space limitations, epistemic modalities will not be discussed in this study. They are not found to be extended to other domains of knowledge-related categories.

(1) a. *tó-zə* t^{h}*ó-tso* ***ra.***
one-CLF:MAN TS-run EVID:DIR
'A (person) ran away.'

b. *ndɛ́* *á-**ra**?*
sense.2SG INTRG-EVID:DIR
'Did you sense (hear) it?'

c. *ŋí* *tí* *tó-lö* *tə-né* *ti* *ndá*
1SG+ERG something one-CLF:GENR UP-stink GN sense.1SG
ra.
EVID:DIR
'I can sense (smell) that something stinks.'

d. *tɕə́tɕə́* t^{h}*əvá* ***ra.***
long.time become EVID:DIR
'(It) has been a long time.'

There are interesting interactions between this evidential marker, the person of the subject, and the volitionality of predicate verbs. Importantly, if the predicate of a clause is a volitional verb, then this marker cannot be used together with a first person subject. Therefore, (2) below is ungrammatical.

(2) **ŋú* *ɛ́-tso* ***ra.***
1SG DS-run EVID:DIR
Intended meaning: 'I ran downstream.'

Explaining why this clause is unacceptable, native speakers said that this is because 'you cannot see yourself running.' However, they all agree that if one is watching a video recording of oneself running, then (2) can be said without any problem. In a similar vein, in an interrogative clause, if the predicate is volitional and the subject is in the second person, this marker cannot be used either, as in (3) (Bai 2019: 237).

(3) **nɛ́* *i* *kətɕɛ́* *ɛtí-lö* *ɛ́-ndzü* ***ra**?*
2SG ERG pancake how.many-CLF:GENR DS-eat.2SG EVID:DIR
Intended meaning: 'How many pancakes did you eat?'

To form a content interrogative clause in Munya, the questioner needs to anticipate the way the question will be answered before he can choose the appropriate evidential or aspect or egophoric marker, and the marker used in interrogatives should in principle be identical to that which will be used in the answering clause. (3) is ungrammatical as it anticipates that the answering clause, which is headed by a volitional predicate, would have a first person subject and a direct evidential marker.

There is no other constraint on the co-occurrence of the direct evidential marker with the type of verb and person of subject. For example, *ra* can occur freely with a first person non-volitional actor (4a), or a second person volitional actor in a declarative clause (4b) (Bai 2019: 237).

(4) a. *ngɛ́ tə-ŋé* ***ra.***
1SG+EXP UP-be.ill EVID:DIR
'I'm ill.'

b. *nɛ́ i ŋú le té kʰɤ-má-seŋa* ***ra.***
2SG ERG 1SG DAT at.all NONS-NEG-listen.to EVID:DIR
'You didn't listen to me at all.'

The direct evidential *ra* may originate from the motion verb which means 'go'. Aside from the fact that the two morphemes are homophonous, another piece of evidence is that *ra* 'go' cannot be followed by the direct evidential. One can say (5) if one saw a cow going downstream (Bai 2019: 238).

(5) *ŋə́mo tó-lö* *a-**rá.***
cow one-CLF:GENR DS-go
'A cow went downstream.'

In this example, *ra* takes the dual function of a motion verb and a direct evidential marker. Evidentials originating from motion verbs are also reported in Tibetan (Oisel 2014) and the Lizu dialect of Ersu (Chirkova 2008), also a Qiangic language.

2.2 *Inferential Evidential*

The inferential evidential auxiliary *sə*, which is also a perfective aspect marker, contrasts, both paradigmatically and functionally, with the imperfective marker *pi* and the direct evidential *ra*. Thus, it can either be analyzed as an aspect marker with an extended evidential sense (which is cross-linguistically quite common for perfects; see Aikhenvald (2004: 112) and Forker (2018)), or an evidential marker, as it also shows the first person effect often found for non-firsthand and inferential evidentials (Aikhenvald 2004: 220). For the purpose of discussion, here I take the second approach, noting that the first analysis is equally viable.

This marker can only be used with dynamic verbs and for past situations. In terms of its evidential sense, it often indicates that the information is based on visual or non-visual sensory evidence or assumption. This function can be best demonstrated by contrasting it with the direct evidential, as in (6) (Bai 2019: 241).

(6) a. *rɔ́* *tɛ́-zɛ* *tʰó-sə* ***ra.***
snake one-CLF:LONG TS-die EVID:DIR
'A snake died.'

b. *rɔ́* *tɛ́-zɛ* *tʰó-sə* ***sə.***
snake one-CLF:LONG TS-die EVID:INF
'A snake died.'

(6a) implies that the speaker saw the whole process of the death of the snake. In contrast, if the speaker only sees a dead snake, she would use (6b), as she is inferring that the snake has died based on observable results.

As was mentioned above, this marker shows the first person effect commonly found for non-firsthand, non-visual or reported evidentials (see Aikhenvald (2004: 219–233) for more discussion). This effect, which essentially denotes the speaker's 'unprepared mind', non-intentional or non-volitional action, can be seen as a kind of mirative overtone of evidentials (Aikhenvald 2004: 195–196; Sun 2018). In Munya, when used together with a first person subject and a volitional predicate, this marker indicates lack of control or inadvertent action on the part of the speaker. Consider the example in (7) (Bai 2019: 249).

(7) *ŋí* *nbətʂ̺á* *tó-lö* *ní-tʰɛ* *no-só*
1SG+ERG worm one-CLF:GENR DOWN-step.on DOWN-kill
sö.
EVID:INF.1SG
'I stepped on a worm and killed it.'

This sentence implies that the speaker stepped on a worm unintentionally and may feel regretful on realizing that the worm is dead. Therefore, it can be said that the inferential evidential in Munya has a mirative sense in a first person volitional environment.

When the predicate is non-volitional, then a first person subject can occur naturally with the inferential evidential without any additional meaning, as in (8).

(8) *məhú ŋí nɛ́ nó-mi sö.*
last.night 1SG+ERG 2SG DOWN-dream EVID:INF.1SG
'I dreamed of you last night.'

2.3 *Reported Evidential*

The reported evidential marker *tə́pi* signals that the information source is hearsay. It consists of the verb *tə́* 'say' and the imperfective aspect auxiliary *pi* (in third-person form). It does not enter into the same paradigm with the direct evidential or the inferential evidential and can be used after either of the two markers. In (9) below, it follows the direct evidential marker.

(9) *nɛ́ ɣɛ tɔ-tsɔ́ ra* ***tə́pi.***
2SG EXP UP-be.hungry EVID:DIR EVID:REP
'It is said that you are hungry.'

When a clause marked by the reported evidential is questioned, the interrogative morpheme *ɛ-* is infixed to the evidential morpheme, as can be seen in the second clause of (10).

(10) *moɕi=nə́tɕʰo kʰɔ lalɔmé tɕípu nyi, lúkɛ ndə́ ti*
PN=PLA.PL very really be.comfortable EGO:AP hotel COP GN
tə-ɛ́-pi?
EVID:REP-INTRG
'The area around Moxi is really comfortable, and do people say there are hotels there?'

In this example, the interrogative marker is actually prefixed to the erstwhile imperfective marker. This shows that even though *tə́pi* has grammaticalized into a reported evidential, it still retains the morphology when it acted as a verb complex. The negator, however, cannot be used in this way—it should be prefixed to the predicate in a clause marked by *tə́pi*.

The reported evidential can have a noun phrase in its scope; in other words, it can function as a non-propositional evidential. In this case, it means 'so called' or 'by the name of'. It is typically used as a further explanation for a newly introduced topic, when the speaker thinks that the addressee is unfamiliar with the topic under discussion. An example is given in (11).

(11) *tɕáma rilé tɕʰó nɔ-ká pi nyi, tɕáma* ***tə́pi*** *ngötʂʰí*
PN era time DOWN-stop IMPF EGO:AP PN EVID:REP chieftain
tó-lö tʰó-ndʐɯ sə nyi.
one-CLF:GENR TS-COP EVID:INF EGO:AP

'At the time when Jiama was in power, (logging) was forbidden—the so-called Jiama was a chieftain.'

This sentence comes from an autobiography. As the author moves to the topic of logging in the past, he mentions the chieftain of the village, Jiama, for the first time. Knowing that the hearer does not know who he is, the narrator provides some further explanation about this person and uses the reported evidential after the name.

Aikhenvald (2021) points out that in some languages where the reported evidential has a noun phrase scope, it can have the meaning of 'doubt'. As seen in (11), this interpretation seems unavailable when *tə́pi* is used as a non-propositional evidential in Munya.

If the author of the hearsay information is specified, then the clause becomes either a direct or indirect speech report. In this case, *tə́pi* should be analyzed as a predicate verb plus an imperfective marker instead of a quotative evidential. This is illustrated in (12).

(12) *otsí* [*ɣɔ́sə* *kʰɯ-tʂ̺ɛ́* *po* *ŋo*] *tə́* *pi.*
3SG+ERG the.day.after.tomorrow NONS-arrive IMPF.1SG EGO:SAP say IMPF
'He says "I will arrive the day after tomorrow".'

This is an example of a direct speech report, as can be seen from the person-marking on the imperfective aspect marker in the embedded clause, which inflects for the original, first person. Here *tə́* 'say' and the imperfective auxiliary *pi* combine into a verb complex, functioning as the predicate of the matrix clause rather than as an evidential marker. Since *tə́* 'say' is a transitive verb, the third person pronominal subject takes the ergative form. This indicates that in Munya, the reported evidential does not take the function of a quotative evidential.

The three evidential markers can all be used in interrogative clauses (this is probably because of the constraints on formulating content questions in Munya, as was discussed in § 2.1) and negative clauses, but no evidential can be used in imperative clauses. When an evidential appears in an interrogative clause, it is the addressee's information source that is presupposed.

3 Egophoricity

As a relatively new linguistic concept, there is yet no commonly agreed definition for egophoric or egophoricity. For example, Tournadre (2008) prefers to characterize egophoric as expressing 'personal knowledge and intention' of the speaker or addressee while Hyslop (2018) defines egophoricity as referring to 'access to knowledge'. The second definition is adopted in Aikhenvald (2021), but she also points out that this account is not clear enough and can include the availability of knowledge to the speaker, privileged access to knowledge, sharing of knowledge, and so on. In this study, we will follow the approach of San Roque et al. (2018), where egophoricity is defined as 'the grammaticalized encoding of the personal or privileged knowledge or involvement of a potential speaker (the primary knower) in a represented event or situation'. As we shall see, this depiction can best capture the functions of egophoricity in Munya.

Following the above definition, two egophoric markers can be identified, an auxiliary *ŋo* and a clause-final particle *nyi*. The former can take an interrogative or a negative prefix, while the latter shows no morphological change. Different from evidential markers, they do not carry any aspect value, and can be used after aspect auxiliaries. *ŋo* is homophonous with the equative copula, and may be grammaticalized from it, but the origin of *nyi* is currently unclear.

The two markers cannot occur together and are partially complementary in their functions. Specifically, the primary function of *ŋo* is to denote the potential speaker's volition or involvement in an event, but it can also be used for information sharing in second person declarative environment. *nyi* is mainly used for information sharing, but it can in addition express speaker's consciousness of and involvement in her action when used in first person declarative clauses. We now take a detailed look at the grammatical properties and functions of these two markers.

3.1 *The Properties and Functions of ŋo*

ŋo is most commonly used in first person declarative and second person interrogative clauses, signaling that the action is carried out volitionally. It is not found to occur with any third person subject. For this reason, it is glossed as EGO:SAP, in which 'sap' stands for 'speech-act participant'. It can either directly follow the predicate verb or be used after an aspect marker. Consider the two examples in (13).

(13) a. *ŋí* *tɕʰintʂʰɛ́* *tó-lö* *kʰɯ-tá* *ŋo.*
1SG+ERG car one-CLF:GENR NONS-buy.1SG EGO:SAP
'I bought a car.'

b. *ɛzə́ tʰó-vɯ pɛ ŋo?*
what TS-do IMPF.2SG EGO:SAP
'What are you doing?'

When *ŋo* is used without an aspect auxiliary before it, one needs to rely on the context to tell if the event has occurred or not. In (13a), since the speaker is talking about his past experience, the addressee knows that the car has already been bought. The speaker can also use this sentence to talk about his plan, in which case it would refer to a future situation. (13b) is a content interrogative clause addressed to a second person singular subject. The subject is omitted, but the person-number information is indexed on the imperfective marker.

Because *ŋo* indicates that the participant is in conscious control over his action, using this marker after non-volitional predicates would cause semantic incongruity. Therefore, both (14a), with a predicate of internal states, and (14b), with an adjectival predicate, are ungrammatical.

(14) a. **ngɛ́ tə-ŋé ŋo.*
1SG+EXP UP-be.ill EGO:SAP
Intended meaning: 'I'm ill.'

b. **nɛ́ tʂʰöntʂʰö̋ ŋo.*
2SG be.hard-working EGO:SAP
Intended meaning: 'You are hard-working.'

ŋo can also be used in the second person declarative environment, albeit less frequently. In this case, the sense of this egophoric marker is information sharing, that is, the speaker informs the addressee of something about herself that the addressee does not know. The relative rarity of this use may be because people generally are more aware of their own intentions and actions than others do, hence conveying the information about the addressee is normally not needed for the speaker. Consider the two examples in (15).

(15) a. *nɛ́ i ɛ́-ndzü ŋo.*
2SG ERG DS-eat.2SG EGO:SAP
'You have already eaten.'

b. *ŋəmɛ kʰɛ́ tú-do kʰu-nyü̋ sü ŋo.*
really words UP-talk NONS-can EVID:INF.2SG EGO:SAP
'You can already speak very well. (Literally: You talked very ably.)'

(15a) is said when the addressee forgets if she already had dinner or not, and the speaker reminds her that she already had it. (15b) is uttered by the speaker to the author after a brief exchange of voice messages over cellphone. In the two examples, the speaker either gives information to or points out something about the addressee that he himself has no knowledge of. The function of the egophoric marker here is therefore to signal the speaker's privileged access to knowledge.

In conclusion, when used in first person declarative or second person interrogative clauses, the function of *ŋo* is to denote the potential speaker's volition and involvement in the action, and when used in second person declarative clauses, its function is information sharing.

3.2 *The Properties and Functions of nyi*

Another egophoric marker is the clause-final particle *nyi*. Compared to *ŋo*, there is less constraint on the use of *nyi*. It can occur with any person and any kind of predicate, including non-volitional verbs and adjectival predicates. This marker is glossed as EGO:AP, in which 'ap' stands for 'all participants'. Two examples are given in (16), where (16a) contains a non-volitional predicate and (16b) an adjectival predicate with a third person subject.

(16) a. *ngɛ́ tə-ŋé sə* ***nyi.***
1SG+EXP UP-be.ill EVID:INF EGO:AP
'I was ill.'

b. *sédʑű katɕʰá* ***nyi.***
policy be.bad EGO:AP
'The policy is very bad.'

While it can occur after a stative verb (17a), it cannot directly follow a dynamic verb. When the predicate verb is dynamic, *nyi* should be used after an aspect marker, as in (17b) (Bai 2019: 248).

(17) a. *nɛ́ i mənyɛ́ sú ú-nyɛ* ***nyi?***
2SG ERG Munya language INTRG-can.2SG EGO:AP
'Can you speak Munya?'

b. *ótsə dʑópu tʰə́va sə* ***nyi.***
3SG king become EVID:INF EGO:AP
'He became the king.'

There are two reasons for analyzing *nyi* as an egophoric marker. The first reason comes from the effect that it has on a clause with a first person subject and a volitional predicate. (18) is adapted from (7), but with *nyi* added:

(18) *ŋí* *nbətʂá* *tó-lö* *ní-tʰɛ* *no-só*
1SG+ERG worm one-CLF:GENR DOWN-stomp DOWN-kill
sö ***nyi.***
EVID:INF.1SG EGO:AP
'I stomped on a worm and killed it.'

Recall that example (7), which does not contain the egophoric particle, indicates that the speaker stepped on the worm by accident. Now with *nyi* added, this sentence implies that the speaker stomped the worm intentionally. Thus, using *nyi* in a first person clause with a volitional predicate signals the speaker's control of and involvement in the event. This shows that *nyi* has the egophoric function.

The interpretation is different if the predicate is non-volitional, in which case *nyi* is used for information sharing. For example, (16a) does not mean the speaker became ill on purpose, but that the speaker thinks the information is previously unknown to the addressee, which prompts the use of *nyi*.

The second reason is that *nyi* denotes privileged access to information known to the speaker when used with non-first-person participants. This can be illustrated with the pair of adjectival predicate clauses in (19) (Bai 2019: 249).

(19) a. *otsə́* *məní* *tő̃me* ***nyi.***
DEM person be.rich EGO:AP
'That person is rich.'

b. *otsə́* *məní* *tő̃me* ***ti·***
DEM person be.rich GN
'That person is rich.'

(19a) would be used if the speaker assumes that the addressee does not share her information, i.e., does not know that the person being talked about is rich. By contrast, (19b), which ends with the gnomic aspect marker, is a plain statement and does not carry this assumption.

To sum up, when used in a clause with a first person participant and a volitional predicate, *nyi* implies that the speaker consciously participates in the event; and when used in other environments, it expresses the speaker's privileged access to information.

TABLE 23.1 The meaning of egophoric markers in relation to the predicate and the person of subject

		Meaning of egophoric marker	
Type of predicate	**Person of subject**	***ŋo***	***nyi***
Volitional	1	volition and involvement	volition and involvement
	2	information sharing	information sharing
	3	NA	information sharing
Non-volitional	1	NA	information sharing
	2	NA	information sharing
	3	NA	information sharing

The functions and properties of these two egophoric markers are summarized in Table 23.1. As can be seen from this table, the primary function of Munya egophoric markers is to indicate information sharing or epistemic authority on the part of the speaker, with the sense of volition and involvement only found with a first person volitional actor.

The two egophoric markers in Munya can have semantic overtones of certainty regardless of whether the focus is on the potential speaker's volition and involvement or on information sharing. In the first case, since the action is carried out volitionally and consciously, it implies that the speaker is certain of her action. In the second case, as the speaker is telling the addressee something that is not yet known to her, it presupposes that the speaker has a high degree of certainty with respect to the information being provided.

4 Mirativity

Mirativity is now viewed as being related to the expectation of knowledge (Aikhenvald 2014; Hyslop 2018), but the idea of establishing it as a cross-linguistically valid grammatical category was initially put forward in DeLancey (1997). It was substantially developed in Aikhenvald (2012), where sudden discovery, revelation or realization, surprise, unprepared mind, counter-expectation, and new information are all subsumed under the label of mirativity. Also, the mirative effects are not restricted to the speaker. In various languages, effects of such a kind relating to the main character in narration or the audience/addressee can also trigger the expression of mirativity (Aikhenvald 2012). In Munya, mirativity can be used to show sudden or deferred realization, counter-expectation, surprise, or new information. In all these situations, the mirative effect is on the part of the speaker or the main characters in narration.

The sense of mirativity in Munya is indicated with the clause-final particle *tʰoŋósə*. While this word can be further parsed into the prefixed equative copula *tʰó-ŋo* 'TS-be' and the perfective aspect auxiliary *sə*, considering that it has a fixed, non-compositional meaning (mirativity) and an invariable, non-breakable form (*sə* cannot inflect for the person-number of subject), it is treated as a grammaticalized lexeme here. In terms of its distribution, it can directly follow stative predicates (examples 20 and 21) or an aspect auxiliary (example 22).

As a first illustration of the use of this marker, consider (20), which was heard multiple times from native speakers:

(20) *pɤ́su* **tʰoŋósə.**
Tibetan.language MIR
'It turns out that it IS Tibetan.'

This was often uttered by Munya speakers as we were discussing the etymology of some words. If I thought that a word was borrowed from Tibetan (usually based on its phonetic form), I would ask them for confirmation. Their first responses were normally negative, asserting that the word in question is a native Munya word. But when I asked them how to say that word in Tibetan, they would ponder for a while, and admit that the word was indeed a Tibetan loan and say (20). The meaning of the mirative marker here is sudden realization or counter-expectation, and the mirative effect is on the part of the speaker (Bai 2019: 255).

(21) is a further illustration of this function.

(21) *reré* **tʰoŋósə.**
be.delicious MIR
'Turns out (the noodles) are delicious.'

The context is that the speaker thought adding vinegar to noodles would not taste good, but when she tasted it, she found that, contrary to her expectation/to her surprise, it was delicious (Bai 2019: 255).

tʰoŋósə can also be used after a speaker has gained certainty about previously uncertain events or situations. The information content triggering the use of the mirative marker may still be new, but not totally unexpected. As an illustration, one day my consultant found that he could not make recordings with his smartphone anymore. He thought it might be because there was no storage left, but was not totally sure. I checked his phone and told him he was right—the SD card was full. After hearing this, he made a phone call to someone explaining the cause of that issue, and uttered (22) (Bai 2019: 256).

(22) *tósə* *pi* ***tʰoŋósə.***
be.full IMPF MIR
'Turns out (the smartphone) is full.'

tʰoŋósə can also be used if the surprise is on the part of a character. (23) below comes from a story (Bai 2019: 257).

(23) *dʑópu=nɛ* *mətsá* *tsəkúː* *otsə́* *dəmú* ***tʰoŋósə*** *nyi*
king=COLL.PL daughter D.M 3SG demoness MIR EGO:AP
'The daughter of the king's family, she turns out to be a demoness!'

The story is about the adventure of three children. After arriving in a new country, one of them married the daughter of a king. However, she turned out to be a demoness who was responsible for the death of several previous kings, a fact which surely came as a surprise. But surprise to whom? Obviously, it cannot be to the narrator, as he knows the story already. If it is to the audience of the story, the egophoric *nyi* would be the more natural choice, which is what we find after the mirative particle. Here the most plausible explanation is that the unexpectedness is on the part of a very general 'character', in other words, anyone who is involved in the fictive world of the story, including the characters in the story and the audience. Using the mirative marker here has the additional effect of making the story more engaging, as it shows that the storyteller is narrating with the perspective of a character in the story in mind rather than simply as an outsider.

As a final illustration of the function of this marker, and also its interaction with evidentiality and epistemic modality, consider (24). Here the mirative marker occurs after the indirect evidential and is then followed by a modality particle *pa* 'possibly'.

(24) *onə́* *ɛɕǘ* *létsɛ* *ɣɤ-rá* *sə* ***tʰoŋósə*** ***pa.***
3PL PN upper.end US-go EVID:INF MIR possibly
'They have probably gone upstream to the upper end of the ɛɕü valley (which is contrary to our previous assumptions).'

Here three speakers are talking about a group of people circumambulating Mount Gongga. Because they have no knowledge of the exact route that the pilgrims took, they can only make conjectures. The indirect evidential is chosen because they do not have firsthand information on the pilgrims' trek. The mirative marker is used as the speakers have already made several assumptions, and the one who utters (24) may think that contrary to previous expectations, they may actually have taken a totally different route. Finally, the modality particle shows that the speaker is uncertain of his inference due to a lack of concrete evidence.

Examples (23) and (24) show that mirativity, evidentiality, egophoricity, and modality are distinct grammatical categories in Munya, and that speakers can combine them in different ways to effectively communicate knowledge-related meanings with considerable nuances.

5 Summary and Discussion

The above analyses demonstrate that evidentiality, egophoricity, and mirativity in Munya each have their own specific functions and can be treated as distinct grammatical categories. The evidential system consists of a direct evidential, an inferential evidential, and a reported evidential. Use of the direct evidential is constrained by the person of the subject and the volitionality of the predicate. The inferential evidential also acts as the perfective aspect and shows first person effects, and the reported evidential can have both a clause and a noun phrase in its scope. Egophorics in Munya can express volition and involvement or epistemic authority on the part of a potential speaker. The first sense is seen in a first person declarative or second person interrogative clause with a volitional predicate, while the second sense is found in other environments. Mirativity in Munya can denote counter-expectation, surprise, and deferred realization. The mirative effects can be on the part of the speaker or of the main characters in narrations.

The fact that the distinctions among the knowledge-related grammatical categories in Munya can be maintained does not mean that they are totally unrelated. The inferential evidential, when used in the first person volitional environment, can have a first person effect, which is essentially a mirative overtone. The two egophoric markers have connotations of certainty, thus overlapping with the domain of modality.

Speakers can use these knowledge-related grammatical categories together to convey complex epistemological meanings. For example, one can use the reported evidential after the direct evidential or the inferential evidential. In this instance, the first evidential marks the information source of the original author, and the second, reported evidential reflects the speaker's source of information. The mirative particle can be used after evidentials, in which case both the speaker's source of information and her expectation of it are coded. The two egophoric markers are incompatible with the direct evidential, but can follow the inferential evidential, or be followed by the reported evidential. Finally, the egophoric markers are not found to co-occur with the mirative particle. This is probably because egophoricity has overtones of certainty, while mirativity denotes surprise and counter-expectation, and the two types of meanings are fundamentally incongruous.

Acknowledgements

My heartfelt thanks for the comments and suggestions made by Anne Storch on an earlier draft of this paper. Special thanks to Mary Chambers for her careful proofreading and revisions.

Abbreviations

1	first person	EVID:INF	inferential evidential
2	second person	EVID:REP	reported evidential
3	third person	EXP	experiencer case
AP	all participants	GN	gnomic aspect
CLF:GENR	general classifier	IMPF	imperfective
CLF:LONG	classifier for long objects	INTRG	interrogative
CLF:MAN	classifier for human	MIR	mirativity
COLL.PL	collective associative plural	NEG	negative
COP	copula	NONS	non-specific direction
D.M	discourse marker	PL	plural
DAT	dative	PLA.PL	place associative plural
DEM	demonstrative	PN	proper noun
DOWN	downward direction	SAP	speech act participants
DS	downstream direction	SG	singular
EGO	egophoricity	TS	translocative direction
ERG	ergative	UP	upward direction
EVID:DIR	direct evidential	US	upstream direction.

References

Aikhenvald, Alexandra Y. (2004). *Evidentiality*. Oxford: Oxford University Press.

Aikhenvald, Alexandra Y. (2011). The grammaticalization of evidentiality. In Heiko Narrog and Bernd Heine (eds.), *The Oxford handbook of grammaticalization*, 602–610. Oxford: Oxford University Press.

Aikhenvald, Alexandra Y. (2012). The essence of mirativity. *Linguistic Typology* 16 (3): 435–485. https://doi.org/10.1515/lingty-2012-0017

Aikhenvald, Alexandra Y. (2014). The grammar of knowledge: A cross-linguistic view of evidentials and the expression of information source. In Alexandra Y. Aikhenvald and R.M.W. Dixon (eds.), *The grammar of knowledge*, 1–51. Oxford: Oxford University Press.

Aikhenvald, Alexandra Y. (2015). Evidentials: Their links with other grammatical categories. *Linguistic Typology* 19 (2): 239–277. https://doi.org/10.1515/lingty-2015-0008

Aikhenvald, Alexandra Y. (2018a). Evidentiality: The framework. In Alexandra Y. Aikhenvald (ed.), *The Oxford handbook of evidentiality*, 1–43. Oxford: Oxford University Press.

Aikhenvald, Alexandra Y. (ed.). (2018b). *The Oxford handbook of evidentiality*. Oxford University Press.

Aikhenvald, Alexandra Y. (2021). *The web of knowledge: Evidentiality at the cross-roads*. Leiden: Brill.

Aikhenvald, Alexandra Y. and R.M.W. Dixon (1998). Evidentials and areal typology: A case study from Amazonia. *Language Sciences* 20: 241–257.

Aikhenvald, Alexandra Y. and R.M.W. Dixon (eds.). (2003). *Studies in Evidentiality*. Amsterdam/Philadelphia: John Benjamins Publishing Company.

Aikhenvald, Alexandra Y. and R.M.W. Dixon (eds.). (2014). *The grammar of knowledge*. Oxford: Oxford University Press.

Aikhenvald, Alexandra Y. and Randy J. LaPolla (2007). New perspectives on evidentials: A View from Tibeto-Burman. *Linguistics of the Tibeto-Burman Area* 30: 1–16.

Bai, Junwei (2019). A grammar of Munya. Doctoral dissertation, James Cook University.

Bai, Junwei (2021). Northern and southern Munya dialects: Towards a historical perspective. *Studia Linguistica* 75 (2): 328–344. https://doi.org/10.1111/stul.12159

Chirkova, Ekaterina. (2008). Essential characteristics of Lizu, a Qiangic language of Western Sichuan [Paper presentation]. *Workshop on Tibeto-Burman Languages of Sichuan.*

DeLancey, Scott. (1997). Mirativity: The grammatical marking of unexpected information. *Linguistic Typology* 1: 33–52.

Forker, Diana (2018). Evidentiality and its relations with other verbal categories. In Alexandra Y. Aikhenvald (ed.), *The Oxford handbook of evidentiality*, 65–84. Oxford: Oxford University Press.

Hyslop, Gwendolyn (2018). Evidentiality in Bodic languages. In Alexandra Y. Aikhenvald (ed.), *The Oxford handbook of evidentiality*, 595–609. Oxford: Oxford University Press.

Oisel, Guillaume (2014). From motion verbs to evidentiality in Tibetan. Conference presentation, *24th Meeting of Southeast Asian Linguistics Society*.

San Roque, Lila, Simeon Floyd and Elisabeth Norcliffe (2018). Egophoricity: An introduction. In Simeon Floyd, Elisabeth Norcliffe and Lila S. Roque (eds.), *Egophoricity*, 1–77. Amsterdam/Philadelphia: John Benjamins Publishing Company.

Sun, Hongkai (1983). 六江流域的民族语言及其系属分类—兼述嘉陵江上游、雅鲁藏布江流域的民族语言 [The nationality languages in the six valleys and their language branches]. *Journal of Nationality Studies* 3: 99–273.

Sun, Jackson T.-S. (2018). Evidentials and person. In Alexandra Y. Aikhenvald (ed.), *The Oxford handbook of evidentiality*, 47–63. Oxford: Oxford University Press.

Tournadre, Nicolas (2008). Argument against the concept of 'conjunct'/ 'disjunct' in Tibetan. In Brigitte Huber, Marianne Volkart and Paul Widmer (eds.), *Chomolangma, Demawend und Kasbek. Festschrift für Roland Bielmeier zu seinem 65 Geburtstag*, 281–308. Halle: International Institute for Tibetan and Buddhist Studies.

CHAPTER 24

Nominal Incorporation in Shiwilu (Kawapanan): Nouns, Classifiers and the Deceased Marker =*ku'*

Pilar Valenzuela

1 Introduction

Shiwilu (a.k.a. Jebero) is a critically endangered language of Northeastern Peru and one of the two members of the Kawapanan family. Shiwilu is fluently spoken by ca. 25 elders, most of who live in and around the town of Jeberos or the neighboring city of Yurimaguas (Alto Amazonas Province, Loreto Region). Today, all Shiwilu speakers are bilingual in Spanish and employ this language in their daily lives almost exclusively. Intergenerational transmission of Shiwilu ceased several decades ago (Valenzuela 2010, 2012).

Shiwilu is a good representative of the Andes-Amazonia transitional zone, in that it exhibits a mixture of phonological and grammatical traits that are typical of the languages of these two regions (Valenzuela 2015, 2018). The present article addresses a phenomenon that is common in Amazonian languages but absent in the Central Andean families Quechuan and Aymaran: nominal incorporation (Dixon and Aikhenvald 1999: 10; Adelaar with Muysken 2004; Aikhenvald 2017: 296). In this work, 'nominal incorporation' is a cover term to designate the process of inserting into the verb a noun, a classifier, or the deceased marker =*ku'*.

Canonical noun incorporation can be defined as "the morphological construction where a nominal lexical element is added to a verbal lexical element; the resulting construction being a verb and a single word" (de Reuse 1994: 2842).[1] Use of this strategy may derive new lexical items, affect the syntactic relations in a clause, or have discourse ramifications (Mithun 1984, 1986, 1994; de Reuse 1994; Gerdts 1998; Aikhenvald 2007). Although noun incorporation is prominent in polysynthetic languages, the two must not be equated: incorporation takes place in languages with different morphological profiles (e.g. several Austronesian languages), and there are polysynthetic languages that lack this feature, strictly speaking (Eskaleut languages) (Mithun 2009; Aikhenvald

1 For a more encompassing definition of noun incorporation, see Johns (2017).

© PILAR VALENZUELA, 2022 | DOI:10.1163/9789004510395_025

2007: 12). Noun incorporation is frequent in the Indigenous languages of North and South America, Austronesia, Northern Australia, and Siberia (Mithun 1994: 5024). Consider the following Shiwilu sentences involving the intransitive verb *iker-* 'ache'.[2] In (1a), without incorporation, the possessed body part is realized as an independent NP and is registered as clausal subject by means of the verbal suffix *-lli*. In (1b), the noun *mutu'* (stripped off possessive marking) is inserted in the verb, which allows the possessor to assume the subject function, as indicated by *-lek*.[3]

(1) a. Mutu'wek ikelli
mutu'=wek *iker-lli*
head=POSS.1SG ache-NFI.3SG
'My head aches.'

b. Ikermutu'lek
iker-mutu'-lek
ache-head-NFI.1SG
'I have a headache.'

Structures resembling (1b) have been analyzed as instances of possessor raising, whereby an erstwhile possessor is 'promoted' to core argument. However, (1a) and (1b) are two separate constructions, effecting distinct meanings

2 The Shiwilu data are given in the phonologically-based official orthography, which includes the following conventions: ⟨e⟩ = /ə/, ⟨d⟩ = /ð̞/, ⟨ll⟩ = /ʎ/, ⟨ñ⟩ = /ɲ/, ⟨ch⟩ = /tʃ/, and ⟨y⟩ = /j/. The diacritic ⟨'⟩ indicates a glottal stop after a vowel, but syllable break after a consonant. Primary stress falls on the first syllable of disyllabic words or the second syllable of words with three or more syllables; the addition of certain affixes results in modifications.

3 The following abbreviations are used throughout this paper: 1 first person, 2 second person, 3 third person, A transitive subject, ABL ablative, ADD additive, ADV adverbial, AFFECT affective (benefactive/malefactive), AND andative, APPL applicative, ASSOC associative, CAUS causative, CL classifier, COM comitative, COMM commiserative, CONT continuous, CONTRST contrastive, COP copula, DECSD deceased, DEPREC deprecatory, DES desiderative, DIM diminutive, DS different subject, E exclusive, EMPH emphatic, FEM female, FOC focus, FRUST frustrative, FUT future, HSY hearsay, I inclusive, IMP imperative, INCORP incorporation, INFL inflection, INSTR instrumental, INT interrogative, intr. intransitive, LOC locative, MASC masculine, MOV movement, NEG negative, NFI non-future indicative, NMLZ nominalization, NP noun phrase, O object, OBL oblique, OUT outward movement, PL plural, POSS possessive, PROG progressive, PTCP participle, REC reciprocal, REF reflexive, REP repetitive, S intransitive subject, SIMIL similative, SG singular, SS same subject, SUBJ subjunctive, SURP surprise, tr. transitive, V verb, VAL valency, VM valency modifier, VOC vocative, w/o without.

or discourse consequences (Gerdts 1998: 86). Roughly speaking, in (1a) the focus is placed on the possessed body part, while in (1b) the focus lies on the affected possessor.

The purpose of this paper is two-fold. First, it provides an account of canonical nominal incorporation in Shiwilu, thus inaugurating the discussion on incorporation in Kawapanan linguistics.[4] Secondly, this paper seeks to expand our knowledge of nominal incorporation in Amazonian languages and beyond.

Before engaging in the analysis of Shiwilu nominal incorporation, selected grammar traits of the language are outlined in § 2, by way of providing the necessary background for the subsequent discussion. The next three sections are structured according to the kind of material that gets incorporated. Section 3 is devoted to noun incorporation, largely along the lines of Mithun (1984). It deals with noun-verb compounds as well as the syntactic and discourse effects of noun incorporation constructions. The incorporation of classifiers is taken up in § 4. After an introduction to the Shiwilu classifier system, this section focuses on compounds and a construction involving classifier incorporation and locative applicativization. Section 5 discusses a highly idiosyncratic feature of Shiwilu, the ability of the deceased marker *=ku'* to appear in the verb. The purpose of § 6 is to demonstrate that incorporated nominals assume different syntactic functions, including transitive subject. The conclusions and final remarks are presented in § 7.

2 Selected Features of Shiwilu Grammar

Shiwilu is agglutinating with some fusion, polysynthetic, and predominantly head-marking. It uses more suffixes than prefixes. Both AVO and AOV are common orders in spontaneous speech. Nonetheless, the language has postpositions and the possessor precedes the possessum; this is compatible with the OV pattern (Dryer 2007). Bendor-Samuel (1981[1958]: 74–81) distinguishes four major word classes: nominal, verb, adverb, and particle. He subdivides nominal into: noun, adjective (including quantifiers and demonstratives), pronoun, and relative; all but pronoun are open classes. Additionally, Shiwilu has classifiers, but lacks noun classes or a gender system.

Shiwilu distinguishes four persons (first exclusive, first inclusive, second, third) and two numbers (minimal and augmented, labeled singular and plural

4 A relatively early record of Shiwilu noun incorporation appears in Rivet and Tastevin (1931: 241). For Shawi, see Hart (1988: 274).

TABLE 24.1 Shiwilu personal pronouns, possessives, and unipersonal verb suffixes

Person	Personal pronouns	Possessives	Unipersonal verb markers
1SG(.E)	kua	=wek	-lek
1SG.I	kenmu'	=mapu'	-lek
2SG	kenma	=pen	-la
3SG	nana	=nen	-lli
1PL.E	kuda	=widek	-llidek
1PL.I	kenmu'wa'	=mapu'wa'	-lekwa'
2PL	kenmama'	=penma'	-lama'
3PL	nawa'	=nenna'	-llina'

TABLE 24.2 Shiwilu bipersonal suffixes, non-future-indicative

	1SG	1SG.I	2SG	1PL.E	1PL.I	2PL
1SG	--	--	-llen			-llenma'
2SG	-lun			-lundek		
3SG	-llun	-llenmu'	-llen	-llundek	-llenmu'wa'	-llenma'
1PL.E	--		-lliden ~ -lliyen			-llidenma' ~ -lliyenma'
2PL	-lama'uku			-lama'ukudek		
3PL	-llinerku	-llinerkenmu'	-llinerken	-llinerkudek	-llinerkenmu'wa'	-llinerkenma'

for simplicity). Table 24.1 presents Shiwilu personal pronouns, possessive modifiers, and the verb 'unipersonal' suffixes corresponding to the non-future indicative (the most frequent inflectional paradigm). 'Unipersonal' suffixes are portmanteau morphemes that encode (tense-)mood and the subject of intransitive verbs, or the subject and object of transitive verbs with a 3rd person object.

'Bipersonal' suffixes convey (tense-)mood and index subject and primary object. They are mandatory on transitive verbs with a 1st or 2nd person O. Table 24.2 contains the bipersonal suffixes corresponding to the non-future indicative. Vertically listed categories refer to the A and horizontal ones to the O.

There are several additional paradigms of verb inflectional suffixes; two of them mark switch-reference (e.g., compare -sik in (10) and -anna' in (12b)). Each paradigm has unipersonal and bipersonal sets.

DES VAL_2 VAL_1 ADV_2 ADV_1 [STEM] all.night.long/at.night $APPL_1$ think.of.doing **$INCORP_1$** $APPL_2$ VM **$INCORP_2$** DIM CONT MOV_1 MOV_2 ADV_1 ADV_2 COMM FRUST 3PL.O NEG INFL

FIGURE 24.1 Structure of the Shiwilu verb

When a 3rd person (patient) object is plural, the verb requires the suffix -*dek*, which precedes the negative marker, if present, and the bipersonal suffix (see (17c)).

Minimally, a verb consists of a root and a unipersonal or bipersonal suffix. However, verbs can be very complex. Bendor-Samuel (1981[1958]) identifies over 25 slots that he organizes into (a) verb expanding prefixes, (b) stem, (c) verb extending suffixes, and (d) inflectional suffix. Verb forms comprising up to ten morphemes can be attested (pp. 88–89). Prefixes include the desiderative, causativizers, the reflexive/reciprocal, and adverbial-like morphemes.

Shiwilu features a prolific applicative system comprising seven constructions with distinct affixes. In 'double applicative' constructions the verb must take the valency modifier -*tu* simultaneously with a dedicated applicative, regardless of the base transitivity value (Valenzuela 2016a).

Depending on the verb to which it applies, the valency modifier -*tu* (-*t* before a vowel) may function as applicative, adding an object (2a), or as antipassive, suppressing an object (2b).

(2) a. pasun- 'stick' > pasun-tu- 'stick to' (7)
b. lli'- 'see'(9) > lli'-tu- 'appear, see' (w/o overt O)

Figure 24.1 schematizes the structure of the Shiwilu verb. Slots for incorporated items are bolded. For further details on the Shiwilu verb and argument encoding, consult Bendor-Samuel (1981[1958]) and Valenzuela (2011a, 2016a).

Argument NPs are unmarked for case. However, when O is the 3rd person, =*ler* may encliticize to the A under certain conditions (roughly, to highlight an unexpected A or to disambiguate the identity of participants). When both A and O are 3rd person, and O precedes A in the clause, =*ler* is mandatory. Although the distribution of =*ler* is superficially ergative, there is no syntacticized ergative-absolutive alignment with regard to the Shiwilu NP (Valenzuela 2011a).

3 Incorporation of Nouns

3.1 *Shiwilu Nouns*

Most Shiwilu nouns, including those conveying body parts or kinship relations, can stand as free words by themselves, without possessive marking or any other additional morphology. The following extract belongs to a narrative centering around *Uwi'lunsha* 'Little Miss Spider', the first Shiwilu woman to learn how to manufacture and wear clothes. A young girl accompanies her father to the jungle, unaware that he plans to get rid of her. Once abandoned in the jungle, the girl is visited in dreams by protective spirits who teach her how to spin the thread and weave clothes. Sometime later, she grows additional limbs and turns into a spider. Example (3) contains three body-part nouns. While *chi'tek* takes possessive morphology, the bare nouns *tanpa'* and *tula* are independent words.

(3) a. Nanek ima…ma'pu'siklinpi'ma asu' chi'tekñiklima ipa' ali'la tanpa' yunsu'pilalli

nanek ima ma'pu'si=kla=inpu=ima asu' ***chi'tek****=nen=kla=ima*

then HSY how=ABL-NEG=HSY this chest=POSS.3SG=ABL=HSY

ipa' ali'la ***tanpa'*** *yunsu'-apa-ila-lli…*

already other arm come.out-CONT-PASS.OUTWARD-NFI.3SG

'Then … who knows how, another arm began to grow out of her chest …'

b. Inkatu' tula a'ñilli, inkatu' tanpa' a'ñilli.

inkatu' ***tula*** *a'ñi-lli inkatu'* ***tanpa'*** *a'ñi-lli*

four thigh have-NFI.3SG four arm have.NFI.3SG

'She had four legs and four arms.' (Author fieldnotes: *Uwi'lunsha*)

Alongside free-standing, alienable nouns, Shiwilu features a set of monosyllabic, inalienably possessed nouns that denotes the body or its parts, i.e., these nouns must take possessive marking to function as words: *pi-* 'body' > *pinen* 'his/her/its body', *tek-* 'skin' > *teknen* 'his/her/its skin', *llin-* 'vine' > *llinen* 'its vine/tail', *mek-* 'leaf' > *meknen* 'its leaf', etc. Most monosyllabic nouns are phonologically reduced versions of semantically equivalent alienable nouns: *chip-****itek*** 'skin', ***lullin*** 'wild vine' or ***llin****tek* 'tail', *lalu****mek*** 'leaf'. Monosyllabic nouns and classifiers often share the same form (see Table 24.3).

3.2 *Incorporation of Free-Standing Nouns*

In a seminal paper, Mithun (1984) puts forward a crosslinguistic typology of noun incorporation constructions focusing on their diachronic development. According to this author, the first type of noun incorporation to arise in a language is lexical compounding, i.e., the combination of a verb stem and a noun stem to yield a complex predicate denoting a recognizable, unitary concept. Typically, incorporated nouns do not refer to a specific entity but narrow the scope of the verb. The purpose of this construction is to create new labels for activities or states that are 'name-worthy' and more specific than those denoted by the verb stems alone. The compounded verbs below involve various body-part nouns. The host verb may be intransitive or transitive.

(4)	a. wa'danpin- 'be crazy'	mutu' 'head'	wa'danpin**mutu'** 'feel dizzy'
	b. nanpi- 'live'	lada 'face'	nanpi**lada**- 'stay up all night'
	c. wellek- 'cry'	kankan 'liver'	wellek-kankan- 'cry in the inside'
	d. u'wa- 'inhale'	netchek 'nose'	uwa'**netchek**- 'suck from the nose'
	e. usu'- 'pull out'	latek 'tooth'	usu'**latek**- 'pull out a tooth'
	f. usu'- 'pull out'	kadu'la 'testicles'	usu'**kadu'la**- 'castrate'
	g. dekpa'-tu- 'cut down'	enchek 'hair'	dekpa'**enchek**tu- 'cut a woman's hair'

Verbs like *pamu'*- 'wash' frequently carry reflexive prefixing and body-part incorporation.

(5)	a. in-pamu'-itekla-	[REF-wash-hand-]	'wash one's hands'
	b. in-pamu'-enchek-	[REF-wash-hair-]	'was one' hair'
	d. in-pamu'-lada-	[REF-wash-eye/face-]	'wash one's face'
	e. in-pamu'-latek-	[REF-wash-tooth-]	'wash one's teeth'[5]

A second type of noun incorporation construction posited by Mithun (1984) involves the manipulation of case, i.e., a change in the syntactic roles of participants, often accompanied by a decrease in or the rearrangement of the verb's valency (Aikhenvald 2017: 298). As expected, this process has concomitant semantic or pragmatic consequences. Body-part nouns incorporate very

5 In preparing manioc beer, Shiwilu women carefully rinse their mouths and rub their teeth with their fingers before chewing the boiled manioc.

often, which allows the possessor to be encoded as a core argument, usually O or S, rather than oblique. This strategy is a means to foreground a participant and is motivated by the general fact that the affected possessor is of greater overall interest than their body part (recall example (1b)). The alternate non-incorporation expression would be favored, for instance, if the speaker seeks to focus on the location of an injury (Mithun 1984, 1994).[6] Sentences (6)–(7) involve the noun *landu'* 'lower part of the leg'. (6) was uttered by a woman who sadly explains that she can no longer walk and work in the garden due to her limp. The speaker's focus is on herself and incorporating *landu'* permits the affected participant to be kept as subject.

(6) Ma'pu'sui'na ikellandu'mu innichi'nek dekkunta'kasu'.
Ma'pu'su'=i'na *iker-**landu'**-amu* *innit-i'n-lek*
how=FOC ache-lower.leg-PTCP.SS.1SG can-NEG-NFI.1SG
dekkunt-a'kasu'
walk-NMLZ.1SG
'Since now I suffer from leg pain, I cannot walk.' (Valenzuela 2012: 95)

In contrast, (7) belongs to the entry for *landu'* in the Shiwilu Dictionary. The focus is now on the body part, where the leech is found.

(7) Tata'lu'tek pasuntullun landu'wekkek.
tata'lu'tek *pasun-tu-llun* ***landu'**=wek=kek*
leech stick-VM-NFI.3SG>1SG lower.leg=POSS.1SG=LOC
'The leech stuck to my lower leg.' (Valenzuela et al. 2013: *landu'*)

In sum, constructions like (6) and (7) are not mere paraphrases of each other but serve different discourse functions.

Incorporated nouns appear in their full form even when compounded or derived (the only attested exception is *wi'wek* 'ear', which adopts the truncated form *wek*). Aikhenvald (2007: 14–15) reports that some languages can incorporate whole NPs (possessive NP, attributive NP, comitative NP). This is not possible in Shiwilu.

A third type of noun incorporation corresponds to the regulation of information in discourse. Its function is to background a participant that is an established part of the scene, incidental, predictable, or devoid of special focus.

6 The predicates in (5) also involve the 'manipulation of case relations' in the sense that *pamu'*- appears in non-incorporation constructions.

Coding this participant with an independent NP might interfere with the flow of information and distract the listener's attention (Mithun 1984: 859, 1994: 5025).[7] Let us examine some instantiations of *pidek* 'house' in a narrative featuring the ancient Shiwilu and Arakayu, the spiritual owner of fish and river animals in general. At the beginning of the story, a group of men are walking in the jungle and catch sight of smoke emanating from a fire. Next, they see a house. Intrigued, they decide to approach the house and find out who lives there. It turns out to be Arakayu, who comes out of his home and welcomes the men. Up to this point, the narrator is building the story. The house, which codes new information, is referred to by two locative phrases.

(8) a. Penwanpasik pidekñik ...
pen-wan-pa-sik ***pidek**-ñik*
fire-HAVE-CONT-PTCP.DS.3SG house-POSS.3SG:LOC
'Somebody was lighting a fire in a house ...'

b. "Enchuku' luwetchunta'wa' den'ipa'tek."
enchuku' luwer-tu-unt-a'wa' den=ipa'=tek
let's.go know-VM-AND-IMP.1PL.I who=perhaps=DEPREC?
'"Let's go meet whoever it might be."'

c. Tanni'ma kawinta'llini'ma yunsu'lli pidekñikla.
t-anna'=ima kawi'=nta'-llina'=ima yunsu'-lli
say-PTCP.SS.3PL=HSY get.close-AND-NFI.3PL=HSY came.out-NFI.3SG
***pidek**=ñikla*
house=POSS.3SG:ABL
'Saying that, they approached (the house) and Arakayu came out of his house (to greet them).' (Valenzuela 2012: 117)

Then a conflict emerges. Spurred on by curiosity to find out what kind of being Arakayu is, the men demand to see his house, to which Arakayu does not agree. Yet the men do not give up and utter the expression in (9) below. This time, *pidek* 'house' is incorporated in the verb, which permits Arakayu to be cast into the core role of O instead of possessor. This choice is motivated by the fact that the men are ultimately interested in Arakayu rather than his house.

7 (6) might be interpreted as an instance of Type 3 noun incorporation. The woman's physical impediment is obvious from the situational context and it could be argued that noun incorporation backgrounds this piece of information.

(9) "Nu'pachi yalli'llen. Yaluwerpidektullen".
nu'pachi ya-lli'-llen *ya-luwer-**pidek**-tu-llen*
then DES-see-NFI.1PL.E>2SG DES-know-house-VM-NFI.1PL.E>2SG
'"We want to visit you. We want to see your house" (lit. We want to know you with regard to your house).' (Valenzuela 2012: 118)

While standing outside Arakayu's house the men spot a river they have not seen before and ask Arakayu for fish. The river turns out to be Pampayacu, the core of Shiwilu ancestral territory. Arakayu calls out to the fish and, to the men's dismay, all sorts of highly valued fish species come to them, along with turtles, dolphins, etc. The men return to their village and spread word about Arakayu. After this encounter, the Shiwilu would visit Arakayu often and ask him for fish, which he would always give them. However, Arakayu remains firm in not letting anyone inside his house. One day, the chief of the Shiwilu invites Arakayu to come to their village on the main day of the carnival. Arakayu accepts the invitation and brings his wife with him. While the couple are dancing the *pandilla* (traditional dance), a group of wicked men decide to burn Arakayu's house. The men conjecture that, once homeless, Arakayu will move out of Pampayacu and they will have all the fish to themselves. This is a crucial moment in the story and, according to the narrator, the consequences affect the well-being of the Shiwilu up to this day.

(10) Nana nu'apasik ima di'serpidektullina'.
Nana nu'-apa-sik *ima di'ser-**pidek**-tu-llina'*
that be.so-CONT-PTCP.DS.3SG HSY burn-house-VM-NFI.3SG>3SG
'While that (the carnival celebration) was taking place, they set the house on fire.'

Once the celebration concludes, Arakayu and his wife return home only to find that their house has been burned down. Arakayu becomes extremely angry and, furious with rage, screams the following.

(11) "¿Kenmama'a'cha u'pidekta'mama'u'kusu' kua musu' nu'tapallenma'?"
kenmama' a'cha *u'-**pidek**-t-a'mama'u'kusu'* *kua musu'*
2PL EMPH.INT do.so-house-VM-NMLZ.2PL>1SG 1SG good
nu'-t-apa-llenma'
be.like-VM-CONT-NFI.1SG>2SPL
'Who the hell are you to do this to my house (lit. doing this to me with regard to my house), even though I treated you well?!' (Valenzuela 2012: 125)

In (11), the incorporation of *pidek* coincides with another instance of direct speech and, more importantly, begins the denouement of the story. Feeling very disappointed and upset, Arakayu decides to leave Pampayacu, as anticipated by the wicked men. However, he takes all the best fish and other river animals with him and makes the lakes dry up. In this way, Shiwilu oral tradition accounts for the relative scarcity of fish and the lack of highly valued river species in their territory. In closing the story, Shiwilu elders recall the events that led to Arakayu's departure with deep sorrow and console each other.

(12) a. "¿Ma'kin nu'tullinerkenmu'wa' chi?" tullina' taserpiku'lusa'.
ma'kin nu'-tu-llinerkenmu'wa' chi tu-llina'
why be.like-VM-NFI.3PL>1PL.I SURP.MASC say-NFI.3PL
taserpi=ku'=lusa'
old.man= DECSD=PL
'"Why did they (wicked men) do this to us?" the late old men said saddened.'

b. Tanna' nerpi'pu', kumarinenna'lek inpilli'iteklatanna', inmusha'itekla-tanna', wellekllina'.
t-anna' nerpi'pu' kumari=nenna'=lek
say-PTCP.SS.3PL sometimes *comadre*[8]=POSS.3PL=COM
*in-pilli'-**itekla**-t-anna' in-musha'-**itekla**-t-anna'*
REC-grab-hand-VM-PTCP.SS.3PL REC-kiss-hand-VM-PTCP.SS.3PL
wellek-llina'
cry-NFI.3PL
'Saying this, sometimes, with their *comadres* they would hold hands, kiss each other on the hands, and cry.' (Valenzuela 2012: 132)

In (12b) *itekla* 'hand' appears incorporated twice. Suffixation of *-tu* makes the inherently intransitive *pilli'*- become transitive (a patient object is added) and the inherently transitive *musha'*- become ditransitive (a locative object is added). Next, prefixation of the reciprocal *in-* takes place. Hence the translations 'hold hands' and 'kiss each other on the hand'. These actions, along with a somewhat formulaic dialogue, are part of what is known as the Shiwilu traditional greeting. The text portion above shows that they are also performed in other contexts.

The fourth and last type of incorporation contemplated in Mithun (1984) involves classifier nouns. While this exact construction is not available in Shiwilu, the incorporation of classifiers is common.

8 In this usage, the Spanish loan *comadre* translates as 'fellow Shiwilu women'.

4 Incorporation of Classifiers

Noun categorization devices have been given a significant amount of attention in Amazonian linguistics (a recent volume on the topic is Aikhenvald and Mihas 2019). Several languages of the region possess classifiers that appear in various morphosyntactic loci, including the verb (Aikhenvald 2000: 149–171, 204–240, 2012: 292–298).

4.1 *Classifiers in Shiwilu*

Shiwilu has a system of over twenty classifiers that combine with nouns, adjectives, demonstratives, quantifiers, interrogative words, and personal pronouns. Furthermore, Shiwilu classifiers may incorporate in the verb. But despite their ability to adhere to various syntactic hosts, Shiwilu classifiers are not grammatically mandatory in any of these contexts.

The semantic organization of Shiwilu classifiers is represented in Table 24.3. First, a distinction is made between animate and inanimate classifiers. Animate classifiers divide into female and male biological gender.[9] Inanimate classifiers are structured according to salient dimensionality, constitution, function, and arrangement. Not all nouns fall under the scope of a classifier, and there is no default classifier (Valenzuela 2016b, 2019a).

Most inanimate classifiers appear to be phonologically reduced versions of free-standing nouns and/or are formally identical to the inalienable, monosyllabic nouns alluded to in § 3.1.

4.2 *Classifier Incorporation*

Like noun incorporation, classifier incorporation is used to create new vocabulary or manage the presentation of information in discourse (Mithun 1994: 5025). The verbs offered below diachronically involve classifier incorporation; synchronically, alternative predicates without the classifier are non-existent. The lexicalizations in (13d)–(13e) contain the classifier *-dan*, which applies to manioc, the main crop of the Shiwilu people.

9 These classifiers exclusively apply to animates, whereas *-lanser* [CL.SKELETON] also applies to inanimates.

TABLE 24.3 Shiwilu classifier system (from Valenzuela 2019a)

PARAMETER				**CLASSIFIER**	**CATEGORY (GLOSS IN PARENTHESIS)**
ANIMACY	ANIMATE	SEX	FEMALE	**-lun**	female (**FEM**) *Shiwilu**lun*** 'Shiwilu woman'
			MALE	**-pen**	male (**MALE**) *Shiwilu**pen*** 'Shiwilu man'
	INANIMATE	DIMENSIONALITY	ONE-DIMENSIONAL (LONG)	**-na(n)**	long, rigid, wooden (**TRUNK**) *pentu**nan*** 'log used as a bridge'
				-la	long, not large, non-wooden (**BONE**) *pinte**lla*** 'cigarette'
				-llin	long, thin, flexible (**VINE**) *du**llin*** 'intestine'
			TWO-DIMENSIONAL (FLAT)	**-mek**	flat, thin, extended (**LEAF**) *ker'**mek*** 'manioc leaf'
				-tek	flat, used to cover or wrap (**SKIN**) *ket**chek*** 'manioc peel'
			THREE-DIMENSIONAL (ROUND, TUBULAR)	**-la**	round, small (**SEED**) *wise**kla*** 'Amazon grape'
				-pi	round, not small (**FRUIT**) *lawa'**pi*** 'jungle cacao fruit'
				-si	tubular (**CANE**) *illapa**si*** 'shotgun barrel'
				-pi	body, bulky entire object (**BODY**) *wa'na**pi*** 'metal object (car, airplane, radio)'
				-du'	bulky w/bumpy surface (**CORNCOB**) *kala**du'*** 'three corncobs, ice-cream bean fruits, war grenades'
				-u'pi	oval, bulky object like the bract of a banana tree (with an overhanging open petal) (**BRACT**)

TABLE 24.3 Shiwilu classifier system (*cont.*)

Parameter	Classifier	Category (gloss in parenthesis)
Constitution	**-dek**	liquid (**LIQUID**) *chiter'**dek*** 'corn drink'
	-lu'	powdery, pasty, land (**SOIL**) *kaset**llu'*** 'sugar'
	-lu'	meat, flesh (**MEAT**) *dekkana**lu'*** 'paca meat'
FUNCTION	**-dan**	elongated, thick tuber (**MANIOC**) *utek**dantu**-* 'harvest manioc'
	-dun	clothing (**CLOTHES**) *pi'pi'**yun**-* 'sew clothes'
DIMENSIONALITY AND CONSTITUTION	-lek	long, made of flesh (**PENIS**) *kala**lek*** 'three snakes, three eels'
	-lanser	skinny animal or person; branches of a dead tree (**SKELETON**) *widunalanser* 'old broom (made from a leafless bush)'
ARRANGEMENT	**-luwa**	elongated, wrapped in leaf, pressed, and tied w/vine fiber (**SHICANA**[10]) *chin**luwa*** 'dish made of salted small fish wrapped in leaf, pressed, tied w/vine fiber, and cooked in the fire'

(13) a. ka**lu'**- (tr.) [-lu' CL.MEAT] 'cook meat in broth or soup'
b. aka'**lu'**- (intr.) [-lu' CL.SOIL] 'mix clay with *apacharama*'[11]
c. dinpa**nan**- (intr.) [-nan CL.TREE.TRUNK] 'for a tree to fall (due to the wind)'
d. utek**dan**-tu- (intr.) [-dan CL.MANIOC] 'harvest manioc'
e. pau**dan**-tu- (tr.) [-dan CL.MANIOC] 'replant (a manioc garden)'

10 *Shicana* is the Spanish term for the Shiwilu dish *chinluwa*. The classifier *-luwa* applies to objects arranged in a similar fashion.

11 Tree bark that is burned, ground, and mixed with clay to make durable pottery.

In contrast, the following compounded verbs are analyzable; i.e., the stems can function as verbs without the classifier.

(14)	a. mu-**pen**-	['be good'-CL.MALE]	'be handsome (a man)'
	b. ñi-**la**-tu-	['exist'-CL.SEED-VM]	'bear a small fruit'
	c. peksa'-**dun**-	['wash'-CL.CLOTHES]	'wash clothes'
	d. pipek-**lu'**-	['carry.on.the.back'-CL.MEAT]	'carry meat on the back'
	e. pankuer-**llin**-tu-	['roll up'-CL.VINE-VM]	'make a skein'
	f. ma-**dek**-tu-	['catch'-CL.LIQUID-VM]	'collect manioc/corn beer'

A small set of compounded verbs consist of an intransitive or transitive stem, the incorporated classifier *-dek* (CL.LIQUID), and the locative applicative *-tu*.

(15)	a. chimi[n]-**dek**-tu-	['die'-CL.LIQUID-LOC.APPL]	'drown'
	b. ekkuan-**dek**-tu-	['spear'-CL.LIQUID-LOC.APPL]	'fish with arrow'
	c. a'-dan-**dek**-tu-	[CAUS-'enter'-CL.LIQUID-LOC.APPL]	'fish with basket'

In (15), the incorporated classifier is syntactically an object but semantically a location. Literally, these verbs translate as 'do x in the water/river.' However, they have undergone lexicalization and constitute the only way to convey the corresponding events.

Analogous complex verbs involving classifier incorporation and locative applicativization are present in the following extract, which brings us back to the story of Arakayu. After cursing the Shiwilu for having burned his house, Arakayu prepares to leave Pampayacu taking the most valued fish species with him. He jumps into the river with his wife, stands in the water, and, submerging himself, disappears laughing. The motivation for incorporating *-dek* might be that the location is evident from the context. But, crucially, these actions represent the resolution of the story.

(16) a. Sekkankatan indi'dektulli sadinlek.
sekkankat-an *in-di'-**dek**-tu-lli*
jump-PTCP.SS.3SG REF-throw-CL.LIQUID-LOC.APPL-NFI.3SG
sadin=lek
his.wife=COM
'Jumping up, he threw himself into the water with his wife.'

b. Wanersu' anudektullina'.
*Waner-su' anu-**dek**-tu-llina'*
stand-NMLZ fall-CL.LIQUID-LOC.APPL-NFI.3PL
'They fell into the water, standing.'

c. Yamer'apila'su'pi'la dankumer'apilalli.
yamer'-ap-il-a'su'=pi'la dankumer'-ap-ila-lli
laugh-CONT-PROG-NMLZ.3SG=same submerge-CONT-PROG-NFI.3SG
'As he was submerging himself in the water he laughed.'

d. Tuna'sik welli.
tuna'-sik wer-lli
become.silent-PTCP.DS.3SG get.lost-NFI.3SG
'Then it became silent and he disappeared.' (Valenzuela 2012: 126)

Let us close this section by examining (17), which contains two reflexive-marked verbs and incorporation of the classifier *-pi* (CL.BODY). The context is as follows. The Shiwilu organize a communal fishing excursion and two little brothers try to join it. However, since the children have the pox, they are rejected and sent away by the adults. As the boys walk away in tears, they come upon a man who asks them why they are crying. Learning about the incident, the man directs the children towards a stream with crystal-clear water and instructs them to drink from it, and then wash and rub their bodies with it.

(17) a. Nana iteklashapenma'lek inshen'anma' ukku'.
Nana itekla=sha=penma'=lek inshen-anma' uk-ku'
that hand=DIM=POSS.2PL=INSTR scoop-PTCP.SS.2PL drink-IMP.PL
'Scoop up this water with your little hands and drink it.'

b. Nu'anma' nanalek'i'la inpamu'piku', inpanka'piku'
*nu'anma' nana=lek=i'la in-pamu'-**pi**-ku'*
then.2PL that=INSTR=SAME REF-wash-CL.BODY-IMP.PL
*in-panka'-**pi**-ku'*
REF-rub-CL.BODY-IMP.PL
'With the same (water) wash and rub your bodies.'

c. "Nanek iñer asu' sa'la' apu'tetchun" itudekllima.
"nanek iñer asu' sa'la' apu'-t-etchun"
there all this pox put.away-VM-FUT.3SG
itu-dek-lli=ima
tell-3PL.O-NFI.3SG>3SG=HSY
'"Then the pox will go away completely", he told them.' (Valenzuela 2012: 111)

Interestingly, incorporated classifiers may be accompanied by derivational morphemes. This is shown in the next two sections.

5 Incorporation of the Deceased Marker =*ku'*

Kawapanan languages (and various genetically unrelated Amazonian languages (Valenzuela 2019b)) have a grammatical marker indicating that the animate entity to which it applies has ceased to exist at the time of utterance or at another point in time established in the discourse. In Shiwilu and Shawi this deceased marker is =*ku'* (Valenzuela 2011b). Especially when referring to a dead human, the addition of =*ku'* is fairly consistent in spontaneous speech and elicitation. Consider the following text portion, where the speaker blames herself for the imminent loss of Shiwilu traditional culture.

(18) a. Kui'na usha'wanek wilaweklusa' a'lek'inpu'dek'amu
kua=i'na usha'-wan-lek wila=wek=lusa'
1SG=FOC guilt-HAVE-NFI.1SG child=POSS.1SG=PL
a'-lek-inpu'-dek-amu
CAUS-ask-NEG-3PL.O-PTCP.SS.1SG
'It's me who is to blame for not teaching my children'

b. iñer ñinchita'kudeksu' napi'ku'lusa'ki,
*iñer ñinchi-t-a'kudeksu' napi'=**ku'**=lusa'=ki*
all know-VM-NMLZ.1PL.E long.ago=DECSD=PL=OBL
'everything we know of the elders who have already passed,'

c. kaikku'lusa'ki,
*kaik=**ku'**=lusa'=ki*
woman's.sister=DECSD=PL=OBL
'of the women already dead,'

d. inetchaku'lusa'ki
*inetcha=**ku'**=lusa'=ki*
paternal.aunt=DECSD=PL=OBL
'of the late (paternal) aunts.'

e. Taker'apilallina' iñer.
taker-ap-ila-llina' *iñer*
die.out-CONT-PROG-NFI.3PL all
'Everyone is dying off.' (Valenzuela 2012: 83)

The deceased marker may also apply to animals and even some plants: *kusher=ku'* 'the pig now dead', *lalansha'=ku'* 'the orange tree now dead'.

It must be clarified that *=ku'* is not a nominal tense marker, comparable to those found in several languages spoken in Amazonia and elsewhere (Aikhenvald 2003: 183–188, 2012: 158–163; Mihas 2014; Rodrigues and Cabral 2012: 521; Campbell 2012: 285–288; Nordlinger and Sadler 2004; among others). This morpheme does not provide any temporal (aspectual/modal/evidential) information, is not productive across different types of nouns or other NP constituents, and is not in a paradigmatic relationship with morphemes coding temporal values. Therefore, *=ku'* cannot be used in expressions like 'my ex-husband', 'my husband who is not present at the moment', 'a dog that was mine but is not anymore', 'a former canoe that is now destroyed, lost or stolen', etc.

At first sight, the deceased marker resembles the classifiers *-lun* (CL.FEM) and *-pen* (CL.MALE):[12] it is a monosyllabic bound root that specifies a property of animate entities, it occurs in multiple morphosyntactic environments, and can incorporate in the verb. Consider (19), where *=ku'* combines with various types of hosts.

(19) a. ami=ku'=lusa' 'late grandmother/old woman'
b. Antuñu=ku' 'the late Antonio'
c. asu'=ku' / nana=ku' 'this / that dead entity'
d. ínkatu'=ku'=lusa' 'four dead entities'
e. dudinpu'=ku'=lusa' 'different types of dead entities'
f. aperku'tek=ku' 'the stingy one (now dead)'
g. enpu'du=ku'=lusa' 'how many dead entities?'

12 Chipewyan (Athabaskan) has a classifier that applies to dead beings (Aikhenvald 2000: 298).

Nonetheless, the deceased marker and classifiers differ in important respects. Crucially, they occupy different positions in the NP, as shown below.

(20) Ñiñi'walunshawekku' malek enpu'nipa' welleklek.

*ñiñi'wa-**lun**-sha=wek=**ku'***	*malek*	*enpu'nipa'*	*wellek-lek*
dog-CL.FEM-DIM=POSS.1SG=DECSD	because.of	much	cry-NFI.1SG

'I cried a lot for my little female dog (now dead).' (Valenzuela et al. 2013: =*ku'*)

Furthermore, only the classifiers can serve an agreement function or be exploited to track participants in discourse (Valenzuela 2016b). =*ku'* may also attach to proper names ((19b)), whereas classifiers cannot.[13]

The deceased marker may be added to different types of verbs: inactive intransitive (21a–b), active intransitive (21c–f), and transitive (21g–h, where it may refer to the A or the O).

(21)

a.	uka-ku'-lli	['have.fever'-DECSD-NFI.3SG]	'he/she (now dead) had fever'
b.	susu'-ku'lli	['grow.up'-DECSD-NFI.3SG]	'he/she (now dead) grew up'
c.	wellek-ku'-lli	['cry'-DECSD-NFI.3SG]	'he/she (now dead) cried'
d.	tu-ku'-lli	['say'-DECSD-NFI.3SG]	'he/she (now dead) said'
e.	tekka'-ku'-lli	['run'-DECSD-NFI.3SG]	'he/she (now dead) ran'
f.	di'-ku'-lli	['kill'-DECSD-NFI.3SG]	'he/she (now dead) killed'
g.	ka'-ku'-lli	['eat'-DECSD-NFI.3SG>3SG]	'he/she (now dead) ate'
h.	lli'-ku'-lek	['see'-DECSD-NFI.1SG>3SG]	'I saw him/her (now dead)'

The next verb forms contain an animate classifier alongside the deceased marker.

(22) a. *uka-**pen-ku'**-lli*
have.fever-CL.MALE-DECSD-NFI.3SG
'the late man had fever'

b. *di'-**lun-ku'**-lli*
kill-CL.FEM-DECSD-NFI.3SG
'the late woman killed (someone)'

13 Though very rare, a language may incorporate proper names (Johns 2017: 18).

In sum, a Shiwilu verb may carry the deceased marker either by itself or in combination with a coreferential animate classifier.

6 Nominal Incorporation and Syntactic Relations

There is a very robust crosslinguistic tendency for incorporated nouns and classifiers to encode non-agentive participants serving as clausal objects or inactive intransitive subjects; additionally, they may correspond to obliques like locative or instrumental. Conversely, it is exceptional for incorporated items to refer to active intransitive subjects or transitive subjects (Mithun 1984: 865; Gerdts 1998: 87; Aikhenvald 2000: 162, 2012: 196, 2017: 378; among others). Notably, this syntactic restriction does not apply to Shiwilu classifier incorporation constructions (Valenzuela 2016b, 2019a).

In (23)–(24) below, inanimate and animate classifiers act as the subjects of active intransitive verbs. The root *di'-* in (24) is intransitive; i.e., the clause cannot have an overt object. The transitive version is *di'-tu-* (see (27)).

(23) Tekka'deklli La'pir'.
*tekka'-**dek**-lli* *La'pir'*
run-CL.LIQUID-NFI.3SG Rumiyacu.river
'The Rumiyacu river has a torrential flow (Lit. 'runs').' (Valenzuela 2019a: 137)

(24) Di'penñi.
*di'-**pen**-lli*
kill-CL.MALE-NFI.3SG
'The man has killed (someone).'

When a single classifier incorporates into a transitive stem, its interpretation as either O or A depends on different factors such as verb semantics, animacy, linguistic and non-linguistic contexts, and speech-act participants' knowledge of the world (Valenzuela 2016b: 368). The next causative expression contains the base *chinku'-* 'cough'. Since the causee must be animate, the incorporated classifier, being inanimate, can only be read as the causer and syntactic A.

(25) A'-chinku'lu'palli.
*a'-chinku'-**lu'**-pa-lli.*
CAUS-cough-CL.SOIL-CONT-NFI.3SG>3SG
'The dust is making him/her cough.' (Valenzuela 2019a: 138)

The expression in (26) is potentially ambiguous since *-mek* may be interpreted as either A or O.

(26) Sekwa'meklli.
*sekwa'-**mek**=lli*
scratch-CL.LEAF-NFI.3SG>3SG
'She/he scratched the leaf.' / 'She/he was scratched by the leaf.' (e.g., the leaf has tiny thorns) (Valenzuela 2019a: 138)

Example (27) contains the transitive verb *di'-tu-* 'kill'. Interestingly, the incorporated animate classifier is necessarily interpreted as realizing the A function.

(27) Di'luntullen.
*di'-**lun**-tu-llen*
kill-CL.FEM-VM-NFI.1SG>2SG
'I (woman) killed you' (talking to a deceased person). / *'I killed you (woman).' (Valenzuela 2019a: 137)

The data in (28) belongs to a narrative from the late 1950s, about a boy who kills a black jaguar. The spear (*rejón* in Spanish) functions as clausal A and the incorporated classifier (*-nan* CL.TRUNK) is selected in semantic agreement with it.

(28) Da'suketñantapilalli rejón.
*da'-suker'-**nan**-tu-apa-ila-lli* *rejón*
ENTERING-pierce-CL.TRUNK-VM-CONT-OUT-NFI.3SG>3SG spear
'The spear pierced (the black jaguar's throat) and penetrated it completely.' (Bendor-Samuel 1981[1958]: 155, in Valenzuela 2019a: 139)

It is possible for two different classifiers to incorporate in a single transitive verb,[14] as illustrated by (29). *Tekkua-* 'be afraid' becomes transitive after taking *-tu*. This suffix is preceded by the classifier representing the O and followed by the one representing the A. (The object NP contains a second instance of *-tek* (CL.SKIN), this time serving a derivational function: *ishek* 'bat' > *ishek-tek* 'vampire'.)

14 These data, though elicited, were carefully confirmed by different native speakers and by the same speakers on separate occasions. Nevertheless, not all speakers find expressions with two incorporated classifiers grammatical (Valenzuela 2016a: 335).

(29) Tekkuatektuluñina' ishektek asu' wilalunlusa'.
*tekkua-**tek**-tu-**lun**-llina'* *ishek-tek* *asu'*
fear-CL.SKIN-VM-CL.FEM-NFI.3PL>3SG bat-CL.SKIN this
wila-lun=lusa'
child-CL.FEM=PL
'These young girls fear vampires.' (Valenzuela 2019a: 140)

Similarly, in (30) below the intransitive *di'ser'-* 'burn' increases its valency after the suffixation of *-tu*. However, this time the incorporated items are a noun and a classifier. The noun corresponds to the O and precedes *-tu;* the classifier corresponds to the A and occurs after *-tu*. The diminutive suffix accompanying the classifier adds a mocking overtone to the expression.

(30) Di'setpidektupenchañina'.
*di'ser'-**pidek**-tu-**pen**-sha-llina'*
burn-house-VM-CL.MALE-DIM-NFI.3PL>3SG
'The little men burned the house.' (with mocking overtone) (Valenzuela 2019a: 140)

In (31), *-tu* functions as locative applicative. The classifier *-mek* (CL.LEAF) metonymically refers to the jungle and serves as O. The male classifier alongside the deceased marker refer to the A. Unexpectedly, both classifiers precede *-tu*.

(31) Tekka'mekpenku'tulli.
*tekka'-mek-**pen-ku'**-tu-lli*
run-CL.LEAF-CL.MALE-DECSD-LOC.APPL-NFI.3SG>3SG
'The late man ran in the jungle.'

Unlike classifiers and the deceased marker, incorporated nouns serving as syntactic A have not (so far) been attested.

7 Conclusions and Final Remarks

Noun incorporation has been attested in numerous Amazonian languages belonging to distinct genetic assemblages including Arawak, Carib, Tupían, Yanomami, Bora, and Takanan (Aikhenvald 2012, 2017). The present study puts Kawapanan on the map of Amazonian languages displaying this interesting feature and expands our knowledge of how incorporation is realized in language. These findings also contribute to a better characterization of the languages from the Andes-Amazonia transitional zone, where noun incorporation seems uncommon. In fact, in a chapter on polysynthetic languages of Lowland Amazonia Aikhenvald (2017: 297) reports that Jivaroan and Urarina, the two languages in her survey that are geographically closest to Kawapanan, lack productive incorporation of any sort. As mentioned in § 1, incorporation is absent in the neighboring Quechuan languages.

Aikhenvald (2012: 194–197) notes that most Amazonian languages only incorporate inalienably possessed nouns, which most often correspond to body parts. Furthermore, the incorporated noun precedes the verb root, even in dominantly suffixing languages. Shiwilu deviates from these generalizations. First, verbs can host nouns that do not convey a body part, such as house, clothes, money, canoe, name, language, and village. One may be argue, nonetheless, that these items semantically imply some type of 'owner'. Secondly, incorporated nouns immediately follow the verb stem, preceding valency-affecting suffixes. Therefore, in compounded verbs the modifier (the noun) follows its head (the verb), while the opposite order is predominant in compounded nouns. All incorporated nouns in the data have inanimate referents; this agrees with the observation that nouns lower in animacy incorporate more easily due to the less central role they play in discourse. Incorporated nouns are almost always realized in full form, even when derived or compounded. The host verb can be transitive or inactive intransitive and the incorporated noun represents the O, S, or a sort of oblique. Noun incorporation does not diminish the clause valency.

Noun and classifier incorporation serve two main purposes: forming new vocabulary for nameworthy concepts and providing speakers with alternative expressions to help regulate the information in discourse (Mithun 1984, 1986, 1994). A function more specific to Shiwilu might be adding agility and excitement to a narrative, since this grammatical strategy coincides with the points of highest tension and drama.

Of special typological interest is the fact that incorporated classifiers, inanimate and animate, can function as clausal O, S (inactive or active), and even A; this characteristic is very rarely attested in the world's languages. Additionally, a transitive verb may host two classifiers, or a noun and a classifier; the O necessarily precedes the A.

Finally, it was shown that the morpheme *=ku'*, indicating that the entity to which it applies has ceased to exist, also incorporates in the verb, either by itself or alongside a coreferential animate classifier. Like classifiers, *=ku'* assumes different syntactic functions when joining the verb, including active intransitive subject and transitive subject.

Acknowledgements

I am truly happy and honored to take part in this Festchrift for Sasha. She is not only a world-renowned linguist from whose work I learn, but has always shown me generosity and kindness. The data in this paper were collected by the present author, between 2007 and 2018, thanks to funds from the National Science Foundation (# 0853285) and Chapman University. Some of the examples come from texts published in Valenzuela (2012) or appear in a Shiwilu dictionary (Valenzuela et al. 2013). I am grateful to the various Shiwilu speakers who generously shared their language with me, especially Mrs. Emérita Guerra Acho, Mrs. Julia Inuma Inuma, Mr. Meneleo Careajano Chota, and Mr. Fernando Lachuma Cachique. All remaining shortcomings are my sole responsibility.

References

Adelaar W.F.H. with Pieter C. Muysken (2004). *The languages of the Andes*. Cambridge: Cambridge University Press.

Aikhenvald, Alexandra Y. (2000). *Classifiers: A Typology of Noun Categorization Devices*. Oxford: Oxford University Press.

Aikhenvald, Alexandra Y. (2003). *A Grammar of Tariana, from Northwest Amazonia*. Cambridge and New York: Cambridge University Press.

Aikhenvald, Alexandra Y. (2007). Typological dimensions in word formation. In Timothy Shopen (ed.), *Language Typology and Syntactic Description, Vol. III: Grammatical Categories and the Lexicon*, 1–65. Cambridge: Cambridge University Press.

Aikhenvald, Alexandra Y. (2012). *The languages of the Amazon*. Oxford: Oxford University Press.

Aikhenvald, Alexandra Y. (2017). Polysynthetic structures of Lowland Amazonia. In Michael Fortescue, Marianne Mithun and Nicholas Evans (eds.), *The Oxford Handbook of Polysynthesis*, 284–311. Oxford: Oxford University Press.

Aikhenvald, Alexandra Y. and Elena Mihas (eds.) (2019). *Genders and classifiers, a cross-linguistic typology*. Oxford: Oxford University Press.

Bendor-Samuel, John T. (1981[1958]). *The structure and function of the verbal piece in the Jebero language*. Lima: Ministerio de Educación and ILV.

Bendor-Samuel, John T. (n.d.). Fieldnotes. Ms.

Campbell, Lyle (2012). Typological characteristics of South American indigenous languages. In Lyle Campbell and Verónica Grondona (eds.), *The Indigenous languages of South America, A comprehensive guide*, 285–288. Berlin: Mouton de Gruyter.

De Reuse, Willem (1994). Noun incorporation. In R. Asher (ed.), *Encyclopedia of Language and Linguistics*, Vol. 5, 2842–2847. Oxford: Pergamon Press.

Dixon, R.M.W. and Alexandra Y. Aikhenvald (1999). Introduction. In R.M.W. Dixon and Alexandra Y. Aikhenvald (eds.), *The Amazonian Languages*, 1–21. Cambridge: Cambridge University Press.

Dryer, Matthew S. (2007). Word order. In Timothy Shopen (ed.), *Language Typology and Syntactic Description, Vol. 1: Clause Structure*, 61–131. Second edition. Cambridge: Cambridge University Press.

Gerdts, Donna B. (1998). Incorporation. In Andrew Spencer and Arnold Zwicky (eds.), *The Handbook of Morphology*, 84–100. Oxford, UK: Basil Blackwell.

Gerds, Donna B. and Stephen Marlett (2008). Introduction: The Form and Function of Denominal Verb Constructions. Special Issue on Denominal Verbs in Languages of the Americas. *International Journal of American Linguistics* 74 (4): 409–422.

Hart, Helen (1988). *Diccionario chayahuita-castellano (Canponanquë nisha nisha nonacaso')*. Yarinacocha: Ministerio de Educación and Instituto Lingüístico de Verano.

Johns, Alana (2017). Noun incorporation. In Martin Everaert and Henk C. Riemsdijk (eds.), *The Wiley Blackwell Companion to Syntax, Second Edition*. John Wiley & Sons, Inc. https://doi.org/10.1002/9781118358733.wbsyncom093

Mihas, Elena (2014). Nominal and verbal temporal morphology in Ashéninka Perené (Arawak). *Acta Linguistica Hafniensia* 45 (1): 1–30. http://dx.doi.org/10.1080/03740463.2014.883724

Mithun, Marianne (1984). The evolution of noun incorporation. *Language* 60 (4): 847–895.

Mithun, Marianne (1986). On the nature of noun incorporation. *Language* 62 (1): 32–38.

Mithun, Marianne (1994). Word-formation: Incorporation. In R.E. Asher (ed.), *The Encyclopedia of Language and Linguistics*, Vol. 9, 5024–5026. Oxford: Pergamon.

Mithun, Marianne (2009). Polysynthesis in the Arctic. In Marc-Antoine Mahieu and Nicole Tersis (eds.), *Variations on Polysynthesis: The Eskimo-Aleut Languages*, 3–17. Amsterdam: John Benjamins.

Nordlinger, Rachel and Louisa Sadler (2004). Nominal tense marking in crosslinguistic perspective. *Language* 80 (4): 776–806.

Rivet, Pierre and Constant Tastevin (1931). Nouvelle contribution à l'étude du groupe Kahuapana. *International Journal of American Linguistics* 6: 227–271.

Rodrigues, Aryon Dall'Igna and Ana Suelly Arruda Câmara Cabral (2012). Tupían. In Lyle Campbell and Verónica Grondona (eds.), *The Indigenous languages of South America, A comprehensive guide*, 495–574. Berlin: Mouton de Gruyter.

Valenzuela, Pilar (2010). Ethnic-racial reclassification and language revitalization among the Shiwilu from Peruvian Amazonia. *International Journal of the Sociology of Language* 202: 117–130.

Valenzuela, Pilar (2011a). Argument Encoding and Pragmatic Marking of the Transitive Subject in Shiwilu (Kawapanan). *International Journal of American Linguistics* 77: 91–120.

Valenzuela, Pilar (2011b). Contribuciones para la reconstrucción del proto-cahuapana: Comparación léxica y gramatical de las lenguas jebero y chayahuita. In W.F.H. Adelaar, P. Valenzuela and R. Zariquiey (eds.), *Estudios en lenguas andinas y amazónicas. Homenaje a Rodolfo Cerrón-Palomino*, 271–304. Lima: PUCP.

Valenzuela, Pilar (2012). *Voces Shiwilu: 400 Años de Resistencia Lingüística en Jeberos.* Lima: Fondo Editorial Pontificia Universidad Católica del Perú.

Valenzuela, Pilar (2015). ¿Qué tan "amazónicas" son las lenguas kawapana? Rasgos centro-andinos y evidencia para una posible sub-área lingüística. *Lexis* 39 (1): 5–56.

Valenzuela, Pilar (2016a). "Simple" and "Double" Applicatives in Shiwilu (Kawapanan). *Studies in Language* 40 (3): 513–550.

Valenzuela, Pilar (2016b). Classifiers in Shiwilu (Kawapanan) in Northwestern Amazonian Perspective. *Anthropological Linguistics* 58 (4): 333–380.

Valenzuela, Pilar (2018). Difusión de rasgos andinos y elementos para una sub-área lingüística intermedia Andes-Amazonia en el norte del Perú. In Alejandra Regúnaga, Silvia Spinelli and María Emilia Orden (eds.), *IV Encuentro Internacional de Lenguas Indígenas Americanas. Libro de Actas*, 657–684. Santa Rosa, Argentina: Universidad Nacional de la Pampa.

Valenzuela, Pilar (2019a). Classifiers in Shiwilu (Kawapanan): Exploring Typologically Salient Properties. Alexandra Aikhenvald and Elena Mihas (eds.), *Genders and classifiers, a cross-linguistic typology*, 67–102. Oxford: Oxford University Press.

Valenzuela, Pilar (2019b). Towards an Andes-Amazonia linguistic sub-area in the Marañón and Huallaga river basins. 22nd Workshop on American Languages, University of California Santa Barbara, May 10–11, 2019.

Valenzuela, Pilar, Meneleo Careajano, Emérita Guerra, Julia Inuma and Fernando Lachuma (2013). *Kirka' Llawer'lla'la' Ñak: Diccionario Shiwilu-Castellano y Castellano-Shiwilu.* Lima: Federación de Comunidades Nativas de Jeberos.

CHAPTER 25

Utilitarian versus Intellectualist Explanations of Lexical Content: A False Dichotomy

N.J. Enfield

Languages vary widely in the degree to which their speakers can name biological distinctions in nature. Members of cultivator societies are able to name up to 500 distinct plant species, while urban dwellers often struggle to name a dozen. How can we explain the depth and breadth of linguistic nomenclature in specific lexical domains? Experts agree that the explanation relates to the cultural context of a language, but in a classic debate in cognitive anthropology, two hypotheses are contrasted. A "utilitarian" view (after Eugene Hunn) holds that people will name distinctions and entities that are culturally/practically useful to them, while an "intellectualist" view (after Brent Berlin) holds that people are intellectually engaged with perceptual and other distinctions that the natural world reveals, and hence will name those distinctions, irrespective of their utility. In this chapter I will argue that these two positions are not in competition. One obvious reason is that they can both be true. More interesting, though, is the need to reframe the debate as being not about the utility or otherwise of the referents (such as various tree species) but the utility *of the words for* those referents. This important distinction will be explicated with reference to field work with speakers of languages in upland Laos.

Like so many forest dwellers worldwide, speakers of the Kri language of Mrkaa Village, a network of hamlets dotted along the snaking Nam Noy River in a remote hilltop valley of Central Laos, have extensive knowledge of the biodiversity of their surroundings.[1] For Kri speakers, the rainforest is their source of food and hardware, and their transport network.

Mrkaa is located deep within the tropical Northern Annamites Rain Forests area, one of the World Wildlife Fund's Global 200 most outstanding and representative areas of biodiversity.[2] During my early fieldwork with Mrkaa speakers

1 Enfield 2009, Zuckerman and Enfield 2021.

2 https://www.worldwildlife.org/ecoregions/im0136. The Northern Annamites Rain Forests area is one of the 867 terrestrial ecoregions recognized by the World Wide Fund for Nature (WWF) (ecoregion code IM0136; ADB/UNEP 2004:68–69), and one of the 'Global 200' subset of ecoregions that are 'outstanding examples of biodiversity' in the world (ADB/UNEP

© N.J. ENFIELD, 2022 | DOI:10.1163/9789004510395_026

I set out to elicit terms for trees and plants. In a single session, I was able to note more than two hundred distinct timber and bamboo species. I found that all Kri speakers—including children—have extensive vocabularies for the many biological distinctions found in their immediate environment: not just the plants but also the fish, reptiles, birds, and insects.

The Kri are typical of many human groups whose lifestyles involve cultivation of plants and close proximity to nature in everyday life.[3] The Warnindhilyagwa people of Groote Eylandt, a low-lying island in the Gulf of Carpentaria off the northeastern tip of Australia's Northern Territory, traditionally engaged in a hunter-gatherer lifestyle. Their considerable knowledge of the plant ecology is encoded in their language, Anindilyakwa, which has at least 199 terms for distinct generic plant taxa (Waddy 1988). On the northwestern plateau along the Columbia River and its tributaries in the northwest of the United States, speakers of the Sahaptin language—also practising a hunter-gatherer livelihood—have at least 213 labels for generic plant taxa (Hunn 1982). These examples are typical of indigenous hunter-gatherer peoples around the world. The mean number of generic plant labels in these languages is around 200, ranging from 137 terms in Lillooet, spoken on the Fraser River in British Columbia, to 310 terms in Seri, an indigenous language of the Gulf of California in Sonora, Mexico.

Two hundred words for plant species is a lot compared to the average urban-dwelling English speaker but it is less than half the size of the vocabularies for plants found in languages spoken by traditional cultivator peoples.[4] In riverine villages straddling the thickly forested borderlands of French Guiana and Brazil, speakers of the Wayampí language have at least 516 generic plant terms. This is around the global average plant vocabulary size for cultivator peoples (Grenand 1980). An even greater number of words for plants is found in the Aguarana language, spoken along the Marañón River—the source of the Amazon—in northern Peru. Aguarana has at least 598 terms for gen-

p72). ADB/UNEP, 2004. *Greater Mekong Subregion Atlas of the Environment.* Asian Development Bank (ADB), Manila, Phillipines, and United Nations Environment Programme (UNEP) Regional Resources Centre for Asia and the Pacific, Pathumthani, Thailand. Manila/Pathumthani: ADB/UNEP.

3 Information on numbers of generic taxa in cited languages is drawn from Berlin (1992: 98–100). These data should be treated with the usual caution reserved for any linguistic data, dependent as we are on field researchers' empirical and analytic skills, standards, and biases.

4 The following data are from Berlin (1992: 96 ff.). Claude Levi-Strauss in *The Savage Mind* (1966: 153–154) noticed that in reports of traditional peoples' knowledge of biology and names for species and varieties, that there was a tendency for people to have "in the order of several hundred" names.

eric plants (Berlin 1976). Some cultivator peoples have fewer labels than this, though hardly less impressively: Quechua speakers in Peru were found to have 238 terms (Felger and Moser 1985; this overlaps with the top of the range of terms among hunter-gatherer peoples). And speakers of Ndumba, living on the northern slopes of Mount Piora in the rugged Kratke Ranges in the Eastern Highlands Province of Papua New Guinea, have at least 385 generic plant terms in their language (Hays 1974). Towards the high end of the scale, there is Hanunóo, an indigenous language of the south of Mindoro Island in the Philippines. Hanunóo has an established total of 956 generic plant terms. And in the Ifugao language of northern Luzon, also in the Philippines, legendary anthropologist Harold Conklin described more than two thousand separate words for distinct plant types.

We can contrast these examples with the most impoverished known human vocabularies for natural kinds. Urban dwellers in industrialized societies typically know only a handful of plant names, and often aren't even able to identify the plants if they see them. A Mayan child has a solid capacity to name nature with far greater breadth and accuracy than the average urban US adult.[5] It is natural to wonder: Why do speakers of languages like Kri in Mrkaa have so many words for types of plants? But this question betrays a certain perspective. We think that Kri speakers know 'so many' words for types of plants because we compare them to a suburban dweller from afar. But relative to the full extent of diversity that exists in their environment, they actually only label a small subset. So, we could just as well ask: Why do they have so *few* words? There are nearly five thousand scientifically documented vascular plants in Laos, and there are well over a thousand in the province of Khammouan, where Mrkaa is situated.[6] There are some sixty thousand known tree species in the world and nearly four hundred thousand vascular plants.[7] Yet few languages name more than a few hundred. Why do people have words for just a subset of the plant life in their environment? And why just *those* plants and not others? One answer—which has been suggested by the anthropologist Brent Berlin—is that people focus on the aspects of nature that we find most striking or noticeable, the aspects that most attract our attention. Different species look different to

5 Not only do urban dwellers know a small number of plants, they also work at a coarser level of distinction; the other question is which level should be treated as 'basic'; "instead of maple and trout, Rosch et al. found that tree and fish operated as basic-level categories for American college students". (Atran and Medin 2008:102 and *passim*).

6 Newman et al. (2007: 4–5).

7 Beech et al. (2017). For all known species see Christenhusz and Byng (2016). For Laos, see Newman et al. (2007) and the 2017 report released by researchers at the Royal Botanic Gardens, Kew, in the United Kingdom: https://stateoftheworldsplants.org/2017/.

us in obvious ways. There are perceptible 'discontinuities' in natural systems. These forms of structure guide our attention to certain distinctions that are found in the world and not others. This is the idea behind Berlin's 'intellectualist hypothesis', the contention that words exist because people have an intellectual interest in the things that those words label (and not necessarily because people have any practical interest in the thing named).

A similar claim that the underlying perceptual structure of the world can guide the selection of distinctions in reality for naming comes from the visual domain of colour. The smooth and continuous gradation of colours in a rainbow suggests that there are no natural points of 'discontinuity' between colours—like the joints in a body—that could lead different languages to have similar naming systems. But we now know that languages are not free to divide up the colour space in unlimited or arbitrary ways. There is, of course, a range of types of system for colour naming. In the Dani language of the Biliem Valley of the tropical Western Highlands of Irian Jaya, Indonesian New Guinea, speakers have the leanest possible lexicon for naming colours: two words, *mili* and *mola*. The word *mili* refers to the 'cool' shades: black, green, blue, or any shade in between. *Mola* is 'warm': white, red, yellow. Many languages around the world have this kind of two-term system for labelling colour. At the other end of the scale, there are languages, for example Italian, that have up to twelve basic words that divide the colour spectrum more finely: *verde* 'green', *azzurro* 'light blue', *viola* 'purple', *blu* 'dark blue', *rosa* 'pink', *giallo* 'yellow', *marrone* 'brown', *arancione* 'orange', *rosso* 'red', *bianco* 'white', *grigio* 'grey', and *nero* 'black'.

Research on colour systems has found that between the extremes of a two-term and a twelve-term system, there is a limited set of possible systems for naming colour (Kay and Maffi 1999). Comparing languages to the simplest two-term system found in Dani, Brent Berlin and Paul Kay famously found that when a language divides the colour space more finely than the simplest two-way divide between warm (white/red/yellow) and cool (black/green/blue), it will do so in a constrained and predictable way. Berlin and Kay described this as a system of evolutionary stages, from Stage I to Stage V (see Kay et al. 1997).

The Dani language, with its two basic colour words meaning white/red/yellow and black/green/blue, is an example of a Stage I language.[8] A stage II language, for example the Ejagham language of Nigeria and Cameroon, builds on this by splitting one of the two categories. Ejagham has a black/green/blue category like Dani but splits the warm category into two: white versus red/yellow.

8 This section with data from languages at the various stages draws on Kay et al. (1997: 37 ff.).

(1) *Ejagham basic colour terms*
ébáré 'white'
ébí 'red/yellow'
ényàgà 'black/green/blue'

The Kwerba language, spoken in the Upper Tor River area of Irian Jaya, is a Stage III system. It has a further split, dividing the red/yellow category into red and yellow (while retaining the compound black/green/blue term):

(2) *Kwerba basic colour terms*
əsiram 'white'
nokonim 'red'
kainanesɛnum 'yellow'
icɛm 'black/green/blue'

The Sirionó language, spoken in the eastern Beni and northwestern Santa Cruz departments of the Bolivian lowlands, is a Stage IV language. It has distinct terms for four fundamental colour categories: white, red, yellow, and black. In this system, the black/green/blue part of the colour space—labelled by a single term in the Kwerba language system—is split into two terms, one for black, the other for the green-blue composite:

(3) *Sirionó basic colour terms*
eshĩ 'white'
eɨrẽɨ̃ 'red'
echo 'yellow'
erondeɨ 'black'
eruba 'green/blue'

Martu-Wangka, spoken in the Western Desert region of Western Australia, is also a Stage IV language, but black/green/blue is split in the other direction, into green versus black/blue:

(4) *Martu-Wangka basic colour terms*
piila-piila 'white'
miji-miji 'red'
karntawarra 'yellow'
yukuri-yukuri 'green'
maru-maru 'black/blue'

Kalam, a Trans-New-Guinea language spoken in the Hagen District of the Western New Guinea Highlands, has a Stage V system, in which the white/red/yellow and black/blue/green spaces are fully split into distinct categories. The result is distinct words for each of the six fundamental colour categories:

(5) *Kalam basic colour terms*

tund	'white'
likañ	'red'
walin	'yellow'
minj-kimemb	'green'
muk	'blue'
mosimb	'black'

Many languages with Stage V systems have more than these six terms. In English, for example, the eleven basic colour terms include the same six fundamental colour categories found in Kalam, along with five secondary terms: *brown, purple, pink, orange, grey*.

There is a lot more to the linguistics of colour reference in the world's languages than this simple stepwise set of distinctions between types of languages from stages I–V. Hundreds of studies of languages around the world have honed and challenged our understanding of the possible kinds of colour system, and these studies have presented counterexamples and refinements to the generalisations just given. Of course, these rarefied systems of basic colour terms contain only a small number of the many words that people can use when talking about colour. English has many words for highly specific colours beyond the eleven just mentioned. We have words like *fuchsia, teal*, and *alizarine*. We can refine our descriptions of colour with phrases like *dark red* or *sky blue*. And we can appeal to common knowledge of the colours that things typically have; e.g., *fire engine red*. But these words are not 'basic' in a technical sense (i.e., being morphologically simple, frequently used, known by all speakers, with agreed-upon reference, etc.).

Going beyond the basic colour terms, there are special situations in which people may use dozens if not hundreds of distinct words for colours, for example in commercial paints, but even allowing non-basic terms, and even allowing the highly specialised vocabulary of the paint industry, the distinctions that languages make in the colour space are extremely small in comparison to the well over two million distinctions in colour that the human eye can discern. Even when we include these highly specialised, technical vocabularies, the total inventory of colour terms in use makes less than a tenth of one percent of the discernible distinctions in colour that the human visual system can make. The everyday basic vocabulary that most people use will be one hundred times less than that again.

The way that humans perceive colour is a crucial part of this story. For humans, colour isn't really that smooth gradient we learn about in the colour spectrum. In human colour perception, we experience certain hues as focal. There is a broad range of colours that can fit the description of *red*, but within that range we can pick out 'real red', something like the colour of arterial blood or a fire engine. The focal nature of certain colours and not others is arguably a basis for the same underlying mechanism of naming that we saw in relation to biological classification earlier. Following the 'intellectualist' hypothesis of naming, the idea would be that because certain colours stand out better to us, we are therefore more likely to be interested in naming them.

The aspects of reality we have considered so far are things we can see. What about a more subjective, less tangible domain? Let's look at words for smells. If European languages are any guide, odours are more difficult to capture in words than experiences in any of the other senses. Researchers have long argued that olfactory abstraction is impossible, and that humans are poor at naming and identifying odours. An online research resource titled the *Cabinet of Grammatical Rarities* published by linguist Frans Plank says that it's hard to find a good vocabulary for smells in any language. But this conclusion has been based on a skewed sample of languages, in which languages like English are over-represented—that is, languages in which odours appear to defy description. English speakers have only a few vague everyday expressions that refer to smells. Possibly the only dedicated, abstract forms of basic reference to odour in English are *It smells* and *It stinks*. These are both extremely broad in meaning, and they both refer to a bad smell of some kind. For good smells, we have the word *fragrant*, but it is not a basic term. Normally, we just say that something *smells good*. And mostly, when we talk about odours, we use metaphors (e.g., extending from flavours such as sweet or minty) or we construct wordy, non-basic descriptions using reference to concrete things that have the smell in question (*smells like a wet dog, old socks, roses, fresh apple pie*, and so on).

But not all languages are like this (see Wnuk et al. 2020). In the 1940s, linguist Herman Aschmann noted the special vocabulary for smells in the Totonac language, spoken along the Gulf of Mexico: "In Totonac there is no general word to indicate that a thing smells. The exact shade of smell must be taken into account and a word chosen giving it." (Aschmann 1946: 187). The distinct terms in Totonac fall under eight headings: 'bad smells', 'sour smells', 'artificial smells', 'air-permeating smells', 'body and animal smells', 'vegetation and good smells', 'medicinal and aromatic smells', 'smells that leave a taste in the mouth'. Totonac speakers use a variety of words based on these categories to refer to smells as diverse as the 'smell of mint, parsley, tobacco and other herbs', the 'savoury smell of garlic', 'smell of mould', 'smell of citrus fruit skins', and 'intense skunk smell'.

There have been similar reports from other languages, including the Seri language of coastal Sonora, Mexico, the Xóõ language of Botswana and Namibia, the Tarok language of plateau Nigeria, the Kapsiki/Higi language of Cameroon and Nigeria, Boholano in the Philippines, the Amis language of Eastern coastal Taiwan, and the Matsigenka and Yora (Yaminahua) languages of Amazonian Peru (see references in Wnuk et al. 2020).

A study of the vocabulary for smells in Jahai (Majid and Burenhult 2014: 269), an indigenous language of upland Peninsular Malaysia spoken by a hunter-gatherer community, found a dozen basic terms for smells, including fairly abstract notions like *cŋəs* 'to smell edible, tasty' and *harim* 'to be fragrant', but also more specific smells like *crŋir* 'to smell roasted', *sʔīŋ* 'to have a smell of human urine', and *plʔɛŋ* 'to have a bloody smell which attracts tigers'. In a controlled experiment and analysis to compare the smell vocabulary of Jahai with that of Dutch, a language that represents the kind of 'standard average European' language that has evidenced the supposed pan-human hopelessness at encoding smells in language, researchers exposed language speakers to 37 different odours (Majid et al. 2018). These included both pleasant smells (e.g., *acetoin* 'butter, cream', *cyclotene hydrate* 'caramel', and *nerol* 'sweet, floral, rose') and unpleasant ones (e.g., *skatole* 'faecal', *trimethyl amine* 'fishy' and *2-methyl-1-butane thiol* 'bloody, sulphurous'). People in the experiment had to smell each odour and simply state what smell it was. The responses from Jahai and Dutch speakers couldn't have been more different. Recall that the Jahai speakers have a set of words that denote smells in an abstract sense. In the experiment, Jahai speakers consistently used these words to describe the test smells. They independently agreed on which Jahai words should be used for each smell. This conformed with Majid and Burenhult's earlier findings about Jahai speakers' tendency to describe smells quickly and without hesitation. They concluded that "contrary to the widely-held belief that people universally struggle to describe odors, Jahai speakers name odors with ease" and "with the same conciseness and level of agreement as colors" (Majid et al. 2018: 4). By contrast, the Dutch speakers struggled with their inadequate vocabulary. Their responses were meandering and vague (Majid and Burenhult 2014: 269). They grappled for ways to describe what they were smelling. Most of the time they named things that might give off the smell (e.g., flowers, ammonia, manure) or a scenario associated with the smell (a house that isn't aired, if you ride along or stand behind a garbage truck). Dutch speakers showed a lower level of agreement with each other than Jahai speakers did. And their words were mostly focused on concrete descriptions. The Dutch language actually does have some abstract smell terms. Five were used in the study—*stinkt* 'smelly', *stinkt niet* 'not smelly', *muf* 'musty', *ranzig* 'rancid smell', and *weeïg* 'sickly smell'—but these made up only two percent of responses in the experiment.

The comparison of Jahai and Dutch shows that odours can be far more expressible in human language than some have supposed. But these findings are relative to a baseline of a language like English, which has almost the most primitive imaginable vocabulary for smells. When compared to English, Jahai or Totonac can be said to have highly refined vocabularies for smell. So, when it comes to capturing our experience of reality, some languages are indeed better than others. But that said, in the context of our capacity for actually *perceiving* distinctions in smells in our surroundings, even the most discerning linguistic systems only discern and label the tiniest subset of reality.[9] Once again, the question arises: why are just *those* odours labelled and not others? Is it because—as Berlin might have it—humans are simply more interested in the distinctions that stand out better to our perceptual systems? Or is it, as Hunn might argue, that we label the smells that have 'practical consequences' in our lives?

These examples show that languages vary, but only within the same narrow range. In the domain of names for plant life in a local environment, there are predictable patterns of variation: urban populations will tend to have only a small number of names for life forms, say a couple of dozen, and will have trouble identifying them in nature; hunter-gatherer communities will have a much larger knowledge set, with people knowing some two hundred or so names for plants they can recognise; and cultivators will be able to name and identify around five hundred distinct types of plant. Words for colours may make finer distinctions in some languages than others, but within strong constraints on the structure and number of distinctions made. And with reference to words for smells, languages will make more distinctions among bad smells, but will only ever make the tiniest fragment of distinctions out of what we can individually perceive. Similar types of constrained diversity are found in other domains of reference.

Why do languages make such fragmentary distinctions in reality compared to how finely we are able to make distinctions through our senses? Why do they do this in similar ways across languages? And why does the observed variation appear to be conditioned by social and cultural practices? For the answer to these questions, we need to ask what language is *good* for. If the true function of

9 See references and discussion in Majid et al. (2017: 407).

language were to capture and communicate our experience of reality, it would have to be better than it is. Instead, the function of linguistic reference isn't to transmit information per se (though it does do that), but to provide for social coordination. The labels found in the words of languages are not for mirroring or depicting reality. Their function is not grounded in individual perception or interest. They are practised solutions to problems of social coordination.

Languages have developed in such a way that they draw on available sources of *mutual prominence*. For people to be readily able to coordinate around something, the two criteria are (1) that it should be somehow prominent, and (2) that this prominence should be assumed to be shared among the people who would coordinate. One of these sources of prominence is our pan-human perceptual system. If something is visually prominent to you, then you can assume it will be visually prominent to everyone else. If that landmark happens to be useful for people in solving a recurrent coordination problem, then it is likely to become encoded in the main tool box of language: the vocabulary. Another source of shared prominence is common cultural interest or values. If we all share an interest in some aspect of reality then we can assume that its prominence will be noticed by all, and thus will be available as a landmark for people to coordinate around. (Sometimes, of course, in a certain cultural context people will have their awareness heightened to certain things that in another cultural context would be overlooked.) Perception and cultural interest are distinct sources of mutual prominence, but clearly, they can combine. Both universal human colour vision and local cultural practices around colour—say in producing paints, dyes, or cosmetics—will interact in charting a collective map for members of a community to coordinate around colours (and the same is true, mutatis mutandis, for smells). Similarly, both human perception of the structures of plants and culture-specific practices of plant collection or cultivation will interact in charting a community-wide map for coordinating around certain plant species.

But what is the mechanism by which the prominent features of the perceptual world in domains from biodiversity to colour to smells and beyond become fixed in the shared conventions of our languages? How does that mechanism allow for both the universal patterns and the diversity that we observe across languages? In relation to how we label the biological world, Berlin posed the question as follows: why is it that "only a small subset of the species diversity in any one local habitat is ever recognized linguistically by local human populations"? (Berlin 1992: 80). As we have mentioned, two explanations are suggested. One is the *intellectualist* view: languages make the distinctions they make because human beings are inherently interested in acknowledging—by naming—the distinctions that are perceptually most prominent in nature.

Words directly reflect this perceptual prominence. Berlin states that "in the categorization of plants and animals by peoples living in traditional societies, there exists a specifiable and partially predictable set of plant and animal taxa that represent the smallest fundamental biological discontinuities easily recognized in any particular habitat. This large but finite set of taxa is special in each system in that its members stand out as beacons on the landscape of biological reality" (Berlin 1992: 53). Another view is *utilitarian*. According to this view, the naming of a plant or animal in a language will be guided by the "practical consequences of knowing or not knowing [that] plant or animal" in the relevant cultural context (Hunn 1982: 834). An obvious problem with this claim is that languages often have words for plants and animals that are of no clear utility to speakers, whether this utility be concerned with the need to pursue, avoid, or be otherwise invested in the ability to identify a life form (Berlin 1992: 80–90). For example, I have found that speakers of Kri have a large vocabulary for bird species, but they do not hunt, breed, catch, or otherwise utilise any birds apart from domesticated chickens.

The intellectualist and utilitarian positions are presented as competing alternatives, applicable not only to explaining why vocabularies of biological classification are the way they are, but also why the lexicon of other perceptual domains such as colour and smell have the properties they have. Which view is correct? I want to argue that the implied dichotomy is a false one. The dichotomy is presented as being about the status of particular *referents*—such as certain plants or animals, or swatches of the perceptual fields of colour or smell—and whether they are labelled because they attract special interest because of some perceptual salience or because the distinctions are of practical use. But this is not the issue. Linguists are not trying to explain why people see the colours that they see or recognize the structures in nature that they recognize. We are trying to explain why the *words* exist. So, with apologies to Hunn, the question is not what the practical consequences are of knowing or not knowing a plant or animal. The question is what are the practical consequences of knowing or not knowing the *word for* it?

It is clearly reasonable to assume that if something is useful to a group of people, those people will probably have a word to refer to it. People will need a label for solving recurrent problems of social coordination around the thing. For example, there is a variety of Cyperacea reed (related to papyrus) that is useful to many Lao-speaking villagers for making floor mats, so it is useful for them to have a word for the plant (in Lao, the word is *phùù3*). The word is needed in order to coordinate social behaviours around that thing (e.g., to say things like 'Shall we go to the swamp tomorrow and collect some Cyperacea reeds?'). But this is not simple or direct evidence for the utilitarian hypothesis.

The utility of the thing is logically quite distinct from the utility of a *word for* the thing. To be sure, the reeds are of practical use to the villagers. But this is not the proximate cause of the word *phùù3* existing in the Lao language. *The word* exists because *the word* is of practical use. In the case of *phùù3*, the referent also happens to be of practical use (which in turn helps to explain why the word is useful, too). But there are plenty of words for plants that are of no direct utility to people who know the word. There is what we might call *indirect* utility. Here is an example of the indirect utility of knowing a particular tree species and being able to distinguish it from others. The word *lkȅȅm* is Kri for the tree *Pterocarya tonkinensis* or Tonkin Wingnut. Why do Kri speakers have a word for this tree? One way to tell is to look at what Kri speakers are doing when they use the word in real life.

In one of my field recordings of conversation in Kri-speaking homes, two Kri-speaking men are talking about where they plan to plant crops in the next year: 'I'm going to chop the vegetation up here and make a fence on the side of that other *lkȅȅm* tree there.'[10] In mentioning this species of tree by name, the man takes it for granted that the other man knows which tree he means. This presupposes that the tree species is perceptually distinct enough to serve as a landmark for people. But nothing here suggests that the tree itself is of any direct use to the men in this conversation, for example as a source of food, building material, or shelter. Nor is this reference motivated by intellectual interest. This example supports Berlin's view that the perceptual salience of the referent is important, but it suggests that the role of this salience is not to satisfy speaker's intellectual curiosity but to provide a shared basis for people to solve social coordination problems. What matters is that the two men can mutually identify a specific tree for the purpose of coordinating their understanding of the location being spoken about. The reference to the tree as a landmark is opportunistic. It works because both speakers share a rich common understanding of the local environment: they are able to distinguish tree species, they can reliably label them, and they are familiar with specific trees in the area. So, for Kri speakers, one payoff of recognizing and remembering tree species and their names is that their locations can be used in communicating about spatial location.

Another example is the phenomenon of calendar plants. In Tafea Province in southern Vanuatu, a hardy coastal shrub known as sea daisy (*Melanthera biflora*) is called *intop asiej in* the Aneityum language. The sea daisy goes into flower at the same time that sea turtles are fat and good to hunt. The flowers

10 From Enfield (2015), paraphrased; the example is from a video-recorded conversation.

have no causal connection to the lives of turtles, they just happen to be reliably correlated in the annual cycle of life. So, if one person says *Look, the sea daisies are flowering*, to an outsider this might appear to be a random observation of no consequence. But to an insider who shares knowledge of the local environment it can mean *We could go turtle-hunting*. The observation of the flowering daisies would be seen as a reason for action, yet it would entail no direct utility of the plant itself. A statement that a certain plant is flowering could have an intended meaning well separated from what its simple, literal meaning would suggest. The Vanuatu sea daisy example suggests that a person's reason to know a word for a certain plant might have nothing to do with their interest in that plant per se, but rather be solely in the service of their interest in hunting turtles.

These examples illustrate how words for life-forms can be of indirect utility. It can be useful to refer to the plant—using an at-hand word in the language—but without the plant itself being useful in a direct sense. We could of course say that its being an index of something else is a form of usefulness. Other cases are less clear. Consider the case of bird species names in Kri. When traveling through Kri territory, whether by boat along rivers and streams, or walking along rainforest footpaths, one frequently encounters native bird life. Often, upon sighting a bird, Kri speakers will point and call out the name of the bird species. In an example I noted while traveling with Kri speakers, a man saw a crested argus (a rather grand type of peafowl) fly overhead and pointed, calling to his companion *vung vaawq!*— the Kri word for this bird. It is a puzzle why the Kri language has many bird species names, for Kri speakers have little use for birds. They have virtually no direct interactions with birds, nor any practical uses for them. Yet somehow in that moment, the word *vung vaawq* 'crested argus' served some kind of function for this speaker. That function was not the obviously helpful one of isolating a referent for some practical purpose (as the word salt does in 'please pass the salt'), nor did it have the indirect utility of referring to something that it secondarily signifies (as when reference to a tree species helps us communicate a location). I can think of two other possibilities for the function that the speaker's act of saying the bird's name to his associate may have served. One is to display expertise ('Look, I know what that bird is called'). Another is simply to share a rare experience with a companion. Neither of these functions would explain the men's knowledge of the bird per se. But they would explain *the word* for it.

The Berlin-Hunn debate sets up a dichotomy between two ways of explaining why human languages have the kinds of vocabularies that they have: either our words are shaped by our sheer intellectual interest in the perceptible world or they reflect the practical consequences of registering certain distinctions in everyday life. It is true that the question may be *distally* concerned with our relationship to aspects of the physical world, such as our sensory perception of it, our intellectual interest in it, or our practical engagement with it, but the *proximal* issue is why the *words* in question are in circulation. The question is, first and foremost, not about our relationship with the world but about our relationships with words. And unlike nature, words are created and sustained by people. As I wrote in *The Utility of Meaning* (Enfield 2015): "If words exist, they have survived. If they have survived, they have been used. And if they have been used, it has been for a reason. ... So, to truly understand a word, we must ask not what it means. Instead, we must ask: What are people's reasons for using it?" That question removes the supposed dichotomy between different possible kinds of relationship that people—at the *individual level* of perceiving agents—might have with a feature of the physical world. It does this by shifting our attention to the relevance of those features of the world *at a social level,* the level at which words operate, as landmarks for coordination among social agents. Seen in this way, the question of why we have the words we have is only secondarily—if at all—one about perception or thought. It is primarily a question of language's social value.

Acknowledgements

This essay is offered to Sasha Aikhenvald, in appreciation of a truly formidable linguist.

I am grateful for comments and input from the editors and reviewers of this chapter; note that it features revised sections of the book *Language versus Reality* (N.J. Enfield, MIT Press, 2022).

References

Aschmann, Herman P. (1946). Totonac Categories of Smell. *Tlalocan* 2: 187–189.

Atran, Scott, and Douglas L. Medin. 2008. *The Native Mind and the Cultural Construction of Nature*. Life and Mind. Cambridge, Mass: MIT Press.

Beech, E., M. Rivers, S. Oldfield and P.P. Smith (2017). GlobalTreeSearch: The first complete global database of tree species and country distributions. *Journal of Sustainable Forestry*, 36 (5): 454–489. https://doi.org/10.1080/10549811.2017.1310049

Berlin, Brent (1976). The Concept of Rank in Ethnobiological Classification: Some Evidence from Aguaruna Folk Botany. *American Ethnologist* 3 (3): 381–399.

Berlin, Brent (1992). *Ethnobiological Classification: Principles of Categorization of Plants and Animals in Traditional Societies*. Princeton, NJ: Princeton University Press.

Christenhusz, Maarten J.M. and James W. Byng (2016). The number of known plants species in the world and its annual increase. *Phytotaxa* 261 (3): 201–217. http://dx.doi.org/10.11646/phytotaxa.261.3.1

Enfield, N.J. (2009). Everyday Ritual in the Residential World. In Gunter Senft and Ellen B. Basso (eds.), *Ritual Communication*, 51–80. Oxford: Berg Publishers.

Enfield, N.J. (2015). *The Utility of Meaning: What Words Mean and Why*. First edition. Oxford Linguistics. Oxford: Oxford University Press.

Felger, R.S. and M.B. Moser (1985). *People of the Desert and Sea*. Tucson: University of Arizona Press.

Grenand, Pierre (1980). *Introduction a l'Étude de l'Univers Wayāpi*. Paris: Societe d'Etudes Linguistiques et Anthropologiques de France.

Hays, Terence Eugene (1974). Mauna: Explorations in Ndumba Ethnobotany. PhD thesis, University of Washington.

Hunn, Eugene (1982). The Utilitarian Factor in Folk Biological Classification. *American Anthropologist* 84 (4): 830–847. https://doi.org/10.1525/aa.1982.84.4.02a00070.

Kay, Paul, Brent Berlin, Luisa Maffi and William Merrifield (1997). Color Naming across Languages. In C.L. Hardin and Luisa Maffi (eds.), *Color Categories in Thought and Language*, 21–56. Cambridge University Press. https://doi.org/10.1017/CBO9780511519819.002.

Kay, Paul and Luisa Maffi (1999). Color Appearance and the Emergence and Evolution of Basic Color Lexicons. *American Anthropologist* 101 (4): 743–760. https://doi.org/10.1525/aa.1999.101.4.743.

Lévi-Strauss, Claude (1966). *The Savage Mind*. Chicago: University of Chicago Press.

Majid, Asifa and Niclas Burenhult (2014). Odors Are Expressible in Language, as Long as You Speak the Right Language. *Cognition* 130 (2): 266–270. https://doi.org/10.1016/j.cognition.2013.11.004.

Majid, Asifa, Laura Speed, Ilja Croijmans, and Artin Arshamian. (2017). What Makes a Better Smeller? *Perception* 46 (3–4): 406–430. https://doi.org/10.1177/0301006616688224.

Majid, Asifa, Niclas Burenhult, Marcus Stensmyr, Josje de Valk and Bill S. Hansson (2018). Olfactory Language and Abstraction across Cultures. *Philosophical Transactions of the Royal Society B: Biological Sciences* 373 (1752): 1–8. https://doi.org/10.1098/rstb.2017.0139.

Newman, M., S. Ketphanh, B. Svengsuksa, P. Thomas, K. Sengdala, V. Lamxay and K. Armstrong (2007). *A checklist of the vascular plants of Lao PDR*. Scotland: Royal Botanic Garden Edinburgh.

Waddy, Julie Anne (1988). *Classification of Plants and Animals from a Groote Eylandt Aboriginal Point of View*. Darwin: Australian National University.

Wnuk, Ewelina, Rujiwan Laophairoj and Asifa Majid (2020). Smell Terms Are Not Rara: A Semantic Investigation of Odor Vocabulary in Thai. *Linguistics* 58 (4): 937–966. https://doi.org/10.1515/ling-2020-0009.

Zuckerman, Charles H.P. and N.J. Enfield (2021). The Unbearable Heaviness of Being Kri: House Construction and Ethnolinguistic Transformation. *Journal of the Royal Anthropological Institute*. In press.

CHAPTER 26

On Language Use beyond the Sentence: The Role of Discourse Markers in Akie

Bernd Heine and Christa König

1 Introduction

It is hard to find a central topic of functional linguistics that has not been dealt with competently in the work of Sasha Aikhenvald, irrespective of whether the topic relates to world-wide comparisons or to the perspective of the descriptive linguist aiming to comprehensively understand the nature of an unknown or little known language. It seems, however, that discourse markers (henceforth: DMs) constitute such a topic. To be sure, DMs have been discussed in her work in one form or another, for example in her grammar of Manambu (Aikhenvald 2008). But so far, they have not figured prominently in her publications, and in the present chapter, devoted to her, we wish to draw her attention to this research topic.

One may wonder, however, what DMs may have to do with 'the art of language', which is the title of this book—note that DMs are widely believed to be a fairly peripheral phenomenon of language use, and even more so of language structure.[1] Referred to in some earlier work as 'disfluencies', 'filled pauses', 'fumbles', 'pleonasms', 'signals', 'signs of poor elocution', 'symptoms', and the like, they tended to be discussed in grammatical treatments only marginally, if at all. It would seem, however, that, if taken in the sense of standing for something special, beyond the ordinary, 'DMs' do have something in common with 'art': they contribute to creating larger texts out of clauses, sentences and other text pieces and to providing hearers or readers with instructions on how these texts are to be interpreted. Research on DMs has therefore developed more recently into a lively field of contemporary linguistics.

The chapter is organized as follows. Section 2 provides an overview of research on DMs, while in Section 3 the Akie language of north-central Tanzania is introduced, which is the main concern of the study. Section 4 is devoted to analyzing the occurrence of a DM of this language in spoken texts. The obser-

1 The term (linguistic) 'discourse' refers generally to language in use and to how language is used in order to enact activities and identities (Bax 2011: 1).

© BERND HEINE AND CHRISTA KÖNIG, 2022 | DOI:10.1163/9789004510395_027

vations made there are then discussed in Section 5, and some conclusions are drawn in the final Section 6.

2 On Discourse Markers

There are a variety of different terms under which DMs are known, such as discourse particles (e.g., Abraham 1991; Schourup 1999; Aijmer 2002; Diewald 2006: 406), pragmatic markers (e.g., Aijmer 2013, 2016; Aijmer and Simon-Vandenbergen 2009; Beeching 2016; Brinton 1996, 2008, 2017; Fraser 1999; Traugott 2016), discourse connectives (Blakemore 1987: 105; Erman and Kotsinas 1993: 79), discourse operators (Gaines 2011; Redeker 1991: 1169), style disjuncts or conjuncts (Quirk et al. 1985: 631–645), speech act adverbials (Aijmer 1997: 3), formulaic theticals (Heine, Kaltenböck and Kuteva 2016: 56–58), discourse organizers (Pons Bordería 1998: 215), or discourse signals (Lamiroy and Swiggers 1991: 123). In grammars of non-European languages, they are frequently subsumed under the label 'interjections'.

DMs have been the subject of many studies (see, e.g., Aijmer 2002; Dér 2010 for convenient overviews; see also Furkó 2014). The most detailed characterization of DMs that we are aware of is provided by Brinton (2017: 8–9, Table 1.1). Examples of DMs in English are *anyway, however, indeed, in fact, instead, okay,* or *what else*. Furthermore, there is a range of English expressions which are DMs in some of their uses but not in others. For example, common DMs are also *now, so, then* and *well,* as well as *I mean, I think* and *you know,* where the former also occur as adverbials and the latter as clauses without complements (see (2) below).

In the course of the last decades the study of discourse markers has developed into a booming field of research. Most of this research has focused on English (e.g., Aijmer 2002; Beeching 2016; Brinton 1996; 2017) and a few other European languages such as French (e.g., Hansen 1998) and Spanish (e.g., Pons Bordería 2018), as well as Korean (e.g., Ahn and Yap 2013; Rhee 2020) and Japanese (e.g., Onodera 2004). But there are also now analyses of DMs in many other languages of the world (see Heine et al. 2021).

There are many definitions and characterizations that have been proposed for DMs. In the following we will rely on the prototypical definition in (1) to narrow down the set of expressions qualifying as DMs (see Heine et al. 2021: 1.1.2, (7), (40)).

(1) Discourse markers are (a) invariable expressions which are (b) semantically and syntactically independent from their environment, (c) set off

> prosodically from the rest of the utterance in some way, and (d) their function is metatextual, being anchored in the situation of discourse and serving the organization of texts, the attitudes of the speaker, and/or speaker-hearer interaction.[2]

This definition shows that DMs contrast sharply in their grammatical structure with grammatical markers as they are used to form sentences. The reason for this contrast has been the subject of a number of controversies; see Heine et al. (2021: Chapter 1) for an overview of these controversies. While the definition is fairly explicit, it is somewhat broader than a number of other definitions that exist, most of which are restricted essentially to one function as their only or their main defining feature, namely to the organization of texts. For example, according to Schiffrin's (1987: 31) classic definition, DMs are "sequentially dependent expressions which bracket units of talk"; for similar definitions see Fraser (1999: 938) and Traugott (2018: 27). However, not all expressions that are generally classified as DMs do in fact "bracket units of talk", or they may do so in some of their uses but not in others.

A number of attempts have been made to argue that DMs constitute a distinct 'category' but such attempts have remained controversial to some extent. In the present chapter we will take the definition in (1) to identify DMs, being aware that this is not the only convention that has been proposed.

We may illustrate the definition with the constructed example in (2) (Traugott 1995: 6; Heine 2019: 412).[3]

(2) a. She spoke well.
b. **Well**, she spoke.

As similar as the two utterances in (2) look, their meanings and structures are far from being the same. In both sentences, *well* is an invariable expression; however, it is a manner adverbial in (2a) but a DM in (2b). The main differences between the two usages of *well* can be sketched as follows, in accordance with the definition in (1). First, in (2a), *well* is part of the meaning of the clause; in (2b), by contrast, *well* is not a semantic part of the clause *she spoke*. Second, the functions of the two are also different: *well* in (2a) is an adverbial qualifying the meaning of the verb, while the function of *well* in (2b) is commonly classified as 'metatextual' (e.g., Traugott 2018: 27; Heine et al. 2021: 8), relating the

2 For a more specific set of grammatical properties defining DMs, see Heine et al. (2021: 1.5, (40)).

3 DMs, like well in (2b), are generally printed in bold in this chapter.

DM immediately to the situation of discourse, that is, the preceding text, the attitudes of the speaker, and/or speaker-hearer interaction.

Third, with regard to syntax, *well* in (2a) is a constituent of the sentence—hence, it belongs to the sentence syntax. In (2b), by contrast, *well* is fairly independent of the syntactic structure of a sentence.

Fourth, whereas *well* in (2a) is integrated into the intonation contour of the sentence, *well* in (2b) is likely to be set off from the rest of the sentence, often occurring "in an independent breath unit carrying a special intonation and stress pattern", as Traugott (1995: 7) puts it. Fifth, *well* in (2a) forms one unit of semantic-pragmatic scope with the verb it modifies, whereas the scope of *well* in (2b) extends beyond the sentence it is associated with. And sixth, there is also a difference in placement: whereas *well* in (2a) is restricted to positions reserved for adverbial constituents, that in (2b) does not show such constraints, even if the position at the left periphery of the sentence is its favorite position (see Heine et al. 2021 for a more detailed discussion).

DMs have been shown to be of world-wide distribution (see Heine et al. 2021). Comparative work on DMs is still in its beginnings but it would seem that they share a number of features in different languages across the world, and that the probabilistic generalizations in (3) in particular can be proposed. While these generalizations do not hold true for all DMs, we hypothesize that there are at least some DMs in a given language to which they apply.

(3) Probabilistic generalizations on some crosslinguistic features of DMs
  a. One of the main text-structuring functions of DMs is to build a macrostructure of discourse.
  b. Even if the organization of texts is one of their main functions, DMs are likely to express other functions in addition or instead.
  c. DMs express, on average, a wider range of functions than other grammatical markers.

In the present chapter we wish to test these generalizations by looking at one particular African language, namely the Akie language of Tanzania. As can be seen in (3), the features to be examined all relate to the functions of DMs. The term 'macrostructure', introduced by van Dijk (1980), refers to the observation made in some form or other in many studies that in the analysis of linguistic discourse two levels of discourse processing are to be distinguished (see Heine 2019 and Haselow 2019 for summarizing discussions), namely a 'microstructure' and a 'macrostructure'. The former is based on knowledge of the propositional-semantic format of text pieces expressing events, states, or relations, most commonly taking the form of sentences, clauses, or phrases. Macrostructure, by contrast, is based on the communicative intents of the speaker and on strategies of discourse processing employed for whole texts, relating the text to the situation of discourse. The two structures complement and interact with one another, both being needed for successful linguistic communication.

The distinction is supported by neurolinguistic findings in that it exhibits some correlations with neural activity relating to the lateralization of the human brain (Haselow 2019; Heine 2019: 426–433; Heine, Kuteva and Kaltenböck 2014, 2015), as captured in the following generalization:

> Whereas the microstructure implicates mainly the left hemisphere of the human brain, building a macrostructure of discourse is a task that cannot be achieved without participation of the right hemisphere.
>
> HEINE 2019: 433, (8)

3 DMs in the Akie Language of Tanzania

The following account is based on the analysis of 35 texts in the Akie language, collected in the Maasai Steppe of north-central Tanzania between 2013 and 2018 within the *DoBeS* (Documentation of Endangered Languages) program of the *VolkswagenStiftung* (Volkswagen Foundation).[4]

Akie, a language of traditional hunter-gatherers, belongs to the Kalenjin cluster of the Southern Nilotic branch of the Nilotic family, the latter being commonly classified as the Eastern Sudanic branch of the Nilo-Saharan phylum (Greenberg 1963; Rottland 1982). The language is spoken in the Kilindi District of Tanga Region and the Kiteto and Simanjiro Districts of Manyara Region of north-central Tanzania, roughly between Handeni to the east and Kibaya and Simanjiro to the west. The Akie people seem to have been living in this area since before the arrival of all their neighbors, such as the Maasai and the Nguu (Ngulu) (Bakken 2004: 38 ff.; Kaare 1996; Schöperle 2011). The language is critically endangered, being spoken by roughly 230 people only (Heine, König and Legère 2014, 2016; Legère 2002, 2006, 2012; Maguire 1948).

Akie is an inflectional, verb-initial (VSO) tone language, having a marked-nominative case system where the two cases, nominative and accusative, are distinguished almost exclusively by tone. Further typological features are a

4 The project, "Akie in Tanzania—documenting a critically endangered language", was directed by Karsten Legère and Christa König. The 35 texts are electronically accessible via https://archive.mpi.nl/tla/islandora/search/akie?type=dismax. 16 of the texts were published in König et al. (2020).

cross-height vowel harmony and a rich inventory of verbal derivations, and also of DMs (König, Heine and Legère 2015a, 2020).

DMs, in fact, constitute a conspicuous feature of Akie speech. On average we found nearly one DM per information unit in our sample of spoken Akie texts.[5] DMs thus belong to the most frequently occurring grammatical elements of the language. Example (4), taken from the *Blessing the Hunting Weapons* ceremony (König et al. 2020: 4.8.1), illustrates their use.[6] There are altogether five DMs (*à*, *icháide*, and *hḿ* occurring three times) in this one information unit.

(4) ***hḿ a*** *kéé táá ko pa ko ng'âm akiée*
DM DM RP still.be.doing NAR go.PERF NAR receive Akie.NOM
chaa ***hḿ icháide hḿ.***
DEM.PROX.PL DM DM DM
'And they (the white people) went and the Akie welcomed them, so it be.' [1/55]

The total number of DMs in the language is unknown; in our text collection and in elicitation tests we found the markers listed in Table 26.1. Many of these markers are etymologically opaque, others are transparently coopted from expressions of sentence grammar, and still others are borrowed from Swahili.[7]

With regard to their contribution to the organization of texts, three main types of DMs can be distinguished, namely (a) retrospective, (b) prospective, and (c) connective DMs (Heine, König and Legère 2017). Each type tends to be associated with a specific set of discourse markers (DMs). Thus, *ikaísha* and *m̀m̀* are paradigm markers of retrospective planning, signaling the end of an event. The DMs *koinákata, ntán, tándeí*, by contrast, signal the beginning of a new episode or event, being prospective DMs. The main function of connective DMs is to create cohesion between different pieces of discourse and here again, two subtypes can be distinguished: on the one hand, there are conjunctive DMs, such as *à, ási, basí, í*, and *koéénа*, which link larger pieces of a text to

5 The term 'information unit' stands for a bounded text segment. It is roughly equivalent to the notion 'prosodic unit', designating a text piece that is typically separated prosodically by intonation features and/or pauses from what precedes and/or follows.

6 The source of the text piece cited is added in parentheses. Thus, example (4) is taken from Text 1, line 55 of König et al. (2020). In the Akie examples presented in this paper, an acute accent (e.g., *á*) marks a high tone. Low tones are unmarked except for grammatical morphemes, such as the DM *à*, where low tone is marked with a grave accent; see König, Heine and Legère (2015a) for more details.

7 Concerning the concept of 'cooptation', see Heine, König and Legère (2017). The relevance of cooptation for DMs is discussed in Heine et al. (2021: 65–72).

TABLE 26.1 Common Akie discourse markers (cf. Heine, König and Legère 2017; H = hearer; IU = information unit).

Marker	Approximate English translation	Typical discourse function	Comments
à	'and'	Introducing a new IU	
áai		Text continuity	
alé	'at that point'	Introducing a new episode	
anasínanu	'Look!'	Drawing H's attention to what follows	
aríí kas ira	'you understand?'	Making sure that H has understood the speaker's account	Lit. 'have you heard (it) today?'
arii sʊwɛ́ íra	'you see?'	Making sure that H has seen what S presents to him or her	Lit. 'have you seen (it) today?'
ási, basí	'so, well'	Pausing, preparing for new IU	Both presumably borrowed from Swahili *basi* 'enough'
dé, dedúo, dúo, ídé		Text continuity	Cf. Maasai *dúóó* 'earlier (the same day)'
eé	'yes'	Confirmation, typically in turn-taking	
hḿ	'and (then)'	Introducing a new IU, text continuity	
í	topic enclitic	Ending a topical IU and preparing for a new IU	
ichayaíde, icháide, yáide	'it is this', 'you should know'	Text continuity	
ikaísha	'it is over'	End of narrative account	< Swahili *ikaisha* 'it is finished'
ɪra	'now'	Text continuity	Lit. 'today'
kitío	'just'	Text continuity	Lit. 'self'
koééna	'then'	Text continuity	
koinákata	'and now'	Highlighting a new event	
koléēna or kokolên	'this is how it is'	Concluding the content of a preceding IU	Lit. 'it is (what) they say'
kɔrɪɔ	'now'	Text continuity	Lit. 'now, presently'
koto	'then'	Text continuity	Lit. 'then'
m̀m̀	'I follow and agree with you'	Confirmation in turn- taking	
náíde	'now'	Text continuity	
nayái	'so it be!'	Concluding agreement	
ntán(o)	'you should know'	Drawing attention to the following IU	
sʊwɛn	'look!'	Drawing attention to the following IU	Lit. 'look!'
tándeí	'look!'	Drawing H's attention to what follows	
yai, yáide	'look!'	Text continuity	

one another. In addition to conjunctive DMs there are also what we propose to call cohesive DMs, such as *áai, dé, ídé, dedúo, dúo, hḿ, icháide, ichayaíde, ɪra, kitío, kɔrɪɔ, náíde, yai,* and *yáide,* which promote text continuity and cohesion of some kind or other. Cohesive DMs are perhaps the most conspicuous feature of Akie linguistic discourse. They can be placed essentially anywhere, including within constituents, and they can be combined or repeated. Thus, in the following text piece containing two information units, the cohesive marker *dé* is repeated three times.

(5)

aá	*ki*	*ínte*	***dé***	*pií*	*ayéng'-uun*	*chaa*	*kií*	*pa*	*kií*
yes	RP	exist	DM	people.NOM	two-NOM	REL.PL	RP	go.PL.PERF	RP

pa	***dé***	***dé***	***dé***	*ólliin*	***dedúo.***
go.PL.PERF	DM	DM	DM	there	DM

'Yes, [at the beginning of mankind] there were only two people who lived ['went']. They just lived there.' (König et al. 2020: 4.2.2, 1–2)[8]

DMs provide Akie speakers with an important tool of metacommunicative planning, serving most of all the organization of texts beyond the clause or the sentence. A quantitative survey conducted by Heine, König and Legère (2017) suggests that both men and women commonly employ discourse markers in structuring their discourse but that there are clear differences between the two sexes: women make less use of DMs and tend to favor a smaller set of the types of markers available. A number of the DMs occur in complementary distribution, being restricted to either male or female speakers. Furthermore, there is also a clear difference between descriptive (procedural) and (fictional) narrative texts: the former are distinctly richer in both tokens and types of DMs and there are also markers found either in the former or the latter only. In sum, the most extensive use of DMs is made by men producing descriptive texts whilst the most parsimonious use can be expected from women presenting fables and other fictional texts.

8 The example is taken from Text 4.2.2 of the text collection in König et al. (2020), occurring at the introduction to the mythical account of how the Akie became hunter-gatherers and the Maasai pastoralists.

4 A Case Study: The Marker *aríí kas ira*

Of all the 25 DMs listed in Table 26.1, our interest in this study is exclusively with *aríí kas ira* 'you understand?'. This marker is transparently derived from the sentence grammar segment *aríí kas ira?* (PERF.2.SG hear today), literally meaning 'have you heard (it) today?'. The marker is similar in both in its form and its functions to the DM *arii sʊwɛ́ íra* (lit. 'have you seen (it) today?') 'you see?'. The two differ, for example, in the fact that the latter is only weakly grammaticalized, having retained its lexical meaning of visual perception.[9] Thus, *arii sʊwɛ́ íra* is largely restricted to usages where the speaker expects the hearer to have visual evidence of the item or event concerned.

The difference in grammaticalization between the two DMs is reflected in their relative frequency of occurrence in our corpus of Akie texts. This corpus of 35 texts consists of a total of 3850 information units, containing 87 occurrences of *aríí kas ira* but only 23 occurrences of *arii sʊwɛ́ íra*. Thus, the former occurs in 2.25 % and the latter in only 0.6 % of all information units,

The DM *aríí kas ira* conforms to the definition that was proposed in (1), with one partial exception: while being on the whole invariable in accordance with (1a), it occasionally shows some variants. Thus, in addition to the canonical form *aríí kas ira*, the form may also be *arɔ́ɔ́ kas ira* (PERF.2.PL hear today) when the speaker addresses more than one hearer, and instead of the perfective (PERF), speakers sometimes use the imperfective (IPFV) form *kas-é ira* (hear-IPFV today). Furthermore, unlike most other DMs in Akie, *aríí kas ira* occurs most of the time as a stand-alone, that is, it does not need a host utterance, and it can form a conversational turn of its own.

The basic meaning of the DM is to ascertain that the hearer has understood the content of the preceding text segment, paraphrasable as 'do you understand?' or 'do you follow me?'. But the DM has been grammaticalized to the extent that it forms a rhetorical question, that is, the speaker does not expect, or does not even want the hearer to respond. In most of its uses it has the function of a text connective, linking two pieces of discourse to one another, as we will see below in more detail. And rather than retrospectively referring to the preceding text piece, it serves more commonly prospectively to draw attention to the following piece, somehow signaling 'now that I have introduced the topic of my talk, be ready for what I have to tell you now'. In sum, depending on the communicative intent of the speaker and the context in which it is used, the DM may present a retrospective, a prospective, or a conjunctive perspective.

9 Concerning the distinction between weakly vs. strongly grammaticalized DMs, see Heine et al. (2021: 2.5.2).

To illustrate the usage of the DM, a text taken from our collection of texts on the myth of origin, entitled *How Heaven and Earth Were Separated*, was selected.[10] In this text, the Akie people explain why they no longer live physically united with God. The ultimate cause of separation is fairly consistently described in their traditions in the following way: heaven and earth used to be connected with a pole (*taláíta*) so people could move freely up to God and vice versa. But one day this pole was cut by ignorant or mischievous members of the society, thereby disconnecting heaven and earth.

The text, consisting of a total of 99 information units, is divided into five episodes. Exemplification in the discussion below is restricted to the DM and the immediately preceding and/or following text piece.

Episode 1: The speaker Bahati Nkuyaki describes the situation of the Akie by observing that in former times there was a pole connecting heaven and earth. The DM in (7) has two functions: on the one hand, it establishes that the preceding text presents the topic of the narrative. On the other hand, it signals the shift from Episode 1 to Episode 2: having provided the background situation of the narrative, the speaker now prepares his audience (henceforth: the hearer) for what is going to follow.

(6) [...] *talaí-í* *kí-í* *néékít* ***dé*** *tóroreitâ*
pole-DEM.PROX.NOM RP-become near DM God.NOM
nákatta
time.that
'[...] [due to] this pole God was nearby at that time.' [4]

(7) ***aríí kas ira.*** [5]

(8) *a-ko* *pwá* ***ira*** *kɔrɪɔ* [...].
and-3.PL come.PL.PERF today now
'And [the Akie] came then [...].' [6]

Episode 2: The Akie then brew beer and pray to God. They leave the beer pot there for God to drink. The DM in (10) then signals the shift to Episode 3.

10 This is text 4.2.1 of the text collection in König et al. (2020). Numbers in square brackets after the text pieces refer to the numbers of information units provided there.

(9) [...] *kéé* *pa* *kéé* *pakaai* *ɓɔɔway-aa* *nen*
3.PL.MP go.PL.PERF 3.PL.MP leave clay.pot.ACC-DEM.HE LOC
íyaa
there
'[...] and they went, they left that clay pot there behind.' [30]

(10) ***arii kas*** [***ira***].[11] [31]

Episode 3: During this episode, God, his wife, and his child come down the pole, drink the beer and move up again to heaven. After God has moved back to heaven, the Akie drink the remainder of the beer. The DM in (12) signals the end of Episode 3.

(11) *asi* *ar-ko* *é* ***dé*** *ko* *ng'óllɛɛ* *dé* *oo-eey-e*
SO PERF-3.SG become DM COP saliva.ACC DM 2.PL-drink-IPFV
ikáá *tóroreita*
GEN.ACC god.ACC
'It is the saliva, that of God, that you drink.'[12] [62]

(12) ***aríi kas ira.*** [63]

Episode 4: The DM in (12) also marks the transition to Episode 4, which now tells how the Akie started quarreling with each other and cut the pole connecting them with heaven; subsequently, God tells them that from now on he will not return back to earth. Episode 4 ends with the Akie concluding that from that time on they can see God only by looking up (see (13)); (14) signals the transition from Episode 4 to the final Episode 5.

(13) *ko* *nɪnyɛ́ɛ́* *niin* *ki* *taak-e* *kitíó* *nen* *óll-iin*
COP 3.SG DEM.DIST.SG 1.PL see-IPFV only LOC LOC.REL-DIST
torróór
on.top
'It is him we see up there,' [80]

(14) ***aríi kas ira.*** [81]

Episode 5: The speaker now summarizes the conclusions of the narrative.

11 The reason why the speaker omits the final element *ira* here is unclear.

12 'God's saliva' is a metaphorical expression for 'beer'.

In sum, the DM *aríí kas ira* imposes a frame for interpreting the text—a text that is central to the belief system of the Akie. The DM provides instructions for the hearer on how to understand the text. The text segment over which the DM has semantic-pragmatic scope is neither a clause nor a sentence but rather a larger piece of text expressing a bounded event, and this piece, referred to here as an 'episode', forms a major building block of the macrostructure of the narrative. Thus, the DM is part of the linguistic machinery that language users employ to design texts—in the wording of Schiffrin (1987: 31), its main function is to "bracket units of talk", and in the present text these units are what we propose to refer to as episodes.

But marking boundaries between distinct units of a text is not the only function of the DM *aríí kas ira*. Another function is to provide the hearer with clues on how to interpret the content of the text. For example, in the narrative *How the Akie Became Hunter-Gatherers* (König et al. 2020: 4.2.2) we are told that the first people on earth were an Akie man and a Maasai man. Both were poor and approached God to provide them with cows. God gave them a container each and asked them to take it home and open it only when they had closed the fence around their homestead, not telling them, however, that once they opened the container cows would come out. The following statement by God is essential for appreciating the content of the narrative.

(15) *alé íí yaat mákasí í*
when 2.SG open container.ACC DM
'When you open the container'

así *ak-ɔɔ sʊwɛ kíí-yaa*
well and-2.PL see.SBJV thing-DEM.HE.ACC
'well, you see the thing,' [47]

tukuni cháá ng'eet-u
things.ACC REL.PL come.out-VEN
'the things which come out.' [48]

(16) ***aríí kas ira***. [49]

With the DM in (16) the speaker wishes to provide the hearer with clues on how to interpret the text, roughly paraphrasable as 'Remember (15) otherwise you might not understand what the narrative is about'. Thus, the DM in (16) mainly serves to facilitate comprehension by relating the preceding to the following text.

But the functions of *aríí kas ira* are not restricted to text structuring; they also extend to usage within smaller segments of the macrostructure. With the usage of the DM in (17), for example, the speaker wants to make sure that the hearer is sufficiently familiar with Akie history to know that formerly the Akie lived further north before they moved to their present location. Thus, in this example the semantic-pragmatic scope of the DM is restricted to the preceding adverbial *oll-ii* 'here'—in other words, the domain of operation of the DM is restricted to one constituent rather than applying to some larger text piece or the text as a whole.[13]

(17) *ai* *oll-ii* ***aríí kas ira***
and LOC.REL-DEM.PROX DM
'And there [in the south—the Akie assume that at some time in the past they migrated from north to south], you understand,' [19]

a-kéé *pa* ***ira*** *kɔrɪɔ* *kéé* *pa* [...].
and-3.PL.MP go.PL.PERF today now 3.PL.MP go.PL.PERF [20]
'[the Akie] went, they went, [...].' [20]

In examples such as (17), the speaker is appealing to the state of world knowledge of the hearer, hence the DM relates to speaker-hearer interaction rather than to text organization (see the definition in (1)).

The role played by speaker-hearer interaction is most obvious in contexts where the DM immediately follows a request or a directive. Thus, in the excerpt of (18), taken from the tale *The Woman and the Monster* (König et al. 2020: 4.7.3), the woman tells the monster and his son:

(18) *o* *rú-iyye-n* *nen* *íyu* *kosi* *kɛ́ɛ́* *am* *ímahoi!*
2.PL sleep-APPL-IMP LOC here so.that 1.PL eat.SBJV medicine.ACC
'stay here so that we take the medicine!' [33]

kas-é ***ira*** ***í.***[14]
hear-IPFV now DM
'you hear [me]?' [34]

13 'Semantic-pragmatic scope' must be distinguished from both the notions 'syntactic scope' and 'structural scope' (see Heine et al. 2020: 1.3.2.1).

14 Note that the speaker uses the imperfective form *kas-é ira* rather than the perfective form (*aríí kas ira*) of the DM. The DM *í* signals topic shifts but unlike *aríí kas ira* it operates on smaller text segments like clauses or phrases.

In such contexts, the main function of the DM appears to be to reinforce the request or directive expressed in the preceding information unit, thus serving the interaction between speaker and hearer rather than the organization of the text.

5 Discussion

According to the definition in (1), the functions of DMs relate to three domains of the situation of discourse, namely (a) text organization, (b) the attitudes of the speaker, and/or (c) speaker-hearer interaction. Of these domains, (a) plays a paramount role and in some theoretical accounts this is the only domain that is considered (cf. Schiffrin 1987: 31; Fraser 1999: 938; Traugott 2018: 27). As we saw in the preceding section, (a) is in fact the predominant domain of usage of the DM *aríí kas ira*: its main function can be seen in providing a scaffold for structuring the discourse examined. For one thing, it divides the discourse into a sequence of text pieces, referred to as episodes, by marking the boundaries that separate episodes. For another thing, it implements an information structure for interpreting the discourse, where the DM signals that the first episode provides topical information that forms the basis for understanding what follows.

But the functions of the DM are not restricted to (a); rather, they also relate to (c), that is, to speaker-hearer interaction. With the use of *aríí kas ira* the speaker establishes a close relationship with the hearer, making sure that the hearer remains attentive. Even if the speaker does not expect an answer—*aríí kas ira* ('do you hear me?') being more or less a rhetorical question, by using the DM s/he is able to strengthen the communicative and social ties with his or her audience.

In more general terms, the functions of the DM *aríí kas ira* that surfaced in Section 4 can be summarized as in (19).

(19) The main functions of the DM
 a. To bracket units of a text
 b. To establish the preceding text segment as the topic for what follows
 c. To provide the hearer with clues on how to interpret the text
 d. To secure the active participation of the hearer

The functions in (19) are not neatly separated from one another; rather, it is typically more than one of the functions that are involved in a given usage of the DM, where one of the functions is foregrounded while the others are backgrounded. For example, we saw in Section 4 that the DM in (7) expresses its canonical function of signalling the shift from one episode to another, but its main function in this context appears to be to establish that what precedes presents the topic of and the background for what the narrative is about. Which of the functions is highlighted is contingent on the nature of the context in which the DM is used. For example, (19b) is likely to be highlighted at the end of the first phase of a narrative text after the speaker has presented all the background information that is needed for the hearer to understand and appreciate the following text. (19d) surfaces most clearly in contexts where the speaker wishes to urge the hearer to perform the action described in the preceding text segment, especially if that text segment is phrased as an imperative speech act.

6 Conclusions

Discourse markers appear to be a ubiquitous phenomenon in the languages of the world, but there are differences in the extent to which they are used. Akie can be called a DM-prominent language in that it exhibits both a great variety of markers and an extensive use of them. At the same time there are also differences among interlocutors of the language in where and how frequently discourse markers are employed, as we saw in Section 3. This also applies to the marker *aríí kas ira*, which was the topic of the present chapter. Some speakers, like our main consultant Bahati Nkuyaki, use it fairly generously, while others make more parsimonious use of it. The functions identified in the preceding sections, however, do not seem to differ greatly from one speaker to another.

Over the last decades the study of discourse markers has developed into a booming field of research. It is predominantly European languages—above all English—and some of the languages of eastern Asia, in particular Korean and Japanese, that have figured prominently in this research, but there are also a number of other languages in various parts of the world that have been the subject of work on discourse markers. This research has greatly informed our knowledge of how meaning is structured in the intersection of semantics and pragmatics. In Section 2, three generalizations on the functions of discourse markers were proposed and the main goal of this chapter was to test these generalizations by looking in more detail at an African language, and more specifically at one particular discourse marker of that language.

The findings presented on the Akie language of north-central Tanzania are in fact in support of these generalizations, suggesting, first, that the analysis of discourse markers requires a perspective that is not restricted to clauses, sentences, and other discourse fragments but rather has the global structure of discourse in its scope. Second, even if many discourse markers have been shown to be instrumental in building a macrostructure of discourse, their usage also extends to smaller parts of a discourse and to functions beyond those of text organization. As we saw in Section 4, one domain of usage of the Akie marker *aríí kas ira* is that of speaker-hearer interaction, helping the speaker to establish a communicatively appropriate and close relationship with the hearer. And finally, we also found confirmation of the observation made independently in a number of studies that, as a rule, discourse markers cannot reasonably be reduced to one core function but rather tend to be polysemous, at least distinctly more so than other grammatical markers.

The goal of the chapter was a modest one, being highly restricted both in its scope and its data base. But, as was observed in Section 2, comparative work on discourse markers is still in its beginnings and it is hoped that the observations made here will contribute to encouraging such work on the nature and the usage of discourse markers.

Acknowledgements

The present study is the result of field research carried out by the authors jointly with our colleague and friend Karsten Legère in north-central Tanzania between 2013 and 2018 within the *DoBeS* (Documentation of Endangered Languages) program of the *VolkswagenStiftung* (Volkswagen Foundation). We wish to thank the foundation for all the support it gave us, and our gratitude is especially due to Karsten Legère, who initiated and directed our project.

During our research in Tanzania, we were able to rely on the hospitality provided to us by the United Republic of Tanzania in general and the Akie people in particular, who gave us the feeling of being at home. Our deeply felt gratitude is due to all Akie people for all their kindness, patience, and understanding, and most of all to our main consultants Bahati Nkuyaki and Nkoiseyyo Kalisya. Bahati, especially, turned out to be a treasure for our research: with his deep knowledge of the Akie language and culture he made us aware of how rich the culture of a traditional hunter-gatherer society can be.

Abbreviations

1, 2, 3	first, second, third person	MP	middle past
ACC	accusative	NOM	nominative
APPL	applicative	NAR	narrative
COP	copula	PERF	perfective
DEM	demonstrative	PL	plural
DIST	distal	PROX	proximative
DM	discourse marker	REL	relative clause marker
HE	hearer-proximal	RP	remote past
IPFV	imperfective	SBJV	subjunctive
IP	imperative	SG	singular
LOC	locative marker	VEN	venitive marker

References

Abraham, Werner (1991). The grammaticization of the German modal particles. In Elizabeth Closs Traugott and Bernd Heine (eds.), *Approaches to Grammaticalization*. Volume 2 (Typological Studies in Language, 19), 331–380. Amsterdam/Philadelphia: Benjamins.

Ahn, Mikyung and Foong Ha Yap (2013). Negotiating common ground in discourse: a diachronic and discourse analysis of *maliya* in Korean. *Language Sciences* 37 (1): 36–51.

Aijmer, Karin (1997). "I think"—an English modal particle. In Toril Swan and Olaf Jansen Westvik (eds.), *Modality in Germanic Languages. Historical and Comparative Perspectives*, 1–47. Berlin & New York: Mouton de Gruyter.

Aijmer, Karin (2002). *English Discourse Particles: Evidence from a Corpus*. Amsterdam & Philadelphia: John Benjamins.

Aijmer, Karin (2013). *Understanding Pragmatic Markers: A Variational Pragmatic Approach*. Edinburgh: Edinburgh University Press.

Aijmer, Karin (2016). Pragmatic markers as constructions: The case of anyway. In Gunther Kaltenböck, Evelien Keizer and Arne Lohmann (eds.), *Outside the Clause*. (Studies in Language Companion Series, 178), 29–57. Amsterdam, Philadelphia: Benjamins.

Aijmer, Karin and Anne-Marie Simon-Vandenbergen (2009). Pragmatic markers. In Jan-Ola Östman and Jef Verschueren (eds.), *Handbook of Pragmatics*, 1–29. Amsterdam: John Benjamins.

Aikhenvald, Alexandra Y. (2008). *The Manambu Language of East Sepik, Papua New Guinea*. Oxford: Oxford University Press.

Bakken, Marianne Hovind (2004). Becoming Visible: Economic and Social Transformation and Marginalization of Akie Hunters and Gatherers in Northern Tanzania. MPhil. dissertation, University of Oslo, Department of Social Anthropology.

Bax, Stephen (2011). *Discourse and Genre: Analysing Language in Context.* Basingstoke: Palgrave Macmillan.

Beeching, Kate (2016). *Pragmatic Markers in British English.* Cambridge: Cambridge University Press.

Blakemore, Diane (1987). *Semantic Constraints on Relevance.* Oxford: Blackwell.

Brinton, Laurel J. (1996). *Pragmatic Markers in English: Grammaticalization and Discourse Functions* (Topics in English Linguistics 19). Berlin & New York: Mouton de Gruyter.

Brinton, Laurel J. (2008). *The Comment Clause in English: Syntactic Origins and Pragmatic Development* (Studies in English Language). Cambridge: Cambridge University Press.

Brinton, Laurel J. (2017). *The Evolution of Pragmatic Markers in English: Pathways of Change.* Cambridge: Cambridge University Press.

Dér, Csilla Ilona (2010). On the status of discourse markers. *Acta Linguistica Hungarica* 57, 1: 3–28.

Diewald, Gabriele (2006). Discourse particles and modal particles as grammatical elements. In Kerstin Fischer (ed.), *Approaches to Discourse Particles.* (Studies in Pragmatics, 1), 403–425. Amsterdam: Elsevier.

Erman, Britt and Ulla-Britt Kotsinas (1993). Pragmaticalization: the case of *ba* and *you know. Studier i modern sprakvetenskap* 10: 76–92.

Fraser, Bruce (1999). What are discourse markers? *Journal of Pragmatics* 31: 931–952.

Furkó, Bálint Péter (2014). Cooptation over grammaticalization. *Argumentum* 10: 289–300.

Gaines, Philip (2011). The multifunctionality of discourse operator *okay*: Evidence from a police interview. *Journal of Pragmatics* 43: 3291–3315.

Greenberg, Joseph H. (1963). *The Languages of Africa.* The Hague: Mouton.

Hansen, Maj-Britt Mosegaard (1998). *The Function of Discourse Particles. A Study with Special Reference to Spoken Standard French.* Amsterdam & Philadelphia: John Benjamins.

Haselow, Alexander (2019). Discourse markers and brain lateralization: Evidence for dual language processing from neurological disorders. Typescript.

Heine, Bernd (2019). Some observations on the dualistic nature of discourse processing. *Folia Linguistica* 53 (2): 411–442.

Heine, Bernd, Gunther Kaltenböck and Tania Kuteva (2016). On insubordination and cooptation. In Nicholas Evans and Honoré Watanabe (eds.), *Insubordination* (Typological Studies in Language), 39–63. Amsterdam, Philadelphia: Benjamins.

Heine, Bernd, Gunther Kaltenböck, Tania Kuteva and Haiping Long (2013). An outline of discourse grammar. In Shannon Bischoff and Carmen Jany (eds.), *Functional Approaches to Language*, 175–233. Berlin: Mouton de Gruyter.

Heine, Bernd, Gunther Kaltenböck, Tania Kuteva and Haiping Long (2015). On Some Correlations between Grammar and Brain Lateralization. *Oxford Handbooks Online in Linguistics*. New York: Oxford University Press.

Heine, Bernd, Gunther Kaltenböck, Tania Kuteva and Haiping Long (2017). Cooptation as a discourse strategy. *Linguistics* 55: 1–43.

Heine, Bernd, Gunther Kaltenböck, Tania Kuteva and Haiping Long (2021). *The Rise of Discourse Markers*. Cambridge: Cambridge University Press.

Heine, Bernd, Christa König and Karsten Legère (2014). What does it mean to be an endangered language? The state of Akie, a Tanzanian language. In Iwona Kraska-Szlenk and Beata Wójtowicz (eds.), *Current Research in African Studies: Papers in Honour of Mwalimu Dr. Eugeniusz Rzewuski*, 107–122. Warsaw: Dom Wydawniczy Elipsa.

Heine, Bernd, Christa König and Karsten Legère (2016). Reacting to language endangerment: The Akie of north-central Tanzania. In Martin Pütz and Luna Filipović (eds.), *Endangered Languages: Issues of Ecology, Policy and Documentation. (LAUD Proceedings 2014)* (IMPACT: Studies in Language and Society.), 313–333. Amsterdam, Philadelphia: John Benjamins.

Heine, Bernd, Christa König and Karsten Legère (2017). A text study of discourse markers in Akie, a Southern Nilotic language of Tanzania. In Raija Kramer and Roland Kießling (eds.), *Mechthildian Approaches to Afrikanistik: Advances in Language Based Research on Africa, Festschrift für Mechthild Reh*, 147–167. Cologne: Rüdiger Köppe.

Heine, Bernd, Tania Kuteva and Gunther Kaltenböck (2014). Discourse Grammar, the dual process model, and brain lateralization: Some correlations. *Language & Cognition* 6 (1): 146–180.

Kaare, Bwire Timothy Maarwa (1996). The Symbolic Construction of Community Identity of the Akie Huntergatherers of Northern Tanzania. PhD. dissertation, London School of Economics and Political Science.

König, Christa, Bernd Heine, Karsten Legère and Ingo Heine (2020). *The Akie Language of Tanzania: Texts and Dictionary*. Cologne: Rüdiger Köppe.

König, Christa, Bernd Heine and Karsten Legère (2015a). *The Akie Language of Tanzania: A Sketch of Discourse Grammar*. Tokyo: Research Institute for Languages and Cultures of Asia and Africa (Tokyo University of Foreign Studies).

König, Christa, Bernd Heine and Karsten Legère (2015b). Discourse markers in Akie, a Southern Nilotic Language of Tanzania. In Osamu Hieda (ed.), *Information Structure and Nilotic Languages* (Studies in Nilotic Linguistics, 10), 117–139. Tokyo: Tokyo University of Foreign Studies, Research Institute for Languages and Cultures of Asia and Africa.

König, Christa, Bernd Heine, Karsten Legère and Ingo Heine (2020). *The Akie Language of Tanzania: Texts and Dictionary*. Cologne: Rüdiger Köppe.

Lamiroy, Béatrice and P. Swiggers (1991). Imperatives as discourse signals. In Suzanne Fleischman and L.R. Waugh (eds.), *Discourse-Pragmatics and the Verb: the Evidence from Romance*, 121–146. London: Routledge.

Legère, Karsten (2002). The "Languages of Tanzania" project: Background, sources and problems. *Africa & Asia* 2: 163–186.

Legère, Karsten (2006). Language endangerment in Tanzania: Identifying and maintaining endangered languages. *South African Journal of African Languages* 26 (3): 99–112.

Legère, Karsten (2012). Endangered Languages in Africa: Focus on Tanzania's Ngasa and Akie. In Xu Shixuan, Tjeerd de Graaf and Cecilia Brassett (eds.), *Issues of Language Endangerment* (Book Series of the 16th World Congress of the IUAES), 89–102. Beijing: Chinese Academy of Sciences.

Maguire, R.A.J. (1948). Il-Torobo, Being some notes on the various types of Dorobo found in the Masai reserve of Tanganyika territory and contiguous districts. *Tanganyika Notes and Records* 26: 1–28.

Onodera, Noriko Okada (2004). *Japanese Discourse Markers: Synchronic and Diachronic Discourse Analysis* [Pragmatics & Beyond New Series 132]. Amsterdam: John Benjamins.

Pons Bordería, Salvador (1998). Los apelativos *oye* y *mira* o los límites de la conexión. In M.A. Martín Zorraquino and E. Montolío (eds.), *Marcadores discursivos: teoría y práctica*, 213–228. Madrid: Arco.

Pons Bordería, Salvador (2018). Introduction: New insights in grammaticalization studies. In Salvador Pons Bordería and Óscar Loureda Lamas (eds.), *Beyond Grammaticalization and Discourse Markers: New Issues in the Study of Language Change*. (Studies in Pragmatics, 18), 1–16. Leiden, Boston: Brill.

Quirk, Randolph, Sidney Greenbaum, Geoffrey Leech and Jan Svartvik (1985). *A Comprehensive Grammar of the English Language*. London, New York: Longman.

Redeker, Gisela (1991). Linguistic markers of discourse structure. *Linguistics* 29: 1139–1172.

Rhee, Seongha (2020). Pseudo-hortative and the development of the discourse marker *eti poca* ('well, let's see') in Korean. *Journal of Historical Pragmatics* 21 (1): 53–82.

Rottland, Franz (1982). Die südnilotischen Sprachen: Beschreibung, Vergleichung und Rekonstruktion (Kölner Beiträge zur Afrikanistik, vol. 7). Berlin: D. Reimer.

Schiffrin, Deborah (1987). *Discourse Markers* (Studies in Interactional Sociolinguistics, 5.) Cambridge: Cambridge University Press.

Schöperle, Florian (2011). The Economics of Akie Identity: Adaptation and Change among a Hunter-Gatherer People in Tanzania. MA thesis, African Studies Centre, University of Leiden.

Schourup, Lawrence (1999). Discourse markers. *Lingua* 107: 227–265.

Simon-Vandenbergen, Anne-Marie and Dominique Willems (2011). Crosslinguistic data as evidence in the grammaticalization debate: The case of discourse markers. *Linguistics* 49 (2): 333–364.

Traugott, Elizabeth Closs (1995). The role of the development of discourse markers in a theory of grammaticalization. Paper presented at the International Conference of Historical Linguistics XII, Manchester 1995.

Traugott, Elizabeth Closs (2016). On the rise of types of clause-final pragmatic markers in English. *Journal of Historical Pragmatics* 17: 26–54.

Traugott, Elizabeth Closs (2018). Modeling language change with constructional networks. In Pons Bordería, Salvador and Óscar Loureda Lamas (eds.), *Beyond Grammaticalization and Discourse Markers: New Issues in the Study of Language Change* (Studies in Pragmatics, 18), 17–50. Leiden, Boston: Brill.

van Dijk, Teun A. (1980). *Macrostructures: An Interdisciplinary Study of Global Structures in Discourse, Interaction, and Cognition*. Hillsdale, New Jersey: Erlbaum.

CHAPTER 27

The Semantics of Adverbial Clause Linking in Mongolic Languages: Evaluation of Events and Relations between Them

Elena Skribnik

1 Introduction

This chapter, corresponding to some of Alexandra Aikhenvald's manifold interests (e.g. Dixon and Aikhenvald 2009), presents some results of research on adverbial clauses in three major Mongolic languages: Khalkha (Kh.), Buryat (B.), and Kalmyk (K.). Clause linking is understood as a system of grammatical means employed to code syntactic and semantic relations, and sometimes also the information status of clauses (i.a. Lehmann 1988; Dixon and Aikhenvald 2009; Givón 2001; Cristofaro 2003; Muravyev 2017). Concrete complex constructions, i.e. form-meaning correspondences, are mostly bi-clausal (e.g. 'A when/because/therefore/in order to B', 'A-*cognition/communication* that B', 'A⊃NP that B'), but there also are some tri-clausal ones (e.g. constructions of intermediacy 'A between B and C / from B till C, A'; inference and interpretation 'A-*infer* B on the base of C'; 'B A-*means/presupposes* that C'; comparison 'B is A-*better/worse* than C'; etc.). Such basic units, with their individual semantics, combinable in discourse/text into rather long chains ('clause complex', Matthiessen 2002; 'combinations of clauses', Longacre 2007), are to be described as an inventory (constructicon) for each language individually.

Mongolic languages have a long literary tradition that goes back to the 13th century, when the written Mongolian script (known as the 'Old Script', derived from the Ancient Uighur alphabet) was introduced (Janhunen 2003: 30–31). For the three languages in this study Cyrillic-based orthographies were introduced in the 1930s–1940s after a short period during which the Latin script was used. Examples in this paper are presented in a straightforward Latin transliteration of the official Cyrillic orthography, disregarding phonetic nuances. All examples, unless otherwise indicated, are taken from the online corpora;[1] my

1 Khalkha National Corpus, http://web-corpora.net/MongolianCorpus/search/index.php?interface_language=en; Buryat National Corpus, http://web-corpora.net/BuryatCorpus/search/

© ELENA SKRIBNIK, 2022 | DOI:10.1163/9789004510395_028

sincere gratitude goes to Dolgor Guntseseg (Khalkha), Nadezhda Darzhaeva (Buryat) and Olga Seesing (Kalmyk) for help with language data, its glossing and translation, and to Jeremy Bradley for helpful comments.

All three Mongolic languages under study are agglutinating postfixal languages with vowel harmony. The basic constituent order is AOV/SV (strict in Buryat and Khalkha, less strict in Kalmyk); NPs are head-final; dependent clauses always precede the main ones. Mongolic clause linking is predominantly non-finite through extensive systems of converbs as well as participles/action nouns with different connectors (case markers, postpositions, particles). Constructions with postpositions are the most numerous, individual semantics of postpositions providing the variety of relations expressed and the choice of a non-finite form adding temporal and aspectual characteristics. Non-finite complements of postpositions can carry NOM, GEN or ABL, or rarely DLOC cases. Non-finite clauses employ differential subject marking (NOM vs. GEN in Buryat, NOM vs. GEN vs. ACC in Khalkha and Kalmyk) for information structuring (Guntsetseg 2016; Skribnik and Darzhaeva 2016: 36–46; Seesing 2013: 44–53); personal or reflexive possessive markers for agreement and switch-reference are placed either on non-finites or on postpositions.

The number of different constructions identified in each semantic subtype of adverbial clauses is noteworthy: temporal (Kh. 103, B. 65, K. 52), causal (Kh. 24, B. 22, K. 20), conditional (Kh. 6, B. 4, K. 4), concessive (Kh. 9, B. 3, K. 4), manner (Kh. 20, B. 10, K. 4), etc. This suggests some additional semantic features that are not, or are less consistently, coded in complex constructions in better-known European languages; the dominant factor is evaluation.

Evaluation is defined as a linguistic expression of a speaker's value judgement concerning a person, an object or an event using criteria based on certain standards. There exists an extensive literature on evaluation in psychology, cognitive studies, and linguistics, defining evaluation (also 'appraisal' or 'stance') as an operation, describing its linguistic expression, classifying its types, and listing different dimensions/categories of evaluation (see Bednarek 2009 for a detailed comparative overview). One of the differentiations that Bednarek (2009) lists concerns types of evaluation targets, e.g., texts/processes/natural phenomena on the one hand, and people and their behaviour on the other (or events, objects, and agents/actions). The dimensions of evaluation, both generalized GOOD/BAD (referring to the idea of evaluation itself, without presupposing any concrete dimension; semantic primes after Wierzbicka (1996:

?interface_language=en, and Kalmyk National Corpus: http://web-corpora.net/KalmykCorpus/search/?interface_language-en.

35)) and more complex ones based on aesthetic, ethical and other standards (morality, beauty, utility, desirability, novelty, predictability, efficiency, feasibility, etc.—Malrieu 1999: 131; Bednarek 2009; White 2011), can correlate with types of targets (e.g., ethical standards are hardly applicable to natural phenomena/processes). Evaluation can also be multi-dimensional (Malrieu 1999: 69, 131).

This highly complex domain is still unevenly researched: "what is needed is an investigation into linguistic evaluations of events and a classification of the meanings expressed in their evaluation" (Bednarek 2009: 156). In this paper I will deal with evaluation not only of events (processes, actions), but also of relations between them, showing what is grammaticalized in adverbial constructicons in Mongolic languages and to what extent.

In what follows, Section 1 gives an overview of evaluation in Mongolic temporal constructions; Sections 2 and 3 pertain to logical relations and manner respectively. The conclusion sums up the distribution of evaluative dimensions across different semantic types of adverbial constructions.

2 Evaluation in Temporal Constructions

Temporal constructions (TC) in the languages under description show both the common Mongolic inventory as well as individual elaborations of the temporal domain. In addition to the three major groups of anteriority, simultaneity, and posteriority (general or specialized, e.g. immediate, co-extensive, with a terminal or initial boundary, etc. (see Kortmann 1998; Longacre 2007; Givón 2001)), the intermediacy group ('between B and C, A' (Givón 2001: 330)) is also present. Neutral TCs are opposed to those indicating evaluation; the prevalent evaluative dimension, 'expectancy' (first of all 'contrary to expectations'), is coded in all three major groups of TC. One additional dimension is 'utility' ('using the moment when'). General evaluation in terms of GOOD/BAD is irrelevant here. The intermediacy group contains very few constructions, none evaluated, so it will not be discussed further.

Connectors in evaluated TCs are mostly postpositions, grammaticalized from nouns with appropriate semantics; but there are also constructions with common Mongolic converbs among them.

2.1 *Anteriority*[2]*/Temporal Succession*

In this group, all three languages have at least one TC encoding 'succession contrary to expectations'. In Buryat there are several such constructions; some are polysemantic with 'mirative' meaning ('contrary to expectations') in certain contexts, like the terminative converb in *-tAr*; some are more specialized. For instance, the polyfunctional converb in *-tAr* denotes not only a terminal boundary, but also unexpected succession (comments on (2)) or simultaneity (1)—in contexts with a continuous event in the dependent clause and a punctiliar event in the main clause:

(1) *Eži-n-gee* *jüüme* *hura-xaa* *baj-**tar-n'***
mother-GEN-REFL thing ask-CVB.PURP AUX-CVB.TERM-3POSS
trubka-jaa *tabi-žarxi-ba*
receiver-REFL put-INTENS-PST[3SG]
[Buryat] '(Her) mother was intending to ask her something, but (she) threw down the receiver.'

The converb in *-tAr* builds an interesting opposition with the form of the past participle with obligatory possessive marking (its same-subject reflexive form in *-hAn-AA* functions practically as a converb). If *-tAr* codes unexpected succession, *-hAn-AA* denotes a change of phases, sometimes abrupt, in a flow of a (single) complex of events, so that it often means something like 'expected, normal succession'. Compare:

(2) *Xaluun hajxan üder-nüüd xodo_baj-**han-aa*** *ol'bon una-han*
warm good day-PL last-PTCP.PST-REFL cold fall-PTCP.PST
baj-gaa
AUX-PST[3SG]
[Buryat] 'Nice warm days continued for some time, (and then) it became cold.'

Here replacement of *baj-han-aa* by *baj-tar-aa* is possible with a pronounced semantic change: with *-han-aa* it refers to autumn, while with *-tar-aa* it refers to unexpected turn of events, for instance cold days in early summer.

There are also TCs specialized on unexpected succession, e.g. *-n ge-xe-de* (-POSS), an idiomatized combination of a general temporal form *-xA-dA*(-POSS) (PTCP.FUT-DLOC with optional possessive marking) and a periphrastic form *-n*

2 Anteriority of the dependent clause event in relation to the main clause event: *after* B, A.

ge- (a modal converb and the auxiliary quotative verb *ge-* 'say') denoting an action that has started but was not necessarily completed:

(3) *Fed'ka ojlgomžo-güj-göör uragšaa alxa-**n***
NAME caution-NEG-INS forward step-CVB.MOD
ge-xe-d-ee, *nege xün-höö toro-žo*
AUX-PTCP.FUT-DLOC-REFL one man-ABL stumble-CVB
una-ša-ba
fall-INTENS-PST[3SG]
[Buryat] 'Fed'ka stepped carelessly forward, (but) stumbled on someone and fell down.'

With cognitive verbs or verbs of visual perception and motion in the dependent clause, all constructions of unexpected succession, as well as the form in *-hAn-AA*, express sudden discovery/realization (the scheme *veni, vidi, comprehendi, dixi*, i.e. a prototypical pre-mirative context (Skribnik 1999)):

(4) *Malaan-aj xara-**n*** ***ge-xe-de,*** *dombo-n'*
NAME-GEN look-CVB.MOD AUX-PTCP.FUT-DLOC-REFL jug-3POSS
xoohon baj-ba
empty be -PST[3SG]
[Buryat] 'When Malaan looked in, (it turned out that) the jug was empty.'

In Khalkha, the semantics of the converb in *-snAA* (the same structure as the Buryat *-han-AA*, i.e. PTCP.PST-REFL) was previously described in aspectual terms: "quasiconverbial structure ... used in the function of a conjunct converb indicating an action that is not yet completed before the following action begins" (Janhunen 2012: 171 with reference to Brosig p.c.). Our data shows that it codes an unexpected succession, i.e., semantically corresponds to the Buryat *-tAr*, not *-hAn-AA*; this meaning can also be stressed lexically (e.g., with *genet* 'suddenly'):

(5) *Dolgor egč-ee geed güj-**snee** genet zogso-v*
NAME sister-VOC say.CVB.PRF run-CVB.MIR suddenly stand-PST
[Khalkha] '"Sister Dolgor!" (he) cried and ran, but suddenly stopped.'

As for the terminal converb, in Khalkha the form in *-tAl* does not express unexpected succession, but the Kalmyk *-tl* does: it is one of the contextual readings of this converb with a punctiliar event in the main clause (Seesing 2013: 73–74). Note that Kalmyk has no form analogous to B. *-han-AA* and Kh. *-snAA*.

(6) *Bičkn küükn pojezd dor jov-**tl**, pojezd köndr-vä*
little girl train under go-CVB.TERM train roll-PST[3SG]
[Kalmyk] 'As the little girl got under the train, the train started (suddenly) to move.'

All in all, this data shows different developments in the three languages: the common Mongolic terminal converb has unexpected succession among its meanings in Buryat and Kalmyk, but not in Khalkha; the forms B. *-hAn-AA* / Kh. *-snAA* have opposite meanings in these two languages (though both are tied to the expression of expectancy) and have no cognate forms in Kalmyk.

2.2 *Posteriority*

In the posteriority group (*before* B, A), at least one construction expresses 'precedence with unexpected succession'. For instance, out of ca. 15 Buryat posteriority constructions there are two expressing an opposition between 'normal/expected posteriority' ((7), PTCP.FUT-GEN-POSS + *urda* 'before') and 'unexpected posteriority' ((8), PTCP.FUT-ABL-POSS + *urid* 'before').

(7) *Ed'eel-**x-yn-gee** **urda** gar-aa ugaa!*
eat-PTCP.FUT-GEN-REFL POSTP hand-REFL wash.IMP
[Buryat] 'Wash your hands before you eat!'

(8) *Üüde tonšo-**xo-hoo-mni** **urid** tajla-žarxi-ba*
door knock-PTCP.FUT-ABL-POSS.1SG POSTP open-INTENS-PST[3SG]
[Buryat] '(She) had opened the door before I knocked.'

Replacing the connector in (7) with the one in (8) and vice versa results in ungrammatical sentences, thus this is not a contextual reading induced by lexicon and world knowledge.

While the Buryat constructions are set apart both by postpositions and case markers, in Kalmyk there are two postpositions, *urd* and *ömn*, that build four constructions differentiated by case forms of the future participle, GEN vs. ABL; both ablative variants denote 'posteriority with unexpected succession' as in (10), while genitive variants describe a normal flow of events as in (9) (Seesing 2013: 133–135), e.g., with *urd*:

(9) *äärm-d duu-gd-**x-in** **urd** bagš bol-ad*
army-DLOC call-PASS-PTCP.FUT-GEN POSTP teacher AUX-CVB
ködl-lä
work-DIR.EVID.PST[3SG]
[Kalmyk] 'Before (he) was called up in the army, (he) worked as a teacher.'

(10) *Čirä-hi-n'* ***üz-x-äs-n*** ***urd*** *terü-g*
face-ACC-3POSS see-PTCP.FUT-ABL-REFL POSTP s/he-ACC
tan'-v
know-PST[3SG]
[Kalmyk] '(She) recognized him (even) before (she) saw his face.'

In Khalkha there are already three posteriority postpositions with such case variations: *ömnö, urd,* and *ur'd* 'before'; as in Kalmyk, the genitive variants are neutral/expected (11), while the ablative variants are 'mirative' (12):

(11) *Üür* ***caj-x-yn*** ***ömnö*** *xojor najz tür*
dawn brighten-PTCP.FUT-GEN POSTP two friend short
dug_xij-lee
doze-DIR.EVID.PST3SG
[Khalkha] (Having talked all night long,) 'Before the sunrise the two friends dozed a little.'

(12) *Üür* ***caj-x-aas*** ***ömnö*** *Tömör mordo-n*
dawn brighten-PTCP.FUT-ABL POSTP NAME ride-CVB
jav-žee
go-INDIR.EVID.PST3SG
[Khalkha] 'Tömör rode off (even) before the sunrise.'

One more specialized construction with a complex postposition *davaan deer* 'just before' denotes that an unexpected event of the main clause makes the dependent event impossible:

(13) *Dalantaj üg* ***xele-x-ijn*** ***davaan deer*** *xonx žingene-v3SG*
NAME word say-PTCP.FUT-GEN POSTP bell ring-PST
[Khalkha] 'Before Dalantay could say a word, the bell rang.'

2.3 *Simultaneity*

Simultaneity TCs demonstrate evaluation in two dimensions: 'expectancy' and 'utility'. 'Contrary to expectation'-TCs are mostly continuous-punctiliar (span—event). For example, the Kalmyk TC with the postposition *cagla* (*cag* 'time' + COM) presents a continuous dependent event as a background for an unexpected punctiliar event in the main clause (Seesing 2013: 122–123):

(14) *Kesg züsn tuul' kel-äd suu-**sn** **cagla** gentkn kün*
many kind tale tell-CVB.PRF sit-PTCP.PST POSTP suddenly man
du harh-sn bol-ad od-v
voice come-PTCP.PST become-CVB.PRF AUX-PST[3SG]
[Kalmyk] 'While (he) was sitting and telling different tales, suddenly somebody's voice was heard.'

Many simultaneity connectors function not only in temporal adverbials, but also in manner and attendant circumstance adverbials, and thus will be discussed in Section 3.

In TCs with the simultaneity and the 'utility' evaluation co-expressed, one continuous event is presented as an opportunity to carry out some action (usually positively evaluated) while it lasts, e.g., the Buryat postposition *hambaanda* 'while (using an opportunity)' (from *hambaan* 'convenience, opportunity' + DLOC):

(15) *noxoj-goo xori-**xo** **hambaanda-n'** šamduu-xan*
dog-REFL hold-PTCP.FUT POSTP-3POSS hasty-DIM
ger-te-n' oro-bo
house-DLOC-3POSS enter-PST[3SG]
[Buryat] '(Using the opportunity) While (she) held her dog, (he) went inside hastily.'

In Khalkha this meaning is expressed by a postposition *dalimaar* (from *dalim* 'convenient moment, chance' + INS):

(16) *Ažl-aar java-**x** **dalimaar** aldar-t Venec ge-gč-ijg*
work-INS go-PTCP.FUT POSTP fame-ADJ Venice say-PTCP.FOC-ACC
üz-sen
see-PST
[Khalkha] 'I have seen the famous Venice thanks to (using the time of having) a business trip.'

Kalmyk has two such constructions, with the postpositions *xöön* and *deer*, differentiating the time reference of the dependent event: opportunity already existing at the time of utterance (*deer*) or expected in the future (*xöön*) (Seesing 2013: 126–127).

3 Evaluation in Constructions of Logical Relations (Cause/Reason, Purpose)

The logical relations domain includes the major groups cause/reason, purpose, condition, and concessivity, as well as some minor ones. Only the first two groups will be discussed here, as concessive relations are built on expectancy per definition (the dependent clause event is such that the main clause event would not be expected), and the semantic differences between Mongolic concessive constructions seem to involve rather the strength of expectations. In the conditional group the differences seem to be more epistemic in nature.

3.1 *Causal Constructions*

Causal constructions, both in common Mongolic and as developed in individual languages, within subtypes like cause, reason or sanction (Hengeveld 1998; Dixon 2009; Hetterle 2015), also express evaluation in general terms of GOOD/BAD (i.e. they can be applied both to natural phenomena and human actions, allowing different contextual readings). Evaluation can apply to the cause, the effect, or the relationship as a whole. As already mentioned, among 24 causal constructions in Khalkha there are three with positive and five with negative evaluation, while in Kalmyk there are three negative and five positive causal constructions, and in Buryat two negative and three positive.

Additionally, all three languages can express quantitatively evaluated cause ('A because of intensive/long/frequent B', but in Khalkha also 'minor, often trivial B and its strong effect A'), peripherally also 'expectancy' and 'utility'.

Similarly to TCs, the expression of evaluation relies primarily on the semantics of postpositions, grammaticalized from nouns with positive or negative semantics: B. *urmanda* 'because; for (positive)' < *urman* 'good mood' + DLOC; Kh. *ačaar* 'because (positive)' < *ač* 'favour, grace, benefit' + INS; Kh. *uršgaar*, K. *uršgar* 'because (negative)' < *uršig* 'misfortune, nuisance, troublesome matter' + INS; B. *jexe-de* 'because (intensive)' < *jexe* 'big, strong; large size, strength' + DLOC; etc. Still, some connectors consisting of conventionalized sequences of morphemes are not so transparent, e.g., Kh. *-či(x)-xa-d l* 'because (unexpectedly intensive effect A of a minor cause B)': the intensive *Aktionsart* suffix *-čix-* plus the general temporal form *-xA-d* 'when' (PTCP.FUT-DLOC) followed by the focus particle *l*. Examples:

(17) Kalmyk: 'B > positive A'

Ert	*har-sn*	***küčär***	*bidn*	*cag-la-rn*	*ir-ü-vid*
early	leave-PTCP.PST	POSTP	we	time-COM-REFL	come-PST-1PL

'Thanks to having left early, we arrived on time.'

(18) Buryat: 'very positive B > even more positive A'
*Tarilga-jaa sag bolzor soo-n' düürge-**hen-ejn-gee***
harvest-REFL period POSTP-3POSS finish-PTCP.PST-GEN-REFL
***urmanda** bulta xüxi-xe baj-gaa-bdi*
POSTP all have_fun-PTCP.FUT AUX-PST-1PL
'As (we) finished harvesting in time, we all were (planning) to celebrate.'

(19) Khalkha: 'B > positive A + without B, no A'
*Pürevmaa fitness-eer xičeelle-**sn-ij** **ačaar** alx-dag*
NAME fitness-INS exercise-PTCP.PST-GEN POSTP step-PTCP.HAB
bol-žee
become-INDIR.EVID.PST
'Thanks to doing fitness exercises, Pürevmaa started to walk (again).'

(20) Buryat: 'negative B > negative A'
Xeden xün-ej ažal-d-aa xar'uusalga-güj-göör
several man-GEN work-DLOC-REFL responsibility-NEG-INS
*xanda-**han-aj** **gemeer** avtobus iiteree haata-na geeše-b?*
handle-PTCP.PST-GEN POSTP bus so be_late-PRS DIP-Q[3SG]
'The bus is so late because several people are careless in their work, isn't it?'

(21) Kalmyk: 'uncontrolled and unexpected negative B > (mostly negative) A'
*Enžl xavr haŋ bol-**sn** **uršgar** nidnäk-äs-n*
this_year spring hot become-PTCP.PST POSTP last_year-ABL-REFL
zövär bah urhc av-gd-x-mn
very small harvest take-PASS-PTCP.FUT-DIP3SG
'Because the spring was (too) hot this year, the harvest will be (lit. taken) considerably less than that of the last year.'

(22) Khalkha: 'negative B > even more negative A'
*Osl-yg nuucal-**sn-y** **uršgaar** 5 xün am'-ia*
accident-ACC hide-PTCP.PST-GEN POSTP 5 person life-REFL
alda-v
lose-PST
'Five people died because [the mine administration] had concealed the accident.' (The miners did not get medical help immediately.)

Note that inherently positive lexical items (e.g., 'help' or 'heal') cannot be used in constructions of negative semantics and vice versa (?'thanks to his death').

Examples of causal constructions with quantitative evaluation:

(23) Buryat: 'intensive B > A':
*Tere xübüün aj-**han-ajn-gaa** **jexede** aman-d-aa*
this boy be_afraid-PTCP.PST-GEN-REFL POSTP mouth-DLOC-REFL
xurga-jaa xeed, ab'aa-güj zogso-šo-bo
finger-REFL put.CVB.PRF sound-NEG stand-INTENS-PST[3SG]
'This boy, as he was (so very much) afraid, put his finger in his mouth and became silent.'

(24) Khalkha: 'minor/trivial B > (unexpectedly) intensive A'
Gadaad-yn xen neg irgen, ner devšigč-ijn dansan-d
foreign-GEN who one citizen name allocation-GEN account-DLOC
*100 am dollar xij-**čix-sen** **baj-xa-d** l*
100 Amer. dollar make-INTENS-PTCP.PST AUX-PTCP.FUT-DLOC FOC
una-na
fall-FUT
'A candidate will be excluded from elections (lit. fall) (just) because a foreigner transferred 100 dollars to her private account.'

Examples of less frequent dimensions in this semantic group: 'utility' (25) and 'expectancy' (26, 27):

(25) Buryat: '(by a good chance that) B > A'
*Jere-**hen-ej-xii-je** xar-aa-güj-göö xara-ža…*
come-PTCP.PST-GEN-NMLZ-ACC see-PTCP.PRS-NEG-REFL see-CVB
'Due to the fact that (we) came here, (we) have seen what we had never seen (before) …'

(26) Buryat: 'B > A, and it is unusual':
*Manaj X'aagt-yn zon songol-oor xele-**deg** **aad,** bur'aad*
our NAME-GEN people NAME-INS speak-PTCP.HAB PTL Buryat
xele zaa-xa-n' jexe xüšeer xünde
language teach-PTCP.FUT-POSS3 very difficult
baj-dag
be-PTCP.HAB[3SG]
'As our Kyakhta people speak the Tsongol dialect, it's very difficult to teach them (the literary) Buryat.'

(27) Kalmyk: 'justification B of A that deviates from social norms or individual habits':
*Bolv bi eck-in-n' surh-s-**ar** am ald-ž*
but 1SG father-GEN-POSS3 ask-PTCP.PST-INS mouth loose-CVB
du har-d-go bilä-v
sound go_out-PTCP.HAB-NEG AUX:PST-1SG
'(It was against my principles.) But I did not say a word because my father asked me (not to do it).'

See also (21) and (24).

3.2 Evaluation in Purposive Constructions

Purposive relations presuppose intention (Verstraete 2008); the main clause subjects are predominantly human/animate and evaluation is based on emotion and cognition. As a consequence, evaluative dimensions found in this group are 'goal significance', 'desirability'/ 'emotional involvement', and 'complexity'/'necessity to make an effort'; 'expectancy' is marginal. If simple neutral 'purpose-cum-motion' constructions are built by several same-subject converbs, more complex goals, including evaluated ones, can be different-subject and are expressed either by non-finite clauses with postpositions or by finite clauses with connectors on the base of the auxiliary quotation verb B., Kh. *ge-* / K. *gi-*. Buryat has the highest number of 11 specialized purposive constructions. Note that many postpositions build both purpose and reason constructions, differentiated only by temporal characteristics of non-finite forms (PTCP.PST = reason, PTCP.FUT = purpose), so that their semantics can be generalized as 'motivation'.

The common Mongolic postposition B. *tülöö* / K. *tölä* / Kh. *tölöö* 'for' in combination with the future participle expresses a desirable goal; but in Kalmyk it is positive, in Khalkha highly positive and strongly motivating, and in Buryat not easy to achieve. A Khalkha example:

(28) *magadgüj udm-aa tasla-**x-güj-n** **tölöö***
maybe progeny-REFL break-PTCP.FUT-NEG-GEN POSTP
xan'-taj bol-son.
spouse-PROPR become-PTCP.PST
[Khalkha] 'Maybe I got married in order to continue my lineage (lit. not to interrupt my progeny).'

In Kalmyk the postposition *tust* 'in order to' (< *tus* 'benefit, favour' + DLOC) expresses a highly desirable goal worth the effort described in the main clause:

(29) *Äämšgtä gem xör-**x-in** **tust** jamr profilaktičesk*
horrible disease prevent-PTCP.FUT-GEN POSTP which prophylactic
ködlmš kücä-gd-žä-x-in tuskar son'ms-v-idn
work complete-PASS-CONT-PTCP.FUT-GEN about wonder-PST-1PL
[Kalmyk] 'We wanted to know which prophylactic measures were being taken to prevent the horrible disease.'

Buryat has two constructions with an interesting opposition, with postpositions *urmanda* 'because; for' (see Section 2.1 (18)) and *talaanda* 'for' (< *talaan* 'luck, happiness' + DLOC). The former denotes a goal so important to the subject that s/he is ready to carry out the less attractive action of the main clause:

(30) *Mori una-**x-yn** **urmanda** Lodon* ⟨…⟩ *xašarag-uud-yje*
horse ride-PTCP.FUT-GEN POSTP NAME heifer-PL-ACC
aduul-dag jum
tend-PTCP.HAB DIP[3SG]
[Buryat] 'Lodon is tending heifers (only) in order to ride horses.'

The second construction involves evaluation from two different points of view: it denotes a goal attractive to the main clause subject, but the means to achieve it are seen by the speaker as unusual or as breaching the social norms; as a result, this construction is not used in the 1st person:

(31) *Gorod-oj zon ööhedy-göö seng-üül-**x-in** **talaanda***
city-GEN people self.PL-REFL amuse-CAUS-PTCP.FUT-GEN POSTP
üxibüü-tej bolo-xojoo ašaarxa-dag
child-PROPR become-CVB.PURP feel_burdened-PTCP.HAB[3SG/PL]
[Buryat] 'The city people do not burden themselves with children, just in order to enjoy themselves.'

Negatively evaluated goals are expressed by constructions with the postpositions B. *tülöö* / K. *tölä* / Kh. *tölöö* 'for' and B. *tula*(*da*) / K., Kh. *tul*(*d*) 'because; for' and negation suffixes on non-finite forms.

There are also specialized constructions expressing undesirable events that can be prevented by main clause actions, e.g. in Buryat with one of imperative forms and the connector *geže* (auxiliary quotation verb *ge-* + CVB.IPF):

(32) … *tani-han* *xün-de* *xara-gda-š-**uuža-b*** ***geže***
know-PTCP.PST man-DLOC see-PASS-INTENS-IMP-1SG SAY-CVB.IPF
⟨…⟩ *xojš-oo* *uragš-aa* *xaraašal-na*
back-REFL forward-REFL look_around-PRS[3SG]
[Buryat] '(He) looks back and forth in order not to be noticed by acquaintances' (lit. saying I should not be noticed).

4 Evaluation in Constructions of Manner and Attendant Circumstance

In this semantic group only one evaluative dimension is represented, namely 'expectancy': neutral constructions are in opposition to 'mirative', where either the manner or the main action is presented as unexpected, unusual, not matching the norms or typical patterns of behaviour; the 'conforming' constructions are probably not yet fully grammaticalized.

Buryat has a unique converb of 'unusual manner' (Sanžeev 1962: 291) in *-mgAšAA*, often denoting an unusual position in which an action is carried out; the most frequent forms are 'standing' (e.g., when milking a cow), 'lying' (e.g., when putting shoes on) or 'sitting' (e.g., when picking flowers):

(33) *Dagba arajxan terge-d-ee ahalda-ža ürd-eed,*
NAME somehow wagon-DLOC-REFL grasp-CVB manage-CVB
*xebte-**mgešee*** *boožo-d-oo* *ahalda-ba*
lie-CVB.MIR reins-DLOC-REFL grasp-PST[3SG]
[Buryat] 'Dagba, having barely managed to reach his wagon, lying grasped the reins.'

In Khalkha this meaning is expressed by a postpositional construction with *čigeer* 'in an unusual way' (from *čig* 'straight; direction'+ INS):

(34) *Bi … avsan dotr-oo nuugd-**san*** ***čigeer*** *čagna-laa*
1SG coffin inside-REFL hide-PTCP.PST POSTP listen-DIR.PST.EVID
[Khalkha] 'I listened hiding in the coffin.'

(35) *Suu-**gaa*** ***čigeer*** *morin xuur-aa deer gegč dalaj-n …*
sit-PTCP.PRS POSTP morin khuur-REFL up so raise-CVB
[Khalkha] 'Sitting, (he) raises his morin khuur (a musical instrument) so high' (musicians usually stand up for this).

One more type of expectancy evaluation is presented in Kalmyk and Buryat (but not in Khalkha). Kalmyk has a construction with the postposition *kevär* (*kev* 'look; form; pattern'+ INS) denoting that the manner/attending circumstance still continues contrary to the speaker's expectations:

(36) *Bičg dörvlžl-ž xuhl-gd-**sn** **kevär-n***
letter fold_in_four-CVB fold-PASS-PTCP.PST POSTP-REFL
bääh-ä
be-PTCP.PRS[3SG]
[Kalmyk] 'The letter was lying there (still) folded in four' (it should have been opened).

Buryat has two such constructions, with the postpositions *zandaa* (from *zan* 'behaviour, habit') and the polysemantic *mürtöö* (from *mür* 'path, track'), both in the dative-locative case with reflexive marking. The former, like K. *kevär*, expresses unexpected continuation:

(37) *Andrej buruu xara-**han** **zandaa:** —Xülise,— geže*
NAME wrong see-PTCP.PST POSTP forgive.IMP COMP
šebene-be
whisper-PST[3SG]
[Buryat] 'Andrey, (still) looking away, whispered "Forgive me …"'

In contrast to this, the *mürtöö* construction evaluates the continuing attendant circumstance as normal and expected, but the main clause action as unexpected or improper:

(38) *Nege düšööd naha-taj haališan gente ün'ee-gee haa-ža*
one 40 age-PROPR milkmaid suddenly cow-REFL milk-CVB
*huu-**han** **mürtöö** oro-lso-bo*
sit-PTCP.PST POSTP enter-SOC-PST [3SG]
[Buryat] 'One milkmaid, about forty years old, (still) sitting and milking her cow, suddenly interfered (lit. entered—into our discussion).'

Finally, the negative converbs (B. *-ngüj*, K. *-lgo*, Kh. *-lgüj*) must be mentioned here, as they often indicate the non-occurrence of some event expected by the speaker (negative circumstance):

(39) *... xen-ej-šje n'uur xara-**ngüj** ed'eel-še-ne.*
who-GEN-PTL face look-CVB.NEG eat-INTENS-PRS[3SG]
[Buryat] 'He attacked his food, not even looking at anyone.'

(40) *Zärmdän ju xälä-s-än med-**lgo** har-dg*
sometimes what see-PTCP.PST-REFL know-CVB.NEG leave-PTCP.HAB
bilä-v
be.PST.EVID-1SG
[Kalmyk] 'Sometimes I would leave (the cinema) without knowing what I've seen.'

Conformity to norms and expectations can be expressed lexically, by nouns like 'custom', 'rule', and similar, usually in the instrumental case, e.g., Buryat *gurimaar* (from *gurim* 'custom, habit' + INS): *bur'aad gurimaar* 'in the Buryat tradition'. Used with participles, such nouns also tend to be grammaticalized as postpositions:

(41) *Šobdog lama šojro xajalsa-**dag** **gurimaar**, mün le*
NAME debate exchange-PTCP.HAB POSTP also
duula-n hagad, dajanša-da xar'uusa-ba
listen-CVB hardly RANK-DLOC answer-PST.3SG
[Buryat] 'Shobdog-lama, in the way (arguments) are exchanged in a lamaistic debate, also answered the Dayansha[3] hardly waiting for him to finish (lit. hardly listening).'

Similarly, in Khalkha (*žuram* 'order; rule' + INS):

(42) *Ixes deedes-ee xündetge-**x** **žurmaar** zočil-loo.*
grand majesty-REFL respect-PTCP.FUT POSTP visit- DIR.EVID.PST
[Khalkha] '(They) visited Their Majesties (following the conventions and) paying them respect.'

Consider also Kalmyk *avjasar* 'according to' (*avjas* 'habit, custom' + INS):

3 A rank of a Buddhist monk, lit. 'contemplator'.

(43) *Maj-in 7-d bidn kesg žil-in turšart toxr-****sn***
May-GEN 7-DLOC 1PL many year-GEN POSTP establish-PTCP.PST
avjasar *radio-n ödr tömdgl-žä-nä-vidn*
POSTP radio-GEN day celebrate-CONT-PRS-1PL
'On May 7 we celebrate the Day of Radio, the way it was established for many years.'

5 Conclusions

As the data shows, the two main evaluative dimensions present in Mongolic adverbial constructions are generalized GOOD/BAD (with contextual readings) and 'expectancy' (comparison of coded relations with the natural order of things, social norms and individual expectations, with the value 'contrary to expectations', or 'mirativity', dominating). Positive and negative evaluation is more elaborated in causal and purposive constructions (cf. Eng. *thanks to, lest*), whereas expectancy coding has a strong position in temporal and manner constructions (unusual sequence of events or unusual manner). Causal and purposive constructions together also allow quantitative evaluation ('intensive cause' or 'efforts to reach the goal'). Conditional and concessive constructions have their own differentiating parameters, not evaluative.

The semantics of evaluation are mostly based on the semantics of postpositions (i.e., lexical nouns they are grammaticalized from); 'mirativity' meaning can be supported by pre-mirative contexts (*veni, vidi, comprehendi, dixi*) and lexical means ('suddenly'). As for the lexicon used here, negative constructions do not allow inherently positive lexical items (e.g. 'help') and vice versa.

These observations present several topics for future research: first, how the regular expression of the meaning 'contrary to expectations' in non-finite predicates correlates with the grammaticalization of mirativity in the finite verb, prominent in the Mongolic languages under study (e.g., Skribnik and Seesing 2014: 168–169). The second task would lie in the framework of cultural linguistics: "... many grammatical phenomena are best understood as governed by cultural schemata rather than universal innate or emergent cognitive schemata. [...] linguists cannot rely solely upon their own intuitions about the semantics of complex domains, but should instead attempt to discover which concepts have particular relevance for speakers" (Palmer 2006: 14). Why do Mongolic languages, when coding events and their sequences, constantly evaluate and compare them to social norms and individual expectations?

Acknowledgements

I would like to express my deeply felt gratitude to the Fritz Thyssen Foundation for supporting the projects "Digitales Konstruktikon dreier mongolischer Sprachen (Temporalkonstruktionen)" (Az. 10.11.2.068) and "Constructions with adverbial clauses in Mongolic languages (Khalkha, Buryat, Kalmyk)" (Az. 10.14. 2.082).

Abbreviations

The glossing of the examples, with a few marginal exceptions, follows the Leipzig Glossing Rules.

3POSS	possessive marker 3SG/PL	MIR	mirative
ACC	accusative	MOD	modal (converb)
ADJ	adjective (derivative)	NEG	negation
AUX	auxiliary	NMLZ	nominalizer suffix
CAUS	causative	NOM	nominative
COM	comitative	PASS	passive
COMP	complementizer	PL	plural
CONT	continuative (derivative)	POSS	possessive marker
CVB	converb	POSTP	postposition
DIR.EVID.PST	direct evidential past	PROPR	proprietive
DIM	diminutive	PRS	present tense
DIP	discourse particle	PST	past tense
DLOC	dative-locative	PTL	particle
FOC	focus	PTCP	participle
FUT	future tense	PURP	purposive
GEN	genitive	Q	question marker
HAB	habitive	REFL	reflexive possessive markers
INDIR.EVID.PST	indirect evidential past		
IMP	imperative	SG	singular
IPF	imperfective	SOC	sociative (voice)
INTENS	intensive (derivative)	TERM	terminative (converb)
INS	instrumental case	VOC	vocative

References

Bednarek, Monika (2009). Dimensions of evaluation: cognitive and linguistic perspectives. *Pragmatics & Cognition* 17 (1): 146–175.

Cristofaro, Sonja (2003). *Subordination.* Oxford: Oxford University Press.

Dixon, R.M.W. (2009). The Semantics of Clause Linking in Typological Perspective. In Dixon and Aikhenvald (2009), 1–55.

Dixon, R.M.W. and Alexandra Aikhenvald (eds.) (2009). *The Semantics of Clause Linking: A Cross-Linguistic Typology*. Oxford: Oxford University Press.

Givón, Talmy (2001). *Syntax: An introduction.* Vol. 2. Amsterdam & Philadelphia: John Benjamins (new edition of *Syntax: A functional-typological introduction*, 1984).

Guntsetseg, Dolgor (2016). *Differential Case Marking in Mongolian* (Tunguso-Sibirica 39). Wiesbaden: Harrassowitz.

Hengeveld, Kees (1998). Adverbial clauses in the languages of Europe. In Johan van der Auwera (ed.), *Adverbial constructions in the languages of Europe*, 335–419. Berlin & New York: Mouton de Gruyter.

Hetterle, Katja (2015). *Adverbial clauses in cross-linguistic perspective*. Berlin & Boston: Mouton De Gruyter.

Janhunen, Juha (ed.) (2003). *The Mongolic Languages*. London & New York: Routledge.

Janhunen, Juha (2012). *Mongolian.* (London Oriental and African language library 19.) Amsterdam: John Benjamins.

Kortmann, Bernd (1998). Adverbial subordinators in the languages of Europe. In Johan van der Auwera (ed.), *Adverbial constructions in the languages of Europe*, 457–562. Berlin & New York: Mouton de Gruyter.

Lehmann, Christian (1988). Towards a typology of clause linkage. In John Haiman and Sandra A. Thompson (eds.), *Clause combining in grammar and discourse*, 181–226. Amsterdam & Philadelphia: Benjamins.

Longacre, Robert E. (2007). Sentences as combinations of clauses. In Timothy Shopen (ed.). *Language typology and syntactic description. Vol. 2: Complex constructions*, 372–420. Cambridge University Press. (New edition of Shopen 1985).

Malrieu, Jean-Pierre (1999). *Evaluative Semantics. Cognition, Language and Ideology*. London & New York: Routledge.

Matthiessen, Christian M.I.M. (2002). Combining clauses into clause complexes: a multi-faceted view. In Joan Bybee and Michael Noonan (eds.), *Complex sentences in grammar and discourse: Essays in honor of Sandra A. Thompson*, 235–319. Amsterdam & Philadelphia: John Benjamins.

Muravyev (2017) = Муравьев, Н. А. *Таксис и таксисные формы в языках мира: таксономия и типология*. Дисс. на соискание ученой степени кандидата филологических наук. Москва: МГУ.

Palmer, Gary (2006). When does cognitive linguistics become cultural? Case studies in

Tagalog voice and Shona noun classifiers. In June Luchjenbroers (ed.), *Cognitive Linguistics Investigations: Across languages, fields and philosophical boundaries*, 13–45. Amsterdam/Philadelphia: John Benjamins Publishing Company.

Sanžeev (ed.) (1962) = *Грамматика бурятского языка: Фонетика и морфология* / Под ред. Г. Д. Санжеева.—Москва: Изд-во восточной литературы.

Seesing, Olga (2013). *Die temporalen Infinitkonstruktionen im Kalmückischen*. (Tunguso-Sibirica 34.) Harrasowitz Verlag: Wiesbaden.

Skribnik, Elena (1999). Miratives and pre-mirative contexts in West-Siberian languages. In *ALT III. Third Biennal Conference of the Association for Linguistic Typology*. Programme and Abstracts. University of Amsterdam, 25–28 August 1999. P. 32.

Skribnik and Darzhaeva (2016) = Скрибник Е. К., Даржаева Н. Б. *Грамматика бурятского языка. Синтаксис сложного (полипредикативного) предложения*. Т. I.—Улан-Удэ: Изд-во БНЦ СО РАН.

Skribnik, Elena and Olga Seesing (2014). Evidentiality in Kalmyk. In Alexandra Y. Aikhenvald and R.M.W. Dixon, *The Grammar of Knowledge: A Cross-Linguistic Typology*, 148–170. Oxford: Oxford University Press.

Verstraete, Jean-Christophe (2008). The status of purpose, reason and intended endpoint in the typology of complex sentences. *Linguistics* 46: 757–788.

White, Peter R.R. (2011). Appraisal. In Jan Zienkowski, Jan-Ola Ostman, Jef Verschueren (eds.), *Discursive pragmatics* (Handbook of Pragmatics Highlights, vol. 8), 14–36. Amsterdam & Philadelphia: John Benjamins Publishing Company.

Wierzbicka, Anna (1996). *Semantics: Primes and Universals*. Oxford: Oxford University Press.

Index

Printed in the United States
by Baker & Taylor Publisher Services